WORLD TRADE ORGANIZATION

Dispute Settlement Reports

2018
Volume X

Pages 5247-5864

THE WTO DISPUTE SETTLEMENT REPORTS

The *Dispute Settlement Reports* of the World Trade Organization (the "WTO") include panel and Appellate Body reports, as well as arbitration awards, in disputes concerning the rights and obligations of WTO Members under the provisions of the *Marrakesh Agreement Establishing the World Trade Organization*. The *Dispute Settlement Reports* are available in English. Volumes comprising one or more complete cases contain a cumulative list of published disputes. The cumulative list for cases that cover more than one volume is to be found in the first volume for that case.

This volume may be cited as DSR 2018:X

CAMBRIDGE
UNIVERSITY PRESS

University Printing House, Cambridge CB2 8BS, United Kingdom

One Liberty Plaza, 20th Floor, New York, NY 10006, USA

477 Williamstown Road, Port Melbourne, VIC 3207, Australia

314–321, 3rd Floor, Plot 3, Splendor Forum, Jasola District Centre,
New Delhi – 110025, India

79 Anson Road, #06–04/06, Singapore 079906

Cambridge University Press is part of the University of Cambridge.

It furthers the University's mission by disseminating knowledge in the pursuit of
education, learning, and research at the highest international levels of excellence.

www.cambridge.org
Information on this title: www.cambridge.org/9781108834667
DOI: 10.1017/9781108876407

First published 2020

Printed in the United Kingdom by TJ International Ltd. Padstow Cornwall

A catalogue record for this publication is available from the British Library.

ISBN 978-1-108-83466-7 Hardback

TABLE OF CONTENTS

Page

AUSTRALIA - CERTAIN MEASURES CONCERNING TRADEMARKS, GEOGRAPHICAL INDICATIONS AND OTHER PLAIN PACKAGING REQUIREMENTS APPLICABLE TO TOBACCO PRODUCTS AND PACKAGING

Reports of the Panels[*] [a]
WT/DS458/R, WT/DS467/R
and Add.1 and Supp.1[b]

SCI redacted, as indicated [[***]]

*Adopted by the Dispute Settlement Body
on 27 August 2018*

Report of the Panel[*] [a]
WT/DS435/R
and Add.1 and Supp.1[b]

SCI redacted, as indicated [[***]]

Appealed on 19 July 2018

Report of the Panel[*] [a]
WT/DS441/R
and Add.1 and Supp.1[b]

SCI redacted, as indicated [[***]]

Appealed on 23 August 2018

---

[*]   These Panel Reports are in the form of a single document constituting four separate Panel Reports: WT/DS435/R, WT/DS441/R, WT/DS458/R and WT/DS467/R. The cover page, preliminary pages, sections 1 through 7, appendices, and annexes are common to all four Panel Reports. Section 8 on page HND-5225 of Volume IX contains the Panel's conclusions and recommendations in the Panel Report WT/DS435/R; section 8 on page DOM-5226 of Volume IX contains the Panel's conclusions and recommendations in the Panel Report WT/DS441/R; section 8 on pages CUB-5228 of Volume IX contains the Panel's conclusions and recommendations in the Panel Report WT/DS458/R; and section 8 on page IDN-5230 of Volume IX contains the Panel's conclusions and recommendations in the Panel Report WT/DS467/R.

[a]   The Panel's findings on the Trips Agreement can be found in DSR 2018:IX, starting at section 7.3.

[b]   Annexes A to C and Suppl.1 can be found in this volume.

LIST OF ANNEXES

ANNEX A

WORKING PROCEDURES OF THE PANEL

Contents		Page
Annex A-1	Working Procedures of the Panel	5252
Annex A-2	Additional Working Procedures Concerning Strictly Confidential Information	5262

ANNEX B

ARGUMENTS OF THE PARTIES

Contents		Page
Annex B-1	Integrated executive summary of the arguments of Honduras	5267
Annex B-2	Integrated executive summary of the arguments of the Dominican Republic	5313
Annex B-3	Integrated executive summary of the arguments of Cuba	5357
Annex B-4	Integrated executive summary of the arguments of Indonesia	5382
Annex B-5	Integrated executive summary of the arguments of Australia	5410

ANNEX C

ARGUMENTS OF THE THIRD PARTIES

Contents		Page
Annex C-1	Executive summary of the arguments of Argentina	5460
Annex C-2	Executive summary of the arguments of Brazil	5468
Annex C-3	Executive summary of the arguments of Canada	5475
Annex C-4	Executive summary of the arguments of China	5479
Annex C-5	Executive summary of the arguments of the European Union	5485
Annex C-6	Executive summary of the arguments of Guatemala	5491
Annex C-7	Executive summary of the arguments of Japan	5499

LIST OF APPENDICES

ANNEX A

WORKING PROCEDURES OF THE PANEL

Contents		Page
Annex A-1	Working Procedures of the Panel	5252
Annex A-2	Additional Working Procedures Concerning Strictly Confidential Information	5262

ANNEX A-1

WORKING PROCEDURES OF THE PANEL[1]

*Adopted on 17 June 2014,
as Amended on 1 October 2014 and 15 December 2014*[2]

1.   In its proceedings, the Panel shall follow the relevant provisions of the Understanding on Rules and Procedures Governing the Settlement of Disputes (DSU). In addition, the following Working Procedures shall apply.

2.   Pursuant to Article 9.3 of the DSU, the timetables in DS434, DS435, DS441, DS458 and DS467 are harmonized. The Panel shall, to the greatest possible extent, conduct a single panel process, with a single record, resulting in separate reports contained in a single document, taking into account the rights of all Members concerned and in such a manner that the rights that parties or third parties would otherwise have enjoyed are in no way impaired.

General

3.   The deliberations of the Panel and the documents submitted to it shall be kept confidential. Nothing in the DSU or in these Working Procedures shall preclude a party to the disputes (hereafter "party") or a third party to the disputes (hereafter "third party") from disclosing statements of its own positions to the public. Members shall treat as confidential information submitted to the Panel by another Member which the submitting Member has designated as confidential. Where a party or third party submits a confidential version of its written

---

[1]   The panels established in DS434, DS435, DS441, DS458 and DS467 are referred to collectively in these Working Procedures as "the Panel".
[2]   These Working Procedures were originally adopted on 17 June 2014. They were amended on 1 October 2014 and 15 December 2014.

submissions to the Panel, it shall also, upon request of a Member, provide a non-confidential summary of the information contained in its submissions that could be disclosed to the public. Further to a joint request by the parties, the Panel adopted additional procedures for the protection of Strictly Confidential Information (SCI).[3]

3*bis*. Any document submitted, and information otherwise conveyed to the Panel by a party or third party, including Strictly Confidential Information ("SCI"),[4] that is not otherwise in the public domain, shall only be used by any other party or third party, including their outside advisers and experts, for the purposes of these disputes and for no other purpose. In particular, any document submitted, and information otherwise conveyed to the Panel, including SCI, shall not be used by any other party, third party, and/or their outside advisers and experts, in connection with any other proceedings in which Australia's Tobacco Plain Packaging Act 2011 (Cth) is under challenge ("related proceedings"). Any document submitted, and information otherwise conveyed to the Panel, excluding SCI, may be disclosed to a claimant and/or its employees, or to a company affiliated to a claimant and/or the employees of an affiliated company ("claimant") in related proceedings, only for the purposes of consulting or seeking advice from the claimant as an outside adviser or expert in preparing a party's or third party's argument or evidence in these disputes.

4.   The Panel shall meet in closed session. The parties, and Members having notified their interest in the disputes to the Dispute Settlement Body in accordance with Article 10 of the DSU, shall be present at the meetings only when invited by the Panel to appear before it.

5.   Each party and third party has the right to determine the composition of its own delegation when meeting with the Panel. Each party and third party shall have the responsibility for all members of its own delegation and shall ensure that each member of such delegation acts in accordance with the DSU and these Working Procedures, particularly with regard to the confidentiality of the proceedings.

5*bis*. Notwithstanding paragraph 5, a claimant in related proceedings shall not be permitted to attend substantive meetings of the Panel, except if attendance is for the purposes of giving expert evidence on behalf of a party or third party.

Submissions

6.   Before the first substantive meeting of the Panel with the parties, each party shall submit a written submission in which it presents the facts of the case and its arguments, in accordance with the timetable adopted by the Panel. Each party shall also submit to the Panel, prior to the second substantive meeting of

---

[3]   See the Additional Procedures Concerning Strictly Confidential Information, adopted on 1 October 2014, and as amended on 15 December 2014.
[4]   As defined in the Additional Procedures Concerning Strictly Confidential Information referred to in paragraph 3.

the Panel, a written rebuttal, in accordance with the timetable adopted by the Panel.

7.   A party shall submit any request for a preliminary ruling at the earliest possible opportunity and in any event no later than in its first written submission to the Panel. If a complainant requests such a ruling, Australia shall submit its response to the request in its first written submission. If Australia requests such a ruling, the complainant or complainants shall submit their response to the request prior to the first substantive meeting of the Panel, at a time to be determined by the Panel in light of the request. Exceptions to this procedure shall be granted upon a showing of good cause.

8.   In each dispute, each party shall submit all factual evidence to the Panel no later than during the first substantive meeting, except with respect to evidence necessary for purposes of rebuttals, answers to questions or comments on answers provided by the other party. Exceptions to this procedure shall be granted upon a showing of good cause. Where such exception has been granted, the Panel shall accord the other party a period of time for comment, as appropriate, on any new factual evidence submitted during or after the first substantive meeting.

9.   A party wishing to incorporate by reference or rely upon arguments and/or evidence submitted by another party or third party may do so provided that it clearly identifies the specific arguments and/or evidence it refers to and their source.

10.   Where the original language of exhibits is not a WTO working language, the submitting party or third party shall submit a translation into the WTO working language of the submission at the same time. The Panel may grant reasonable extensions of time for the translation of such exhibits upon a showing of good cause. Any objection as to the accuracy of a translation should be raised promptly in writing, no later than the next filing or meeting (whichever occurs earlier) following the submission which contains the translation in question. Any objection shall be accompanied by a detailed explanation of the grounds of objection and an alternative translation.

11.   In order to facilitate the work of the Panel, each party and third party is invited to make its submissions in accordance with the WTO Editorial Guide for Panel Submissions attached as Annex 1, to the extent that it is practical to do so.

12.   To facilitate the maintenance of the record of the dispute and maximize the clarity of submissions, each party and third party shall sequentially number its exhibits throughout the course of the dispute. For example, exhibits submitted by Ukraine could be numbered UKR-1, UKR-2, etc. If the last exhibit in connection with the first submission was numbered UKR-5, the first exhibit of the next submission thus would be numbered UKR-6. To avoid duplication of exhibits, the parties may submit joint exhibits by numbering them accordingly, for example as JE-1, JE-2, etc. Each party may also cross-refer to an exhibit submitted by another party by using the number attributed to the exhibit by the

party who initially submitted it. Each party is also invited to provide a list of exhibits together with the relevant submission.

13.   In the interest of full transparency and harmonization of the timetable in DS434, DS435, DS441, DS458 and DS467, each party is encouraged to make its written communications to the Panel, including written submissions, any preliminary submissions and written answers to questions available to the parties in the other disputes at the time that they are submitted to the Panel.

14.   In the interest of full transparency and harmonization of the timetable in DS434, DS435, DS441, DS458 and DS467, each party is encouraged to make its written submission in advance of the first substantive meeting with the Panel, as well as its written rebuttal in advance of the second substantive meeting with the Panel[5], available to the third parties in the other disputes at the time that they are submitted to the Panel.

Questions

15.   The Panel may at any time pose questions to the parties and third parties, orally or in writing, including prior to each substantive meeting.

Substantive meetings

16.   Each party shall provide to the Panel the list of members of its delegation in advance of each meeting with the Panel and no later than 5.00 p.m. on the fifth working day preceding the first day of the meeting.

17.   In the interest of full transparency and harmonization of the timetable in DS434, DS435, DS441, DS458 and DS467, the parties agree that the substantive meetings referred to in paragraphs 18 and 19 shall take place in the presence of the parties to all five disputes.

18.   The first substantive meeting of the Panel with the parties shall be conducted as follows:

    a.   The Panel shall first invite each complainant to make an opening statement to present its case, in the order in which the disputes were filed. Subsequently, the Panel shall invite Australia to present its point of view. Before each party takes the floor, it shall provide the Panel and other participants at the meeting with a provisional written version of its statement. In the event that interpretation is needed, each party shall provide additional copies for the interpreters, through the Panel Secretary. Each party shall make available to the Panel, the other parties and the third parties[6]

---

[5]   Third parties' access to the parties' written rebuttals shall be subject to the Additional Procedures Concerning Strictly Confidential Information, adopted on 1 October 2014, and as amended on 15 December 2014.

[6]   Third parties' access to the final version of the parties' opening statements at the Panel's first substantive meeting shall be subject to the Additional Procedures Concerning Strictly Confidential Information, adopted on 1 October 2014, and as amended on 15 December 2014.

the final version of its opening statement, preferably at the end of the session at which the opening statement is delivered, and in any event no later than 9.00 a.m. on the first working day following that session.

b.   After the conclusion of the statements, the Panel shall give each party the opportunity to ask each other questions or make comments, through the Panel. Each party shall then have an opportunity to answer these questions orally. Each party shall send in writing, within a timeframe to be determined by the Panel, any questions to the other parties to which it wishes to receive a response in writing. Each party shall be invited to respond in writing to the other party's written questions within a deadline to be determined by the Panel.

c.   The Panel may subsequently pose questions to the parties. Each party shall then have an opportunity to answer these questions orally. The Panel shall send in writing, within a deadline to be determined by it, any questions to the parties to which it wishes to receive a response in writing. Each party shall be invited to respond in writing to such questions within a deadline to be determined by the Panel.

d.   Once the questioning has concluded, the Panel shall afford each party an opportunity to present a brief closing statement, with the complainants presenting their statements first, in the order in which the disputes were filed. Each party shall make available to the Panel, the other parties and the third parties[7] the final version of its closing statement, preferably at the end of the meeting, and in any event no later than 5.00 p.m. on the first working day following the meeting.

19.   The second substantive meeting of the Panel with the parties shall be conducted as follows:

a.   The Panel shall ask Australia if it wishes to avail itself of the right to present its case first. If so, the Panel shall invite Australia to present its opening statement, followed by the complainants, in the reverse order to that in which the disputes were filed. If Australia chooses not to avail itself of that right, the Panel shall invite the complainants to present their opening statement first, in the reverse order to that in which the disputes were filed. Before each party takes the floor, it shall provide the Panel and other participants at the meeting with a provisional written version of its

---

[7]   Third parties' access to the final version of the parties' closing statements at the Panel's first substantive meeting shall be subject to the Additional Procedures Concerning Strictly Confidential Information, adopted on 1 October 2014, and as amended on 15 December 2014.

statement. In the event that interpretation is needed, each party shall provide additional copies for the interpreters, through the Panel Secretary. Each party shall make available to the Panel, the other parties and the third parties[8] the final version of its opening statement, preferably at the end of the meeting, and in any event no later than 5.00 p.m. on the first working day following the meeting.

b. After the conclusion of the statements, the Panel shall give each party the opportunity to ask each other questions or make comments, through the Panel. Each party shall then have an opportunity to answer these questions orally. Each party shall send in writing, within a deadline to be determined by the Panel, any questions to the other parties to which it wishes to receive a response in writing. Each party shall be invited to respond in writing to the other parties' written questions within a deadline to be determined by the Panel.

c. The Panel may subsequently pose questions to the parties. Each party shall then have an opportunity to answer these questions orally. The Panel shall send in writing, within a deadline to be determined by it, any questions to the parties to which it wishes to receive a response in writing. Each party shall be invited to respond in writing to such questions within a deadline to be determined by the Panel.

d. Once the questioning has concluded, the Panel shall afford each party an opportunity to present a brief closing statement, with the party that presented its opening statement first, presenting its closing statement first. Each party shall make available to the Panel, the other parties and the third parties[9] the final version of its closing statement, preferably at the end of the meeting, and in any event no later than 5.00 p.m. on the first working day following the meeting.

---

[8] Third parties' access to the final version of the parties' opening statements at the Panel's second substantive meeting shall be subject to the Additional Procedures Concerning Strictly Confidential Information, adopted on 1 October 2014, and as amended on 15 December 2014.

[9] Third parties' access to the final version of the parties' closing statements at the Panel's second substantive meeting shall be subject to the Additional Procedures Concerning Strictly Confidential Information, adopted on 1 October 2014, and as amended on 15 December 2014.

Third parties

20.   In the interest of full transparency and harmonization of the timetable in DS434, DS435, DS441, DS458 and DS467, a complaining party's first written submission in one dispute shall be deemed to be an exercise of its third party rights in the other four disputes. Arguments presented as a third party only shall be clearly identified as such.

21.   The Panel shall invite each third party to transmit to the Panel a written submission prior to the first substantive meeting of the Panel with the parties, in accordance with the timetable adopted by the Panel. Each third party is encouraged to submit a single submission, clearly identifying the dispute(s) to which its views relate. Third party written submissions shall not exceed 50 pages per third party irrespective of whether a third party chooses to submit a single written submission.

22.   In the interest of full transparency and harmonization of the timetable in DS434, DS435, DS441, DS458 and DS467, each third party is encouraged to make its written submission to the Panel available to the parties and third parties in the other disputes, at the time that it is submitted to the Panel.

23.   Each third party shall also be invited to present its views orally during a session of the first substantive meeting, set aside for that purpose, in a statement the duration of which shall be set by the Panel prior to that session. In the interest of full transparency and harmonization of the timetable in DS434, DS435, DS441, DS458 and DS467, the parties agree to allow all third parties having expressed interest in one or more of the five disputes to be present during the entirety of the third party session, and third parties to each of these disputes are encouraged to allow their presentations and responses to questions during the third party session to take place in the presence of the parties and third parties in the other disputes.

24.   Each third party shall provide to the Panel the list of members of its delegation in advance of this session and no later than 5.00 p.m. on the fifth working day preceding this session.

25.   The third-party session shall be conducted as follows:

    a.   The Panel shall first hear the arguments of the third parties, in alphabetical order.

    b.   Third parties present at the third-party session and intending to present their views orally at that session, shall provide the Panel, the parties and all other third parties with provisional written versions of their statements before they take the floor. Third parties shall make available to the Panel, the parties and other third parties the final versions of their statements, preferably at the end of the session, and in any event no later than 5.00 p.m. on the first working day following the session.

    c.   After the third parties have made their statements, the parties may be given the opportunity, through the Panel, to ask the third parties questions for clarification on any matter raised in the third parties' submissions or statements. Each party shall send in writing, within a timeframe to be determined by the Panel, any questions to a third party to which it wishes to receive a response in writing.

d.   The Panel may subsequently pose questions to the third parties. Each third party shall then have an opportunity to answer these questions orally. The Panel shall send in writing, within a timeframe to be determined by it, any questions to the third parties to which it wishes to receive a response in writing. Each third party shall be invited to respond in writing to such questions within a deadline to be determined by the Panel.

Descriptive part

26.   The description of the arguments of the parties and third parties in the descriptive part of the Panel reports shall consist of executive summaries provided by the parties and third parties, which shall be annexed as addenda to the reports. These executive summaries shall not in any way serve as a substitute for the submissions of the parties and third parties in the Panel's examination of the case.

27.   Each party shall submit an integrated executive summary of the facts and arguments as presented to the Panel in its written submissions and oral statements, in accordance with the timetable adopted by the Panel. This integrated summary may include a summary of responses to questions. The integrated executive summary submitted by each complainant shall not exceed 30 pages. The integrated executive summary submitted by Australia shall not exceed 40 pages. The Panel will not summarize in the descriptive part of its report, or annex to its report, the parties' responses to questions.

28.   Each third party shall submit an executive summary of its arguments as presented in its written submission and statement in accordance with the timetable adopted by the Panel. This summary may also include a summary of responses to questions, where relevant. The executive summary to be provided by each third party shall not exceed 5 pages.

Interim review

29.   Following issuance of the interim reports, each party may submit a written request to review precise aspects of the interim report in the respective dispute and request a further meeting with the Panel, in accordance with the timetable adopted by the Panel. The right to request such a meeting shall be exercised no later than at the time the written request for review is submitted.

30.   In the event that no further meeting with the Panel is requested, each party may submit written comments on the other party's written request for review, in accordance with the timetable to be adopted by the Panel. Such comments shall be limited to commenting on the other parties' written requests for review.

31.   The interim reports, as well as the final reports prior to their official circulation, shall be kept strictly confidential and shall not be disclosed.

Service of documents

32.   The following procedures regarding service of documents shall apply:

   a.   Each party and third party shall submit all documents to the Panel by filing them with the DS Registry (office No. 2047).

   b.   Each party and third party shall file its documents with the DS Registry and serve copies on the other parties (and third parties where appropriate) by 5.00 p.m. (Geneva time) on the due dates established by the Panel.

   c.   Each party and third party shall file with the DS Registry eight (8) paper copies of all documents it submits to the Panel, except executive summaries submitted in accordance with paragraphs 27 and 28 above, and exhibits. Exhibits may be provided on CD-ROM or DVD. In this case, six (6) CD-ROMs or DVD and two (2) paper copies of such exhibits shall be filed. The paper copies of such exhibits shall be filed no later than 5 p.m. (Geneva time) on the first working day following the due date established by the Panel for the documents to be submitted. The DS Registrar shall stamp the documents with the date and time of the filing.

   d.   Each party and third party shall also provide an electronic copy of all documents it submits to the Panel on the due date, in PDF and in Microsoft Word format, either on a CD-ROM, a DVD, or as an e-mail attachment. If the electronic copy is provided by e-mail, it should be addressed to ****@*wto.org*, with a copy to ****.****@*wto.org*, ****.****@*wto.org*, ****.****@*wto.org*, ****.****@*wto.org*, ****.****@*wto.org* and ****.****@*wto.org*. If a CD-ROM or DVD is provided, it shall be filed with the DS Registry. The electronic PDF version shall constitute the official version for the purposes of the record of the dispute.

   e.   Each party shall serve any document submitted to the Panel directly on the other party to the dispute. Each party shall, in addition, serve on all third parties having notified their interest in the dispute its written submissions in advance of the first substantive meeting with the Panel.

   f.   Each third party shall serve any document submitted to the Panel directly on all of the parties and on those other third parties having notified their interest in the same dispute. Each party and third party shall confirm, in writing, that copies have been served as required at the time it provides each document to the Panel.

   g.   A party or third party may submit its documents to a party or third party in electronic format only.

h.   The procedure described in subparagraph g. shall also apply to submissions filed pursuant to paragraphs 13, 14 and 22.

i.   The Panel shall provide the parties with an electronic version of the descriptive part, the interim report and the final report, as well as of other documents as appropriate. When the Panel transmits to the parties or third parties both paper and electronic versions of a document, the paper version shall constitute the official version for the purposes of the record of the dispute.

33.   The Panel reserves the right to modify these procedures as necessary, after consultation with the parties.

ANNEX A-2

ADDITIONAL WORKING PROCEDURES CONCERNING STRICTLY CONFIDENTIAL INFORMATION[1]

Adopted on 1 October 2014,
as amended on 15 December 2014

The following procedures apply to strictly confidential information (SCI) submitted in the course of the Panel proceedings.

1.   For the purposes of these proceedings, Strictly Confidential Information (SCI) means any financial, commercial or government confidential information: (a) that is clearly designated as such by the party or third party submitting it; (b) that is not otherwise accessible to the general public; and (c) that is commercially sensitive or, in the case of government confidential information, the release of which could reasonably be considered to cause or threaten to cause harm to the public interest, including by impairing the ability of the government to conduct its work. Each party and third party shall act in good faith and exercise restraint in designating information as SCI. The Panel shall have the right to intervene in any manner that it deems appropriate, if it is of the view that restraint in the designation of SCI is not being exercised. If a party, or the Panel, contests the designation of information as SCI, the party or third party designating the information shall provide reasons for the designation within three (3) working days. After giving the parties an opportunity to comment on the justification provided within three (3) working days, the Panel shall decide on the designation of the information.

2.   As required by paragraph 3 of the Working Procedures of the Panel[2], the deliberations of the Panel and the documents submitted to it shall be kept confidential. Further, as required by Article 18.2 of the DSU a party or third party having access to information designated as SCI submitted in these Panel proceedings shall treat it as confidential and shall not disclose that information other than to those persons authorized to receive it pursuant to these working procedures. Each party and third party is responsible for ensuring that its employees, outside advisers and experts comply with these Additional Working Procedures to protect SCI.

---

[1]   These additional procedures were originally adopted on 1 October 2014 in accordance with the Panel's Working Procedures adopted on 17 June 2014, as amended on 1 October 2014. These additional procedures are hereby amended in accordance with the Panel's Working Procedures as further amended on 15 December 2014.
[2]   Adopted on 17 June 2014, as amended on 1 October 2014, and as further amended on 15 December 2014.

3.   Panel Members and employees of the WTO Secretariat assigned to the present dispute shall have access to SCI submitted in these proceedings. Employees of the Governments of Ukraine, Honduras, Dominican Republic, Cuba, Indonesia, and Australia shall have access to SCI submitted in these Panel proceedings to the extent necessary for their involvement in their official capacity in DS434, DS435, DS441, DS458 or DS467 proceedings. Subject to paragraph 4 of the Working Procedures of the Panel, parties may give access to SCI to outside advisers and experts providing assistance to the parties in these proceedings and their clerical staff. SCI, whether submitted as part of a document or in oral form to the Panel, shall not be disclosed to employees, officers or commercial agents of an enterprise engaged in the tobacco industry, including in the production, export or import of tobacco products, or employees or officers of an industry association of such enterprises, unless the information is business confidential information that pertains exclusively to the enterprise of which the person is an employee, officer or commercial agent.

4.   Third parties to these Panel proceedings shall receive the confidential versions of the first written submissions of the parties to the Panel and redacted versions of exhibits to the first written submissions of the parties where those exhibits contain SCI. In addition, third parties shall receive the parties' written rebuttals, the final version of the parties' opening and closing statements at the Panel's first and second substantive meetings, and any exhibits to these, with the understanding that third parties shall receive redacted versions of such rebuttals, statements or exhibits where these contain SCI.

5.   The redacted versions of the parties' written rebuttals and statements mentioned in paragraph 4, as well as any exhibits thereto or to the parties' first written submissions, containing SCI shall be sufficient to convey a reasonable understanding of the nature of the information at issue. Employees of the Governments of third parties to any of the above listed disputes, and their outside advisers, may request access to the non-redacted version of an exhibit to a party's first written submission containing SCI for the purpose of participating effectively in the Panel proceeding. The Panel, in consultation with the parties, shall decide whether to grant access to such SCI, taking into consideration the sensitivity of the information and the need for the third party to see the information in order to ensure that their interests as a third party are fully taken into account. If granted, the third party's access to such SCI will take place on the premises of the WTO Secretariat, unless good cause is shown for an alternative arrangement. Third parties shall be entitled to review, but not to copy, the SCI accessed on the premises of the WTO Secretariat.

6.   Each party and third party shall maintain a list of the names of all outside advisers and experts provided with access to SCI. The list shall be updated when additional outside advisers or experts are provided with access to SCI.

7.   A party or third party submitting or referring to SCI in any document submitted to the Panel (including in any exhibits) shall mark the cover and the first page of the document containing any such information with the words "Contains Strictly Confidential Information". The specific information in

question shall be enclosed in double brackets, as follows: [[xx.xxx.xx]], and the notation "Contains Strictly Confidential Information" shall be marked at the top of each page containing the SCI. In the case of an oral statement containing SCI, the party or third party making such a statement shall inform the Panel before making it that the statement will contain SCI, and the Panel will ensure that only persons authorized to have access to SCI pursuant to these Additional Working Procedures are in the room to hear that statement.

8.   Any SCI that is submitted in binary-encoded form shall be clearly marked with the statement "Strictly Confidential Information" on a label on the storage medium, and clearly marked with the statement "Strictly Confidential Information" in the binary-encoded files.

9.   The parties, third parties, the Panel, the WTO Secretariat, and any others permitted to have access to documents containing SCI under the terms of these Additional Working Procedures shall store all documents containing SCI so as to prevent unauthorized access to such information.

10.   The Panel will not disclose in its report any information designated as SCI under these Additional Working Procedures. The Panel may, however, make statements of conclusion based on such information. Before the Panel makes its final report(s) publicly available, the Panel shall give each party or third party an opportunity to ensure that any information it has designated as SCI is not contained in the report(s).

11.   At the conclusion of the dispute[3], and within a period to be fixed by the Panel, each party shall return all documents (including electronic material) containing SCI, submitted during the Panel proceedings, to the party that submitted such documents, certify in writing to the Panel and the other parties that all such documents have been destroyed, or otherwise protect the SCI against public disclosure, consistent with the party's obligations under its domestic laws. The WTO Secretariat shall have the right to retain one copy of each of the documents containing SCI for the archives of the WTO.

12.   If a party formally notifies the DSB of its decision to appeal pursuant to Article 16.4 of the DSU, the Secretariat will inform the Appellate Body of these procedures and will transmit to the Appellate Body any SCI governed by these procedures, including any submissions containing information designated as SCI under these working procedures. Such transmission shall occur separately from the rest of the Panel record, to the extent possible.

---

[3]   Where this is defined as when (a) the Panel or Appellate Body report is adopted by the DSB, or the DSB decides by consensus not to adopt the Panel or the Appellate Body report; (b) the authority for the establishment of the Panel lapses under Article 12.12 of the DSU; or (c) a mutually satisfactory solution is notified to the DSB under Article 3.6 of the DSU.

13.   At the request of a party, and in consultation with the other parties, the Panel may apply these working procedures or an amended form of these working procedures to protect information that does not fall within the scope of the information set out in paragraph 1. The Panel may, with the consent of the parties, waive any part of these procedures.

ANNEX B

ARGUMENTS OF THE PARTIES

Contents		Page
Annex B-1	Integrated executive summary of the arguments of Honduras	5267
Annex B-2	Integrated executive summary of the arguments of the Dominican Republic	5313
Annex B-3	Integrated executive summary of the arguments of Cuba	5357
Annex B-4	Integrated executive summary of the arguments of Indonesia	5382
Annex B-5	Integrated executive summary of the arguments of Australia	5410

ANNEX B-1

INTEGRATED EXECUTIVE SUMMARY OF THE ARGUMENTS OF HONDURAS

I.   INTRODUCTION

1.   This dispute is about whether Australia has breached its WTO obligations through the means by which it has sought to change consumer behaviour relating to smoking. The dispute is *not* about whether smoking is dangerous or whether it affects the health of many people in Australia and around the world – it is and it does. Similarly, the dispute is *not* about whether governments have the right to regulate tobacco products and to take measures to decrease smoking prevalence and consumption – clearly they do. Indeed, Honduras has itself implemented comprehensive tobacco regulation measures and shares Australia's goal of reducing smoking prevalence and tobacco consumption. Honduras certainly does not wish to constrain a government's ability to regulate tobacco products in a WTO-consistent manner where necessary and justifiable. Honduras differs with Australia on the critical point that no matter how legitimate the objective that a WTO Member pursues through domestic regulation, it must also respect its WTO obligations. Honduras considers the means chosen to fulfill Australia's smoking reduction objective are unlawful, ineffective and disproportionate.

2.   Australia maintains the "plain packaging measures" at issue in this dispute through the following legal instruments: (i) the Tobacco Plain Packaging Act 2011, Act No. 148 of 2011, "An Act to discourage the use of tobacco products, and for related purposes" (*"TPP Act"*); (ii) the Tobacco Plain Packaging Regulations 2011 (Select Legislative Instrument 2011, No. 263), as amended by the Tobacco Plain Packaging Amendment Regulation 2012 (No. 1)

(Select Legislative Instrument 2012, No. 29) ("*TPP Regulations*"); and (iii) the Trade Marks Amendment (Tobacco Plain Packaging) Act 2011, Act No. 149 of 2011, "An Act to amend the Trade Marks Act 1995, and for related purposes" ("*Trade Marks Amendment Act 2011*").

3.   The plain packaging measures impose a number of requirements that seek to standardize the presentation of the product and the packaging of tobacco products in Australia. Most notably, Australia's TPP Act provides that "[n]o trade mark may appear anywhere on a tobacco product" other than as permitted by the TPP Regulations. The TPP Act also provides, *inter alia*, that "[n]o trade mark may appear anywhere on the retail packaging of tobacco products", permitting the appearance of only the brand, variant, business or company name and other marks pursuant to the relevant legislative requirements. The appearance of the brand name is regulated by the TPP Act and the TPP Regulations. The TPP Act further requires that tobacco product packages be "drab dark brown" (specified as Pantone 448C in the Regulations) in a matte finish, with no other colours, logos or brand features visible on the package, other than the brand and variant name in a standardised form and font below the graphic health warnings ("GHWs"). Tobacco product packaging will continue to contain GHWs, which are increasing from 30 to 75 percent of the front surface of each package and continue to cover 90 per cent of the back surface of the package. The TPP Act and TPP Regulations also regulate the physical features of retail tobacco packaging, imposing a standardised type and size of packaging. Cigarette packs and cartons must have a standardised shape with no decorative elements, and cigarette packs must have flip-top openings. The lining of cigarette packs must only be foil backed with paper or a material allowed by the TPP Regulations. Similar standardisation requirements are imposed on cigars and their packaging.

4.   As explained in greater detail below, Honduras claims that Australia's plain packaging measures are inconsistent with its obligations under the Agreement on Trade-Related Aspects of Intellectual Property Rights ("TRIPS Agreement") and the Agreement on Technical Barriers to Trade ("TBT Agreement").

5.   The tobacco sector is an essential part of Honduras' economy. Internationally, the high quality tobacco grown by Honduras is becoming more and more in demand to manufacture cigars. This favours cigar exports, which generate large amounts of local employment in specific areas of the country, such as the Department of El Paraíso situated in Honduras' eastern region. The tobacco industry produces benefits in the primary and secondary sectors of the tobacco value and supply chain. In 2011, Honduras' cigar exports amounted to USD 80 million, while cigarette exports totalled USD 30 million. In the period 2006-2010, the Honduran tobacco sector made annual contributions of 0.4 per cent to the country's Gross Domestic Product. Moreover, the tobacco sector generates almost 14,000 direct and indirect jobs in Honduras. Honduras aspires to develop high-value tobacco-related trademarks and geographical indications ("GIs") in the future. Indeed, the loss of the opportunity to compete on the basis

of high-value brands, including in the cigar segment, is one of the reasons why Honduras has decided to initiate this dispute.

6.   As a general matter, it must also be noted that the World Health Organization's Framework Convention on Tobacco Control ("FCTC") does not require that Parties implement plain packaging measures in their jurisdiction. Article 11 of the FCTC requires Parties to adopt and implement effective measures to ensure that tobacco product packaging and labelling do not promote a tobacco product "by any means that are false, misleading, deceptive or likely to create an erroneous impression". There is no reference to plain packaging in Article 11 of the FCTC. Article 13 of the FCTC requires Parties to undertake a comprehensive ban of all tobacco advertising, promotion and sponsorship, in accordance with their constitution or constitutional principles. There is no reference to plain packaging in Article 13 of the FCTC. Neither do the FCTC Guidelines for Article 11 and Article 13 impose any obligation to adopt plain packaging. These non-binding Guidelines merely suggest that Parties "should consider" the adoption of plain packaging. The record shows that, at the time these Guidelines were considered for adoption, the WHO's legal counsel noted that "restricting or eliminating registered trademarks might be seen in some jurisdictions as an infringement of those trademark rights" and that "the situation was not the same in all countries since it depended on national law and the international obligations of the State concerned". The "consideration" that the Guidelines recommend should clearly include an examination of whether such measures would be consistent with the Party's obligations under international law, such as the obligations under the WTO Agreements for those Parties also Members of the WTO. Honduras notes that the FCTC itself requests Parties to adopt "effective" and "evidence-based" tobacco control measures. In Article 2.1, the FCTC provides that "stricter requirements" that go beyond what is required by the FCTC, like plain packaging, must be "in accordance with international law", which includes WTO law.

II.   AUSTRALIA'S PLAIN PACKAGING MEASURES VIOLATE THE TRIPS AGREEMENT

A.   Introduction

7.   The importance of intellectual property rights to modern society and the global economy is evident. Intellectual property rights are present in the goods and services that are bought and sold on a daily basis. Trademark protection is thus an essential part ofthe multilateral trading system. Trademarks are an essential instrument of fair competition. Intellectual property rights are private rights that WTO Members must protect. Part II, Section 2 of the TRIPS Agreement imposes a number of obligations on Members in terms of the protection of a special category of intellectual property rights, trademarks. In so doing, the TRIPS Agreement disciplines the regulatory freedom of Members. The TRIPS Agreement reflects a number of principles of trademark protection that are fundamental, namely, that the functional criterion of "distinctiveness" is

the essence of the trademark; that the validity and protectability of a trademark is to be examined on an individual basis and not as part of a group based on, for example, the type of trademark or the nature of the product; that trademarks are private and exclusive rights the scope of protection and power of enforcement of which depend on the action or inaction of the trademark owner; that "use" of the mark is essential to the creation, maintenance and enforcement of trademark rights; that trademarks are to be protected "as is" and thus in the form that they are registered and used; and that trademarks are important elements of "fair competition" in the market. These different principles are reflected in the text of the TRIPS Agreement. It is this text that forms the basis of Honduras' claims. Australia's plain packaging measures are inconsistent with each of these principles and thus violate the TRIPS Agreement because they deny the functional nature of trademarks as signs to distinguish products.

8.   In response to practically all of Honduras' claims under the TRIPS Agreement, Australia argues that the acceptance of Honduras' arguments would mean that WTO Members will no longer be able to regulate or ban the sale of products that pose risks to health or to adopt comprehensive advertising bans for tobacco products because such general product or advertising bans would violate the TRIPS Agreement. These concerns are without merit. The TRIPS Agreement provides ample flexibility and policy space to Members to deal with trademarks that pose concerns from a public health perspective both at the stage of registration and thereafter when the trademark is used on a product in the market. There is no need to eviscerate trademark rights in order to regulate products that may be harmful to health. The fact that the sale of products can be restricted or prohibited is clear from Article 19.1 of the TRIPS Agreement, which explicitly recognises that Members may adopt measures banning products, even though these measures may affect incidentally the use of the trademarks for those products. Furthermore, to the extent that it is the trademark rather than the product that is a cause of concerns, the TRIPS Agreement provides broad regulatory authority to deal with such trademark-specific concerns based on an individual assessment of the mark. Article 6*quinquies*(B) of the Paris Convention and Article 15.2 of the TRIPS Agreement (relating to registration and validity of trademarks), and Article 20 (in so far as it concerns flexibility for use-related requirements) allow Members to take measures to deal with specific trademarks that are considered to be misleading or deceptive for example. Thus, contrary to Australia's assertions, Honduras' interpretation of the TRIPS Agreement does not lead to the conclusion that the TRIPS Agreement prevents restrictions on the sale of addictive and/or dangerous products. Australia's general rebuttal arguments erroneously suggesting that Honduras is developing an absolute and positive "right to use" argument that would unduly restrict regulatory policy are in error, and merely seek to divert the Panel's attention from the proper scrutiny of the consistency of the plain packaging measures with WTO law. The TRIPS Agreement does not prevent Members from regulating the product or banning product advertisements. As evidenced by the Australian advertisement ban in place since 1992, trademarks can still

maintain their distinctiveness, and trademark rights can still be enforced when allowed to be used on products, even under a general ban on advertising.

B. Australia's Plain Packaging Measures are Inconsistent with Article 15.4 of the TRIPS Agreement

9.   Honduras submits that Australia's trademark restrictions on tobacco products and retail packaging violate Article 15.4, read in the context of Article 15.1 of the TRIPS Agreement, by preventing inherently non-distinctive signs from ever acquiring distinctiveness through use. A sign that is not distinctive, either inherently or as a result of its use, cannot be registered as a "trademark". Under the plain packaging measures, the nature of the goods (namely, tobacco products) to which the sign is to be applied, is the reason for not permitting the use of the non-inherently distinctive sign. Therefore, the nature of the goods forms an obstacle to the registration of those otherwise non-inherently distinctive signs as "trademarks" in violation of Article 15.4 of the TRIPS Agreement.

10.   Article 15.4 provides that "[t]he nature of the goods or services to which a trademark is to be applied shall in no case form an obstacle to registration of the trademark". The "goods" at issue are "tobacco products" that are defined in Section 4 of the *TPP Act* and fall within the scope of the plain packaging measures. Article 15.1 defines the term "trademark" in a broad manner as: "[a]ny sign, or any combination of signs, capable of distinguishing the goods or services of one undertaking from those of other undertakings". Importantly, Article 15.1, third sentence, further establishes that "[w]here signs are not inherently capable of distinguishing the relevant goods ..., Members may make registrability *depend on distinctiveness acquired through use*" (emphasis added). Thus, use is a critical condition precedent for the registration of such signs, explicitly recognised in the TRIPS Agreement. In fact, use is the *only* means by which an inherently non-distinctive sign may acquire distinctiveness for a particular product. Inhibiting use, by definition, poses an obstacle to the ability of non-distinctive signs to acquire distinctiveness and, as a result, to become eligible for registration.

11.   According to Article 15.1 (third sentence), WTO Members "may" make registrability of inherently non-distinctive marks dependent on distinctiveness acquired through use. Australia has exercised this option in its *Trade Marks Act 1995*, which focuses heavily on use permeating all aspects of the "life cycle" of a trademark in Australia. It is thus clear that the assessment of distinctiveness of an inherently non-distinctive mark under Australia's *Trade Marks Act 1995* would necessarily have to focus upon *the extent of the use* of this mark prior to the filing date of the application for its registration. The extent of use would thus be determinative of whether the mark would be registered.

12.   In light of the above background, the plain packaging trademark restrictions, by prohibiting the use of non-word marks (such as design, figurative, or composite marks), make it impossible for an applicant to acquire distinctiveness through actual and extensive use. This prohibition of the use of non-inherently distinctive signs applies only to tobacco products. Australia,

therefore, has created an obstacle to registration based on the nature of the goods in a manner inconsistent with Article 15.4 of the TRIPS Agreement.

13.   Australia has not presented any evidence showing that non-inherently distinctive signs that acquire distinctiveness through use can be registered as trademarks for tobacco products. Instead, Australia attempted to rebut Honduras' claim by making general assertions that are not supported by the text of the TRIPS Agreement and that misrepresent the effect of the plain packaging measures under Australian law. First, Australia alleged that the complainants confuse a "sign" with a "trademark", and it asserts that a non-inherently distinctive "sign" that has not yet acquired distinctiveness through use is not a "trademark" and must not be registered as such. This argument is based on circular reasoning and an overly formalistic interpretation of the terms in Article 15.4, isolated from their context. Article 15 focuses on *signs* that either are distinctive or acquire distinctiveness through use and therefore can be registered as *trademarks* and obtain the protection guaranteed by the TRIPS Agreement. The focus of Honduras, and other complainants, on *signs* and whether these signs can be registered as trademarks, without the nature of the product to which they apply being an obstacle to eventual registration, is thus entirely appropriate and consistent with the text and context of Article 15.4. Second, Australia made an unsubstantiated assertion that Section 28 of the *TPP Act* ensures that the operation of the Act does not prevent trademark owners from registering their marks. Australia has never adequately explained how this provision ensures that, under the plain packaging measures, an owner is allowed to register an *inherently non-distinctive sign* in connection with a tobacco product as a trademark. Section 28 does not address the fundamental obligation under Australia's trademark law that only signs that are distinctive merit trademark protection. In particular, pursuant to Section 41(3) of the *Trade Mark Act 1995,* non-inherently distinctive signs will not be able to be registered and protected in Australia *unless they have been used in Australia to such an extent that they do in fact distinguish the goods to which they apply.* Section 28 of the *TPP Act* does not address matters regulated by Section 41(3) of the *Trade Mark Act* – it mainly protects against the loss of registration or protection that could otherwise have been the consequence of the requirement of genuine use of the trademark for maintaining registration and protection.

C.   Australia's Plain Packaging Measures are Inconsistent with Article 16.1 and are not Justified under Article 17 of the TRIPS Agreement

14.   Australia's plain packaging measures violate Article 16.1 of the TRIPS Agreement, which sets forth the minimum guaranteed level of protection to be provided to owners of registered trademarks, namely the exclusive right of the owners to enjoin unauthorised third-party uses of their registered trademarks. The scope of protection guaranteed under Article 16.1 depends on the owner's ability to use its mark and the resulting strength of the mark in the marketplace. The more use is made of the mark, the stronger the mark; and the stronger the

mark, the greater its scope of protection vis-à-vis unauthorised third-party uses. These fundamental principles are commonly recognised, including in Australia's own legislation, which emphasises the importance of the use of trademarks. The inherent dependence of the use of trademark to afford protection to the trademark has been acknowledged by many third parties and authoritative IP associations, including the International Association for the Protection of Intellectual Property ("AIPPI") and MARQUES. Based on a survey of its domestic AIPPI chapters, the Association adopted a Resolution in September 2013 stating: "The continuous and extensive use of a trademark can have an effect on its scope of protection (see, e.g. Article 16 (2) and (3) TRIPS with express reference to Article 6bis Paris Convention), and can contribute to the notoriety, reputation and/or the goodwill/value of the mark. In consequence, a restriction in the nature of plain packaging amounts to a serious impairment of the trademark rights and can cause considerable damage to the trademark right holder". MARQUES, the leading European trademark association, noted in its *amicus curiae* brief that, "[a] measure that prevents the mark from maintaining its scope of protection or from growing its notoriety and strength through use as intended is thus inconsistent with the rights conferred on registered trademark owners under Article 16.1 TRIPS. For certain marks that are not inherently distinctive, like colours for example, a measure that prevents them from being used, like standardized packaging, could actually lead to these marks becoming 'generic' again". The link between use and distinctiveness/scope of protection of a trademark has also been explicitly acknowledged by the panel in *EC – Trademarks and Geographical Indications (Australia)*.

15.   Australia's plain packaging measures significantly reduce – if not completely eliminate – the ability of the owners of tobacco-related trademarks to prevent their unauthorised third-party use by prohibiting the use of a wide array of trademarks on tobacco products and packaging that were previously used to distinguish tobacco products, in a manner inconsistent with Article 16.1. The courts will find that there is no likelihood of confusion because the trademark has lost much of its strength as a result of mandatory non-use. This, in turn, will lead to a further weakening of the distinctiveness of the trademark as similar signs on similar products will likely be allowed to be used. This means that it is not just the original prohibition on use that weakens the trademark and its scope of protection; rather this prohibition allows further encroachment on the previously protected "territory" of the trademark leading to what Professor Dinwoodie in his expert report finding that plain packaging violates Article 16.1 referred to as "death by a thousand cuts". Article 16 requires Members to grant private rights of enforcement and protection in order to allow the trademark owner to protect the distinctiveness of the trademark. The strength of the mark and the level of protection are to be determined by the actions of the trademark owners exercising their private rights. Plain packaging reduces protection below this minimum guaranteed level.

16.   The most plausible situation in which an infringement could occur is with respect to the use of a similar trademark (e.g. a different word mark with a

similar combination of colours or design elements) on a similar product (e.g. electronic cigarettes or various tobacco accessories). The reduced ability of consumers to recognize the original trademark will make it easier for an unauthorised third party to demonstrate that its use is not likely to deceive or cause confusion with the original mark, and, therefore, does not constitute an infringement of this mark. Consequently, the plain packaging measures prevent the owners of duly registered tobacco-related trademarks from enforcing their rights under Article 16.1, by enjoining unauthorised third-party uses.

17.   However, Honduras does not rule out that there could be a violation of Article 16.1 under other scenarios of infringements contemplated under this provision, in particular the use of identical signs, such as colours or design elements, on similar goods. As the distinctiveness of tobacco-related trademarks recedes and their protection weakens, it is likely that a usurper would be able to encroach more closely on the registrant's marks, possibly even including word-marks. The more distinctive a mark, the higher degree of protection it enjoys. The measures will have an even stronger effect on non-inherently distinctive signs registered as trademarks, as the distinctiveness of these signs (acquired through use) will (without their use) be even more weakened in the eyes of consumers. Such marks will inevitably lose their protection.

18.   Australia did not respond to Honduras' arguments on the importance of the use of the mark to the strength of the trademark and thus to its scope of protection and the minimum guaranteed enforcement rights under Article 16.1 of the TRIPS Agreement. Instead, Australia addressed Honduras' claim at an upstream, abstract level, by claiming that Article 16.1 confers only a negative right to prevent the use of similar signs by third parties and not a "positive right to use" a trademark. In Australia's view, Article 16.1 does not concern "the public regulatory relationship between owners of trademarks and sovereign governments". A slight variation of the above argument is Australia's contention that Article 16.1 does not create the "right of confusion", and that Article 16.1 does not serve to protect the "economic function" of trademarks to distinguish the goods, because this would have otherwise implied the existence of a "positive right to use". Honduras does not consider that the use of labels such as "negative rights" or "positive right to use" are helpful for the Panel's work of interpreting and applying Article 16.1. These labels do not reflect treaty language and are thus not helpful to discerning the meaning of WTO provisions. More importantly, Honduras has never asserted that there exists an absolute positive right to use trademarks that results from their registration. Article 16 imposes an obligation on Members to guarantee a minimum level of private rights to trademark owners that allows them to successfully protect the distinctiveness and source-indicating function of their marks in the context of infringement proceedings. The TRIPS-obligation of WTO Members is to guarantee that the registered trademark owner will be able to successfully do so, if he so wishes. A measure that undermines negative enforcement rights of trademark holders under Article 16.1 by diminishing the distinctive power of all trademarks registered with respect to a specific product (such as *in casu* plain

packaging) would necessarily violate this provision that seeks to protect the distinctiveness of the trademark.

19.   Similarly, Honduras has never argued that Article 16.1 creates a "right to confusion". Rather, Honduras noted that the "likelihood of confusion" is a normative assessment that is relevant in the context of any infringement proceeding. The strength of the mark, as determined by the extent to which the mark is used in trade, is a key aspect of such a "likelihood of confusion" assessment, as are the other key factors of the infringement analysis, such as the similarity of signs and similarity of products.

20.   Section 28 of the TPP Act on which Australia relies to argue that the "negative" rights of trademark owners are not affected does not address the problem of the erosion of distinctiveness, and consequently the scope of protection, of registered tobacco-related trademarks resulting from the operation of *the TPP Act*. Similarly, Section 28 does not regulate the issue of the maintenance of protection of tobacco-related marks vis-à-vis their potential use by third parties.

21.   In light of the above, Australia's limited rebuttal fails to address the arguments of Honduras and thus Honduras' *prima facie* case of a violation of Article 16.1 stands. In the event the Panel finds the plain packaging trademark restrictions are inconsistent with Article 16.1, Honduras submits that these measures cannot be justified under Article 17 of the TRIPS Agreement. The plain packaging measures do not constitute "limited exceptions", and they fail to take into account the legitimate interests of the owners of tobacco-related trademarks in using their original trademarks in connection with the relevant goods. In any event, Australia did not invoke the exception under Article 17.

D.   Australia's Plain Packaging Measures are Inconsistent with Article 2.1 of the TRIPS Agreement and Article 6quinquies A(1) of the Paris Convention

22.   Honduras further submits that the trademark restrictions are inconsistent with Article 6*quinquies* of the Paris Convention, incorporated into the TRIPS Agreement through Article 2.1 thereof. Pursuant to this provision, a trademark registered in the country of origin, a WTO Member must be accepted for filing and protected "as is" in other WTO Members (i.e. "*telle quelle*" principle). This essentially means that WTO Members may not require that a trademark, already registered in the country of origin, be modified or altered as a condition for acceptance for filing *and protection* in their territory. WTO Members are obliged to accept for filing and to protect a trademark in the original form in which it was registered in the country of origin.

23.   The plain packaging measures are inconsistent with Article 6*quinquies*(A)(1) of the Paris Convention incorporated through Article 2.1 of the TRIPS Agreement, because Australia fails to protect, in its original form, every tobacco-related trademark that has been previously registered in the country of origin. From a practical perspective, the obligation to afford "protection"

necessarily requires Members to allow some minimal use of trademarks in the course of trade, since use is of crucial importance for the acquisition, scope, maintenance and enforcement of trademark rights. This is true in particular for design (image) marks and composite marks, the protection of which may inherently depend on use, but also for word-marks. Moreover, the TRIPS Agreement itself, in its preamble and footnote 3, recognises that the term "protection" under Article 6*quinquies*(A)(1) also applies to the use of the trademark.

24.   In response to Honduras' claim, Australia asserts that the requirement under Article 6*quinquies*(A)(1) that a trademark "be accepted for filing and protected as is" refers merely to the protection conferred as a result of the registration, and does not set minimum standards with respect to how that trademark is to be protected. Australia's response is based on its erroneous understanding of the legal standard under Article 6*quinquies*(A)(1), the nature of this provision within the TRIPS framework, as well as of Honduras' claim. First, Article 6*quinquies*(A)(1) establishes two *independent* obligations: (i) to accept for filing "as is", and then (ii) to protect "as is" every trademark duly registered in the country of origin. Australia reads out from the scope of Article 6*quinquies*(A)(1) the terms "*protected* as is" by suggesting that Members satisfy the above two obligations by merely allowing the registration of trademarks "as is". Australia's interpretation is, therefore, inconsistent with the principle of the effective treaty interpretation, recognised by the Appellate Body in previous disputes. Australia's contention that Honduras' claim is based on "the right to use" argument is also incorrect. Honduras has not argued that the terms of Article 6*quinquies* A(1) create a "right to use". Rather, in Honduras' view, the ability to use a trademark is an integral part of the availability, acquisition, scope, maintenance and enforcement of trademark rights, and is, therefore, of crucial importance for the effective "protection" of a trademark "as is". This link between use and protection is recognized by the TRIPS Agreement and Australia's own legislation. Australia has never disputed this link.

E.   **Australia's Plain Packaging Measures are Inconsistent with Article 20 of the TRIPS Agreement**

1.   **The plain packaging measures are special requirements that unjustifiably encumber the use of trademarks in the course of trade**

25.   Australia's plain packaging trademark restrictions are inconsistent with Article 20 of the TRIPS Agreement, which provides that "the use of a trademark in the course of trade shall not be unjustifiably encumbered by special requirements, such as ... use in a special form or use in a manner detrimental to its capability to distinguish the goods or services of one undertaking from those of other undertakings".

26.   The plain packaging trademark restrictions constitute the "ultimate encumbrance", because they prohibit the use of almost all trademarks on tobacco

products and packaging in the course of trade (i.e. retail trade), and to the extent that they permit certain word-marks, such as brand and variant names, they require use of such marks in a highly regularised, standardised form and font.

27.   The plain packaging measures encumber the use of a trademark "by special requirements". This is so because the plain packaging measures impose requirements specifically and directly on the use of trademarks. In fact, the measures' trademark restrictions fall under two of the three examples of "special requirements" listed in Article 20: (a) the use of a trademark in a special form; and (b) the use in a manner detrimental to the capability of a trademark to distinguish the goods of one undertaking from those of other undertakings. The trademark restrictions prescribe the use of a tobacco-related trademark in a special form, as they only allow the display of particular types of word-marks (the brand and variant name in a standardized format) on tobacco products and retail packaging. All other types of trademarks (e.g. design (image) marks and composite marks) cannot be displayed on tobacco products and packaging. In addition, the plain packaging trademark restrictions prescribe "use in a manner *detrimental to the capability of a trademark to distinguish the goods* of one undertaking from those of other undertakings". One of the core objectives of the plain packaging measures is to make all retail packages for tobacco products plain – i.e. by definition non-distinctive.

28.   The plain packaging measures encumber the use of the trademark "in the course of trade" because they prohibit the use of certain tobacco-related trademarks (i.e. design (or image) marks and composite marks) and prescribe how word marks can be used on tobacco products and packaging "in retail sale which is undeniably encumbering the use of the trademark "in the course of trade".

29.   The special requirements imposed by the plain packaging measures are "unjustifiable" by their very nature, because they deviate from the default rule under the TRIPS Agreement that trademarks must be regulated based on their individual features. The text and context of Article 20 confirm this basic approach under the TRIPS Agreement. Trademark rights, in terms of trademark acquisition, registration, maintenance and enforcement, are acquired on individual basis. This is precisely why the term "*a* trademark" is used in its singular form in Article 20 as well as most other provisions of the Agreement. The plain packaging trademark restrictions are not of a limited nature, addressing only the specific feature of the allegedly problematic tobacco-related trademark, or a narrow group of these trademarks. The plain packaging measures constitute an indiscriminate restriction on all trademarks on tobacco products and packaging, regardless of whether these trademarks undermine Australia's public health objective. Australia itself expressly acknowledged that it does not have any concerns about the specific trademarks that are prevented from being used by the plain packaging measures thus confirming the "unjustifiable" nature of the measures.

30.   Moreover, by prohibiting the use of all tobacco-related trademarks, other than those prescribed by the *TPP Act*, the plain packaging measures eviscerate

the substance of the trademark protection stipulated in the TRIPS Agreement. In other words, these measures defeat the fundamental principle of the TRIPS Agreement that, in normal circumstances, trademarks must be used in the course of trade so as to enable them to fulfil their core function to distinguish products of different undertakings. Such measures are manifestly "unreasonable", constitute an abusive exercise of a Member's right in a way that disregards Members' obligation to provide effective and adequate protection of intellectual property rights and, therefore, amount to an encumbrance that is "unjustifiable" by its very nature and inconsistent with Article 20 of the TRIPS Agreement. For these reasons, the plain packaging trademark restrictions encumber the use of trademarks in the course of trade. They are by their very nature unjustifiable and, consequently, inconsistent with Article 20 of the TRIPS Agreement.

31.   *In the alternative*, should the Panel disagree with Honduras' view that the plain packaging trademark restrictions are unjustifiable *by their very nature*, Australia failed to satisfy its burden of demonstrating that its measures are justifiable under Article 20 of the TRIPS Agreement. Article 20 is a provision that consists of both "prohibitive" and "exception/qualification" elements. It fulfils a dual function of disciplining "special requirements", while, at the same time, providing Members with the ability to "justify" measures that are necessary for achieving their legitimate objectives, and consistent with the text, context and object and purpose of the TRIPS Agreement. The text, context, as well as the negotiating history of Article 20 confirm that the normal situation is that of unencumbered use.

32.   In considering whether Australia's plain packaging trademark restrictions are justifiable, the Panel should strike an appropriate balance between the interests of effective and adequate protection of trademarks and Australia's right to regulate public health, which are both recognised by the TRIPS Agreement. In Honduras' view, this balance should be achieved by determining whether the measures: (i) make a material contribution to the achievement of their public policy objective; and (ii) constitute the least-restrictive, least trademark encumbering means to achieve this objective in the light of other options that are reasonably available. In varying permutations, these two criteria have been applied for decades – from the GATT 1947 to current WTO law – to delimit the scope of the regulatory autonomy of the GATT/WTO Member in each particular case.

33.   Honduras' test of "unjustifiably" is supported by the ordinary meaning of this term, which denotes measures that are "necessary", "proportionate" and "supported by evidence". In Honduras' view, a measure that does not contribute to achieving its objective, however legitimate the objective is, cannot be properly characterised as "necessary" or "supported by evidence". Similarly, if the legitimate objective of the measure can be achieved by a less-restrictive measure that makes the same, or even higher, degree of contribution to the objective, and is reasonably available, the challenged measure cannot properly be characterised as "proportionate". Honduras' interpretation of the term "unjustifiably" is also supported by the context of Article 20, and the object and

purpose of the TRIPS Agreement, expressed, *inter alia*, in the preamble and Articles 7 and 8.1. These instruments call for a "balanced" approach to regulating the use of trademarks, taking into account the interests of trademark protection, even when adopting measures necessary to protect public health. As explained below, the evidence confirms that the plain packaging measures fail to contribute to the public health objective of reducing smoking prevalence and are for that reason as well "unjustifiable". Less trademark-restrictive alternative measures are reasonably available to Australia and should have been preferred.

2. Australia's response to Honduras' claim is based on its erroneous interpretation of Article 20 of the TRIPS Agreement and must be rejected

34.   Australia responded to Honduras' arguments by advancing several unreasonable interpretations of the legal standard under Article 20 of the TRIPS Agreement, which deprive this provision of any substance. Australia argued that: (i) Article 20 disciplines only use-related "requirements" but not use-related "prohibitions"; (ii) the only "relevant use" of a trademark protected under Article 20 is the use of a trademark to distinguish the goods of different undertakings, which is sufficient to identify the commercial source of the product at issue; and (iii) as long as a special requirement encumbering the use of trademarks has a "rational connection" to a Member's legitimate objective, it must be considered as "justifiable". In addition, Australia asserted that the plain packaging measures are not related to the use of a trademark "in the course of trade" because, *inter alia*, the practical effect of Australian States' retail display ban is that consumers have no opportunity to see tobacco packages or products at the point of sale and thus "in the course of trade". All these arguments are untenable, flawed and based on the erroneous interpretation of Article 20. They must, therefore, be rejected.

(a)   Special requirements on use include prohibitions

35.   Australia suggests that a Member enjoys an absolute freedom to prohibit the use of a trademark in the course of trade. Under Australia's logic, Article 20 covers limited restrictions (encumbering requirements), but not complete restrictions (prohibitions). Such a proposition does not make any sense. Australia's lack of textual support for its approach is clear from its avoidance of any interpretation based on the ordinary meaning of the terms of Article 20. Australia attempts to distinguish between "requirements" and "prohibitions" so that limited restrictions are covered, but that the ultimate encumbrance would be excluded. This interpretation is not consistent with the ordinary meaning of the term "requirements", which includes limitations as well as prohibitions. Honduras also notes that the plain packaging measures fall under two of the three examples of "special requirements" mentioned explicitly in Article 20, which confirms that the measures at issue can be properly characterised as "special requirements" that encumber the use of a trademark within the meaning of Article 20. Many third parties agree with Honduras' reading of Article 20, in

particular the term "special requirement", and do not support Australia's categorical view that a prohibition on use cannot be deemed to be a "special requirement".

36.   Australia also raised alleged "systemic implications" of a contrary interpretation of Article 20, by asserting that, if Article 20 encompasses also measures that prohibit the use of a trademark, this could lead to the conclusion, for example, that prohibitions on advertising in print or broadcast media fall within the scope of Article 20. This argument is without merit. A general regulatory measure, such as an advertising ban, is not a "special requirement" on the use of a trademark, as it does not address distinctive elements of a trademark, and its application is not limited to a particular aspect of trademarks. The term "special" highlights that Article 20 is concerned with trademark requirements that "specifically" impact the conditions for the use of the trademark, by imposing requirements on the commercial use of the trademark. Requirements that incidentally affect the use of a trademark but are unrelated to the mark, such as general advertising bans, are not "special requirements" for the purpose of Article 20. Nor would this general measure fall under any of the examples of special requirements set out in Article 20.

(b)   The TRIPS Agreement does not distinguish between the source-identification and other functions that trademarks may fulfil in the market

37.   Australia further argues that the only "relevant use" of a trademark protected under Article 20 is the use of a trademark to distinguish the goods of different undertakings, which is "sufficient to identify" the commercial source of the product at issue. In this context, Australia suggests that the only trademarks that are *necessary* to distinguish products are clearly presented word-marks – other trademarks fulfils the alleged "advertising function", which is not protected by Article 20. Honduras questions the legal basis on which Australia attempts to bifurcate a trademark to argue that it is only a word-mark, but not a figurative element (design or image mark), that merits protection under Article 20. First, the TRIPS Agreement provides protection for trademarks writ large. It does not draw a distinction between first-class trademarks and second-class trademarks. Trademarks are defined in Article 15.1 of the TRIPS Agreement as any sign, or any combination of signs, capable of distinguishing the goods of one undertaking from those of other undertakings. These signs include figurative elements, which must be eligible for registration as a trademark, and once registered, deserve to be protected under the TRIPS Agreement. Second, Australia errs in trying to distinguish between word-marks and figurative elements in terms of their "neutrally distinguishing function". There is no basis in the TRIPS Agreement or in international intellectual property law generally for asserting that word-marks distinguish products in a neutral manner whereas figurative elements do not, such that non-word marks do not merit the same protection as long as there are other (word) marks that can be used to distinguish products. For example, the TRIPS Agreement does not permit the unauthorised

use of certain trademarks such as figurative marks or elements in a manner inconsistent with Article 16.1, simply because the trademark owner may still be able to use other trademarks such as word-marks that are sufficient to distinguish his products. It is not clear why such an artificial distinction would be valid under Article 20. All trademarks merit the same protection and that protection does not depend on whether the trademark is "necessary" to distinguish a product or not. Third, Honduras disagrees with Australia that Article 20 would always require a complainant to demonstrate that a challenged measure encumbers by special requirements the use of a trademark to *distinguish the goods*. The text of Article 20 makes it clear that, as long as a measure is a "special requirement" that unjustifiably encumbers the use of a trademark in the course of trade, such as a requirement to use the mark together with another mark, it is inconsistent with this provision. Whether a consumer can still distinguish the product does not save such a special requirement. Finally, Honduras notes that Australia's argument is in clear contradiction with its recognition that the different functions that trademarks may fulfill in the market cannot be separated in practice. This means logically that a measure cannot encumber, for example, the alleged "advertising function" of a trademark without also encumbering the "source identification" function of the trademark. Australia's distinction based on the alleged functions of trademarks is not supported by the text of the TRIPS Agreement and does not make logical or practical sense.

(c)   "Unjustifiably" requires more than a mere "rational connection", otherwise Article 20 would not set forth a meaningful discipline

38.   Australia initially argued that special requirements that are covered by Article 20 can nonetheless be "justifiable" encumbrances if there is a "rational connection" between those measures and the pursuit of a Member's public policy objective. Australia tried to rely on WTO case law interpreting the term "unjustifiable discrimination" in the chapeau of Article XX of the GATT 1994 to argue that there is no reason why the term "unjustifiably" would have a significantly different meaning in the context of Article 20 of the TRIPS Agreement than it does in the context of the chapeau of Article XX of the GATT 1994.

39.   Australia's reliance on WTO case law interpreting the terms in the chapeau of Article XX of the GATT 1994 is misplaced. In particular, Honduras considers that: (i) the chapeau of Article XX of the GATT 1994 is an entirely different context, where the term "unjustifiable" is used in combination with terms that are not present in Article 20, such as the terms "arbitrary or unjustifiable discrimination between countries where the same conditions prevail"; (ii) the chapeau of Article XX is part and parcel of a larger two-tiered holistic test, whereas the test of "unjustifiably" under Article 20 is the only tool to "weigh and balance" Members' rights and obligations under the TRIPS Agreement; (iii) Article XX of the GATT 1994 sets out "General Exceptions", whereas Article 20 of the TRIPS Agreement contains a mixture of an affirmative

obligation and permissive elements. In any event, Australia is incorrect in suggesting that, under the chapeau of Article XX of the GATT 1994, discrimination may be justifiable merely because there is a "rational connection" with the policy objective in question. In WTO jurisprudence, the Appellate Body has considered the factor of a "rational connection" as merely one element in a "cumulative" assessment of "unjustifiable discrimination", which involved the analysis of many other factors that Australia failed to address.

40.   It is telling that most third parties, even those generally supportive of Australia's tobacco-control measures, disagree with Australia and agree with Honduras' interpretation of the term "unjustifiably". Probably in the light of this lack of support for its untenable argument, Australia has amended its argument in the course of the proceedings. Australia now agrees that the assessment of the contribution of the measure to the stated objective is an important element of this test, although it still disputes that less restrictive reasonably available alternative measures must also be considered within this test.

(d)   The plain packaging trademark restrictions encumber the use of a trademark "in the course of trade"

41.   Australia adopts an overly narrow reading of the term "in the course of trade" in Article 20, and argues that the plain packaging measures do not encumber the use of a trademark in the "course of trade" because in most Australian States the retail display ban in combination with the general advertising ban prevents a consumer from seeing the trademark until after the point of sale. Australia states, *inter alia*, that the "course of trade" culminates at the point of sale and that insofar as a measure might affect the presentation and use of a trademark after the point of sale, this effect would fall outside the scope of Article 20. In Honduras' view, the term "in the course of trade" in Article 20, but also in Articles 16.1 and 10*bis*, is simply included to distinguish commercial use of trademarks from non-commercial use of trademarks. For example, trademarks are not used "in the course of trade" when trademarks are mentioned in Honduras' submissions. However, use of a trademark in wholesale or retail trade, is undoubtedly "commercial use" of a trademark or use "in the course of trade". This view is based on the ordinary meaning of the terms "course of trade" and "commerce"; it is shared by many third parties, as well as by commentators on the TRIPS Agreement including Australia's own expert. Furthermore, as a matter of fact, Australia errs when it over-states the effects of the retail display ban on the use of trademarks in the "course of trade". In fact, Australia acknowledges that the display ban is not implemented nation-wide without exceptions, as specialist tobacconist shops in the Australian States of Victoria and Western Australia are not subject to the ban. Australia also accepts that even where a display ban is in place, customers can still view the tobacco packaging and products before the purchase is completed.

3. Conclusion

42. In light of the foregoing, Australia failed to rebut Honduras' legal arguments that the plain packaging trademark restrictions are special requirements that unjustifiably encumber the use of a wide array of trademark elements on tobacco products and retail packaging in the course of trade, in a manner inconsistent with Article 20 of the TRIPS Agreement.

F. Australia's Plain Packaging Measures are Inconsistent with Article 10bis of the Paris Convention as Incorporated into the TRIPS Agreement by Article 2.1 of the TRIPS Agreement

43. Australia's plain packaging measures are inconsistent with Articles 10*bis*(1) and 10*bis*(3)(iii) of the Paris Convention because they require the kind of anti-competitive and misleading actions that Australia is under a legal obligation to prevent. Article 10*bis*(1) requires Members to provide "effective protection against unfair competition" resulting from the use of marks on products. Article 10*bis*(1) does not specify the means by which WTO Members can provide this "effective protection". This discretion notwithstanding, the key requirement is that when "unfair competition" exists, some form of "effective protection" must be provided. This key requirement is violated when a Member enacts a domestic law that encourages or requires private economic operators to act in a manner amounting to "unfair competition". This is because, by definition, where a Member encourages or requires acts of unfair competition, that Member cannot be said to be "assur[ing] ... effective protection" against such acts. Nothing in the wording of Article 10*bis* excludes private economic operators acting pursuant to government regulation from the relevant disciplines. Indeed, the panel decision in *Mexico – Telecommunications* supports Honduras' position. Honduras considers that the plain packaging measures violate Article 10*bis*(1) by requiring private economic operators to adopt a uniform trade dress. In this manner, both the trademark restrictions and formatting restrictions of the plain packaging measures oblige manufacturers of tobacco products to compete in the Australian market in a manner that eliminates the possibility of achieving or maintaining product differentiation. This inability to achieve or maintain product differentiation systematically affects premium products and their producers more than lower quality products and producers. This behaviour, referred to as "downtrading", *ex ante* and deliberately, skews conditions of competition to the advantage of producers providing low-price products and to the disadvantage of producers providing high-price products. This direct, and profoundly asymmetrical, impact of Australia's plain packaging measures on the competitive dynamics in the market constitutes "unfair competition" in the Australian market.

44. Honduras' second claim is under Article 10*bis*(3)(iii). This provision is a more specific manifestation of the requirement under Article 10*bis*(1) to ensure effective protection against unfair competition. Article 10*bis*(3)(iii) provides a specific example of conditions of unfair competition that Members are required to provide protection against. Under Article 10*bis*(3)(iii), Members are to

provide protection against unfair competition that consists in "indications or allegations the use of which in the course of trade is liable to mislead the public" as to, *inter alia*, the nature and characteristics of the goods. Australia's plain packaging measures amount to "indications or allegations" through both affirmative indications (the uniformity of the required packaging) and omissions (the mandated absence of distinguishing features). Honduras notes that Australia has not disputed the argument that the packaging adopted by market participants, in response to Australia's legislation, amount to such indications and allegations. These indications or allegations are that all tobacco products are the same, of the same or similar quality, and of the same physical properties. Moreover, these misleading indications or allegations are being used in the "course of trade". Contrary to Australia's allegations, the "course of trade" does not culminate at the point of sale. Any intended post-sale use of the product by the consumer – such as smoking or the mere display – can influence and affect a subsequent purchase of the product by the consumer or by another person. Consumers are liable to be misled because they have come to understand over time that differently packed and differently branded (tobacco) products have different objective physical characteristics. Through experience, consumers also come to associate particular trademarks and imagery with particular quality of the product. Therefore, the removal of the brand imagery, as well as the imposition of uniform packaging design and stick requirements will induce in the minds of consumers the erroneous belief that all tobacco products are essentially the same and that there are no quality differences between them. This belief is factually incorrect because not all products are of the same or similar quality. As a result of the required indications, as well as equally relevant "omissions", consumers are being "misled" in violation of Article 10*bis*(3)(iii).

G.   Australia's Plain Packaging Measures are Inconsistent with Article 22.2(b) of the TRIPS Agreement

45.   Australia's plain packaging measures are inconsistent with Article 22.2(b) of the TRIPS Agreement because Australia fails to provide the legal means, in respect of GIs, for interested parties to prevent "use which constitutes an act of unfair competition". Article 22.2(b) applies the disciplines of Article 10*bis* of the Paris Convention "[i]n respect of geographical indications". The use of the term "[i]n respect of" GIs is broader than use "of" GIs. Under Article 22.2(b), any circumstance relating to the use "[i]n respect of" GIs that has a bearing on competition and results in unfair competition within the meaning of Article 10*bis* must be subject to legal remedies that an interested party can pursue in a WTO Member's system. These severe limitations on the use of GIs prevent GI owners from communicating, through their GIs, differences in quality, taste and other physical characteristics to their consumers and to the broader public. Therefore, consumers of tobacco products will gain the erroneous impression that all tobacco products from all geographical origins are the same and have the same characteristics. This perception, and its resulting impact on competition, is not "fair" because it causes detriment to owners of existing GIs who have invested

time and resources into establishing their GIs as well as of future owners of potential GIs, because they will be unable to develop and establish GIs in the Australian market. This unfair competitive outcome is the outcome exactly intended by the Australian legislator; it is therefore not merely an incidental effect of legitimate regulation, but rather the very legislative purpose of the measure.

H. Australia's Plain Packaging Measures are Inconsistent with Article 24.3 of the TRIPS Agreement

46.   Australia's plain packaging measures are inconsistent with Article 24.3, because Australia has diminished the level of protection of GIs that existed in Australia prior to 1995. The term "geographical indication" includes anything that identifies a good as originating in a particular territory, region or locality, even if the indication is not a topographical term. Consumer perception is critically important to allow a GI to enjoy effective protection. Article 24.3 requires that Members do not diminish a particular level of protection *as a whole*, rather than specific GIs, because the term "that existed" in the French and Spanish versions grammatically refers only to the "level of protection", rather than the "geographical indications". The argument to the contrary is incorrect from both a legal and policy perspective.

47.   Australia's plain packaging measures have reduced the protection afforded to GIs that existed in Australia immediately prior to 1 January 1995. Prior to that date, Australian law permitted owners of GIs to use and maintain already established GIs on their products; to use a word or non-word indication so as to develop GIs by placing these indications on the product; to avail themselves of legal remedies against misleading use; and to obtain a so-called certification mark. Australia has diminished the protection resulting from the above factors because, first, the plain packaging measures make it impossible to use, develop and maintain a word-based GI other than the name of a country. Second, as a result of the plain packaging measures, it is no longer possible to use, develop and maintain a non-word GI. This is because the plain packaging measures do not permit any design elements on the part of the pack not reserved for the GHWs.

48.   Australia's argument that the protection of GIs refers only to negative rights (rights to prevent third parties' illegal use of GIs) is incorrect and, in any event, irrelevant. To the extent that Australian law prior to 1995 included the possibility of GI owners to use the GI – regardless of whether that possibility is labelled a "right to use" (which Australia argues did not exist prior to 1995) or "ability to use" (which Australia accepts existed prior to 1995) – that possibility must be preserved and may not be rolled-back, by virtue of Article 24.3. Hence, Australia's distinction between the "right to use" and the "ability to use" is irrelevant. Furthermore, Australia is wrong in arguing that the words "[i]n implementing this Section" in Article 24.3 limit the application of Article 24.3 only to measures enacted for the sole and explicit purpose of implementation of Section 3 of the TRIPS Agreement. Australia's formalistic argument not only has

no legal basis, but would also open up easy means of circumventing the GI-disciplines of the TRIPS Agreement.

III.   AUSTRALIA'S PLAIN PACKAGING MEASURES VIOLATE THE TBT AGREEMENT

A.   The Plain Packaging Measures are Inconsistent with Article 2.2 of the TBT Agreement

1.   The plain packaging measures constitute technical regulations within the meaning of Annex 1.1 of the TBT Agreement

49.   The plain packaging measures as a whole, i.e. the trademark restrictions and the format restrictions, constitute technical regulations, since they satisfy all three elements of the definition of "technical regulations" of Annex 1.1 of the TBT Agreement identified by the Appellate Body: (i) the measures apply to an identifiable product or group of products; (ii) the measures lays down product characteristics; and (iii) compliance with the product characteristics is mandatory.

50.   Australia argues that the trademark restrictions of the plain packaging measures fall outside the scope of Article 2.2 of the TBT Agreement because this provision does not apply to the "exploitation of intellectual property rights". Australia's contention must be rejected as it lacks any basis in the TBT Agreement. Nothing in the definition of "technical regulation" of Annex 1.1 of the TBT Agreement indicates that a measure, otherwise qualifying as a technical regulation, would fall outside the scope of the TBT Agreement because it also affects the use of intellectual property rights. Honduras notes that Articles 1.4 and 1.5 of the TBT Agreement set out express exceptions to the scope of this Agreement, none of which relate to the protection of intellectual property rights.

2.   The objective pursued by Australia through the plain packaging measures is to reduce smoking prevalence

51.   The determination of the objective pursued by Australia through the plain packaging measures is a critical element in the Panel's assessment of Honduras' claims. Section 3.1 of the *TPP Act* provides that the objective pursued by Australia through the plain packaging measures is to improve public health by reducing smoking prevalence in Australia. Section 3.1(a) of the *TPP Act* stipulates that the objects of the legislation are to "improve public health by" changing smoking behavior related to smoking initiation, cessation, and relapse. The stated aim of the measures is to contribute to reducing smoking prevalence to 10% by 2018 and to halve the smoking rate among Torres Strait Islanders and aboriginals. Section 3.2 of the *TPP Act* determines the *mechanisms* to achieve this objective: (i) reduce the appeal of tobacco products; (ii) increase the effectiveness of health warnings on the retail packaging; and (iii) reduce the ability of the retail packaging to mislead consumers about the harmful effects of

tobacco products. Australia has confirmed that the "objective" of the measures is to be found in Section 3.1, and not in Section 3.2 of the *TPP Act*. These mechanisms are thus not legally relevant for purposes of examining the legitimacy of the objective, the measures' degree of contribution to the fulfilment of the objective, or the identification of alternative measures that provide an equivalent contribution to the smoking reduction objective of the *TPP Act*. The relevant evidence to be considered concerns the effect of the measures on smoking behaviour and the degree to which the plain packaging measures contribute to reducing smoking as intended. Honduras supports the adoption of tobacco-control measures to improve public health by reducing smoking prevalence, as reflected by the fact that Honduras itself has adopted a series of these measures. In this context, Honduras does not dispute the legitimacy of Australia's public health objective.

3. **The plain packaging measures are more trade restrictive than necessary to fulfil a legitimate objective, taking account of the risks of non-fulfilment**

(a) **The plain packaging measures are trade-restrictive**

52. The Appellate Body has found that, under Article 2.2 of the TBT Agreement, a measure is trade restrictive if it has a "limiting effect on trade". The concept of trade-restrictiveness does not require the demonstration of actual trade effects, as the focus is on the competitive opportunities available to the imported product. In Honduras' view, the measures' design, structure and architecture confirm the trade restrictive nature of the plain packaging measures. In so far as necessary, evidence of downtrading resulting from the introduction of the plain packaging measures confirms the distortion of the conditions of competition imposed by the plain packaging measures. The plain packaging measures are trade restrictive by nature because they affect the competitive opportunities of imported tobacco products in various ways.

53. First, the plain packaging measures severely limit brand differentiation, that is, the producers' ability to rely on brand packaging to distinguish their products from those of their competitors. This, in turn, affects competitive opportunities of tobacco producers because they are no longer able to communicate to consumers the quality and reputation of their products. Given that trademarks are essential to fair competition and are important instruments of competition, it is clear that prohibiting trademarks from fulfilling this competition enhancing role distorts the conditions of competition in the market. In order to confirm this point, Honduras submitted empirical evidence demonstrating that a downward substitution effect has taken place in the Australian market after the entry into force of the plain packaging measures. This situation, also known as downtrading, is the logical consequence of a market with reduced brand differentiation.

54. Second, the plain packaging measures are trade-restrictive because they entail significant compliance costs. The entry into force of the plain packaging

measures logically meant that foreign producers wishing to continue supplying the Australian market needed to adapt their manufacturing processes applicable to packaging of tobacco products and of tobacco products themselves. This, in turn, compelled those foreign producers to bear certain adaptation costs. Australia's own authorities recognised that plain packaging "will involve some upfront costs to adjust manufacturing processes for the Australian market". In Australia's own Post-Implementation Review, the costs for producers were estimated to be about AUD 69 million. These compliance costs are significant under any metric. These compliance costs are prohibitive for small producers in developing countries seeking to enter an already dark market with no expectation of high profitability as a result of the competition-distorting nature of the plain packaging measures and absent any possibility of communication of the brand logos.

55.   Third, the plain packaging measures are also trade-restrictive because they restrict access to the Australian market and distort conditions of competition. As explained in the expert reports of Professor Damien Neven, the measures produce certain communication and price effects that make access to the Australian tobacco market almost impossible. By imposing these barriers on market access, the plain packaging measures affect competitive opportunities of tobacco products, have a limiting effect on trade, create a disincentive to import into Australia, and have identifiable negative consequences on the importation of tobacco products, all of which are circumstances that qualify as trade restrictions according to previous panels and the Appellate Body.

(b)   The plain packaging measures make no contribution to Australia's objective

56.   As indicated below, the available evidence demonstrates that the plain packaging measures have failed, now more than two and a half years after their introduction, to change actual smoking behaviour. Similarly, there is no evidence that plain packaging is apt to product any effect on smoking behaviour at some point in the future. The plain packaging measures, therefore, fail to make any contribution to Australia's objective. In Honduras' opinion, the issues of trade restrictiveness and contribution are two different considerations that must be examined separately when conducting a weighing and balancing exercise under Article 2.2 of the TBT Agreement. Contrary to Australia's rebuttal argument that any measure that is effective in reducing consumption will be trade restrictive and *vice versa*, Honduras considers that Australia unduly seeks to collapse these two different factors of the weighing and balancing test. The issue of trade restrictiveness must be assessed in terms of whether the challenged measures affect competitive opportunities, involve compliance costs or act as a disincentive to export to Australia. The focus is on the nature, architecture and design of the measures. In contrast, the question of contribution is examined by looking at the evidence of the actual contribution to the specific objective. A measure can be effective in reducing consumption without imposing WTO-inconsistent barriers to trade.

(c)   The risks of non-fulfilment of the plain packaging measures does not change the analysis

57.   Article 2.2 of the TBT Agreement requires that the risks of non-fulfilment be included in the analysis of whether the measures are more trade restrictive than necessary. The analysis of the risks of non-fulfilment consists of examining two aspects: (i) the nature of the risks at issue; and (ii) the gravity of the consequences that would arise from non-fulfilment of the objective pursued by the Member through the challenged measure. On the first element, Honduras recognises that the risks at issue, health risks that arise from tobacco smoking, are of great importance to any society. On the second element, Honduras argues that it is clear that Australia was in a position to achieve its desired reduction of tobacco prevalence without the introduction of the plain packaging measures given the pre-existing and continued decline in smoking prevalence. In addition, as the evidence showed that the measures are not effective in reducing smoking, including the "risks of non-fulfilment" does not affect the outcome of the weighing and balancing exercise. Australia's smoking rates have been declining consistently for years as a result of Australia's numerous tobacco-control measures. In this connection, Australia's Cancer Council Victoria noted in 2009 that even without plain packaging Australia could reduce its smoking rate to 10 percent by 2020.

B.   Honduras Provides Several Reasonably Available Alternative Measures that are WTO-Consistent and Provide an at Least Equivalent Degree of Contribution to the Objective of Reducing Smoking while being less Trade Restrictive

58.   Honduras presents four reasonably available alternative measures which produce an at least "equivalent contribution" to the objective of reducing smoking and which are less trade restrictive and/or entirely WTO consistent.

59.   First, Honduras proposes an increase in the minimum legal purchasing age ("MLPA") from 18 to 21. This measure has the effect of removing cigarettes from the social network of secondary school students, given that, unlike adults, adolescents frequently obtain cigarettes from friends of their same age. In addition, smoking during adolescence substantially elevates the risk for regular adult smoking, and thus intervening at this age is key to preventing adult smoking. In many jurisdictions, raising the MLPA for cigarettes from 16 to 18, and in one case (i.e. the town of Needham in Massachusetts) from 18 to 21, led to substantial decreases in smoking rates. Raising the MLPA to 21 is also supported by the expert of Honduras and the Dominican Republic, Professor Steinberg. Following a request from the US Food and Drug Administration, a committee of the US Institute of Medicine ("IOM") published a report on the public health implications of raising the MLPA for tobacco products in the United States to 21 and 25 years. Honduras' expert, Professor Steinberg presented to the committee in April 2014 on adolescent and young adult cognitive and psychosocial development and decision-making, and was also selected to provide an independent review of the committee's draft report. In its

final version of the report, made public on 12 March 2015, the IOM agreed with Professor Steinberg's recommendation that raising the MLPA for tobacco products would help prevent initiation of tobacco use among adolescents. Raising the MLPA is not a technical regulation and does not distort competitive opportunities for foreign producers in any way given that it does not affect product differentiation and does not impose any compliance costs. It also respects intellectual property rights. It is thus a WTO-consistent and less trade-restrictive alternative that provides at least an equivalent contribution.

60.   Second, Honduras proposes the increase of tobacco taxes. The effectiveness of tax measures in reducing smoking rates, including among young people, is recognised by the WHO and scholars which consider it to be "the single most effective tobacco control instrument". Australia itself acknowledges the effectiveness of these measures, as it has already implemented tobacco excise increases, albeit insufficiently. Australia fails to rebut the fact highlighted in Honduras' submissions that its tobacco taxes are below the WHO recommendation of 70% of the retail price of the products. Australia argues that it has attempted to increase taxation toward that level but blames industry pricing policies for its failure to reach that goal. This, of course, is no defence: Australia cannot blame its own regulatory failure on the industry when the industry is merely implementing common and well-understood pricing policies. Further, regulatory practice in other Members belies Australia's contentions as fifty-four other FCTC Parties reached the 70% goal by 2015. Furthermore, an additional twenty-five Parties have a higher overall tax level than Australia's 56.76%, even if they have not reached the 70% goal. Thus, Australia ranks 80th out of 180 FCTC Parties in respect of the single most effective tobacco-control instrument. It is thus disingenuous for Australia to argue that it cannot do better or that tobacco tax increases are not an available and effective alternative measure. A non-discriminatory tax increase is a WTO-consistent and less trade-restrictive measure. It is not a technical regulation and does not impose any compliance costs. In addition, this measure does not affect competitive opportunities of imported tobacco products, nor does it restrict the ability of tobacco producers to compete in the Australian market by using brand packaging to signal quality and reputation to consumers. It also respects intellectual property rights. The important advantage of tax increases is that they would not only encourage cessation and prevent relapse, but would also reduce smoking initiation, which is an important action to prevent young persons from becoming adult chronic smokers. Finally, the proposed tax increase is also reasonably available to Australia and would actually raise additional revenue for the Australian Government. It does not involve substantial technical difficulties or prohibitive costs.

61.   Third, Honduras proposes a mechanism to vet tobacco product packaging prior to marketing and commercialisation of tobacco products. This pre-vetting mechanism, developed in the expert report of Mr. Shavin Q.C., is a less-restrictive alternative measure in the event the Panel finds that the alternatives in question must operate though the same causal pathway as plain packaging and

affect the same "mechanisms" set out in Section 3.2 of the *TPP Act*. In combination with the Australian Consumer Law's protection against misleading or deceptive aspects of tobacco packaging as enforced by the Australian Consumer and Competition Commission, this mechanism would provide an equivalent contribution as plain packaging. The pre-vetting mechanism would be designed to prohibit, even before they are placed on the market, any problematic packaging or product feature based on a compulsory pre-notification process. Such a pre-vetting mechanism would by definition be less trade restrictive because it would require an *individualised* assessment of the signs and design features of each trademark before the trademark is allowed on the Australian market. Similar pre-vetting mechanisms already exist in Australia and Honduras is proposing a user-pay system which will not entail an undue burden for the Australian Government.

62.   Fourth, Honduras proposes improved social marketing campaigns to reach youth with anti-smoking messages and information in formats that would be familiar to them. This alternative is supported by the expert report of Professor Keller who explains that Australia's recent anti-smoking campaigns, ongoing since 2011, have been found to be ineffective in a series of reviews by the Australian Government. Professor Keller proposes concrete improvements to Australia's campaigns that would increase their effectiveness. Honduras considers that this alternative measure is a WTO-consistent and less trade-restrictive alternative that does not impose any costs on producers and that does not distort competitive opportunities for foreign producers while making an equivalent contribution to Australia's objective as any contribution that plain packaging may make. It also respects intellectual property rights and it is clearly an alternative that is reasonably available to Australia.

63.   Honduras has rebutted Australia's various arguments aimed at undermining the validity of the alternative measures proposed by Honduras. Australia contends that, in order for an alternative measure to be valid, it is not sufficient for the measure to achieve Australia's objective of reducing smoking prevalence, it must also employ the same mechanisms used by the plain packaging measures, namely to reduce the appeal of tobacco products, increase the effectiveness of GHWs, and eliminate producers' ability to mislead consumers through packaging. Honduras disagrees with Australia's approach. In *US – COOL (Article 21.5 – Canada and Mexico)*, the Appellate Body addressed the very argument advanced by Australia in these proceedings. It noted that "a proposed alternative measure may achieve an equivalent degree of contribution in ways different from the technical regulation at issue". In light of this precedent, Honduras contends that the proposed alternative measures are valid for purposes of Article 2.2 because, even if they do not incorporate the same mechanisms as the plain packaging measures, they are more effective at reducing smoking prevalence.

64.   Australia also invokes the Appellate Body's findings in *Brazil – Retreaded Tyres* as support for its argument that, because the plain packaging measures are part of a comprehensive suite of measures, they cannot be replaced

with alternative measures. Honduras has explained that Australia's arguments are without merit. Unlike the facts addressed by the Appellate Body in *Brazil – Retreaded Tyres*, the plain packaging measures are neither a key element nor a pillar in Australia's tobacco strategy. Given that plain packaging does not work in a synergistic manner with Australia's other tobacco-control measures, its removal would not undermine the functioning of Australia's other measures.

C.   **Australia's Legal Rebuttal Arguments are Without Merit and Aim at Avoiding Proper Scrutiny of the Lack of Contribution of the Plain Packaging Measures**

65.   To respond to the claims under the TBT Agreement, Australia's defence has been to try to avoid any scrutiny of whether the plain packaging measures actually make a contribution to the health objective of reducing smoking. Australia develops the untenable position that the TRIPS Agreement is *lex specialis* for trademarks and that the plain packaging measures' prohibition on the use of trademarks is thus not covered by the disciplines of the TBT Agreement, but only by those of the TRIPS Agreement. However, at the same time, under Australia's reading of the TRIPS Agreement, measures prohibiting or restricting the use of trademarks are not subject to any of the disciplines of the TRIPS Agreement. In effect, therefore, Australia is arguing that there is actually no WTO discipline that applies to its plain packaging measures. This argument is not credible in light of the obvious applicability of the TBT Agreement to technical regulations (such as Australia's plain packaging measures) that involve packaging and labelling and the well-established fact in WTO jurisprudence that there may be overlapping disciplines in different WTO agreements that apply to the same measure. In addition, Australia develops three sets of arguments with a view to trying to avoid a review of its plain packaging measures and their lack of contribution to achieving Australia's objective of smoking reduction.

66.   First, Australia argues that the complainants failed to demonstrate that the stringent set of requirements imposed by the plain packaging measures are trade restrictive, hoping that the Panel would examine trade restrictiveness as a threshold question rather than examining this concept as part of its weighing and balancing exercise under Article 2.2 of the TBT Agreement as the Appellate Body has explained is required. Australia argues that the plain packaging measures are not trade restrictive because Honduras and the other complainants have not demonstrated that overall trade in tobacco products has declined following the imposition of the measures. Australia's argument, which is based on the oft-rejected notion that "actual trade" effects must be used to arrive at a determination of trade restrictiveness, is wrong. Actual trade effects are not required to be demonstrated. Trade restrictiveness is not a threshold question – it is part and parcel of the weighing and balancing test. In any case, the "limiting condition" to sell into the Australian market that the plain packaging measures impose is difficult to deny. The plain packaging measures adversely affect the conditions of competition for tobacco products. Furthermore, a measure can be trade restrictive even just for a distinct segment of the category of products

covered by the technical regulation, such as for premium tobacco products. It is not necessary to demonstrate that "overall", for the entire product category, and for every single product, trade has been reduced, or is likely to be adversely affected. Nothing in the TBT Agreement supports the notion that restrictiveness exists only if a measure affects all segments of a product and all WTO Members that export that product. Such interpretation would severely undermine the value of WTO rules. A country specialising in one particular segment of a product must be able to challenge a restrictive technical regulation under Article 2.2 even if the measure does not affect other product segments or other countries. Actually, according to WTO case law, a country may challenge a restrictive measure even if it does not actually produce the product in question.

67.   Second, Australia tries to move the goal posts by focusing on the mechanisms of the measures, such as reducing the appeal of the product etc., instead of the effectiveness of the measures on achieving its objective of reducing smoking and by further suggesting that the Panel can only examine the effects over time, i.e. in the next generation. Australia seeks to convince the Panel that speculative studies about the plain packaging measures' possible effects on perceptions and intentions, coupled with abstract theories on human behaviour are as informative, or even more informative, than data showing that, after three years of actual operation of the measures, smoking behaviour has not changed. Australia's measures may have been enacted with the best of intentions, but the reality is that they have failed to produce any effect on decreasing smoking, and are not likely to do so today, in the near future, in the next generation, or in generations to come. The speculative studies and theories were simply wrong. Moreover, the Appellate Body has clarified that it is not so that a measure which is only intended to produce effects "over time" escapes scrutiny and does not need to be supported by positive evidence. Established WTO jurisprudence holds that even technical regulations intended to produce effects in the future must be shown to be "apt" to make a material contribution. This demonstration could consist of "quantitative projections in the future, or qualitative reasoning based on a set of hypotheses that are tested and supported by sufficient evidence". Conjecture or mere speculation is therefore clearly insufficient.

68.   Third, Australia seeks refuge in the "safe haven" that Article 2.5 of the TBT Agreement potentially offers technical regulations adopted in accordance with international standards. Honduras notes that, in the four years that preceded Australia's first written submission in this dispute, Australia never argued that the FCTC Guidelines constituted an international standard that must be used as the basis for Members' technical regulations on tobacco products. In 2011, Australia notified its plain packaging measures under Article 2.9.2 of the TBT Agreement, the same way that other WTO Members notified similar plain packaging measures. In so doing, Australia itself recognised that no relevant international standard exists in connection with plain packaging since Article 2.9.2 of the TBT Agreement is a type of notification made only whenever a relevant international standard does not exist. This shows that Australia and the

other notifying Members are of the view that no relevant international standard exists for tobacco plain packaging. It is odd that Australia is now arguing that its plain packaging measures are ostensibly being applied in accordance with an "international standard".

69.   Australia argues that the Guidelines adopted by the FCTC's Conference of the Parties ("FCTC COP") are an "international standard" and that measures taken in accordance with this standard are thus deemed to be WTO-consistent. Honduras considers that the plain packaging measures do not satisfy the requirements of Article 2.5 of the TBT Agreement and, therefore, they do not benefit from the rebuttable presumption offered by this provision. First, the provisions of the FCTC Guidelines cited by Australia do not meet the definition of "standard" provided in Annex 1.2 of the TBT Agreement, which refers to a document "for common and repeated use". The FCTC Guidelines lack the necessary precision to be susceptible of common and repeated use. Each country wishing to implement these FCTC Guidelines must decide individually how to implement the various suggestions concerning plain packaging. The lack of prescriptiveness of the FCTC Guidelines becomes clear when contrasted against standards issued by recognised standardizing bodies, such as ISO, an example of which is ISO standard 3394. Second, the FCTC Guidelines are not "international" standards because the body that approved them, the FCTC COP, is not an international standardising body. More specifically, the FCTC COP is not an international standardising body since it lacks recognised standardisation activities. Article 23.5 of the FCTC indicates that the functions of the FCTC COP relate generally to promoting and facilitating the implementation of the FCTC, as well as other coordination activities. Nothing in Article 23.5 indicates that the FCTC is responsible for preparing and adopting international standards in connection with tobacco packaging.

70.   In sum, the FCTC Guidelines are not a "standard", and the body that prepared the FCTC Guidelines – the FCTC COP – lacks recognised activities in standardisation. According to the Appellate Body, an instrument that does not satisfy these two key requirements does not constitute a "relevant international standard". The FCTC COP's mandate does not include the development of new standards, as compared to other established international standard-setting bodies like the CODEX or the ISO. In fact, the differences between these different entities' objectives, role and functioning are so significant that it is almost impossible to compare them with the FCTC. Nothing in Articles 23, 24 and 25 of the FCTC concerning the COP and the FCTC Secretariat suggests that a body was set up by the FCTC with the capacity to act as a standardising body for tobacco-control measures. Indeed, nowhere in the FCTC do the drafters contemplate the development of tobacco product standards. Thus, by the terms of the FCTC, the COP does not engage in activities in standardisation. Also in the context of Indonesia's claim under Article 2.9 of the TBT Agreement relating to the United States' ban on clove cigarettes, which was based on the COP Partial Guidelines to Article 9 and 10, the panel found that "the first condition

set out in Article 2.9 of the TBT Agreement for the application of the obligations therein [i.e. the absence of a relevant international standard] is fulfilled".

IV. POSITIVE EVIDENCE PRESENTED BY HONDURAS CONFIRMS THAT THE PLAIN PACKAGING MEASURES HAVE NOT MADE A CONTRIBUTION TO REDUCING SMOKING AND ARE NOT CAPABLE OF MAKING ANY CONTRIBUTION IN THE FUTURE

71.   As the Appellate Body stated in *Brazil – Retreated Tyres*, a demonstration of a measure's contribution can be made by resorting to evidence or data, pertaining to the past or the present, that establish that the measure at issue makes a material contribution to the protection of public health. Australia has failed to present such evidence. In contrast, the evidence presented by Honduras and the other complainants demonstrates the lack of contribution of the measures to changing smoking behaviour. Certainly, the Appellate Body has also said that this is not the only type of demonstration that could establish such a contribution, suggesting that certain (environmental) measures may take time to produce their effects. Accordingly, a panel might also conclude that a measure is "necessary" on the basis of a demonstration that the measure is "apt" to produce a material contribution to the achievement of its objective. According to the Appellate Body, this demonstration could consist of "quantitative projections in the future, or qualitative reasoning based on a set of hypotheses that are tested and supported by sufficient evidence". Speculation does not suffice.

72.   Honduras presents both quantitative and qualitative analyses based on scientifically sound methodologies in the form of: (i) post-implementation market and sales data as well as survey evidence; (ii) medical science; (iii) social science; (iv) a critique of the plain packaging literature relied on by Australia; (v) a critique of the lack of cigar evidence; and (vi) data on illicit trade.

73.   As discussed below, Professor Klick conducted a unique longitudinal study of smoking behaviour before and after the introduction of plain packaging in Australia of a representative sample of Australian consumers and a counterfactual group of consumers in New Zealand. In addition, at the request of Honduras, Professor Klick analysed tracking surveys organised by Australia and certain State agencies, including the National Tobacco Plain Packaging Tracking Survey ("NTPPTS") conducted by the Cancer Council Victoria with the support of the Australian Government. He also examined the results of the tobacco tracking survey conducted by Cancer Council New South Wales which tracks the effects of tobacco control measures in New South Wales, the most populous State of Australia. Professor Klick examined wholesale and retail sales data from before and after the implementation of the plain packaging measures. All of the data point in the same direction that Australia's plain packaging measures failed to change smoking behaviour and did not lead to a reduction in smoking as intended. In addition, Honduras and the other complainants present a qualitative analysis of the scientific and medical evidence that shows that trademarks (and

packaging) are not among the drivers of smoking behaviour, and that prohibiting or restricting them will thus not contribute to Australia's objective of reducing smoking prevalence. Quantitative analysis of the competition-distorting effects of Australia's plain packaging measures further supports the conclusion that the measures are not apt to contribute to the reduction of smoking.

A.   **Tracking Survey Analyses as Corroborated by Wholesale and Retail Sales Data Confirm the Lack of Contribution of the Plain Packaging Measures**

74.   Honduras considers that the best available evidence of whether the plain packaging measures are contributing to their stated objective to reduce smoking prevalence to 10% by 2018 consists of real world data following implementation of the measures in 2012. Professor Klick finds, through his analyses, that the data from across multiple varied sources provide consistent evidence that plain packaging has not achieved Australia's objective of reducing smoking.

1.   **Longitudinal Survey/Market analysis comparing Australia and New Zealand before and after plain packaging was introduced shows no effect on smoking behaviour**

75.   Professor Klick conducted a unique longitudinal study of the smoking behaviour before and after the introduction of plain packaging in Australia of a representative sample of Australian consumers and a counterfactual group of consumers in New Zealand. The study was based on survey data collected by Roy Morgan Research, a consulting firm that also conducts survey work for the Australian Government, and involved a large representative sample of consumers in Australia and New Zealand which were followed over 6 waves. The results of the survey are discussed in Professor Klick's Survey/Market Report. The study showed that during the first 16 months of their application, the plain packaging measures did not have any impact on consumers' smoking behaviour. The study is the only longitudinal dataset available that has tested the actual impact of Australia's plain packaging measures by comparing smoking behaviour in Australia to smoking behaviour in a relevant comparator – New Zealand – over a period immediately preceding and immediately following the implementation of plain packaging in Australia. New Zealand provides the optimal control group because of the great similarity with Australia in respect of smoking metrics, regulatory environment, and seasonality. The study by Professor Klick confirms that plain packaging has not contributed to the reduction of smoking in Australia. Professor Klick's findings based on the survey responses is supported by his analysis of industry wholesale shipment data (technically referred to as Exchange of Sales ("EOS") data) and retail sales data collected by well established companies like Nielsen and Aztec in Australia and New Zealand. The survey data, wholesale data and retail sales data all tell the same story: there is no indication that smoking declined as a result of plain packaging in Australia given that the same or higher declines in smoking are

found in New Zealand. Based on these survey data and observed sales data, there is no evidence that plain packaging reduces smoking.

76.   In his Rebuttal Report and his Supplemental Rebuttal Report, Professor Klick disproves Australia's critique of his unique longitudinal study. In particular, he shows that the results of the Survey/Market Report were not vitiated by a lack of a proper pre-period for the comparison, and that New Zealand is a proper counterfactual jurisdiction to Australia. Professor Klick shows through various controls and alternative modelling choices that the early roll-out of plain packaging in October-November 2012 did not affect his pre-period. In addition, he confirms that New Zealand consumers provide a proper comparison group because of the great similarity between New Zealand and Australia and, in particular, because the smoking rates in the two countries are highly correlated. Professor Klick controls for any changes in taxation in both jurisdictions by controlling for price. After all, if taxes have an effect on consumption, it will be through their price effects. By controlling for price developments in both countries, Professor Klick eliminates the risk that the results are affected by changes in taxes in New Zealand introduced soon after plain packaging was implemented in Australia. Professor Klick also applies the Instrumental Variable technique to ensure that his analysis of the wholesale and retail market data is not undermined by the issue of endogeneity of price. He thus addresses all of the criticisms lodged against his Survey/Market analysis by Australia and its experts. Professor Klick updates his analysis of the retail sales data and EOS data up to September 2015 and concludes that his findings stand. Professor Klick concludes that, even controlling for the points raised by Australia's experts, the analysis of the updated sales data confirms the conclusions in his original report: "Updated wholesale sales data and retail sales data point in the same direction and confirm, once again, the findings from the Roy Morgan longitudinal survey data presented in my Original Report, namely that plain packaging has failed to advance the public health goals that motivated its adoption ... The facts are clear. It is not correct that fewer people are smoking or that people are smoking less as a result of the plain packaging measures".

2.   **Australia's own National Tobacco Plain Packaging Tracking Survey shows the lack of effect of the measures on reducing smoking**

77.   In his Supplemental Rebuttal Report Professor Klick also examines data from Australia's national tracking survey, the NTPPTS. With funding by the Australian Department of Health, the NTPPTS was conducted by the Centre for Behavioral Research in Cancer at the request of the Cancer Council Victoria ("CCV") to assess the effects of plain packaging in Australia. The survey entailed a continuous cross-sectional baseline survey of about 100 interviews per week conducted from 9 April 2012 to 30 March 2014. A follow-up survey of baseline participants then took place approximately four weeks after the initial survey, with the follow-up surveys conducted from 7 May 2012 to 4 May 2014. The NTPPTS is not longitudinal in nature. That is, the survey does not follow

the same group of people over a period of time. The NTPPTS "cross-sectional" approach interviews different people in a series of surveys conducted over time. First, considering smoking status, Professor Klick's analyses find no statistically significant impact of plain packaging to reduce smoking status, and these findings hold when Professor Klick varies his model in a number of ways. Second, considering smoking consumption, Professor Klick finds that plain packaging had no effect on reducing the number of cigarettes smoked per day when considering similar variables and analyses as mentioned for smoking status. Plain packaging did not reduce the number of cigarettes smoked per day by daily smokers or all smokers, or even when allowing for quitting/relapse (by including the responses of those stating that they currently smoke 0 cigarettes per day). He thus finds that "there is no statistically significant reduction in any smoking indicator". Australia's own NTPPTS dataset confirms his previous conclusions about plain packaging, namely that the measures have had no impact on reducing smoking or changing smoking behaviour as Australia intended.

78.   The NTPPTS data covered only current smokers and is thus incomplete. Therefore, Professor Klick analysed prevalence data from the New South Wales ("NSW") Population Health Survey reflecting prevalence data until 2014 in Australia's most populous State. Professor Klick analyses this dataset because Australia itself had referred to it as the relevant dataset to assess changes in smoking prevalence in New South Wales. The same conclusion is drawn based on this dataset, namely that plain packaging has not been effective in reducing smoking.

79.   Professor Klick, in this Supplemental Rebuttal Report, also demonstrates that any claims based on the NTPPTS data relating to Australia's three non-behavioural "specific mechanisms" that plain packaging is producing its intended effects are unsubstantiated. Professor Klick reviews the relevant studies published in the special edition of the journal "Tobacco Control" dedicated to the NTPPTS results and shows that the favourable results are largely found through the authors' "cherry-picking" the questions and data that suit their goals. Professor Klick's analysis of the data set related to these "mechanisms" shows that the data do not support the affirmative conclusions even regarding the impact of plain packaging on the "mechanisms". To illustrate that the authors have cherry-picked their favoured results, Professor Klick points to other, closely related questions for each of Australia's three mechanisms to show that these survey data point in multiple directions and do not provide a clear basis for the study's authors to draw their unequivocal conclusions that the plain packaging measures are working. Professor Klick finds that "the data and indicators point in multiple directions but that they do not support any affirmative conclusion that plain packaging is systematically contributing to any meaningful change in the perceptions or intentions of smokers or recent quitters". It is noteworthy that Professor Klick's conclusions – that there are no changes in the behavioural metrics – are also confirmed by Scollo et al., one of the Australian post-implementation studies based on the NTPPTS data. That study is the only study that even discusses data on actual consumption.

Interestingly – and revealingly – Australia never cites this study in its first written submission. The authors of that paper conclude the following regarding the impact of plain packaging in Australia: "Among daily cigarette smokers, there was no change in consumption between pre-PP and the transition phase or PP year 1 period ... Nor was any change detected when mean daily consumption was analysed among regular smokers ... Mean daily consumption also did not change from the pre-PP to subsequent two phases among current smokers ... Furthermore consumption did not change from pre-PP to the subsequent two phases among current smokers of brands of any market segment". Thus, the study by Scollo et al. confirms that plain packaging did not affect actual consumption of tobacco.

3. The tobacco tracking survey conducted in Australia's most populous State confirms that plain packaging did not lead to a reduction in smoking and failed to change smoking behaviour

80.   The New South Wales' Cancer Institute has conducted a continuous, cross-sectional tobacco tracking survey – the Cancer Institute Tobacco Tracking Survey ("CITTS") – of a representative sample of the population in the most populous State in Australia since 2006. This survey collects relevant data on actual smoking behaviours as well as other, less relevant data on indicators related to intentions and perceptions. Professor Klick's Second Supplemental Rebuttal Report provides an analysis of the CITTS data. Professor Klick's conclusions are the same as he drew from his analysis of the Australia-wide NTPPTS: the data does not show that smoking has decreased or quitting has increased since the introduction of plain packaging. With respect to direct data on actual smoking behaviour, Professor Klick analysed the smoking status and consumption levels of the survey participants. His analyses, when controlling for the relevant variables and considering either an October 2012 or a December 2012 implementation date, show that the data do not support the conclusion that plain packaging has led to a decline in actual smoking. In addition, Professor Klick found that the non-behavioural indicators on intentions and perceptions point in multiple directions. Professor Klick finds that "[a] neutral and objective analysis is forced to acknowledge that there are a number of these soft metrics that go in either direction, and none of them provides credible evidence of a reduction in actual smoking behaviour in any event".

4. Australia's criticism of the smoking-related conclusions drawn by Professor Klick are without merit

81.   Professor Klick responds to criticisms by Australia's experts to various aspects of his analyses, including his analyses of the prevalence data from the NSW Population Health Survey and the data from the NTPPTS and the CITTS. Professor Klick shows that Australia's criticisms are entirely unwarranted and unfounded as a matter of econometric practice and judgment, and that they are often at odds with points the Australian experts have made in the proceeding. For example, Australia asserts that his analysis of the survey data including

Australia's own NTPPTS and the CITTS do not permit conclusions to be drawn about smoking prevalence because these datasets do not reflect data of young smokers below the age of 18. Professor Klick is of course well aware of this limitation. That is why he also analyses the NSW Population Health Survey which does reflect, as per Australia's own acknowledgement, prevalence data covering also young smokers. In addition, the actual sales data that Professor Klick examined to corroborate his conclusions also make no distinction based on the age of the consumer and can thus be assumed to accurately reflect the effects of the measures on initiation and quitting. Professor Klick also finds support for his conclusions in another dataset relied on by both Australia and the complainants, the Roy Morgan Single Source Survey ("RMSS") which provides individual survey data about smoking status (smoker v non-smoker) from January 2000 to June 2015. Professor Klick finds that the conclusion based upon the RMSS data is consistent with the conclusions drawn from all of the other available datasets, including the NSW Population Health Survey. Namely, there is no evidence that plain packaging led to a systematic improvement in smoking outcomes.

82.   Finally, as Professor Klick points out, it is disconcerting to see that Australia is actually trying to minimise the clear behavioural results of the NTPPTS that it had itself developed simply because the results do not suit the argument. In addition, Australia has conducted a similar plain packaging tracking survey for youth, known as the "School-Based Surveys" but has refused to provide the results of those surveys for purposes of analysis by the Panel and the complainants in this dispute. Australia's complaint that the complainants have not provided evidence on the effect of the plain packaging measures on initiation and prevalence is therefore not only incorrect, as explained above, but it is also disingenuous and self-serving as Australia refused to make that evidence available for analysis which only it had in possession. That is telling of the weakness of Australia's case.

83.   The analyses in all of Professor Klick's reports is clear, namely that there is no evidence that plain packaging has improved any actual smoking outcomes. Australia ignores the fact that this conclusion is amazingly robust across a wide variety of data sources, and it is robust to various modelling assumptions. Survey data as well as updated wholesale and retail sales data running until October 2015 corroborate that there is no evidence that plain packaging has led to a decline in smoking.

5.   Conclusion

84.   In conclusion, after three years, the plain packaging measures have not had any positive effect on changing smoking behaviours and reducing smoking. Professor Klick's analyses withstand all of the critique levelled at them, and the conclusion based on his unique longitudinal survey data, as well as on survey data collected by Australia and certain of its States, which are also corroborated by retail and wholesale market data, remains robust to various modelling choices. Professor Klick concludes as follows: "[M]y analyses of all of the

available data, confirm that actual smoking behavior in Australia has not declined following the introduction of plain packaging. This conclusion is the same regardless of whether these metrics are derived from self-reported smoking status in surveys, the NSW prevalence data, or market data. Further, the survey data from the NTPPTS regarding smoker perceptions and intentions do not indicate a systematic improvement, from a public health policy perspective, after plain packaging came into effect. Therefore, as shown by all of my earlier reports, data from across multiple varied sources provide consistent evidence that plain packaging has not achieved Australia's objective of reducing smoking and changing behaviors".

B.   Expert Analyses based on the Known Drivers of Smoking Confirm that Plain Packaging is Not Apt To Contribute To the Reduction of Smoking Since Packaging and Trademarks Are Not Driving Smoking Behaviour

85.   In addition to the facts relating to the first three years of application of the plain packaging measures, as discussed in the reports of Professor Klick, Honduras also presents expert analyses of the medical science regarding smoking initiation, cessation and relapse which confirm that trademarks and packaging are not the drivers of smoking. This qualitative evidence about the drivers of smoking demonstrates that the plain packaging measures, which deal with trademarks and packaging, are not capable of contributing to reducing smoking in any meaningful manner because they do not address these drivers.

86.   With respect to initiation, Professor Steinberg addresses the science relating to adolescent behaviour and applies it to the plain packaging measures. He reviews the key factors that drive smoking initiation by youth – a form of risk-taking behaviour. He notes that these factors, which are different from those driving adult decision-making processes, include psychological characteristics, interpersonal influences and community context (including price and availability of tobacco products). In Professor Steinberg's opinion, plain packaging cannot have any impact on the important causes leading to smoking initiation for youth and, therefore, cannot have any impact on the goal of reducing smoking by youth. Australia and its experts do not dispute the complex nature of the drivers of initiation. But Australia attempts to shoehorn product packaging into this list by referring vaguely to "comprehensive" models of the drivers of initiation. This is unwarranted and inconsistent with the well-established list of drivers of smoking behaviour, which does not include trademarks or packaging. In this context, Honduras notes that the risks and harmful effects of tobacco consumption are well-known in Australia by adults and youths alike. Australia seems to agree with this fact. Professor Steinberg notes that youth are well aware of the risks of smoking and that measures to raise awareness or knowledge are unnecessary and thus ineffective because there is no information deficit to overcome.

87.   With respect to cessation and relapse behaviours, Dr. Satel provides her views on the complex drivers including "pharmacological, psychological, social,

and environmental factors", which Australia also does not contest. Dr. Satel finds that cessation and avoidance of relapse are promoted by motivation and commitment, a supportive social environment and self-efficacy, but she finds no credible evidence that branding, logos or packaging impact smoking behaviours. Further, she shows that a cigarette or cigarette pack itself is a conditioned cue and can drive cravings to smoke whether sold in branded or plain packaging. These views are also supported by Professor Fischer in her expert report. In particular, Professor Fischer explains that "[a] tangled web of factors interact in a dynamic fashion to either promote or undermine quitting or smoking cessation at any point in time ... Branded tobacco packaging, hypothesised as a smoking-related cue that impedes quit attempts, promotes relapse, and undermines cessation, has never been implicated in smoking-behaviour research as associated with any of these outcomes". Plain packaging is not apt to increase cessation or to prevent relapse.

88.   This inaptitude of the plain packaging measures is confirmed by marketing experts such as Professor Steenkamp and Professor Winer. Both experts conclude that packaging, as an aspect of the "P" of "product" in the Marketing Mix, in a mature, declining market does not drive or increase aggregate demand for the product. Dedicated advertising instruments are largely ineffective in increasing sales for primary or secondary demand. The necessary corollary is that, if the demand-stimulating power of dedicated advertising media is already so small, the effect of a non-dedicated instrument, such as brand packaging, should be even smaller. The sales and survey data discussed above confirm the views of these marketing experts that, in the highly regulated Australian market where advertising is already prohibited, packaging and trademarks does not affect aggregate demand.

C.   **An Analysis of the Behavioural Science Relied on by Australia and its Experts Confirms that these Intention-Based Theories are of Limited Relevance, have been Contradicted by the Facts, and have not been Properly Tested in Any of the Studies Done to Date**

89.   Faced with the overwhelming evidence that the plain packaging measures are having no positive effect whatsoever, Australia has taken the position that plain packaging will operate through a causal pathway that will have its effect "over time", i.e. over a generation or more. Its behavioural theory is that the measures will, first, reduce the appeal of tobacco products, increase the noticeability of GHWs and the perceptions about the harm of smoking which in turn, second, will lead to a behavioural change of reducing smoking. Honduras contests Australia's reliance on behavioural theories to justify its measures in the light of the facts on the record which show that three years after the measures were implemented, they have failed to change smoking behaviour as intended. It does not make sense to speculate about the effects of a measure based on theories about how consumers will react, when actual data exist. It certainly makes no sense to refer to a theory for justifying measures when the facts actually prove the theory wrong or reveal that the theory has been misapplied or

misinterpreted. However, that is exactly what Australia is doing. Moreover, Honduras points out that also analyses by the U.S. Surgeon General confirm that it is inappropriate to rely on behavioural intentions at the expense of empirical and behavioural data. This demonstrates that intentional theories themselves are not sufficient to form the basis for policy decisions.

90.   In any case, Australia inappropriately relies on intentions- and appeal-based metrics to conjure a strained argument that plain packaging will one distant day have an effect on smoking behaviour, even though such behaviour is entirely absent today. Honduras, along with the Dominican Republic and Indonesia, consulted Professor Ajzen who is a leading behavioural scientist that developed the Theory of Planned Behaviour ("TPD"), which grew out of his earlier theory, the Theory of Reasoned Action ("TRA"). Importantly, it is in large part based on this TRA and related theories that Australia has unsuccessfully tried to justify its plain packaging measures.

91.   Professor Ajzen concludes that Australia and its experts' understanding of the role and relevance of behavioural science theories is flawed. He also finds that the tobacco-control researchers appear to misunderstand important aspects of the theories that invalidate their predictions of the effectiveness on the plain packaging measures to reduce smoking consumption and prevalence. Professor Ajzen notes that Australia posits a causal chain whereby its implementation of plain packaging is designed to impact on three non-behavioural mechanisms which in turn are supposed to impact smoking behaviour. Thus, instead of conducting or relying on research that shows that plain packaging changes behaviour, Australia argues that the research shows plain packaging will impact the non-behavioural mechanisms and then attempts to rely on behavioural theories to "bridge the evidentiary gap" between the mechanisms and the behaviour at issue. Australia points to the TRA and the Affect Heuristic. However, as Professor Ajzen explains, this attempt is illegitimate and fails to meet the scientific standards of those theories.

92.   The fundamental flaw with Australia's presentation of the behavioural theories is that it relies on the theories to prove the link between the non-behavioural intentions, beliefs and attitudes, and the ultimate behaviour. This reliance is misplaced because only well-conducted empirical research can prove or disprove such a link. While the theories may generate hypotheses, these hypotheses must be rigorously and empirically tested to determine their legitimacy. Further, given that smoking behaviour is an addictive behaviour, the research shows that in this context, even more than in other contexts, intentions cannot predict smoking behaviour effectively. Professor Ajzen notes that "no behaviour theory, including the Theories of Reasoned Action and Planned Behaviour, can establish or prove that non-behavioural mechanisms are causally linked to, as well as being good predictors of, any particular future behaviour. These propositions can only be confirmed by empirical research".

93.   Professor Ajzen develops the same critique of Australia's view of the attitude-behaviour relation. That is, Australia's expert Professor Fong simply states that there is "extensive" research connecting attitudes to behaviour, but he

does not discuss any of it and fails to verify that any potential relation between the two concepts remains valid with respect to smoking behaviour. Professor Ajzen states that Professor Fong's assertion "is belied by research on the attitude behaviour relation that goes back at least 80 years. Contrary to Professor Fong's assertion, this longstanding body of research suggests that people's attitudes toward a non-behavioural target (i.e. tobacco products) do not reliably predict their behaviour (i.e. smoking) with respect to the target. Consequently, the attitude-behaviour research would lead us to hypothesize that a change in tobacco packaging, even if it affects the appeal of tobacco products, is *unlikely* to change smoking behaviour".

D.   An Objective Review of the Speculative Studies Testing People's Response to Plain Packaging Shows That These Studies Fail To Address The Relevant Behaviour and Are Methodologically Flawed

94.   Australia has consistently relied on a number of studies that were published prior to the adoption of the plain packaging measures to test people's reaction to a possible plain packaging environment. The relevance of these studies, if any, has been overtaken by subsequent data on the actual response by consumers to plain packaging in Australia that reveal an entirely different picture. In any case, already at the time the studies were published, some of the tobacco-control researchers themselves acknowledged that the conclusions drawn in these studies about the positive contribution of plain packaging to changing smoking behaviour were "speculative" at best. Despite the limited relevance of these speculative studies to the dispute, Honduras presents expert evidence to show that these studies generally undertaken by the same set of tobacco-control researchers fail to provide a sound basis for Australia's measures.

95.   In this respect, Honduras notes that the Panel's task is to make an objective assessment of the matter, including an assessment of the quantitative, qualitative and scientific evidence put before the Panel by the parties. The jurisprudence does not support the notion that as soon as a measure is based on a number of peer-reviewed studies not involving data from the actual operation of the measure, it can be considered as being based on scientific evidence. In this case, the real world data from three years of application of the measures demonstrate that the measures have not been effective and are not likely to ever be effective. In addition, Honduras considers that the Appellate Body found that "respectable scientific evidence" must have the "necessary scientific and methodological rigour to be considered reputable science". The standard set by the Appellate Body is a substantive one: does the evidence have the "necessary scientific and methodological rigour" to be considered reputable science and does the science warrant the particular measure? This test is not met simply by referring to the fact that studies speculating about the effect of a measure are peer-reviewed and published in a journal. That would in effect prevent any review by a panel of the "scientific" nature of certain evidence as it would simply have to accept any study's conclusions as soon as it gets past peer-review

and is published. With that substantive standard in mind, Honduras consulted a number of experts to examine the studies relied on by Australia.

96.   First, Professor Inman and his colleagues conducted an independent "peer review" of the studies that were previously published in dedicated health and tobacco control journals. The Peer Review Project was designed to emulate a peer-review process in a high-quality social science journal, examining whether the plain packaging studies relied on by Australia were of sufficient quality to be included in a such a journal. The original Peer Review Project report concluded that none of the plain packaging studies would be published in a high-quality journal because they would fail a rigorous peer review process. Based on their comprehensive review process, Professor Inman's research concludes that "the plain packaging literature as a whole falls short of providing compelling evidence on the effect of plain packaging on the demand for tobacco products". Even though Australia's experts themselves, such as Professor Fong, rely on research from the field of consumer behaviour to argue that plain packaging will be effective, Australia nevertheless criticises the Peer Review Project for applying criteria from research into consumer behaviour. In his rebuttal of the criticisms made by Australia's experts, Professor Inman concludes that "Australia's experts have largely failed to engage with the substance of the arguments put forward" and focused on minor issues.

97.   Second, Professor Kleijnen conducted a systematic analysis of the quality of this literature across four key aspects of validity in social science research (construct validity, internal validity, external validity, and conclusion validity). His research concludes that "there is not a single study outcome that has a 'low risk of bias' on all four aspects of validity". Australia's experts failed to identify a single error in the systematic review's assessment of the plain packaging studies. Australia's experts have not engaged in a methodical discussion of the results of the systematic review and the piecemeal responses that were given do not change the assessment that the evidence base regarding the potential impact of plain packaging on reducing smoking prevalence or tobacco consumption is unreliable and lacks credibility. It is noteworthy that in Australia's own Post-Implementation Review, Australia did not discuss these "experimental" studies in the context of its assessment of the impact of the plain packaging measures on public health but considered them merely in the introductory background section relating to the adoption of the measures. This confirms the lack of relevance of these pre-implementation studies.

E.   **An Analysis of the Problem of Illicit Tobacco Trade in Australia Confirms the Likelihood that Plain Packaging Will Further Stimulate Illicit Trade in Australia**

98.   Honduras points to the problem of illicit trade in tobacco products as a result of plain packaging. Honduras' experts Professors Chaudhry, Murray and Zimmerman, as well as analysis by KPMG, reveal that illicit trade has become more of a problem in the plain packaging environment of Australia. As with the other post-implementation data, updated data on illicit trade from KPMG

confirms that illicit trade has continued to worsen during the time that plain packaging has been in place.

F.   Australia Has Failed to Present Any Evidence of The Effect of Plain Packaging on Cigar Consumption

99.   Australia adopted the plain packaging measures with practically no evidence on cigars. While Australia relied on certain studies concerning the supposed effectiveness of plain packs, these studies examined the effects on cigarette packaging, not cigar packaging. Unfortunately, the complete lack of evidence on cigars did not stop Australia from adopting the *TPP Act* for all tobacco products. A few months after the adoption of the plain packaging measures, the Australian Government attempted to produce some evidence on cigars. This attempt failed. As documented in the Peer Review Project, the GfK Bluemoon study, which consisted of interviews with eight cigar smokers, is beset by multiple methodological failings that render it entirely unreliable. In 2015, years after the adoption of the plain packaging measures, Australia made another attempt at generating *ex post* evidence concerning the effects of plain packaging on cigar consumption. Australia's efforts resulted in one additional study, conducted by Miller et al. (2015). This *ex-post* evidence on cigars suffered from serious methodological flaws and limited sample sizes. For example, the study interview is based on a sample of only 10 regular premium smokers, and the two focus groups with occasional premium cigar and premium cigarillo smokers have a sample of 14 participants.

100.   As a cigar-producing country, Honduras is astonished that, in 2011, Australia adopted a highly-restrictive measure affecting cigars despite the absence of any evidentiary support for its application to cigars. Australia's efforts to obtain *ex post* evidence are, as a matter of principle and in fact, inadequate. No country should be allowed to *first* adopt a trade-restrictive measure and *then* seek evidence to support it. In any event, both of Australia's *ex post* studies suffer from various flaws that deprive them of any evidentiary value. Consequently, Honduras reiterates that Australia has not demonstrated that plain packaging can make any contribution to the reduction of the prevalence of cigar smoking.

G.   Australia is Unable to Rebut the Empirical and Theoretical Evidence Presented by Honduras and the Other Complainants

101.   Faced with the empirical evidence that fails to show any impact of Australia's measures on actual smoking behaviours, Australia argues that this evidence is not relevant because the measures are expected to produce results only "over time" and in combination with other measures. However, this argument is self-serving and not supported by any evidence. The speculative studies relied on by Australia purport to demonstrate an immediate positive contribution of plain packaging mainly in terms of perceptions, attitudes and intentions related to smoking behaviour. The "effects" of plain packaging presented in these studies took only the short time of the survey to become

apparent. Similarly, the study of calls to the Australian Quitline following the measures' implementation, which is relied on by Australia, also suggested that there was an immediate effect of the measures, with those researchers concluding that Australia's measures were "now supported by evidence of an immediate impact of this legislation". The tobacco-control experts consulted by Professor Pechey in her study also predicted a decline of 1-3% in smoking rates in the first two years of the measure. Even though there were these purported immediate impacts, Australia now argues that the measures will only produce effects "over time" and that they will take a generation for the measures to have an effect. In addition to the fact that this contradicts its objective of reducing smoking to 10% by 2018 (and thus not "over time" for the next generation), Australia does not support this speculation with any qualitative or quantitative evidence, as required.

102.   Indeed, in *Brazil – Retreaded Tyres*, the Appellate Body noted that it may prove difficult in the short term "to isolate the contribution to public health or environmental objectives of one specific measure from those attributable to the other measures that are part of the same comprehensive policy" and that "results obtained from certain actions – for instance, measures adopted in order to attenuate global warming and climate change or certain preventive actions to reduce the incidence of diseases that may manifest themselves only after a certain period of time – can only be evaluated with the benefit of time". In this respect, however, it is important to recall that the Appellate Body in *Brazil – Retreaded Tyres* found that the panel sought to verify a number of hypotheses on the basis of the evidence adduced by the parties and found them to be logically sound and supported by sufficient evidence. The above time-related considerations of the Appellate Body therefore were made to justify the panel's mainly "qualitative" approach to examining the contribution of the measure, not to absolve the parties from providing evidence or allowing parties to disregard the actual empirical evidence of the impact of a measure by pointing to abstract general theories. As noted before, the last sentence of this oft-quoted paragraph makes clear that a demonstration of a likely future contribution must still be based on "quantitative projections in the future, or qualitative reasoning based on a set of hypotheses that are tested and supported by sufficient evidence".

103.   The actual operation of the measures and its actual impact are still the preferred evidence to consider if such evidence exists and if the measures have been in place for a reasonable period of time. In fact, in its Technical Report accompanying the NTPPTS, which covered a period until May 2014, Australia referred to this two-year period that passed as a "medium term" impact. The nature, quantity and quality of evidence existing at the time that the analysis is made determine what evidence the Panel must rely on. In this case, reliable and probative empirical evidence of the lack of actual impact of the measures three years after their introduction is available and must be given primacy in the analysis.

104.   Furthermore,it is widely accepted in the tobacco-control context that what is known about "shock communications" is that they sometimes have an

immediate, short-term effect which is difficult to sustain in the long term. In fact, researchers, tobacco-control experts and the FCTC itself all agree that health communications such as GHWs are subject to "wear out" after repeated exposures and have their largest impact in the early days of their release in a jurisdiction. Australia's plain packaging measures have now been in place for three years, and if they were going to have some relevant effect, this change in behaviour would have been visible by now. However, there is no evidence of such an effect. Indeed there is already evidence of an expected wear-out effect of plain packaging in Australia, which entirely undermines Australia's claim that the measures will have a long-term impact. Similarly, the evidence that Australia cites regarding increased calls to the Australian Quitline following the implementation of plain packaging shows that the effect was only temporary and that the number of calls returned to the level prior to the introduction of plain packaging within six months. Accordingly, there is no basis for believing that these measures, which have not had even a short-term effect on smoking behaviours, would have a long-term effect.

105.   Finally, the fact that the plain packaging measures do not deal with the drivers of smoking further demonstrates that there is no credible basis for expecting that the measures will be able to have any long-term effect. As explained by Honduras by reference to academic articles and reports as well as the expert reports of, among others, Professor Steinberg, Professor Fischer and Dr. Satel, the multi-causal model that is understood to drive smoking behaviour does not include trademarks or packaging as a reason why people start smoking, continue to smoke or relapse after a failed quit attempt. As trademarks and packaging are not even factors, let alone genuine and substantial factors, of smoking initiation and continued consumption of tobacco products, there is no basis to assume that Australia's plain packaging measures will reduce smoking in either the short or the long term.

106.   In sum, Australia has not presented any "quantitative projections" and has not developed any "qualitative reasoning based on a set of hypotheses that are tested and supported by sufficient evidence produced" in support of its assertion that the plain packaging measures will produce effects over time. Australia simply urges the Panel to accept the speculative assertion that "over time" smoking will go down as a result of the measures. However, the Panel's conclusion should not be based on speculation and conjecture but on positive evidence that is objectively assessed. Australia is right that over time smoking is expected to go down, as it has been going down for the last 40 years. That is the trend that even Australia and its experts have acknowledged exists. For example, Gartner et al., in research funded by the Australian National Health and Medical Research Council and published in the Tobacco Control journal, forecast that under a *status quo* scenario where no new tobacco-control measures were implemented and in which smoking initiation and cessation rates remained at 2007 levels (which the authors thought for smoking initiation rates may be overly pessimistic), smoking prevalence would decline to 18.3% in 2010 and 14.1% in 2020. A failure to account for this pre-existing trend will falsely bias

any estimation of the effects of new tobacco-control measures on smoking metrics. Therefore, the fact that smoking prevalence has gone down does not say anything about the relationship between the reduction in smoking prevalence and plain packaging. The relevant question is whether this trade-restrictive measure actually contributes, or is apt to contribute, to the further reduction of smoking, or rather is an unnecessary element of the suite of measures and thus an unjustifiable encumbrance or an unnecessary obstacle to trade.

107.   On the basis of the evidence before the Panel, it is clear that there is no such contributing relationship as the trend of the decline in smoking trend is simply continuing without any additional contribution from the plain packaging measures.

H.   Australia's Post-Implementation Review Fails to Present Evidence of the Effectiveness of the Plain Packaging Measures

108.   More than three years after it implemented the plain packaging measures, and after having failed to conduct the required pre-implementation impact assessment, Australia released its Post-Implementation Review ("PIR") of the plain packaging measures on 26 February 2016.

109.   The PIR fails to objectively examine the many data sources that Australia had at its disposal for assessing whether plain packaging contributed to the objective of reducing smoking. The PIR uncritically summarises post-implementation studies that were published back in March 2015. The PIR does not objectively examine these studies' findings in light of Australia's objective to reduce smoking. The PIR ignores the relevant information on the effects of plain packaging on smoking behaviour that were revealed, among others, through the NTPPTS that it helped to organise.

110.   The only piece of "new" evidence relating to the impact of the measures on health, consists of an expert report by Dr. Chipty, the same economic consultant that supported Australia in the context of this WTO dispute. It is not credible that the same economic consultant hired to support the Australian Government's litigation objectives can provide an objective analysis of the effectiveness of the measures to Australia's Department of Health. In addition, Dr. Chipty's expert report for the PIR is simply a compilation of the RMSS-related sections of her WTO reports. Although the Australian Government is very well aware of the many different ways in which the RMSS data has been interpreted by the complainants' experts and of their critical comments of Dr. Chipty's approach, the PIR acts as if this debate never took place. The Department of Health is part of the Australian Government and could have been expected to critically review the expert report of Dr. Chipty taking some of these alternative readings into consideration. It did not do so. Nor did it seek to put the claims of Dr. Chipty based on this one dataset in the context of other datasets supporting contrary conclusions.

111.   In sum, Honduras considers that the this long-awaited PIR only serves to highlights the weakness of Australia's evidence base for tobacco plain packaging

as it uses the same avoidance tactics relied upon by Australia in the context of this WTO dispute. The PIR focuses on whether plain packaging achieves the "mechanisms" rather than on whether plain packaging achieves the acknowledged objective of reducing smoking. Unfortunately, the PIR does not attempt to conduct a critical analysis of the information available so as to assess objectively the effectiveness of plain packaging. The PIR was intended to assess "the effectiveness and efficiency of the tobacco plain packaging measures to meet its objective [i.e., of improving public health, by ultimately reducing smoking] in order to determine if it is an appropriate regulatory mechanism". Unfortunately, the PIR does not provide a robust assessment of this important question. Instead, it avoids addressing this issue head-on. Where it does attempt to address the issue, its conclusions are equivocal. It rightly notes that the declines in national smoking prevalence cannot be "entirely attributable to plain packaging given the range of tobacco control measures in place in Australia". And even the "new" expert analysis by Dr. Chipty on which Australia relies is not actually specific to plain packaging as it allegedly "shows that the 2012 packaging changes (plain packaging combined with GHWs) have contributed to declines in smoking prevalence, even at this early time after implementation". Honduras questions the accuracy of the decline found to exist by Dr. Chipty due to methodological concerns about the analysis, which is similar to the analysis presented by Dr. Chipty and rebutted by Honduras and the other complainants in the WTO dispute. Nevertheless, even assuming this figure is correct (*quod non*), the conclusion is that the decline is attributable to the "packaging changes" as a combination of plain packaging and the GHWs. The PIR does not answer the relevant question about what is the contribution of plain packaging alone to the decline in smoking prevalence.

I.   CONCLUSION

112.   Reliable and probative data of three years of application of the Australian tobacco plain packaging measures exists. It shows that the measures have not been effective. Analysis of the actual sales and consumption data and the tracking survey data confirm this lack of contribution of the plain packaging measures. These are the facts that Australia would like the Panel to ignore. Honduras considers that there is no basis in law or in the facts of this case to justify Australia's suggestion to disregard this evidence in favour of speculative theories. Australia does not present any empirical data of its own to show that the plain packaging measures are contributing to reducing smoking prevalence or changing smoking behaviour. It has failed to rebut the probative evidence presented by Honduras and the complainants that demonstrated clearly that the measures have failed.

113.   Honduras' evidence demonstrates that the plain packaging measures do not make a contribution to Australia's objective. Honduras' evidence approach is in line with established WTO jurisprudence and does not jeopardise a Member's freedom to regulate to protect health. Faced with this overwhelming evidence, Australia has resorted to the argument that more time is needed to see an impact.

However, this is an inadequate response. Studies that Australia has relied upon in these proceedings suggest that plain packaging would have an immediate shock effect. That shock effect was supposed to lead to more quit attempts and less smoking initiation. Clearly this has not occurred. In the light of this lack of an immediate effect, Australia is now arguing that the effect of the plain packaging measures will only be manifested in the long-term. This argument not only has no factual basis, it also flies in the face of common sense. A more likely outcome, which is consistent with what experts have claimed in respect of other tobacco-control policies, is that plain packaging would be most effective (if effective at all) immediately after its introduction. It is to be expected that any impact that a policy intervention like plain packaging might have would wear-out over time as a result of consumers' repeated exposure to the new pack. Indeed, as noted above, researchers are already observing this expected wear-out effect of the plain packaging measures in Australia. Accordingly, in light of the evidence on the lack of impact of plain packaging reducing actual tobacco consumption to date and of this wear-out effect, Australia's assertion that plain packaging will have effects on smoking behaviour at some uncertain point in the future when it has not had any effect in the first three years that it has been in place is entirely speculative and untenable.

114.   For all of the above reasons, Honduras requests the Panel to find that Australia's plain packaging measures are inconsistent with the following provisions of the TRIPS Agreement:

- Article 20 of the TRIPS Agreement because the plain packaging measures are special requirements that unjustifiably encumber the use of tobacco-related trademarks in the course of trade;

- Article 16.1 of the TRIPS Agreement because these measures prevent the owner of a registered tobacco-related trademark from enjoying the exclusive rights conferred by the trademark – namely the right to enjoin unauthorised use of the trademark by third parties – and are not justified under Article 17 of the TRIPS Agreement;

- Articles 15.4 of the TRIPS Agreement because the nature of the goods to which a trademark is to be applied – i.e., tobacco products – forms an obstacle to the registration of inherently non-distinctive trademarks in Australia;

- Article 2.1 of the TRIPS Agreement, which incorporates provisions of the Paris Convention, in particular Article 6*quinquies* of the Paris Convention, because a trademark duly registered in the country of origin outside Australia is not protected "as is" – i.e., in its original format; and Article 10*bis* of the Paris Convention, because: (a) the plain packaging measures give rise to a situation of "unfair competition" by *ex ante* and systematically skewing the conditions of competition to the detriment of high-end products and producers and to the

> advantage of lower-end products and producers; and (b) the
> plain packaging measures require producers to make
> "indications or allegations the use of which in the course of trade
> is liable to mislead the public as to the nature, the manufacturing
> process, the characteristics, the suitability for their purpose, or
> the quantity, of the goods";
>
> - Article 24.3 of the TRIPS Agreement because the plain
>   packaging measures diminish the protection afforded to GIs that
>   existed in Australia immediately prior to 1 January 1995; and
>
> - Article 22.2(b) of the TRIPS Agreement because Australia fails
>   to provide the legal means for interested parties to prevent use,
>   with respect to GIs, constituting an act of unfair competition
>   under Article 10*bis*(3)(iii) of the Paris Convention.

115.   Australia's plain packaging measures are also inconsistent with Article 2.2 of the TBT Agreement as they are more trade-restrictive than necessary to fulfil Australia's legitimate objective of reducing smoking prevalence, taking account of the risks of non-fulfilment.

116.   Honduras requests the Panel to recommend, in accordance with Article 19.1 of the DSU, that the DSB request Australia to bring the measures at issue into conformity with the TRIPS Agreement and the TBT Agreement.

ANNEX B-2

INTEGRATED EXECUTIVE SUMMARY OF THE ARGUMENTS OF THE DOMINICAN REPUBLIC

I.   INTRODUCTION

1.   More than 3 years ago, on 1 December 2012, Australia implemented sweeping measures to eliminate differentiation among tobacco products by banning all design features (including those of trademarks and geographical indications ("GIs")) on tobacco retail packaging and the tobacco products themselves. Australia claimed that these features induce people to smoke, and that by banning them, smoking would reduce in Australia.

2.   Over the course of these proceedings, the Dominican Republic (the "DR") and its experts have shown that this premise is fundamentally flawed. The totality of evidence, ranging from post-implementation to predictive evidence, shows that these plain packaging ("PP") measures do not, and will not, contribute to their objective of reducing smoking in Australia. The measures serve only to deny competitive opportunities owed to Australia's trading partners and undermine the system of international trade that Australia has pledged to uphold because of its WTO membership.

3.   Many developing countries resisted – but ultimately accepted – the legal protections for intellectual property ("IP") that developed nations insisted upon in the Uruguay Round negotiations, skeptical of the benefits that IP rights could bring to their economies. Nonetheless, now that the DR has transformed itself from an exporter of unprocessed tobacco leaf into the world's leading producer and exporter of premium branded cigars, the protection of trademarks and GIs has taken on considerable importance to its exports. Yet, through the PP measures, Australia effectively abandons the rules that it and other developed nations insisted upon. The PP measures seek, by legislative design, to denude trademarks of their basic functions and to eliminate tobacco-related GIs, rendering meaningless the trademark and GI protections contained in the *TRIPS Agreement*, without public health benefit.

4.   The DR fully supports a WTO Member's right to take effective public health measures. In the present proceedings, the DR has shown that Australia could replace the ineffective PP measures by tobacco control measures that are both effective and consistent with Australia's obligations under the *TRIPS Agreement* and the *TBT Agreement*.

II.   THE LEGAL CLAIMS AND ARGUMENTS

A.   Legal Claims under the *TRIPS Agreement*

1.   The PP measures are inconsistent with Article 15.4[1]

5.   Article 15.4 of the *TRIPS Agreement* provides that "[t]he nature of the goods or services to which a trademark is to be applied shall in no case form an obstacle to registration of the trademark". Thus, to the extent that a WTO Member imposes obstacles or impediments to registration of a trademark due to the essential quality or constitution of the good or service with which a sign is linked, it violates Article 15.4.

6.   Under the PP measures, the use of all signs on tobacco products is prohibited or greatly restricted. In this situation, there is no opportunity for a non-inherently distinctive sign for tobacco products to gain distinctiveness through use and, consequently, no possibility of registering such a sign as a trademark for tobacco products. The impediment to registering such signs as trademarks in Australia is due to the nature of the products with which the sign is linked, i.e., tobacco products. This violates Article 15.4.

7.   Australia errs when it asserts that non-inherently distinctive signs are not "trademarks", and therefore that such signs are not covered by the scope of Article 15.4. In fact, Article 15.1 defines a "trademark" as a sign that must be "*capable* of distinguishing the goods or services of one undertaking from those of other undertakings",[2] and Australia's argument impermissibly reads the term "capable" out of that definition. Article 6*quinquies*(B) of the *Paris Convention* provides relevant context, clarifying that the term "trademark" encompasses signs that are not inherently distinctive and that have not acquired distinctiveness through use.

8.   Australia argues that, if accepted, the DR's interpretation of Article 15.4 would require that Members guarantee the right to sell and advertise products in their territory, regardless of the nature of those products. This is incorrect. The DR has explained that restrictions on the availability of, or trade in, a good or service are disciplined by, *inter alia*, the GATT 1994 or the GATS, not the trademark provisions of the *TRIPS Agreement*.

2.   The PP measures are inconsistent with Article 16.1[3]

9.   Article 16.1 of the *TRIPS Agreement* requires that WTO Members provide registered trademark owners: (i) the exclusive right to prevent all (ii)

---

[1]   *See* DR's FWS, Section VI.E; DR's SWS, Section III.A; DR's response to PQs 172, 195; DR's comments on AUS' response to PQ 172.

[2]   Emphasis added.

[3]   *See* DR's FWS, Section VI.F; DR's SWS, Section III.B; DR's SCS, para. 21; DR's response to PQs 29, 30, 32, 94, 95, 96, 172; DR's comments on AUS' response to PQs 172 and 185.

unauthorized use (iii) in the course of trade of (iv) identical or similar signs, (v) for goods or services that are identical or similar to those in respect of which the trademark is registered, (vi) where such use would result in a likelihood of confusion.

10.   By prohibiting or restricting the use of trademarks for tobacco products, the PP measures diminish or eliminate, depending on the circumstances, the distinctiveness and recognition of such trademarks. This breaks the connection for consumers between the trademark and the product for which it was registered, rendering it practically impossible for a trademark owner to demonstrate that unauthorized use of an identical or similar mark on similar goods causes a likelihood of confusion. Consequently, the trademark owner's ability to exercise the exclusive rights guaranteed under Article 16.1 is diminished, or even eliminated, as a result of the PP measures.

11.   Australia responds by mischaracterizing the DR's argument as asserting that Article 16.1 requires Members to guarantee a "right to use" trademarks.[4] More generally, Australia's standard response to the DR's claims under the *TRIPS Agreement* is that such claims are based on the proposition that the *TRIPS Agreement* affords a "right to use" trademarks (and GIs). Australia thereby creates a "straw man" that it proceeds to knock down. The DR has never asserted that the *TRIPS Agreement* grants a "right" of use. Rather, the DR, like most third parties, understands that "use" permeates the *TRIPS Agreement* provisions relating to trademark and GI protection. It is uncontested that the basic function of a trademark is to distinguish goods and services in the course of trade. Fulfillment of this basic function creates competitive opportunities for goods and services, and is the very purpose of international trademark protection. Unless a trademark is used on the goods and services in the course of trade, it simply cannot fulfill its basic function.

12.   In focusing wrongly on a "right to use" argument, Australia fails to engage substantively with the DR's actual argument, which is concerned with the inability to *enforce* the trademark rights protected by Article 16.1.

3.   The PP measures are inconsistent with Article 16.3[5]

13.   In its capacity as a third party in DS458 and DS467, the DR has explained that to acquire and maintain the status of a mark as "well-known", and therefore to enjoy the additional protections of Article 16.3 of the *TRIPS Agreement*, consumers must know and recognize the mark.

14.   The PP measures violate Article 16.3, because (i) they remove the "negative rights" that were previously accorded to marks that achieved well-known status (*i.e.*, rights that go above and beyond those accorded under Article

---

4   *See* AUS' FWS, para. 315.
5   *See* DR's FWS, section VI.G, DR's SWS, Section III.C; DR's SCS, para. 21; DR's response to PQ 31; DR's comments on AUS' response to PQ 172.

16.1) prior to the imposition of PP; and (ii) they render it impossible for any other registered trademarks on tobacco products to acquire that status going forward, and to thereby exercise the rights accorded by Article 16.3. Thus, because of the PP measures, trademarks cannot acquire and maintain the level of knowledge critical to "well-known" status.

4. The PP measures are inconsistent with Article 10*bis* of the *Paris Convention*[6]

15.   The obligations in Article 10*bis* of the *Paris Convention* are incorporated into the *TRIPS Agreement* through Article 2.1. Article 10*bis*(1) establishes a general obligation to ensure effective protection against unfair competition. In turn, Article 10*bis*(3) requires Members to prohibit three particular types of private acts of unfair competition, in particular, under Article 10*bis*(3)(3), "indications or allegations the use of which in the course of trade is liable to mislead the public as to the nature, the manufacturing process, the characteristics, the suitability for their purpose, or the quantity, of the goods".

16.   The PP measures require competitors to present their tobacco products in a uniform manner that prevents differentiation, and is intentionally meant to give the misleading impression that all brands are the same, and that each is "the least appealing" and the "lowest quality". In reality, there are significant variations in the quality and characteristics of tobacco used in different cigar and cigarette brands, and, for cigars in particular, between hand- and factory-made products. Indeed, the DR's successful development of a premium cigar industry is premised on the existence of such differences in quality, as recognized by both consumers and experts.

17.   Thus, the PP measures compel private acts that are liable to mislead consumers as to the nature, the manufacturing process, and the characteristics of tobacco products, in violation of Article 10*bis*(3)(3). Thus, rather than preventing unfair competition, Australia is mandating it,. The DR has further shown that no other Australian measure can be used to cure the acts of unfair competition compelled by the *PP Act*.

18.   In response to Australia's arguments, the DR has clarified that it does not contend that the PP measures are *themselves* "acts" of unfair competition. Rather, the DR has explained how, as a result of the PP measures, Australia mandates *private acts* of unfair competition in the *presentation* of tobacco products to consumers and, thereby, fails to assure effective protection against such unfair competition. Moreover, the DR has explained that, under Article 10*bis*(1) and (3), the intention of the commercial actor is not relevant to whether its act involves unfair competition, and Australia's contention to the contrary is erroneous.

---

[6]   *See* DR's FWS, Section VI.I; DR's SWS, Section III.E; DR's SCS, para. 22; DR response to PQs 15, 16, 17, 18, 19, 20, 22, 177; DR's comments on AUS' response to PQ 185.

19.   With particular respect to Article 10*bis*(3)(3), and in response to Australia's erroneously narrow interpretation of the phrase "in the course of trade", the DR has demonstrated that this phrase refers to commercial activities generally, rather than to a period of time that culminates at the point of sale of an individual product to the consumer.

5.   The PP measures are inconsistent with Article 22.2(b)[7]

20.   Article 22.2(b) of the *TRIPS Agreement* disciplines acts of unfair competition, within the meaning of Article 10*bis* of the *Paris Convention*, with respect to GIs, and establishes an obligation to provide legal means for interested parties to prevent such acts. Acts of unfair competition include acts that diminish consumers' understanding of the qualities, reputation, or other characteristics expected from a good with a particular origin. Article 22.2(b) covers uses of any types of indications, designations, or presentations.

21.   As a result of the PP measures, producers are unable to signal the geographical origin of the product in a way that links the origin with the qualities of the product, thereby limiting consumer information. Moreover, the compulsory presentation of cigars without GIs serves to mislead consumers. Consumers generally will be led to believe erroneously that the geographical origin of the product makes no difference to the quality or characteristics of the products.

22.   Under the PP measures, premium Dominican and Cuban cigar makers who meet their local requirements concerning use of the "*Cigarro Dominicano*" or "*Habanos*" GIs are limited in Australia to simply identifying their products as having been manufactured in the DR or Cuba. This is the same manner in which *every* cigar manufactured in the DR or Cuba is identified as a product of that country, *regardless of quality or other characteristics*. Thus, by requiring all cigar producers to identify their products with respect only to the country of manufacture, and not the additional elements associated with GIs, the PP measures mandate the use of indications that are, *inter alia*, liable to mislead as to the different characteristics of different products coming from the same country.

23.   In sum, through the mandatory use of plain packaging and the prohibition on use of GIs, competitors are compelled to use "indications or allegations ... which in the course of trade [are] liable to mislead the public as to the nature ... [or] characteristics" of the tobacco products, within the meaning of Article 10*bis*(3)(3) of the *Paris Convention*. As such, in violation of Article 22.2(b) of the *TRIPS Agreement*, Australia fails to "provide the legal means for interested parties" to prevent uses of designations or presentations on packaging that constitute such an act of unfair competition.

---

[7]   *See* DR's FWS, Section VI.J; DR's SWS, Section III.F; DR's response to PQ 44, 45, 47, 49, 50, 54, 87, 174, 177, 178; DR's comments on AUS' response to PQ 175.

6. The PP measures are inconsistent with Article 24.3[8]

24. Article 24.3 of the *TRIPS Agreement* provides that "[i]n implementing this Section, a Member shall not diminish the protection of geographical indications that existed in that Member immediately prior to the date of entry into force of the WTO Agreement", *i.e.*, 1 January 1995 for Australia. A Member's obligations under Article 24.3 apply to the actions it takes to give effect to Articles 22 to 24 of the *TRIPS Agreement*, as well as any acts or omissions by which a Member fails to do so, wholly or partially.

25. Article 24.3 is a standstill provision with respect to the *system* of protection of GIs that existed at the relevant time, as confirmed by the Spanish and French versions. Footnote 3 of the *TRIPS Agreement* provides context clarifying that the word "protection" includes "matters affecting the acquisition, scope, maintenance and enforcement of intellectual property rights". Thus, the relevant system of "protection" includes, where applicable in a given Member prior to 1995, the ability of indications to become GIs *(i.e.*, acquisition), and to maintain and enforce their GI status.

26. For these reasons, Australia's contention that Article 24.3 grandfathers only *individual GIs*, rather than a system of GI protection, is inconsistent with the text of the provision and the relevant context. Moreover, Australia's interpretation would have the absurd effect of benefitting GIs from developed countries, to the disadvantage of developing country GIs. That is because, in 1995, developed countries made greater use of GIs than developing countries. Establishing such discrimination against GIs from developing countries cannot have been the intent of the drafters.

27. By allowing use of GIs, within the meaning of Article 22.1, on tobacco products prior to 1995, Australia provided a level of protection that allowed for indications to acquire, maintain and ultimately enforce, their status as a GI. However, through the PP measures, Australia severely diminished such protection, since interested parties are no longer able to acquire, maintain, or enforce their status as GIs as they were before. Thus, the PP measures violate Article 24.3.

7. The PP measures are inconsistent with Article 20[9]

28. Article 20 of the *TRIPS Agreement* protects "[t]he use of a trademark in the course of trade" against "unjustifiable" encumbrances by "special requirements". In disciplining government action that encumbers trademark use, Article 20 recognizes "use" as essential to a trademark's ability to fulfill its basic

---

[8] *See* DR's FWS, Section VI.K; DR's SWS, Section III.G; DR's response to PQs 43, 44, 48, 51, 113, 179, 180, 181.

[9] *See* DR's FWS, Section VI.H; DR's SWS, Section III.D; DR's responses to PQs 38, 39, 99, 167, 169; DR's comments on AUS' responses to PQs 166, 170; DR's FOS, paras. 9-11; DR's SOS, paras. 6-11.

function of distinguishing goods and services in commerce in terms of their quality, characteristics, and reputation, and ensures the treaty's object and purpose of protecting trademarks.

a. The use of trademarks is "encumbered by special requirements" imposed under the PP measures[10]

29. Article 20 applies to measures that "encumber[] by special requirements". A "special requirement" is a condition mandated by a government (the "requirement") that is "unusual" or "out of the ordinary" ("special"), either because: it prescribes "use" of a trademark in a manner that departs from the usual treatment of a trademark; or it applies to trademarks used in connection with a particular good or service; or both.[11] "Special requirements" *directly* regulate the use of a trademark itself, and are to be distinguished from requirements that *incidentally* affect the use of trademarks, through, for instance, the regulation of a good or a service bearing a trademark.[12]

30. The verb "encumber" means "hamper ... burden", to "act as a ... restraint", or to "obstruct",[13] and refers to the *effect* a "special requirement" has on "[t]he use of a trademark". Encumbrances must therefore have the *effect* of hampering or obstructing the ability to use a trademark as registered (or, if not registered, as the owner would otherwise use it). If a "special requirement" has the effect of "encumber[ing]" trademark use, it must be justifiable.

31. Although the parties agree on the meaning of these words, disagreement remains on whether Article 20 covers (i) only certain encumbrances on trademark use and (ii) "prohibitions" on use.

32. *First*, Australia submits that Article 20 applies only to certain encumbrances on the use of trademarks, namely, those that prevent the commercial source of a good or service from being distinguished. For Australia, since only word marks are "necessary"[14] to distinguish commercial source, the use of trademark design features as part of figurative and composite marks is effectively excluded from Article 20. Australia contends that the use of trademark design features is not needed to distinguish the commercial source. Contrary to Australia's position, it is well established, including in Australia law, that trademarks may differentiate the commercial source of goods and services in terms of quality, characteristics, and reputation. Trademark design features are

---

[10] *See* DR's FWS, paras. 347-367; DR's SWS, paras. 96-127; DR's response to PQs 104, 108, 172; DR's comments on AUS' response to PQ 170; DR's FOS, paras. 13-17; DR's SOS, paras. 12-20.
[11] OED Online, "requirement, *n*"., Exhibit DR-81; OED Online, "special *adj*", Exhibit DR-82, "[o]f such a kind as to exceed or excel in some way that which is usual or common; exceptional in character, quality, or degree".
[12] *See* Panel Report, *Indonesia – Autos*, paras. 14.273 and 14.278.
[13] *See* AUS'FWS, para. 347; Cuba's FWS, para. 310; DR's FWS, para. 349; Honduras' FWS, para. 283; Indonesia's FWS, para. 272 and Ukraine's FWS, para. 329. *See also* OED Online, "encumber, *v*.", Exhibit DR-83.
[14] AUS' SWS, paras. 129 and 130.

expressly included as part of the definition of a trademark under Article 15.1, and are, hence, regarded as literally integral to the differentiating function of trademarks. Under Article 20, if special requirements encumber – that is, hamper, impede, restrain, and obstruct – the use of any feature of any trademark, the encumbrance must be justifiable. There is no basis to consider that Article 20 does not to apply to measures that interfere with the use of trademark design features.

33.   *Second*, Australia submits that a measure is subject to Article 20 solely if it encumbers "*how* a trademark is used ... not *whether* it is used".[15] Thus, on Australia's view, Article 20 does not apply to *prohibitions* on trademark use. Australia's interpretation is not supported by Article 20, which, again, asks only whether "*[t]he use* of a trademark [is *being*] *encumbered*". A prohibition plainly encumbers the use a trademark. Further, each of the examples in Article 20 describes an encumbrance that undermines a trademark's "capability to distinguish" goods and services in commerce: a prohibition is the most extreme example of interference with this function.

34.   Applying the proper legal interpretation, the PP measures severely "encumber" three distinct groups of trademarks on tobacco packaging and products. In particular: (i) *word marks* must appear in standardized format, and in the case of cigarette sticks, are banned entirely; (ii) the word components of *composite marks* must appear in standardized format, and the figurative components of composite marks are banned entirely; and (iii) *figurative marks* are banned entirely.[16]

b.   The PP measures encumber the use of trademarks "in the course of trade"[17]

35.   As discussed above, the "course of trade" includes trademark use as part of the commercial sale of goods, and includes trademark use on retail packaging, and on the good itself.

36.   Australia seeks to limit the scope of Article 20 by arguing that, if a trademark is not *seen* until *after* a sale, it is not "used" in the "course of trade". For Australia, the point-of-sale bans in Australia remove the PP measures from the scope of Article 20. Australia's argument is unduly restrictive. Retail packaging for consumer goods need not be *seen* on the store shelf for the use of a trademark on packaging to be part of the course of trade. This would imply

---

[15] AUS' response to PQ 100, para. 48 (emphasis original).

[16] A *word* mark consists simply of a particular word with no design features forming part of the registered trademark; a *composite* – or combination – mark is a combination of both word and figurative marks. Composite marks include unaccompanied stylized word marks (*e.g.*, a brand name in a particular typeface), as well as stylized word marks that include other design features; a *figurative* mark is comprised exclusively of image constituents, including colours, designs and figurative elements.

[17] *See* DR's SWS, paras. 128-141; DR's response to PQ 87; DR's FOS, paras. 18-20.

that remote purchases, where goods are not *seen* before purchase, are not part of the course of trade. Trademarks are applied to retail packaging and goods as an integral part of a commercial sale, and the use of a trademark on packaging is a routine part of the course of trade.

37.   Even if the Panel accepted Australia's flawed interpretation, it should still conclude that the PP measures encumber use "in the course of trade" because (i) under an exception to the point-of-sale display ban, specialist tobacconist shops in the states of Victoria and Western Australia are not subject to the display ban; and (ii) even where such bans are in operation in Australia, the consumer is still able to see and inspect the product, and its packaging, *before* the transaction is complete.

c.   The word "unjustifiably" imposes a multi-factored standard[18]

38.   According to the dictionary meaning, an encumbrance is "unjustifiabl[e]" if it is not rational, reasonable, proper, defensible or warranted.[19] Read in light of its context, and the object and purpose of Article 20, the "justifiability" of an encumbrance must be assessed on the basis of five factors: (1) the nature and extent of the encumbrance; (2) the importance of the objective pursued; (3) the features of particular trademarks that are considered to mislead or otherwise cause people to smoke; and (4) the connection between the objective and the encumbrance, including (i) the extent to which the measure contributes to its objective, and (ii) whether an alternative measure would make the same contribution to the objective with a lesser degree of encumbrance.

39.   In reaching this position, the DR has taken into account *the interests that Article 20 seeks to protect* and its *objective*.[20] The particular *interest protected* under Article 20 is "[t]he use of trademarks", and the *objective of the provision in protecting* that interest is safeguarding, to the greatest extent possible, the ability of a trademark to fulfill its basic function of distinguishing goods or services, without prejudicing the ability of a Member to achieve other legitimate objectives. This interpretation reflects the importance ascribed by the drafters to protecting the use of a trademark, allowing it to fulfill its basic function of distinguishing goods based on their qualities, reputation and characteristics.

> i.   The nature and extent of the encumbrance on use[21]

40.   Reflecting the express discipline on trademark "use", a panel must determine the nature and extent of the interference with use, and the consequence for the trademark's ability to fulfill its basic function. The nature

---

[18]   *See* DR's FWS, Section VI.H; DR's SWS, paras. 142-153; DR's response to PQ 108.
[19]   *See* DR's FWS, para. 379.
[20]   EU's response to PQ 17 to third parties, para. 102.
[21]   *See* DR's FWS, paras. 418-419; DR's SWS, paras. 181-204; DR's response to PQs 64 and 108; DR's SOS, paras. 21-26.

and extent of the encumbrance defines the prejudice to the protected treaty interest (*i.e.*, "[t]he use of a trademark") that must be justifiable under Article 20. For example, as discussed below, the nature of the encumbrance may require individual assessment of the specific features of a trademark that motivate the Member's decision to interfere with use. As another example, a minimal encumbrance on use would be more easily justified than a severe encumbrance.

41.   As explained in paragraph 34 above, the PP measures impose *severe* encumbrances on three distinct categories of trademarks. The contribution made by the PP measures to reducing smoking must therefore be commensurate with the extent of the severe encumbrances, in terms of both the likelihood of a contribution materializing, and the extent of the contribution.

ii.   The objective pursued[22]

42.   With respect to the second factor, the parties agree that an encumbrance must pursue a *legitimate objective* to be justifiable. Section 3(1)(a) of the *PP Act* establishes that the objective of the PP measures is to reduce the number of people that smoke, by reducing initiation, increasing cessation, and reducing relapse, and to reduce exposure to tobacco smoke. Section 3(2) of the *PP Act* sets out the *means* to achieve the objective, namely: (i) reducing the appeal of tobacco products; (ii) increasing the effectiveness of graphic health warnings ("GHWs"); and (iii) reducing the ability of retail packaging to mislead consumers about the harmful effects of tobacco.

43.   Section 3(1)(b) of the *PP Act* adds a second objective, namely, to give effect to certain of Australia's "obligations" as a party to the Framework Convention on Tobacco Control ("FCTC"). However, the FCTC does not "oblige" members to adopt plain packaging. Also, it is not "legitimate" for a Member to invoke an obligation under a separate international agreement to justify the imposition of WTO-inconsistent restrictions.

iii.   The individualized nature of trademarks and
trademark protection[23]

44.   The third factor reflects the *individual nature of trademarks and trademark protection* – under both the *TRIPS Agreement* and the *Paris Convention*. All aspects of trademark regulation – registration,[24] protection,[25] invalidation[26] – proceed on the basis of individualized processes that consider the specific features of a trademark. In his authoritative guide to the *Paris Convention*, Bodenhausen explains that, in assessing registration and

---

[22]   *See* DR's FWS, paras. 420-425; DR's SWS, paras. 271-288; DR's response to PQ 108; DR's FOS, paras. 38-43.

[23]   *See* DR's FWS, paras. 394-415; DR's SWS, paras. 205-267; DR's response to PQs 93, 108; DR's comments on AUS' responses to DR's Question 1; DR's FOS, paras. 27-36.

[24]   *TRIPS Agreement*, Article 15.

[25]   *TRIPS Agreement*, Article 16.

[26]   *See e.g.* Article 6*quinquies*B of the *Paris Convention*.

invalidation, each trademark must be considered "on its individual merits".[27] Likewise, where a Member interferes with the *use* of a trademark to address allegedly harmful effects of the features of that trademark – in this case, causing people to smoke – it must review the trademark "on its individual merits".[28] The design features of each trademark are unique, and the encumbrances imposed by Australia relate to considerations that *vary from individual trademark to individual trademark* – some design features of some trademarks may give rise to Australia's regulatory concerns, while others do not.

45.   A Member cannot be allowed to exploit a decision on the *use* of a trademark, in order to circumvent the usual requirements of individual consideration that apply to decisions on the *invalidation* of that mark. If a Member currently maintains the registration of a trademark – and has not, based "on its individual merits", invalidated the trademark on the grounds that it is misleading or is otherwise contrary to morality – the Member cannot, under Article 20, deny use of the trademark because of its features, unless it also considers the trademark "on its individual merits".

46.   Australia also concedes that it never attempted to identify which design features of which trademarks are problematic. Australia therefore accepts that it adopted a measure that was, by design, a regulatory "sledgehammer". Australia justifies its actions on the grounds that: (i) the affected trademarks have in common that they are all applied to tobacco products; [29] and (ii) there is a *possibility* that their features might be appealing or misleading.[30] But neither of these arguments excuses Australia's failure to conduct an individual assessment. The first argument conflates the features of a harmful product with those of the trademark. The mere fact that a trademark is applied to a harmful product does not mean that the trademark's features are harmful or misleading. As regards the second argument, as Australia readily admits, *not* all design features of all trademarks for tobacco products serve to make tobacco products more appealing to consumers. Reliance on the *abstract possibility* that the features of some trademarks might give rise to concerns is not "justifiable" conduct on the part of the regulator.

47.   Finally, Australia argues that the panel in *EC – GIs (US)* rejected the need for "individualized assessment" under Article 17 of the *TRIPS Agreement*. Although that panel found that a case-by-case assessment is not *always* required under Article 17, it did *not* find that a case-by-case assessment is *never* required. To the contrary, in addressing the pertinent facts under Article 17, the panel relied on the fact that an individual assessment had been conducted by the

---

[27]   *See* Bodenhausen (1969), Exhibit DR-79, pp. 115-118.
[28]   *See also* Bodenhausen (1969), Exhibit DR-79, pp. 115-118.
[29]   *See e.g.* AUS' FWS, para. 414.
[30]   *See e.g.* AUS' FWS, para. 411.

regulating Member, and hence the legitimate interests of the trademark owner had been respected.[31]

iv.   The "nexus" or connection between the
        encumbrance and objective[32]

48.   All of the parties – including Australia – accept that there must be a "nexus" or connection between the encumbrance and the objective. The disagreement between the parties relates to the nature and extent of the required connection. For Australia, an encumbrance is "unjustifiable" only if there is "no rational connection" between the encumbrance and the objective. However, that proposed standard does not exhaust the circumstances in which an encumbrance is unjustifiable. Rather, the determination of whether a "sufficient" nexus exists must follow an assessment of: (a) the extent of the encumbrance's contribution to the objective; and, if there is a contribution, (b) whether there are alternative measures available that would make an equivalent (or greater) contribution to the objective while imposing a lesser encumbrance on trademark use.

49.   The inclusion of both factors in considering whether a "nexus" is present is supported by a proper reading of Article 20. First, to warrant prejudicing the basic function of a trademark, an encumbrance on use must *contribute* positively to the achievement of the legitimate objective at stake. Otherwise, there is no valid basis to interfere with trademark use in a manner that undermines or defeats the trademark's basic treaty function.[33] Second, Article 20 requires that a Member give effect to the treaty interest it has agreed to protect (*i.e.*, use of a trademark), as far as possible, *without* prejudicing the ability of a Member to contribute to the achievement of other objectives, such as public health. Thus, if an *alternative is available* that would allow both the use of the trademark to a greater extent and make an equivalent contribution to the achievement of the other objective, the Member must opt for that alternative. This means that the expressly protected interest of trademark use and the achievement of another legitimate objective are reconciled in a justifiable, defensible and rational manner. The trademark can be used as far as possible, while still accommodating the Member's imperative of contributing to another legitimate objective to the same extent. Put differently, interfering with trademark use is not justifiable if an alternative measure can achieve the desired objective with lesser or no harm to trademark use.

50.   Australia dismisses consideration of both contribution and alternative measures, because these factors are part of a "necessity" analysis. For Australia,

---

[31]   *See e.g.* Panel Report, *EC – GIs (US)*, para. 7.673 ff.
[32]   *See* DR's FWS, paras. 425-427; DR's SWS, paras. 289-294; DR's response to PQ 108; DR's FOS, paras. 44-56.
[33]   Canada's TP submission, para. 87; Singapore's TP statement, paras. 16-17; EU's response to PQ 19 to third parties, para. 89; Nicaragua's response to PQ 19 to third parties; Singapore's response to PQ 19 to third parties, first bullet; Taiwan's response to PQ 17 to third parties; Uruguay's response to PQ 19 to third parties.

the standard of "justifiable" must be interpreted in "*contradistinction*" to the standard of "necessity". Australia concedes that "[i]n most cases, there will be an array of possible measures" that could be deployed. However, for Australia, it is justifiable (rational, reasonable, proper, defensible or warranted) for a Member to adopt a measure that does most violence to the ability of a trademark to fulfill its basic treaty function without even considering alternatives.

51.   The DR disagrees. The treaty interpreter cannot begin with a contextual argument that relies on an assumption that the word "unjustifiably" must be interpreted in *opposition* ("contradistinction") to the word "unnecessary" and, for that reason, arbitrarily exclude some elements of a necessity test. The interpretive exercise begins with the meaning of the word actually used – here, "unjustifiably". With its focus on creating contextual opposition to a necessity test, Australia fails to give the word "unjustifiably" its ordinary meaning and fails to explain why the word "unjustifiably" excludes consideration of the contribution and alternatives. Australia and the DR agree that the word "unjustifiably" must be understood in light of the context of the chapeau of Article XX of the GATT 1994, which refers to "unjustifiable and arbitrary" discrimination. In *EC – Seal Products*, the Appellate Body found that the word "unjustifiable" under the chapeau allows for consideration of a broad range of factors.[34] In other cases, the standard included consideration of *alternative measures*.[35] Citing to the earlier case law in *US - Gasoline*,[36] *US – Shrimp*,[37] the panel in *China – Rare Earths* found that "discrimination may ... be arbitrary or unjustifiable in cases where it is avoidable and foreseeable, [that is] where alternative measures exist which would have avoided or at least diminished the discriminatory treatment".[38] In the chapeau, the term "unjustifiable and arbitrary" plays a small part in the overall justification of a GATT-inconsistent measure; whereas, under Article 20 of the *TRIPS Agreement*, "unjustifiably" is the entire basis upon which a panel must assess the justification of an encumbering measure.[39] In these circumstances, the word "justifiable" in Article 20 cannot involve a lesser standard than the same word in the chapeau of Article XX.

(1)   The PP measures fail to contribute to reducing smoking behaviour

52.   The DR turns now to the application of the legal standard of contribution. The evidence in this dispute shows a *lack of contribution* and ranges from pre-implementation predictions about how the PP measures would work to post-

---

[34]   Appellate Body Report, *EC – Seal Products*, para. 5.306.
[35]   DR's response to PQ 108, paras. 166-167, referring to Appellate Body Report, *US – Gasoline*, pp. 26-28; Appellate Body Report, *US – Shrimp*, para. 171 and Panel Report, *China – Rare Earths*, para. 7.354 and footnote 549.
[36]   Appellate Body Report, *US – Gasoline*, p. 25.
[37]   Appellate Body Report, *US – Shrimp*, para. 172.
[38]   Panel Report, *China – Rare Earths*, para. 7.354 (emphasis original; emphasis added), referring to Appellate Body Report, *US – Gasoline*, pp. 28-29.
[39]   *See* DR's FOS, para. 50. *See also* China's TP submission, para. 52.

implementation evidence showing how it has actually operated. The totality of the evidence shows that the PP measures do not, and will not, contribute to their objective of reducing smoking in Australia. Before summarizing the evidence, the DR outlines the principles to be applied when assessing this evidence.

(a) Approach to the evidence[40]

53.   There is substantial common ground between the parties about how the Panel should approach its assessment of the evidence. In particular, there seems agreement about four principles. *First*, tobacco control measures must be *evaluated rigorously*, including post-implementation evidence, ideally using different types of data, analytical techniques, and in light of accepted behavioural theories. This principle is formulated in the WHO IARC Handbook on Methods for Evaluating Tobacco Control Policies, which recognizes that a policy might not work "when implemented under real-world conditions".[41] *Second*, this evaluation must be based on the *totality of evidence*, covering pre- and post-implementation evidence. This principle pleads against any "cherry picking" among – and certainly within – the available datasets. *Third*, when pre- and post-implementation evidence point in different directions, evidence of what actually happened is more important than predictions about what might happen. Australia agrees that it would be "appropriate to *disregard* evidence of predicted behaviour if the evidence of actual behaviour was clearly *inconsistent* with those predictions".[42] Australia and the complainants, therefore, rely on post-implementation evidence as a "consistency check" to confirm or reject predictions. *Fourth*, in its responses to the Panel's second set of questions, Australia accepts that sufficient time has passed to assess whether the PP measures have changed smoking behaviour.

54.   Despite this common ground, an important area of disagreement remains – how the Panel should scrutinize the probative value of scientific evidence. For Australia, if the *formal source* of evidence is acceptable, the substantive content of this evidence is beyond criticism and must be accepted as probative by a panel. The DR disagrees. In addition to the credibility of the source, panels must assess whether scientific evidence has "the necessary scientific and methodological rigour".[43] Evidence from a respected source may lack the necessary scientific and methodological rigour, for instance, if its findings are contradicted by the underlying data.

---

[40]   *See* DR's comments on Australia's response to PQ 196, paras. 337- 376.
[41]   WHO-IARC Handbook (2008), Exhibit DOM-368, p. 9.
[42]   AUS' response to PQ 205, para. 403 (emphasis added).
[43]   Appellate Body Report, *US – Continued Suspension*, para. 591.

(b)   Consideration of the evidence

(i)   Post-implementation evidence

55.   An objective assessment of the totality of post-implementation evidence yields an unambiguous and consistent conclusion: the PP measures have failed to change either the antecedents of smoking behaviour or smoking behaviour itself. The only behavioural effect that has consistently emerged is downtrading by consumers from higher-priced to low-priced cigarettes.

1)   Antecedents[44]

56.   Australia and its experts predicted that the PP measures would set in motion a causal chain of effects leading, *via* the three *mechanisms* specified in the *PP Act* (appeal of tobacco products, GHW effectiveness, and deception), to changes in downstream *antecedents* of smoking (*e.g.*, beliefs, attitudes, and intentions towards smoking) and, ultimately, changes in these antecedents would change *smoking behaviour*. In its first submission, Australia urged the Panel to evaluate the PP measures in light of its impact on the antecedents, and claimed that the measures had led to important changes in these antecedents.

57.   To test Australia's assertions, the Panel asked Australia and the Australian tobacco control entities that had gathered the data to provide the underlying data. Some of the data was provided, and some was not. Six datasets have been made available, in whole or in part: the National Plain Packaging Tracking Survey ("NPPTS"), the ITC survey, the New South Wales Tracking Survey ("CITTS"), Personal Pack Display ("PPD"), calls to the Quitline, and cigar data. The datasets were all developed by Australia's tobacco control community and show the real-world effects of the PP measures on multiple variables related to the mechanisms, downstream antecedents, and actual smoking. Despite the Panel's request, Cancer Council Victoria ("CCV") and Cancer Council Queensland refused to provide an anonymized version of the results of a survey of the impact of the PP measures on young Australians, the so-called Schools-based Survey ("SBS").

58.   Applying a rigourous and transparent analytical approach, the DR's experts, Professors Icek Ajzen, Ali Hortaçsu, John A. List, and Azeem M. Shaikh (Ajzen et al.), and Honduras' expert, Professor John Klick, have found consistent results across the six datasets. These results show that the PP measures, even combined with larger GHWs, have failed to change the posited antecedents of smoking behaviour, and have failed to change smoking behaviour.

---

[44]   *See* DR comments on AUS' response to PQ 196, paras. 388-435. *See also* (First) Data Expert Report, Exhibit DOM/IDN-2; Second Data Expert Report, DOM/IDN-4; (First) Data Expert Rebuttal Report, Exhibit DOM/IDN-6; Second Data Expert Rebuttal Report, Exhibit DOM/IDN-8; Ajzen Response to Panel Questions 146, 202, and 203, Exhibit DOM/HND/IDN-6; Third Ajzen Report, Exhibit DOM/IDN-5.

59.   *NPPTS dataset.* To assess the real-world impact of the PP measures, Australia commissioned a large-scale survey of the Australian population. The NPPTS results were assessed by several papers published, in April 2015, by the same group of CCV authors, in a special issue of the journal *Tobacco Control.* With pre-publication access to these papers, Australia relied extensively on them in its first submission in March 2015 to claim that the PP measures are working as intended. Australia, again, relied heavily on these papers in its domestic Post-Implementation Review ("PIR"), published on 26 February 2016.[45]

60.   After examining the full NPPTS dataset in the WTO proceedings, using the computer code provided by the authors of the published papers, Ajzen et al. reached a very different conclusion from that of the authors. *First,* Ajzen et al. found that the papers in *Tobacco Control* "painted an *inaccurate and misleading picture* of the [NPPTS] results".[46] For instance, the papers greatly underreported the data, omitting to report results for 28 out of 50 variables, with 89% of the unreported results showing *no PP effects.* Further, although the same authors prepared different papers on the NPPTS dataset, they used different analytical techniques, without explanation. The choice of different techniques in each paper gives an inflated impression of the number of statistically significant results showing a PP effect. To give one example, Ajzen et al. found that *each* of the pro-PP results reported in Durkin et al. (2015) *disappeared* when the analytical approach applied in Wakefield et al. (2015) was used instead. Ajzen et al. also showed that the techniques used in Durkin et al. (2015) suffered from fundamental shortcomings and that when *any* one of these shortcomings was corrected, *all* the pro-PP results likewise disappeared.

61.   *Second,* analyzing the totality of NPPTS data, Ajzen et al. "found a pattern of poor results, showing that the policy has failed to set in motion Australia's hypothesized chain of effects to change smoking behavior".[47] Even with respect to the impact on the mechanisms, the results were disappointing. The pack changes produced mixed effects on the appeal variables: although they reduced the appeal of the *pack,* the effects weakened and then disappeared as one moves to the appeal of the *product* and the *brand,* and then to the appeal of *smoking.* Regarding the impact on GHWs, although people noticed the enlarged GHW more, they had no greater knowledge of the diseases caused by smoking, and did not attribute more motivation to quit to the GHWs. Finally, the pack changes failed to generate any sustained effects in terms of reducing deception.

62.   Further, the obvious changes in pack appeal and the noticeability of a much enlarged GHW, failed to produce *any* sustained changes in downstream antecedents, including enjoyment of smoking, concerns about the health effects of smoking, perceptions of the health risks from smoking, smoking intentions

---

[45]   Australian Government Department of Health, "Post-Implementation Review – Tobacco Plain Packaging 2016" ("PIR"), Exhibit AUS-624.
[46]   First Data Expert Rebuttal Report, Exhibit DOM/IDN-6, para. 3 (emphasis added).
[47]   First Data Expert Rebuttal Report, Exhibit DOM/IDN-6, para. 2.

and other quit-related variables (thoughts about quitting, firm date to quit, stubbing out, foregoing cigarettes, limiting cigarettes, quitting importance, quit attempts, aids for quitting). Quit attempts even declined in a statistically significant manner. Given these results, there was, unsurprisingly, no impact on smoking behaviours (consumption, cessation, or relapse).

63.   Confronted with these findings, Australia's assessment of the relevance of the NPPTS changed dramatically, at least in the WTO proceedings. Australia *stopped citing* these papers; *never defended* them against the serial shortcomings identified by Ajzen et al.; and *never challenged* the analytical techniques applied, or the results obtained by, Ajzen et al. Instead, Ausralia's *sole* response was to *denigrate* the quality of its own NPPTS, claiming that the NPPTS, which cost Australian taxpayers more than A$3 million, is not suitable for measuring most of the variables it was designed to measure. Notably, this alleged shortcoming was *not* mentioned in the Technical Report accompanying the NPPTS; it was *not* mentioned by the authors of the published papers examining the NPPTS results; it was *not* mentioned by Australia in relying on the NPPTS results presented in those papers earlier in these proceedings. Even in the PIR, in which Australia once again relied on the NPPTS results presented in the published papers, Australia did *not* even mention its newfound criticisms in the NPPTS. Ajzen et al. have explained why Australia's latest efforts to denigrate the quality of its own NPPTS dataset are misplaced and unfounded.

64.   *ITC dataset*. Australia relied on a published paper, Yong et al. (2015), that uses the ITC dataset to assess the impact of the PP measures. Although the authors (who include Professor Geoffrey Fong, one of Australia's experts) were unwilling to provide the Panel with the full dataset that they analyzed, they provided the parts on which they had chosen to report. In their an*alysi*s of that partial dataset, using the same analytical approach as the authors and their computer code, Ajzen et al. reached a similar conclusion to the one they reached using the full NPPTS dataset. The PP measures failed to set in motion the predicted chain of effects in the antecedents of smoking, even leading to a small *decline* in quit intentions and quit interest. Further, even the partial dataset shared by the authors reveals that the paper by Yong et al. (2015) misrepresents the ITC data, and suffers from underreporting of results that are not favourable to the PP measures.

65.   Australia's response parallels its response to Ajzen et al.'s NPPTS analysis. Although Professor Fong co-authored Yong et al. (2015), neither he nor Australia have defended Yong et al. (2015) against the serious criticisms made, nor have they contested the results obtained by Ajzen et al.. Instead, Australia's response was, again, to stop citing this paper and to denigrate the ITC dataset itself, claiming that it provides a "biased" sample. Ajzen et al. have shown that this criticism is incorrect and contradicted by the data. Surprisingly, in its PIR, Australia again relies on the ITC results presented in Yong et al. (2015), without mentioning the alleged "bias" in the data or any of the shortcomings in the paper identified by Ajzen et al.

66.   *CITTS dataset*. At the start of the proceedings, Australia relied on Dunlop et al. (2014), which examined the New South Wales CITTS dataset. However, the DR's request for full access to this dataset was declined, and the Cancer Institute New South Wales ("CINSW") provided selective information. In particular, CINSW declined to provide the raw data for the entire survey, and it provided a redacted version of its questionnaire; upon further request, it refused to provide the full questionnaire. Honduras and its experts have shown, first, that Dunlop et al. (2014) "cherry-picked" the CITTS data to assess and, second, that the CITTS dataset does not show that the PP measures have increased the effectiveness of GHWs, or have changed quitting intentions.[48] In response, as it did with the NPPTS and ITC datasets, Australia again opted to denigrate the quality and relevance of the dataset, claiming that alleged limitations in the CITTS data were so serious that they "rais[ed] questions about conclusions drawn from analyses that employ these data".[49] However, in its PIR, Australia again relies on Dunlop et al. (2014) – without denigrating the CITTS dataset.

67.   *Calls to the Quitline and Personal Pack Display*. Australia has placed reliance on published papers that use the data on actual calls to the Quitline (Young et al. (2014)) and on Personal Pack Display (PPD) (Zacher et al. (2015)). By reference to Young et al. (2014), Australia has claimed that the PP measures led to a sustained increase in calls to the Quitline and, by reference to Zacher et al. (2015), it has claimed sustained pack avoidant behaviour (*i.e.*, people taking steps to avoid seeing the gruesome GHWs). However, Australia consistently misstates the results of these papers and ignores the wear-out of the PP effects.

68.   Young et al. (2014) found that calls to the Quitline initially spiked following the introduction of the PP measures, with calls then rapidly dropping to pre-implementation levels. Ajzen et al. confirmed these results. Likewise, Zacher et al. (2015) found that there was an initial increase in pack avoidant behaviours but that these effects also wore out, which the authors said was expected. Again, Ajzen et al. confirmed these findings. The only effect still observed one year after implementation was a small decline in outdoor smoking in selected venues in two cities. However, Zacher et al. (2015) correctly explained that this decline could not be generalized to the population, and could not be linked to the PP measures because it could have been caused by a host of unrelated factors for which the analysis did not control.

69.   *Cigar-based dataset.* A single study by Miller et al. (2015) in the special issue of *Tobacco Control* assessed the effects of the PP measures on cigar smoking. With access to the full dataset, Ajzen et al. found that this study suffers from serious methodological shortcomings. Ajzen et al. also explained that the dataset shows, if anything, that the PP measures did not set in motion the chain of effects expected to lead to a change in cigar smoking. Australia and its experts

---

[48]   Klick Second Supplemental Rebuttal Report, Exhibit HND-165, para. 57.
[49]   Supplementary expert report of F. Chaloupka, Exhibit AUS-590, para. 24.

have chosen *not* to contest any of these arguments, and simply ignore these findings.

70.   *SBS survey.* To evaluate the impact of the PP measures on young people, Australia commissioned the SBS survey. The SBS dataset forms the basis for two papers published in the special issue of *Tobacco Control*: White, Williams, and Wakefield (2015) and White et al. (2015). As Australia had relied on these papers, the Panel sought the underlying data in an anonymized format. However, the authors, the entities commissioned by Australia to conduct the survey, and Australia itself, refused to provide any of the data, even though it would be protected by special confidentiality procedures. No valid basis has been offered to justify this refusal. Similar datasets on youth smoking are *publicly* available in the EU and the United States.[50] Australia has not responded to these arguments.

71.   Without access to the data, it is impossible to make an objective assessment of the findings in the two papers. To illustrate the need for access to the underlying data, the DR recalls that, with access to the NPPTS and ITC datasets, Ajzen et al. have shown that the published analyses of these datasets give an "inaccurate and misleading picture" of the datasets. In its PIR, Australia also acknowledges the critical importance of having access to underlying datasets in order to verify conclusions asserted based on that data.[51] With respect to the SBS data, even without the ability to assess the underlying dataset in full, as summarized in paragraph 92-93 below, the selection of results that the authors have chosen to publish shows disappointing results and supports the complainants' position.

> 2)   Smoking behaviour – prevalence, consumption, and downtrading[52]

72.   The complainants and their experts have analyzed the rich empirical record regarding the operation of plain packaging in the three years following its implementation. They found that the PP measures are not effective in reducing smoking, but have caused downtrading from higher-priced to low-priced cigarettes.

73.   To conduct these analyses, the complainants have relied on several experts: Professor John List; Professors David Afshartous, Marcus Hagedorn, Ashok Kaul and Michael Wolf (collectively "IPE"); and Professor John Klick. Applying complementary methodological approaches to multiple datasets, the

---

[50]   DR's response to PQ 134 and footnote 10.
[51]   Australia dismisses certain assertions made in the PIR consultations because the underlying data "was not provided and is not publicly available". Hence, it said, "the Department is unable to verify the claims made in relation to this dataset". Australia's PIR, Exhibit AUS-624, paras. 136 and 138.
[52]   *See* DR Comments on AUS' response to PQ 196, paras. 436-539. *See also* IPE Report, DR-100; Updated IPE Report, Exhibit DOM-303; Second Updated IPE Report, Exhibit DOM-361; Third Updated IPE Report, Exhibit DOM-375; List Supplemental Report, Exhibit DOM/IDN-3; Presentation by Professor List at the FOH, Appendix 2 to the DR's FOS; Presentation by Professor List at the SOH, Appendix 2 to the DR's SOS.

complainants' experts have assessed the effects of the PP measures on a variety of important metrics: smoking prevalence; tobacco sales (as a proxy for consumption); smoking incidence (the proportion of smokers who stopped smoking during a survey period); and downward substitution or "downtrading" (switching from higher-priced to low-priced tobacco products).

74.   In undertaking their assessments, the experts have adhered to fundamental principles of scientific inquiry. To ensure that their findings are not artifacts of any particular data or model, the experts have developed a total of seven distinct types of empirical methods and used seven datasets, reporting results across a wide range of specifications and applying an array of robustness checks Table 1, below, summarises the complainants' approach to post-implementation empirics relating to smoking behaviour (prevalence, consumption, downtrading). As Table 1 shows, the complainants have arrived at their results by: (i) utilizing all available datasets that report relevant behavioural metrics;[53] (ii) covering different tobacco products; (iii) covering relevant population subgroups; and (iv) applying a multitude of complementary and well-established empirical methods. In addition, the complainants assessed alternative starting dates for plain packaging. Finally, consistent with the principles of scientific inquiry, the experts have remained receptive to constructive criticism by peers. In an effort to improve the quality of the analysis, they have responded to criticism offered by Australia's experts with principled adjustments to their approaches.

Table 1:   The complainants' approach to post-implementation evidence on smoking behaviour

Topic	Dataset	Metric	Subgroup	Analysis	Finding
Prevalence				Statistical trend analysis	No PP effect
				Time-series regression	No PP effect
	RMSS	Prevalence	All	ARIMA	No PP effect
				One-stage micro-econometric probit	No PP effect
				Two-stage micro-econometric probit	No PP effect

---

[53]   The complainants analysed the best available datasets, including long-term cross-sectional surveys on smoking prevalence and incidence (RMSS and Professor Klick's Roy Morgan Research survey); wholesale data covering the entire Australian market (IMS) as a proxy for smoking consumption; and retail databases tracking actual sales by end-customers (Nielsen and Aztec) as another proxy for smoking consumption; wholesale data covering the entire market in New Zealand (EOS) as a proxy for smoking consumption; and on retail databases tracking actual sales by end-customers (Nielsen) as another proxy for smoking consumption.

Topic	Dataset	Metric	Subgroup	Analysis	Finding
	RMSS	Prevalence	Minors	Statistical trend analysis	No PP effect
				Two-stage micro-econometric probit	No PP effect
	RMSS	Prevalence	Young adults	Statistical trend analysis	No PP effect
				Two-stage micro-econometric probit	No PP effect
	RMSS	Prevalence	Minors and young adults	Two-stage micro-econometric probit	No PP effect
	RMSS	Cigar prevalence	All	Time-series regression	No PP effect
				ARIMA	No PP effect
Smoking incidence	Roy Morgan	Prevalence	All	Difference-in-difference estimation	No PP effect
	IMS	Consumption	All	Time-series regression	No PP effect
				ARIMA	No PP effect
				Event analysis	No PP effect
	Aztec	Consumption	All	Time-series regression	No PP effect
				ARIMA	No PP effect
Sales				Event analysis	No PP effect
	Nielsen	Consumption	All	Time-series regression	No PP effect
				ARIMA	No PP effect
				Difference-in-difference estimation	No PP effect
	EOS	Consumption	All	Difference-in-difference estimation	No PP effect
	IMs	Consumption	All	Time-series regression	Down-trading effect
				ARIMA	Down-trading effect
				Event study	Down-trading effect
Downtrading	RMSS	Prevalence	All	One-stage micro-econometric probit	Down-trading effect
	Aztec	Consumption	All	Time-series regression	Down-trading effect
				ARIMA	Down-trading effect
				Event analysis	Down-trading effect

75.   Until the second hearing, Australia and its experts had insisted that not enough time had elapsed to detect an effect on smoking behaviour. However, confronted with the disappointing results on the antecedents, Australia and its experts abruptly changed course, claiming, based on Dr. Chipty's analysis, to have found a statistically significant effect of plain packaging on smoking behaviour. Australia, therefore, urged the Panel to evaluate plain packaging in light of its impact on actual smoking behaviour, "regardless" of the evidence on the antecedents.[54] This is a remarkable U-turn by any standard within a mere period of four months.

76.   Further, Dr. Chipty's few favourable results are compromised by at least four critical methodological errors. Correcting for them, one at a time or all at once, *reverses* Dr. Chipty's results. *First*, although Australia's other expert, Professor Scharfstein, considered this approach incorrect, Dr. Chipty applies a single, uninterrupted linear trend over the entire 2001-2015 period. In so doing, she introduces a fundamental model mis-specification by failing to control for breaks in the secular trend of smoking over time. *Second*, although Dr Chipty agrees with the need for a "nationally representative sample", she refuses to control for important instances of sample reweighting, undertaken by Roy Morgan Research itself, to ensure that the sample remains representative of the Australian population. *Third*, Dr. Chipty insists on the use of *tax dummies* as a control variable for tobacco costliness, and rejects superior control variables, such as actual prices or tax levels, despite the fact that these variables track the increased costliness of smoking much more closely. Dr. Chipty's approach accounts for only 60 percent of the total excise tax increases, and even less of total price increases. *Fourth*, when calculating standard errors, Dr. Chipty's approach does not comply with the scientifically appropriate standards implemented by the complainants' experts. Dr. Chipty's approach results in "false positives" (*i.e.*, reporting a PP effect, when in reality there is none) almost *four times more often* than the approach used by the complainants' experts.

77.   Throughout these proceedings, Dr. Chipty has been inconsistent in her modeling choices. For example, her finding of a PP effect when applying a modification of Professor List's two-stage model requires, *inter alia*, an abridged observation period (*2006-2015*) and the use of *prices* as a control variable for tobacco costliness. However, in modifying IPE's models, Dr. Chipty applies an extended observation period (*2001-2015*) and explicitly rejects prices as a control variable in favour of *tax dummies*. Hence, the sole consistency in Dr. Chipty's approach is her application of whatever combination of modeling choices enables her to find a PP effect.

78.   Dr. Chipty has consistently argued that econometric models of smoking behaviour are flawed if they *fail* to find that excise tax increases cause a statistically significant *reduction* in prevalence and consumption. Dr. Chipty

---

[54]   Australia's response to Panel Question 196, para. 238.

repeatedly described as "*nonsensical*" any model output suggesting that a tax increase leads to an *increase* in prevalence or consumption.[55] Yet, in her final two reports in these proceedings, Dr. Chipty produced – but did not report – just such a "*nonsensical*" outcome herself: a statistically significant *positive* coefficient for the 2013 excise tax increase. The DR has shown that this "nonsensical" result is critical to her conclusion that the PP measures reduced consumption.

79.   Finally, the DR notes that Australia commissioned Dr. Chipty to prepare a new report for its PIR, using the RMSS dataset familiar to the Panel. Dr. Chipty's PIR Report provides a flawed and misleading assessment based on a narrow and self-serving selection of datasets, behavioural metrics, and methodologies presented in the WTO proceedings. Conveniently, Australia fails to mention in the PIR that Dr. Chipty's PIR analysis – largely recycled from the WTO proceedings with a few novel tweaks – has been subject to detailed criticisms by the complainants' experts, such as her failure to control for breaks in the secular smoking trend, or reweighting. Dr. Chipty's PIR Report ignores these criticisms altogether. In the WTO, the DR has shown that correcting for these flaws reverses Dr. Chipty's findings of PP effects. Furthermore, the DR identified important inconsistencies between Dr. Chipty's WTO work and her PIR report, which she has left unexplained.

3)   Australia's PIR

80.   On 26 February 2016, Australia submitted its PIR of the PP measures to assess the effectiveness of the PP measures.[56] Australia's PIR Guidelines state that the evidence used in a PIR should be "gathered *rigorously* and presented in a *balanced fashion*".[57]

81.   However, Australia fails to respect the guidelines, providing a one-sided and misleading impression of the evidence. Australia recycles its own initial argument and evidence to the Panel, without addressing the serious flaws identified in that argument and evidence. In fact, Australia's description of the evidence in the PIR often cannot be reconciled with – and sometimes even contradicts – the later positions that Australia took in the WTO. For example, whereas Australia has denigrated the NPPTS and ITC datasets in the WTO, it relied on them once again in the PIR.

82.   In response, Australia said that the evidence addressed in the PIR is more limited than that addressed in the WTO.[58] This cannot explain why Australia assessed evidence one way in the WTO and a different way in the PIR. In any

---

[55]   Supplementary expert report of T. Chipty, Exhibit AUS-535, para. 39; Supplementary expert report of T. Chipty, Exhibit AUS-586, para. 33a; Supplementary Expert Report of T. Chipty, Exhibit AUS-605, footnote 45.
[56]   PIR, Exhibit AUS-624.
[57]   PIR Guidelines, p. 5 (emphasis added).
[58]   *See* Letter from Australia to the Panel (22 March 2016).

event, the PIR addresses virtually all of the datasets under consideration by the Panel.[59] With its own access to this data, Australia could have conducted a "rigorous" and "balanced" review (e.g., rather than perpetuate the errors in the *Tobacco Control* papers, Australia could have analyzed the full NPPTS dataset using techniques free from flaws and inconsistencies). Remarkably, Australia even urges the Panel to disregard its PIR in favor of its WTO argument and evidence. However, the Panel must assess all of the evidence before it, including the PIR.

(ii)　　Evidence predicting the effects of the PP measures

1)　　Pre-implementation PP research[60]

83.　　Australia relies on a body of papers that sought to predict the impact of plain packaging using hypothetical plain packs in a research setting. These studies suggested that the PP measures would have an almost immediate impact on factors such as knowledge of health risks, smoking intentions, and smoking behaviour. None of this actually occurred in a real-world setting.

84.　　To assess the scientific rigour of these papers, the DR and Honduras commissioned two independent reviews. *First*, in the Peer Review Project, each paper was submitted to peer review by two independent reviewers, replicating the real-world peer review process for leading journals in the field of consumer behaviour.[61] *Second*, applying an existing assessment tool, a separate group of experts in social science research methodology conducted a systematic review.[62] Both groups reached a consistent conclusion: the PP literature contains serious and pervasive flaws such that it does not provide a reliable research basis for public policy. For both reviews, the detailed assessment of each PP paper was made available to Australia.

85.　　Australia provided a limited response to both sets of reviews. For the handful of flaws on which Professor Fong did initially comment, he never

---

[59]　Australia has previously said that the "evidence available for consideration in the post-implementation review is necessarily *more limited* than the evidence available to the Panel in this dispute [...]". *See* Australia's response to Panel Question 149, para. 34 (emphasis added).

[60]　*See* DR Comments on AUS' response to PQ 196, paras. 540-581. *See also* the following expert reports: Peer Review Project, Exhibit DR/HON-3; Peer Review Rebuttal Report, Exhibit DOM/HND-17; Peer Review Second Rebuttal Report, Exhibit DOM/HND-17; Systematic Review, Exhibit DOM/HON-4 Systematic Review Rebuttal Report, Exhibit DOM/HND-13; Systematic Review Second Rebuttal Report, Exhibit DOM/HND-18.

[61]　Professor Jeff Inman (University of Pittsburgh) served in the role of editor and his team of six reviewers consisted of: Professor Marc Fischer (Mannheim University), Professor Rik Pieters (Tilburg University), Professor Debra Ringold (Willamette University), Professor Alan Sawyer (University of Florida), Professor Luk Warlop (KU Leuven), and Professor Klaus Wertenbroch (INSEAD).

[62]　The Systematic Review was led by Professor Jos Kleijnen, Director of Kleijnen Systematic Reviews, who was supported by Professor Alan Bryman (University of Leicester) and Professor Michael Bosnjak (University of Mannheim).

addressed the responses given by the Systematic Review and Peer Review teams, which highlighted that Professor Fong's responses were selective, incorrect, and misleading. For the large majority of PP studies, Australia and its experts simply ignored the criticisms. At the same time, they continued to rely on the studies, including in the PIR, as if they were unaware that serious concerns had been raised about their scientific reliability.

86.   Instead of contesting the criticisms, Australia and Professor Fong argued that the papers must be assessed against lower scientific standards and even that they should be immune from criticism because they were "peer reviewed". Both arguments are unconvincing. *First*, Professor Fong has entirely failed to explain *why* tobacco control research should be held to lower scientific standards than any other area in social science; and, if so, *which* of the basic scientific standards he thinks may be violated in tobacco control research. *Second*, the fallibility of the peer review process is well-recognized both within and outside the scientific world. The facts before the Panel confirm this. Ajzen et al. have, for instance, demonstrated that, despite peer review, the NPPTS-based papers in *Tobacco Control* are not reliable.

87.   In a final attempt to divert attention from the flaws in the papers, Australia and its experts insist that the overall direction of the PP literature should be trusted, regardless of the pervasive and systematic flaws. Australia's approach violates the generally accepted principle that any proper literature review starts with an assessment of the quality of the relevant studies. As the DR's experts have said, this approach is critical because, "if the building blocks are defective, the house does not stand".[63] Indeed, convergence may be the result of flaws in the underlying studies, including systematic flaws of the type identified in the PP studies that bias the results in one direction.

88.   The stark divergence between the predicted and real-word impact of plain packaging confirms that the pre-PP "building blocks" upon which the policy was based are, indeed, "defective". The papers vastly overestimated the effect of plain packaging on the three mechanisms, on downstream antecedents, as well as on smoking behaviour. Significantly, none of the PP papers correctly predicted that plain packaging would have no effect on critical antecedents of smoking and on actual smoking behaviour in Australia.

2)   Initiation[64]

89.   To understand youth smoking behaviour, the DR consulted Professor Laurence Steinberg, a leading authority on adolescent risk-taking behaviour. He has explained that, as a result of brain development, adolescents are particularly

---

[63]   Systematic Review Second Rebuttal Report, Exhibit DOM/HND-18, para. 4.
[64]   *See* DR Comments on AUS' response to PQ 196, paras. 582-610. *See also* Steinberg Initiation Report, Exhibit DR/HON-6; Steinberg Rebuttal Report, Exhibit DR/HON-10; Third Steinberg Report, Exhibit DOM/HND-15; (Steinberg) Response to Panel Question 159, Exhibit DOM/HND-20.

sensitive to (short-term) rewards (*e.g.*, social status) and give less importance to (long-term) costs (*e.g.*, health risks). Therefore, although they are well aware of the risks, adolescents are attracted to risky behaviours (such as smoking) associated with adulthood because of the social rewards from peers of engaging in the *behaviour* itself, and not because of any *packaging* features.

90.   Australia's experts (Professors Slovic and Biglan) have expressed agreement with many of Professor Steinberg's views on the factors influencing youth initiation, including that young people have a higher propensity to engage in risk-taking behaviours (such as smoking); that "it is highly improbable that an adolescent who is interested in smoking will decline a cigarette from a friend because of the packaging";[65] and that "young people do not pay attention to risk information".[66]

91.   Despite this agreement, Australia and its experts maintain that the PP measures will reduce smoking initiation among adolescents by *eliminating the appeal* (so-called "positive perceptions and associations"[67] or "strong positive affect"[68]) created by pack design elements, and by *increasing knowledge* about the health risks of smoking. However, as Professor Steinberg and Professor Ajzen have explained, the published results of Australia's SBS contradict both arguments, a contradiction Australia's experts have not addressed.

92.   *First*, White, Williams, and Wakefield (2015) showed that, pre-PP, branded packaging (with a 30% GHW) did *not* create any of the supposed positive perceptions. To the contrary, *prior to PP*, branded packs in Australia, including the most popular brands among adolescents, were viewed as *un*appealing with *negative* associations ("ugly", "daggy (uncool)", "gross", and "disgusting"). Thus, pre-PP *branded* packaging already created precisely the negative associations for which Australia deemed it necessary to introduce *plain* packaging. The published SBS results show that, since the pack changes, the already-negative appeal ratings have become only *slightly* more negative.

93.   *Second*, the pack changes have not increased the already high level of awareness of the health risks of smoking, nor have they induced adolescents to read or think more about warnings, to forgo cigarettes more, or to think more about quitting (White et al. (2015)).

94.   When confronted with these results, Australia criticized the DR's experts for focusing unduly on the published results from the SBS data, even though this is the only dataset commissioned by Australia to evaluate the impact of the PP measures on adolescents.[69]

---

[65]   Expert Report of P. Slovic, Exhibit AUS-12, para. 111.
[66]   Expert Report of P. Slovic, Exhibit AUS-12, para. 110.
[67]   AUS' FWS, paras. 8, 157, 158.
[68]   Expert Report of P. Slovic, Exhibit AUS-12, paras. 13 and 83 (strong positive affect), 14, 104, and 111 (cachet); Second Expert Report of P. Slovic, Exhibit AUS-532, paras. 3 (strong positive affect), 4, 85, and 87 (cachet, designed to be popular).
[69]   AUS' response to PQ 196, para. 268, (b), (c).

3) Cessation and relapse[70]

95.   To understand cessation and relapse behaviours, the DR consulted Professor Gabriele Fischer, psychiatrist and medical director of the addiction clinic at the Medical University of Vienna. She has explained that the drivers of cessation and relapse behaviours are well documented and do not include the design of retail packaging. Cessation is mainly driven by factors such as health concerns, self-efficacy, motivation to quit, and low tobacco dependence. Relapse is often associated with negative emotions, background stress, and tobacco dependence.

96.   Australia's expert, Dr. Brandon, disagrees because, in his view, plain packs are *weaker smoking cues* than branded packs. He acknowledges that his argument lacks empirical support, but believes that plain packs are *less* salient to smokers and might have *lower* contingency with smoking compared to branded packs.

97.   Professor Fischer explains why this argument lacks merit. Dr. Brandon's *own* research finds that unbranded and unappealing objects (like unbranded cigarettes, ashtrays, matches, and even environmental tobacco) are *highly salient* and *highly contingent* with nicotine delivery. Dr. Brandon has explained that largely *unbranded* cigarettes are the *strongest* cue. Further, cue reactivity research confirms that making cues more "personal" (for instance, through branding) does *not* increase cue strength. Despite numerous opportunities, Dr. Brandon chose never to respond to these arguments.

98.   As Professor Fischer explains, all packs, whatever their appearance, are subject to the same conditioning process among smokers, and have the same close connection to smoking. After a short period of adaptation by smokers, newly designed packs simply acquire the same cue status as old packs. The post-implementation evidence is consistent with Dr. Fischer's predictions, and it contradicts those of Dr. Brandon. Australia's new packs have had no impact on antecedents of smoking or actual quitting and relapse. There was an initial spike in calls to the Quitline. However, consistent with Professor Fischer's position, when smokers had become familiar with the pack changes, that initial effect quickly vanished.

4) Marketing[71]

99.   The DR's marketing expert – Professor Jan-Benedict Steenkamp – predicted that the PP measures would have no impact on tobacco prevalence and consumption: instead, the removal of branding would reduce product

---

[70]   *See* DR comments on AUS' response to PQ 196, paras. 611-628. *See also* Fischer Cessation and Relapse Report, Exhibit DR/HON-7; Fischer Rebuttal Report, Exhibit DR/HON-11, Third Fischer Report, Exhibit DOM/HON-18.

[71]   *See* DR Comments on Australia's response to PQ 196, paras. 629-641. *See* also the following expert reports: Steenkamp Branding Report, Exhibit DR/HON-5; Steenkamp Rebuttal Report, Exhibit DOM/HND-14; Steenkamp Second Rebuttal Report, Exhibit DOM/HND-19.

differentiation in the marketplace, which would reduce consumer brand loyalty, leading to a likelihood of increased brand-switching to cheaper products.

100.   Australia and its experts – Professors Tavassoli and Dubé – disagree. They argue that the PP measures will have a strong effect on prevalence and consumption. Professor Tavassoli predicted there would be *no* brand switching effects, though Professor Dubé refused to make any predictions.   Their prediction that primary demand will inevitably fall rests on an analogy between traditional mass media advertising and Australia's plain packaging.

101.   Professor Steenkamp outlined the reasons why retail packaging, in particular Australia's packaging, that is dominated by large and repulsive GHWs, cannot be equated with traditional advertising.[72] Australia's marketing expert, Professor Dubé, seems to agree. He explained that traditional advertising and packaging are distinct, used in a "different context", and that he is "not aware of any evidence" that the consumption effects of advertising "provide an appropriate analogy for the likely effects of tobacco plain packaging".[73]

102.   Assessments of the effects of plain packaging by the tobacco control community – including the U.S. Surgeon General reports – confirm that the effects of traditional advertising and packaging on consumer demand cannot be simply equated. Rather than drawing conclusions based on the effects of advertising, leading tobacco control scholars rely on evidence drawn from *plain-packaging-specific* research. They have also emphasized the need for post-implementation research into the actual effects of plain packaging to examine whether the predictions actually hold in the real world.

103.   Evidence from Australia confirms that Australia's simple analogy is misplaced: pre-PP branded packaging, even with smaller health warnings, had *negative* appeal. Thus, partially branded packaging, with GHWs, did not have the *same effects* as traditional advertising, which conveys strongly *positive* messages.

104.   Significantly, Australia and its experts failed to provide a single convincing example illustrating the alleged causal link between pack appeal and smoking. At the first meeting, Australia offered examples of packaging such as Fantasia, Sobranie, and Vibes – which Australia considers to be *highly appealing*. However, the DR showed that virtually *no one in Australia smokes* these highly appealing brands. Australia also referred to Longbeach and Peter Jackson, but, according to its own research, these two brands have among the *least appealing* packaging, and yet they are amongst the *most smoked* in Australia, including among youth.

105.   Australia appears to recognize that its analogy with traditional advertising is even less credible when packaging is dominated by large and repulsive GHWs. Throughout the proceedings, Australia and its experts displayed

---

[72]   Steenkamp Rebuttal Report, Exhibit DOM/HND-14, Section 3.3.2.
[73]   Expert Report of Jean-Pierre Dubé, AUS-11, para. 11.

numerous images of branded packaging and even tobacco advertising. Significantly, *not a single* image displayed a package with the dominant GHWs required in Australia.

106. The post-implementation evidence described above also *confirms* Professor Steenkamp's predictions, and contradicts those of Australia's experts: the PP measures have resulted in a marked increase in downtrading, with no change in smoking prevalence or consumption.

5)   Behavioural Theory[74]

107. Australia and its experts started the proceedings relying on a "causal chain model" that sought to link the *appeal* of tobacco packaging to *smoking behaviour*, using behavioural theories. They argued that behavioural theories reliably predict that when the *appeal* of tobacco products is changed, the antecedents of smoking behaviour, and then smoking behaviour itself, will also change. In other words, Australia used behavioural theories to bridge the gap between evidence of a change in pack appeal and evidence of a change in smoking behaviour.

108. In terms of specific behavioural theories, Professor Fong relied on *attitude-behaviour literature*, stating that "[s]ocial psychological theories, notably the '*Theory of Reasoned Action*' (Fishbein & Ajzen, 1975), and research arising from such theories, have demonstrated clearly that attitudes are indeed related to behaviour".[75] He alleged that it is, therefore, "*straightforward* to conclude that, if plain packaging lowers the *appeal* of tobacco products, this would lead to a reduced likelihood of *behaviours* such as starting to smoke and continuing smoking".[76] Professor Slovic, in turn, relied on his *Affect Heuristic* theory to claim that, by reducing "positive affect", the PP measures would increase the perceived risks of smoking and lower its perceived benefits, which, ultimately, would decrease smoking behaviour, in particular among youth.

109. To review these arguments, the DR sought the advice of Professor Icek Ajzen, who has been identified as the number 1 ranked psychologist in the field of behavioural theory, and who developed the *Theory of Reasoned Action* and its successor, the *Theory of Planned Behavior*. Professor Ajzen explained that Australia's arguments rest on fundamental misconceptions regarding behavioural theories, including – but not limited to – his own theories. He emphasized that behavioural theories cannot *prove* a link between the appeal of packaging and

---

[74]   *See* DR Comments on AUS' response to PQ 196, paras. 642-669. *See also* Ajzen Behavioral Report, Exhibit DOM/HON/IND-3; Presentation by Professor Ajzen of "Examination of Australia's Reliance on Behavioral Theories to Support its Tobacco Plain Packaging Legislation", Exhibit DR/HON/IND-3; Ajzen Supplemental Report, Exhibit DR/HON/IND-4; Ajzen Response, Exhibit DOM/HND/IDN-5; Ajzen, Response to Questions 146, 202, and 203 by the Panel, Exhibit DOM/HND/IDN-6; Presentation given by Professor Ajzen at the SOH, Appendix 1 to the DR's SOS.
[75]   Export Report of G. Fong, para. 252 (emphasis added).
[76]   Expert Report of G. Fong, Exhibit AUS-14, para. 32 (emphasis and underlining added).

behaviour. Rather, when properly applied, theories can generate useful *hypotheses* that must be confirmed or rejected empirically.

110.   Professor Ajzen explained why a correct understanding of behavioural theories leads to the prediction that the PP measures are unlikely to be effective. The long-standing attitude-behaviour research suggests that people's attitudes toward a non-behavioural target (packaging) do not reliably predict their behaviour with respect to the target (smoking). For plain packaging to change smoking behaviour, it would have to set in motion a chain of effects, leading from pack changes, through to attitudes toward the pack, brands and products, to perceptions and beliefs about the health risks of smoking, on to attitudes and intentions with respect to smoking, and ultimately to actual smoking behaviour. Professor Ajzen considered it unlikely that Australia's pack changes would carry all the way through across this causal chain, but emphasized that this was ultimately an empirical question.

111.   Together with Professors Hortaçsu, List and Shaikh, Professor Ajzen subsequently examined his predictions – and those of Australia's experts – in light of the post-implementation evidence. As summarized above, Australia's predictions based on behavioural theories are incorrect: although the pack changes reduced pack *appeal* to some extent and people *noticed* the much-enlarged GHWs more, neither the downstream antecedents to behaviour nor smoking behaviours changed. The outcome that Professor Fong thought it "straightforward"[77] to assume – namely, if pack appeal changes, the antecedents of behaviour and behaviour will change – *has not* materialized in the real world. Equally, contrary to Professor Slovic's assessment, the *pre*-PP packs did not have "strong positive affect", and the plain packs have not increased perceived risks or lowered perceived benefits of smoking.

112.   A major reason for the failure of the PP measures can be seen in Australia's own NPPTS data: the assumed relationship (correlation) between the *appeal of tobacco products* on one hand, and multiple *downstream antecedents and smoking behaviours* on the other, is lacking. Using the NPPTS dataset, Ajzen et al. examined 130 possible correlations between the appeal of tobacco products and downstream antecedents of smoking behaviour or smoking behaviour itself. Out of the 130 possible relationships examined, *not one* showed a significant correlation in the expected direction.

113.   In response, Australia downplayed the role of behavioural theories. Australia and its experts stopped mentioning Professor Ajzen's behavioural theories, except to say they had never really relied on them. The conceptual framework underlying plain packaging was no longer founded in behavioural theory but in the *PP Act* itself. Finally, Professors Fong and Slovic never attempted to explain the inconsistency between their theory-based predictions and the post-implementation evidence.

---

[77]   Expert Report of G. Fong, Exhibit AUS-14, para. 32.

> (iii)   Australia's assertions of a future contribution are not supported by sufficient evidence[78]

114.   Although Australia argues that the effects of the PP measures will be most significant in the longer term, it has provided surprisingly few details on the hypotheses that underlie this argument, and it has provided even less evidentiary support. As the Appellate Body has insisted, the pathway to alleged future effects must be "based on a set of *hypotheses* that are *tested* and *supported* by sufficient evidence".[79]

115.   Australia has proposed different hypotheses, one to explain the delayed effect of the PP measures on initiation and quitting (a hypothesis based on a "delayed contribution" to reducing initiation and increasing quitting) and another to explain the delayed ability of econometric techniques to detect these changes in population-level prevalence and consumption data (a "delayed detection" hypothesis). These hypotheses are either not tested or, when they are, contradicted by the evidence. Thus, the alleged pathway to long-term effects is not supported by any, let alone sufficient, evidence.

116.   Before addressing the hypotheses, it bears noting that Australia's long term effects argument assumes that the effects of the PP measures will *strengthen* over time. However, it is well-documented that a person's reaction to a novel package is strongest on first exposure, and weakens as he or she becomes more familiar with the new pack. This "wear-off" phenomenon is well-documented by tobacco control scholars, including with regard to tobacco packaging (in relation to both GHWs and plain packaging) and is confirmed by the post-implementation data. That data shows that, before smoking behaviour ever changed, the few initial reactions in downstream antecedents (*e.g.*, calls to the Quitline, pack concealment) wore out. As Professor Ajzen explained, if people have already adapted to the new packaging, and their negative reactions have worn out without behavioural change occurring, there is no reason to expect that behaviour will change in the future.

117.   Relying on Professor Slovic, Australia rejected the possibility of "wear out", arguing that, because there was no branding on the pack, "there is simply nothing to wear out".[80] Professor Ajzen explained that this "mystifying argument" was based on a fundamental misunderstanding of wear-out. Australia then stopped relying on this argument and, instead, accepted that the NPPTS data shows that some effects have indeed worn out.

118.   *"Delayed contribution" hypothesis*. Australia's first set of hypotheses is that the largest impact on reducing initiation and quitting will be delayed until the long term. With regard to initiation, without much, if any, explanation or evidence, Australia hypothesizes that the effect of the PP measures will be most

---

[78]   *See* DR's Comments on AUS' response to PQ 200.
[79]   Appellate Body Report, *Brazil – Retreaded Tyres*, para. 149 (emphasis added).
[80]   AUS' SWS, para. 503.

pronounced in the long-term because "it will take time for the cohort of children who have not been exposed to fully-branded tobacco packaging to reach adolescence".[81] There is a fundamental problem with this proposition. Australia expressly assumes that the pre-PP branded packaging created strong *positive* associations with smoking for the current generation, and that it will take until the next generation for these positive associations to disappear. However, the SBS data show that Australia's pre-PP packs with GHWs already led young people to form strongly *negative* associations with smoking. Further, although Australia argues that the alleged positive associations stem from the lingering effects of traditional advertising, the current generation has never been exposed to traditional advertising, because it was banned almost 25 years ago.

119.   With regard to the delayed impact on quitting, Australia's explanation has amounted to little more than the following: "*multiple* quit attempts" are often necessary before a smoker is successfully able to quit.[82] Hence, the effects on quitting will take time to arise. Again, Australia's proposition is contradicted by the evidence. Australia's NPPTS dataset shows that *none* of the dozen quit-related variables, including quit attempts, changed in the direction envisaged by the PP measures. In fact, instead of leading to an *increase* in quit attempts, the pack changes led to *fewer* quit attempts.

120.   *"Delayed detection" hypothesis.* Australia's alternative hypothesis is that econometric techniques are not capable of detecting the initial contribution of the PP measures to reducing smoking behaviour, because the impact on initiation and cessation is too small to detect, but will grow. Professor List's results contradict Australia's hypothesis: the RMSS prevalence data do not reveal any statistically significant PP effect on smoking prevalence amongst youth. Dr. Chipty has not countered these findings with any empirical work of her own. Further, by the end of the proceedings, Australia no longer asserted that insufficient time had passed to detect changes in prevalence and consumption. Instead, Dr. Chipty explained that the "discussion of power [to detect] is no longer crucial".[83]

(iv)   Conclusion [84]

121.   At the outset of the proceedings, the DR's experts explained, through the prism of their respective expertise, why the PP measures would be an ineffective tobacco control instrument, and were not founded on a credible scientific basis. As a wealth of post-implementation evidence has become available, the initial predictions made by the DR's experts have, one by one, been confirmed by what has happened in the real world. Furthermore, the many diverse pieces of

---

[81]   AUS' SWS, para. 496.
[82]   AUS' FWS', para. 670 and Annex E, para. 12.
[83]   Supplementary Expert Report of T. Chipty, Exhibit AUS-591, para. 2.f.
[84]   *See* DR Comments on AUS response to PQ 196, paras. 670-684.

evidence before the Panel fit together in a coherent and consistent way with the DR's argument and evidence.

122.   In contrast, the different pieces of evidence cannot be fit together in a coherent and consistent way with Australia's arguments. The picture that emerges from those arguments is muddled and incoherent, across the board. The expert predictions do not fit either with the evidence on the antecedents or with the evidence on smoking behaviour; and the evidence on the antecedents and smoking behaviour do not fit with Australia's arguments. In an effort to force all of the pieces to fit together, Australia has been compelled to change its arguments, making the later arguments inconsistent with the earlier ones. Behavioural theories no longer provide the answer; antecedents, like intentions, are no longer the best way to assess the PP measures; the NPPTS and ITC datasets are no longer reliable; the published *Tobacco Control* papers no longer provide a comprehensive evaluation of the PP measures; and, instead, the evidence on actual smoking behaviour now does matter – at least on Dr. Chipty's selective and erroneous assessment – whereas before it did not.

123.   The consistency and coherence between the totality of the evidence and the complainants' arguments, coupled with the inconsistency and incoherence between the totality of the evidence and Australia's arguments, speaks volumes. The conclusion to be drawn from the evidence is clear: the PP measures do not and will not change smoking behaviour in Australia.

(2)   Less restrictive alternative measures

(a)   The proposed alternatives

124.   Should the Panel find that the PP measures do make a contribution, the DR proposes four alternatives. Through these alternatives, the DR shows its commitment to ensuring that Australia can take effective tobacco control measures. The alternatives are: (1) an increase in the minimum legal purchase age ("MLPA") from 18 to 21 years; (2) an increase in the rate of excise taxation; (3) enhanced social marketing campaigns; and (4) a pre-vetting mechanism to review the trademark and form features on the packaging of tobacco products and the products themselves. Whether considered alone or in combination, these alternatives: (1) are less encumbering of the use of trademarks than the PP measures (that is, they are less trademark restrictive); (2) make an equivalent or greater contribution to the reduction of smoking prevalence and consumption than the PP measures; and (3) are reasonably available to Australia as alternative measures. For the PP measures, the evidence supports nothing more than a conclusion that a contribution would be, at best, *negligible* in size, with a *very low likelihood* of materializing, and at an indeterminate time in the *long-term*; on the other hand, the alternatives have a much *higher likelihood* of making a *significant contribution* to Australia's objective, both *immediately and in the future* over the long term.

125.   Importantly, Australia does not contest that the proposed alternatives would contribute to reducing smoking, especially among the target group –

youth. For instance, as regards an *increase in taxation*, Australia accepts that taxation is "the single most effective policy for reducing tobacco use".[85] In his own words, Australia's expert, Professor Chaloupka, has found that research "consistently demonstrate[s] the effectiveness of higher tobacco taxes in discouraging *initiation* and uptake of tobacco use among young people, promoting *cessation* among adult tobacco uses, and reducing *consumption* among continuing users, with relatively *larger effects on tobacco use among the young and the poor*".[86] An increase in taxation has an almost immediate effect that carries over to the long-term, with the long-term elasticity higher than the short-term elasticity.[87]

126.   Australia has also not contested the DR's evidence that an *increase in the minimum legal purchasing age* from 18 to 21 would secure a "large" reduction (25 percent) in smoking among 15-17 year-olds; and a "medium" reduction (15 percent) in smoking among those less than 15 years old and among 18-20 year-olds.[88] Translating these figures into prevalence rates, an increase in the MLPA from 18 to 21 would result in a 12 percent decrease in long-term overall prevalence rates.[89] Thus, raising the MLPA to 21 would make a contribution to reducing smoking that is much *greater* than any contribution that the PP measures might one day make, and it is certain to have an effect on youth smoking in the short term that necessarily entails long-term impacts.

127.   Australia has not addressed the alternative measures proposed by the DR under Article 20, because it incorrectly assumes that the provision does not require the consideration of alternatives. It nonetheless makes arguments about the alternatives in its arguments under Article 2.2 of the *TBT Agreement*, which the DR addresses here.

(b)   Australia's interpretative arguments are unfounded

128.   Australia objects to the proposed alternatives on two interpretative grounds: first, a strengthened version of an existing measure "is not a valid 'alternative'";[90] and, second, even if an existing measure could be an alternative, an alternative must employ a mechanism that is the same as that employed by the challenged measure.[91]

129.   As regards the first argument, Australia mischaracterizes findings of the panel and Appellate Body in *Brazil – Retreaded Tyres*, when it states that they

---

[85]   AUS' FWS, para. 719.
[86]   Supplementary expert report of F. Chaloupka, Exhibit AUS-582, para. 29 (emphasis added).
[87]   *See* Gallet and List (2003), Exhibit DR-120, p. 824; Bardsley and Olekalns (1999), Exhibit DR-122, p. 237, Figure 5; H. Ross and F. J. Chaloupka, "Economic Policies for tobacco control in developing Countries", *Salud Publica Mexico* 2006;48 suppl 1: S116-S117, Exhibit DR-118; Chaloupka and Hu (2000), Exhibit DR-121, p. 251.
[88]   IOM Report, Exhibit DR-232, p. 7-11.
[89]   IOM Report, Exhibit DR-232, p. S-6.
[90]   AUS' response to PQ 148, para. 21.
[91]   AUS' response to PQ 148, paras. 22 and 23.

found that "a proposed alternative measure that has already been implemented, *in whole or in part*, or is in the process of being implemented", is not a "valid" alternative.[92] In fact, the words "in whole or in part" do not feature in any of the panel and Appellate Body findings. In that dispute, as an alternative to a ban on the import of retreaded tyres, the European Union proposed measures that were not new and had been, or were being, fully implemented by Brazil. The proposed alternative measures were not *strengthened* versions of existing measures, as the alternatives proposed in this dispute are. Finally, Australia's argument that strengthened versions of existing measures cannot serve as alternatives is directly contradicted by findings of the panel in *China – Rare Earths*.[93]

130.   Australia's second argument – that an alternative cannot make an equivalent contribution if it works through a mechanism *different* from that employed by the challenged measure – is squarely contradicted by the Appellate Body in *US – COOL (Article 21.5)*, which found that an alternative measure need not make its contribution through the *same means* or *mechanism* as the challenged measure.[94]

(c)   Australia's factual arguments on the alternatives are unfounded [95]

131.   While Australia does not contest that the proposed alternatives would contribute to reducing smoking, it argues, as a factual matter, that the alternatives do not make an equivalent contribution. In particular, Australia submits, in not more than a few lines repeated throughout its submissions, that replacing the PP measures with an increase in the MLPA, an increase in excise tax, or improved social marketing (i) "*would result in a more limited set of mechanisms at work*"; (ii) would, thereby, reduce "*the ability of Australia to influence the broadest range of consumers and potential consumers*"; and (iii) would reduce synergies with other tobacco control measures.[96] All three arguments fail.

132.   As to Australia's *first argument* – that the alternatives would reduce the set of mechanisms at work – Australia suggests that the PP measures involve *new policy mechanisms*, whereas the alternatives involve a *strengthening of existing mechanisms,* implying that, without the PP measures, fewer policy mechanisms would be at work. The DR disagrees.

133.   *First*, Australia misconceives the issue: the issue is not the *number of mechanisms* at work, but the *degree of the contribution* that results from the operation of the measures. *Second*, Australia's suggestion that the PP measures entail new policy mechanisms is inconsistent with its own characterization of the

---

[92]   AUS' response to PQ 148, para. 21.
[93]   Panel Report, *China – Rare Earths*, para. 7.186.
[94]   Appellate Body Report, *US – COOL (Article 21.5)*, para. 5.215.
[95]   *See* DR's Comments on AUS' response to PQ 148, paras. 72-115.
[96]   Australia's response to Panel Question 148, para. 27 (emphasis added).

PP measures throughout these proceedings. Australia has argued that the PP measures involve an *extension of an existing policy mechanism*, that is, its prohibitions on the advertising, marketing, and promotion, which are also designed to reduce the appeal of tobacco products. Likewise, the other two mechanisms through which the PP measures were expected to operate (GHW effectiveness and reducing deception) are extensions of existing policy mechanisms (e.g., GHWs, social marketing, and the general prohibition on deceptive conduct). It is, therefore, simply not correct that the PP measures involve the addition of any *new* policy mechanisms to its comprehensive tobacco control strategy. The proposed alternatives are, therefore, equivalent to the PP measures in this respect: they all represent an extension of existing policy mechanisms. Therefore, replacing the PP measures with the alternatives would not reduce "the set of policy mechanisms at work".

134.   Australia's *second argument* is that the alternatives would reduce the *ability of Australia to influence the broadest range of consumers and potential consumers*. However, this argument is explicitly premised on Australia's first argument that the PP measures involve *new* policy mechanisms that would be eliminated from its tobacco control strategy if the PP measures were replaced by the alternatives. However, as just outlined, this is not accurate: the three policy mechanisms allegedly operating under the PP measures would continue to operate through other tobacco control measures.

135.   The evidence also shows that the PP measures have led to little or no incremental change in the operation of the mechanisms: product appeal was already negative, and has not much changed; people were already well informed about the health risks of smoking, and this has not changed; people do not seem, therefore, to have been deceived about these health risks, and deception levels have also not changed. Unsurprisingly, these disappointing changes in the policy mechanisms have not led to any change in antecedents closer to smoking behaviour (e.g., intentions), nor in actual smoking.

136.   In contrast, for the proposed alternatives, there is strong evidence that the existing policy mechanisms could be strengthened further, with favourable results. For instance, the MLPA relies on extending an access-based policy mechanism that is much more effective than plain packaging, because *banning young people from smoking is preferable to allowing them to smoke from packs that are less visually appealing*. Likewise, an increase in taxation works through a policy mechanism that is regarded, including by the tobacco control community itself, as the single most effective tobacco control measure, including to reduce youth smoking. In sum, the proposed alternatives are a much more effective means of influencing the broadest possible range of people than the PP measures. As a result, replacing the PP measures by the alternatives would strengthen – rather than weaken – the ability of Australia to influence the broadest range of consumers.

137. Finally, Australia's *third argument* is that, if the PP measures were replaced by the proposed alternatives, synergies with other tobacco control measures would be lost.[97] The essence of this argument seems to be that the PP measures contribute indirectly to reducing smoking by making taxation and social marketing campaigns *more effective*. To support its argument, Australia has mentioned only one study, which is not about plain packaging but about point-of-sale advertising and its synergies with price measures. Australia has not explained how these findings can be extrapolated to plain packaging. Of course, the alleged synergies, if any, between Australia's point-of-sale advertising bans and other tobacco control measures would not be diminished by the replacement of the PP measures. Further, the PP-specific evidence directly contradicts Australia's position, showing that, post implementation, taxation has not become more effective. Finally, Australia fails to take into account that the proposed alternative measures would themselves lead to enhanced synergies.

B. Legal Claims under the *TBT Agreement*

1. The *TBT Agreement* applies to the PP measures, as a whole[98]

138. The Appellate Body has established a three-part test for determining the threshold question of whether a measure, as "an integrated whole"[99], is a "technical regulation" under Annex 1.1 of the *TBT Agreement*. The PP measures satisfy all three elements of the test: *First*, they apply to an "*identifiable group of products*", *i.e.*, tobacco products;[100] *second*, they "*lay down*" product characteristics – in both a permissive and prohibitive manner – for tobacco products and their packaging relating to whether and/or how trademarks may appear on cigars and cigarettes; independently, they qualify as *packaging, marking, and labelling requirements*; *third*, compliance with the requirements under the PP measures is strictly mandatory.[101]

139. Australia seeks to exclude the PP measures' "trademark requirements"[102] from the Panel's consideration under the *TBT Agreement* on the ground that the *TRIPS Agreement* governs the "trademark requirements". However, WTO obligations in different covered agreements apply cumulatively, unless the contrary is expressed or there is a conflict. Since neither exists, both Article 2.2

---

[97] AUS' response to PQ 148, para. 26.
[98] *See* DR's FWS, paras. 934-949; DR's SWS, paras. 815-841; DR's responses to PQs 62, 89, 115; DR's comments on AUS' responses to PQ 145; DR's FOS, paras. 57-58.
[99] Appellate Body Report *EC – Seal Products*, para. 5.28-5.29. *See also* Appellate Body Report, *EC – Asbestos*, para. 64. *See also* Appellate Body Report, *US – COOL (Article 21.5)*, paras. 5.239 and 5.241
[100] DR's FWS, paras. 939-940.
[101] DR's FWS, paras. 948-949.
[102] In contrast to the "form requirements" which regulate the form of products and packaging, "trademark requirements" regulate whether and how trademarks are displayed on tobacco products and packaging.

of the *TBT Agreement* and Article 20 of the *TRIPS Agreement* apply to the PP measures.

2. The PP measures are not in accordance with international standards[103]

140.   Australia invokes Article 2.5 of the *TBT Agreement* to argue that the PP measures are "in accordance with relevant international standards" and therefore "shall be rebuttably presumed not to create an unnecessary obstacle to international trade". By "international standards", Australia refers to two guidelines for the implementation of Articles 11 and 13 of the Framework Convention on Tobacco Control ("FCTC Guidelines"), adopted by the FCTC Conference of the Parties ("FCTC COP"). Both Guidelines recommend that FCTC Parties "consider" the adoption of plain packaging.

141.   Australia's own actions call into question whether even Australia considers that it meets the Article 2.5 conditions. For instance, on notifying its PP measures to the TBT Committee, Australia[104] ticked the box indicating that "a relevant international standard does *not* exist or the technical content of a proposed technical regulation is *not* in accordance with the technical content of relevant international standards".

142.   Although the parties agree that successful invocation of Article 2.5 establishes a rebuttable presumption of compliance with Article 2.2, the DR contests Australia's assertion that the conditions that give rise to the presumption under Article 2.5 have been satisfied; and, moreover, the nature of the presumption that would arise if they have been.

143.   *First*, although the FCTC Guidelines pursue a worthy objective, they were not prepared by a relevant "international standardizing body" under the *TBT Agreement*,[105] and therefore do not constitute an "international standard". Bearing in mind the role "international standards" play in furthering the objective of the *TBT Agreement* to facilitate international trade,[106] a body like the FCTC COP, whose very purpose is to end international trade in tobacco products, does not qualify as an international standardizing body.[107]

144.   Equally, the FCTC COP does not comply with at least three of the six principles applicable to international standardizing bodies set out in the TBT Committee Decision.[108] The FCTC COP is not "open",[109] nor is it "impartial"[110]

---

[103]   *See* DR's SWS, paras. 814-920; DR's responses to PQs 66, 67,68,69,70, 130, 131, 136, 150, 163; DR's comments on AUS' responses to PQs 147, 150, 162, 163; DR's SOS, paras. 27-33.

[104]   *See* G/TBT/N/AUS/67 (8 April 2011).

[105]   *See* Appellate Body Report, *US – Tuna II (Mexico)*, para. 359.

[106]   Appellate Body Report, *EC – Sardines*, paras. 214-215; *see* Second Triennial Review of the Agreement on International Standards, Contribution by Australia: document G/TBT/W/139, para. 8.

[107]   *See e.g.* FCTC, Exhibit JE-19, Articles 3, 7, 23, 22.1(b)(iii) and 26.3, Part III.

[108]   Decisions and Recommendations adopted by the WTO Committee on Technical Barriers to Trade since 1 January 1995, G/TBT/1/Rev.12 (21 January 2015)

because, to implement the treaty, parties to the FCTC must follow *preordained policy choices that privilege* particular interests and perspectives.[111]

145. Nor does the FCTC COP meet the requirements of the principle of "effectiveness and relevance",[112] which requires that international standards be underpinned by a proper scientific base. When first requested by the DR to provide the "scientific basis" for the FCTC Guidelines, the FCTC Secretariat refused.[113] When the Panel requested this same information, the FCTC Secretariat cited only *one piece of scientific research on plain packaging*, comprising a methodologically flawed *single-page* study which reached *mixed conclusions* about the merits of the policy.[114] The activities of the FCTC COP contrast greatly with those of bodies that are widely-accepted as international standardizing bodies, like the International Organization for Standardization and the Codex Alimentarius Commission, which are open, and impartial, and adhere to science-driven agendas. To further underscore the lack of status of the FCTC COP as an international standardizing body, the WHO and FCTC Secretariat emphasized in their joint Communication to the Panel the standardizing activities of the WHO – the FCTC COP's umbrella organization – even though that organization conducts no standardizing activities in relation to tobacco.[115]

146. *Second*, the FCTC Guidelines are not "standards" under Article 1.2 of the *TBT Agreement* because they are not amenable to "common and repeated use". To perform their role of harmonizing and facilitating trade, international standards must be sufficiently precise to ensure that domestic measures can simply adopt them without variation. Failing the required precision, the content of national regulation inevitably varies, undermining the objective of harmonizing the terms of international trade.

147. The FCTC Guidelines lack the necessary precision to be an international standard. For instance, the *packaging requirements* do not specify standardized terms in respect of: the type face, the font colour, and the font size for the brand and variant name; the background colour of the packaging; the location of the brand and variant name on the packaging; the size or shape of the packaging; the type of opening mechanism; and the materials to be used (e.g., hard or soft pack). For *individual cigars*, the Guidelines lack specificity in terms of: the type face, the font colour, and the font size for the brand, variant and country name; and the background colour of the cigar band. Finally, in the absence of *any*

---

[109] *See TBT Committee Decision*, p. 47.
[110] *See TBT Committee Decision*, p. 48.
[111] Appellate Body Report, *US – Tuna II (Mexico)*, para. 376. For example, to participate in the FCTC COP, a tobacco-growing country, like the DR, must accept, on accession, efforts to shift agricultural production to other crops that may not be as economically fruitful.
[112] *See TBT Committee Decision*, p. 48.
[113] Letter from the Dominican Republic to the Head of the FCTC Secretariat (25 April 2014), Exhibit DR-46.
[114] *See* Expert Report of G. Fong, Exhibit AUS-14, paras. 333-334.
[115] *See* WHO/FCTC Communication.

FCTC Guidelines recommending the prohibition on the use of brand and variant names *on cigarette sticks*, Australia has nonetheless prohibited their use.

148.   *Third*, even if the FCTC Guidelines were international standards, the PP measures are not "in accordance with" them because the required high degree of correspondence between a Member's technical regulation and an international standard is missing.[116] A technical regulation is "in accordance with" an international standard if it "*embod[ies]* the international standard *completely* and, for practical purposes, *convert[s]* it into a municipal standard".[117] The text of Article 2.5 of the *TBT Agreement* requires that a "technical regulation", and not some sub-element of it, be "in accordance with" an international standard. Therefore, contrary to Australia's argument, it is not appropriate to atomize a technical regulation into elements that are in accordance with an international standard and elements that are not.

149.   As explained above, the FCTC Guidelines leave a high degree of discretion to domestic regulators in implementing them domestically. Further, the PP measures ban the use of brand names on cigarettes, which is not part of the Guidelines. As a result, the PP measures are not in accordance with the FCTC Guidelines.

150.   Therefore, because Australia has not demonstrated that the FCTC Guidelines are "international standards" or that the PP measures are "in accordance with" them, it cannot benefit from a rebuttable presumption of compliance under Article 2.2.

151.   Even if the Panel were to disagree, the presumption accorded under Article 2.5 has been rebutted by the DR. Contrary to Australia's argument, the presumption relates to the factors that must be considered under an Article 2.2 analysis, including the challenged measure's trade-restrictiveness, its contribution, the risk non-fulfilment would create, and the existence of alternatives that are reasonably available. However, the precise nature and content of the presumption arising in a particular case depends on whether and how a particular international standard addresses the Article 2.2 factors. In this dispute, at most, the FCTC Guidelines address whether the PP measures "contribute" to the achievement of its objectives.[118] However, as regards the contribution, the Panel record confirms that the FCTC COP lacked a sufficient evidentiary basis to support the conclusion that plain packaging would likely reduce smoking: as already noted, at the time the FCTC Guidelines were adopted, the scientific basis for the Guidelines comprised a single study on plain packaging, comprising a single page, with mixed results.[119] Moreover, any predictive evidence relied on in formulating those Guidelines has since been

---

[116]   *See* Appellate Body Report, *EC – Hormones*, para. 163.
[117]   *See* DR's response to PQ 66, paras. 310-311, referring to Appellate Body Report, *EC – Hormones*, paras. 170-171 (emphases added).
[118]   *See below* paras. 152-163.
[119]   DR's SWS, para. 544. *See also* Expert Report of G. Fong, Exhibit AUS-14, paras. 333-334.

overtaken by the more probative post-implementation evidence provided by the complainants in this dispute. As regards the reasonable availability of alternatives, the FCTC Guidelines do not consider or weigh *at all* the relative merits of the PP measures and proposed alternative measures. Indeed, it would be anathema to the objectives of the FCTC to identify the measure(s) that will have the *least* restrictive effects on trade in tobacco products, because the FCTC seeks to end trade in tobacco products by *maximizing* the restrictive effects on trade.

3. The PP measures are inconsistent with Article 2.2[120]

152. Article 2.2 requires a holistic weighing and balancing of the following factors under a "necessity" analysis: (a) the trade restrictiveness of the challenged measure; (b) the contribution the measure makes to the legitimate objective; (c) the risks non-fulfilment would create; and (d) the reasonably available alternative measures.[121] Since many of these factors have been discussed in the analysis of the Article 20 TRIPS claims, the DR focuses here on the distinct aspects of the Article 2.2 analysis.

a. The PP measures are highly trade restrictive[122]

153. Under Article 2.2, "trade-restrictiveness" refers to a limitation on competitive opportunities on internationally-traded goods. The assessment must take into account the opportunities relative to "the situation prior to the enactment of" the challenged measures. WTO obligations do not protect existing trade flows, but opportunities to engage in international trade, including future opportunities to develop and expand exports.[123] Thus, to succeed in demonstrating "trade restrictiveness", a complainant is not required to prove the actual trade effects of a measure, but rather a limitation on competitive opportunities. A measure's effect on competitive opportunities is to be determined by reference to its design, architecture, structure and operation.

154. For Australia, a limitation on competitive opportunities requires that there be an *overall* decrease in actual volumes of imports of tobacco products *as whole*. Australia illustrates its argument through a reference to a technical regulation affecting different car segments.[124] Under that example, a technical regulation that *entirely eliminates* competitive opportunities in the *most valuable*

---

[120] *See* DR's FWS, paras. 952-954; DR's SWS, paras. 922-923; DR's responses to PQs 117, 118, 121, 165; DR's comments on AUS' responses to PQs, 151, 152.

[121] *See* Appellate Body Reports, *US – Tuna II (Mexico)*, paras. 318, 320, 322; *US – COOL*, paras. 374, 376.

[122] *See* DR's FWS, paras. 957-963; DR's SWS, paras. 924-961; DR's responses to PQs 152, 153; DR's comments on AUS' responses to PQs 152, 154, 165; DR's FOS, paras. 59-62; DR's SOS, paras. 34-36.

[123] Appellate Body Report, *Korea – Alcohol*, para. 112*ff*.

[124] *See* AUS' SWS, paras. 385-396.

market segment does not restrict trade, because "offsetting" sales of cheaper cars means that overall trade volumes do not fall.

155.   The DR disagrees. Article 2.2 obliges a Member to ensure that *none* of the goods subject to a technical regulation is subject to an unnecessary trade restriction. Thus, if a Member imposes an unnecessary trade restriction on some of the goods subject to a technical regulation, it cannot "offset" that improper treatment by imposing no unnecessary restrictions on trade in other goods subject to that regulation, or by creating competitive opportunities in respect of those other goods. A note prepared by the WTO TBT Committee supports the interpretation that an effect on trade may be measured by reference to a measure's effect on "a specific product, group of products or products in general".[125]

156.   Australia also argues that, although trade restrictions affecting particular market segments are not disciplined under Article 2.2, they are disciplined if they involve discrimination on grounds of origin under Article 2.1 of the *TBT Agreement*.[126] However, whether a measure restricts trade in goods in the overall market or in particular segments, the restriction may be prohibited under WTO law both as discriminatory under Article 2.1 or as unnecessary under Article 2.2. There is no basis to conclude that the drafters intended to prohibit restrictions on trade in goods sold in particular market segments when the restrictions were discriminatory, but to permit such restrictions when they were unnecessary.

157.   Applying the correct legal standard, the PP measures are trade-restrictive because they limit competitive opportunities for all tobacco products, in particular the opportunity for producers to differentiate competing offerings in the marketplace, which has an impact on consumer loyalty and willingness to pay a premium for a differentiated product.

158.   Although unnecessary, the DR has also presented uncontested empirical evidence showing the adverse trade effects entailed by this loss of competitive opportunities. In particular, the PP measures have led consumers to switch from more expensive to cheaper tobacco products (i.e., downtrading). A measure that limits the ability to trade in more expensive tobacco products is a value-based restriction on international trade in those goods. Countries seek to maximize export revenues, and a measure that induces consumers to switch to cheaper products suppresses export revenues. Thus, even if a showing of trade effects were required, the DR has established that the PP measures have had such effects.

---

[125]   *See e.g.* G/TBT/W/2/Rev.1 (21 June 1995), p. 7 and G/TBT/M/2 (4 October 1995).
[126]   DR's response to PQ 154, para. 57*ff.*

b.   The alternatives proposed by the DR are less trade restrictive than the PP measures[127]

159.   Under Article 2.2, a complainant must show that a proposed alternative is "less *trade* restrictive" than the challenged measure (as opposed to less "trade*mark*" restrictive under Article 20). Were the Panel to reach consideration of alternatives, it would have disagreed with the complainants that the PP measures do not contribute to reducing smoking behaviour. On that assumption, the loss of competitive opportunities entailed by the PP measures leads to *two* distinct types of trade-restrictive effects: (1) a reduction in overall sales of tobacco products due to an assumed impact on consumers that either quit smoking or do not start; and (2) a reduction in sales of more expensive tobacco products in favour of cheaper ones (i.e., value-based downtrading), which arises due to an impact on consumers that continue to smoke but smoke cheaper cigarettes.

160.   Each of the alternatives is less trade restrictive than the PP measures. With respect to the *volume effects*, the PP measures and the alternatives would reduce tobacco sales to an *equivalent* extent or, as necessary, the alternatives could be calibrated to do so.[128] In terms of *value effects* (or downtrading), the alternatives would be less trade-restrictive: the MLPA does not lead continuing smokers to swap more expensive tobacco products for cheaper ones; an increase in taxation has a lesser effect on downtrading, and Australia has failed to demonstrate otherwise; social marketing does not lead to downtrading; and pre-vetting would lead to less downtrading, because fewer distinguishing elements would be removed from the packaging. Finally, in terms of their *treatment under the covered agreement*, whereas the PP measures are disciplined as a technical regulation that restricts international trade and they "encumber the use of trademarks", increased taxation, MLPA and social marketing are not trade/IP restrictive under any of the disciplines in the covered agreements.

c.   The PP measures are more trade restrictive than necessary "taking into account the risks non-fulfillment would create"[129]

161.   Article 2.2 requires that a panel take account of the "risks non-fulfilment would create", which requires consideration of: first, the nature of the risks at issue; and second, the gravity of the consequences that would arise from non-fulfilment of the legitimate objective.[130] By its terms, the nature of the risks

---

[127] *See* DR's FWS, paras. 972-978; DR's SWS, paras. 966-990; DR's response to PQs 63, 151, 152, 153, 157, 165; DR's comments on AUS' responses to PQ 151, 152, 154, 158.

[128] *See above* paras. 153-158 for discussion by the DR on the trade-restrictiveness of the PP measures.

[129] *See* DR's FWS, paras. 1025-1031; DR's SWS, paras. 991-1011; DR's response to PQ 65.

[130] Appellate Body Report, *US – Tuna II*, para. 321. *See also* Appellate Body Report, *US – COOL (Article 21.5)*, para. 5.215.

enquires into (i) the possibility or likelihood of (ii) a negative event occurring – i.e., the failure to achieve, in whole or in part, the desired objective. The gravity of the risks relates to the seriousness of the consequences that flow from the negative event materializing.

162.   As regards the *nature of the risks* under the PP measures, the economic data shows that the PP measures have not reduced smoking and have not, therefore, fulfilled their objective; the evidence from the NPPTS also suggests that the PP measures are not even having the intended effects on the mechanisms by which the PP measures are ultimately supposed to reduce smoking. Thus, the best-case scenario still involves a *considerable risk of non-fulfilment* of the objective of reducing smoking because of the uncertainties over whether the PP measures will ever reduce smoking. By contrast, the *alternative measures* proposed by the DR collectively involve *no risk* of non-fulfilment, but rather involve the *certainty* that they would reduce smoking behaviour in the population in general, and among young people in particular, both in the short- and the long-term.

163.   As to the *gravity of the risks* of non-fulfilment, Australia does not contest that the gravity of the risks as between the PP measures and the alternatives is identical.

III.   REQUESTS FOR FINDINGS

164.   To conclude, the DR respectfully requests the Panel to find that Australia's PP measures violate Article 2.2 of the *TBT Agreement* and the following provisions of the *TRIPS Agreement*: Articles 15.4, 16.1, 20, 2.1 (and Article 10*bis* of the *Paris Convention*), Article 22.2(b) and Article 24.3. The DR requests that, pursuant to Article 19.1 of the DSU, the Panel recommend to the Dispute Settlement Body that it request Australia to bring its PP measures into conformity with its obligations under the *TRIPS Agreement* (including the substantive provisions of the *Paris Convention*, as incorporated into the *TRIPS Agreement*) and the *TBT Agreement*.

ANNEX B-3

INTEGRATED EXECUTIVE SUMMARY OF THE ARGUMENTS OF CUBA[*]

I. INTRODUCTION AND IMPORTANCE OF THE PRESENT DISPUTE FOR CUBA

1.   This dispute settlement proceeding is the first that Cuba has initiated against another WTO Member. The decision to bring this complaint against Australia follows thorough reflection and analysis by the Cuban authorities.

2.   The Cuban Government attaches great importance to public health and fully accepts that tobacco consumption has serious consequences for public health. Cuba does not wish to interfere unduly with the ability of WTO Members to undertake effective actions in the field of tobacco control, since it considers that every country has the sovereign right and overriding duty to implement measures geared to safeguarding the health of its population.

3.   At the same time, however, every WTO Member must respect the commitments it has undertaken multilaterally and, in addition, adequately take into account the socio-economic implications they will have for small and vulnerable developing economies before implementing them. Cuba is not seeking to challenge Australia's right to protect the health of its population, but to demonstrate that plain packaging (PP) constitutes an unjustified and unnecessary restriction on trade which infringes the brand protection recognized in international intellectual property agreements, inasmuch as it hinders the identification and characterization of products by consumers and prohibits the use of distinctive signs, warranty seals and appellations of origin.

4.   Cuba opposes the plain packaging ("PP") established by Australia on 1 December 2012 (the PP measures) because it considers that there is no convincing evidence that it has generated, or will generate, tangible public health benefits in Australia; because it is disproportionate; and because it will have a significant detrimental effect on Cuba's cigar industry as well as on the intellectual property that Cuba has built up over generations.

5.   By standardizing the appearance of packaging, the application of these measures represents the total dilution of the distinctive characteristics of the identifying marks of tobacco industry products. This hinders the differentiation and characterization of products by consumers on the basis of brand preference, by eliminating trademark functions such as "distinguishing one product or service from another", "indication of origin" and "identification of quality".

---

[*]   Original Spanish.

6.   It is for this reason that Cuba initiated this dispute. Cuba bases its action to defend large hand-made (hereinafter LHM) cigars on the social, historical, cultural and economic impact involved for the country. Cuban premium cigars embody a wealth of traditional knowledge, culture, history and Cuban characteristics such that the sector in and of itself is a bulwark of the country's identity associated with a history stretching back over more than five centuries. A large number of women, elderly people, rural workers etc. are linked with the sector, and other family members depend economically upon them, so that it is the essential economic pillar for various regions of Cuba such as the province of Pinar del Río. Account has also been taken of the singularity of this product, identified through the distinctive signs of Industrial Property as an emblematic Cuban product, such as the Habanos geographical mark and appellation of origin, the Cuban Government Warranty Seal and the tobacco manufacturers' marks, some of which date back over a century and are also protected as works of art historically associated with this same geographical origin.

7.   Ever since its cultivation began in Cuba even prior to colonization, twist tobacco has been part of our historical and cultural traditions. It is the only custom of the indigenous population of the island to have been documented by the first Spaniards when they arrived in 1492. The twist tobacco harvesters were probably the first workers' association to acquire social representation in Cuba and organized the first protests *and* uprisings against the Spanish colonial regime as early as the 17th century. The tobacco strippers and twisters spearheaded important struggles in the history of the Cuban workers' and union movement. Twist tobacco cultivation is rooted in Cuba's cultural life and has attracted priority attention from social anthropologists. The greatest of these, Fernando Ortiz, who is known as the third discoverer of Cuba owing to his invaluable contributions to the study of Afro-Cuban traditions, wrote his classic essay, "Cuban Counterpoint: Tobacco and Sugar", in the first half of the 20th century. In this study the author describes and analyses the social and cultural factors associated with these two Cuban products.

8.   In 2009, Cuban LHM cigars were presented to UNESCO as the intangible heritage of the Cuban nation, and the tobacco factory collective readings (Lecturas de Tabaqueria) are part of the cultural heritage of the Cuban nation as "an illustration of the permanent cultural dialogue between tobacco workers and the surrounding society, and recognized as an important expression of the nation's intangible cultural heritage".

9.   Cuban corporations hold 50 separate trademarks which are registered in Australia under Class 34 of the International Classification (the Class relating to tobacco products) (the Cuban Class 34 trademarks). A full list of the 50 registered trademarks is set out in Annex 1 to Cuba's first written submission. Many of these trademarks have been in use since the mid-19th century and are associated with considerable goodwill. Indeed, several have been recognized as "well-known marks" by courts and jurisdictions as varied as the Dominican Republic, France, Spain, Mexico and the United States.

10.   Cuba has also developed a geographical indication for its LHM cigar products. The *"Denominación de Origen Protegida (DOP) Habanos"* (the Habanos GI) is a coloured composite mark consisting of the word "Habanos", the suffix "DOP" and an image of chevrons forming a leaf. The Habanos GI is protected in major export markets. The current composite mark has been in use since 1994 but the term Habanos has been used and protected for a much longer period. A more detailed account of the development of this geographical indication is set out in Annex 1 to Cuba's first written submission. The Habanos GI is used to designate cigars that: (1) have been produced in Cuba according to stringent and comprehensive quality standards; and (2) contain certain varieties of Cuban black tobacco grown in specific regions of Cuba.

11.   The applicable quality standards, and the use of the Habanos GI, are currently regulated by the "Consejo Regulador de la Denominación de Origen Protegida Habanos" (Regulatory Board of the Cuban Tobacco Appellation of Origin). The Consejo Regulador acts pursuant to Resolution No. 201/2009, promulgated by the Agriculture Ministry of the Republic of Cuba. The stringent requirements imposed by the Consejo Regulador are meant to ensure that the authentic and special quality claimed for Cuban hand-made cigars is present in every product that bears the Habanos GI. Like many geographical indications, the Habanos GI is used to designate a product which reflects the cultural heritage of the place where it is produced and which is made from natural materials according to traditional methods.

12.   Cuba also requires that an official seal be affixed on all tobacco products exported from Cuba (the Cuban Government Warranty Seal). The Cuban Government Warranty Seal was first used in 1889 pursuant to a Spanish Royal Decree. The current design can be traced back to legislation promulgated by the Republic of Cuba in 1912. It provides an assurance of authenticity to consumers and also allows for tracking and tracing by Cuban exporters. Like the Cuban Class 34 trademarks and the Habanos GI, the Cuban Government Warranty Seal is protected under trademark and unfair competition laws in export markets.

13.   The Warranty Seal and Habanos GI are reproduced below in an easy-to-view format:

Habanos GI   Warranty Seal

14.   Cuban LHM cigars have an unsurpassed reputation for quality. They typically command a significant price premium over competing tobacco products and are regularly ranked by critics among the best cigars in the world.

15.   That reputation is a product of the collective investment by the Cuban people over generations; it arises from a combination of the natural environment in Cuba and the know-how and techniques used by Cuban tobacco growers and cigar makers. Cuba has made every effort to preserve a method of production in which the LHM cigars are made entirely by hand by highly skilled workers. The economic implications of following these traditional methods of production are significant: in broad terms, a machine-made cigar factory employing 100 people could produce 670,000 cigars a day, while an equivalent Cuban hand-made cigar factory would only produce 9,000 cigars in the same time frame.

16.   Consumers all over the world are willing to pay a premium for Cuba's long experience in producing its LHM cigars, and this makes the use of these traditional methods of manufacture worthwhile. However, with the distortion caused to Cuban intellectual property (in particular, the Cuban Class 34 trademarks, the Habanos GI and the Cuban Government Warranty Seal), Australia's measures will affect the Cuban industry's ability to charge that premium, to maintain customer loyalty and to sustain its commitment to these methods of manufacture.

17.   If Australia's plain packaging measures are replicated across major export markets, such as the European Union, Cuban exporters will no longer be able to compete on the basis of quality, which will have a significant adverse impact on its tobacco industry. At the same time, any adverse effect on its tobacco industry will have significant negative effects on the Cuban economy as a whole, since:

    a.   Tobacco products consistently account for more than 5% of Cuba's total exports (by value). As a small and vulnerable economy with limited export opportunities, Cuba would be significantly affected by the loss of these exports. Tobacco is one of the few agricultural crops which can be cultivated profitably in Cuba. This is because of the value addition created locally and the significant value that inheres in the Cuban intellectual property associated with these products.

    b.   Cuba has 465 tobacco production units and employs more than 200,000 people in the tobacco sector. In percentage terms, the tobacco sector accounts for 4% of the economically active population in Cuba. To put that figure in context, a similar proportion of the economically active population in Switzerland is engaged in the banking sector.[1]

---

[1]   Swiss Bankers Association – The Economic Significance of the Swiss Financial Centre, Exhibit CUB-14, First Written Submission of Cuba.

c.   Production employees in hand-made cigar factories have dedicated years of effort to acquiring specialized skills. These employees will not be able to transfer their skills to other sectors if, as a result of plain packaging and in a situation where Cuban tobacco products are perceived to be indistinguishable from non-Cuban tobacco products, consumers abroad are unwilling to pay a premium for Cuban exports.

d.   The population within certain regions such as that of San Luis in Pinar del Río province and the Florencia region in Ciego de Ávila province are heavily dependent on the tobacco sector. Tobacco has been grown in those regions for hundreds of years.

e.   The profits earned from tobacco exports also generate tax and dividend revenues for the Cuban Government. Those revenues allow the Cuban Government to meet the needs of the Cuban population as a whole.

f.   Cuba is currently unable to abandon the twist tobacco industry, which for the time being is one of its most important exportable products, particularly in the context of an economic, trade and financial blockade applied by the United States, which prevents access to markets for goods, services and credit to boost the country's economic development.

18.   Australia's response to these concerns about intellectual property protection appears to be that it continues to protect Cuban trademarks because: (1) they can be placed on the Australian trademarks register in their original form; and (2) Cuban trademark holders have the ability to prevent third parties from using Cuban trademarks on tobacco products. But that response does not go anywhere near to addressing the real issue. Third parties cannot use Cuban trademarks in their original form on tobacco packaging because that would amount to a breach of Australian plain packaging laws. It follows that Australia grants a right to Cuban trademark holders which is entirely illusory because Cuban trademark owners cannot take advantage of those trademarks by using them in their original and recognizable form. Australia's regime has been created solely for the purpose of maintaining the appearance that Australia continues to protect trademarks of tobacco products, but it actually provides no genuine protection for such trademarks.

II.   EFFECTIVENESS OF PLAIN PACKAGING

19.   Cuba questions the esoteric theories invoked by Australia with regard to the impact PP may have on consumer behaviour, culminating in the *"affect heuristic theory"* and the *"conditioned cue reactivity"* to tobacco trademarks. It is not appropriate for the Panel to rely on these theories, particularly in a context where the data show that PP did not contribute to a decline in the prevalence of the smoking habit. Moreover, Cuba considers that a behavioural theory can be developed to justify any conclusion (including conclusions that clearly

contradict each other). Therefore, the Panel should be extremely cautious when evaluating such theories. The simple question facing the Panel is whether Australia's public health objective is less likely to be achieved by the packaging shown below in Photograph 1 (a pack of LHM cigars with a health warning, but without the effect of other aspects of the PP measures) than by the packaging in Photograph 2 (a pack of LHM cigars with a health warning and with the effect of the PP measures). The question is whether the difference between the two is sufficiently great to justify the PP measures.

Figure 1:

Figure 2:

20.　The reply is obviously "no". Cuba maintains that the dominant and unattractive graphic health warnings (which must compulsorily be placed on all tobacco packaging) would effectively eliminate the aesthetic appeal of packaging. It therefore follows that any additional standardization of the appearance of tobacco packs (in the residual portion which occupies, for example, 25% of the front face and 10% of the back face of cigarette packs) cannot have a dissuasive effect on the decision to take up a behaviour that is both risky and the object of widespread social disapproval in Australia.

21.　The Panel could only agree with Australia if it were overwhelmingly and clearly supported by the data and evidence. That is undoubtedly not the case. The post-implementation data on prevalence and consumption in the Australian market show that PP has not reduced rates of smoking since its introduction in December 2012.

22.　Different types of analysis on various sources of information indicate that PP has failed in reducing the smoking and tobacco consumption rate. The only effect that PP has had is to accelerate the current trend towards down-trading (i.e. consumer migration towards lower-priced products or brands) in certain segments of the Australian tobacco market. This is an unforeseen consequence of the PP measures which, far from reducing smoking and tobacco consumption rates, carries a genuine risk of generating adverse consequences for public health. The acceleration of down-trading is consistent with Cuba's concerns in relation to the future effect of PP.

23.　Moreover, the studies relied upon by Australia provide no solid basis for concluding that PP measures will reduce tobacco use. None of these studies measures actual consumption of tobacco by individuals; instead, they use substitute variables. This shortcoming is explicitly recognized in the so-called Chantler Report. In addition, these studies used research models which give rise to considerable doubt about the reliability of any conclusion reached. The great majority of these studies do not evaluate the impact of PP in the real world.

24.   Consequently, PP measures cannot "justify" the total "encumbrance" imposed on Cuban trademarks for the purposes of Article 20 of the TRIPS Agreement. By the same token, the PP measures are much more restrictive than necessary to fulfil Australia's objective of reducing the prevalence of the smoking habit, and therefore violate Article 2.2 of the TBT Agreement.

25.   In its second written submission, Australia continues suggesting that the use of trademarks and geographical indications for LHM cigars made in Cuba makes them more attractive to children and adolescents. In this connection, Cuba wishes to emphasize that the Australian authorities are entitled to prohibit alcoholic beverages that are especially attractive to minors. However, no Australian authority has at any time suggested that trademarks and geographical indications can no longer be shown on premium alcoholic beverages, for example on bottles of the brand of champagne illustrated below:

Figure 3:

III.   PLAIN PACKAGING MEASURES AND THEIR IMPACT ON CUBAN LHM CIGARS

26.   Cuba wishes to draw the Panel's attention to the recent phenomenon of so-called parallel imports of Cuban LHM cigars into Australia. This was made possible by the compulsory withdrawal of the Cuban Government Warranty Seal which must be carried by all LHM cigars exported from Cuba. Prior to the PP measures, consumers who purchased LHM cigars only acquired products with an authentic and intact warranty seal. Normally, consumers would never purchase Cuban LHM cigars without the warranty seal because Cuban LHM cigars are luxury premium products which carry a high unit price. However, the

PP measures have made it impossible to market the product with the warranty seal, thus enabling parallel traders to purchase Cuban LHM cigars outside Australia and to repackage them in PP-compliant packs, albeit without the warranty seal. Prior to the introduction of the PP measures, parallel imports did not occur on a major scale, since they always require repackaging of the cigars and, hence, the breaking of the warranty seal without the possibility of affixing a new one. While consumers would not normally purchase Cuban LHM cigars without an intact warranty seal, all Cuban LHM cigars currently marketed in Australia have no warranty seal, and this has created an opportunity for parallel imports.

27.   There is a major risk that the handling of the product by third parties not subject to any control by the Cuban industry or the latter's strict standards of quality will affect the quality of the cigars, and this will definitely affect the presentation of the product within the package. Moreover, this practice will entail a reduction in consumer prices (since the ability to offer lower prices to consumers is the raison d'être of parallel trade).

IV.   THE PLAIN PACKAGING MEASURES VIOLATE ARTICLE 20 OF THE TRIPS AGREEMENT

28.   The PP measures adopted by Australia violate Article 20 of the TRIPS Agreement because they unjustifiably encumber the use of tobacco product trademarks in the course of trade through the establishment of special requirements. That provision places limits on the ability of WTO Members to restrict the use of trademarks by commercial actors in the course of trade.

A.   The plain packaging measures are a special requirement

29.   The PP measures impose a set of conditions that must be complied with by commercial actors involved in the manufacture and distribution of tobacco products in Australia. Australia's measures, therefore, impose "requirements".

30.   The requirements arising from the PP measures are "special", since they affect only trademarks used on tobacco products. Equivalent requirements are not applied to trademarks in general or to trademarks used in connection with other types of products.

B.   The plain packaging measures encumber the use of a tobacco-related trademark in the ordinary course of trade

31.   The relevant ordinary meaning of the term "encumber" is "to hamper, impede, act as a check or restraint". Encumbrances have the effect of restricting the display of a trademark and limiting its ability to distinguish goods from competing goods.

32.   That is precisely the effect of the restrictions imposed by Australia on the display of trademarks. These restrictions involve "impediments", "checks" and "restraints" on the use and display of trademarks by trademark owners and they

limit the capacity of trademarks to distinguish specific tobacco products from other tobacco products.

33. The PP measures prohibit the use of trademarks at the point of sale. To the extent that the use of specific trademarks is permitted (e.g. mark and variety names), the PP measures require the use of such marks in a specific form and typeset. These are "*special requirements*" for the use of a trademark "*in a manner detrimental to its capability to distinguish the goods or services of one undertaking from those of other undertakings*". This implies the imposition of an encumbrance on the use of trademarks "*in the course of trade*".

34. Australia submits that the PP measures do not affect the use of trademarks "*in the course of trade*" because Australia is a "dark market" and, therefore, the packaging is not visible before the conclusion of the operation. This interpretation is unacceptably limited and out of line with the ordinary meaning of the term (as used in other articles; e.g. Article 16.1 of the TRIPS Agreement and subparagraph 3 of Article 10bis of the Paris Convention). Rather, the term "*in the course of trade*" refers more broadly to any use "in trade" or any "commercial use" of the mark.

35. The correct interpretation of Article 20 requires that, once it is established that a measure imposes special requirements constraining trademark use, the burden of justifying those special requirements shifts to the implementing WTO Member. This is so because: (i) the imposition of encumbrances on trademark use should only be permitted in exceptional circumstances; and (ii) it is inappropriate to require a complainant to identify and refute a justification of which it may be unaware or which may not be particularized.

C. The plain packaging measures are unjustifiable

1. The PP measures make no contribution to Australia's objective of reducing tobacco consumption levels

36. Cuba maintains that the special requirements imposed by Australia on the use of tobacco trademarks are ineffective because they fail to achieve the legitimate aim of causing a reduction in smoking prevalence. Cuba bases this submission primarily on the post-implementation data from the Australian market, which demonstrate that Australia's measures have not had the desired effect. Moreover, Cuba goes further and shows that Australia's measure is not based on a cogent and robust rationale.

37. As Cuba explained in detail in section IV.A of its first written submission, the post-implementation evidence establishes that the PP measures, including the trademark restrictions, have not caused any discernible reduction in prevalence rates (or tobacco consumption levels) in Australia. In particular, they have not led to material changes in prevalence or consumption relative to the rates observed in New Zealand, and they have not altered smoking prevalence rates for minors or young adults. Moreover, sales of LHM cigars, as evidenced in the Pacific Cigar Co. Ltd. (PCC) data, have remained steady and

rates of cigar smoking, as measured in the Roy Morgan survey data, have not been altered by the implementation of the PP measures.

38.   The evidence shows that the "special requirements" established by the PP measures have been ineffective in connection with tobacco use in general. Moreover, even if such evidence were available, it is unlikely that the prohibition on the use of Cuban-owned trademarks, such as Cohíba and Habanos on LHM cigars would have an impact on the prevalence of smoking in Australia.[2]

39.   In addition, Cuba argues that Australia's justification for the trademark restrictions suffers from material flaws.

40.   To begin with, the body of literature offered in support of Australia's measures consists of studies which suffer from a number of horizontal limitations.

41.   Australia's claim that PP will reduce the appeal of packaging and thereby alter smoking decisions suffers from a number of shortcomings. Australia's claim that PP will increase the effectiveness of Graphic Health Warnings (GHWs) and thereby reduce smoking rates is also flawed. Finally, the claim that plain packaging reduces the ability of packaging to mislead consumers about the harmful effects of smoking cannot justify Australia's PP measures. For all of these reasons, Cuba submits that the trademark restrictions are ineffective as they are not supported by a defensible rationale. Consequently, for this reason as well, they are unjustifiable.

42.   Lastly, Cuba wishes to mention that, on 26 February 2016, Australia notified the Panel of the results of its post-implementation review. The review concludes that the PP measures are meeting its objective of improving public health in Australia. On 21 March 2016, Cuba informed the Panel that it endorsed the comments submitted by Honduras in relation to Australia's post-implementation review. Those comments, in essence, indicate that the conclusion put forward in the post-implementation review is based on certain evidence which has been shown to lack validity by the complainants in this dispute.

2.   Alternative less restrictive measures that would have enabled it to achieve its objective were available to Australia

43.   If the Panel concludes, contrary to Cuba's position, that the trademark restrictions have been effective in reducing prevalence rates and per capita consumption levels in Australia, such changes can be obtained through alternative measures less encumbering on trademark use.

44.   The alternative measures in question are the following:

---

[2]   Habanos is both a trademark and a geographical indication.

a. An increase in the level of excise tax on tobacco products. This would suffice to bring down prevalence rates and per capita consumption levels by the modest amounts that the PP measures might possibly achieve. It is obvious that specific excise tax increases do not affect the ability of tobacco trademark owners to use their rights.

b. Pre-vetting of packaging design features. This would suffice to replicate any benefits of PP. There is no evidence that all of the design features of tobacco product packaging and trademarks cause changes in smoking behaviour, and it would therefore be enough, by means of a pre-vetting regime, to identify and eliminate only those specific packaging features that may affect smoking behaviour (without severely curtailing the ability of manufacturers to distinguish their products from other products from different sources by means of trademarks).

c. An increase in the age at which tobacco products can be purchased legally would make at least an equivalent contribution to reducing prevalence rates and, by removing tobacco products from adolescents' social networks, would be particularly effective in reducing prevalence among the young.

d. Improved social campaigns for tobacco control. To this end, it would be necessary to remedy the flaws present in Australia's current social marketing campaigns and there would be no impact on the intellectual property rights of tobacco trademark owners.

D.   Australia has failed to rebut Cuba's *prima facie* case in relation to Article 20 of the Trips Agreement

45.   Australia argues that "the scope of the 'special requirements' at issue [in Article XX] does not include the respects in which the tobacco plain packaging measure prohibits the use of certain trademarks on tobacco retail packaging and products". According to Australia, Article 20 prevents only measures that impose positive obligations upon the trademark owner, but does not prevent measures in the form of prohibitions on use.

46.   Australia's argument is erroneous. The term "requirement" is broader than the term "prohibition", but unquestionably also includes prohibitions. "To prohibit" is nothing other than "to require, negatively" that something be done or not done. Furthermore, the PP measure imposes both negative and positive requirements through the prohibition on use of all trademarks, on the one hand, and by requiring, for example, the use of trade names in a specific format and typeface. Accordingly, the PP measure establishes a series of positive and negative requirements on trademark use.

47.   Australia also argues erroneously that the role of trademarks is limited to the identification of the manufacturer. While one of the main functions of a trademark is to guarantee the origin of goods and services, this is not its only

purpose. The body of international jurisprudence on trademarks clearly indicates that trademarks have a set of important functions that go far beyond merely indicating the origin of the product (such as distinguishing the goods of the trademark owner from those of other traders). This is specifically applicable to luxury premium brands, such as the Cuban LHM cigars marketed in Australia.

48.   Trademarks have important quality, communication and investment functions, in addition to their function of indicating origin. In the case of Cuban cigars, their prestige is communicated by the mark and by its association with Cuba. Lastly, trademarks have an investment function. The investment function consists in the use of the trademark to acquire or preserve a reputation which maintains customer loyalty over a prolonged period of time.

49.   Australia's arguments overlook these essential and broader functions of trademarks. Instead, they focus and limit the role of trademarks to their narrow historical function as a mere factor in differentiating the trademark owner from other producers in terms of a difference of origin.

50.   Australia attempts to argue that its PP measures are "justifiable" by making a distinction between what it calls the "*essential source identification function*" of a trademark and what it calls the "*advertising function*" of trademarks. According to Australia, the PP measures respect the "*essential source identification*" because they permit the use of the trademark name (in a standardized source and without graphic elements) and simply prohibit "*unacceptable advertising*".

51.   Cuba totally disagrees with Australia when it argues that the use on product packaging of trademarks including figurative elements and colours is not protected by Article 20 of the TRIPS Agreement. Both types of trademark (i.e. those which only contain text and those which contain figurative elements) are independently protected by the TRIPS Agreement (Articles 15.1, 22 and 23 of the TRIPS Agreement). It is also obvious that a trademark that cannot be used is incapable of fulfilling its *essential source identification function*; thus, the PP measures impede the primary function of a trademark. Many WTO Members regulate or prohibit advertising of products such as alcoholic beverages, health products and tobacco. However, no WTO Member other than Australia has implemented a prohibition on the use of trademarks in product packaging.

52.   In addition, the graphic elements play a fundamental role in source identification. By way of example, the complete version of the Cohíba trademark refers to the indigenous people of Cuba, the Taínos Indians smoking the "cuaba" which was an ancestral ceremony prior to the arrival of Christopher Columbus. The graphic element of the trademark, which alludes to the cultural inheritance in which the product has its roots, is at least as important for the function of source identification, if not more so, than the name itself.

53.   It is not reasonable to assume that the presence of this figurative element on a box of cigars with 75% or 90% health warnings will negatively affect Australia's public health objective (and certainly not in a context where the

evidence shows that the PP measures have not increased the effectiveness of health warnings and have not had any impact on actual smoking behaviour).

54.   In addition, the use of a complete trademark (i.e. one with figurative elements) on a box of cigars with 75% and 90% graphic health warnings can never be considered as inadequate or subject to "justified encumbrances" in a WTO context. Trade can only take place if a minimum level of communication is possible whereby the seller can inform the buyer of the qualities and origin of his product, as well as the differences with other products. In a "dark market", the display of the trademark on the package is the only way of communicating this information to the consumer. Australia describes this as "*promotion*" instead of communication, but this ignores what really happens when a Cuban cigar is placed on the market with a trademark on the packaging, especially in the context of the existing regulations in Australia, which restrict the display of trademarks to a very small space on the packages. In these circumstances, the seller seeks primarily to communicate to the buyer the quality, origin, tradition and characteristics of the product, as well as the differences with other similar products. This is the real reason why trademarks and geographical indications have been created and are protected by WTO rules. However, and as explained by Australia itself, the effect and the objective of the PP measures is precisely to do away with any variability between the packaging of different tobacco products and to "*eliminate*" the opportunity for a manufacturer to differentiate his products by means of the tobacco packaging. In doing so, Australia invalidates the essential function of protection of the trademark in the context of international trade. What the display of trademarks in the limited space remaining on the tobacco package does not do is to incite smoking.

E.   **Trademarks are of essential importance for the creation of brand image and for differentiating premium tobacco products**

55.   Cuban LHM cigars are not "standardized" low quality tobacco products. LHM cigars are luxury products and, as with other luxury products, the creation of brand image through the use of trademarks is fundamental for commercial prestige and for economic value.

56.   As Cuba has explained, the incomparable reputation and prestigious brand status of Cuban LHM cigars are derived from a collective investment by the Cuban people over many generations. They result from a combination of Cuba's natural environment and the know–how and techniques used by Cuban tobacco producers, as well as highly skilled cigar manufacturers, who produce them entirely by hand.

57.   Strict regulations and standards are scrupulously applied to maintain the quality of Cuban LHM cigars. For this reason, consumers throughout the world correctly regard Cuban cigars as a product of the highest quality, a status which the Cuban cigar manufacturers have sought to protect by investing substantially in the creation of the brand image of LHM cigars, over a prolonged period and with specific trademarks that have been used for more than a century

(e.g. Partagás – 1845; Hoyo de Monterrey – 1865; Romeo Y Julieta – 1875; Bolívar – 1902).

58.   In this connection, Cuba considers it useful to picture the devastating impact that similar measures, even without health warnings, would have on other high–end products, such as champagne. **Figure 4** below shows a label with a trademark and a geographical indication. **Figure 5** shows how the label would look under the PP measures.

Figure 4: *Bollinger Special Cuvée champagne label.* On this label, the trademark is "Bollinger Special Cuvée" and the geographical indication is "Champagne"	***Figure 5:*** *The label that Bollinger Special Cuvée champagne would have if it were subject to the PP measure (without the health warning).*

59.   Any WTO Member which sought to introduce such PP measures would face strong opposition from a series of developed WTO Members, particularly from the European Union, but also from Australia and the United States. They would argue that it is unthinkable that such a measure is in any way compliant with the TRIPS Agreement since it would jeopardize the essential aim that the TRIPS Agreement seeks to achieve. Cuba agrees with this and stresses firmly that the conclusion should be the same under the scenario which concerns us. That conclusion cannot be different simply because the products affected by this case are high–end LHM cigars, instead of high–end alcoholic beverages, and because the country with a leading market position is a small developing country like Cuba.

60.   Australia itself has recognized the high value segment occupied by Cuban LHM cigars and commented in its first written submission that cigars are "increasingly associated with an upscale status, luxury, affluence, sophistication and style". It is not by chance that consumers have come to view Cuban cigars as an upscale, luxury product; the perceived value and quality of these cigars derive from the years of investment made in trademarks and the considerable goodwill and utility associated with such trademarks.

61.   In this context, it is totally erroneous and also incoherent for Australia to argue that trademarks do not distinguish products in terms of their "quality, characteristics, and reputation". On the contrary, the essential purpose of these trademarks is to communicate the traditions, culture and investment that contribute to the quality of the world–renowned Cuban cigars. Consumers do not pay a significantly higher price in recognition of a producer's identity; consumers pay the higher price because they subscribe to the brand offer communicated by a trademark.

62.   This far–reaching "encumbrance" is unjustified because it is not necessary, reasonable or rational, in the light of Australia's public health objective, to reduce smoking prevalence. The PP measures are ineffective, alternative measures exist that would be more effective and would entail no encumbrance on trademarks, such as: an increase in excise tax, pre–vetting of packaging design features or increasing the minimum legal purchase age.

V.   THE PLAIN PACKAGING MEASURES VIOLATE ARTICLE 24.3 OF THE TRIPS AGREEMENT

63.   Cuba submits that the PP measures violate Article 24.3 of the TRIPS Agreement because they have the effect of diminishing the level of protection afforded to Cuban geographical indications compared with the level of protection that existed in Australia prior to 1 January 1995. Specifically, Cuba emphasizes that the use of the Habanos geographical indication on the retail packaging of Cuban LHM cigars was permitted under Australian domestic law prior to 1 January 1995, whereas the use of that specific geographical indication on the retail packaging is currently prohibited.

64.   Contrary to Australia's allegations, Cuba has shown that the Habanos geographical indication has since 1968 gained a reputation in Australia which is covered by protection against fraudulent imitation (passing off) under the ordinary law on injury, and Australia has admitted that this could imply protection for geographical indications for the purposes of Article 24.3 of the TRIPS Agreement.[3]

65.   Cuba points out that Article 24.3 imposes an obligation on Australia and other Members not to diminish the level of protection afforded to specific

---

[3]   Australia's second written submission, paras. 70 and 71.

geographical indications, compared with the level of protection that existed prior to the conclusion of the TRIPS Agreement. Given this obligation, Cuba maintains that insofar as the pre-existing protection in a Member includes the right to use geographical indications, the Member cannot subsequently diminish that protection through a prohibition on the use of geographical indications.

VI. THE PLAIN PACKAGING MEASURES ARE INCONSISTENT WITH ARTICLE 10*BIS* OF THE PARIS CONVENTION READ IN CONJUNCTION WITH ARTICLE 2.1 OF THE TRIPS AGREEMENT

66. Cuba has made a *prima facie* case that the PP measures violate Article 10*bis* of the Paris Convention incorporated into the TRIPS Agreement by its Article 2.1. Article 10*bis* (1) requires Members to provide "effective protection against unfair competition" resulting from trademark use on products.

67. Specifically, under Article 10*bis* (3) (i) Members must prohibit "all acts of such a nature as to create confusion by any means whatever with the establishment, the goods or the industrial or commercial activities, of a competitor"; and under Article 10*bis* (3) (iii) prohibit indications or allegations "the use of which in the course of trade is liable to mislead the public" as to the nature and characteristics of the goods. Australia's plain packaging measure eliminates all the distinctive elements of tobacco packaging with the exception of the brand and variant name, which may only be printed in the prescribed typeface and size. Consequently, the Australian PP measure requires companies to follow the anti-competitive practices that Australia is obliged to prevent under Article 10*bis* of the Paris Convention. PP deliberately creates confusion and liability to mislead the public, aspects which Members have an obligation to prevent.

68. The PP measures also violate Article 10*bis* because they require traders to mislead consumers into believing that different products are similar. Owing to the major similarities in the appearance of packaging and products, consumers will have difficulty in identifying premium tobacco products and will probably reach the mistaken conclusion that all cigars (whether made industrially or by hand) and all cigarettes are interchangeable. The resulting situation is harmful to the producers of premium products because, despite having made considerable investments in quality, it is highly unlikely that they will be rewarded by consumers for having made such investments. This is particularly unjust in the case of beneficiaries of geographical indications, such as the Cuban producers of LHM cigars, since the social, economic and cultural investments made over many years will go unrewarded.

69. The PP measures create unfair competition because they jeopardize the capacity of Cuban producers to protect themselves against trade in counterfeit goods. To guarantee the authenticity of its exports, Cuba requires that every box of cigars: (1) has a label affixed to it with the Habanos geographical indication; (2) carries an ink seal indicating the factory, as well as the month and the year of

production; and (3) is sealed with the Cuban Government Warranty Seal. By preventing the use of these forms of protection, the PP measures make it easier for counterfeiters to repackage fake Cuban cigars or non-Cuban cigars as authentic Cuban cigars, and in this way to divert goods to the detriment of Cuba.

70.   As mentioned above, the Cuban Government Warranty Seal is a distinctive characteristic of Cuban cigars with a history dating back to 1889. Apart from playing a unique and irreplaceable role in guaranteeing the authenticity of Cuban LHM cigars, the Cuban Government Warranty Seal is also a geographical indication within the meaning of Article 22.1 of the TRIPS Agreement, since its function is to guarantee Cuban origin. Consequently, all the arguments put forward by Cuba in relation to geographical indications in this proceeding are also applicable to the Cuban Government Warranty Seal.

71.   Cuba's position in this matter is further supported by the Panel Report in *Mexico – Telecoms*. In that case, the Panel examined a WTO Member's obligation to put in place "appropriate measures" aimed at preventing "anti-competitive practices".

VII.   THE PLAIN PACKAGING MEASURES VIOLATE ARTICLE 2.2 OF THE TBT AGREEMENT

72.   The PP measures are inconsistent with Article 2.2 of the TBT Agreement given that they constitute a technical regulation more trade-restrictive than necessary to fulfil a legitimate objective.

A.   The Plain Packaging measures are trade-restrictive in the light of their design, structure and operation

73.   The trade restrictiveness of the PP measures is evidenced by the design, structure and operation of the measures themselves. As has been explained, Cuban cigars are luxury products for which the trademarks and their association with Cuba through the geographical indication are essential. Australia explains in its second written submission that the PP measures seek to eliminate the opportunity for manufacturers to use the tobacco packaging in order to promote their products, and to remove all variability between tobacco packages. The inevitable consequence is that consumers will change from luxury premium products to standardized products of lower quality.

74.   Australia appears to argue that this significant restrictive effect on competitive opportunities for Cuban cigars is not important (and that it is not trade-restrictive) if demand shifts to other imported products. Obviously, however, it is important and the trade-restrictive effect for our country is quite clear. Cuba is unaware of any principle under WTO rules which allows a *de facto* restriction on trade with a country to be justified by an increase in imports from another country. This is not surprising because such a principle would run counter to the most-favoured-nation principle. Thus, Cuba's interpretation leaves totally unchanged the distinction between subparagraph 1 of Article 2.1 and

subparagraph 2 of Article 2. Cuba's position in this respect is also supported by the TBT Committee's recommendations approved on 4 October 1995.

75.   Cuba submits that Australia is mistaken in stating that, in order to be trade-restrictive, its PP measures must have a "limiting effect on overall trade" in tobacco products. The key issue in gauging trade restrictiveness is whether the measure has had an adverse effect on competitive opportunities for imported products, by discouraging exports to Australia and creating uncertainties for exporters. As Professor Damien Neven establishes, the PP measures have a negative impact on this variable.

76.   Moreover, in order to be able to have access to the Australian market, the PP measures require exporters to adapt their production processes to specific and detailed requirements; this implies some significant adjustment and compliance costs, which inherently entails a restriction on trade. This is also supported by the TBT Committee in its recommendations on the concept of significant effect on trade.

77.   One particularly significant change in the production process required by the PP measures is that the Cuban Government Warranty Seal can no longer be affixed on boxes of Cuban LHM cigars marketed in Australia. As has been explained by Cuba, compliance with the PP measures requires that the original sealed box produced in Cuba be opened so that the cigars can be repackaged in boxes that comply with the PP measures, after the cigars have been handled in order to substitute the cigar bands as well. Naturally, this also implies that it is no longer possible to guarantee that the product has not been handled between the moment it left the factory in Cuba and the moment the consumer opens the box.

78.   In addition, the Panel should take into account the design, structure and operation of the PP measures when gauging the trade-restrictive nature of those measures. Australia itself has explained that the PP measures are designed to eliminate the opportunity for a manufacturer to use tobacco products in order to promote its products and to remove all variability between tobacco packages. The measure is inherently trade-restrictive. In the case of luxury products, such as Cuban LHM cigars, this measure will have disastrous consequences, since trademarks and geographical indications are essential for highlighting the association of the products with Cuba and with its history as a country that manufactures and exports cigars, as well as in order to differentiate these products from the rest. This is especially important in the context of a "dark market", such as occurs in the case of tobacco products in Australia.

79.   In this connection, we must emphasize that it is no coincidence that Article 23 of the TRIPS Agreement introduces additional protection for geographical indications of wines and alcoholic beverages. Such protection is particularly important for wines and alcoholic beverages because they belong to a product category for which consumers value product differentiation in terms of geographical origin, quality and tradition much more than for other products. Cuban LHM cigars fall within this same category, and a measure that is

specifically designed to remove all variability in tobacco packaging and to eliminate the last opportunity for communicating tradition and quality is inherently trade restrictive for Cuba.

80.   Finally, we must emphasize that Australia itself acknowledged that the PP measures are trade-restrictive (and that they are not based on any relevant international standard) when it notified them under Article 2.9.2 of the TBT Agreement.

B.   The PP measures are more trade-restrictive than necessary given that alternative measures were available to Australia

81.   Cuba's argument is that the PP measures are ineffective since they are incapable of reducing tobacco consumption levels in Australia. Cuba includes in this section its previous arguments outlined in the context of Article 20 of the TRIPS Agreement in relation to the reasons why the PP measures will not contribute to Australia's objective.

82.   Even if the Panel were to conclude that the PP measures do make some contribution to Australia's objective, Cuba maintains that various alternative measures were available to Australia which would achieve the same degree of contribution. The alternative measures are the same as were explained previously in Cuba's claim under Article 20 of the TRIPS Agreement. *Pro memoria*, those alternative measures are: (i) an increase in excise duties on tobacco products; (ii) pre-vetting of the packaging design features; (iii) an increase in the minimum age for legally purchasing tobacco products; and (iv) improved social marketing campaigns for tobacco control.

83.   Cuba wishes to point out that the Australian Office of Best Practice Regulation (OBPR) found no justification for the PP measures. In fact, on 23 April 2009, in a letter to the Australian Department of Health and Ageing (DHA), the OBPR not only informed the DHA that the Regulation Impact Statement did not comply with the principles established by Australia's Best Practice Regulation Handbook, but also stated that it was "*having trouble determining what the problem is and how significant it is. It is mentioned in the second paragraph that there has been a decline in tobacco consumption over the past 15 years among young people and over the past 30 years for the population as a whole. It appears then that current programmes are achieving their objectives and that there are no clear reasons for other initiatives.*"[4]

C.   The plain packaging measures were not adopted in accordance with the relevant international standards

84.   Australia seeks to rely on Article 2.5 of the TBT Agreement, which provides that, when an approved technical standard exists, with a legitimate aim,

---

[4]   Australian Government, Office of Best Practice Regulation, *Draft RIS for the Tobacco Control Act* (23 April 2009), Annex HON-12, p. 3.

in accordance with the relevant international standards, there will be a rebuttable presumption that the obstacle to international trade is not unnecessary. However, the FCTC Guidelines are not a relevant international standard, first because they do not meet the definition of a "standard", and secondly because the Conference of the Parties (COP) of the FCTC is not a recognized international standardizing body.

1. The FCTC Guidelines are not standards

85.   In order for the Guidelines to be equivalent to a standard, they must meet the definition established in Annex 1.2 to the TBT Agreement, which indicates that standards must provide "*guidelines or characteristics for products or related processes and production methods*" for "*common and repeated use*". Obviously, this refers to "*common and repeated use*" by producers and the fact that they are not binding on producers. An excellent example of the above is provided by the ISO standards, which are appropriate for "*common and repeated use*" by producers and which are not binding, but which enable a producer to achieve a certain level of quality, safety or technical compatibility in a "standardized manner". An illustrative example is standard ISO 3394 on dimensions of rigid rectangular packages, previously cited by Honduras.

86.   Unlike those standards, the FCTC Guidelines are completely different and seek to encourage the authorities to impose binding technical standards on producers. The FCTC Guidelines are not, and have never been claimed to be, binding technical standards to be observed directly by a producer. It is for that reason that the FCTC Guidelines are also neither precise nor prescriptive: they are policy recommendations for regulators and legislators, not detailed technical guides for producers.

2. The FCTC COP has no recognized activities in standardization

87.   Cuba and Australia agree that there are two requirements that must be satisfied in order for a body to be classified as one with "*recognized activities in standardization*". First, standardization must be one of the functions of the body in question (Australia refers to this as the "*normative dimension*"). Secondly, WTO Members must be aware or have reason to expect that the international body in question is engaged in standardization activities (Australia refers to this as the "*factual dimension*").

88.   The FCTC COP is not a standardizing body in the normative sense because the documentary framework on which it is based says nothing about it being a standardizing body. Moreover, it cannot be asserted that WTO Members are aware or have reason to expect that the FCTC COP is engaged in standardizing activities. The text of the FCTC makes it clear that it is a "framework convention" concerning which even sceptical States agree in their understanding that it does not oblige them to take any specific action.

89.   For these reasons, Australia's invocation of the rebuttable presumption contained in Article 2.5 of the TBT Agreement is inappropriate.

VIII. THE PLAIN PACKAGING MEASURES ARE INCONSISTENT WITH ARTICLE IX:4 OF THE GATT 1994

90.   Cuba maintains that the PP measures are inconsistent with Article IX:4 of the GATT 1994 because, by preventing Cuban LHM cigars from displaying the "Habanos" geographical indication, the value of those products is materially reduced.

91.   The material reduction in value results from the fact that the "Habanos" geographical indication is part of the information that helps to give consumers certainty as to the authenticity of the product; in other words, it assures consumers that the product is genuine and not of illicit origin. Australia's measures prevent certain information from being displayed, which creates consumer uncertainty as to whether the product they are acquiring is genuine. This is a well-known benefit of the "Habanos" geographical indication.

92.   In addition, the material reduction in value is also due to the fact that, by preventing Cuban LHM cigars from displaying the "Habanos" geographical indication, Australia's measures limit the ability of Cuban exporters to maintain the price premium in respect of these products.

93.   Cuba duly substantiated these factual assertions by means of various exhibits, including Exhibits CUB-10, CUB-31, CUB-34, CUB-36 and JE-24(50).

94.   Australia is mistaken in alleging that Article IX:4 of the GATT 1994 requires a particular burden of proof. As Cuba has made clear throughout this dispute, the establishment of a *prima facie* case of violation under Article IX:4 is subject to the same general rules established by the Appellate Body, to the effect that "[a] *prima facie* case must be based on 'evidence and legal argument' put forward by the complaining party".[5]

95.   It should be mentioned that, in Cuba's opinion, the "value" of a product may be reduced either quantitatively or qualitatively. Cuba has already established the reasons why the value of the product is reduced in quantitative terms. With regard to the reduction of value in qualitative terms, Cuba observes that the ordinary meaning of the term "value" is "degree of utility or ability of things to satisfy needs or procure well-being or enjoyment".[6] In line with this meaning, the value of the "Habanos" geographical indication may also be measured in qualitative terms owing to its important utility for satisfying a specific need, i.e., its usefulness as an important tool for determining the

---

[5]   Appellate Body Report, *US – Gambling*, para. 140 (citing Appellate Body Report, *US – Wool Shirts and Blouses*, p. 16).

[6]   Diccionario de la Real Academia Española, available at: *http://dle.rae.es/?id=bJeLxWG*.

authenticity of the product. Affecting this "value" of the "Habanos" geographical indication in qualitative terms would also substantiate Cuba's claim under Article IX:4 that the PP measures materially reduce the value of Cuban LHM cigars.

96.   The "Habanos" geographical indication is one of the main elements of the reputation of Cuban LHM cigars as high-quality products with a long tradition. As Cuba established in its opening oral statement at the Panel's second meeting, Cuba considers that the impact of a prohibition on the use of the "Habanos" geographical indication is similar to a prohibition of the use of the term "champagne" for wine from the Champagne region. Nobody would question that such a prohibition on the term "champagne" would have a material and considerable impact on the higher prices that champagne wines command compared with other sparkling wines. Even though the impact on prices might not be immediate, it would inevitably occur with the passage of time. The specific intention of the geographical indications used to demonstrate the quality and tradition of luxury products is to differentiate such products from other "standard" products.

97.   The replacement of the Habanos geographical indication with the words "Made in Cuba", "Hand-made" and "Pacific Cigar Company", which is the text that currently appears on the PP of Cuban cigars in Australia is clearly insufficient to communicate the association with Cuban origin and with the long tradition of tobacco growing and cigar manufacturing that is transmitted by the use of the Habanos geographical indication.

98.   Moreover, not all Cuban cigars meet the requirements for the use of the Habanos geographical indication - this indication is reserved exclusively for the best Cuban cigars which satisfy strict quality standards. On the contrary, the expressions "Made in Cuba", "Hand-made" and "Pacific Cigar Company" that currently appear on the PP of Cuban cigars in Australia cover a much broader category of cigars than those which meet the requirements for inclusion in the Habanos geographical indication. Consequently, these terms are incapable of communicating the same information about origin, tradition and quality as the Habanos geographical indication.

IX.   OTHER LEGAL CLAIMS

99.   Cuba has also endorsed the following claims submitted by the other co-complainants:

   a.   Article 15.4 of the TRIPS Agreement, which states that the nature of the goods or services to which a trademark is to be applied shall in no case form an obstacle to registration of the trademark;

   b.   Article 16.1 of the TRIPS Agreement, which provides that the owner of a registered trademark shall have the exclusive right to prevent all third parties not having the owner's authorization from using in the course of trade identical or similar signs for goods or services which are identical or similar;

c.   Article 16.3 of the TRIPS Agreement, which establishes increased protection for well-known trademarks in respect of which the trademark owner has the right to prevent unauthorized use, even when the trademark is used on goods that are not similar;

d.   Article 22.2(b) of the TRIPS Agreement, which provides that, in respect of geographical indications, WTO Members shall provide the legal means for interested parties to prevent any use which constitutes an act of unfair competition within the meaning of Article 10bis of the Paris Convention (1967).

e.   Article 6*quinquies* of the Paris Convention (in relation to Article 2 of the TRIPS Agreement), which states that every trademark registered in the country of origin shall be accepted for filing and protected as is in the other countries of the Union.

X.   DEFENCE UNDER ARTICLE XX OF THE GATT 1994

100.   Australia cannot invoke a defence under Article XX of the GATT 1994, since the PP measures cannot be defined as "necessary" to the achievement of Australia's public health objective of reducing smoking prevalence. In accordance with the established jurisprudence of the WTO, in order for a measure to be "necessary" a series of factors must be met, including (i) the "contribution of the measure to the realization of the ends pursued"; and (ii) the availability of alternative WTO-consistent measures which could reasonably be expected to be applied by Australia. With regard to the first factor, the evidence shows that the PP measures have not contributed to reducing smoking during the first three years following implementation. As regards the second factor, alternative measures exist, as was observed in paragraph 44, which could be effective in achieving Australia's objective.

XI.   CONCLUSION

101.   For the reasons set out above, Cuba reiterates its request that the Panel find that:

a.   The PP measures violate Article 20 of the TRIPS Agreement.

b.   The PP measures violate Article 24.3 of the TRIPS Agreement.

c.   The PP measures violate Article 10bis of the Paris Convention (read in conjunction with Article 2.1 of the TRIPS Agreement).

d.   The PP measures violate Article 2.2 of the TBT Agreement.

e.   The PP measures violate Article IX:4 of the GATT 1994.

f.   The PP measures violate Articles 15.4, 16.1, 16.3 and 22.2(b) of the TRIPS Agreement and Article 6*quinquies* of the Paris Convention (read in conjunction with Article 2.1 of the TRIPS Agreement).

102.   Cuba requests the Panel to recommend, in accordance with Article 19.1 of the Dispute Settlement Understanding, that the Dispute Settlement Body request Australia to bring the measures at issue into conformity with the TRIPS Agreement, the TBT Agreement and the GATT 1994 within a reasonable period of time.

ANNEX B-4

INTEGRATED EXECUTIVE SUMMARY OF THE ARGUMENTS
OF INDONESIA

I.   INTRODUCTION

1.   On 1 December 2012 Australia banned or in some cases severely restricted the use of all trademarks, geographical indications ("GIs"), distinctive colors, and other design features on tobacco products and packaging. It also required that (i) those parts of tobacco packaging not already covered by large graphic health warnings ("GHWs") be covered in a uniform, matt finish and a drab, dark brown color; and (ii) the brand (e.g. "Marlboro") and variant (e.g. menthol) names appear in a uniform typeface, size, color, and placement on the package. These so-called "plain packaging" ("PP") requirements are radical and without precedent. No other Member of the World Trade Organization ("WTO") has ever required a maker of a legal product to remove its trademarks, GIs, trade dress, logos, and other branding from products prior to sale at the retail level.

2.   Indonesia has a very strong interest in this case. Indonesia initiated this proceeding because PP threatens the export opportunities for its cigarette industry, in particular its clove cigarette industry. That industry accounts for approximately 1.66 percent of Indonesia's total gross domestic product. Clove cigarettes are integral to the Indonesian economy. It is Indonesia's second largest industry and employs over 6 million people. More than half of Indonesia's citizens live in rural areas where agriculture and the clove cigarette industry are the main sources of income. Indonesia exports its cigarettes all over the world, including to Australia, and exported approximately $700 million in tobacco products in 2013. Indonesia brings this dispute to protect its interests in these exports.

3.   The WTO provides wide latitude to Members to pursue legitimate public policy objectives such as smoking prevention. As a result, none of the complainants in these disputes challenge Australia's right to restrict tobacco products advertising, labeling requirements, point-of-sale restrictions, mandatory health warnings, and the numerous other measures taken by Australia to reduce the consumption[1] of tobacco products and lower smoking prevalence[2] rates within its borders. In particular, Indonesia is *not* challenging requirements

---

[1]   Tobacco "consumption" represents the total amount of tobacco consumed, usually expressed in terms of the number of "sticks" sold.

[2]   Tobacco "prevalence" measures the number of people who smoke within a given population. It is usually expressed as a percentage.

regarding GHW. In fact, Indonesia recently adopted its own set of rules requiring GHWs on tobacco products.[3]

4.   The issue before the Panel is *not* whether tobacco is harmful or should be regulated. Rather, the issue is whether changes to the image and appearance of tobacco packaging (i.e. the small portion of cigarette packages not already covered by GHWs in Australia) and individual cigars and cigarettes are consistent with Australia's WTO obligations.

II.   FACTUAL BACKGROUND

A.   Regulation Of Tobacco Products And Packaging In Australia Prior To 1 December 2012

5.   It is important to view PP in light of the existing regulatory environment in which the measures were adopted and the array of tobacco marketing restrictions that were already in place at the time PP was implemented. None of these other tobacco control policies are at issue in this dispute.

6.   Australia is a "dark market", which means that it prohibits all forms of tobacco advertising and promotion.[4] In 1973 the Australian government began to phase out radio and TV advertising of tobacco products, and a full ban came into effect on 1 September 1976. In December 1990 a ban on print advertising (newspapers and magazines) became effective as part of the *Tobacco Products Advertisements (Prohibition) Act*. The 1992 *Tobacco Advertising Prohibition ("TAP") Act* stipulated additional restrictions, including bans on advertisements in the form of films, outdoor advertisements and sponsorships.

7.   Australia has required health warnings on tobacco packages since 1973.[5] In 1985 additional health warnings were introduced and became more prominent on the packages. The *Trade Practices (Consumer Product Information Standards) (Tobacco) Regulations 2004* required that packages for most tobacco products (except, for example, individually wrapped cigars) carry GHWs and a series of rotating messages regarding the health risks of smoking.[6]

8.   As of 1 March 2006 all packages were required to have pictorial health warnings covering 30 percent of the front of the pack and 90 percent of the back of the pack. Concurrent with its move to PP, Australia substantially increased the size of its GHWs under the *Competition and Consumer (Tobacco) Information Standard 2011* (the "Information Standard"). For cigarette packs, the required size of the warning statement and graphic increased from 30 percent to

---

[3]   See Australian Broadcasting Commission News, "Indonesia pushes for graphic health warnings on cigarettes", (25 June 2014).
[4]   Indonesia's first written submission, para. 54.
[5]   Indonesia's first written submission, para. 57.
[6]   *Ibid.*

75 percent of the front surface.[7] For cigar tubes, warning statements must occupy 95 percent of the total length of the outer surface and extend to at least 60 percent of the circumference of the outer surface.[8]

9.   At the state and local levels, Australia has also implemented bans on the consumption of tobacco products in certain areas and under certain circumstances ("smoking bans"), normally in public places. The Australian states and territories where smoking bans are in effect cover more than 99 percent of Australia's total population in terms of residency.[9]

10.   Tobacco products are heavily taxed in Australia. From 1999 until March 2010, the excise tax was increased twice per year in line with overall inflation – from 0.18872 cents per stick to 0.26220 cents per stick. On 1 August 2013 Australia further announced additional increases in tobacco taxation over the coming years. Four additional excise taxes of 12.5 percent each were announced for 1 December 2013, 1 September 2014, 1 September 2015 and 1 September 2016.[10]

11.   Anti-smoking mass media campaigns are also prevalent in Australia.[11] Among these are social marketing campaigns, which consist of public service messages targeted at specific segments of the population that are communicated through a range of media channels (e.g. television, radio, print, health and social networks, and digital media).

12.   In attempting to build a case that regulation of tobacco packaging was needed, Australia has repeated concerns with tobacco packaging that are decades old.[12] The Post Implementation Review ("PIR") repeats these claims in Section1.3, citing tobacco company documents and practices dating back more than 20 years.[13] What the PIR fails to mention is that as a result of many of the policies described above, many of these problems were no longer relevant when PP was adopted.

B.   Overview Of PP In Australia

1.   The *T/PP Act* and accompanying regulations

13.   The *Tobacco Plain Packaging Act 2011* ("*T/PP Act*") passed both Houses of Parliament on 21 November 2011 and received Royal Assent on 1 December 2011.[14] The *Tobacco Plain Packaging Regulations 2011* ("*T/PP Regulations*")

---

[7]   Indonesia's first written submission, para. 58.
[8]   *Ibid.*
[9]   Indonesia's first written submission, para. 62.
[10]   Indonesia's first written submission, para. 67.
[11]   Indonesia's first written submission, para. 69.
[12]   Indonesia's comments on the PIR, para. 8.
[13]   Australian Department of Health and Ageing, "Post – Implementation Review: Tobacco Plain Packaging 2016," ("PIR") (March 2016), Exhibit AUS-624, paras. 20-22.
[14]   Indonesia's first written submission, para. 73.

were promulgated on 7 December *2011*.[15] Under the terms of the PP measures, all tobacco packages had to be manufactured in compliance with the PP requirements as of 1 October 2012.[16] Retail outlets were given an additional two months to exhaust their inventories of non-compliant packages, but, as of 1 December 2012, all tobacco products sold at retail outlets had to comply with the PP measures.[17]

a.   Trademark and mark-related requirements

14.   Section 20 of the *T/PP Act* prohibits the use of any mark or trademark on the retail packaging of tobacco products, other than as expressly permitted. The appearance of brand, business, company, or variant names is strictly regulated, with detailed conditions regarding position and appearance.[18] The *T/PP Regulations* provide that the following may appear on retail packaging: origin marks, calibration marks, a measurement mark and trade description, a bar code, a fire risk statement, a locally made product statement, and a name and address.[19]

15.   Section 26 of the *T/PP Act* prohibits the use of trademarks and marks anywhere on a tobacco product, other than as permitted by the Regulations. Section 3.1.2 of the *T/PP Regulations* permits a cigarette to be marked only with an alphanumeric code. Division 3.2 of the *T/PP Regulations* imposes similar requirements on cigars and bidis.

b.   Format/appearance requirements

16.   Section 18 of the *T/PP Act* imposes uniform requirements for the physical shape or features of tobacco product retail packaging. Packaging must have no "decorative ridges, embossing, bulges or other irregularities of shape or texture, or any other embellishments, other than as permitted by the regulations".[20] Cigarette packs and cartons may be made only from cardboard and must be rigid and perfectly rectangular without any distinctive features.[21] The manner in which packs and cartons are opened is also regulated, eliminating alternative designs for product opening.[22] The *T/PP Regulations* also set out ranges of dimensions with which cigarette packs must comply.[23] For cigars, tubes must be cylindrical and rigid with both ends tapered or rounded.[24]

---

[15]   *Ibid.*
[16]   See *T/PP Act*, Section 2; *T/PP Regulations*, Section 1.1.2.
[17]   *T/PP Act*, Section 2.
[18]   *T/PP Act*, Section 21.
[19]   *T/PP Regulations*, Division 2.3.
[20]   *T/PP Act*, Section 18(1); see also *T/PP Regulations*, Section 2.1.6.
[21]   *T/PP Act*, Section 18(2)(a)-(c). *T/PP Regulations*, Section 2.1.2.
[22]   In respect of cigarette packs, their only opening can be a flip-top lid, hinged at the back of the pack. *T/PP Regulations*, Section 2.1.2.
[23]   See *T/PP Regulations*, Section 2.1.1(1) and *T/PP Act*, Section 18(3)(b)-(d).
[24]   *T/PP Regulations*, Section 2.1.4.

17. Section 19 of the *T/PP Act* imposes strict limitations on the color and finish of retail packaging of tobacco products. The *T/PP Regulations* also standardize the appearance of tobacco products. Under sections 3.1.1(1), all cigarettes, regardless of brand, must look alike.[25]

2. Trade Mark Amendment Act

18. Along with the passage of the *T/PP Act*, the Australian parliament passed the *Trade Marks Amendment (Tobacco Plain Packaging) Act 2011* ("*TM Amendment Act*"). The *TM Amendment Act* gives broad power to the regulator under the *T/PP Act* to modify Australian trademark law and allows for regulations to override specific trademark protections in relation to tobacco products, where such protections are otherwise of general application to any trademarks for all other, non-tobacco products.

3. The objective of plain packaging

19. According to Australia, PP's overall objective is to contribute to "reducing the smoking rate {prevalence} among the Australian population to 10 per cent by 2018, and halving the smoking rate among Aboriginal and Torres Strait Islander people".[26] Thus, PP's objective is to protect health by reducing smoking prevalence. Australia believes PP will contribute to fulfilling these objectives in the following manner:

> It is the intention of the Parliament to contribute to achieving the objects in subsection (1) *by regulating the retail packaging and appearance of tobacco products in order to*:
>
> (a) reduce the appeal of tobacco products to consumers; and
>
> (b) increase the effectiveness of health warnings on the retail packaging of tobacco products; and
>
> (c) reduce the ability of the retail packaging of tobacco products to mislead consumers about the harmful effects of smoking or using tobacco products.[27]

20. After taking conflicting positions on the question, Australia confirmed that these "mechanisms" are not themselves objectives of the *T/PP Act*.[28]

21. Australia also has indicated that an additional objective of PP is to fulfil certain alleged "requirements" of the Framework Convention on Tobacco Control, most recently in the PIR.[29] The FCTC does *not* require parties to adopt PP measures and certainly not PP measures that prohibit all trademarks, GIs,

---

[25] *T/PP Regulations*, Section 3.1.3. Section 3.1.3 of the *T/PP Regulations* similarly requires that any filter tip must be white.

[26] Consultation Paper on the plain packaging Bill Exposure Draft, p. 1.

[27] *T/PP Act*, Section 3(2) (emphasis added).

[28] Australia's response to Question No. 1 from the Dominican Republic.

[29] Indonesia's comments on PIR, paras. 10-13 .

trade dress, logos, and other branding on tobacco products themselves, in addition to their packaging. Rather, Article 11 permits packaging that promotes a tobacco product as long as it is not "false, misleading, deceptive or likely to create an erroneous impression". Article 13 requires Parties to comprehensively ban all tobacco advertising, promotion and sponsorship.

22.   The guidelines for Articles 11 and 13 recommend that parties to the Convention merely "*consider adopting*" PP but do not require them to do so. The non-binding nature of these recommendations is highlighted by the fact that PP is not integral to the WHO's evaluation of countries' compliance with the FCTC.[30] Indeed, the WHO gave Australia a perfect 10 out of 10 score for compliance with direct and indirect bans on advertising, sponsorship and promotion in 2011 *before* Australia had implemented PP.[31] Thus, adopting PP does not advance Australia's compliance with its FCTC obligations.

C.   Requirements On 1 December 2012

23.   Smoking prevalence for daily smokers in Australia aged 14 years and over fell by almost 10 percentage points from 24.3 percent in 1991 to 15.1 percent in 2010.[32] Observed smoking prevalence declined steadily from 2006 onward at an annual rate of about 0.59 percentage points. Cancer Council Victoria determined that a combination of tax increases and increased spending on social media campaigns and other tobacco control measures would reduce smoking prevalence to just under 10 percent by 2020 even *without* implementing PP.[33]

24.   Had Australia not been in such a hurry to adopt PP, prevalence rates were on a clear trend to accomplish the same prevalence target as that set for PP within the same period of time. In fact, given the well-documented effect of tax increases on tobacco prevalence rates, and given the four additional tax increases beginning 1 December 2013, Australia might well have exceeded its objectives without PP.

D.   Tobacco Prevalence In Australia Since Plain Packaging Requirements Were Implemented On 1 December 2012

25.   At the time of its passage, PP was hailed by its supporters as a "crucial step" in Australia's anti-smoking effort.[34] Australians and the international

---

[30]   Compliance with the FCTC is included in the WHO's Tobacco Control Country Profiles. World Health Organization, "FCTC Surveillance and Monitoring", Exhibit IND-34. These country profiles include an evaluation of several measures included in the FCTC, including health warnings on tobacco products and bans on advertising, sponsorship and promotion.

[31]   World Health Organization, "Report on the Global Tobacco Epidemic, 2011: Country Profile - Australia", (2011), Exhibit IND-35.

[32]   See Indonesia's first written submission, para. 109 and Table VI.1: Tobacco Key Facts and Figures.

[33]   Indonesia's first written submission, para. 111.

[34]   Explanatory Memorandum to the *Tobacco Plain Packaging Bill 2011*.

trading community were told that PP would "slash smoking rates . . . make significant inroads into reducing rates of smoking initiation and consumption . . . [and have] enormous potential to cut smoking rates."[35]

26.   More than three years have elapsed since the PP measures took effect. This is a significant period within which it is reasonable to expect that, if PP were going to cut prevalence rates, those effects would be discernible by now.

27.   Since implementation, there have been numerous quantitative studies examining PP's impact on smoking prevalence and consumption. These studies: (1) were undertaken by independent teams of researchers; (2) adopt several standard econometric techniques; and (3) are based on the different long-term, large-scale datasets covering pre- and post-implementation prevalence, consumption and sales data, respectively.

28.   None of the studies comparing prevalence data before and after the implementation of PP has found that PP has made a material contribution toward a reduction in smoking prevalence. Not only has PP failed to account for any sustained decrease in prevalence, some state-level surveys have indicated that smoking prevalence in those states has *increased*. By every analytical assessment, PP has not made *any* measurable contribution toward reducing smoking prevalence in Australia. What it is contributing to is a shift in consumption from branded, more expensive tobacco products, to cheaper products and illicit products.

29.   Australia commissioned the National Plain Packaging Tracking Survey ("NPPTS") for the express purpose of evaluating the effectiveness of Australia's PP measures.[36] The NPPTS was a "national, monthly tracking survey of smokers and recent quitters undertaken by the Centre for Behavioral Research in Cancer, Cancer Council Victoria ("CCV"), and funded by the DHA.[37] The Australian Government called the NPPTS the "key survey" for the PIR.[38]

30.   In April 2015, Professor Wakefield and her CCV team of five co-authors published a series of papers in *Tobacco Control* presenting the NPPTS results. These papers make favourable findings and conclusions on the impact that the PP measures have had on the posited antecedents of smoking behaviour.[39]

31.   During the course of this dispute, complainants' experts were given full access to the NPPTS dataset, and the authors' computer code. Complainants experts identified several serious flaws in the analysis performed by the co-authors of the published papers, including "a *pattern of poor* results," which Professor Wakefield and her co-authors simply chose not to report in their

---

[35]   D. Hill, "Tobacco Industry has much to Fear: Plain Packaging will Slash Smoking Rates – and Cigarette Makers Know It," *The Sydney Morning Herald* (8 April 2011).
[36]   NPPTS Technical Report, Exhibit DOM-307, p. 6; PIR, para. 69.
[37]   PIR, para. 69.
[38]   Commonwealth of Australia, Proof Committee Hansard, Finance Administration Legislation Committee, Estimates (26 May 2015 and 2 June 2015), Exhibit DOM-371, p. 85.
[39]   Indonesia's comments on the PIR, para. 14.

papers.[40] The overwhelming majority of the unreported results showed the PP measures had little to no lasting effect on the variables being measured. Quit attempts even show a small but statistically significant *decline*. These flaws lead to the conclusion that the published papers "painted an *inaccurate and misleading picture* of the [NPPTS] results", suffering from severe underreporting.[41]

32.   In response to these findings, Australia took the surprising approach of indicting its own NPPTS survey, claiming that it was ill-suited for assessing the impact of the PP measures – a view previously unreported by Australia, the entities collecting the data, or the authors relying on the datasets in peer-reviewed publications.[42] Conveniently, Australia still views the NPPTS dataset as well-suited – and even a "powerful tool" – for evaluating the impact of the PP measures on the very few variables that *do* show an impact from PP.[43] However, the survey is now regarded as suitable for evaluating the impact on the vast majority of NPPTS variables, virtually all of which happen to be unaffected by the pack changes. [44] As the Dominican Republic so aptly explained, apparently "Australia paid A\$3 million for a survey that was allegedly not suited to measuring the vast majority of the variables it was designed to measure.[45]

33.   Despite Australia's own misgivings about the suitability of the NPPTS for evaluating the effectiveness of PP, the PIR relies extensively on its questionable findings, as well as those of other studies that the complainants have substantively refuted throughout this dispute.[46] Indonesia notes there is *nothing new* in the study findings reported in the PIR. Australia continues to contort the survey data by whatever means necessary in order to create support for its foregone conclusion that PP is working.

III.   LEGAL CLAIMS

A.   Australia's PP Measures Violate The TRIPS Agreement

34.   Australia's PP measures are inconsistent with several of Australia's obligations under the TRIPS Agreement. Of particular importance in discerning the protections provided by the TRIPS Agreement is how trademarks function and the centrality of use to trademark protection.

---

[40] Indonesia's comments on the PIR, para. 15.
[41] First Data Expert Rebuttal Report, Exhibit DOM/IDN-6, para. 3 (emphasis added).
[42] Indonesia's comments on the PIR, para. 17.
[43] Australia's response to Panel Question No. 198, para. 291.
[44] Australia's response to Panel questions 196, paras. 224-225. See also, First Data Expert Rebuttal Report, Exhibit DOM/IDN-6, paras. 8-9 and 36-38.
[45] Indonesia's comments on the PIR, para. 17.
[46] PIR, paras. 69-98.

1. Trademarks and TRIPS

35. Article 15.1 of the TRIPS Agreement defines "trademark" as "{a}ny sign, or combination of signs, capable of distinguishing the goods or services of one undertaking from those of other undertakings, shall be capable of constituting a trademark". Words, letters, names, logos, images, colors, numbers, the shape of goods or packaging, sounds, and any combination thereof, can all serve as trademarks.[47] Indeed, one product may carry several of these signs and each one can be individually registered as a trademark.

36. For purposes of Indonesia's TRIPS claims, we refer to two categories of trademarks. The first category contains word marks, which includes letters or characters making up the name of a brand. The second category encompasses non-word marks, which includes device, figurative or stylized marks like logos and combined marks containing stylized letters, shape marks, and color marks.

37. The function of trademarks is understood as distinguishing goods and services of one undertaking from another in the course of trade. Every trademark owner has a legitimate interest in preserving the distinctiveness, or capacity to distinguish, of its trademark so that it can perform that function.[48]

38. The panel in *EC – Trademarks and GIs* ("*EC – GIs*") highlights the connection between a trademark owner's use of "its own trademark in connection with the relevant goods and services of its own and authorized undertakings" and the legitimate interest of the trademark owner to "preserve the distinctiveness or capacity to distinguish" the trademark "so that it can perform" its function.[49] Put differently, a trademark that cannot be used can no longer serve its function of "distinguishing goods and services of undertakings in the course of trade".[50] This is exactly what Australia's PP measures do – by severely limiting the use of trademarks, PP guts the function of trademarks and consequently denies the protections guaranteed by the TRIPS Agreement.

a. Trademarks function to differentiate products and promote competition

39. As Article 15.1 of the TRIPS Agreement reflects, the principal function of a trademark is to differentiate the goods and services of one company from that of another. Put simply, the distinguishing function of a trademark is to communicate quality and other qualitative product characteristics. Australia asserts that word marks alone are capable of distinguishing the goods to which they apply.[51] However, word marks are seldom, if ever, *used* in the plain format in which they are registered. They are invariably used in conjunction with

---

[47] Indonesia's first written submission, para. 128.
[48] Panel Report, *EC—Trademarks and GIs (Australia)*, para. 7.664 (emphasis added).
[49] Panel Report, *EC—Trademarks and GIs, (Australia)*, para. 7.664.
[50] *Ibid.*
[51] Indonesia's second written submission, para. 100.

typeface, color, size, placement, and design elements that contribute to the distinctiveness of the product. Contrary to arguments made by Australia, the distinguishing function is protected with respect to *all* trademarks – including purely figurative marks.

40.   The *EC – GIs* panel also acknowledged that the ability to distinguish is important for both trademark owners *and* consumers. The panel observed that "{c}onsumers have a legitimate interest in being able to *distinguish* the goods and services of one undertaking from those of another, and to avoid confusion".[52]

41.   Australia argues that there is an alternate, subversive function of trademarks – that is, advertising and promotion.[53] Australia argues that because trademarks are used in advertising and promotion, and because Members may restrict product advertising and promotion that may harm consumers, Australia may also restrict the use of trademarks *on the products themselves*.[54]

42.   However, Australia improperly conflates the use of trademarks on packaging with advertising or promotion. Indeed, "it is *not* the received wisdom in marketing to regard brand packaging as a dedicated advertising medium, and for good reason".[55] Branded packaging "falls short on key dimensions of function, reach, versatility, size and interactivity when pitted against advertising instruments".[56] It is for these reasons that branded packaging is seen by marketing professionals as part of the product itself, rather than advertising and promotion.[57]

b.   Centrality of use to trademarks

43.   A trademark owner's ability to use its trademark underlies the ability of a trademark to perform its distinguishing function. Therefore, use is a cornerstone of trademark protection. In this respect, trademarks are unique among intellectual property rights. A patent, for example, is valuable to its owner even it sits on a shelf unused. Owners of patents can stop infringement without any need to show that they have used it. In contrast, use is central to trademarks and "a trademark owner…registers a mark primarily to be able to use it".[58] Without use, a trademark has no social or economic value and over time will lose its distinctiveness and can no longer be protected.

44.   Although registration of a trademark confers certain protections, the *raison d'etre* of trademarks is their ability to distinguish goods, which is attained

---

[52]   Panel Report, *EC – Trademarks and Geographical Indications (Australia)*, para. 7.675 (emphasis supplied).
[53]   Indonesia's second written submission, para. 24, fn. 31.
[54]   Australia's first written submission, paras. 210-11.
[55]   Indonesia's second written submission, para. 27.
[56]   *Ibid.*
[57]   *Ibid.*
[58]   Indonesia's first written submission, para. 137.

through use.[59] The importance of use is reflected in its central role in trademark registration and protection. Some countries like the United States have use-based registration system in which use of a mark is required before it can be registered. Other countries like Australia have a registration-based system in which prior use is not required before registration. However, even in registration-based systems, use plays an important role in trademark law. This is true of Australia's trademark law.[60] Under Section 17 of the Australian *Trade Marks Act 1995*, the definition of a trademark is "a sign used, or intended to be used to distinguish goods or services dealt with or provided in the course of trade by a person from goods or services so dealt with or provided by any other person".[61] Accordingly, an applicant for trademark registration must be using or intend to use the trademark. Non-use of a trademark is grounds for cancelation of a registration in Australia.[62] Australia recognized the importance of use in its system and included a provision in the *T/PP Act* that circumvents its own registration requirements and allows for registration of tobacco trademarks despite the inability to use them.[63]

45.   Use also plays an important role in the scope of protection and enforcement of trademarks. Australian courts have repeatedly noted the importance of use in infringement actions.[64] When determining whether a mark is infringing upon a registered mark, Australian courts take note of the manner in which both marks are actually used in the marketplace and how those marks are perceived by consumers. Thus the ability to use a trademark increases its owner's ability to enforce the right of exclusive use against others that use their marks without authorization.

46.   For these reasons, Indonesia argues that the TRIPS Agreement contemplates a *minimum* opportunity to use a trademark in the course of trade.[65] This minimum opportunity of use is based on the text of the TRIPS Agreement and is supported by the text, context, and the object and purpose of the treaty and is not unlimited. However, without a minimum opportunity of use, the provisions of the TRIPS Agreement relating to trademarks would be utterly meaningless. As Indonesia will discuss in the context of Articles 16.1 and 16.3 below, use is essential for the enforcement of the private rights WTO Members are required to provide to trademark owners under the TRIPS Agreement. This is true even in jurisdictions, such as Australia, in which there is no statutory "right to use" a trademark.[66]

---

[59] Indonesia's first written submission, para. 138.
[60] Indonesia's first written submission, para. 141.
[61] *Trade Marks Act 1995: An Act relating to trade marks*, No. 119 of 1995, as amended, ("*Trademarks Act 1995*").
[62] *Trademarks Act 1995*, Sections 27(1), 92(4).
[63] *T/PP Act*, Section 28.
[64] See Indonesia's second written submission, para. 16 and Section II.D.
[65] Indonesia's second written submission, para. 13.
[66] Indonesia's second written submission, para. 71.

47.   The fact that the TRIPS Agreement does not offer mark holders an absolute "right to use" does not diminish the importance that use plays in protecting intellectual property rights. A registered trademark, without any opportunity of use in the marketplace, has no value.[67] The object and purpose of the TRIPS Agreement, as expressed in its Preamble, is to provide "adequate standards and principles concerning the availability, scope, and *use* of trade-related intellectual property rights".[68] An interpretation of the rights conferred upon owners of registered trademarks that does not include any opportunity to use the trademark in connection with the goods and services that it is meant to distinguish completely contradicts the object and purpose of the treaty.

c.   "In the course of trade" includes a broad range of uses

48.   The phrase "in the course of trade" is relevant to several of Indonesia's claims as it appears in Article 10*bis*(3) of the Paris Convention, as well as Articles 16.1 and 20 of the TRIPS Agreement.[69] Australia has argued that "in the course of trade" is narrow and ends at the point of sale."[70] Australia's interpretation of this phrase is based on a fictional divide between "pre-sale" and "post-sale" use of a trademark that is fundamentally inconsistent with the text, context, and the object and purpose of the TRIPS Agreement.[71]

49.   "In the course of trade" refers to activities conducted in a commercial context as opposed to private use. It does *not* end at the point of sale. The use of a registered trademark on a billboard, in a television commercial, or on promotional correspondence would constitute use of a trademark "in the course of trade" even though there is no immediate sales transaction involved in these commercial activities. In this regard, Indonesia agrees with the European Union's statement in its third party submission.[72]

50.   Even if Australia were correct that use of a trademark "in the course of trade" ceases at the point of sale, Australia has failed to account for the fact that trademarks are "used" on packaging *from the point of manufacture* and Australia's PP measures apply restrictions on the use of trademarks on tobacco products and their packaging at every stage of the value chain, including "selling or supplying", "purchasing", "packaging", and "manufacturing".[73]

---

[67]   As counsel for Indonesia noted during the First Substantive Meeting, trademarks derive their value from use in the marketplace. This is in contrast to patents, which retain their value even if they are locked away in a cabinet and not used by their owners.

[68]   Emphasis supplied.

[69]   Indonesia's second written submission, paras. 28-29.

[70]   Australia's first written submission, para. 311.

[71]   Indonesia's first written submission, para. 270.

[72]   EU's third party submission, para. 23.

[73]   See *T/PP Act*, Exhibit JE-1, Sections 31-35

2. The TRIPS Agreement does not include a general exception for public health measures

51.   Australia repeatedly overstates the level of deference accorded to public health measures by the TRIPS Agreement. In so doing, Australia glosses over the mandate that public health measures must be balanced with the obligations of the TRIPS Agreement and the interests of owners of intellectual property.

a.   TRIPS Article 8.1

52.   Australia argued that Members have a "sovereign right to regulate the use of trademarks in furtherance of public policy objectives (as acknowledged in the principle set forth in Article 8.1)".[74] This is simply incorrect. The plain text of Article 8.1 requires that public health measures must be *both* necessary and consistent with the provisions of the TRIPS Agreement. Australia invoked Article 8.1 and thus bears the burden of proving that PP is "necessary" to protect public health. While Australia has alleged that its PP measures will contribute to its health objective of reducing smoking, Australia has not put forward sufficient argument and evidence to prove that the PP measures meet the criteria to be considered "necessary" to protect public health. Thus, it is not clear to Indonesia that Article 8.1 should be assumed to apply in this case at all. Even if it does apply, Australia has mischaracterized the meaning that the Panel should ascribe to this provision. Under the TRIPS Agreement a Member's right to regulate public health must be balanced with the obligation to protect intellectual property rights, such as trademarks and geographical indications.

b.   TRIPS Article 19.1

53.   Australia has stated that Article 19 allows it to regulate, and even prohibit, the use of trademarks.[75] Contrary to Australia's interpretation, Article 19.1 is intended to protect trademarks from being invalidated. Trademarks can only be invalidated if they are unused for at least three years, and then only if non-use is not due to measures regulating the underlying product. The oft-cited example of the type of measure contemplated by Article 19 is the pharmaceutical product that has not yet been approved for sale.[76] The agreement *does not* contemplate a scenario in which a Member opts to regulate trademarks as a blatant *substitute* for restricting the sale of a potentially dangerous consumer product.[77] Thus, Australia's reliance of Article 19.1 as a defense for its prohibition on the use of certain trademarks is misguided.

---

[74]   Australia's first written submission, para. 374.
[75]   Indonesia's second written submission, para. 44.
[76]   Indonesia's second written submission, para. 45.
[77]   Indonesia's response to Q.95 from the Panel, para. 23.

c.   The Doha Declaration

54.   In Australia's view, "the [Doha] Declaration states that the TRIPS Agreement 'does not and should not prevent members from taking measures to protect public health', and 'reaffirm{s} the right of WTO members to use, to the full, the provisions in the TRIPS Agreement, which provide flexibility for this purpose'".[78] Indonesia notes that this statement is consistent with the language of Article 8.1 and does not expand the level of deference to be accorded to public health measures under the TRIPS Agreement. The Doha Declaration merely serves to underscore the fact that the TRIPS Agreement, as originally drafted, provides ample latitude to Members to take measures to protect public health that are consistent with the obligations therein.

2.   Plain Packaging Violates Article 2.1 Of The TRIPS Agreement

55.   Pursuant to Article 2.1 of the TRIPS Agreement, Australia is required to comply with Article 10*bis* of the Paris Convention for the Protection of Industrial Property (1967). Article 10*bis* of the Paris Convention requires Australia to provide effective protection against unfair competition. Australia violates Article 10*bis* by compelling conduct through its PP measures that it is required to prohibit. Specifically, PP creates confusion between competitors' tobacco products and misleads consumers about the characteristics of tobacco products.

56.   Article 2.1 incorporates certain provisions of the Paris Convention into the TRIPS Agreement. WTO Members must comply with these obligations even if they are not parties to the Paris Convention.[79] Under Article 10*bis*, as incorporated by TRIPS Article 2.1, WTO Members have a general obligation to provide "effective protection against unfair competition". The article describes unfair competition as "{a}ny act of competition contrary to honest practices in industrial or commercial matters". In order to protect against unfair competition, WTO Members must at a minimum ensure effective protection against the three kinds of acts described in 10*bis*, including creating confusion regarding the goods or commercial activities of a competitor; and misleading the public as to the nature, manufacturing process, or characteristics of goods.

57.   Australia does exactly the opposite. PP compels competitors to present their goods in identical trade dress and with limited descriptive words. In so doing, they force competitors to present their goods in a manner that creates confusion. For example, there are a number of similar variations of word marks for tobacco products that are already registered in Australia. The word marks themselves are, in many cases, insufficient to differentiate one brand from

---

[78]   Australia's first written submission, para. 382.
[79]   Indonesia's first written submission, para. 152.

another. Indonesia provided an illustrative list of such word marks in its first written submission.[80]

58.   The fact that word marks alone are insufficient to differentiate competing products is especially true under Australia's PP measures, which require all word marks to be presented in an identical format. But for the use of word marks, retail packaging under the PP measures are stripped of *all* distinguishing characteristics and the word marks themselves are stripped of any distinguishing style features. This is particularly problematic in Australia's dark market, where there is little opportunity for consumers to make a careful examination of tobacco packaging.[81]

59.   The confusion among brands created by PP frustrates the purpose of 10*bis* to protect competitors, especially those in the mid-priced and premium segment of the market, against unfair competition. Denied the means to distinguish their products from competitors, manufacturers have no incentive to compete on quality and are driven to compete on price. This is because consumers have no basis other than price upon which to make purchasing decisions absent the "information channel"[82] that trademarked and fully branded packaging provides.

60.   Additionally, the nearly identical appearance of competing tobacco products is liable to mislead consumers that all tobacco products on the market share the same quality, characteristics and reputation. Indeed, this was the express intent of Australia's PP measures. Australia selected the specific packaging requirements of its PP measures precisely because they convey the message to consumers that all tobacco products are – in the words of the GfK Bluemoon study – the "lowest quality".[83]

61.   In short, Australia's PP measures rob tobacco product manufacturers of the ability to distinguish their products based on quality and "commoditize" the tobacco market. Australia sought to ensure that manufacturers *cannot* distinguish their products or compete on the basis of consumer perceptions of quality. Therefore, PP violates Article 2.1 by failing to provide effective protection against legally mandated unfair competition.

3.   Plain Packaging Violates Article 15.4 Of The TRIPS Agreement

62.   Article 15.4 of the TRIPS Agreement imposes an affirmative obligation on WTO Members not to prevent the registration of trademarks based on the nature of the goods and services to which the trademark will be applied.[84] This

---

[80]   Indonesia's first written submission, para. 166.
[81]   Indonesia's second written submission, para. 49.
[82]   Indonesia's first written submission, para. 168.
[83]   Indonesia's first written submission, para. 174.
[84]   Indonesia's first written submission, para. 185.

requirement is clearly understood when looked at in the context and scope of Article 15. [85]

63.　　In *US - Section 211* the Appellate Body stated that Article 15.1 "embodies a definition of what can constitute a trademark".[86] Under this provision Members must guarantee that signs that are "distinctive" are "eligible for registration as trademarks within their domestic legislation". It also states that Members may make the registrability of non-inherently distinctive signs "depend on distinctiveness acquired through use". That said, Article 15.1 does not require that any sign "capable of registration" actually be registered. Registration can be further conditioned based on the text of Articles 15.2, 15.3 and 15.4.[87] Under Article 15.2, Members may deny registration of a trademark on "other grounds" (even if they are distinctive) "provided they do not derogate from the provisions of the Paris Convention (1967)". Under Article 15.3, Members may also make registrability depend on use. However, Article 15.4 makes clear that a denial of registration based on "other grounds" under Article 15.2 may not be justified based on "the nature of the goods or services to which a trademark is to be applied".

64.　　In light of this framework, Australia has failed to properly implement its obligations under Article 15 of the TRIPS Agreement. Australia, through its *Trade Marks Act 1995*, requires the registrability of non-inherently distinctive marks to depend on use.[88] Under this act, the registration of non-inherently distinctive marks will be rejected if "the applicant has not *used* the trade mark before the filing date in respect of the application to such an extent that the trade mark does in fact distinguish the designated goods or services as being those of the applicant".[89] Use with respect to goods is defined by the statute as use of the mark "upon, or in physical or other relation to the goods".[90]

65.　　At the same time, under the PP measures, Australia prohibits the use of non-inherently distinctive signs related to tobacco products. When a Member requires prior use in order to register non-inherently distinctive marks, as Australia has done, but at the same time restricts the ability of a trademark applicant to use a sign related to a particular class of goods in order to acquire distinctiveness, it violates Article 15.4 of the TRIPS Agreement. Australia has created an "obstacle to the registration of the trademark" related to the "nature of the good or services to which a trademark is to be applied".

66.　　Australia argued that: (i) Article 15.4 does not create a "right to use" a sign on any product;[91] (ii) the complainants' interpretation of Article 15.1 and

---

[85]　Indonesia's first written submission, para. 186.
[86]　Appellate Body Report, *US - Section 211 Appropriations Act*, para. 154.
[87]　Appellate Body Report, *US - Section 211 Appropriations Act*, paras. 155-64.
[88]　*Trade Marks Act 1995*, Exhibit JE-6, Sections 41(1)-(3).
[89]　*Trade Marks Act 1995*, Exhibit JE-6, Section 41(2) and 41(3).
[90]　*Trade Marks Act 1995*, Exhibit JE-6, Section 7(4).
[91]　Australia's first written submission, paras. 299-300.

15.4 would impair the ability of governments to regulate the promotion and sale of dangerous products and result in an undoing of almost all tobacco control measures adopted by WTO Members around the world;[92] and (iii) non-inherently distinctive signs that have not achieved distinctiveness through use are not "trademarks eligible for registration" and, therefore, are not subject to the disciplines of Article 15.4.

67.   Indonesia agrees with Australia that Article 15.4 of the TRIPS Agreement does not create a "right to use" a trademark. Indonesia further notes that Article 15.4 does not impede the ability of Members to regulate *goods* in their respective territories. However, when a Member elects to make registrability of trademarks depend upon use (as they are permitted to do under Article 15.1), they are bound by Article 15.4 to not prohibit the use of such trademarks based on the nature of the goods to which they are applied. This is precisely what Australia has done in its *TPP Act*, which Australia itself admits.[93]

68.   Consequently, Australia's PP measures violate Article 15.4 of the TRIPS Agreement.

4.   Plain Packaging Violates Article 16.1 Of The TRIPS Agreement

69.   TRIPS Article 16.1 provides that Members must afford protection to the owners of registered trademarks against the unauthorized use of those marks by third parties. Members need only extend protections against unauthorized use to trademark owners when (i) the owner's trademark is validly registered in accordance with national law; (ii) the third party's mark is being used on identical or related goods; and (iii) the third party's mark is being used in a manner that is likely to create confusion.[94] The TRIPS Agreement does not provide a standard for "likelihood of confusion," and therefore it is left to each WTO Members to implement the obligation in its domestic laws.

70.   Under Australian jurisprudence, a likelihood of confusion is established when marks are deceptively similar such that a consumer is unable to recall the difference between two marks.[95] This "impression-based" comparison does not envision a side-by-side comparison, but rather an assessment of what a reasonable person would remember about a trademark. The owner of a trademark registered in Australia seeking to prevent unauthorized third party use on the basis of deceptive similarity must establish that a consumer of ordinary intelligence would have difficultly distinguishing between the two marks, separately, based on his or her recollection.

---

[92]   Australia's first written submission, para. 306 and fn. 498.
[93]   Australia's first written submission, para. 307.
[94]   Indonesia's first written submission, para. 205.
[95]   Indonesia's first written submission, paras. 207-212.

71.   Australia's PP measures undermine the ability of a trademark owner to prevent a "likelihood of confusion" with nearly identical marks. In addition, PP impairs the distinctiveness of marks and, therefore, the ability of mark owners to prevent the use of similar or identical marks on similar or identical goods. In such cases "evidence of actual confusion" based on the use of trademarks in the market "is given great weight".[96] Indeed, trademark owners who can show that consumers are actually confused by similar uses of marks have a much greater likelihood of success in exercising their "exclusive" rights as compared to trademark owners who are unable to offer such evidence. Even when such evidence is not available, the courts in Australia will draw conclusions about how trademarks might be used in the marketplace under normal conditions. By prohibiting the use of trademarks on tobacco products, PP creates a very real legal bias against the owners of tobacco trademarks who want to exercise their "negative" rights of exclusion.

72.   Indonesia separately argued that Australia's PP measures require trademarks that are permitted on tobacco packaging to appear in a manner that is likely to result in confusion in violation of Article 16.1.[97] Owners of registered tobacco product trademarks find themselves legally required to present their trademarks in a manner that is deceptively similar to those of other tobacco brands. Australia's PP measures increase the risk of consumer confusion that Article 16.1 is intended to prevent through private right of action.

73.   Australia's *only* rebuttal is that the PP measures do not require certain word marks to appear in a manner that is likely to result in confusion because "the Registrar has determined that these trademarks are in fact capable of distinguishing the goods of the trademark applicant from the goods of other persons".[98] However, the fact that a trademark is registered does not preclude its use in a manner that might result in confusion with another registered trademark. The *Trade Marks Act 1995* provides the Registrar with the authority to revoke the registration of a trademark if "it is reasonable to revoke the registration, taking account of all the circumstances",[99] including "any *use* that has been made of the trade mark" as well as "any past, current or proposed legal proceedings relating to the trade mark".[100] Thus, the mere fact of registration does not preclude the possibility of later revocation based on confusing *use* of the trademark.

74.   Moreover, the manner and context in which trademarks are used – including their trade dress – is an important element of trademark infringement actions in Australia.[101] Under the "imperfect recollection" test, Australian courts

---

[96]   Indonesia's second written submission, para. 81.
[97]   Indonesia's first written submission, paras. 214-19.
[98]   Indonesia's first written submission, p. 66, Table V.1.
[99]   *Trade Marks Act 1995*, s 84(1)(b), Exhibit JE-6, p. 83.
[100]   *Trade Marks Act 1995*, s 84(3)(a)-(b), Exhibit JE-6, pp. 83-84 (emphasis supplied).
[101]   Indonesia's second written submission, para. 97.

draw conclusions about what a consumer would *recall* about marks and compare how marks *are used or intended to be used* in the marketplace.[102] In the case of word marks, Australian courts have taken judicial notice of the fact "that as a matter of common experience, people often do not read words carefully and do not pronounce them distinctly".[103] Given the PP measures' propensity for creating a likelihood of confusion, Australia violates TRIPS Article 16.1.

5.   Plain Packaging Violates Article 16.3 Of The TRIPS Agreement

75.   TRIPS Article 16.3 requires Members to give trademark owners a private right of action when: (i) a registered, well-known mark, (ii) is used by an unauthorized third party, (iii) on non-similar goods or services, (iv) such use indicates a connection with the trademark owner, and (v) such use is likely to damage the trademark owner's interests. This protection includes refusing or canceling the registration of infringing marks and prohibiting their use.

76.   The purpose of Article 16.3 is to preserve the commercial value of a well-known mark in connection with a particular good or service. This is often thought of as protection against dilution. Dilution of a well-known mark usually results in "depreciation of the goodwill attached to it, even in cases where there is no likelihood of confusion."[104]

77.   Australia argued that its PP measures have not impaired the rights accorded to owners of well-known marks under Article 16.3 because these are "negative" rights only, and Australia is not obligated to refrain from taking action that would impact the well-known status of marks.[105] Australia presented no rebuttal argument to the complainants' claim that Article 16.3 obliges Members to protect well-known marks from dilution,[106] and it did not rebut the complainants' statement of Australian jurisprudence regarding the process by which marks become well-known.

78.   Accordingly, the Panel should find that Australia's PP measures undermine the rights conferred by Article 16.3 of the TRIPS Agreement by ensuring that well-known tobacco trademarks lose their protected status, as defined by Australian jurisprudence, and by preventing other tobacco trademarks from attaining the recognition necessary to achieve the heightened level of protection accorded to well-known marks.

---

[102]   Indonesia's second written submission, para. 76.
[103]   Indonesia's second written submission, para. 97.
[104]   Indonesia's first written submission, para. 229.
[105]   Australia's first written submission, para. 325.
[106]   Australia's first written submission, fn. 517.

6.   Plain Packaging Violates Article 20 Of The TRIPS Agreement

79.   TRIPS Article 20 prohibits Members from adopting "special requirements" that "encumber" the use of a trademark "in the course of trade" without justification.

a.   Australia's PP measures are "special requirements"

80.   "Special requirements" are those mandated requirements that: 1) apply to a limited product class; 2) apply only for a particular purpose; or 3) are distinct from those that apply generally or "usually". Australia did not dispute that the PP measures impose "special requirements".[107] Therefore, this element of Article 20 is satisfied.

b.   Australia's PP requirements encumber the use of a trademark in the course of trade

81.   As discussed above, Australia's PP requirements affect the use of trademarks in the course of trade by setting requirements on their use at every phase of the value chain.[108]

82.   Australia's PP requirements encumber use of a trademark in the course of trade by preventing the use of figurative marks, stylized marks, most word marks, and combined marks of one or more of the above on retail packaging and tobacco products themselves. Furthermore, word marks permitted to appear on the packaging must appear in a particular typeface, size, capitalization, and color.

83.   Australia responded with a circular argument, claiming that a prohibition on use cannot be covered by Article 20 because there *is* no use in the course of trade. On the contrary, the use of the term "such as" in Article 20 makes it clear that the specified examples are not a closed list and a wide range of special requirements could be covered by Article 20, so long as they encumber use of a trademark in the course of trade. There is no support in the language of Article 20 for the view that a special requirement *prohibiting* use in the course of trade is excluded from the scope of Article 20.

84.   Australia's interpretation would create an untenable situation where the TRIPS Agreement would allow Members total freedom to impose a prohibition on the use of a trademark without any justification or explanation. And yet Members would be required to provide a justification and explanation for far less intrusive limitations on the use of a trademark.[109]

---

[107]   Australia's first written submission, paras. 79, 120-121.
[108]   See *T/PP Act*, Sections 31-35.
[109]   Indonesia's second written submission, para. 125.

c.   Australia's PP requirements "unjustifiably" encumber use of trademarks in the course of trade

85.   Article 20 prohibits Members from "unjustifiably" encumbering the use of trademarks in the course of trade. An Article 20 analysis of "unjustifiable" requires use of a sliding scale – measures that impose a high degree of encumbrance also impose a higher burden on the respondent to justify the measure. Radical and unprecedented encumbrances, such as those imposed by PP, require more evidence to prove that the burden is "warranted" and "supported", whereas a minor encumbrance (i.e. use with a health warning and limitations on size or placement) could be justified with less rigorous evidence.

86.   Each type of special requirement and its related encumbrance must also be evaluated and "justified" independently. It would be inappropriate to use evidence that may support one type of encumbrance (i.e. a limitation on the use of certain colors) to justify the imposition of a different type of encumbrance (mandating a certain typeface) or a range of encumbrances across the board.

87.   Australia has assumed that *any* trademark element located *anywhere* has the effect of persuading people to smoke. At every turn Australia has crafted its PP requirements to impose some of the most extreme encumbrances, without attempting to determine whether any other approach, such as allowing manufacturers to use their preferred typeface and size, could satisfy PP's purposes. This approach is unsubstantiated and is certainly unjustified. There was *no* credible evidence that the specific marks (i.e. stylized marks in their registered typeface, larger font size, etc.) used on tobacco products and their retail packaging had that effect, nor was there *any* credible evidence more generally that every trademark element does so equally.

88.   By every measure of post-implementation data, there is no evidence that PP is contributing to a decrease in prevalence in Australia, much less at a level sufficient to justify the draconian and unprecedented encumbrances imposed on figurative marks, stylized marks, and word marks. Studies by multiple researchers using different analytical approaches have failed to find any empirical evidence that Australia's PP measures are reducing prevalence in the general population or among youth, who were predicted to be particularly affected by PP. After more than three years of PP there is *no* evidence that it is having a positive impact on consumer behavior. None of the predictions about the effect of PP have proven to be correct. PP has failed to bring about the declines in tobacco prevalence predicted by its proponents. It is not working and is not likely to work and, therefore, unjustifiably encumbers the use of trademarks in violation of TRIPS Article 20.

7. Plain Packaging Violates Articles 22.2(b) And 24.3 Of The TRIPS Agreement

89.   Indonesia supports the arguments presented by the Dominican Republic and the Honduras with respect to Australia's violation of Articles 22.2(b) and 24.3 of the TRIPS Agreement.[110]

B. Plain Packaging Violates Article 2.2 Of The TBT Agreement

90.   In order to establish a violation of Article 2.2 of the TBT Agreement, panels and the Appellate Body have held that a complainant must prove that: (1) the objective of the challenged measure is not "legitimate"; or (2) the technical regulation is more trade-restrictive than is necessary to achieve that legitimate objective, bearing in the mind the risks that non-fulfillment would create. Because the TBT Agreement only applies to technical regulations, complainants must also prove that the challenged measure is a "technical regulation". Indonesia will address this question first.

1. Australia's PP measures are "technical regulations"

91.   The Appellate Body has established a three-tier test for determining whether a measure is a "technical regulation" under the TBT Agreement: 1) the document must apply to an identifiable product or group of products; 2) the document must lay down one or more characteristics of the product, prescribed in either a positive or a negative form; and 3) compliance with the product characteristics must be mandatory.[111]

92.   While Australia conceded that the "format requirements" (which specify the physical appearance of tobacco packs and tobacco products themselves) are technical regulations subject to the disciplines of the TBT Agreement, Australia mistakenly claimed that the "trademark requirements" (which address the use of trademarks on tobacco products and their packaging) are not.[112] In response, Indonesia countered that Annex 1.1 of the TBT Agreement indicates that a technical regulation:

> . . . may also include or *deal exclusively with terminology, symbols, packaging, marking or labeling* requirements as they apply to a product, process or production method. (emphasis added)

In a finding that was not appealed, the WTO panel in *EC – GIs* clarified that a document that sets requirements for product labels lays down a product

---

[110]   See Dominican Republic's first written submission, Section VI.J and VI. K and Honduras' first written submission, Section VI.

[111]   Appellate Body Report, *EC – Sardines*, para. 176 (citing Appellate Body Report, *EC – Asbestos*, paras. 66-70).

[112]   Indonesia's second written submission, para. 211.

characteristic.[113] It also is not in dispute that compliance with the PP requirements is mandatory. [114] Therefore, all aspects of Australia's PP measures are technical regulations subject to the TBT Agreement.

2. Australia's PP measures are not in accordance with an international standard within the meaning of Article 2.5 of the TBT Agreement

a. The FCTC COP is not an international standardizing body

93.   Australia has asserted, without providing evidence, that the FCTC COP and its Guidelines satisfy the requirements in *US – Tuna II (Mexico)* to qualify as an "international standards organization" and "international standards" respectively. An "international standard" exists where there is: (i) a standard; (ii) adopted by an international standardizing/standards organization; and (iii) that is made available to the public.[115]

94.   In order to be considered an "international standardizing/standards organization", an organization must have "recognized activities in standardization".[116] In examining whether an international body has "recognized activities in standardization", evidence of recognition by WTO Members is relevant".[117] Such recognition does not exist among WTO Members with respect to the FCTC. In total, 19 WTO Members, including 15 who have signed or ratified the FCTC, did not agree that the FCTC Guidelines are an international standard.[118] Contrary to Australia's argument, there is no "recognition" of the standardization activities at the FCTC among WTO Members. Furthermore, no document published by the relevant organizations (WHO, WTO) describes the FCTC COP as a standard-setting organization and while the FCTC assigned a number of specific functions to the COP, none was the development of product standards.[119]

95.   Whether the body adopting a measure adheres to the principles of transparency, openness, impartiality and consensus contained in the TBT Committee Decision on Principles for the Development of International Standards, Guides and Recommendations with Relation to Articles 2, 5, and Annex 3 to the Agreement (the "TBT Committee Decision") is also relevant to the analysis of whether an organization is an international standardizing body.[120]

---

[113]   Indonesia's first written submission, para. 387.
[114]   *T/PP Act*, Chapter 5, Part 2, p. 89-100.
[115]   Indonesia's response to Q.66 from the Panel, para. 75.
[116]   Appellate Body Report, *US – Tuna II (Mexico)*, paras. 356-359
[117]   Appellate Body Report, *US – Tuna II (Mexico)*, para. 363.
[118]   See Indonesia's second written submission, paras. 239-240.
[119]   Indonesia's second written submission, para. 244.
[120]   Appellate Body Report, *US – Tuna II (Mexico)*, paras. 373-378.

96.   The FCTC COP did not, as Australia claims, recommend PP "by consensus".[121] The COP could only reach consensus to recommend *considering* PP, which means there was *no* consensus to recommend adopting PP as part of Members' obligations under Articles 11 and 13.

97.   The FCTC Guidelines do not result in "common or repeated use". A Party may "consider" adopting PP and decide to adopt it or it may "consider" adopting PP and reject the policy. These are widely divergent outcomes that could not possibly be considered "common" use.

98.   No tobacco manufacturer has voluntarily adopted PP. The requirements of FCTC Articles 11 and 13 with respect to packaging and advertising are mandatory for Parties to the FCTC; i.e. they are not "voluntary".[122] The Guidelines for Articles 11 and 13 make recommendations on how Parties should implement the "mandatory" provisions of Articles 11 and 13. To date the only "use" of the Guidelines has been by Australia, which imposed PP by adopting a mandatory technical regulation. Indonesia is not aware of a single instance where a standard was considered to exist, yet had not been used voluntarily in even a single commercial instance. In this regard the FCTC Guidelines contrast sharply with other international standards.

99.   Finally, the FCTC COP is not open or transparent.[123] The Rules of Procedure for the COP establishes the criteria for obtaining observer status and provides that it is only open to "{o}ther international and regional nongovernmental organizations whose aims and activities are in conformity with the spirit, purpose and principles of the Convention . . . ."[124] The COP's rules for designating only like-minded observers means that deliberations in which observers participate are not open on a non-discriminatory basis.

100.   In addition, FCTC Guidelines for Article 5.3 ("Guidelines 5.3") address interaction with tobacco companies. The Guidelines 5.3 are replete with admonitions to Parties to avoid any interaction with tobacco companies, protect policies from "commercial and other vested interests of the tobacco industry", and consider that there is a "fundamental and irreconcilable conflict between the tobacco industry's interests and public health policy interests".[125] The Guidelines directly conflict with the TBT Committee Decision provisions regarding transparency.[126] There is no analogous set of guidelines in existence in any other recognized standard-setting body prohibiting engagement with industry.[127]

101.   Finally, the FCTC COP bears no resemblance to other standardizing organizations, such as the Joint Food and Agriculture Organization

---

[121]   Indonesia's second written submission, para. 225.
[122]   Indonesia's second written submission, para. 229.
[123]   Indonesia's second written submission, paras. 230-241.
[124]   Indonesia's second written submission, para. 231.
[125]   Indonesia's second written submission, paras. 236-237.
[126]   TBT Committee Decision, Article 2.1 (G/TBT/1/Rev.9, p. 37). (emphasis supplied)
[127]   Indonesia's second written submission, para. 248.

("FAO")/WHO Codex Alimentarius Commission ("Codex") or the International Standards Organization ("ISO"). The FCTC's far more amorphous guidelines for implementation of either Article 11 or 13 lack the requisite scientific or technical underpinnings, as well as a transparent and well-articulated standard-setting process (which is understandable given that it is not, and never was intended to be, a standard-setting organization) that would permit any consideration of its work product as a "relevant international standard" within the meaning of Article 2.5 of the TBT Agreement.

b.   Australia's PP measures are not "in accordance with" the FCTC Guidelines

102.   For all of the reasons described above, the Panel should find that the FCTC Guidelines for Articles 11 and 13 are not international standards and the Panel's analysis of Australia's claims under Article 2.5 should end here. Alternatively, if the Panel concludes that an international standard does exist, Indonesia argued that Australia's PP measures are not "in accordance with" that international standard because they go well beyond what is recommended in the Guidelines.

103.   Interpretations of SPS Article 3.2 have held that a measure must fully "conform to" or "comply with" all aspects of the relevant international standard, *without exceeding* the "rules, guidelines or characteristics" established by the standard.[128] The Appellate Body has held that a measure that exceeds the requirements of an international standard does not conform to that standard and *is not entitled to any presumption of consistency.*[129]

104.   Australia's PP measures are not "in accordance with" the purported standard allegedly established in the Guidelines for Articles 11 and 13. First, Australia has previously informed the WTO that its PP measures are not "in accordance with" an international standard in its notification to the TBT Committee under Article 2.9.2.[130] Furthermore, the vague language of the FCTC Guidelines does not provide a level of specificity sufficient for there to be the required "*degree of correspondence* between the Member's technical regulation and the international standard, such that the technical regulation '*embod{ies}* the international standard *completely* and, for practical purposes, *convert{s}* it into a municipal standard'".[131]

105.   Moreover, Australia's PP measures go beyond the Guidelines for Article 11 and 13, which eliminates any presumption that might attach pursuant to TBT Article 2.5. The Guidelines for both Article 11 and 13 do not include requirements, such as prohibiting use of the manufacturer's name on tobacco products themselves, imposing restrictions on wrappers inside of tobacco packs,

---

[128]   Indonesia's second written submission, para. 255.
[129]   Appellate Body Report, *US/Canada — Continued Suspension*, para. 694. (emphasis added)
[130]   Indonesia's second written submission, para. 256.
[131]   *Ibid.*

or such details as the location and orientation of information permitted to appear on tobacco packaging and the number of times certain information may appear on a pack, all of which are mandated by Australia's PP measures.[132] Because Australia's PP measures exceed the requirements described in the Guidelines for Articles 11 and 13, they do not enjoy any presumption of consistency under Article 2.5 with respect to Article 2.2 of the TBT Agreement.

3. Australia's PP requirements are more trade restrictive than necessary and create an unnecessary obstacle to trade in violation of TBT Article 2.2

106. Indonesia agrees that measures to reduce smoking prevalence have the potential to protect public health and is not challenging the legitimacy of the objective pursued by Australia's PP measures. In *US – Tuna II (Mexico)* the Appellate Body concluded that an analysis of the consistency of a measure with Article 2.2 involves a "relational analysis" of: the trade-restrictiveness of the technical regulation; the degree of contribution that it makes to the achievement of a legitimate objective; and the risks non-fulfillment would create.[133] Indonesia argued that Australia's PP measures do not make a contribution toward this legitimate objective, are trade restrictive, and less trade restrictive alternatives are available, all of which indicate that Australia's PP measures are more trade restrictive than necessary.

a. Australia's PP requirements are trade restrictive

107. Australia's PP measures prevent tobacco companies from using trademarks to distinguish their tobacco products from those of competitors and in many cases demand premium pricing. By stripping away the most identifiable elements of branding (colors, shapes, typefaces, etc.), PP "commoditizes" tobacco products and price becomes the primary form of competition.

108. The inability of foreign tobacco product manufacturers to establish their brand identity in Australia in order to compete against domestic competitors makes it difficult to overcome the existing domestic brand bias. Australia's PP measures are thus trade restrictive because they limit competitive opportunities in the Australian market by imposing restrictions on the right to use trademarks and other aspects of brand identity that are necessary to compete against domestic brands.

b. Australia's PP measures fail to make a meaningful contribution to the legitimate objective of reducing smoking prevalence

109. The Appellate Body has clarified in the context of Article XX(b) of the GATT 1994 that "a contribution exists when there is *a genuine relationship of*

---

[132] *T/PP Act* (JE-1), pp. 22-27.
[133] Appellate Body Report, *US – Tuna II*, para. 318, Appellate Body Report *US – COOL*, para. 374.

ends and means between the objective pursued and the measure at issue".[134] In assessing whether Australia's PP measures have had an "ends and means" relationship with a reduction in smoking prevalence, it is useful to begin with an understanding of the trend in smoking prevalence prior to the introduction of PP. Australia's own health data show that smoking prevalence had fallen consistently from 24.3 percent in 2001 to 15.1 percent in 2010.[135] Observed smoking prevalence declined steadily from 2006 at an annual rate of about 0.59 percentage points. In order for there to be an "ends and means" relationship between Australia's PP measures and a reduction in smoking prevalence, PP would need to have reduced prevalence *beyond* the rate that was already occurring – if not, it was and is "unnecessary".

110.   Underlying PP is a belief that any design element that might appear on a pack or cigarette/cigar presumptively has the effect of persuading people to smoke when they otherwise would not. At the time PP was adopted by Australia, there was no credible evidence that the specific design elements used on tobacco products and their packaging had that effect, nor was there any credible evidence more generally that every design element regulated by PP did so. Post-implementation data continues to show that PP has had no effect on smoking prevalence rates in Australia, even three years after it went into effect, and is unlikely to do so in the future.

c.   Less restrictive alternatives are available

111.   Even if PP had made some tiny contribution to its objective, there are less trade-restrictive alternatives that make an equivalent or greater contribution to reducing prevalence than PP. These include excise tax increases, increased spending on social marketing campaigns, raising the minimum legal purchase age, and a pre-vetting mechanism.[136]

112.   Australia has claimed that the first three of these alternatives cannot be considered "alternatives" because they are already in use in Australia.[137] However, Australia is misstating the circumstances in *Brazil – Retreaded Tyres*. In that case, certain measures proposed as LRAs were found not to be valid "alternatives" because they were implemented as part of a comprehensive approach to address a risk to human, plant and animal life and health.[138] However, the panel did not reach this conclusion in the abstract. Brazil had put extensive factual evidence on the record in that case showing that if imported retreaded tires were allowed in the Brazilian market, they would have displaced local retreading of used tires, leading to an increase in waste tires (unrecycled

---

[134]   Appellate Body Report, *Brazil –Retreaded Tyres*, para. 145 (emphasis added).
[135]   Indonesia's first written submission, para. 408.
[136]   Indonesia's first written submission, paras. 430-457.
[137]   Australia's first written submission, paras. 703-717.
[138]   Indonesia's second written submission, para. 289.

tires) in Brazil.[139] Accordingly, the panel concluded that domestic retreading of tires in Brazil could have been adversely affected in the absence of the import ban on foreign retreaded tires. In the instant case, Australia has provided no evidence (and certainly nothing comparable to the evidence developed by Brazil) showing that excise taxes, social marketing campaigns, or the minimum legal purchase age would be *less effective* in the absence of the PP measures.

113.   Complainants are not arguing that existing tobacco control measures – like taxation, social marketing campaigns, or the LMPA – would serve as alternatives in their present form. In each instance complainants have proposed modifications of those policies such that they would become a new measure not currently in effect in Australia. For example, the fact that Australia raised its LMPA from 16 to 18 *almost 20 years ago* has no bearing on the positive effects that a rise from 18 to 21 *now* could generate.[140] Also, implementing the structural programmatic changes to social marketing campaigns would result in new, more effective, programs that would make an increased contribution to reducing prevalence.[141]

114.   Furthermore, the LRAs proposed by complainants are less trade-restrictive than PP because they do not diminish competitive opportunities by eliminating the ability of manufacturers to distinguish their product from those of other suppliers.

115.   Based on the analysis above, the PP measures violate Article 2.2 of the TBT Agreement.

IV.   REQUEST FOR FINDINGS

116.   Indonesia requested the Panel find that Australia's *Trade Marks Amendment (Tobacco Plain Packaging) Act 2011*, *Tobacco PP Act 2011*, and *Tobacco Plain Packaging Regulations* 2011, collectively and individually, violate Australia's obligations under Article 2.2 of the TBT Agreement and Articles 2.1, 15.4, 16.1, 16.3, 20, 22(b) and 24.3 of the TRIPS Agreement.

---

[139]   Panel Report, *Brazil – Retreaded Tyres*, para. 7.142.
[140]   Australia's first written submission, para. 710.
[141]   Indonesia's second written submission, para. 289.

ANNEX B-5

INTEGRATED EXECUTIVE SUMMARY OF THE ARGUMENTS
OF AUSTRALIA

I.   INTRODUCTION

1.   For the reasons set out in Australia's written submissions, oral statements, responses to questions from the Panel, and comments on the complainants' responses, the complainants' claims that the tobacco plain packaging measure is inconsistent with Australia's obligations under the covered agreements are unfounded both in law and in fact.

2.   As a matter of law, the complainants' claims either rely on clear distortions and misinterpretations of the relevant provisions of the TRIPS Agreement, the TBT Agreement, and the GATT 1994, or otherwise fail to satisfy the legal requirements for establishing a claim of violation under those provisions.

3.   Moreover, even if the Panel were to find that the complainants have established the *prima facie* applicability of the relevant legal provisions, the complainants have failed to prove their claims of violation as a matter of evidence.

4.   Under the two principal provisions at issue in this dispute – Article 20 of the TRIPS Agreement and Article 2.2 of the TBT Agreement – the complainants have assumed the burden of proving that the tobacco plain packaging measure will make *no* contribution to its public health objectives. The qualitative and quantitative evidence before the Panel, and the complainants' own contradictory arguments regarding the effects of the measure, demonstrate that the complainants have failed to discharge this burden.

5.   In recognition of this failure, the complainants have attempted throughout their submissions to shift their legal burden to Australia by suggesting that Australia must positively demonstrate that the tobacco plain packaging measure has resulted in immediately observable and quantifiable declines in smoking prevalence and consumption in the limited period of time since the measure's implementation. Not only does this argument fundamentally ignore the nature of the tobacco plain packaging measure as a long-term public health measure that forms an integral part of a comprehensive suite of tobacco control measures, and the nature of tobacco use as a complex public health problem that requires a comprehensive response, it also constitutes an additional error of law that infects the complainants' arguments.

6.   In light of the complainants' failure to prove that the tobacco plain packaging measure is inconsistent with Australia's obligations under the covered agreements, the Panel should reject the complainants' claims in their entirety.

II.   SUMMARY OF THE RELEVANT CONTEXT FOR ASSESSING AUSTRALIA'S TOBACCO PLAIN PACKAGING MEASURE

7.   This dispute concerns a Member's right to regulate the advertising and promotion of tobacco – a unique, highly addictive product that kills half of its long-term users; is the world's leading cause of preventable morbidity and mortality; is globally responsible for the deaths of nearly 6,000,000 people annually, including 600,000 non-smokers exposed to second-hand smoke; for which there is no safe level of use or safe level of exposure; and which harms nearly every organ in the body.[1]

8.   In Australia, tobacco use is a leading cause of preventable disease and premature death. Over 15,000 Australians die each year from smoking-related diseases.[2]

9.   To combat the global epidemic of tobacco use,[3] the FCTC requires comprehensive tobacco control strategies in recognition that they are the most effective means of reducing the incidence and prevalence of smoking.[4] To be effective, such comprehensive strategies must cover all aspects of supply and demand; apply to all tobacco products; optimize synergies between complementary measures; and be continually refreshed and revised.[5]

10.   Australia's comprehensive suite of tobacco control measures includes: measures that have progressively restricted advertising of tobacco products; graphic health warnings; increased excise taxes; restrictions on youth access; retail and point-of-sale-display bans; bans on smoking in public places; support for cessation; and anti-smoking social marketing campaigns and public education campaigns.[6] The tobacco plain packaging measure was introduced to prohibit one of the last remaining avenues for the advertising and promotion of tobacco products to consumers and potential consumers in Australia: the retail packaging of tobacco products and the product itself.[7]

11.   The measure achieves this objective by prohibiting the display of design features on the retail packaging of tobacco products, including trademarks (other

---

[1]   Australia's first written submission, Part II.A, paras. 23-24, 27-30, and Part II.B, para. 32.
[2]   Australia's first written submission, Part II.C, para. 34; Australia's opening statement at the first substantive meeting of the Panel, para. 7.
[3]   Australia's first written submission, Part II.B, para. 31; Australia's opening statement at the second substantive meeting of the Panel, paras. 17-18.
[4]   Australia's first written submission, Part II.D, paras. 38, 46-49; Australia's second written submission, para. 250; Australia's opening statement at the second substantive meeting of the Panel, para. 8; Australia's comments on responses to Panel Question No. 6, paras. 34-36.
[5]   Australia's first written submission, Part II.D, paras. 38-49; Australia's opening statement at the second substantive meeting of the Panel, paras. 9-10; Australia's comments on responses to Panel Question No. 6, paras. 34-36.
[6]   Australia's first written submission, Part II.D.2 and Part II.D.3; Australia's second written submission, para. 552; Australia's opening statement at the second substantive meeting of the Panel, para. 9.
[7]   Australia's first written submission, Part II.D.3.

than brand, business or company name or variant name), logos, symbols, imagery, colours and promotional text; imposing certain restrictions on the shape and finish of the retail packaging of tobacco products; and imposing certain other requirements related to the appearance of tobacco products.[8] To ensure that tobacco companies are still able to distinguish their products from other products in the marketplace, the measure permits the use of brand, business or company name and variant names on retail packaging, including names that are trademarked, in a standardised form.[9] These requirements apply to all tobacco products.[10]

12.   Australia's decision to implement the tobacco plain packaging measure was based upon an extensive body of supporting scientific evidence,[11] and the explicit recommendation of the FCTC Guidelines to adopt tobacco plain packaging as a means of implementing Parties' obligations under the FCTC.[12] Numerous other countries, including Ireland, the United Kingdom, France, Hungary, New Zealand, Norway, Chile and Singapore, have now adopted or are considering adopting their own tobacco plain packaging measures, consistent with the FCTC Guidelines, to improve public health in their respective jurisdictions.[13]

13.   The synergies between Australia's comprehensive and complementary tobacco control measures are critical.[14] For example, tobacco plain packaging works together with excise tax increases to address youth initiation across each of its stages, including the early stages of experimentation with tobacco use.[15] Similarly, tobacco plain packaging enhances the effectiveness of Australia's social marketing campaigns, which are otherwise undermined by tobacco product marketing.[16] Tobacco plain packaging also increases the effectiveness of graphic health warnings, and the enhanced graphic health warnings reinforce the messages conveyed in anti-tobacco social marketing campaigns, and do so at a

---

[8]   Australia's first written submission, Part II.G.2.
[9]   Australia's first written submission, Part II.G.2; Australia's second written submission, Part II.C.5(c); Australia's opening statement at the first substantive meeting of the Panel, paras. 50-54.
[10]   Australia's first written submission, Part II.G.2(e).
[11]   Australia's first written submission, Part II.E.3 and Part II.I.3; Australia's second written submission, Parts II.C.5(b) and III.D.3.
[12]   Australia's first written submission, Part II.F; Australia's second written submission, paras. 242-245; Australia's opening statement at the second substantive meeting of the Panel, para. 11.
[13]   Australia's comments on responses to Panel Question No. 163, paras. 117-118; Australia's second written submission, paras. 245-249; Australia's opening statement at the second substantive meeting of the Panel, para. 11.
[14]   Australia's opening statement at the first substantive meeting of the Panel, paras. 16-17; Australia's opening statement at the second substantive meeting of the Panel, para. 10; Australia's response to Panel Question No. 158, para. 73; Australia's comments on responses to Panel Question No. 161, paras. 107-111.
[15]   Australia's comments on responses to Panel Question No. 161, para. 108.
[16]   Australia's comments on responses to Panel Question No. 161, para. 110.

particularly important time – namely, the point of consumption.[17] Such measures therefore complement, rather than act as a substitute for, each other.[18]

14.   Australia's comprehensive tobacco control strategy has resulted in a decline in the prevalence rates of smoking in Australia.[19] Prevalence in Australia is now the lowest it has been for many decades, with substantial declines occurring during the period in which tobacco plain packaging has been in force.[20]

15.   The most recent NDSHS, which covers the period 2010-2013, showed a notable decline in prevalence rates. Rates of daily smoking declined from 15.9% to 13.3% among Australians aged 18 or older and, significantly, from 15.1% to 12.8% among Australians aged 14 or older.[21] This drop in prevalence of 2 to 3 percentage points translates to 200,000 fewer daily smokers, aged 14 or older.[22] Similarly, under the Australian Bureau of Statistics 2014-15 wave of the National Health Survey, daily smoking among Australians aged 18 and over was 14.5% in 2014-15, down from 16.1% in 2011-12.[23] These results are consistent with other evidence before the Panel showing significant declines in smoking prevalence following the introduction of the tobacco plain packaging measure.

16.   Recent data on smoking prevalence taken from the Roy Morgan monthly survey confirms a substantial reduction in prevalence. While Roy Morgan uses different survey methodologies, the pattern of rapid decline in prevalence is significant and consistent. Overall prevalence for Australian smokers aged 14 and over declined from 18.7% in the period from January to June 2012 (prior to the introduction of tobacco plain packaging) to 16.2% in the first six months of 2015.[24] Prevalence among Australians aged 14-24 also declined, from 16.7% to 14.1%. This translates to approximately 492,000 fewer smokers aged 14 and over, including approximately 86,000 fewer youth and young adult smokers.[25]

17.   Since the complainants have assumed the burden of establishing that the tobacco plain packaging measure is incapable of contributing to Australia's public health objectives, they must demonstrate that *none* of the significant declines in smoking prevalence and consumption that have occurred since the

[17]   Australia's opening statement at the second substantive meeting of the Panel, para. 10; Australia's comments on responses to Panel Question No. 161, para. 110.
[18]   Australia's opening statement at the second substantive meeting of the Panel, para. 10; Australia's second written submission, Part III.F; Australia's opening statement at the second substantive meeting of the Panel, paras. 9-10, 154-155.
[19]   Australia's first written submission, Part II.C, para. 36 and Figure 1; Part II.D, para. 53, Figure 3; Australia's opening statement at the second substantive meeting of the Panel, paras. 12-15.
[20]   Australia's first written submission, Part II.C, para. 36; Australia's opening statement at the second substantive meeting of the Panel, paras. 12-15.
[21]   Australia's first written submission, Part II.C, para. 36; Australia's response to Panel Question No. 199, para. 310; Australia's opening statement at the second substantive meeting, para. 12.
[22]   Australia's opening statement at the second substantive meeting of the Panel, para. 12.
[23]   Australia's response to Panel Question No. 199, para. 389.
[24]   Australia's opening statement at the second substantive meeting of the Panel, para. 14.
[25]   *Ibid.*

measure's introduction can be attributed to the tobacco plain packaging measure; and that the measure is incapable of making *any* contribution to reducing the use of, and exposure to, tobacco products in the future.

18. As Australia has established in its submissions throughout these proceedings, the complainants have failed entirely to discharge this burden. Because the complainants' failure to discharge this burden is fatal to the complainants' principal claims under Article 20 of the TRIPS Agreement and Article 2.2 of the TBT Agreement, Australia will summarise the relevant arguments and evidence concerning the measure's contribution to its public health objectives before addressing the other deficiencies in the complainants' claims.

III. THE COMPLAINANTS HAVE FAILED TO DEMONSTRATE THAT THE TOBACCO PLAIN PACKAGING MEASURE IS INCAPABLE OF CONTRIBUTING TO ITS OBJECTIVES

19. Australia has witnessed an acceleration in the significant decline in smoking prevalence since the introduction of tobacco plain packaging as part of a comprehensive suite of tobacco control measures in late 2012, as the following graph shows.[26]

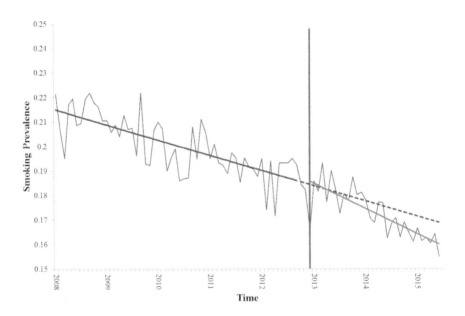

---

[26] Australia's response to Panel Question No. 196, para. 222.

20.   In the same period, the consumption of tobacco products also fell. Average per capita monthly sales in the twelve months to September 2015 fell by more than 15% as compared to the equivalent twelve months prior to the introduction of the measure.[27]

21.   Nevertheless, the complainants claim that there is insufficient evidence to satisfy the Panel that the tobacco plain packaging measure will ever contribute to its public health objectives. While it is the complainants that bear the burden of proving this argument, Australia has demonstrated that, properly analysed, the weight of the qualitative and quantitative evidence before the Panel overwhelmingly supports the conclusion that the measure is apt to contribute to reducing the use of tobacco products, and exposure to tobacco smoke.

A.   **The complainants have failed to establish on the basis of the qualitative evidence before the Panel that the measure is incapable of contributing to its objectives or is unjustifiable**

22.   Throughout the course of these proceedings, Australia has submitted a large body of qualitative evidence that supports the conclusion that tobacco plain packaging is apt to contribute to reducing the use of tobacco products and exposure to tobacco smoke. As Australia has explained, there are multiple hypotheses that are "tested and supported by sufficient evidence"[28] which justify the conclusion that the measure is apt to contribute to Australia's public health objectives.

23.   The complainants have failed to discredit any of this evidence. The complainants' assertion that tobacco plain packaging is incapable of contributing to its objectives amounts, at most, to a request that the Panel take a different view of this evidence. This is insufficient as a matter of law to establish that there is no credible evidentiary support for the conclusion that tobacco plain packaging is capable of contributing to its objectives.

1.   **The complainants have failed to sever the clear link between advertising and smoking-related behaviours**

24.   The evidence shows that there is a clear link between advertising and smoking-related behaviours and that because retail packaging represents a medium for advertising and promoting tobacco products, the tobacco plain packaging measure is capable of affecting smoking-related behaviours. The clear weight of scientific evidence supports this link. This evidence dates back to the 1980s, and includes successive, eminent reports of United States Surgeons General, the World Health Organization, the United States National Cancer Institute, and the United States Institute of Medicine.[29] These reports have

---

[27]   Australia's comments on responses to Panel Question No. 146, para. 14.

[28]   Appellate Body Report, *Brazil – Retreaded Tyres*, para. 151.

[29]   Australia's first written submission, para. 64; Australia's second written submission, paras. 217-236, citing Expert Report of F. Chaloupka, Exhibit AUS-9.

consistently concluded that tobacco companies deliberately target their marketing and advertising to young people to "lure them into starting smoking".[30]

25.   There can be no real dispute that advertising increases primary demand for tobacco products. While the complainants have attempted to dispute this, their evidence fails genuinely to contest the proposition that tobacco advertising causes people to smoke.[31]

2.   The complainants' argument that tobacco product packaging does not constitute advertising or promotion is implausible

26.   Australia has placed a significant amount of qualitative evidence on the Panel record which demonstrates that retail tobacco packaging advertises and promotes tobacco products.[32] This evidence includes marketing theory and practice,[33] as well as evidence from the tobacco industry itself, which views the package as a "billboard"[34] and acknowledges that "tobacco companies, like other consumer goods companies, see branded packaging as one of the tools of advertising."[35] In short: branded packaging functions as a form of advertising and promotion, which increase primary demand for tobacco products.[36]

27.   The complainants have disputed this proposition, relying on two key arguments. First, that packaging cannot be advertising because it does not fit within a textbook definition of "promotion". Second, that even if packaging does generally function as advertising, it cannot serve this function in the context of Australia's dark market. Both of these arguments are without foundation.

(a)   Packaging is advertising

28.   Branded packaging plays a powerful role in consumer decision-making, a proposition supported by evidence from the tobacco industry and Australia and the complainants' marketing experts.

---

[30]   Australia's first written submission, Part II.E, paras. 62-63, citing Teague, Exhibit AUS-69; R.J. Reynolds, Exhibit AUS-70; and *USA et al v. Philip Morris USA Inc., et al*, Exhibit AUS-71.

[31]   Australia's first written submission, paras. 621-626; Australia's second written submission, paras. 214-226.

[32]   Australia's first written submission, Part II.E; Australia's opening statement at the first substantive meeting of the Panel, paras. 26-55, and accompanying Powerpoint presentation; Australia's second written submission, paras. 227-236.

[33]   Australia's first written submission, Part II.E.2(b), citing Expert Report of N. Tavassoli, Exhibit AUS-10; and Expert Report of J.P. Dubé, Exhibit AUS-11.

[34]   Australia's first written submission, Part II.E.2(a) and (c); Australia's second written submission, para. 231. See also, *JT International SA v Commonwealth of Australia*, Exhibit AUS-84.

[35]   Australia's opening statement at the second substantive meeting of the Panel, para. 32, citing Chantler, Exhibit AUS-81, para. 3.22.

[36]   Australia's first written submission, paras. 70-84; Australia's second written submission, paras. 227-236.

29.   Extensive evidence before the Panel demonstrates that the tobacco industry has developed and exploited tobacco packaging for decades as "one of the tools of advertising" tobacco products,[37] including cigars,[38] to project positive images that appeal to specific demographic groups, especially young smokers.[39]

30.   Australia has submitted expert marketing evidence, including the reports of Professors Dubé and Tavassoli,[40] which explains the role packaging plays in appealing to consumers and influencing consumer responses, including purchase and consumption behaviour.[41] The complainants' contention that packaging does not function as a form of advertising is directly contradicted by the complainants' own submissions[42] and the expert report of Professor Steenkamp,[43] who acknowledges that advertising plays a powerful role in consumer decision-making.[44]

(b)   Tobacco packaging functions as advertising in Australia's dark market

31.   Even if packaging is advertising, the complainants have asserted that because Australia is a "dark market",[45] packaging cannot possibly perform an advertising function.

32.   This argument is contradicted by evidence from the tobacco industry itself showing that tobacco packaging became an increasingly important form of advertising and promoting tobacco products precisely *because* of Australia's

---

[37]   Australia's first written submission, Part II.E.2, citing Chantler, Exhibit AUS-81; Philip Morris, Exhibit AUS-82; R.J. Reynolds, Exhibit AUS-83; and *JT International SA v Commonwealth of Australia*, Exhibit AUS-84; Australia's second written submission, paras. 227-231; Australia's opening statement at the first substantive meeting of the Panel, paras. 26-55, and accompanying Powerpoint presentation.

[38]   Australia's first written submission, Part II.E.2, paras. 74, 82, citing Hammar, Exhibit AUS-87, Exhibit AUS-98, and Exhibit AUS-99; Swedish Match, Exhibit AUS-100; Miller et al, Exhibit AUS-102; and Swedish Match, Exhibit AUS-103.

[39]   Australia's first written submission, paras. 66-86; Australia's second written submission, paras. 222-230 citing United States Surgeon General, Exhibit AUS-76; and WHO, Exhibit AUS-80.

[40]   Australia's first written submission, Part II.E.2, paras. 70-72, citing Expert Report of N. Tavassoli, Exhibit AUS-10, and Expert Report of J.P. Dubé, Exhibit AUS-11.

[41]   Australia's first written submission, Part II.E.2, paras. 70-84, citing Expert Report of N. Tavassoli, Exhibit AUS-10; Expert Report of J.P. Dubé, Exhibit AUS-11; Expert Report of P. Slovic, Exhibit AUS-12; Expert Report of A. Biglan, Exhibit AUS-13; Expert Report of G. Fong, Exhibit AUS-14. See also, Centre for Tobacco Control Research Core, Exhibit AUS-90; Hammond, Exhibit AUS-91; and United States Surgeon General, Exhibit AUS-76.

[42]   Cuba's first written submission, para. 197.

[43]   Australia's opening statement at the second substantive meeting of the Panel, paras. 41-42, citing Expert Report of J. Steenkamp, Exhibit DOM/HND-14, para. 92.

[44]   Australia's response to Panel Question No. 204, para. 390; Australia's opening statement at the second substantive meeting of the Panel, paras. 37-46; Australia's comments on responses to Panel Question No. 197, para. 310.

[45]   Australia's first written submission, para.8, fn 3: Australia is a "dark market" because it has a highly restricted regulatory environment for tobacco advertising and promotion.

dark market.[46] Indeed, reviews of Australian tobacco industry documents[47] show that the tobacco industry in Australia researched and adopted packaging design changes because they generate positive imagery that appeals to its target markets, notwithstanding Australia's general ban on advertising. The complainants have not even attempted to respond to this evidence.

33.   The importance of packaging in a dark market is confirmed by the expert opinions of Professors Dubé and Tavassoli, who explained that Australia's dark market likely *enhances*, rather than diminishes, the ability of tobacco packaging to serve as an effective advertising vehicle.[48] Indeed, absent tobacco plain packaging, the surfaces, shape, size, structure, materials and texture of tobacco packaging[49] could all serve an advertising and promotion function, including through the use of branding, and figurative and design elements.[50]

34.   Based on the complainants' own propositions and evidence, the tobacco plain packaging measure has clearly affected consumer behaviour in ways consistent with the packaging of tobacco products functioning as advertising. For example, the complainants contend that the absence of branded packaging in Australia's dark market has already altered consumers' behaviour by causing "downtrading".[51] According to the complainants' expert, Professor Steenkamp, this has occurred because removing branding reduces consumers' willingness to pay for tobacco products in general, and premium products in particular, and also reduces brand loyalty.[52] Professor Steenkamp opines that tobacco plain packaging "reduces the contribution of branding to the 'intangible benefits' for both premium and value brands" that may be conveyed to consumers, particularly of premium products.[53]

35.   If branded packaging (even with a dominant graphic health warning) has the effect of promoting the "intangible benefits" of a tobacco product, increasing a consumer's willingness to pay for that product, and making consumers more loyal to their brand in the context of Australia's dark market, there is no serious dispute that tobacco packaging functions as advertising. Moreover, if, as the complainants contend, these "intangible benefits" can no longer be conveyed to

---

[46]   Australia's first written submission, Part II.E.2, para. 83, citing Philip Morris, Exhibit AUS-96.

[47]   Australia's first written submission, paras. 83-84, see also Expert Report of A. Biglan, Exhibit AUS-13, paras. 69-75; Expert Report of P. Slovic, Exhibit AUS-12, paras. 60-83; and Expert Report of N. Tavassoli, Exhibit AUS-588, paras. 42-49.

[48]   Australia's opening statement at the second substantive meeting of the Panel, paras. 38-39, citing Expert Report of J.P Dubé, Exhibit AUS-583, Section VI; and Expert Report of N. Tavassoli, Exhibit AUS-588.

[49]   Australia's first written submission, paras. 125-131.

[50]   Australia's response to Panel Question No. 204, paras. 392-399, citing Expert Report of N. Tavassoli, Exhibit AUS-588, paras. 6-8, 20-27

[51]   Australia's second written submission, paras. 409-412.

[52]   Australia's opening statement at the second substantive meeting of the Panel, paras. 41-42, citing Expert Report of J. Steenkamp, Exhibit DOM/HND-14, paras. 96-97.

[53]   Australia's opening statement at the second substantive meeting of the Panel, paras. 40-44, citing Expert Report of J. Steenkamp, Exhibit DOM/HND-14, para. 93.

consumers as a result of tobacco plain packaging, then by their own admission, Australia has eliminated a means of advertising tobacco products.[54]

3. The complainants have failed to refute that tobacco plain packaging is capable of affecting smoking-related behaviours by standardising tobacco products

36. If the Panel is satisfied that the tobacco plain packaging measure has eliminated an avenue for advertising tobacco products, the overwhelming weight of the evidence demonstrating that advertising increases smoking is a sufficient basis for the Panel to conclude that the measure is capable of contributing to Australia's public health objectives and is not unjustifiable.

37. However, and without prejudice to the burden of proof, Australia has advanced a number of other bases upon which the Panel can be satisfied that the measure is apt to contribute to Australia's public health objectives. Each of these core bases of scientific inquiry – namely, behavioural science, marketing, and economics – provides a separate hypothesis "tested and supported by sufficient evidence"[55] for the same conclusion: that by standardising the appearance of retail tobacco packaging and products,[56] the tobacco plain packaging measure is capable of affecting smoking related-behaviours[57] and will contribute to discouraging smoking initiation and relapse, encouraging quitting, and reducing people's exposure to smoke from tobacco products.[58]

(a) Behavioural science

38. The premise of tobacco plain packaging is that by reducing the appeal of tobacco products, increasing the effectiveness of graphic health warnings, and removing the ability of packaging to mislead, tobacco plain packaging will lead to behavioural change.[59] This premise is supported by behavioural psychology,[60] as well as by the complainants' own evidence, which confirms that tobacco plain packaging has reduced the appeal of tobacco products and increased the effectiveness of graphic health warnings,[61] and that these effects were durable.[62]

---

[54] Australia's opening statement at the second substantive meeting of the Panel, para. 42.

[55] Appellate Body Report, *Brazil – Retreaded Tyres*, para. 151.

[56] Australia's second written submission, Part II.C.5(a) and (c).

[57] Australia's first written submission, Part II.I.4; Australia's second written submission, paras. 237-255; Australia's opening statement at the second substantive meeting of the Panel, paras. 34-46.

[58] Australia's opening statement at the second substantive meeting of the Panel, paras. 49-63; Australia's second written submission, paras. 227-236, 444-459 and 476-481.

[59] *Tobacco Plain Packaging Act*, Exhibit AUS-1, section 3.

[60] Australia's first written submission, Part II.I.3; Australia's second written submission, Part III.D.3; Australia's opening statement at the second substantive meeting of the Panel, paras. 49-63.

[61] Australia's opening statement at the second substantive meeting of the Panel, para. 51; Australia's response to Panel Question No. 196, paras. 228-233, citing Expert Report of I. Ajzen et al, Exhibit DOM/IDN-2, Table 1A, p. 22 and Table 2A, p. 26; and Expert Report of I. Ajzen et al, Exhibit DOM/IDN-4, Table 1, p. 6.

39.   As Australia stated at the second substantive meeting of the Panel, these are important concessions on the part of the complainants. By accepting that the measure has reduced the appeal of tobacco products and increased the noticeability of graphic health warnings, the complainants' own experts have confirmed the findings of many of the published studies which were undertaken to investigate the effects of tobacco plain packaging, including experimental evidence.[63] These concessions represent a remarkable evolution from the complainants' early arguments that the body of literature supporting the tobacco plain packaging measure was biased, unpublishable and unavailing.[64] The complainants' own evidence affirms the correctness and utility of at least 50 studies on the Panel record.[65]

40.   Australia has submitted several reports by behavioural experts (including Professor Slovic, Professor Fong, Dr Biglan, and Dr Brandon)[66] that have established that, by reducing the appeal of tobacco products, increasing the effectiveness of graphic health warnings, and reducing the ability of the pack to mislead, the tobacco plain packaging measure will result in behavioural change,[67] such as reduced smoking initiation[68] and relapse, and increased quitting.[69] This evidence is also consistent with the conclusions of Advocate General Kokott of the European Court of Justice in her recently released opinion on tobacco plain packaging,[70] as well as the substantial body of evidence on the

---

[62]   Australia's opening statement at the second substantive meeting of the Panel, para. 51, citing Expert Report of I. Ajzen et al, Exhibit DOM/IDN–2, Table 1A (final column), p. 22 and Table 2A (final column), p. 26.

[63]   Australia's opening statement at the second substantive meeting of the Panel, paras. 65-68, citing, in particular, Thrasher et al, Exhibit AUS-229; and Wakefield et al, Exhibit AUS-149.

[64]   Australia's opening statement at the second substantive meeting of the Panel, paras. 65-67; Australia's comments on responses to Panel Question No. 197, para. 351.

[65]   Australia's opening statement at the second substantive meeting of the Panel, paras. 65-67.

[66]   Australia's first written submission, paras. 78 and 98, citing Expert Report of P. Slovic, Exhibit AUS-12; Expert Report of A. Biglan, Exhibit AUS-13; Expert Report of G. Fong, Exhibit AUS-14; Expert Report of T. Brandon, Exhibit AUS-15; Australia's second written submission, citing Expert Report of A. Biglan, Exhibit AUS-533; Expert Report of G. Fong, Exhibit AUS-531; Expert Report of P. Slovic, Exhibit AUS-532; and Expert Report of T. Brandon, Exhibit AUS-534; Australia's response to Panel Question No. 196, para. 249, citing Expert Report of G. Fong, Exhibit AUS-585.

[67]   Australia's first written submission, Part II.I.3; Australia's second written submission, paras. 452-459; Australia's opening statement at the second substantive meeting of the Panel, paras. 49-63.

[68]   Australia's first written submission, paras. 92-96, 161; Australia's response to Panel Question No. 196, para. 260, citing Expert Reports of P. Slovic, Exhibit AUS-12, paras. 26, 46-51, 60-67, and Exhibit AUS-532, paras. 77-80; Expert Reports of A. Biglan, Exhibit AUS-13, paras. 32-51, 177-178, and Exhibit AUS-533, paras. 6-15; Expert Report of G. Fong, Exhibit AUS-14, paras. 141-179; Expert Report of N. Tavassoli, Exhibit AUS-10, paras. 50-53, 68, 78-85; and Expert Report of J. Samet, Exhibit AUS-7, para. 125; Australia response to Panel Question No. 196, para. 268.

[69]   Australia's first written submission, paras. 97-102, 201-205, citing Expert Report of A. Biglan, Exhibit AUS-13; Australia's opening statement at the second substantive meeting of the Panel, para. 68; Australia's response to Panel Question No. 196, para. 276, citing Expert Reports of T. Brandon, Exhibit AUS-15, and Exhibit AUS-534.

[70]   Australia's comments on responses to Panel Question No. 159, para. 98, citing the Opinion of Advocate General Kokott, Exhibit AUS-608.

effects of tobacco marketing and advertising;[71] and the tobacco industry's own marketing strategies.[72]

41.   In seeking to contest that the tobacco plain packaging measure will alter smoking behaviour through these mechanisms, the complainants have relied principally on the evidence of Professor Ajzen. Professor Ajzen, relying on his own theoretical construct of human behaviour, claims that there is no evidence of the measure's effects moving from appeal through to intentions and then behaviour. In reaching this conclusion, Professor Ajzen ignores the evidence of changes in intentions revealed in post-implementation studies[73] and changes in behaviour revealed in the evidence.[74] Professor Ajzen instead focuses on surveys that are not designed to pick up the effects of the measure on the cohort at which it is primarily directed – youth who have not yet initiated smoking.

42.   Professor Ajzen's view that the appeal of tobacco products is not related to smoking behaviour[75] is contradicted by decades of research on the effects of tobacco marketing on smoking behaviour, the tobacco industry's own internal research, the complainants' own arguments on "downtrading", and, in the words of the Quebec Superior Court, flies "furiously in the face of common sense and normal business practice."[76]

43.   Further, there are many accepted approaches to determining the effect of appeal on behaviour that do not rely on Professor Ajzen's particular theory, including those explained by Professor Slovic,[77] Professor Fong[78] and Dr Biglan[79] in their expert reports for Australia.

44.   The totality of the significant volume of public health literature and experimental evidence, and the opinions of Australia's experts in behavioural psychology, combined with the complainants' own arguments, means there cannot be any serious question that the tobacco plain packaging measure has reduced the appeal of tobacco products and increased the effectiveness of graphic health warnings, and thus that the mechanisms through which the measure is designed to work are in place.

---

[71]   Australia's first written submission, paras. 87-102; Australia's second written submission, paras. 217-236.

[72]   Australia's first written submission, paras. 73-74, 77, 80-83, 85, 95; Australia's second written submission, paras. 221-222, 227-233.

[73]   Australia's first written submission, para. 355, citing Young et al, Exhibit AUS-214.

[74]   Australia's first written submission, para. 202, citing Zacher et al, Exhibit AUS-222; and Zacher et al, Exhibit AUS-223. See also, Expert Report of T. Chipty, Exhibit AUS-591, p. 33, Table 5.

[75]   Powerpoint presentation of I. Ajzen displayed during Dominican Republic's opening statement at the second substantive meeting of the Panel, slide 10.

[76]   Australia's closing statement at the first substantive meeting of the Panel, para. 5 and fn 2.

[77]   Australia's second written submission, paras. 454-455, citing Expert Reports of P. Slovic, Exhibit AUS-12 and Exhibit AUS-532.

[78]   Australia's second written submission, para. 453, citing Expert Report of G. Fong, Exhibit AUS-14.

[79]   Australia's second written submission, para. 456, citing Expert Reports of A. Biglan, Exhibit AUS-13 and Exhibit AUS-533.

45.   Accordingly, behavioural science provides credible hypotheses, tested and supported by sufficient evidence, that demonstrate that the measure will contribute to its public health objectives. The evidence submitted by the complainants on this point has not only failed to rebut Australia's arguments, but has in fact confirmed that the tobacco plain packaging measure is working as intended.

(b)   Marketing

46.   Marketing science also confirms the link between the impact of tobacco plain packaging on product appeal and smoking behaviour.[80] As outlined in paras. 28-35, both Australia and the complainants' marketing experts agree that packaging has the power to influence a consumer's perception of the quality and characteristics of tobacco products.

47.   On this basis, Professor Dubé explained that the adoption of standardised packaging would likely reduce the perceived quality of tobacco products and reduce consumers' willingness to pay for them.[81] His assessment of the likely effects of tobacco plain packaging was confirmed by the findings of the Tracking Survey.[82] Professor Dubé's view is that because tobacco plain packaging reduces the desirability of tobacco brands, and reduces consumers' willingness to pay across all price segments (propositions accepted by the complainants' marketing expert, Professor Steenkamp),[83] there will be a reduction in total primary demand for tobacco products as a result of the measure.

(c)   Economics

48.   Finally, the field of economics offers a straightforward explanation as to why reducing the appeal of tobacco products and increasing the effectiveness of health warnings on tobacco packaging will lead to changes in smoking behaviour.[84] This analysis depends upon three propositions. All three propositions are substantiated by the complainants' own experts.

49.   First, it is agreed between the economic experts that

---

[80]   Australia's first written submission, paras. 55, 70-84; Australia's opening statement at the second substantive meeting of the Panel, paras. 37-46, citing Expert Reports of J.P. Dubé, Exhibit AUS-11 and Exhibit AUS-583; and Expert Reports of M. Katz, Exhibit AUS-18, and Exhibit AUS-584.

[81]   Australia's opening statement at the second substantive meeting of the Panel, para. 59, citing Expert Report of J.P. Dubé, Exhibit AUS-11, paras. 25-37.

[82]   Australia's opening statement at the second substantive meeting of the Panel, para. 51, citing Expert Report of I. Ajzen et al, Exhibit DOM/IDN–2, Table 1A p. 22.

[83]   Australia's opening statement at the second substantive meeting of the Panel, para.60, citing Expert Report of J. Steenkamp, Exhibit DOM/HND-14, paras. 92-93.

[84]   Australia's second written submission, paras. 479-480; Australia's opening statement at the first substantive meeting of the Panel, paras. 61-63.

> if one believes that plain packaging will both reduce the appeal of
> tobacco products and increase their prices, then one does not need
> a model to assess plain packaging's impact ... the conclusion is
> immediate because both of these effects push consumption down.[85]

50.   Second, and as outlined above at paras. 38-41, it is agreed that the 2012 tobacco packaging changes have reduced the appeal of tobacco products as intended by the measure.[86]

51.   Third, it is agreed that since the introduction of tobacco plain packaging, prices for tobacco products have increased.[87] The complainants' expert, Professor Klick, and Australia's expert, Professor Katz, have both considered this phenomenon. Professor Klick's view is that tobacco plain packaging appears to have caused tobacco prices to rise.[88] Professor Katz in his reports has provided a theoretical explanation for why this is so, as well as empirical evidence demonstrating this fact.[89]Thus, where the tobacco plain packaging measure has reduced the appeal of tobacco products, and the price of tobacco products has increased since the measure's introduction, the clear prediction of economics is that demand for tobacco products will fall.

52.   Indeed, a fall in demand is precisely what has been observed in the data. As described above at paras. 14-16 and 19-20, smoking prevalence and tobacco consumption have both fallen since the introduction of the tobacco plain packaging measure. Given the strength of the theoretical underpinning for the measure, it would be perverse to find that *none* of the observed declines in prevalence and consumption since the introduction of tobacco plain packaging are attributable to that measure.

4.   Conclusion

53.   The qualitative evidence strongly supports the conclusion that tobacco plain packaging has made and is capable of making a contribution to Australia's public health objectives. Indeed, the evidence upon which Australia relies in support of the tobacco plain packaging measure "reflects at least the majority view, and potentially the unanimous view" within the international scientific

---

[85]   Australia's comments on responses to Panel Question No. 197, paras. 297-298, citing Expert Report of D. Neven, Exhibit HON-123, para. 73.
[86]   See Australia's first written submission, paras. 148-162; Australia's opening statement at second substantive meeting of the Panel, para. 65.
[87]   Australia's second written submission, para. 412; Australia's response to Panel Question No. 151, para. 42; Australia's comments on response to Panel Question No. 197, paras. 294-298.
[88]   Australia's response to Panel Question No. 151, para. 42, citing Expert Report of J. Klick, Exhibit HND-122, fn 71.
[89]   Australia's comments on response to Panel Question No. 197, paras. 294-298, citing Expert Reports of M. Katz, Exhibit AUS-18, and Exhibit AUS-584.

community.[90] Each of the separate hypotheses outlined above leads to the same conclusion: the tobacco plain packaging measure is apt to contribute to Australia's objectives to improve public health by discouraging initiation of tobacco use; encouraging cessation; discouraging relapse; and reducing people's exposure to tobacco smoke.

B.   **The complainants have failed to establish on the basis of the quantitative evidence before the Panel that the measure is incapable of contributing to its objectives or is unjustifiable**

54.   The post-implementation quantitative evidence is consistent with the substantial body of qualitative evidence in demonstrating that tobacco plain packaging is apt to contribute to Australia's public health objectives.

55.   The fact that smoking prevalence and tobacco consumption have declined to their lowest levels in decades since the introduction of the tobacco plain packaging measure provides quantitative evidence, consistent with the qualitative evidence presented above, that the tobacco plain packaging measure is capable of contributing to reducing smoking behaviour.

56.   In the face of this quantitative evidence, the complainants have, in relation to datasets of varying quality, attempted to isolate the specific effects of Australia's tobacco packaging changes from all of the other tobacco control measures that Australia has adopted. The complainants rely on an asserted inability to demonstrate a positive effect from those changes as evidence that the measure has not contributed and will not contribute to its public health objectives.[91]

57.   In doing so, the complainants disregard the relevant legal and evidentiary standards for assessing the contribution of a measure to its public health objectives.[92] In particular, the complainants' arguments ignore the Appellate Body's findings in *Brazil – Retreaded Tyres* that:

> ... certain complex public health or environmental problems may be tackled only with a comprehensive policy comprising a multiplicity of interacting measures. In the short term, it may prove difficult to isolate the contribution to public health or environmental objectives of one specific measure from those attributable to the other measures that are part of the same

---

[90]   Australia's second written submission, paras. 271-272; Australia's response to Panel Question No. 206; Australia's comments on the complainants' responses to Panel Question No. 206; Panel Report, *US – Clove Cigarettes*, para. 7.401.
[91]   See, e.g. Dominican Republic's response to Panel Question No. 126, para. 273; Honduras' response to Panel Question No. 124, p. 35.
[92]   Australia's second written submission, paras. 434-439.

comprehensive policy. Moreover, the results obtained from certain actions ... can only be evaluated with the benefit of time.[93]

58.   Tobacco plain packaging is clearly such a measure and should be approached in the way recommended by the Appellate Body. The complainants cannot discharge their burden merely by asserting that at this point in time they are unable to isolate the specific effects of the measure in the data.

59.   Further, even if the evidence established that at this point, the measure has had no discernible effect on smoking initiation, quitting, relapse or smoking around others in its first three years of implementation (which it does not), such evidence would be insufficient to establish that the measure is not apt to contribute to its public health objectives in the future. Tobacco plain packaging is a long term public health measure that, for the reasons explained below, will take time for its full effects to become apparent. In addition, the measure's immediate effects may be difficult to isolate in the short term in the datasets that are available. Finally, the complainants' attempts to demonstrate that there is no effect from tobacco plain packaging on smoking behaviour that can be discerned and isolated in the current data sets have failed. The complainants' quantitative evidence is deeply flawed and when these flaws are corrected, the quantitative evidence is consistent with tobacco plain packaging already having an effect.

1.   Tobacco plain packaging is a long term measure

60.   Throughout these proceedings, the complainants have contended that whether or not an effect of the measure can be isolated within the short time since its implementation is dispositive. Contrary to the complainants' arguments,[94] the tobacco plain packaging measure was always expected to have its greatest effects in the long term[95] – a fact explicitly acknowledged at the time of the measure's introduction.[96] This is due to the time required for the cohort of children who have never been exposed to fully-branded tobacco packaging to reach adolescence and therefore to be included in national health surveys; and the nature of tobacco addiction.[97]

61.   In these circumstances, even if the complainants had succeeded in establishing that the measure has had no effect at this point in time (which they have not), this would not be sufficient to discharge the complainants' burden.

---

[93]   Australia's second written submission, para. 436; Appellate Body Report, *Brazil – Retreaded Tyres*, para. 151.
[94]   See, e.g., the Dominican Republic's response to Panel Question No. 126, para. 283; Honduras' response to Panel Question No. 126, p. 37; Indonesia's Response to Panel Question No. 126, para. 77.
[95]   Australia's first written submission, para. 12; Australia's second written submission, paras. 495-499; Australia's opening statement at the second substantive meeting of the Panel, para. 20; Australia's response to Panel Question No. 200, para. 320.
[96]   Australia's first written submission, para. 670, Annexure E, paras. 11-17; Australia's second written submission, paras. 489, 492-505;
[97]   Australia's first written submission, para. 670, Annexure E, para. 12; Australia's second written submission, paras. 495-496.

The complainants must instead establish that not only has the tobacco plain packaging measure not worked to date, it will never work.

2. The immediate effects of the measure may be difficult to discern in the data

62. The complainants' claimed inability to isolate a statistically significant effect on smoking prevalence or tobacco consumption that is attributable to the tobacco plain packaging measure in the short time since the measure's implementation does not in itself establish that the measure is not already working.[98] Time is required for the effects of tobacco control measures, like tobacco plain packaging, to be detected and isolated in the data.[99] As Professor Chaloupka demonstrated, it took four years before statistically significant effects of the introduction of graphic health warnings in Canada could be discerned in the relevant data.[100]

63. As Dr Chipty and Professor Scharfstein explain, there is significant scope for the policy to be working exactly as intended but for its effects to prove difficult to isolate in the data in the short-term.[101] Australia has addressed the complainants' experts' attempts to respond to some aspects of this evidence.[102] In other respects, the complainants and their experts have simply failed to respond at all to the evidence of Australia's experts.[103]

64. The complainants' related contention that the effects of the tobacco plain packaging measure will "wear out" over time is equally unfounded and contrary to the available evidence.[104] The complainants' own evidence establishes that the reduced appeal associated with tobacco plain packaging did not wear out.[105] Further, a number of post-implementation studies reveal that tobacco plain packaging has had certain effects on smoking behaviour, including a significant and *lasting* reduction in smoking at outdoor venues where children are

---

[98] Australia's second written submission, paras. 495-499; Australia's comments on responses to Panel Question No. 197, para. 211, citing Expert Reports of T. Chipty, Exhibit AUS-586, paras. 34-40, and Exhibit AUS-591, paras. 47-52.

[99] Australia's first written submission, Annexure E, paras. 12, 14-15; Australia's second written submission, paras. 492-505; Australia's response to Panel Question No. 200, paras. 319-341.

[100] Australia's first written submission, Annexure E, para. 16; Australia's response to Panel Question No. 126, para. 160, fn 38; Australia's second written submission, para. 497; Australia's response to Panel Question No. 200, paras. 333-335, citing Expert Report of F. Chaloupka, Exhibit AUS-9, paras. 89-96; Australia's comments on responses to Panel Question No. 197, paras. 262-267.

[101] Australia's first written submission, Annexure E, paras. 14-15 and 23-45; Australia's response to Panel Question No. 4, paras. 3-12; Australia's response to Panel Question No. 200, paras. 329-332.

[102] Australia's response to Panel Question No. 200, paras. 329-332.

[103] Australia's comments on responses to Panel Question No. 197, para. 213, fn 341, citing Expert Report of D. Scharfstein, Exhibit AUS-587.

[104] Australia's second written submission, paras. 501-505; Australia's response to Panel Question No. 196, paras. 243-247; Australia's comments on responses to Panel Question No. 197, paras. 377-380; Australia's comments on responses to Panel Question No. 203, paras. 395-400.

[105] Australia's comments on responses to Panel Question No. 203, para. 398.

present.[106] The expert reports of Professors Slovic and Dubé clearly demonstrate that the permanent *absence* of features designed to appeal to consumers and potential consumers does not "wear out" – tobacco packaging does not become more appealing in the continued absence of such features.[107] Professor Chaloupka's evidence establishes that, in fact, the impact of tobacco plain packaging is likely to *grow* over time.[108]

3. The post-implementation quantitative evidence supports the proposition that the measure is working

65. Australia has explained at paras. 56-65 above that a claimed inability to isolate a plain packaging effect in the limited period since the measure's implementation is insufficient to discharge the complainants' legal burden. However, assuming *arguendo* that such a conclusion would be determinative of whether the measure is apt to contribute to its public health objectives, the evidence before the Panel is plainly insufficient to demonstrate that the measure has *in fact* made no contribution to its public health objectives since its introduction. Indeed, properly analysed, the evidence indicates that the measure is already working.

66. In particular, Australia's evidence including that of Dr Chipty shows that the 2012 packaging changes have made a statistically significant contribution to reductions in smoking prevalence and tobacco consumption. Dr Chipty has also demonstrated that small reasoned corrections to the models originally proposed by the complainants produce results showing a statistically significant plain packaging effect.

67. The complainants' experts have responded to this evidence by abandoning the models they originally advocated and creating multiple new models with more restrictive assumptions;[109] making unfounded criticisms of Australia's expert, including criticising her adoption of approaches to the data that they themselves originally endorsed;[110] falsely asserting that Australia has only responded to a narrow subset of the complainants' empirical evidence;[111] and reporting their results in ways that are more restrictive than the approach originally advocated by the complainants earlier in these proceedings.[112]

---

[106] Australia's second written submission, para. 464, citing Zacher et al, Exhibit AUS-223.
[107] Australia's second written submission, paras. 502-504; Australia's comments on responses to Panel Question No. 203, para. 398.
[108] Australia's comments on responses to Panel Question No. 197, para. 380.
[109] Australia's opening statement at the second substantive meeting of the Panel, paras. 105-108; Australia's response to Panel Question No. 196, paras. 185, 188-220; Australia's comments on responses to Panel Question No. 197, paras. 229-233, 238-244, 245-247.
[110] Australia's comments on responses to Panel Question No. 197, paras. 223-54.
[111] Australia's comment on response to Panel Question No. 197, paras. 220-225.
[112] Australia's opening statement at the second substantive meeting of the Panel, paras. 90-104; Australia's comments on responses to Panel Question No. 197, paras. 255-261.

4. Conclusion

68. Accordingly, the complainants have no credible basis for asserting that they have demonstrated on the basis of "consistent and clear" evidence that the tobacco plain packaging measure has "not worked" and will not work in the future.[113] Rather, the quantitative data upon which the complainants rely are entirely consistent with the measure having contributed to reducing smoking prevalence and tobacco consumption in the limited period since its implementation. The assessment of the available post-implementation quantitative data thus confirms that the complainants have failed to discharge their burden of establishing that the tobacco plain packaging measure has not contributed and is not apt to contribute to its objectives.

IV. THE COMPLAINANTS HAVE FAILED TO DEMONSTRATE THAT THE TOBACCO PLAIN PACKAGING MEASURE IS INCONSISTENT WITH THE TRIPS AGREEMENT

69. The complainants' claims under the TRIPS Agreement are based on interpretations of the relevant provisions that find no basis in the ordinary meaning of these provisions, properly interpreted in their context and in light of the object and purpose of the Agreement. Rather, their claims are based on theories of "interests" that supposedly "pervade" the TRIPS Agreement, and on attempts to rewrite various provisions of the TRIPS Agreement to create rights and obligations that do not exist in the text itself.

A. The complainants have failed to demonstrate that the measure is inconsistent with Article 20 of the TRIPS Agreement

70. The complainants have failed to establish a *prima facie* case that the tobacco plain packaging measure imposes "special requirements" that "encumber" the "use of a trademark in the course of trade". In particular, the complainants have failed to demonstrate how any special requirements imposed by the measure encumber the use of a trademark to distinguish the goods or services of one undertaking from those of other undertakings in the course of trade and have therefore failed to demonstrate the threshold applicability of Article 20. Even if the complainants have established a *prima facie* case of applicability, they have failed to demonstrate that any encumbrance imposed by the tobacco plain packaging measure has been imposed "unjustifiably".

---

[113] Australia's comments on responses to Panel Question No. 197, paras. 257, 259-261.

1. **The complainants have failed to establish that the measure encumbers by special requirements the use of trademarks in the course of trade**

(a) **The relevant "use" of a trademark under Article 20 of the TRIPS Agreement is the use of a trademark to distinguish the goods or services of one undertaking from those of other undertakings**

71.   All parties appear to agree that, to establish a violation of Article 20, a complainant must demonstrate that any special requirements imposed by the measure at issue "encumber" the "use" of a trademark in the course of trade. The parties further appear to agree that Article 15.1 of the TRIPS Agreement provides the basis for identifying the relevant "use" of a trademark under Article 20;[114] and that this "use" is the use of a trademark to distinguish the goods or services of one undertaking from those of other undertakings.[115] To demonstrate that a measure encumbers the "use" of a trademark in the course of trade under Article 20, a complainant must therefore demonstrate that the measure encumbers the use of a trademark "to *distinguish* the goods or services of one undertaking from those of other undertakings".

72.   Until the second substantive meeting of the Panel, however, the parties appeared to disagree on what it means for trademarks to "distinguish" the goods of one undertaking from those of other undertakings. The complainants argued that the relevant "use" of a trademark under Article 20 also encompasses the use of a trademark to "distinguish" products "in terms of their quality, characteristics, and reputation".[116] This proposition has no interpretative foundation. Nothing in the text of Article 15.1 refers to the use of trademarks to distinguish products in terms of their "quality, characteristics, and reputation", or even implies such a use. Rather, the formula is taken from a *different* section of the TRIPS Agreement – Section 3 – which pertains to geographical indications.[117]

73.   In an evolution of their position,[118] the complainants now appear to accept Australia's understanding of which "use" of a trademark is relevant under Article 20 and which "uses" are not. While the complainants' formula of

---

[114] See Dominican Republic's first written submission, para. 248; Indonesia's first written submission, para. 132; Honduras' first written submission, para. 155; Cuba's response to Panel Question No. 87.

[115] Australia's second written submission, para. 86.

[116] Dominican Republic's first written submission, paras. 14, 240; Dominican Republic's response to Panel Question No. 87, para. 4; Honduras' first written submission, para. 144; Indonesia's response to Panel Question No. 87, para. 2.

[117] Australia's second written submission, paras. 97-103; Australia's comments on the complainants' responses to Panel Question Nos. 167 and 168, para. 127.

[118] See in particular the Dominican Republic's opening statement at the second substantive meeting of the Panel, para. 7; the Dominican Republic's response to Panel Question No. 167; Australia's comments on responses to Panel Question Nos. 167 and 168, paras. 127-129.

"quality, characteristics, and reputation" appeared to be simply a euphemism for the use of trademarks to advertise and promote tobacco products,[119] in the course of the proceedings the complainants recharacterised their notion of "quality, characteristics, and reputation", as referring to the "consistency" function of trademarks.[120] The parties now appear to agree that it is the ability of a trademark to convey a *consistency* of quality, rather than any particular *perceived* quality ("high quality", "value", "masculine", "feminine", etc.) that may be relevant to the source distinguishing function of trademarks described by Article 15.1 of the TRIPS Agreement.

(b)   The use of trademarks to advertise and promote the trademarked product is not a relevant "use" of trademarks under Article 20 of the TRIPS Agreement

74.   In addition to distinguishing the products of one undertaking from those of other undertakings, it is widely recognised that trademarks serve an advertising function by conveying certain associations with the trademarked product.[121] Particularly in the case of a largely undifferentiated consumer product like tobacco products, trademark owners carefully calibrate the associations conveyed by the trademark to appeal to different market segments.[122]

75.   While the use of trademarks to advertise and promote a product is an acknowledged function of trademarks, no party (or third party) has advanced an argument as to why this should be considered a relevant "use" of trademarks under Article 20. It therefore appears to be common ground that limiting the use of trademarks to increase the perceived appeal of tobacco products is not an "encumbrance" upon the use of trademarks that falls within the scope of Article 20. It follows that evidence pertaining to such a limitation, at which the tobacco plain packaging measure is directed, is not relevant to establishing a *prima facie* case of inconsistency under this provision.

(c)   The complainants have not even attempted to demonstrate that the tobacco plain packaging measure encumbers the relevant use of trademarks in the course of trade

76.   The existence of an encumbrance is an *evidentiary* question. While the complainants have placed massive quantities of expert evidence on the record of

---

[119]   Australia's second written submission, para. 118; Australia's comments on responses to Panel Question Nos. 167 and 168, para. 128.

[120]   Dominican Republic's opening statement at the second substantive meeting of the Panel, para. 7; Australia's comments on the complainants' responses to Panel Question Nos. 167 and 168, para. 130.

[121]   Australia's second written submission, para. 91. See also Expert Report of N. Tavassoli, Exhibit AUS-10, para. 34.

[122]   See Expert Report of N. Tavassoli, Exhibit AUS-10, Sections 2.1-2.4; Australia's first written submission, paras. 71-82, 85-86, and exhibits cited therein.

this dispute, including commissioning numerous studies and empirical analyses specifically for these proceedings, they have failed to adduce any relevant evidence.[123] In particular, they have offered no evidence at all that any special requirements established by the tobacco plain packaging measure encumber the use of trademarks to distinguish the tobacco products of one undertaking from those of other undertakings – even in response to the Panel's specific question asking them to identify such evidence.[124] The complainants' inability to identify any empirical evidence to support this contention, which is a key element of their claim under Article 20, is also notable in the light of their insistence that the Panel focus exclusively on post-implementation empirical evidence to assess the effectiveness of the tobacco plain packaging measure.[125]

77.   Absent such empirical evidence, the Dominican Republic and Indonesia fall back on their arguments concerning "downtrading" as "evidence" that the permitted use of brand and variant names on retail tobacco packaging does not "adequately distinguish commercial source, quality, characteristics, and reputation."[126] However, the complainants' downtrading theory is based on the inability of tobacco companies to use figurative elements and other design features to create *perceived* differences between "premium" and "value" brands.[127] As all parties agree, the use of trademarks to advertise and promote a product (e.g. by creating perceptions or positive associations with the product) is not part of the source distinguishing function of trademarks protected under Article 20. The complainants' downtrading assertions, even if proven, therefore in no way discharge their task of demonstrating that the tobacco plain packaging measure encumbers the source distinguishing function of a trademark.[128]

78.   In the absence of any evidence, the complainants essentially argue that because Article 15.1 of the TRIPS Agreement provides that "[a]ny sign, or any combination of signs", including "figurative elements and combinations of colours", shall be "eligible for registration as trademarks", any limitation on the use of colours, figurative elements, and other signs that are eligible for registration as trademarks constitutes an encumbrance on the capability to

---

[123]   Australia's second written submission, paras. 121-128; Australia's comments on responses to Panel Question Nos. 167 and 168, paras. 133-136, 141; Dominican Republic's response to Panel Question No. 206, para. 313; Honduras' response to Panel Question No. 206; Cuba's response to Panel Question No. 206.

[124]   See Dominican Republic's response to Panel Question No. 167, para. 185; Cuba's response to Panel Question No. 168; Honduras' response to Panel Question No. 168; and Indonesia's response to Panel Question No. 168, paras. 32-34.

[125]   Australia's comments on responses to Panel Question Nos. 167 and 168, paras. 136; Dominican Republic's response to Panel Question No. 206, para. 313; Honduras' response to Panel Question No. 206; Cuba's response to Panel Question No. 206.

[126]   Dominican Republic's response to Panel Question No. 167, para. 185; Indonesia's response to Panel Question No. 168, para. 31.

[127]   See para. 33 above; Expert Report of J. Steenkamp, Exhibit DR-HON-5, paras. 62, 64; Dominican Republic's response to Panel Question No. 169, para. 194.

[128]   Australia's comments on responses to Panel Question Nos. 167 and 168, paras. 137-138.

distinguish the goods of one undertaking from those of other undertakings.[129] Such an argument in no way discharges the complainants' burden of demonstrating that any special requirements established by the tobacco plain packaging measure encumber the use of a trademark to distinguish the products of one undertaking from those of another in the course of trade.[130]

2. Article 20 does not encompass the prohibitive elements of the tobacco plain packaging measure

79.   Article 20 of the TRIPS Agreement does not encompass the aspects of the tobacco plain packaging measure which prohibit the use of trademarks on tobacco packaging and products. Properly interpreted in context, Article 20 concerns special requirements that encumber *how* a trademark may be used when municipal law otherwise permits the use of trademarks.[131] A contrary interpretation of Article 20 has the potential to bring within its scope a variety of measures that, in Australia's view, were never intended to be covered by the TRIPS Agreement, such as advertising restrictions and point-of-sale restrictions.[132] The complainants appear to agree with Australia that Article 20 was not meant to cover these types of measures,[133] arguing that the term "special requirements" does not encompass measures that only "incidentally" affect the use of trademarks.[134] It is on this basis that the complainants seek to explain the application of Article 20 to the tobacco plain packaging measure, but not to other measures. The complainants have provided no interpretative basis for this distinction.[135] All third parties that address this issue agree that there is no basis for the distinction.[136] Nor can the complainants articulate how such a distinction would operate in practice.

---

[129] Dominican Republic's first written submission, paras. 365-366; Dominican Republic's response to Panel Question No. 167, para. 170; Honduras' responses to Panel Question Nos. 87 and 168; Cuba's response to Panel Question No. 87; Indonesia's response to Panel Question No. 87.

[130] Australia's comments on responses to Panel Question Nos. 167 and 168, paras. 139-141.

[131] Australia's first written submission, paras. 338-345.

[132] Australia's second written submission, paras. 132-139.

[133] See Honduras' opening statement at the first substantive meeting of the Panel, para. 27. See also Dominican Republic's opening statement at the first substantive meeting of the Panel, para. 16.

[134] See Dominican Republic's response to Panel Question No. 38; see also Indonesia's response to Panel Question No. 38; Honduras' response to Panel Question No. 38.

[135] See, e.g. Dominican Republic's response to Panel Question No. 95; Dominican Republic's opening statement at the first substantive meeting of the Panel, paras. 15-17; Honduras' response to Panel Question No. 38; Honduras' opening statement at the first substantive meeting of the Panel, paras. 23-26; Indonesia's response to Panel Question Nos. 95, 96. See Australia's first written submission, para. 341; Australia's response to Panel Question No. 38; Australia's second written submission, paras. 134-142; Australia's comments on responses to Panel Question No. 172, paras. 155-159.

[136] See also Norway's third party response to Panel Question No. 13; South Africa's third party response to Panel Question No. 13; Chinese Taipei's third party response to Panel Question No. 13; New Zealand's third party response to Panel Question No. 13; Canada's third party response to Panel Question No. 13.

80.   However, assuming *arguendo* that the special requirements include both the prohibitive and permissive aspects of the measure, and considering the tobacco plain packaging measure as a whole, the fact remains that the complainants have failed to adduce any evidence to demonstrate that the measure encumbers the ability of the permitted word mark, in a standardised form, to distinguish the product of one undertaking from those of other undertakings.[137]

3.   The complainants' interpretation of the term "unjustifiably" is unfounded

81.   Even if the Panel were to find that the complainants have proven that the tobacco plain packaging measure encumbers by special requirements a relevant use of trademarks in the course of trade, the complainants have failed to prove that Australia has imposed this encumbrance "unjustifiably".

82.   All parties appear to agree that, in order to be found not "unjustifiable", the encumbrance must be imposed in pursuit of a *legitimate objective*.[138] The legitimacy of Australia's public health objectives has not been questioned in this dispute. All parties also appear to agree that, in order to be found not "unjustifiable", there must be a *nexus* between the encumbrance imposed by the special requirements and its legitimate objective,[139] and this connection must be one that is rational or reasonable.

83.   However, the Dominican Republic, Honduras, Cuba and a minority of the third parties believe that in order to be found not "unjustifiable", the encumbrance must be the *least-restrictive option available* to accomplish the Member's legitimate objective, in light of *reasonably available alternatives* that would make an equal or greater degree of contribution to the fulfilment of that objective while imposing a lesser degree of encumbrance upon the use of trademarks[140] – a test that is functionally equivalent to a standard of "necessity". Further, the complainants argue that any interpretation of the term "unjustifiably" must take into account "the nature of trademarks and trademark protection". It is on this basis that the complainants argue that Australia was required to undertake an "individualised assessment" of the "specific features" of particular trademarks.

---

[137] Australia's first written submission, para. 344; Australia's second written submission, para. 213 and fn. 211.

[138] Australia's first written submission, para. 366; Dominican Republic's first written submission, para. 743; Honduras' first written submission, para. 296; Cuba's first written submission, paras. 319-320; Indonesia's response to Panel Question No. 108.

[139] Australia's first written submission, paras. 370-383; Dominican Republic's first written submission, para. 388; Honduras' first written submission, para. 296; Cuba's first written submission, paras. 317-318; Indonesia's response to Panel Question No. 108.

[140] See, e.g. Honduras' response to Panel Question No. 108; Dominican Republic's first written submission, para. 743; Cuba's first written submission, paras. 356-362.

(a)   The term "unjustifiably" requires a rational connection between any encumbrance upon the use of trademarks resulting from the measure and the pursuit of a legitimate objective

84.   The ordinary meaning of the term "unjustifiably" focuses on the rationality or reasonableness of the connection between the encumbrance imposed by a measure and the measure's legitimate public policy objective.[141] Under a rational connection standard, the relevant inquiry is whether the complainants have shown that the relationship between the encumbrance imposed by the measure and the measure's objective is not one that is within the range of rational or reasonable outcomes.[142]

85.   All parties appear to agree that an encumbrance that "goes against" or "cannot be reconciled with" its objective is one that is neither rational nor reasonable.[143] There is no credible evidence or argument before the Panel that the tobacco plain packaging measure will undermine its public health objectives and the complainants abandoned this argument at the first hearing.[144] In order to prove a violation of Article 20, the complaining Member must demonstrate that the responding Member has "*unjustifiably* encumbered" the use of a trademark in the course of trade.[145] As with any affirmative obligation, it is the complaining Member that bears the burden of proving that the obligation has been violated.[146] Thus, the complainants must demonstrate that any encumbrance imposed by the measure is incapable of contributing to its objectives in order to discharge their burden of proof.[147]

(b)   The term "unjustifiably" is not functionally equivalent to a standard of "necessity"

86.   The majority of the third parties agree with Australia that the term "unjustifiably" requires an evaluation of the rationality or reasonableness of the relationship between the encumbrance and its objective, and that this term cannot be understood as equivalent to a standard of "necessity".[148] And yet, the

---

[141]   See Australia's first written submission, paras. 370-383.

[142]   Australia's second written submission, para. 149.

[143]   Dominican Republic's first written submission, para. 737; Honduras' first written submission, para. 297; Cuba's first written submission, para. 319; Indonesia's first written submission, para. 360; Australia's response to Panel Question No. 105, paras. 62-66; Australia's second written submission, para. 150.

[144]   Expert Report of J. List, Exhibit DR/IND-1, para. 16. See also Expert Report of J. Klick, Exhibit HON-118, fn 24; cited in Australia's second written submission, para. 150.

[145]   See, e.g. Dominican Republic's response to Panel Question No. 104, para. 113; Australia's second written submission, paras. 156-157.

[146]   See Australia's first written submission, paras. 427-430; Australia's second written submission, paras. 154-157.

[147]   Australia's second written submission, para. 151.

[148]   See New Zealand's third party written submission, paras. 61-63; Singapore's third party written submission, paras. 52-53; Norway's third party written submission, para. 59; Uruguay's third party written submission, paras. 52-53; Argentina's third party written submission, para. 10; European

complainants have treated their analysis of whether the tobacco plain packaging measure is "unjustifiable" under Article 20 of the TRIPS Agreement as essentially interchangeable with their analysis of whether the measure is "more trade-restrictive than necessary" under Article 2.2 of the TBT Agreement. Such an approach ignores the ordinary meaning of the term "unjustifiable" and represents an attempt by the complainants to rewrite Article 20 to say something that it does not.

i.   The term "unjustifiably" does not require a "weighing and balancing" analysis

87.   The relevant inquiry under a proper interpretation of the term "unjustifiably" is whether there is a rational relationship between the encumbrance imposed by the measure and the pursuit of a legitimate public policy objective, rather than a relational analysis of various factors that are more appropriately considered within the context of a "necessity" analysis.[149]

88.   The *Declaration on the TRIPS Agreement and Public Health* serves to underscore that the term "unjustifiably" in Article 20 provides Members with a wide degree of latitude to implement measures to protect public health and, unlike the term "necessary", contemplates a range of possible outcomes that are "able to be shown to be just, reasonable, or correct" or that are "within the limits of reason". In this relevant context, it is not a panel's function to "weigh and balance" the considerations, including public health considerations, that the Member took into account when crafting the measure at issue in order to substitute the panel's own assessment for that of the implementing Member.[150] Rather, the panel's function is to evaluate whether the complaining Member has demonstrated that an encumbrance upon the use of trademarks resulting from the measure at issue is "unjustifiable".

ii.   The term "unjustifiably" does not impose a standard of "least restrictiveness"

89.   Interpreting the term "unjustifiably" to include a requirement of "least restrictiveness" would render this term functionally equivalent to a standard of "necessity".[151] The term "necessary" requires an evaluation of whether the measure at issue was the least restrictive means of accomplishing the Member's legitimate objective in light of other reasonably-available alternative measures that would have made an equal or greater degree of contribution to that objective.[152] The fact that Article 20 does not use the term "necessary", which

---

Union's third party written submission, paras. 24-37; China's third party written submission, para. 49; Japan's third party written submission, para. 19.

[149]   Australia's first written submission, paras. 384-408; Australia's response to Panel Question No. 105, paras. 65-66; Australia's second written submission, paras. 159-164.

[150]   Australia's second written submission, para. 163.

[151]   Australia's first written submission, paras. 396-408.

[152]   Australia's second written submission, para. 167.

had a well-established meaning in the GATT *acquis* prior to the Uruguay Round,[153] as the basis for its standard of justification must be given interpretative effect,[154] and indicates that Article 20 does not impose a requirement of "least restrictiveness".

90.   The complainants' argument that the term "unjustifiably" should be interpreted to impose a requirement of "least restrictiveness" is based on a contextual argument. In essence, the complainants argue that because trademark owners have a "legitimate interest" in using their trademarks under Article 17 of the TRIPS Agreement or a "protected treaty interest" in the use of trademarks, the term "unjustifiably" in Article 20 must be interpreted to encompass a requirement of "least restrictiveness".[155]

iii.   The context of Article 17

91.   The complainants have offered no explanation for why the context provided by Article 17 would require the Panel to read the requirements of that provision into Article 20. The contextual relevance of Article 17 to the interpretation of Article 20 is primarily by way of contrast.[156] It is contextually significant that the TRIPS Agreement does not address encumbrances upon the use of trademarks as "exceptions" to the "rights conferred" by a trademark. This confirms that the TRIPS Agreement does not confer upon trademark owners a right to use their trademarks, as the parties have now agreed.[157] Furthermore, the fact that Article 20 does not require Members to "take into account the legitimate interests of the owner of the trademark", in contrast to Article 17, strongly suggests that the drafters of the TRIPS Agreement did not consider this to be a relevant or necessary requirement in the case of measures that impose an encumbrance upon the use of a trademark.[158]

92.   The obligation in Article 17 – to "take account of" the "legitimate interests" of trademark owners when establishing exceptions to the rights of exclusion conferred by a trademark – is a limited affirmative obligation and does not mean that a Member must not prejudice those legitimate interests.[159] It provides no basis for the complainants' argument that a trademark owner's legitimate interest is an "interest" that must be "pervasive" in the interpretation

---

[153]   Australia's first written submission, para. 392; Australia's second written submission, para. 168.
[154]   See Australia's first written submission, para. 394 and fn 575; Australia's second written submission, paras. 169-171.
[155]   Australia's second written submission, para. 172.
[156]   See Australia's response to Panel Question No. 99; Australia's second written submission, paras. 179-185.
[157]   Australia's second written submission, para. 180; See, however, Cuba's response to Panel Question No. 99.
[158]   Australia's second written submission, para. 182; See also, e.g. Singapore's third party written submission, para. 49; New Zealand's third party response to Panel Question No. 14; Canada's third party response to Panel Question No. 14; Norway's third party response to Panel Question No. 14.
[159]   Australia's second written submission, para. 184.

of the Agreement's trademark provisions.[160] If anything, it is the *absence* of a comparable obligation in Article 20 that provides the more relevant context for the interpretation of the term "unjustifiably".

iv. "Protected Treaty Interest"

93. In a closely related argument, the complainants refer to the use of trademarks as a "protected treaty interest" or "protected interest" and suggest that because the drafters of the TRIPS Agreement chose to "protect" this "interest" in Article 20, this provision must be interpreted to require the least possible intrusion upon the use of trademarks.[161]

94. This approach is not supported by a proper interpretation of Article 20 in accordance with the Vienna Convention. It is neither based on the context of Article 20 nor on a consideration of the object and purpose of the TRIPS Agreement. The object and purpose of the TRIPS Agreement is to promote the "effective and adequate protection of intellectual property *rights*".[162] All parties agree that these rights do not include a "right" to use trademarks.

95. The obligation set forth in Article 20 of the TRIPS Agreement is that Members may not encumber by special requirements the use of trademarks in the course of trade "unjustifiably".[163] For the reasons that Australia has explained, the term "unjustifiably", properly interpreted, is not equivalent to a standard of "necessity" and does not impose a requirement of "least restrictiveness". The complainants' arguments about "protected treaty interests", whatever their interpretative relevance, do not support a different conclusion.

v. The jurisprudence under the chapeau to Article XX

96. Finally, the complainants' reliance on prior panel and Appellate Body reports interpreting the chapeau to Article XX of the GATT 1994 to support their interpretation of the term "unjustifiably" are based on misguided analogies between Article XX of the GATT 1994 and Article 20 of the TRIPS Agreement.

97. The jurisprudence concerning the meaning of the term "unjustifiable" in the chapeau to Article XX of the GATT 1994 confirms that the term "unjustifiably" concerns the rationality or reasonableness of the connection between the encumbrance and its objective.[164] The complainants, on the other hand, have sought to find support in this jurisprudence for their contention that the ordinary meaning of the term "unjustifiably" is equivalent to a standard of

---

[160] *Ibid.*
[161] See, e.g. Dominican Republic's response to Panel Question Nos. 108 and 89, para. 26; Indonesia's response to Panel Question No. 99.
[162] Australia's second written submission, para. 187.
[163] Australia's second written submission, para. 193.
[164] Australia's second written submission, paras. 195, 199.

"necessity".[165]   Article 20 of the TRIPS Agreement is not an exceptions provision, and there is no basis to transpose the structure and functions of Article XX of the GATT 1994 into Article 20 of the TRIPS Agreement, as the Dominican Republic argues. The term "unjustifiably" in Article 20 of the TRIPS Agreement does not take on a different meaning merely because it stands by itself, whereas it is only one element of the legal inquiry under a different and unrelated provision of the covered agreements.[166] Moreover, the examples that the complainants cite in support of their arguments that a measure must be the "least-restrictive" in order to be "not unjustifiable" reflect the application by panels and the Appellate Body of the *entire* standard set forth in the chapeau, i.e. "a means of arbitrary or unjustifiable discrimination between countries where the same conditions prevail, or a disguised restriction on international trade".[167]

(c)   The term "unjustifiably" does not require an "individualised assessment"

98.   The complainants, the Dominican Republic in particular, argue that any interpretation of the term "unjustifiably" must take into account "the nature of trademarks and trademark protection",[168] as the basis for the assertion that the term "unjustifiably" requires an "individualised assessment" of the "specific features" of individual trademarks, at least in some cases.[169]

99.   The Dominican Republic's "individualised assessment" argument has no interpretative basis. The Dominican Republic has made clear that the foundation for its argument is its theory of "legitimate interests",[170] which Australia has already refuted at paras. 91-92 above, rather than the ordinary meaning of the term "unjustifiably". The Dominican Republic has not identified anything in the context of Article 20 or in the object and purpose of the TRIPS Agreement that would support this asserted requirement.[171]

100.   The Dominican Republic's "individualised assessment" argument appears to be based on the proposition that because trademarks are registered and enforced on an individual basis, it follows that any encumbrance upon the use of trademarks must be justified on an individual basis, at least if the rationale for the encumbrance relates to the "specific features" of trademarks.[172] Contrary to the Dominican Republic's assertions, the panel's findings in *EC – Trademarks*

---

[165]   See, e.g. Dominican Republic's opening statement at the first substantive meeting of the Panel, paras. 49-50; Australia's second written submission, para. 196.

[166]   Australia's second written submission, para. 197.

[167]   Australia's second written submission, para. 198.

[168]   Dominican Republic's response to Panel Question No. 89, para. 25; Dominican Republic's opening statement at the first substantive meeting of the Panel, paras. 27-29.

[169]   Dominican Republic's response to Panel Question Nos. 99, para. 69, and 108, paras. 127-131; Honduras also makes this argument: see Honduras' first written submission, paras. 289-291, 309.

[170]   Dominican Republic's response to Panel Question No. 99, para. 69.

[171]   Australia's second written submission, para. 201.

[172]   Australia's second written submission, para. 202.

and Geographical Indications (US) provide no support for this approach. The panel found that even though the regulation at issue required a case-by-case analysis of the geographical indication at the time of registration, "nothing in the text of Article 17 indicates that a case-by-case analysis is a requirement under the TRIPS Agreement."[173]

101. Further, an entire *category* of trademarks might possess some feature that is relevant to the objective of a measure covered by Article 20. Nothing in Article 20 of the TRIPS Agreement implies that any sort of "individualised assessment" is required, under *any* circumstance. Whether or not a measure covered by Article 20 is "unjustifiable" will depend upon the rationale of the measure as it relates to the affected category of trademarks as a whole.[174]

      i.   The complainants' "individualised assessment" argument is based on a misunderstanding or mischaracterisation of the manner in which the tobacco plain packaging measure operates

102. The premise of the complainants' "individualised assessment" argument is that the concern underlying the tobacco plain packaging measure is that there are "specific features" of particular trademarks that increase the appeal of tobacco products, detract from the effectiveness of graphic health warnings, and mislead consumers as to the harms of tobacco use. The complainants appear to believe that the term "unjustifiably" requires Australia to identify every trademark used in Australia in connection with tobacco products, and then evaluate each trademark against a set of criteria that would allow Australia to determine whether or not that particular trademark implicates Australia's public health concerns.[175]

103. The premise of the complainants' argument is incorrect. The premise of the tobacco plain packaging measure is not that "specific features" of particular trademarks increase the appeal of tobacco products, detract from the effectiveness of graphic health warnings, or mislead consumers as to the harms of tobacco use. The premise of the tobacco plain packaging measure is that requiring a standardised, plain appearance for retail tobacco packaging eliminates, or at least significantly curtails, the ability of tobacco companies to use the package as a vehicle for advertising and promoting the product, which in turn reduces the appeal of tobacco products, increases the effectiveness of graphic health warnings and reduces the ability of the package to mislead. This goal has nothing to do with the "specific features" of trademarks and, instead, has "everything to do with features of the product inside the packaging", namely

---

[173] Panel Report, *EC – Trademarks and Geographical Indications (US)*, para. 7.672 (emphasis added), cited in Australia's second written submission, para. 202.
[174] Australia's second written submission, para. 203-204.
[175] Australia's second written submission, para. 288.

that it is a consumer product that is uniquely hazardous to human health. Allowing tobacco companies to use figurative elements and other non-standardised design elements on the package can only serve to increase the appeal of the package relative to a package design that does not permit the use of these elements.[176]

104.   The Dominican Republic concedes that no "individualised assessment" is required when the measure does not seek to address concerns about the "specific features" of trademarks, even under its erroneous interpretation of the term "unjustifiably".[177]

105.   For these reasons, no purpose would be served by examining the "specific features" of particular trademarks because those features in isolation are irrelevant to the policy decision to require all tobacco products to be sold in a standardised, plain package.[178] The complainants' "individualised assessment" argument therefore provides no basis for finding that the tobacco plain packaging measure is "unjustifiable".[179]

4.   The complainants have failed to prove that any encumbrance resulting from the measure is "unjustifiable"

(a)   By requiring a standardised, plain appearance for tobacco products and packaging, the measure contributes to its objective of improving public health

106.   The tobacco plain packaging measure lays out detailed requirements that specify the standardised, plain appearance of tobacco products and retail packaging, including by prohibiting the use of *all* signs, whether or not any of those signs are also trademarks. The measure prohibits the use of trademarks (other than trademarked brand and variant names) not because they are trademarks, but because the use of these signs would re-introduce opportunities for advertising and promoting the product. At the same time, the measure permits the use of brand and variant names in a standardised format because these particular signs distinguish the tobacco products of one undertaking from those of other undertakings. The tobacco plain packaging measure thus reduces the ability of tobacco companies to use retail tobacco packaging to advertise and promote tobacco products, while preserving the ability of tobacco companies to use trademarks to distinguish their products from those of other undertakings.[180]

107.   The "encumbrance" upon the use of trademarks, if any, that the Panel must evaluate in relation to a legal standard of "unjustifiability" is necessarily an "encumbrance" that results from the special requirements just described. As

---

[176]   Australia's second written submission, paras. 289-294; 296-298.
[177]   Dominican Republic's response to Panel Question No. 108, paras. 133-134.
[178]   Australia's second written submission, para. 295.
[179]   Australia's second written submission, para. 299.
[180]   Australia's second written submission, para. 210-212.

explained above, Australia does not consider that the prohibitive aspects of the tobacco plain packaging measure are "special requirements" that are encompassed by Article 20 of the TRIPS Agreement.[181] However, assuming, *arguendo,* that the special requirements at issue include both the permissive and prohibitive aspects of the measure relating to the use of trademarks, the issue before the Panel is whether the complainants have demonstrated that any encumbrance resulting from these special requirements, when viewed as a whole,[182] is "unjustifiable". Even if the use of trade marks to advertise and promote a product were encompassed by "use" within the meaning of Article 20, the complainants have failed to prove that it is "unjustifiable" for Australia to encumber the use of trademarks to advertise and promote tobacco products.

(b)   The evidence on the record demonstrates that encumbering the use of trademarks to advertise and promote tobacco products is capable of contributing to the measure's objectives

108.   Without prejudice to the burden of proof, Australia has outlined significant evidence at Part III above, including reports of eminent public health institutions such as the United States Surgeons General, the WHO, the United States National Cancer Institute, and the United States Institute of Medicine, which clearly demonstrates that the tobacco plain packaging measure, and any encumbrance it imposes, *is* capable of contributing to its public health objectives. This evidence shows that: (i) there is a clear link between advertising and smoking-related behaviours; (ii) retail packaging is a recognised form of advertising and promotion, and also affects smoking-related behaviours; and (iii) because retail tobacco packaging represents a medium for advertising and promoting tobacco products, the restriction of the advertising and promotional use of trademarks on retail tobacco packaging is capable of affecting smoking-related behaviours, just as other restrictions on tobacco advertising and promotion have been shown to do.[183]

109.   Therefore, there is clearly a rational connection between any encumbrance imposed by the tobacco plain packaging measure and its public health objectives.

(c)   The complainants have failed to show that any encumbrance upon the use of trademarks resulting from the measure is not capable of contributing to its objectives

110.   The complainants bear the burden of demonstrating that any encumbrance upon the use of trademarks in the course of trade resulting from the tobacco plain packaging measure is "unjustifiable". Having abandoned the

---

[181]   See para. 78 above.
[182]   Australia's second written submission, para. 213 and fn. 211, citing Appellate Body Report, *EC – Asbestos,* para. 64; Appellate Body Report, *EC – Seal Products,* para. 5.193.
[183]   Australia's second written submission, paras. 159-178.

proposition at the first substantive meeting of the Panel that the tobacco plain packaging measure would "backfire" or "go against" its objectives, i.e. that it would lead to an *increase* in tobacco prevalence and consumption, the complainants therefore bear the burden of demonstrating that any encumbrance upon the use of trademarks resulting from the tobacco plain packaging measure is not capable of contributing to the measure's legitimate public health objectives. As Australia has demonstrated at Part III above, the complainants have failed to discharge this burden.

5.   Conclusion

111.   The complainants have failed to show that the tobacco plain packaging measure is inconsistent with Article 20 of the TRIPS Agreement. The complainants have failed to show that the measure encumbers by special requirements the relevant "use" of a trademark to distinguish the goods of one undertaking from those of other undertakings in the course of trade, and have therefore failed to establish the threshold applicability of Article 20. The use of trademarks to advertise and promote tobacco products is not a relevant "use" of trademarks under Article 20. Any encumbrance upon this use is therefore irrelevant to establishing the applicability of Article 20.

112.   The complainants have failed to provide a coherent interpretative or factual basis for their assertion that the prohibitive elements of the tobacco plain packaging measure are "special requirements" that fall within the scope of Article 20, while other widely-adopted measures that affect the use of a trademark do not. Assuming arguendo that these prohibitive elements do fall within the scope of Article 20, the complainants have failed to demonstrate that the measure as a whole encumbers the relevant use of a trademark.

113.   Even if the Panel finds that the complainants have established an encumbrance on the use of a trademark, they have failed to demonstrate that any encumbrance upon the use of trademarks in the course of trade resulting from the special requirements at issue has been imposed "unjustifiably". Specifically, the complainants have failed to demonstrate that any such encumbrance goes against or is otherwise not capable of contributing to its objectives and therefore that there is no rational connection between the encumbrance and the objective. There is, in fact, overwhelming evidence to demonstrate that tobacco plain packaging *is* capable of contributing to the legitimate public health objectives set forth in the TPP Act. By requiring the standardisation of the appearance of retail tobacco packaging and of the product itself, there is a clear rational connection between the encumbrance and the public health objectives of the measure, and the complainants have failed to demonstrate otherwise.

114.   For the sake of completeness, Australia notes that the Panel would need to reach the same conclusion even if it were to accept the position of some parties that the term "unjustifiably" requires the Panel to "weigh and balance" the extent to which the tobacco plain packaging measure encumbers a relevant use of trademarks, the extent to which it is capable of making a contribution to its

public health objectives, and the importance of the public health objectives that the measure seeks to fulfil.

115.   The tobacco plain packaging measure preserves the ability of tobacco companies to use trademarks to distinguish their products from those of other undertakings, while curtailing the use of retail tobacco packaging to advertise and promote tobacco products, detract from the effectiveness of graphic health warnings, and mislead consumers as to the harms of tobacco use in order to achieve a vital public policy objective. If the Panel were to "weigh and balance" these factors, there is no question that Australia's tobacco plain packaging measure is not unjustifiable.

116.   Thus, under any conceivable interpretation of the term "unjustifiably", the complainants have failed to discharge their burden of proving that any encumbrance upon the use of trademarks in the course of trade resulting from the special requirements imposed by the tobacco plain packaging measure is "unjustifiable". The Panel must therefore reject the complainants' claims under Article 20 of the TRIPS Agreement.[184]

B.   The complainants acknowledge that there is no "right of use" under the TRIPS Agreement, and so their claims under Articles 2.1, 15.4, 16.1, 16.3, 22.2(b) and 24.3 must fail

117.   The   complainants'   claims   under   Articles 2.1   (incorporating Article 6*quinquies* A(1) and Article 10*bis* of the Paris Convention), 15.4, 16.1, 16.3, 22.2(b) and 24.3 of the TRIPS Agreement, all of which are dependent on a "right of use", are fundamentally flawed and must be dismissed by the Panel. The defects in the complainants' claims are summarised below.

118.   In   relation   to   Article 2.1   of   the   TRIPS Agreement,   incorporating Article 6*quinquies* A(1) of the Paris Convention, Honduras maintains that Members are required to "ensur[e] that trademark owners can 'use' their trademarks"[185] in order for those trademarks to be "accepted for filing and protected as is", despite Honduras' express acknowledgment that trademark owners have no positive right to use those trademarks. Honduras has failed to demonstrate that Australia's tobacco plain packaging measure prevents the registration of trademarks that are registered in the territory of another Member based on their form and therefore, that the tobacco plain packaging measure is inconsistent   with   Article 2.1   of   the   TRIPS Agreement   incorporating Article 6*quinquies* A(1) of the Paris Convention.

---

[184]   Australia's second written submission, paras. 301-306. Australia does not separately address the complainants'   arguments   concerning   "less   restrictive   alternatives"   under   Article 20   of   the TRIPS Agreement because this is clearly not required under a legal standard of "unjustifiability". See paras. 89-90 above. Australia notes, however, that the "less restrictive alternatives" that the complainants purport to identify in this context are the same that they identify in connection with their TBT claims, addressed at Part E below.

[185]   Honduras' first written submission, para. 266.

119.   In relation to Article 15.4, the complainants argue that Members must guarantee (or at least not prevent) the use of all signs that are not yet "capable of distinguishing" goods, so that these "non-inherently distinctive" signs may then potentially become distinctive in the future, so that they may constitute a trademark that is then eligible for registration. The complainants' interpretation of Article 15.4 fundamentally confuses the concepts of "signs" and "trademarks".[186] A proper interpretation of Article 15.4 makes clear that a Member can regulate a product in a way that may restrict or prohibit the use of a trademark in its territory, as long as a Member does not refuse to register that trademark based on the nature of a product.[187] The complainants have failed to establish that under the tobacco plain packaging measure, Australia refuses to register trademarks based on the nature of the underlying product, and therefore that the measure is inconsistent with Article 15.4.

120.   In relation to Article 16.1, the complainants argue that Members must ensure that trademarks can be used in order to ensure that a "likelihood of confusion" is created in the market, so that trademark owners have increased opportunities to exercise their right of exclusion to prevent this confusion. These arguments, besides being nonsensical, cannot be reconciled with the complainants' admission that Article 16.1 obliges Members to confer only negative rights of exclusion on trademark owners.[188] The complainants have therefore failed to demonstrate that the tobacco plain packaging measure is inconsistent with Article 16.1 of the TRIPS Agreement.

121.   In relation to Article 16.3, Indonesia argues that Members are under an obligation to guarantee (or at least not prevent) trademark owners to use their trademarks in order to "maintain" their well-known status or to "become" well known in the future.[189] However, the rights conferred under Article 16.3 of the TRIPS Agreement (and Article 6bis of the Paris Convention) are negative rights of exclusion.[190] Properly interpreted, Article 16.3 protects well known registered trademarks – not trademarks that may become well known in the future or trademarks that were once well known.[191] The tobacco plain packaging measure in no way prevents a trademark owner from availing itself of the protections that

---

[186]   Australia's first written submission, paras. 303-305; Australia's second written submission, para. 25.

[187]   Australia's first written submission, paras. 244-246, 298-301. See also Singapore's third party written submission, paras. 23-26; Norway's third party written submission, paras. 27-30; New Zealand's third party written submission, paras. 17-25; Uruguay's third party written submission, para. 50; Argentina's third party written submission, para. 22; Canada's third party written submission, paras. 35-43; South Africa's third party oral statement at the first substantive meeting of the Panel, paras. 3.3-3.5.

[188]   Australia's second written submission, para. 14.

[189]   See Australia's second written submission, para. 33.

[190]   See Expert Report of C. Correa, Exhibit AUS-16, para. 18.

[191]   See Australia's first written submission, paras. 324-325. See also Canada's third party written submission, paras. 54-57; New Zealand's third party written submission, paras. 34-39; Singapore's third party written submission, paras. 31-34; Uruguay's third party written submission, paras. 46, 107.

are afforded to owners of registered well known trademarks in accordance with Article 16.3.[192]

122.   In   relation   to   Article 2.1,   incorporating   Article 10*bis*   of   the Paris Convention, the complainants argue that Members must allow the use of signs and trademarks on tobacco packaging because the omission of these signs and trademarks is liable to confuse and mislead consumers and constitutes an act of unfair competition. However, Article 10*bis* actually requires that Members assure effective protection against "particular deeds" of "dishonest" or "untruthful" commercial "rivalry" – i.e. attempts by a market actor to gain a commercial advantage over a rival market actor that are liable to influence consumers on the basis of false or misleading representations.[193] Australia provides a range of legal mechanisms for affected private parties to prevent or obtain redress for false or misleading representations,[194] and thus gives effect to its obligations under Article 10*bis*. The tobacco plain packaging measure has no impact on the availability of these legal mechanisms,[195] and the complainants have not suggested otherwise. Instead, the complainants maintain that the tobacco plain packaging measure violates Article 10*bis* because the measure allegedly "compels" private actors to engage in acts of unfair competition.[196] Even assuming that government regulations that compel private actors to behave in certain ways were to fall within the scope of Article 10*bis*, the complainants have failed to demonstrate either that the measure compels acts of competition or that the measure compels acts of competition that are unfair.[197] Accordingly, the complainants' unfair competition claims should be dismissed in their entirety.

123.   In relation to Article 22.2(b) of the TRIPS Agreement, the complainants argue that the provision requires Members to guarantee the use of geographical indications so that consumers are not misled into thinking that all tobacco products from all geographical origins are the same, so as to constitute an act of unfair competition. The complainants' interpretation of Article 22.2(b) is contrary to its plain text, which makes clear that the nature of protection provided is negative[198] and requires Members to provide the legal means for interested parties to prevent any act of using a geographical indication that constitutes an act of unfair competition (as defined by Article 10*bis* of the Paris Convention).[199] Australia provides a range of legal mechanisms for

---

[192]   Australia's first written submission, para. 331.
[193]   See Australia's first written submission, paras. 446-449.
[194]   See Australia's first written submission, para. 458.
[195]   See Australia's first written submission, para. 459.
[196]   Indonesia's first written submission, paras. 151, 161-168, 178-181; Cuba's first written submission, paras. 383-388; Dominican Republic's first written submission, paras. 854-856, 875-879, 883; Honduras' first written submission, paras. 687-690, 694.
[197]   Australia's second written submission, paras. 41-44.
[198]   Australia's first written submission, paras. 479-485.
[199]   Australia's first written submission, paras. 469-472, 480-482, 485; Australia's second written submission, para. 67.

interested parties to prevent any such act by third parties.[200] The complainants have failed to demonstrate that the tobacco plain packaging measure is inconsistent with Article 22.2(b) of the TRIPS Agreement.[201]

124. Finally, in relation to Article 24.3 of the TRIPS Agreement, the complainants argue that Members are obligated to allow geographical indications to be used in a manner that will "allow for indications to acquire, maintain, or enforce their status as geographical indications".[202] The complainants' claims that the tobacco plain packaging measure is inconsistent with this provision are based on the existence of an asserted protected "right of use" in relation to geographical indications under Australian law at the time of entry into force of the TRIPS Agreement. As the complainants have now correctly acknowledged that no "right to use" geographical indications existed under Australian law prior to 1 January 1995,[203] the complainants' claims under Article 24.3 of the TRIPS Agreement must be dismissed.[204]

125. In sum, and as Australia has demonstrated in its written submissions,[205] each of the complainants' claims under Article 2.1 (incorporating Article 6*quinquies* A(1) and Article 10*bis* of the Paris Convention), 15.4, 16.1, 16.3, 22.2(b) and 24.3 of the TRIPS Agreement hinges upon the existence of a positive "right of use" with respect to signs, registered trademarks and geographical indications. As the complainants themselves have expressly acknowledged that there is no such "right of use", and given that the complainants have offered no legal justification or evidence in support of their claims, their claims under each of these provisions must fail.

V. THE COMPLAINANTS HAVE FAILED TO ESTABLISH A *PRIMA FACIE* CASE THAT THE TOBACCO PLAIN PACKAGING MEASURE IS INCONSISTENT WITH ARTICLE 2.2 OF THE TBT AGREEMENT

126. The complainants' claims under Article 2.2 of the TBT Agreement fail at the threshold. The tobacco plain packaging measure is entitled to the presumption in Article 2.5 that it does not constitute an unnecessary obstacle to international trade, and the complainants have failed to rebut that presumption with the type of evidence required.[206] Even if the complainants' claims were found to overcome that fundamental hurdle, the complainants have also failed to

---

[200] Australia's first written submission, paras. 486-487.

[201] See Australia's first written submission, paras. 477-487.

[202] Dominican Republic's response to Panel Question No. 48, para. 216.

[203] See Dominican Republic's response to Panel Question No. 48, para. 213; Indonesia's response to Panel Question No. 48, citing its response to Panel Question No. 44.

[204] See Australia's second written submission, para. 69.

[205] Australia's first written submission, Part IV.B and Part IV.C; Australia's second written submission, Part II.B.

[206] Australia's response to Panel Question No. 162; Australia's second written submission, paras. 347-356; Australia's response to Panel Question No. 67, paras. 161-164.

establish a *prima facie* case that the tobacco plain packaging measure is trade-restrictive *at all*, let alone that it is *more* trade-restrictive than necessary having regard to the contribution it makes to its public health objectives and the risks that non-fulfilment of those objectives would create.

A. The complainants have failed to rebut the presumption in Article 2.5 of the TBT Agreement that the measure is not an unnecessary obstacle to international trade

127. Australia enacted its tobacco plain packaging measure in accordance with the FCTC Guidelines, which set out the relevant international standard for the plain packaging of tobacco products.[207] A technical regulation adopted for a legitimate objective in accordance with the relevant international standard benefits from the presumption in Article 2.5 of the TBT Agreement, whereby it is rebuttably presumed not to constitute an unnecessary obstacle to international trade under Article 2.2.[208] The presumption reflects one of the central purposes of the TBT Agreement, to incentivise Members to adopt and use relevant international standards, in order to harmonise technical regulations, on as wide a basis as possible.

128. The FCTC – one of the most widely embraced treaties in the United Nations system – explicitly recommends the implementation of tobacco plain packaging in the FCTC Guidelines for Article 11 (concerning the packaging and labelling of tobacco products) and Article 13 (concerning tobacco advertising, promotion, and sponsorship).[209] The FCTC Guidelines for Article 11 recognise that:

> [Tobacco plain packaging] may increase the noticeability and effectiveness of health warnings and messages, prevent the package from detracting attention from them, and address the industry package design techniques that may suggest that some products are less harmful than others.[210]

129. The FCTC Guidelines reflect the international scientific consensus[211] on the comprehensive range of tobacco control measures, including tobacco plain packaging, that countries should enact in order to address the grave and serious health impact of tobacco consumption and are relied on by the 180 Parties to the FCTC in implementing their own tobacco control measures.

---

[207] Australia's first written submission, paras. 567-582; Australia's second written submission, paras. 316-345; Australia's responses to Panel Question No. 128, No. 129, Nos. 135, No. 150.
[208] Australia's first written submission, paras. 567-582.
[209] WHO, Exhibit AUS-109, Article s 11, p. 63 and 13, pp. 99-100.
[210] WHO, Exhibit AUS-109, Article 11, p. 63.
[211] Panel Report, *US – Clove Cigarettes*, para. 7.414, cited in Australia's second written submission, para. 271.

130.   Consistent with the criteria for determining what is an "international standard" for the purposes of Article 2.5,[212] Australia has demonstrated that the FCTC Guidelines are: standards within the meaning of the TBT Agreement;[213] have been adopted by the FCTC COP, which is an "international standardizing body or organization" that has "recognised activities in standardization[214] and whose membership is open to the relevant bodies of at least all Members";[215] and have been made available to the public.[216]

131.   For these reasons, Australia has demonstrated that the FCTC Guidelines are an international standard that is "relevant" to the tobacco plain packaging measure, which has been adopted "in accordance with" those Guidelines.[217] The FCTC Guidelines were developed by working groups in which FCTC Parties (including at least one of the complainants) participated, were adopted by the FCTC COP, and were based on "available scientific evidence and the experience of the Parties themselves in implementing tobacco control measures."[218] The FCTC Guidelines provide "guidelines" for "common and repeated use" by the FCTC Parties, concerning the characteristics of a "product" (tobacco), and related "processes and production methods" (manufacture and sale of tobacco products).[219]

132.   The complainants contend that the FCTC Guidelines are not "international standards", on two bases. First, the complainants maintain that the FCTC COP is not an "international standardizing body". As Australia has demonstrated, this claim is without merit: the FCTC COP has "recognized activities in standardization", as is evidenced by the COP's role in developing guidelines for testing and measuring contents and emissions of tobacco products, and for the regulation of those contents and emissions.[220] Second, the complainants argue that in order to be considered an international standard, it must be sufficiently "precise" so as to be relied upon for "common and repeated use", within the meaning of the definition of a standard in Annex 1.2 of the TBT Agreement. This contention has no legal basis in the TBT Agreement.[221] Moreover, the FCTC Guidelines are capable of and are in fact being relied upon

---

[212]   Panel Report, *US – Tuna II (Mexico)*, para. 7.664, cited in Australia's first written submission, para. 570.

[213]   Australia's first written submission, paras. 571-574.

[214]   Australia's second written submission, paras. 333-341; Australia's response to Panel Question No. 128

[215]   Australia's first written submission, paras. 575-579; Australia's second written submission, para. 316, citing Appellate Body Report, *US – Tuna II (Mexico)*, para. 359.

[216]   Australia's first written submission, para. 580.

[217]   Australia's first written submission, para. 582; Australia's second written submission, paras. 316-318.

[218]   WHO, Exhibit AUS-42, para. 19. See also Australia's first written submission, paras. 103-113.

[219]   Australia's first written submission, para. 573; Australia's second written submission, para. 316.

[220]   Australia's second written submission, paras. 333-341.

[221]   Australia's second written submission, paras. 321-323; Australia's response to Panel Question No. 163, para. 101; Australia's comments on responses to Panel Question No. 163, para. 119.

for "common and repeated use".[222] In particular, Ireland, the United Kingdom, France, Hungary, New Zealand, Norway and Chile, have now either adopted or proposed their own tobacco plain packaging measures in reliance on the FCTC Guidelines.[223]

133.   The complainants also argue that if some element of Australia's measure goes beyond the international standard, then those aspects of Australia's measure that are consistent with the FCTC Guidelines should be deprived of the benefit of the presumption under Article 2.5. Not only is there no factual basis for this argument, given that Australia's measure is clearly in accordance with the properly identified scope of the FCTC Guidelines,[224] there is also no legal basis for this argument in the text of Article 2.5 of the TBT Agreement.[225]

134.   Given that the tobacco plain packaging measure benefits from the presumption in Article 2.5 that it does not constitute an "unnecessary obstacle to international trade" within the meaning of Article 2.2, and the complainants have failed to adduce any evidence of the type that would be required to rebut this presumption,[226] the Panel need not proceed further in its analysis of the complainants' claim under Article 2.2 of the TBT Agreement.

B.   The complainants have failed to make a *prima facie* case that the measure is trade-restrictive under Article 2.2 of the TBT Agreement

135.   Notwithstanding their failure to rebut the presumption established by Article 2.5, the complainants' claims under Article 2.2 would fail in any event because they have not established a *prima facie* case that the tobacco plain packaging measure is "trade-restrictive" under a proper interpretation of that provision.

1.   The complainants' claims of trade-restrictiveness fail as a matter of law

136.   Properly interpreted, the terms "trade-restrictive" and "obstacle to international trade" in Article 2.2 require the complainants to establish that the tobacco plain packaging measure will result, or has resulted, in a limiting effect on international trade in tobacco products.[227]

---

[222]   Australia's second written submission, paras. 324-327. Australia's response to Panel Question No. 163; Australia's comments on responses to Panel Question No. 163.

[223]   Australia's response to Panel Question No. 163.

[224]   Australia's response to Panel Question No. 135.

[225]   Australia's responses to Panel Question Nos. 135 and 150.

[226]   Australia's response to Panel Question No. 162; Australia's second written submission, paras. 347-356; Australia's response to Panel Question No. 67, paras. 161-164.

[227]   Australia's second written submission, paras. 363-398; Australia's first written submission, paras. 521-530; Australia's response to Panel Question No. 117, paras. 110-113; Australia's comments on responses to Panel Question Nos. 151 and 165, paras. 37-49.

137.   The complainants' claims of trade-restrictiveness do not even attempt to meet this fundamental requirement. The complainants have instead tried to expand the standard of trade-restrictiveness to an abstract and meaningless concept of a "limitation on competitive opportunities"[228] in order to accommodate their principal claim:[229] that the design, structure and operation of the tobacco plain packaging measure has a limiting effect on the *ability to use design features* on tobacco packaging to advertise and promote tobacco products.[230] The complainants further contend that a "limitation on competitive opportunities" solely within a particular product segment or solely for a particular Member[231] suffices to demonstrate a measure's traderestrictiveness, even where the measure *enhances* overall trade in that product.[232]

138.   The complainants' proposed "limitation on competitive opportunities" standard of trade-restrictiveness cannot be reconciled with either the text of Article 2.2 or the jurisprudence of the Appellate Body and thus fails as a matter of law.[233]

2.   The complainants' claims of trade-restrictiveness fail as a matter of evidence

139.   The complainants' alternative bases for claiming that the tobacco plain packaging measure is trade-restrictive fail for a lack of evidence. None of the complainants has substantiated its claims that the tobacco plain packaging measure entails compliance costs, or increases barriers to market entry, such as to constitute a limiting effect on international trade in tobacco products.[234]

140.   The complainants' only attempt to establish actual trade effects is their argument that the tobacco plain packaging measure has caused "downtrading" in the Australian market by shifting demand for tobacco products from higher-priced to lower-priced products. Even if the Panel were to find that downtrading is attributable in part to the tobacco plain packaging measure,[235] that fact alone would be insufficient to demonstrate a limiting effect on overall trade in tobacco

---

[228]   Australia's second written submission, paras. 370-374; Australia's comments on responses to Panel Question Nos. 151 and 165, paras. 40-49.

[229]   Australia's comments on responses to Panel Question Nos. 151 and 165, paras. 43-45, 54-55.

[230]   Australia's opening statement at the second substantive meeting of the Panel, paras. 157-158; Australia's comments on responses to Panel Question Nos. 151 and 165, paras. 43-44. 54-55.

[231]   Australia's second written submission, paras. 383-385, 397; Australia's response to Panel Question No. 154; Australia's comments on responses to Panel Question Nos. 151 and 165, para. 63.

[232]   Australia's second written submission, paras. 383-397.

[233]   Australia's second written submission, paras. 363-398; Australia's first written submission, paras. 521-530; Australia's response to Panel Question No. 117, paras. 110-113; Australia's comments on responses to Panel Question Nos. 151 and 165, paras. 37-49.

[234]   Australia's first written submission, paras. 547-561; Australia's response to Panel Question No. 155.

[235]   Australia's first written submission, paras. 542-545; Australia's second written submission, paras. 414-420.

products, with respect to either the volume or value of trade.[236] An alleged decrease in sales in the premium segment alone does not establish a limiting effect on the *volume* of overall trade in tobacco products. Moreover, the uncontested evidence before the Panel is that real weighted prices of cigarettes have increased since the introduction of the tobacco plain packaging measure; and the complainants' own experts accept that the measure has *caused* prices to increase.[237] The complainants' downtrading claims thus also fail to establish a limiting effect on the *value* of overall trade in tobacco products.

141. The complainants acknowledge that evidence of actual trade effects may be required when a qualitative assessment of a non-discriminatory technical regulation fails to establish any trade-restrictive effects.[238] However, not one of the complainants has introduced a single piece of evidence demonstrating that tobacco producers in their countries have experienced a decrease in export volumes, prices, revenues or profits in Australia attributable to the tobacco plain packaging measure.[239] Given the resources at the complainants' disposal, it is reasonable to assume that if such evidence supported their claims this would have been provided to the Panel.[240]

142. The complainants have thus failed entirely – as a matter of both law and fact – to demonstrate any credible basis on which to conclude that Australia's measure is trade-restrictive within the meaning of Article 2.2. Accordingly, the Panel need not proceed further in its analysis.

C. **The complainants have failed to establish that the measure is incapable of contributing to its objectives**

143. In the unlikely event that the Panel were to consider that the complainants have made a *prima facie* case that the tobacco plain packaging measure is "trade-restrictive" under a proper interpretation of that term, the complainants have failed in their attempt to establish that the tobacco plain packaging measure is not capable of contributing to its objectives of reducing the use of and exposure to tobacco products in Australia.

144. As outlined in Part III above, the overwhelming weight of the qualitative evidence unequivocally establishes that, by prohibiting tobacco packaging from being used to advertise and promote tobacco products – and thereby reducing the appeal of tobacco products, increasing the effectiveness of graphic health warnings, and reducing the ability of tobacco packaging to mislead consumers – the tobacco plain packaging measure is capable of discouraging smoking

---

[236] Australia's first written submission, paras. 533-541; Australia's second written submission, paras. 407, 409-413.

[237] Australia's comments on responses to Panel Question Nos. 151 and 165, paras. 59-60.

[238] See, e.g. Dominican Republic's and Honduras' responses to Panel Question No. 117.

[239] Australia's response to Panel Question No. 117, paras. 122-123; Australia's opening statement at the second substantive meeting of the Panel, para. 149.

[240] Australia's opening statement at the second substantive meeting of the Panel, para. 149.

initiation and relapse, encouraging cessation, and reducing people's exposure to tobacco products. The quantitative evidence corroborates this conclusion, and is consistent with the tobacco plain packaging measure operating synergistically with other elements of Australia's comprehensive tobacco control policy to reduce further the use of tobacco products and exposure to tobacco smoke in Australia. Moreover, the complainants' own concessions and evidence clearly establish that the measure is apt to contribute to achieving its objectives.

145.   The complainants have thus failed entirely to discharge their burden of establishing that the tobacco plain packaging measure is incapable of contributing to its public health objectives.

D.   The complainants have failed to establish that the risks arising from non-fulfilment of the measure's objectives are not grave

146.   The grave risks to public health that would arise from non-fulfilment of the objectives of the tobacco plain packaging measure overwhelmingly weigh in favour of a finding that the tobacco plain packaging measure is no more trade-restrictive than necessary to achieve those objectives within the meaning of Article 2.2. In an attempt to persuade the Panel of the counter-intuitive proposition that those risks would be anything other than serious and grave, the complainants have once again misconstrued the relevant legal standard.[241]

147.   To this end, the Dominican Republic and Indonesia have fundamentally misinterpreted the nature of the relevant risks that the Panel must assess. Contrary to the plain text of Article 2.2, which makes clear that this aspect of the holistic analysis requires the Panel to assess the "risks non-fulfilment would create" – i.e. the risks that would arise *assuming* non-fulfilment of the tobacco plain packaging measure's objectives – both complainants argue that the Panel must instead assess the *likelihood* of the measure not fulfilling its objectives.[242] Honduras also makes the preposterous argument that because Australia has adopted a comprehensive approach to tobacco control that has successfully reduced smoking prevalence and consumption, the consequences of not *further* reducing tobacco-related premature deaths and serious disease through the tobacco plain packaging measure would not be grave.[243]

148.   Properly interpreted, the risks that would arise from the non-fulfilment of the public health objectives of the tobacco plain packaging measure are significant and grave, and the consequences would include increased tobacco-related deaths and disease in Australia.[244] This is affirmed by the

---

[241]   Australia's second written submission, para. 527.
[242]   Australia's second written submission, paras. 532, 541-542; Australia's comments on responses to Panel Question No. 157, paras. 86-94.
[243]   Australia's second written submission, paras. 545-547.
[244]   Australia's second written submission, paras. 531-540, 543-544; Australia's first written submission, paras. 683-694; Australia's comments on responses to Panel Question No. 157, paras. 86-90.

acknowledgment by Honduras and the Dominican Republic, respectively, that the nature of the serious health risks at issue is a "paramount" concern to any society,[245] and that the consequences of not fulfilling the measure's objectives "would be serious and grave",[246] providing unequivocal support for the conclusion that the tobacco plain packaging measure is no more trade-restrictive than necessary to fulfil its legitimate objectives.

E.   **The complainants have failed to propose alternative measures that establish that the tobacco plain packaging measure is more trade-restrictive than necessary**

149.   Finally, were the Panel to continue its holistic analysis under Article 2.2, notwithstanding the complainants' failure to establish that the tobacco plain packaging measure is trade-restrictive under a proper interpretation,[247] the complainants have failed to discharge their burden of proposing reasonably available alternatives that are less trade-restrictive than the tobacco plain packaging measure, and that are capable of making an equivalent contribution to its public health objectives.[248]

150.   In particular, three of the complainants' four purported "alternatives" – an increase in excise tax, an increase in the minimum legal purchase age for tobacco products, and improved social marketing campaigns – are not alternatives at all, as they constitute variations on *existing* elements of Australia's comprehensive tobacco control policy.[249] Consistent with the findings in *Brazil – Retreaded Tyres*, such measures cannot be a *substitute* for the tobacco plain packaging measure,[250] particularly given the importance of a comprehensive approach to tobacco control.[251] Rather, any such substitution would narrow the range of mechanisms deployed in Australia's comprehensive tobacco control policy, thereby limiting its ability to impact the broadest range of consumers and potential consumers possible and undermining the effectiveness of existing tobacco control measures.[252] This would weaken Australia's comprehensive

---

[245]   Australia's second written submission, para. 540; Honduras' first written submission, para. 891.

[246]   Australia's second written submission, para. 543; Dominican Republic's first written submission, para. 1029.

[247]   Appellate Body Report, *US – Tuna II (Mexico)*, para. 322, fn 647.

[248]   Australia's first written submission, paras. 700-742; Australia's second written submission, paras. 550-569; Australia's response to Panel Question No. 157, paras. 68-71; Australia's comments on responses to Panel Question No. 157, paras. 74-95.

[249]   Australia's first written submission, paras. 703-706; Australia's second written submission, paras. 551-554; Australia's response to Panel Question No. 64, paras. 142-144; Australia's response to Panel Question No. 148, para. 21.

[250]   Appellate Body Report, *Brazil – Retreaded Tyres,* paras. 159, 172.

[251]   Australia's first written submission, paras. 38-49; Australia's comments on responses to Panel Question No. 159, para. 100.

[252]   Australia's response to Panel Question No. 64, paras. 141-144; Australia's second written submission, para. 562; Australia's response to Panel Question No. 148, paras. 26-27; Australia's comments on responses to Panel Question No. 159, para. 102.

tobacco control policy by reducing the synergies between its components, as well as its total effect.[253] The complainants have failed to demonstrate that, within this policy context, any of their three proposed variations to existing measures would (or could) make an *equivalent* degree of contribution to the objectives of the tobacco plain packaging measure.[254]

151. Furthermore, the complainants' criticisms of Australia's existing measures are entirely unfounded, given that Australia: is a world leader in its use of excise as a tobacco control measure[255] – a fact that Honduras has expressly acknowledged;[256] has in place an extensive and dynamic range of policies to restrict youth access to tobacco;[257] and is a world leader in its use of social marketing campaigns as a tobacco control strategy.[258]

152. With respect to the only actual *alternative* measure the complainants propose – a pre-vetting scheme – the complainants have failed to provide any credible evidence or argument to support their implausible assertion that the scheme would make "an equivalent or greater contribution" to that of the tobacco plain packaging measure when its purpose is to eliminate the standardisation of tobacco packaging,[259] and reinstate tobacco packaging as a vehicle for advertising and promoting tobacco products.[260] In any event, a pre-vetting scheme is not "reasonably available" due to the prohibitive costs and burdens it would entail.[261]

153. Moreover, the complainants have failed to discharge their burden of proposing alternatives that are *less* trade-restrictive than the tobacco plain packaging measure.[262] Under the complainants' abstract "limitation on competitive opportunities" test, their alternatives are in fact *more* trade-

---

[253] Australia's first written submission, para. 706; Australia's response to Panel Question No. 64, paras. 142-144; Australia's response to Panel Question No. 69, para. 181; Australia's second written submission, paras. 553-554; Australia's response to Panel Question No. 148, paras. 23-27; Australia's response to Panel Question No. 157, paras. 38-40; Australia's response to Panel Question No. 158; Australia's comments on responses to Panel Question No. 161, paras. 107-111.

[254] Australia's first written submission, paras. 718-724; Australia's second written submission, paras. 556-562; Australia's response to Panel Question No. 139, para. 41; Australia's comments on responses to Panel Question No. 157, paras. 74-80; Australia's comments on responses to Panel Question Nos. 151 and 165, paras. 56-57.

[255] Australia's response to Panel Question No. 158.

[256] Australia's response to Panel Question No. 158, para. 87.

[257] Australia's first written submission, paras. 709-711.

[258] Australia's first written submission, paras. 713-717; Australia's comments on responses to Panel Question No. 157, para. 79.

[259] Australia's first written submission, para. 728; Australia's second written submission, para. 564.

[260] Australia's first written submission, para. 728; Australia's second written submission, paras. 564-569; Australia's response to Panel Question No. 157; Australia's comments on responses to Panel Question No. 157, paras. 84-85.

[261] Australia's first written submission, paras. 725-728, 736, 740; Australia's opening statement at the second substantive meeting of the Panel, para. 155; Australia's response to Panel Question No. 157; Australia's comments on responses to Panel Question No. 157, paras. 81-83.

[262] Australia's first written submission, paras. 734-736, 740; Australia's second written submission, para. 563.

restrictive than the tobacco plain packaging measure[263] – a conclusion the complainants have sought to obscure through various contrived arguments.[264] Furthermore, under a proper interpretation of trade-restrictiveness, the complainants explicitly assume that their alternatives would be *equally* restrictive of the volume of trade in tobacco products in order to make an equivalent contribution to the objectives of the tobacco plain packaging measure.[265] There is no basis in WTO jurisprudence for preferring an *equally* trade-restrictive alternative to the measure at issue.[266]

154.   Thus, an assessment of the complainants' proposed alternative measures reinforces the conclusion that the tobacco plain packaging measure is no "more trade-restrictive than necessary" to fulfil its legitimate objectives under Article 2.2 of the TBT Agreement.

VI.   CUBA HAS FAILED TO ESTABLISH A *PRIMA FACIE* CASE UNDER ARTICLE IX:4 OF THE GATT 1994

155.   The basis of Cuba's claim that the tobacco plain packaging measure is inconsistent with Article IX:4 of the GATT 1994 is that the prohibition on the use of the mark "Habanos" on the packaging of Cuba's large hand-made cigars ("LHM") materially reduces their value.

156.   This argument is entirely without merit, because: (i) Cuba has failed to establish that measures affecting marks other than country of origin marks fall within the scope of Article IX;[267] (ii) even assuming, *arguendo,* that other marks, such as the mark "Habanos" fell within scope, the Appellate Body has unambiguously confirmed that Article IX only disciplines measures that *require* marks of origin, not measures that prohibit such markings;[268] and (iii) Cuba has failed to substantiate its assertion that there has been any reduction in the value of Cuban LHM cigars since the introduction of the tobacco plain packaging measure, let alone to demonstrate a "material" reduction that is attributable to the

---

[263]   Australia's first written submission, paras. 734-736, 740; Australia's second written submission, para. 563; Australia's opening statement at the second substantive meeting of the Panel, para. 156; Australia's response to Panel Question No. 151, paras. 45-51; Australia's comments on responses to Panel Question Nos. 151 and 165, para. 61; Australia's comments on the Dominican Republic's response to Panel Question No. 153, paras. 68-69.

[264]   Australia's comments on responses to Panel Question Nos. 151 and 165, paras. 50-55.

[265]   Australia's opening statement at the second substantive meeting of the Panel, para. 157; Australia's response to Panel Question No. 151, para. 40; Australia's comments on responses to Panel Question Nos. 151 and 165, para. 58.

[266]   Australia's comments on responses to Panel Question Nos. 151 and 165, para. 58.

[267]   Australia's first written submission, paras. 750-751; Australia's response to Panel Question No. 83; Canada's third party written submission, para. 104.

[268]   Australia's second written submission, paras. 577-578; Australia's response to Panel Question No. 133; Appellate Body Report, *US – COOL (Article 21.5 – Canada and Mexico)*, para. 5.356; Australia's first written submission, paras. 745-749.

prohibition on the use of the mark "Habanos".[269] Each of these factors is fatal to Cuba's argument.

157.   Even assuming, *arguendo*, that the tobacco plain packaging measure were somehow found provisionally inconsistent with Article IX:4, the measure would benefit from the exception under Article XX(b).[270]

158.   Given that Cuba has failed to establish a *prima facie* case that the tobacco plain packaging measure is inconsistent with Article IX:4 of the GATT 1994, Cuba's claim must be rejected in its entirety.

VII.   CONCLUSION

159.   For the reasons stated herein and explained more fully in Australia's written submissions, oral statements, responses to questions from the Panel, and comments on the complainants' responses, each of the complainants' claims in this dispute is unfounded both in law and fact.

160.   Moreover, the complainants' claims and arguments in this case have disturbing implications for all WTO Members considering the adoption of public health measures and for the WTO dispute settlement system itself.[271] The improbable standard[272] by which the complainants have asked the Panel to evaluate Australia's tobacco plain packaging measure has no foundation in WTO law and ignores entirely the policy context in which public health policymakers discharge their important responsibilities.[273] The complainants' claims and arguments in this case threaten the essential right of a WTO Member, as consistently recognised by prior panels and the Appellate Body, to decide the level of protection it seeks to achieve when it comes to protecting the lives and wellbeing of its citizens.[274]

---

[269]   Australia's second written submission, paras. 579-585; Australia's response to Panel Question No. 137.

[270]   Australia's second written submission, paras. 586-595; Australia's first written submission, paras. 754-761.

[271]   Australia's closing statement at the second substantive meeting of the Panel.

[272]   Australia's closing statement at the second substantive meeting of the Panel, paras. 7-22.

[273]   Australia's closing statement at the second substantive meeting of the Panel, paras. 15-20, 27-35.

[274]   Australia's closing statement at the second substantive meeting of the Panel, paras. 30-32.

161.   Tobacco plain packaging is a legitimate public health measure, based upon an extensive body of scientific evidence and the explicit recommendations of the Parties to the FCTC. The evidence demonstrates that the measure is already contributing to achieving Australia's public health objectives and its effects are likely to grow over the long term. The complainants have failed to demonstrate that this effective tobacco control measure is inconsistent with Australia's obligations under the covered agreements. Australia therefore respectfully requests that the Panel reject the complainants' claims under Articles 2.1 (incorporating Article 6*quinquies* A(1) and Article 10*bis* of the Paris Convention), 15.4, 16.1, 16.3, 20, 22.2(b), and 24.3 of the TRIPS Agreement, Article 2.2 of the TBT Agreement,[275] and Article IX:4 of the GATT 1994 in their entirety.

---

[275] Australia notes that in their respective requests for the establishment of a Panel the complainants made claims under Article 2.1 of the TBT Agreement and Article III:4 of the GATT 1994 (national treatment). The complainants have not pursued these claims in any of their written or oral submissions in these proceedings. These claims must therefore be considered to have been abandoned by the complainants.

ANNEX C

ARGUMENTS OF THE THIRD PARTIES

ANNEX C-1

EXECUTIVE SUMMARY OF THE ARGUMENTS
OF ARGENTINA[*]

1.   Argentina believes that Australia's plain packaging measure is designed to safeguard public health, forms part of the campaign to discourage people from smoking and was introduced in exercise of the State's regulatory powers. The promotion of tobacco and advertising campaigns for tobacco are among the major threats to public health.

2.   Argentina sees Article 8 of the TRIPS Agreement as an express recognition of the scope that Members retain under that Agreement to adopt laws and regulations for public policy purposes, including the protection of public health.

3.   Furthermore, the Doha Declaration on the TRIPS Agreement and Public Health, approved by WTO Members in November 2001[1], provides a relevant interpretative framework for the scope of certain Articles of the TRIPS Agreement.

4.   The above-mentioned Declaration not only establishes that the Agreement does not and should not prevent WTO Members from taking measures to protect public health, it also reaffirms the right of Members to use, to the full, the provisions of the Agreement which provide flexibility for this purpose. It also advocates a balance between States' powers to pursue health policies and the intellectual property rights established in the TRIPS Agreement.

5.   Argentina also notes that the Doha Declaration reflects the consensus among WTO Member countries in favour of directly applying the principles of interpretation of international law to the TRIPS Agreement. Paragraph 5(a) of the Declaration emphasizes the importance of rules such as Article 8 of the TRIPS Agreement in interpreting the provisions of the Agreement in the light of Article 31 of the Vienna Convention on the Law of Treaties, which states that treaties shall be interpreted in the light of their object and purpose.[2]

6.   As regards the interpretation of the scope of Article 20 of the TRIPS Agreement in relation to the principles established in TRIPS Article 8.1, Argentina considers that the Panel should bear in mind that this instrument

---

[*]   Original Spanish.
[1]   WTO Ministerial Conference, Declaration on the TRIPS Agreement and Public Health (WT/MIN(01)/DEC/2, 20 November 2001).
[2]   *Ibid.*

should be implemented in a manner supportive of Members' right to protect public health.

7. Without prejudice to the foregoing, Argentina believes that the standardization of the elements of the trademark (colour, logo, etc.), as provided for by the plain packaging measure, may limit its distinctiveness within the meaning of Article 15.1. Such standardization, together with a significant reduction in the distinguishing variables of a trademark, may lead to a certain amount of confusion for the consumer.

8. In addition, both Australia and a number of third parties[3] have elaborated upon aspects of the advertising function of cigarette and tobacco packaging, given that these are high-exposure products which consumers carry around with them and display in various settings. For this reason, it has been said that tobacco product packaging plays an important role in communicating a trademark and is one of a range of marketing measures aimed at various types of consumer. In particular, emphasis has been placed on how cigarette product packaging contributes to encouraging young people to take up smoking. It follows, by converse implication, that the absence of the above-mentioned elements of the trademark which make it attractive, in addition to health warnings, may make plain packaging an effective measure for achieving the objectives pursued.

9. In Argentina's view, the prohibition contained in Article 15.4 of the TRIPS Agreement refers to the registration of a trademark, while the plain packaging measure prescribes the modalities for the use of the registered trademark. Consequently, Argentina does not consider Article 15.4 of the TRIPS Agreement to refer to the enjoyment of rights, but merely to their availability. Nevertheless, Argentina imagines that one of the main objectives of registration, particularly in those countries in which registration is constitutive, is the actual use of the registered trademark.

10. Regarding the interpretation of Article 16 of the TRIPS Agreement, in particular Articles 16.1 and 16.3, Argentina understands, as the Appellate Body has pointed out[4], that the rights conferred by these Articles are rights of exclusion granted to the owner of the trademark to "*prevent third parties from using in the course of trade identical or similar signs*". Argentina recalls that the purposes of trademark registration include preventing a third party from either

---

[3] Norway's third party submission, para. 123. Without prejudice to the Panel's acceptance of unsolicited submissions in these proceedings, the issue was also addressed by the World Health Organization in its *amicus curiae* submission dated 16 February 2015, p. 9.

[4] *US – Section 211 Appropriations Act*, paras. 186-188 (WT/DS176/AB/R) "*[...] Article 16 confers on the owner of a registered trademark an internationally agreed minimum level of "exclusive rights" that all WTO Members must guarantee in their domestic legislation. These exclusive rights protect the owner against infringement of the registered trademark by unauthorized third parties.*"

registering or using a trademark, and it is to these exclusive rights to trademarks that the Articles in question refer.

11.   It is Argentina's understanding that by virtue of the requirements established by the Plain Packaging Act for the use of a trademark, a new sign is created that is different from the registered trademark, and this is why two different signs have coexisted in Australia for the same trademark ever since the Plain Packaging Act entered into force: a registered sign of restricted use and an unregistered sign the use of which is prescribed.

12.   Argentina considers this situation to be particularly relevant in the cases referred to in Article 16.1 and 16.3 of the TRIPS Agreement and agrees with Japan that the right conferred on the trademark owner is a right to exclude.[5]

13.   Argentina also notes that although tobacco plain packaging ensures a standardized form[6] of trademark use, this use may be subject to variations in the colours, sizes and fonts used, which could lead to a proliferation of prescribed trademarks that differ from country to country. Argentina therefore believes that the use of the trademark in the prescribed form should enjoy the same protection as the registered trademark, as the trademark may otherwise be vulnerable to unauthorized use.

14.   Regarding the issue of geographical indications, Argentina is of the view that Article 24.3 of the TRIPS Agreement should be analysed grammatically. The Spanish version of this Article states that the purpose of the obligation not to diminish protection is "*la protección de las indicaciones geográficas que existía en él inmediatamente antes de la fecha de entrada en vigor del Acuerdo sobre la OMC*". In this analysis, "*protección*" is the nucleus and "*de las indicaciones geográficas* ... " the indirect modifier. Consequently, Argentina disagrees with Australia and believes that the purpose of the obligation not to diminish protection concerns the protection of geographical indications in general.

15.   This interpretation is corroborated by the French version of the Article: "*Lorsqu'il mettra en oeuvre la présente section, un Membre ne diminuera pas la protection des indications géographiques qui existait dans ce Membre immédiatement avant la date d'entrée en vigueur de l'Accord sur l'OMC.*" Here again, the reference is clearly to the protection of geographical indications in general. Indeed, if the text referred to particular geographical indications, it would use the plural "*qui existaient*".

16.   As regards the TBT Agreement's applicability to this case, Argentina considers that, in conformity with the Appellate Body's analysis in the case cited by Australia, *EC - Bananas III*[7], where a measure is addressed by two or more

---

[5]   Japan's third party submission, para. 4.
[6]   In accordance with Article 46 of the Guidelines for implementation of Article 11 of the WHO Framework Convention on Tobacco Control.
[7]   Australia's first written submission, para. 511.

covered agreements, it is the norm that deals specifically and in detail with the particular subject matter that should be applied. In this respect, Argentina agrees with Australia that the appropriate legal framework for analysing an alleged trademark restriction is the TRIPS Agreement and not the TBT Agreement.

17.   However, should the Panel be of the opinion that the TBT Agreement applies to this case, Argentina would submit that the complainants' claim requires that the Panel examine whether the technical regulation that regulates the physical aspect of the plain packaging is necessary under Article 2.2 of the TBT Agreement. In this respect, Argentina recalls that the issue of necessity has been analysed[8] in previous cases, and it was understood that the jurisprudence under Article XX of the GATT 1994 was relevant to the interpretation of the term "necessary" under the TBT Agreement.

18.   Article 2.2 of the TBT Agreement establishes that "technical regulations shall not be more trade-restrictive than necessary to fulfil a legitimate objective … ". In fact, the rule itself includes, among the legitimate objectives, "protection of human health or safety". Moreover, the Panel in *US — Clove Cigarettes* " ... *considered it to be self-evident that the objective of reducing youth smoking is a "legitimate" one*".[9]

19.   Argentina is of the view that it might be useful, in carrying out an analysis to determine whether or not a measure is inconsistent under Article 2.2 of the TBT Agreement, to bear in mind that the Article can be split into two sentences, the first of which provides that: "*Members shall ensure that technical regulations are not prepared, adopted or applied with a view to or with the effect of creating unnecessary obstacles to international trade*".

20.   The second sentence states that: "*For this purpose, technical regulations shall not be more trade-restrictive than necessary to fulfil a legitimate objective, taking account of the risks non-fulfilment would create*".

21.   As regards the legitimate objectives, this Article provides a non-exhaustive list that expressly includes those mentioned below:

> "*Such legitimate objectives are, inter alia: national security requirements; the prevention of deceptive practices; protection of human health or safety, animal or plant life or health, or the environment. In assessing such risks, relevant elements of consideration are, inter alia: available scientific and technical information, related processing technology or intended end-uses of products*".

22.   In order to determine whether a measure violates the provisions of Article 2.2, we need to consider the following points:

---

[8]   Panel Report, *US - Clove Cigarettes*, paras. 7.353-7.368.
[9]   Panel Report, *US - Clove Cigarettes*, para. 7.347.

(a)   The link between the first and second sentence: the provisions contained in the first and second sentences do not refer to different obligations, but to the same obligation. In *US - Clove Cigarettes*, the Panel stated that it sufficed to note that the second sentence was introduced by the words "for this purpose", thereby establishing a direct link between the two sentences and implying that the second explained the meaning of the first.[10]

(b)   In both *US - Clove Cigarettes*[11] and *US - Tuna II*, the Panel established a two-step review mechanism to analyse the compliance of the challenged technical regulations with the provisions of Article 2.2. Under that mechanism, to determine whether a technical regulation was in conformity with the said provisions, the Panel had to:

    (i)   ascertain whether that regulation pursued or fulfilled a legitimate objective;

    (ii)   if that were the case, examine whether the provisions of the regulation were more trade-restrictive than necessary to fulfil that objective, taking into account the risks non-fulfilment would create.

(c)   The notion of "necessity" is reflected in both the first and second sentences of Article 2.2, through the reference in the first sentence to "unnecessary obstacles to international trade", and in the second sentence to "not ... more trade-restrictive than necessary". As the Appellate Body observed in US – Tuna II (Mexico), the assessment of "necessity", in the context of Article 2.2, involves a "relational analysis" of the following factors:

    (i)   the trade restrictiveness of the technical regulation;

    (ii)   the degree of contribution that it makes to the achievement of a legitimate objective;

    (iii) the nature of the risks at issue and the gravity of the consequences that would arise from non-fulfilment of the objective(s) pursued by the Member through the measure.

23.   In a particular case, a panel's determination of what is considered "necessary" will be based on a consideration of all these factors.

24.   By its terms, Article 2.2 of the TBT Agreement requires an assessment of the necessity of the trade restrictiveness of the measure at issue. In this regard, the Appellate Body in *US – Tuna II (Mexico)* defined "trade-restrictive" to mean "having a limiting effect on trade". Moreover, it found that the reference in Article 2.2 to "unnecessary obstacles" implied that "some" trade restrictiveness

---

[10]   Document WT/DS406/R, fn 618.
[11]   Document WT/DS406/R.

was allowed and, further, that what was actually prohibited were those restrictions on international trade that "exceed what is necessary to achieve the degree of contribution that a technical regulation makes to the achievement of a legitimate objective".

25.   In *US - Tuna*, the Panel stated that the burden rested with Mexico, as the complainant, to demonstrate that the conditions were met to conclude that a violation of Article 2.2 of the TBT Agreement existed.[12]

26.   In *US - Tuna II (Mexico)*, the Appellate Body found that the term "fulfil" was concerned with the degree of contribution that the technical regulation makes towards the achievement of the legitimate objective.[13] This finding was based on the wording of the sixth recital[14] of the preamble to the TBT Agreement, which provides that, subject to certain qualifications, a Member shall not be prevented from taking measures necessary to achieve its legitimate objectives "at the levels it considers appropriate".

27.   Argentina agrees that the objective of protecting public health is legitimate *per se* and that, although the objective of reducing the attractiveness of products is not in itself legitimate, it is so in this dispute, given the harmful nature of tobacco products.

28.   As for the value that should be assigned to the WHO Guidelines, Argentina agrees with the Panel in *US - Clove Cigarettes* that the Guidelines "are non-binding on parties"[15] and that "the WHO Partial Guidelines do not necessarily apply directly to the particular regulatory needs of a particular country."[16] It also agrees that these Guidelines, "'drawing on the best available scientific evidence and the experience of Parties', do show a growing consensus within the international community to strengthen tobacco-control policies … ".[17]

29.   Lastly, with regard to the differences in the interpretation of the term "unjustifiable", found in the *chapeau* of Article XX of the GATT 1994, and the term "unjustifiably", in Article 20 of the TRIPS Agreement, and bearing in mind the difference in the regulatory structure of Article XX of the GATT 1994 and Article 20 of the TRIPS Agreement, Argentina wishes to emphasize, above all, that, in its view, each of the above-mentioned articles, as well as the terminology

---

[12]   Document WT/DS381/R.
[13]   Appellate Body Report, *US – Tuna II (Mexico)*, para. 315.
[14]   The sixth recital reads as follows: "*Recognizing that no country should be prevented from taking measures necessary to ensure the quality of its exports, or for the protection of human, animal or plant life or health, of the environment, or for the prevention of deceptive practices, at the levels it considers appropriate, subject to the requirement that they are not applied in a manner which would constitute a means of arbitrary or unjustifiable discrimination between countries where the same conditions prevail or a disguised restriction on international trade, and are otherwise in accordance with the provisions of this Agreement*[.]"
[15]   *United States – Measures Affecting the Production and Sale of Clove Cigarettes*, WT/DS406/R, para. 7.230.
[16]   *Ibid.*
[17]   *Ibid.*

used therein, should be interpreted in the light of the Agreement in which it appears.

30.   Accordingly, Argentina believes that the notion of "unjustifiable impediment" should be interpreted in the light of the provisions of the TRIPS Agreement, taking into account the Agreement's objectives and purposes in accordance with the Doha Declaration, without extrapolating the application of Article XX of the GATT.

ANNEX C-2

EXECUTIVE SUMMARY OF THE ARGUMENTS
OF BRAZIL

I.   THE FCTC AS A GLOBAL PUBLIC HEALTH TREATY

1.   The WHO Framework Convention on Tobacco Control (FCTC) became the first global public health treaty and is nowadays considered the most widely embraced treaty in the United Nations' history with 180 Parties. The FCTC recognizes that the spread of the tobacco epidemic is a global problem with serious consequences for public health. Scientific evidence has unequivocally established that tobacco consumption and exposure to tobacco smoke cause death, disease and disability. Furthermore, as tobacco use may have severe economic impact on health systems, it poses a heavier burden on developing and least developed countries. Accordingly, the FCTC calls for the widest possible international cooperation to achieve an effective, appropriate and comprehensive international response. Brazil believes that the effective implementation of the FCTC represents an important legacy to present and future generations. In this sense, it is important to bear in mind that the Convention is above all an evidence-based treaty that reaffirms the right of all people to the highest standards of health.

2.   Since its entry into force, the FCTC has been providing governments with important guidance and cooperation opportunities to enhance their national tobacco-control policies., Article 2.1 of the FCTC encourages Parties to implement measures beyond those required by its provisions and protocols, even to impose stricter requirements, as long as they are consistent with the Convention and are in accordance with international law. Brazil is also convinced that it is of great importance to maintain tobacco control efforts up-to-date with any changes in the tobacco market and with new control strategies, as well as to continuously base it on current and relevant scientific, technical and economic considerations.

II.   ARTICLE 2.1 OF THE FCTC AND THE GUIDELINES OF THE CONFERENCE OF PARTIES

3.   Under Article 2.1 of the FCTC, Parties are not merely allowed to exceed the Convention in terms of measures for tobacco control, but they are encouraged to do so, especially when read in the context of other provisions. For example, Article 5.1 of the FCTC, under "General Obligations", establishes that "[e]ach Party shall develop, implement, periodically update and review comprehensive multisectoral national tobacco control strategies, plans and programmes in accordance with this Convention and the protocols to which it is a Party". Moreover, the second part of Article 2.1 makes clear that "(…) nothing

in these instruments shall prevent a Party from imposing stricter requirements (…)". The preamble of the Convention deems it necessary both "to be alert to any efforts by the tobacco industry to undermine or subvert tobacco control efforts" and to "promote measures of tobacco control based on current and relevant scientific, technical and economic considerations".

4.   Brazil believes that FCTC guidelines should be taken into consideration as relevant context, especially if such guidelines are to be qualified as relevant international standards under Article 2.5 of the TBT Agreement. In the US-Clove Cigarettes dispute, for example, the Panel clearly expressed its awareness of the "important international efforts to curb smoking within the context of the WHO FCTC and its WHO Partial Guidelines" and considered the FCTC guidelines relevant to its understanding that the existence of "extensive scientific evidence supporting the conclusion that banning clove and other flavoured cigarettes could contribute to reducing youth smoking". This view was shared by the Appellate Body, which also recognized the importance of Members' efforts on tobacco control in the World Health Organization and expressed its belief that nothing in the Covered Agreements is to be interpreted as preventing Members from devising and implementing public health policies generally, and tobacco-control policies in particular.

5.   At the same time that Article 2.1 of the FCTC requires that measures going beyond the Convention are to be in accordance with international law, which naturally includes international trade law, WTO Covered Agreements fully recognize and respect the sovereign right of Members to take regulatory measures in response to legitimate public health concerns.

III.   THE WTO RECOGNIZES MEMBERS' RIGHT TO PROTECT PUBLIC HEALTH

6.   As recognized at the 4th Ministerial Meeting of the WTO in Doha 2001, nothing in the WTO rules prevents its Members from taking measures for the protection of human life or health, at the levels they consider appropriate, provided that such measures are (i) neither applied in a manner which would constitute a means of arbitrary or unjustifiable discrimination between countries where the same conditions prevail, (ii) nor represent a disguised restriction on international trade, (iii) otherwise in accordance with the provisions of the WTO Agreements.

7.   Specifically in what concerns commitments under the TRIPS Agreement, WTO Members adopted the Declaration on the TRIPS Agreement and Public Health at the Doha Ministerial Conference, where they agreed that such Agreement does not and should not prevent members from taking measures to protect public health. At the same time, the right of Members to use, to the full, the provisions in the TRIPS Agreement, which provide flexibility for such purpose, was reaffirmed. WTO Members recognized that these flexibilities included, among others, the imperative of having each provision of the TRIPS Agreement read in the light of its object and purpose (Articles 7 and 8), when

applying the customary rules of interpretation of public international law. Brazil agrees that the protection of human health is of utmost importance and that the Covered Agreements in general and the TRIPS Agreement in particular afford Members enough policy space to pursue such objective. Nonetheless, Brazil believes that in pursuing its public policies objectives, Members must take into consideration the rights and obligations under the WTO, and the need to ensure a proper balance between them.

IV.   USE OF A REGISTERED TRADEMARK IN THE COURSE OF TRADE

8.   The very fact that trademarks are protected under the WTO evidences that such intellectual property is important to the multilateral trading system, particularly in what concerns fair competition and market access. As emphasized in the Amicus curiae brief of Brazil's National Confederation of Industry (CNI), trademarks are important assets to companies that have long-term plans to grow on a worldwide scale. Likewise, the Brazilian Intellectual Property Association (ABPI) recalled that considerable investments are made into the creation, development and protection of trademarks, as they are deemed essential to the success of business operations domestically and abroad.

9.   Although the use of a registered trademark in the course of trade is not an automatic step following registration (as there could be several government requirements to be fulfilled beforehand), Brazil understands that the registration of a trademark does entail an expectation of use, and a very legitimate one, that would not only give concrete expression to the protection conferred under TRIPS Agreement to trademarks, but also ensure that they can fulfill their socio-economic function. As the Panel in the EC-Geographical Indications dispute affirmed, the function of trademarks, as described in Article 15.1 of the TRIPS Agreement, can be understood as distinguishing goods and services of undertakings in the course of trade. Accordingly, every trademark owner has a legitimate interest in preserving the distinctiveness, or capacity to distinguish, of his trademark so that it can perform that function. If the function of a trademark is to distinguish goods and services, then such function can only be fulfilled if: (i) third parties are prevented from using identical/similar signs for identical/similar goods or services where such use would result in a likelihood of confusion and (ii) the trademark is actually used in the course of trade. Accordingly, the TRIPS Agreement expressly grants owners of registered trademarks exclusive rights in relation to the first condition (Article 16.1) and, in relation to the second condition, it prohibits Members from unjustifiably encumbering the use of a trademark in the course of trade with special requirements (Article 20). Brazil is aware that nowhere in the TRIPS Agreement is found a provision such as "the owner of a registered trademark shall have the right to use it in the course of trade". Yet, it also seems clear that Article 20 not only recognizes the importance of use of a trademark in the course of trade for it to fulfill its socio-economic function, but it also protects such use from special requirements that would otherwise unjustifiably encumber it.

V. ARTICLE 20 OF THE TRIPS AGREEMENT PROTECTS REGISTERED TRADEMARKS FROM HAVING ITS USE UNJUSTIFIABLY ENCUMBERED BY SPECIAL REQUIREMENTS

10. Brazil understands that Article 20 of the TRIPS Agreement establishes a clear obligation on WTO Members not to unjustifiably encumber the use of a trademark in the course of trade with special requirements. This obligation takes into account the importance of use for a trademark to fulfill its socio-economic function, but at the same time, if read jointly with Article 8.1, it does not prevent Members from adopting measures to protect public health. In this sense, if a WTO Member believes that another Member has adopted a measure inconsistent with the obligation under Article 20, it would have to adduce evidence on its favor, whereas the respondent would still need to demonstrate otherwise.

11. In Brazil's view, the term "special requirements" under Article 20 would not be restricted to requirements specifically applicable to individual trademarks, so that any horizontal requirement would be automatically deemed unjustifiable, thus inconsistent with this provision. Brazil understands that the term "special requirements" in Article 20 may also refer to requirements applicable to a group of related trademarks, not just to an individual trademark. Consequently, the fact that a measure at issue is horizontal does not seem to be in itself proof of violation of Article 20 of the TRIPS Agreement.

12. Brazil is also not convinced that the prohibition of use of trademarks would be out of the scope of Article 20 of the TRIPS Agreement. This article provides a non-exhaustive list of examples of special requirements (introduced by the term "such as") that could represent an encumbrance to the use of trademarks, and this list per se does not exclude prohibition of use from the scope of the Article. According to dictionary definition, Brazil understands that "encumbering the use" would be equivalent to "impeding the use", thus prohibitions do seem to be a form of encumbrance – probably the most radical one if compared to the examples provided in Article 20. Furthermore, if prohibition of use was deemed to be out of the scope of Article 20, then a loophole in the TRIPS Agreement could be created, whereby it would be possible to circumvent the obligation of no-unjustifiable-encumbrance by prohibiting the use of trademarks altogether.

V.1 Interpretation of the expression "use of a trademark in the course of trade"

13. Brazil does not consider that the fact that a market for a given product is considered "dark" (i.e. the consumers only see the product after the purchase, that is, after the course of trade is concluded) has a bearing in the scope of Article 20. The expression "use of a trademark in the course of trade" under Article 20 of the TRIPS Agreement is better understood as an opposition to other uses of a trademark which are of no concern to the WTO, such as use in letterheads, promotional material and advertisement, or even under sponsorship

contracts. If jointly read with Article 15, the expression "use of a trademark in the course of trade" seems to restrict the scope of the provision to the situation where trademarks are applied to goods or services in order to distinguish goods and services of one undertaking from those of others. Thus, the scope of Article 20, particularly in what concerns the expression "use of a trademark in the course of trade", is not subject to when or whether consumers actually get in direct contact with products and their trademarks.

V.2 The assessment of whether an encumbrance posed by a measure at issue is unjustifiable

14.   For Brazil, the term "unjustifiably" as expressed in Article 20 of the TRIPS Agreement is associated with the term "encumbered" and not with the expression "special requirements". Therefore, what seems to be central to the analysis of consistency with Article 20 is not so much whether a measure is unjustifiable, but whether the encumbrance it poses to the use of a trademark is unjustifiable. Accordingly, Brazil believes that, when assessing whether a special requirement unjustifiably encumbers the use of a trademark in the course of trade, it may not suffice to demonstrate the lack of a rational connection between the measure at issue and a certain policy objective. Rather, complainants would have to demonstrate that the encumbrance posed by the measure is not commensurate with the importance of the objective pursued. Likewise, it would not suffice for the respondent to explain the reasons for adopting a given requirement: it would also have to adduce evidence in order to prove there is a balance between the importance of the objective pursued and the encumbrance posed by its measure. Consequently, if the encumbrance posed by a special requirement is demonstrated to be excessive in relation to the importance of the objective pursued, it would probably not be justifiable at the same time.

15.   The term "unjustifiably" aims to achieve a fair balance between a Member's ability to regulate and its obligation to refrain from encumbering how a trademark may be used. Thus, more than the assessment of whether the objective pursued is legitimate and whether there is a rational connection between the measure at issue and such objective, the term "unjustifiably" seems to add to the standard of analysis the question of whether the encumbrance posed by the measure is commensurate/equivalent to the importance of the objective pursued

VI.   TBT AND ARTICLES 2.2 AND 2.5

16.   Brazil understands that a measure may fall under more than one of the Covered Agreements. In this sense, a measure dealing with intellectual property issues may also be a technical regulation within the meaning of the TBT Agreement insofar as it deals with product characteristics, labelling or other TBT-related matters concerning trade in products. The analysis of the TBT Agreement and the TRIPS Agreement should be independent from one another,

as there is not a relationship of lex specialis between them. While the TBT Agreement deals with technical regulations and their effects on the trade of goods, the TRIPS Agreement establishes Intellectual Property Rights in what they relate to trade. They integrate different annexes of the Marrakesh Agreement and deal with substantially different obligations and the inconsistency of the obligations in one of them does not bring about necessarily a violation of the other.

17.   As regards the degree of contribution of a measure to its stated objective, Brazil considers it should be discerned by the design, structure and operation of the measure; the evidence relating to the application of the measure should be taken into account as an objective piece of information. In situations where measures have been only recently implemented, the panel may want to include in its assessment not only evidence of the impacts of actual application of the measure, but also take into account what the measure – in light of its design and structure – may achieve in a longer temporal perspective. Given the fact that the adopted measures are inserted in an overall strategy which contains other measures, the attainment of its stated objectives may sometimes only be fully discerned in the interplay of all elements of the strategy and over the course of time.

18.   The analysis of the measure should start with article 2.5, both in what concerns the compatibility with a relevant international standard as well as with the presence of a legitimate objective. This order of analysis makes procedural sense, because if the two conditions above are fulfilled and not rebutted, a presumption of compatibility with article 2.2 emerges: the measure does not create an unnecessary obstacle to international trade. As regards the objectives, while there may be other legitimate objectives under the TBT Agreement, only those explicitly mentioned in article 2.2 will generate a rebuttable presumption.

19.   Article 2.5, second sentence, establishes a rebuttable presumption of compatibility with Article 2.2 for those technical regulations prepared, adopted or applied to fulfil a legitimate objective and that are in accordance with relevant international standards. Brazil understands that the nature of the second sentence of Article 2.5 is not of an exception, but of a conditioned procedural right. The relevant implication of this conclusion is that the responding party is required only to establish – on a *prima facie* basis - that the challenged measure is in accordance with an international standard and fulfils a legitimate objective: the burden is then shifted to the complaining party to demonstrate that the measure either does not comply with these two conditions or does create unnecessary obstacles to international trade. This view is confirmed by the last sentence of Article 2.5. In this sense, Brazil also believes that the jurisprudence of the Appellate Body in *EC – Hormones* regarding the relationship between Articles 3.1, 3.2 and 3.3 of the SPS Agreement can be of relevance in the interpretation of Articles 2.2 and 2.5.

20.   Two requirements must be met in order for a technical regulation to fall under Article 2.5. As regards the first, the technical regulation must be prepared, adopted or applied for one of the legitimate objectives explicitly mentioned in

paragraph 2. Therefore, while there may be other legitimate objectives under the TBT Agreement, only "national security requirements; the prevention of deceptive practices; protection of human health or safety, animal or plant life or health, or the environment" may generate a rebuttable presumption for measures under Article 2.5. With respect to the second requirement, related to the concept of "international standardizing bodies", Brazil would like to recall that, contrary to the SPS Agreement (Annex A (3)), the TBT Agreement does not have a list of international standardizing organizations explicitly listed in its text; the TBT could then be seen as being more welcoming to new standardizing bodies than the SPS Agreement. The jurisprudence in *US – Tuna II* may be useful in determining whether the entity in question is an international standardizing body. In that case, the Appellate Body understood that the body's membership must be open to the relevant bodies of at least all Members, be active in the action of standardization and be recognized as such. These criteria should be addressed, according to the Appellate Body, "in a holistic manner".

CONCLUSION

21.   It is unequivocal that tobacco is a unique product, and that efforts under the FCTC represent the increasing global commitment to counteract the devastating consequences of tobacco consumption and exposure to tobacco smoke. Furthermore, it is recognized that nothing in the WTO's Covered Agreements prevents its Members from taking measures for the protection of human life, including those that may affect intellectual property. Brazil believes that the Panel's interpretations and findings can and should contribute to give proper balance to, on the one hand, policy space for governments in the application of legitimate measures to protect public health, and on the other, rights and obligations under WTO Agreements.

ANNEX C-3

EXECUTIVE SUMMARY OF THE ARGUMENTS
OF CANADA

I.   THE TRIPS AGREEMENT

A.   The role of Articles 7 and 8.1 of the TRIPS Agreement and paragraph 4 of the Doha Declaration on Public Health in the interpretation of the TRIPS Agreement

1.   Articles 7 and 8.1 of the TRIPS Agreement and paragraph 4 of the Doha Declaration on Public Health provide the lens through which the TRIPS Agreement must be interpreted. Paragraph 4 of the Doha Declaration on Public Health elaborates upon the principles and objectives articulated in Articles 7 and 8.1 of the TRIPS Agreement, and comprises part of the relevant interpretive context. The Doha Declaration on Public Health clearly and expressly directs how the provisions of the TRIPS Agreement are to be interpreted. It meets the test set out by the Appellate Body in *US – Clove Cigarettes* as a "subsequent agreement between the parties" within the meaning of Article 31(3)(a) of the Vienna Convention.[1] The Panel therefore needs to take it into account in the interpretation of the provisions of the TRIPS Agreement.

B.   Article 2.1 and Article 10*bis* of the Paris Convention

2.   Canada recalls that the first paragraph of TRIPS Article 2 incorporates by reference certain provisions of the Paris Convention, including Article 10*bis*. Article 10*bis* of the Paris Convention is comprised of two components: an obligation and a definition. The first paragraph establishes the obligation to assure to nationals of the other countries of the Paris Union effective protection against unfair competition. The second and third paragraphs set out a definition of "unfair competition" and an illustrative list of acts, allegations, and indications that are expressly prohibited.

3.   The ordinary meaning of the terms in the context of Article 10*bis* suggests that the phrase "act of competition" is concerned solely with the commercial behaviour of actors competing in the market. Where a Member through its measures is *regulating* the market or its private actors, such measures do not constitute "acts of competition" and fall outside the scope of the definition of "unfair competition" under Article 10*bis*.

---

[1]   Appellate Body Report, *US – Clove Cigarettes*, para. 262.

C. Article 15.4

4.   The complainants confuse two concepts that are distinct under Section 2 of the TRIPS Agreement: 1) registration, and 2) rights that flow from registration. Article 15.4 only obliges Members to ensure that the "nature of the goods" do not form an obstacle to *registration* of the trademark. Article 15.4 neither addresses protections flowing from trademark registration, nor establishes a right to use a registered trademark. Further, contrary to the complainants' assertions, Article 15.4 does *not* guarantee an opportunity, or grant a right, to acquire distinctiveness for non-inherently distinctive signs. This would create a right to use a sign if that sign has the potential to become a trademark, which is *not* a right protected under the TRIPS Agreement. A finding of a right to use a sign or trademark under the TRIPS Agreement would effectively restrict Members' ability to take legitimate measures to protect public health. Members have clearly and unequivocally preserved the freedom to regulate in the interest of protecting public health and this is evident in TRIPS Articles 7 and 8.1, and paragraph 4 of the Doha Declaration on Public Health. The TRIPS Articles in issue, including Article 15.4, must be interpreted in a manner supportive of a Member's right to protect public health.

D. Articles 16.1 and 16.3

5.   The single right conferred on the owner of a registered trademark under Article 16.1 is set out in the first sentence. As confirmed by a previous panel, this right consists *only* of the trademark owner's entitlement to prevent *third parties* from unauthorized use where such use would result in a likelihood of confusion.[2] Contrary to the complainants' arguments, WTO Members are not obliged under Article 16.1, or elsewhere in the TRIPS Agreement, to preserve or strengthen either the mark or the owner's ability to successfully demonstrate a "likelihood of confusion". Underlying the complainants' argument under Article 16.3 is a claim of a right to use a mark in order to acquire or maintain status as a "well-known" mark. Article 16.3 does not establish a right to use a mark. It follows from this that the provision also does not protect a mark's status or ability to acquire status as a "well-known" mark. The complainants' interpretation of Article 16.1 and Article 16.3 is not supported by the text, the negotiating history, case law, or TRIPS Article 8.1 and paragraph 4 of the Doha Declaration on Public Health, and must be rejected.

E. Article 20

6.   Article 20 disciplines certain requirements that Members can impose on *how* a trademark is used. If a panel finds that the measure constitutes a "special requirement"; that "encumbers"; the "use" of a trademark; "in the course of

---

[2]   Panel Report, *EC – Trademarks and Geographical Indications (US)*, fn. 558.

trade" it must then determine whether the measure is "unjustifiable". If a panel finds in the affirmative, then the measure violates Article 20.

7.   In terms of the allocation of the burden of proof to demonstrate that a measure is "unjustifiable", Canada disagrees with the complainants that the burden shifts to the defending Member to prove that a measure is "justifiable". The word "unjustifiably" in the text does not create an exception but rather comprises a component of the affirmative obligation. Therefore the complainants must show, as part of their *prima facie* case, that the Australian measure is "unjustifiable".

8.   It is essential that the test established to determine whether a special requirement is "unjustifiable" safeguards the integrity of the obligation under Article 20 while ensuring regulatory flexibility to protect public health. Having regard for the ordinary meaning of the words, existing case law, and relevant context, including other TRIPS provisions and the Doha Declaration on Public Health, Canada proposes that the elements to be examined in determining whether a requirement is "unjustifiable" under Article 20 constitute the following: 1) whether the objective of the requirement is legitimate. This element involves identifying the objective of the requirement and determining whether it is "legitimate"; 2) whether there is a rational connection between the requirement and the legitimate objective; 3) whether the requirement contributes to the objective; and 4) the extent to which the requirement encumbers how a trademark can be used. Ultimately, a determination of whether the measure in issue is "unjustifiable" must be made on a case-by-case basis taking into account all relevant facts, and weighing and balancing these elements.

II.   THE TBT AGREEMENT - ARTICLES 2.2 AND 2.5

9.   In response to the Parties' arguments regarding the applicability of the TBT and TRIPS Agreements, Canada considers that these agreements are not mutually exclusive – both can apply to the same measure, including a measure that deals with intellectual property.

10.   With respect to Article 2.2, Canada considers that the Appellate Body's findings regarding the assessment of contribution of a measure to its objective in *US – COOL (21.5)* and *Brazil-Retreaded Tyres* are particularly relevant to this case. In particular, that the measure's objective, its characteristics, and the nature, quantity, and quality of evidence that is available will have a bearing on whether the measure's degree of contribution can be assessed in quantitative or qualitative terms, and will influence the degree of precision of that analysis.[3] Further that a panel may rely on a qualitative analysis in assessing the contribution of a measure to the realization of the objective pursued by it[4] and

---

[3]   Appellate Body Report, *US – COOL (Article 21.5 – Canada and Mexico)*, para. 5.211.
[4]   Appellate Body Reports, *Brazil – Retreaded Tyres*, paras. 146, 151-153; and *US – COOL (Article 21.5 – Canada and Mexico)*, para. 5.209.

when dealing with measures that form part of a comprehensive strategy to address a public policy issue, the contribution that any proposed alternative measure would make to the achievement of the objective must be viewed in the light of any decreased effectiveness of other measures within the strategy that could result from substituting the challenged measure.[5]

11.   Further, it is the *overall* degree of contribution that a measure makes to its objective that is relevant in identifying the contribution of the measure in issue, rather than any isolated aspect of contribution; which remains the case even where a measure deploys various methods or techniques that jointly or separately contribute to achieving the objective.[6] Further, a panel may conclude that an alternative measure that might otherwise have been found to make an equivalent degree of contribution to the achievement fails to do so because, for example, the objective is of vital importance, the nature of the risks involve human health, or the severity of the consequences of non-fulfilment of the objective are grave.[7]

12.   A finding by the Panel that the FCTC Guidelines[8] are "relevant international standards" for the purposes of Article 2.5, and the Australian measures are "in accordance" with these standards would create a rebuttable presumption that the measures are not unnecessary obstacles to trade. The standard of proof that the Panel would require of the complainants to demonstrate that the Australian measures violate Article 2.2 must be higher than that required to make out a *prima facie* case as it must reflect such a finding of a rebuttable presumption.

III.   THE GATT 1994 - ARTICLE IX

13.   A "mark of origin" for the purposes of Article IX:4 is not a trademark or a geographical indication. Rather it is a country of origin marking such as "product of Canada" or "made in Canada". Paragraph 4 of Article IX stipulates that a Member's laws and regulations relating to the marking of imported products must permit compliance without, *inter alia*, materially reducing their value. The phrase "permit compliance" in Article IX:4 illustrates the purpose of the provision, which is to discipline *how* compliance with a marking requirement may be prescribed. The provision serves only to limit a Member's laws and regulations relating to marking requirements in terms of *how compliance* with such requirements can be prescribed.

---

[5]   Appellate Body Report, *Brazil – Retreaded Tyres*, para. 172.

[6]   Appellate Body Report, *US – COOL (Article 21.5 – Canada and Mexico)*, para. 5.255.

[7]   *Ibid.*, para. 5.254.

[8]   WHO Framework Convention on Tobacco Control: guidelines for implementation (2013 Edition). (Exhibit AUS-109)

ANNEX C-4

EXECUTIVE SUMMARY OF THE ARGUMENTS
OF CHINA

I.   INTRODUCTION

1.   China first presents its general view that WTO Members are entitled to adopt appropriate measures for protection of public health. Thereafter, China provides observations on the claims made by the complainants under Articles 2.1, 16.1, 16.3, 20, 22.2(b) and 24.3 of the TRIPS Agreement and the claims under Article 2.2 of the TBT Agreement.

II.   WTO MEMBERS MAY TAKE APPROPRIATE MEASURES FOR PROTECTION OF PUBLIC HEALTH

2.   The present disputes involve a general question whether and, if so, to what extent WTO Members may take public health measures under the WTO Agreements. Although trade interests are main concerns under the WTO system which is a multilateral trading system, WTO Agreements recognize and accommodate societal values and interests, such as protection of public health which is "both vital and important in the highest degree"[1]. WTO Members are entitled to take appropriate public health measures. However, Members have no unlimited discretion to adopt public health measures, but should ensure that the measures they take are not WTO-inconsistent.

3.   As to the tobacco plain packaging measures (PP measure) at issue, China shares the view of Australia that tobacco use seriously harms human life and health and notes that the complainants do not take issue with this. As a matter of fact, Chinese government has been developing and applying various effective measures to control tobacco use. China further notes that the scope of the measures being challenged in these disputes is limited. Australia applies a comprehensive range of tobacco control measures. The complainants do not challenge measures other than the PP measure in these disputes. In addition, certain claims aim at only limited aspects of the PP measure. For instance, claims under Articles 16.1, 16.3 and 20 appear to concern only the PP "trademark requirements", and not the PP "form requirements".

---

[1]   Appellate Body Report, *EC – Asbestos,* para. 172.

III. OBSERVATIONS ON CERTAIN CLAIMS UNDER THE TRIPS AGREEMENT

A. Claims Under Article 16.1

4.   The Panel needs to consider whether a trademark owner has rights or interests to use its own trademark and whether its own use of the trademark is a necessary condition for it to effectively exercise the right to prevent unauthorized third party's use conferred by Article 16.1.

5.   The panel in *EC – Trademarks and Geographical Indications (Australia)* stated that every trademark owner has "a legitimate interest in preserving the distinctiveness, or capacity to distinguish, of its trademark so that it can perform that function", including the interest in *using* its own trademark in connection with the relevant goods and services.[2] This statement appears to confirm that the inherent nature of a trademark requires it to be used in the course of trade, being either a right to use or a minimum opportunity of use. Article 20 also supports this interpretation. It implies that the owner of a trademark has a right or legitimate interest to use the trademark in the course of trade; otherwise, WTO Members would be able to take any measures to encumber the use of a trademark as they wish.

6.   China further notes that in cases where a third party uses *similar* signs for identical or similar goods or services, the trademark owner bears the burden of proof to demonstrate that such use of the third party results in a likelihood of confusion. To the extent that the prohibition or strict restriction of use of a trademark necessarily reduces or removes the distinctiveness of that trademark and thus impedes the trademark owner to demonstrate the likelihood of confusion, such measures could be found inconsistent with Article 16.1.

B. Claims Under Article 16.3

7.   In view of the arguments proffered by the parties, the Panel is expected to consider whether the coverage of Article 16.3 would extend to the acquirement and maintaining of the well-known trademark status and whether use is a necessary condition to acquire and maintain the well-known trademark status.

8.   China notes that Article 16.3 provides additional protection to *existing* well-known trademarks, and such protection does not apply to trademarks that may become well known in the future or trademarks that were once well known. Nevertheless, the Panel may wish to consider if it is appropriate to entirely separate the issue of additional protection of well-known trademarks and the issue of the acquirement and maintaining of the well-known trademark status. To give an extreme example, if a Member sets such an extremely high standard that

---

[2]   Panel Report, *EC – Trademarks and Geographical Indications (Australia)*, para.7.664.

no trademark could be qualified as a well-known trademark, the additional protection accorded to well-known trademark would be meaningless.

9.   As to the second question, it appears that use is an important, if not indispensable, way to acquire or maintain the well-known status. As Article 16.2 provides, "[i]n determining whether a trademark is well known, Members shall take account of the knowledge of the trademark in the relevant sector of the public". And it is widely recognized that the duration, extent and geographical area of any use of the mark are highly relevant indicators as to the determination whether or not a mark is well-known by the relevant sector of the public. Therefore, the Panel needs to consider if the PP measure, by prohibiting or strictly restricting the use of tobacco trademarks, necessarily results in that tobacco trademarks cannot acquire or maintain the well-known status and thus are denied the protection accorded under Article 16.3.

C.   Claims Under Article 20

10.   For a measure to be found in violation of Article 20, it should be established that the measure imposes "special requirements" that "unjustifiably" "encumber[s]" "the use of a trademark" "in the course of trade".

11.   "[S]pecial requirements" would include those mandated requirements that: (i) apply to a limited product class; (ii) apply only for a particular purpose; or (iii) are distinct from those that apply generally or "usually". To the extent that the PP measure *prohibits* the use of certain types of trademarks, e.g. figurative trademarks, on *tobacco products and their packaging* and *requires* the use of the brand name/word mark of *tobacco products* in a standardized form and font, it imposes "special requirements" within the scope of Article 20.

12.   As to the meaning of the term "in the course of trade", Australia appears to read this term in a too narrow sense by suggesting that this term refers only to the course of a particular transaction of buying and selling. The same term is used in Articles 16.1 and 24.8 of the TRIPS Agreement as well as Article 10*bis* (3) of the Paris Convention, which is incorporated into the TRIPS Agreement. It is widely accepted that the term means "in commercial activities" or "in commerce", in a broader sense.

13.   In view of the above, it appears to China that the focus of the contention between the parties would be whether the PP measure *unjustifiably* encumbers the use of trademarks in the course of trade. Noting that the meaning of "unjustifiably" under Article 20 has not yet been explored by prior panels and/or the Appellate Body, China makes several observations. First, prohibition of the use of a trademark is not *per se* unjustifiable as suggested by some complainants. Article 20 envisages that the use of a trademark could be prohibited, provided that such prohibition is not unjustifiable. Second, the standard of "unjustifiably" under Article 20 is not necessarily the same as that of "necessary" under Article 2.2 of the TBT Agreement or Article XX of the GATT 1994. The jurisprudence regarding the latter may not be simply transplanted into the former. Third, the underlying test is not merely a question of existence/non-existence of rational

connection between the measure and the policy objectives pursued as Australia appears to suggest, but calls for evaluation on the *extent* of the rational connection. While a special requirement that has no "rational connection" with a legitimate objective is unjustifiable, this does not necessarily mean that a special requirement is justifiable as long as it has *any* extent of "rational connection" with a legitimate objective. This observation initially originates from the ordinary meaning of the term "unjustifiably", which, like the words "just", "reasonable" and "defensible", implies certain discretionary judgement. China takes note that Australia's interpretation of "unjustifiably" under Article 20 essentially relies on the Appellate Body's interpretation of the term "unjustifiable" in the context of Article XX of the GATT 1994.[3] However, the two terms do not necessarily have the same meaning. While Article XX of the GATT 1994 sets out a two-tier test, Article 20 of the TRIPS Agreement contains only a *single* "unjustifiably/justifiably" test which implies that this test would have to bear more functions or set a higher threshold. On the other hand, even the instances identified by the Appellate Body as "unjustifiable" within the meaning of Article XX of the GATT 1994 are not limited to those in which the measure at stake bears no relationship to the legitimate objective. For instance, a measure that is "informal" and "casual" and is not "transparent" and "predictable" was found "unjustifiable".[4]

14.   Based on the above observations, China expects that the Panel will weigh and balance, in a *holistic* manner, all relevant factors, including but not limited to: (i) the policy objective and its importance; (ii) the extent of the rational connection or, in other words, the degree of contribution of the measure to the policy objective; and (iii) the extent of encumbrance imposed by the measure. Given that there are few disputes among the parties with respect to the above factors (i) and (iii), the Panel's examination is expected to concentrate more on the contribution of the trademark requirements to the objective of tobacco control. Both sides put forward extensive evidence to illustrate that the trademark restriction does (not) and can (not) make contribution to that objective. The Panel is expected to objectively assess this factual matter, and when necessary, to exercise its right to seek information under Article 13 of the DSU, including consulting experts to obtain opinions on factual issues concerning scientific or technical matters.

D.   Claims Under Articles 2.1 and 22.2(b)

15.   In China's view, the key contention is the definition of "unfair competition" under the relevant provisions, i.e. whether it must be a result from the market actor's acts or it could also encompass the government regulatory measures.

---

[3]   Australia's first written submission, paras. 366-369.
[4]   Appellate Body Report, *US – Shrimp*, paras. 180 and 181.

16.   The PP measure appears not to be an act of unfair competition within the meaning of Article 10*bis* of the Paris Convention. First, the "act of competition" is defined under Article 10*bis* (2) as any act "contrary to honest practices in industrial or commercial matters". It appears difficult to characterize the acts that are taken by competitors to comply with the legal requirements as acts "contrary to honest". Second, Article 10*bis* (3) provides that three categories of acts "shall be prohibited". The PP measure does not fall within the scope of the second or third category, i.e. false allegations and misleading indications or allegations, nor fall within the scope of the first category which clearly refers to acts of "a competitor".

17.   Alternatively, if the Panel were to interpret "unfair competition" as compassing government regulatory measures and/or its impact on the market, it needs to carefully assess the detailed facts of the dispute, including a range of legal mechanisms available in Australia, so as to determine whether the PP measure compels market actors to engage in acts of unfair competition or Australia fails to assure an effective protection against unfair competition due to the PP measure.

E.   Claims Under Article 24.3

18.   Article 24.3 is a standstill provision which requires that a Member, in addition to comply with the minimum standards established by the provisions of the TRIPS Agreement, shall maintain the existing protection level of geographical indications (GIs) in that Member prior to the entry into force of the WTO Agreement. It thus concerns the pre-existing protection of GIs in *that* Member. Assuming that the protection of GIs under Section 3, Part II of the TRIPS Agreement refers only to negative rights, i.e. rights to prevent third parties' illegal use of GIs, it does not necessarily follows that the pre-existing protection of GIs in a Member is limited to negative rights. To the extent that the pre-existing protection in a Member includes the right to use GIs, the Member is not permitted to diminish the protection by prohibiting the use of GIs. In any event, the complainants need to establish a *prima facie* case that, prior to January 1995, Australian law permits the owners of GIs to *use* established GIs on their products, and/or to *use* a word or non-word indication on their products so as to develop GIs.

IV.   OBSERVATIONS ON CLAIMS UNDER THE TBT AGREEMENT

19.   In order to establish a violation of Article 2.2 of the TBT Agreement, a complainant must first demonstrate that the challenged measure constitutes a "technical regulation" within the meaning of Annex 1:1 of the TBT Agreement. China notes that it is undisputed the "form requirements" imposed by the PP measure are technical regulations. In China's view, the "trademark requirements" also fall within the scope of the definition of a technical regulation as clarified by the Appellate Body in previous cases such as *EC-Asbestos*, *EC-Sardines* and *EC-Seal Products*. These trademark requirements are subject to *not only* the

provisions of the TRIPS Agreement but also the provisions of the TBT Agreement, including Article 2.2.

20.   Article 2.2 of the TBT Agreement sets out a three-tier test of consistency, namely: (i) whether the measure is "trade-restrictive"; (ii) whether the measure fulfills a legitimate objective; and (iii) whether the measure is "not more trade-restrictive than necessary" to fulfill a legitimate objective, taking account of the risks non-fulfilment would create.

21.   As to the first element, what should be assessed is whether the measure has a limiting effect on trade, i.e. importation of tobacco products in the current disputes, rather than whether it results in discrimination between the treatment of imported goods and domestic goods. Like the term "restrictions" in Article XI of the GATT 1994, trade-restrictiveness is of a broad coverage. Furthermore, the limiting effect of restrictions "need not be demonstrated by quantifying the effects of the measure at issue", but "can be demonstrated through the design, architecture, and revealing structure of the measure at issue considered in its relevant context".[5]

22.   As to the second element, the Panel is expected to objectively assess the factual matter whether the PP measures make contribution, and to what extent, to the objective of tobacco control. The Appellate Body has noted that the degree of contribution may be discerned from the *design, structure and operation* of the measure, as well as from evidence relating to the *application* of the measure.[6] The evidence concerning the post-implementation period is not the *only* evidence to establish the contribution, and might not give decisive guidance either.

23.   As to the third element, "a comparison of the challenged measure and possible alternative measures should be undertaken"[7] in most cases. In the context of such "comparative analysis", it may be relevant to consider in particular: (i) whether the proposed alternative measure is less trade-restrictive; (ii) whether it would make an equivalent contribution to the relevant legitimate objective, taking account of the risks non-fulfilment would create; and (iii) whether it is reasonably available.[8] An issue the Panel may need to address is the meaning of the terms "the risks nonfulfilment would create". China considers that the fact that a legitimate objective is of great importance does not, in itself, lead to the conclusion that "the risks non-fulfilment would create" are grave. A panel should assess the importance of the legitimate objective together with the measures that are applied, or the measures proposed by the complainants, to fulfil this objective. In case that a challenged measure does not contribute to the objective or a reasonable available alternative could make greater contribution to the objective, "the risks non-fulfilment would create" are not grave.

---

[5]   Appellate Body Report, *Argentina – Import Measures*, para. 5.217.
[6]   Appellate Body Report, *US – Tuna II (Mexico)*, para. 317.
[7]   *Ibid.*, para. 322.
[8]   *Ibid.*

ANNEX C-5

EXECUTIVE SUMMARY OF THE ARGUMENTS
OF THE EUROPEAN UNION

I. TRIPS

1. The term "unjustifiably" in Article 20 has not yet been clarified by panels or the Appellate Body. The EU view is that as drafted, Article 20 of the TRIPS Agreement provides for a flexible tool of interpretation, that leaves open what degree of justification or deference may be appropriate in particular cases, just as the degree of deference under Article XX of the GATT 1994 is open, in the sense that it depends upon which specific subparagraph of that provision is being applied, and accordingly what nexus is required between the measure and the legitimate objective. How much deference is appropriate in a particular case depends on further contextual considerations, as described below.

2. There are limits on the extent to which case law on the issue of 'unjustifiable discrimination' in Article XX can inform an interpretation of the term "unjustifiably" in Article 20 of the TRIPS. However, the European Union considers that some guidance concerning the meaning of the term 'unjustifiable' in Article 20 of the TRIPS Agreement can be gleaned from prior clarifications by the DSB of the term "unjustifiable discrimination" under the chapeau of Article XX of the GATT 1994.

3. As regards the different tests that have been discussed by the parties, we consider that their nature is the same or very similar with the key difference being a different degree of justification or, more precisely, deference. Properly understood, the five-level structure of the test is just a rationalising heuristic tool. Whether it is used as a tool to intensify judicial control of acts by WTO Members is not determined by the structure of the test but by the degree of judicial restraint practised in applying it. In this sense, more important than the structure of the test is the question which degree of deference to the WTO Member is appropriate in examining a measure under Article 20 of the TRIPS Agreement.

4. In our view, Article 20 of the TRIPS Agreement provides for a flexible tool of interpretation, that leaves open what degree of justification or deference may be appropriate in particular cases, just as the degree of deference under Article XX of the GATT 1994 is open, in the sense that it depends upon which specific subparagraph of that provision is being applied. The concept of "justifiable" is broad, in the sense that it is broad enough to capture the various types of justification, with their various types of nexus, set out in Article XX of the GATT 1994. We are not saying that this necessarily implies a lighter test or more deference than would be the case under Article XX.

5.   While Article 20 of the TRIPS Agreement provides a flexible interpretative tool, capable of capturing the full range of possible justifications, the European Union would like to note that, in this particular case, given that the measure at issue is a technical regulation, we consider that the interpretation and application of Article 20 of the TRIPS Agreement should be contextually informed by Article 2.2 of the TBT Agreement. This means that to the extent Article 20 of the TRIPS Agreement is applicable, such an encumbrance would not be justifiable if at the same time it is inconsistent with Article 2.2 of the TBT Agreement. This would then not give rise to any conflict, nor any question of how any such conflict might need to be resolved.

6.   The provision must also be read in the light of the objectives and principles of the TRIPS Agreement. The provisions of the TRIPS Agreement provide a wide margin of discretion for setting up an intellectual property regime that is capable of responding to public health concerns. We have referred to Article 7 and Article 8 of the TRIPS Agreement in support of our view. These provisions are important for interpreting other provisions of the Agreement, including where measures are taken by Members to meet health objectives. These provisions are relevant context and clarify the object and purpose of the TRIPS Agreement, pursuant to Article 31(1) of the *Vienna Convention on the Law of Treaties*. The European Union recalls also the importance of the Doha Declaration on the TRIPS Agreement and Public Health.

7.   We do not agree with the complainants that the measure at issue can be reasonably characterised as "the ultimate encumbrance". It may be a serious encumbrance, but we do not think that it is the most serious, given that the package may still contain the name of the brand and variant. Furthermore, it seems to us that a general prohibition on use would not have more of an impact on right holders than mandated use contrary to the trademark owner's wishes, although that is a matter that might have to be considered taking into account the fact patterns of particular cases. We do consider, however, that it is an encumbrance that will need to be justified under Article 20 of the TRIPS Agreement.

8.   Article 20 of the TRIPS Agreement, when considered as a whole, is not an exception to a violation. The "unjustifiably" element may be understood as qualifying language that limits the scope of the obligation that is imposed.

9.   As regards the allocation of the burden of proof, splitting up the obligation in Article 20 seems artificial insofar as the obligation is concerned that "[t]he use of a trademark in the course of trade shall not be unjustifiably encumbered by special requirements". It is thus up to the complainant to establish a prima facie case in this respect.

II.   TBT AGREEMENT

A.   Technical Regulation

10.   The European Union considers that the fact that the terminology, symbol, packaging, marking or labelling requirement is also a trademark or a geographical indication does not, without more, take the document outside the scope of Article 2.2 of the TBT Agreement. Article 20 of the TRIPS Agreement and Article 2.2 of the TBT Agreement apply concurrently. The concept of *lex specialis* is a useful analytical tool, but is not to be mechanistically applied. In thinking about which of the two agreements, or specific provisions within them, is to be considered more specific the Panel may wish to consider (1) the overall design and architecture of the WTO Agreement (2) what an appropriate metric of specificity might be and (3) the procedural efficiency with which the dispute might be resolved.

11.   As regards the order of analysis, the European Union considers that the Panel has discretion, and that the Panel would remain within the bounds of that discretion if it would decide to deal first with the claims under the TBT Agreement, and subsequently with the claims under the TRIPS Agreement. Having conducted an analysis under Article 2.2 of the TBT Agreement the Panel may then find itself well-placed to address the claims and arguments of the Parties under Article 20 of the TRIPS Agreement. In doing so, it may find it convenient to refer to earlier parts of its analysis (such as, for example, what the objective of the measure is and whether or not such objective is legitimate), and it may also find that it does not necessarily need to resolve all aspects of the disagreements between the Parties concerning Article 20 of the TRIPS Agreement.

B.   Article 2.5 of the TBT Agreement

12.   The Panel must make an objective assessment of this matter, based on a comprehensive analysis of the nature, content and objectives of the Guidelines. The Panel must consider whether or not the Guidelines are "relevant international standards", taking into account the definition of the term "standard" in Annex 1, paragraph 2 of the TBT Agreement. The Panel should also take into account the TBT Committee Decision on Principles for the Development of International Standards.

13.   We consider that the Guidelines are relevant irrespective of whether or not they are a "relevant international standard" within the meaning of Article 2.5 of the TBT Agreement. That is because Article 2.2 of the TBT Agreement requires the Panel to take into account the "risks non-fulfilment would create". It further requires that, in assessing such risks, relevant elements of consideration are, *inter alia*, available scientific and technical information, related processing technology or intended end-uses of products. The European Union considers that the Guidelines fall within the open category delimited by the final sentence of Article 2.2 of the TBT Agreement.

14.   Thus, given that the objective of the measure is a reduction in the prevalence of smoking, non-fulfilment of the objective would mean no reduction in the prevalence of smoking, or a reduction in prevalence less than that aimed for. As explained by Australia, the "risk" that this would "create" is the risk that the measure would not make any contribution (or would make a lesser contribution) to changing attitudes to smoking in Australia, that is, that it would not make any contribution (or would make a lesser contribution) to the de-normalisation of smoking. In assessing that risk, the Guidelines are "relevant", particularly because they speak precisely to the means by which the relevant international organisation considers that tobacco control can be effectively enhanced. Therefore, they will need to be considered and taken into account by the Panel, irrespective of whether or not they are a "relevant international standard" within the meaning of Article 2.5 of the TBT Agreement. Furthermore, the foregoing analysis confirms that the legitimate public health objective in this case can be defined with specific reference to tobacco and smoking. This means that any alternative measures proposed must also address that specific issue, as opposed to other unrelated public health issues.

C.   Article 2.2 of the TBT Agreement

1.   Trade-restrictive

15.   The terms "obstacles to international trade", "trade-restrictive" and "effect on trade" appear to be used interchangeably in the relevant provisions of the TBT Agreement, and refer to something with a limiting effect on trade. The issue can be addressed both in terms of what the measure is actually causing (although evidence of this, including trade statistics, is not dispositive) and what it is apt to cause. Within the holistic weighing and balancing exercise, it should not be necessary to consider whether or not the trade-restriction is significant, although excessively hypothetical or remote effects would be insufficient. Increased costs, even if absorbed by firms, would generally give rise to a trade-restriction. Trade-restrictiveness is not the same as the impact on competitive opportunities used in the first step of an analysis of whether or not there is *de facto* discrimination, the first concept being about the "size of the cake" and the second concept being about how the cake is divided up (between all market participants). It would be necessary to consider the question of trade-restriction with respect to the trade of all Members, because a highly trade liberalising measure that happened to discriminate between two Members would not be trade-restrictive (although it might breach the rules against unjustified discrimination).

16.   Referring to the recent Appellate Body Report, *US – COOL (Article 21.5 – Canada and Mexico)*, it is to be observed that, in the context of Article 2.2 of the TBT Agreement, it may not always be possible to quantify a particular factor or to do so with precision.

17.   We think that the trade effects of the measure should be measured as a whole, for all Members. It would not be enough for one complainant to

demonstrate that its volume has decreased (the volume of some other complainant or complainants having increased). Consequently, we are not persuaded that the issue of downtrading, without more, demonstrates a trade-restriction, at least insofar as it is simply limited to the observation that the market share of one complainant is increasing at the expense of another.

18.   We see some connection between the discussion about whether or not the measure is trade-restrictive, on the one hand, and the discussion about whether or not the measure makes a contribution to its objective, on the other hand.

2.   The legitimate objectives of the measure at issue

19.   The European Union considers that the overarching objective of improving public health by, over time, reducing the prevalence of smoking, is a legitimate objective. By contrast, the aim of reducing the appeal of products *generally* is not *per se* legitimate. However, the aim of reducing the appeal of *tobacco* products is legitimate, as reflected in the FCTC Guidelines (which, as we have already indicated, should be accorded appropriate weight in the overall assessment), *because* tobacco products are harmful to public health, and protecting public health is *per se* legitimate.

3.   The contribution of the measure at issue to the fulfilment of the legitimate objectives

20.   In the context of Article XX of the GATT 1994, a demonstration of a material contribution to the achievement of its objective can be made by resorting to evidence or data, pertaining to the past or the present. It might also be determined that a measure is necessary on the basis of a demonstration that the measure at issue is apt to produce a material contribution to the achievement of its objective. This demonstration could consist of quantitative projections in the future, or qualitative reasoning based on a set of hypotheses that are tested and supported by sufficient evidence. It should also be possible for Members to defend their measures based on appropriate analysis and/or scientific evaluation in circumstances where, prior to the adoption of the measure, empirical data about its long term effects are not yet known.

21.   We consider that the Parties are entitled to support their arguments also on the basis of the information that has since become available.

22.   We think that packaging is relevant to consumer behaviour, particularly in the context of discouraging initiation, which is especially important for a highly addictive product, such as tobacco. Packaging may be used to convey advertising messages. Advertising is capable of increasing demand, including by influencing adolescent behaviour, also with respect to initiation. Certain packaging may be capable of influencing cessation and relapse behaviour.

4. The alternative measures

23. We consider that the contribution of the alternative measures is to be measured by reference to the contribution to the overarching legitimate objective of improving public health by, over time, reducing the prevalence of smoking. It is not necessary to measure it by reference to the subsidiary aims. In other words, the alternative measures do not have to operate through the same causal pathway as the measure at issue (although in assessing the effectiveness of the measure at issue compared to the alternative measures the Panel will, as already indicated, also take the aims and means into account).

ANNEX C-6

EXECUTIVE SUMMARY OF THE ARGUMENTS
OF GUATEMALA[*]

I.   INTRODUCTION

1.   Guatemala appreciates the opportunity to submit its views with respect to the matters under consideration in the present disputes. Guatemala makes this third party written submission because of its systemic interest in the correct interpretation of the *Agreement on Trade-Related Aspects of Intellectual Property Rights (TRIPS)* and the *Agreement on Technical Barriers to Trade (TBT)*.

2.   In no way is Guatemala questioning Australia's legitimate objectives to improve public health by encouraging people to give up or reduce smoking or using tobacco products as well as by reducing people's exposure to second-hand smoke from tobacco products.

3.   In this submission, Guatemala will not comment upon all legal issues raised in this dispute. Rather, Guatemala will focus on the following:

   a.   The relationship between the TBT and the TRIPS Agreements when assessing the Plain Packaging ("PP") measure;

   b.   The legal interpretation of Articles 19 and 20 of the TRIPS Agreement;

   c.   The scope and application of Article 15.4 of the TRIPS Agreement;

   d.   The relationship between Australia's obligations under the FCTC and those under the WTO Agreements.

4.   Guatemala reserves the possibility to express further its opinion with respect to these as well as other issues at a later stage in the present proceedings. Guatemala hopes that its written and oral submissions may be of assistance to the Panel.

II.   THE RELATIONSHIP BETWEEN THE TBT AND THE TRIPS AGREEMENTS IN ASSESSING THE PP MEASURES

5.   In their First Written Submission, the complainants maintain that the PP Measures are technical regulations within the scope of Art.2.2 of the TBT

---

[*]   Guatemala's written submission is used as its executive summary.

Agreement.[1] Australia contends that its PP Measure should be assessed in a manner that a differentiation must be made between the "physical requirements" and the "trademark requirements" of the measure:

> "The tobacco plain packaging measure establishes: (1) certain requirements as to the usage of trademarks on tobacco packages and products (the "trademark requirements"); and (2) certain requirements as to the physical characteristics of tobacco packages and products (the "physical requirements").[2]

6. According to Australia, the "physical requirements" are technical regulations within the scope of the TBT Agreement.[3] However, the "trademark requirements", in its view, are not technical regulations pursuant to the TBT Agreement and, for this reason, they can only be assessed under Article 20 of the TRIPS Agreement. Australia further contends that Article 20 of the TRIPS Agreement addresses the subject matter more "specifically, and in detail" than Article 2.2 of the TBT Agreement.[4]

7. In Australia's opinion, if the "trademark requirements" were to be considered under both the TRIPS and the TBT Agreements, the panel would be agreeing with the complainants that Article 20 of the TRIPS Agreement and Article 2.2 of the TBT Agreement share "the same subject matter".[5]

8. Australia also argues that even if the Panel were to consider that the requirements affecting the use of trademarks can be "technical regulations" within the scope of the TBT Agreement, Article 20 of the TRIPS Agreement would remain the applicable provision in respect of the trademark requirement imposed by the tobacco plain packaging measure to the exclusion of Article 2.2 of the TBT Agreement.[6]

9. The WTO covered agreements must be interpreted in a coherent and consistent manner. Whenever a measure imposed by a Member falls within the scope of two or more covered agreements, the analysis of such measure should be made in a way that all the covered agreements concerned are taken into account and the obligations contained in each of them are carefully observed. This harmonized view is in accordance with the constituting principles of the WTO, established in Article 2 of the Marrakesh Agreement:

> "The agreements and associated legal instruments included in Annexes 1, 2 and 3 (hereinafter referred to as "Multilateral Trade

---

[1] Cuba's First Written Submission. Section VI.D. (p. 144-150); Indonesia's First Written Submission. Section V.B. (p. 142-175); Dominican Republic First Written Submission, Section V.II. (p. 267-293); Honduras' First Written Submission, Section VII, (p. 163-196).

[2] Australia's First Written Submission, para. 506.

[3] Australia's First Written Submission, para. 507.

[4] Australia's First Written Submission, para. 511.

[5] Australia's First Written Submission, para. 508.

[6] Australia's First Written Submission, para. 511.

Agreements") are integral parts of this Agreement, binding on all Members."

10.   In *US-Anti Dumping and Countervailing Duties (China)*, when addressing a situation in which the application of a covered agreement was being considered to the exclusion of another, the Appellate Body stated that:

> "Such an interpretative approach is difficult to reconcile with the notion that the provisions in the WTO covered agreements should be interpreted in a coherent and consistent manner, giving meaning to all applicable provisions harmoniously. Members have entered into cumulative obligations under the covered agreements and should thus be mindful of their actions under one agreement when taking action under another."[7]

11.   Likewise, the Appellate Body in *Argentina - Footwear (EC)* explained that:

> "..the Panel was correct in saying that "Article XIX of GATT and the Safeguards Agreement must *a fortiori* be read as representing an *inseparable package* of rights and disciplines which have to be considered in conjunction." Yet a treaty interpreter must read all applicable provisions of a treaty in a way that gives meaning to *all* of them, harmoniously. And, an appropriate reading of this *"inseparable package of rights and disciplines"* must, accordingly, be one that gives meaning to *all* the relevant provisions of these two equally binding agreements."[8] (emphasis added).

12.   Guatemala agrees with Australia that each of the Agreements at issue deals with a different "subject matter".[9] The question, however, is whether the measure at issue can be assessed simultaneously under different agreements or, as Australia proposes, the TRIPS Agreement should be considered more specific and, thus, applied to the exclusion of the TBT Agreement.

13.   Guatemala understands Australia's argument as referring to the principle of *lex specialis* derogat *legi generali*. This principle is "inseparably linked with the question of conflict" and does not apply if two agreements "...deal with the same subject from different point of view or [is] applicable in different circumstances, or one provision is more far-reaching that but not inconsistent with, those of the other".[10]

---

[7]   Appellate Body Report, United States – Definitive Anti-Dumping and Countervailing Duties on Certain Products from China, WT/DS379/AB/R, para. 570

[8]   Appellate Body Report, Argentina – Safeguard Measures on Imports of Footwear, WT/DS121/AB/R, para. 81.

[9]   Australia's First Written Submission, paras. 508- 510.

[10]   Panel Report, Indonesia – Certain Measures Affecting the Automobile Industry, WT/DS54/R, WT/DS55/R, WT/DS59/R, WT/DS64/R and Corr.1 and 2, adopted 23 July 1998, footnote 649.

14.   This is the first time that the question of the relationship between the TBT and the TRIPS Agreements arises. In Guatemala's view, however, the TBT Agreement and the TRIPS Agreement, even assuming for the sake of the argument that they might deal with the same subject matter, they do that from a different point of view and apply in different circumstances.

15.   Therefore, Guatemala is not persuaded that the provisions of the TRIPS Agreement are applicable to the exclusion of the provisions of the TBT Agreement.

III.   INTERPRETATION OF ARTICLES 19 AND 20 OF THE TRIPS AGREEMENT

16.   In its written submission, Cuba argues that "Article 20 (of the TRIPS Agreement) sets limits on the ability of WTO Members to constrain the use, by commercial actors, of trademarks in the course of trade."[11] In its view, this is the only provision in the TRIPS Agreement where there is an explicit limit on the ability of States to regulate the use of protected subject matter.[12]

17.   Australia on the other hand, accepts that the PP Measure: "...imposes "special requirements" upon the use of trademarks insofar as it requires that any word trademarks used on retail tobacco packaging must appear in a certain form. However, Australia does not consider that the aspects of the tobacco plain packaging measure that *prohibit the use* of certain trademarks on tobacco products and their retail packaging are "special requirements" that fall within the scope of Article 20"[13] (emphasis added).

18.   Australia appears to interpret Article 20 on the basis of Article 19 of the TRIPS Agreement. In Australia's view, Article 19 "...specifically contemplates that 'government requirements' *may prohibit* the use of a trademark altogether" (emphasis added). Therefore, "if domestic law prohibits the "use" of certain trademarks altogether, then those trademarks are not being 'use[d] ... in the course of trade' and Article 20 is therefore not engaged".[14]

19.   Australia then concludes that "[i]n light of the object and purpose of the TRIPS Agreement, Article 20 is best interpreted as imposing a discipline on how a Member may encumber the use of a trademark in the course of trade when its domestic laws and regulations otherwise do not prohibit the use of that trademark."[15]

20.   Guatemala understands Australia's arguments as proposing that Articles 19 and 20 are mutually exclusive. If a measure imposes a prohibition, Article 19 applies to the exclusion of Article 20.

---

[11]   Cuba's First Written Submission, para. 297.
[12]   *Ibid.*
[13]   Australia's First Written Submission, para. 339.
[14]   Australia's First Written Submission, para. 341.
[15]   Australia's First Written Submission, para. 342.

21.   Guatemala is not persuaded by Australia's interpretation. First, Guatemala understands that Article 19 deals specifically with the "requirement of use" to "maintain a registration" while Article 20 addresses the situation of "other requirements" to the exclusion of the "requirement of use" in Article 19. Moreover, pursuant to Article 19 a special requirement of use to maintain a registration is applicable to the extent that "use *is required* to maintain a registration" (emphasis added). This provision does not deal, however, with general prohibitions to the use or registration of a trademark as Australia apparently is contending.

22.   Second, Article 20 applies provided that the requirement at issue is not a "requirement of use" to "maintain a registration". However, such provision does not appear to be dependent of whether the requirement at issue is an encumbrance or a total prohibition. The ordinary meaning of "encumbrance" is an "impediment...a burden"[16] and "to encumber" is "[h]amper, impede (a person, movement, etc.); act as a check or restraint on".[17] Therefore, Guatemala respectfully submits that the expression "unjustifiably encumbered" also encompasses unjustifiable prohibitions or "impediments" to the use of a trademark.

23.   Finally, from a more general perspective, Guatemala fails to see how Australia's interpretation would justify the fact that the TRIPS Agreement would allow Members to impose a prohibition to the use of a trademark, *without conditions*, while those conditions only would be applicable when a Member imposes encumbrances other than a total prohibition. Put differently, Guatemala is not convinced that the TRIPS Agreement would support the notion that Members have a total freedom to impose prohibitions but not when they impose limitations on the use of trademarks.

IV.   SCOPE AND APPLICATION OF ARTICLE 15.4 OF THE TRIPS AGREEMENT

24.   Article 15.4 of the TRIPS Agreement provides that "[t]he nature of the goods or services to which a trademark is to be applied shall in no case form an obstacle to registration of the trademark". Ukraine contends that "[i] n direct violation of this principle, the TPP Act has rewritten Australia's TM Act in order to create a sub-species of second-class registered trademark protection for tobacco products alone because of the nature of the product to which these trademarks apply."[18]

25.   According to Ukraine, the Australian PP Measure "...prohibits the use of non-inherently distinctive signs. The sole reason for the prohibition on use of such signs on tobacco products and their packaging is the nature of the product".

---

[16]   Shorter Oxford English Dictionary, Sixth Edition, Oxford University Press, 2007, Vol. 1, p. 828.
[17]   *Ibid.*, p. 827.
[18]   Ukraine's First Written Submission, para. 182.

Ukraine adds that "Australia's sole reason for prohibiting the use of trademarks on tobacco products and their packaging is the nature of the product to which the trademark is to be applied."[19]

26.   In response, Australia argues that "[t]he tobacco plain packaging measure is consistent with Article 15.4 because it does not prevent the registration of trademarks based on the nature of the underlying product (i.e. tobacco)."[20] Moreover, Australia indicates that the TPP Act does not prevent an owner from registering a trademark under the Trade Marks Act.[21]

27.   In Guatemala's view, the question before the Panel is whether Australia's regulations "form an obstacle to registration of the trademark" and, in that case, whether such an obstacle is linked to the "nature of the goods or services to which a trademark is to be applied".

28.   From Australia's explanation, Guatemala understands that the registration of trademarks of tobacco products is not prevented by the measures at issue. Rather, Ukraine's argument appears to focus on situations in which a specific sub-category of products, not being inherently distinctive signs, might nevertheless be the subject of registration dependent on use.

29.   If Guatemala understands correctly, Ukraine formulates the proposition that a prohibition on the use of a trademark prevents its registrability (where Article 15.3 would be applicable) and forms an obstacle to registration of the trademark because of the "nature of the goods" (in accordance with Article 15.4).

30.   If that understanding is correct then Guatemala is not persuaded with Ukraine's argument. Guatemala submits that in those very specific situations described above, the alleged obstacle to registration of a trademark would be the lack of use (pursuant to Article 15.3) but not necessarily the "nature of the goods or services to which a trademark is to be applied" (in accordance with Article 15.4).

31.   Guatemala is mindful, however, that the measures at issue limit the use of trademarks and, for that reason, prevents economic operators from registering marks on the basis of its use. Notwithstanding that, Guatemala does not see that this situation would amount to a violation of Article 16.4 of the TRIPS Agreement.

V.   AUSTRALIA'S OBLIGATIONS UNDER THE FCTC AND ITS RELATION TO ITS WTO OBLIGATIONS

32.   Australia argues that it must comply with its obligations under the FCTC. Specifically, Australia refers to Article 11 (concerning the packaging and

---

[19]   Ukraine's First Written Submission, para. 183.
[20]   Australia's First Written Submission, para. 308.
[21]   *Ibid.*

labelling of tobacco products) and Article 13 (concerning tobacco advertising, promotion and sponsorship) of the FCTC.[22] According to Australia, "Article 11 of the FCTC requires Parties to implement measures to eliminate the propensity of tobacco packaging to mislead consumers about the health effects of smoking and to require health warnings on tobacco packaging.* Article 13 requires Parties to implement comprehensive bans on tobacco advertising, promotion and sponsorship" (footnote omitted).[23]

33.   In 2007, the FCTC Conference of Parties adopted nine Guidelines. Among those, one for Article 11, which states the following:

> "Parties *should consider* adopting measures to restrict or prohibit the use of logos, colours, brand images or promotional information on packaging other than brand names and product names displayed in a standard colour and font style (plain packaging)" (emphasis added)[24]

34.   Additionally, Guidelines for Article 13 provides that:

> "Parties *should consider* adopting measures to restrict or prohibit the use of logos, colours, brand images or promotional information on packaging other than brand names and product names displayed in a standard colour and font style (plain packaging)" (emphasis added)[25]

35.   The Dominican Republic advanced the argument that the Implementation Guidelines are of a non-binding nature, and that the Articles 11 and 13 of such Guidelines only offer recommendations to FCTC Parties to "*consider* adopting" plain packaging, but in no way are the Parties obliged to adopt plain packaging.[26]

36.   Guatemala concurs with the Dominican Republic. The expression "should consider" in both Guidelines, which are of a non-binding nature, does not amount to a binding obligation for Australia or any other WTO Member. Therefore, Guatemala does not see a conflict of international obligations.

37.   In *Indonesia – Autos*, the Panel made a reference to situations in which there may be conflicts between two treaties. In particular, that Panel explained the following:

> "In international law for a conflict to exist between two treaties, three conditions have to be satisfied. First, the treaties concerned

---

[22]   Australia's First Written Submission, para. 104.
[23]   *Ibid.*
[24]   *WHO Framework Convention on Tobacco Control: Guidelines for Implementation* (2013 edition) Exhibit AUS-109, Article 11, para. 46.
[25]   *WHO Framework Convention on Tobacco Control: Guidelines for Implementation* (2013 edition) Exhibit AUS-109, Article 13.
[26]   Dominican Republic First Written Submission, para. 187.

must have the same parties. Second, the treaties must cover the same substantive subject matter. Were it otherwise, there would be no possibility of conflict. Third, the provisions must conflict, in the sense that the provisions must impose mutually exclusive obligations ... '[T]echnically speaking, there is a conflict when two (or more) treaty instruments contain obligations which cannot be complied with simultaneously'".[27]

38.   In view of the above, if Australia would have chosen not to implement plain packaging measures, it would still be in compliance with its alleged obligations under the FCTC. As a matter of fact, plain packaging is only one among several measures that implement a comprehensive approach to tobacco control.

39.   Guatemala is also of the view that Members should, and are able to, comply with the FCTC Guidelines, in a manner that such compliance does not compromise their obligations contained in the WTO covered agreements.

---

[27]   Panel Report, Indonesia – Certain Measures Affecting the Automobile Industry, WT/DS54/R, WT/DS55/R, WT/DS59/R, WT/DS64/R and Corr.1 and 2, adopted 23 July 1998, and Corr. 3 and 4, DSR 1998:VI, 220, footnote 649.

ANNEX C-7

EXECUTIVE SUMMARY OF THE ARGUMENTS
OF JAPAN

I.   CHARACTERISTICS OF TRADEMARK PROTECTION UNDER THE TRIPS AGREEMENT

1.   Article 16.1 of the TRIPS Agreement confers on trademark owners a right to exclude others from using the owner's trademark. However, the TRIPS Agreement also makes clear that trademark owners have "legitimate interests" that WTO Members must take into account in certain circumstances, such as when providing limited exceptions to trademark rights, as provided by Article 17 of the TRIPS Agreement. The panel in *EC –Trademarks and Geographical Indications* had identified one such "legitimate interest" as the interest in using one's own trademark.[1] Thus, "the use of a trademark," as part of a trademark owner's legitimate interests, must be taken into account when interpreting the TRIPS Agreement, in particular, when analyzing the "justifiability" of any encumbrance in the context of Article 20 of the TRIPS Agreement.

II.   ARTICLE 20 OF THE TRIPS AGREEMENT

A.   Special Requirements

2.   Article 20 of the TRIPS Agreement is concerned with "special" requirements. Japan understands that the first sentence of Article 20 prohibits Members from imposing different or additional conditions that "unjustifiably" restrict the use of a trademark, in the context of buying or selling goods or services.

3.   In interpreting "special requirements" within the meaning of Article 20, Japan wishes to emphasize that the underlying *raison d'etre* for a trademark is to enable consumers to tell goods and services apart. Article 15 stipulates that trademarks must be "capable of distinguishing the goods or services of one undertaking from those of other undertakings." Because the tobacco plain packaging measure impairs the ability of a trademark owner to distinguish its goods or services from those of other economic operators, there is no doubt that such a prohibition constitutes a "special requirement" within the meaning of Article 20.

---

[1]   Panel Report, *EC –Trademarks and Geographical Indications*, para. 7.664.

4.   Australia agrees that "the tobacco plain packaging measure imposes special requirements on the use of trademarks, at least in some respects."[2] However, Australia argues that "Article 20 is best interpreted as imposing a discipline on how a Member may encumber the use of a trademark in the course of trade when its domestic laws and regulations otherwise do not prohibit the use of that trademark."[3]

5.   Japan disagrees with Australia's interpretation of the scope of Article 20. A prohibition on the use of a trademark is a "special requirement" within the meaning of Article 20. Australia's proposed interpretation would yield outcomes that are counterintuitive. Conditions that interfere with, but do not prohibit, the use of a trademark would only be allowed under Article 20 if such restrictions are justifiable. Yet, under Australia's interpretation, a total prohibition on the use of a trademark would always be allowed without any discipline, even though it effectively deprives the trademark of value.

B.   Unjustifiability

6.   As for the question of whether the plain packaging measure "unjustifiably" encumbers the "use of a trademark in the course of trade", Australia relies on one aspect of the interpretation of the term "unjustifiable" in Article XX of the GATT 1994[4] and concludes that Article 20 of the TRIPS Agreement requires "a rational connection between any special requirements imposed upon a use of trademarks in the course of trade and a legitimate public policy objective."[5]

7.   Japan agrees that, in interpreting the term "unjustifiably" in Article 20 of the TRIPS Agreement, guidance may be drawn from the interpretation of the term "unjustifiable" in the chapeau of GATT Article XX. However, in *EC – Seal Products*, the Appellate Body observed that the question of whether the discrimination can be reconciled with, or is rationally related to, the policy objective is "*one* element in a 'cumulative' assessment of 'unjustifiable discrimination'",[6] and further explained that "[i]n *US – Shrimp*, the Appellate Body relied on *a number of factors* in finding that the measure at issue resulted in arbitrary or unjustifiable discrimination."[7] Further, in *Brazil – Retreaded Tyres*, the Appellate Body found that "[i]n certain cases the effects of the discrimination may be a relevant factor, among others, for determining whether the cause or rationale of the discrimination is acceptable or defensible and, ultimately, whether the discrimination is justifiable."[8] Also, in *US – Shrimp*, the

---

[2]   Australia's first written submission, para. 336.
[3]   *Ibid.*, para. 342.
[4]   Appellate Body Report, *EC – Seal Products*, para. 5.306. Australia also refers to Appellate Body Report, *Brazil – Retreaded Tyres*, paras. 225, 227-228.
[5]   Australia's first written submission, para. 383.
[6]   Appellate Body Report, *EC – Seal Products*, para. 5.306.
[7]   *Ibid.*, para. 5.305 (emphasis added; footnotes omitted).
[8]   Appellate Body Report, *Brazil – Retreaded Tyres*, para. 230.

Appellate Body examined as one of the relevant factors the existence of a reasonably available alternative measure to determine whether the discrimination was unjustifiable.[9]

8. Thus, although the focus of analysis should be "on the cause of the discrimination, or the rationale put forward to explain its existence,"[10] and it is difficult to see how discrimination can be justified if "the rationale for discriminating does not relate to the pursuit of or would go against the objective" of the measure, the determination of whether there is a rational connection between the rationale of discrimination and the policy objective pursued requires the examination of "a number of factors". Such inquiry may also involve the examination of the effect and nature of the means of discrimination adopted to achieve a policy objective and the rational connection of such adopted means to the end pursued.

9. It is also important to note that the analysis required under GATT Article XX, which refers to unjustifiable discrimination, may be narrower in scope than the analysis required under TRIPS Article 20, which need not focus exclusively on the discriminatory aspects of the encumbrance.

10. In Japan's view, a panel reviewing the claim under Article 20 of the TRIPS Agreement must determine whether the nature and extent of the encumbrance on the use of the trademark has a rational connection to the policy objective. In so doing, the following factors may be relevant: Is the encumbrance rationally related to the stated purpose, or does it run contrary to that purpose? Where the policy objective is legitimate, does the encumbrance result from a single and unbending solution applied across a wide range of situations where the problem is more or less present? Is the encumbrance reasonably calibrated to contribute to the policy objective?

11. Japan additionally notes that there is a degree of uncertainty in Australia's description of the objectives of its measure. It is obvious that if the objective of a measure at issue is not precisely identified, it would be impracticable to assess effectively and properly whether the measure is reasonably calibrated to contribute to its policy objective. The first objective ("reduc[ing] the appeal of tobacco products to consumers") as set out in subsection 3(2)(a) of the TPP Act appears to relate to discouraging consumers from smoking no matter whether they are fully informed of the harmful effect of tobacco products. In contrast, the second and third objectives, as set out in subsections 3(2)(b) and 3(2)(c), appear intended to prevent consumers' misunderstanding of the health risk of tobacco products (rather than cause consumers not to smoke even if they fully and accurately understand such risk).[11]

---

[9] Appellate Body Report, *US - Shrimp*, para. 171.
[10] Appellate Body Report, *Brazil – Retreaded Tyres*, para. 226.
[11] The Panel may wish to confirm whether Australia considers that the objective of the plain packaging measure is to prevent consumers' misunderstanding, rather than, to cause Australian

12. With respect to the first objective under subsection 3(2)(a), Japan invites the Panel to ask Australia which aspect(s) of trademarks used on tobacco products are the ones that make tobacco products appeal to consumers and why restrictions on the other aspects of the trademark are warranted. On the other hand, with respect to the latter two objectives under subsections 3(2)(b) and (c), Japan invites the Panel to ask Australia what aspects of the trademarks, in particular, what figurative aspects of the trademarks, give rise to consumers' misunderstanding of the harm of the products in Australia's market. If any figurative aspect of trademarks may give rise to such misunderstanding, Japan would like to invite the Panel to further ask whether and how Australia's position is consistent with the general understanding of the function of trademarks, which is by their nature to distinguish goods or services in the course of trade as provided in Article 15 and is not to contribute to misunderstanding by consumers about the products and their quality.

13. Finally, Japan also believes that Article 8.1 of the TRIPS Agreement makes clear that the measures necessary to protect public health are only permissible if they are "consistent with the provisions of this Agreement." Article 8.1 is not an exception to the Agreement, but an affirmation that the Agreement as a whole already takes into account the ability of Members to take measures pursuant to public policy objectives. Therefore, taking a measure pursuant to public health does not in and of itself make the measure justifiable. To permit otherwise would provide Members with overly broad powers to restrict trademarks.

III.   THE RELATIONSHIP BETWEEN THE TRIPS AND TBT AGREEMENTS

14. Japan disagrees with Australia's argument that "Article 20 of the TRIPS Agreement would apply to the exclusion of Article 2.2 of the TBT Agreement in respect of" the so-called "trademark requirements." Japan also disagrees with Australia's assertion that "Article 20 of the TRIPS Agreement would clearly address this subject matter [i.e. requirements affecting the use of trademarks] more 'specifically, and in detail' as compared to Article 2.2 of the TBT Agreement.[12]

15. In Japan's view, the relationship of different covered agreements must be determined on the basis of objective scrutiny of the relevant provisions of those covered agreements, as any two covered agreements "are both 'integral parts' of the WTO Agreement that are 'binding on all Members."[13]

---

consumers not to smoke even if they fully and accurately understand the health risk of tobacco products (without banning the consumption and sales of tobacco products).
[12]   Australia's first written submission, paras. 508-511.
[13]   Appellate Body Report, *Argentina – Footwear (EC)*, para. 81.

16. In addition, as Australia admits, Article 2.2 of the TBT Agreement "encompasses all manner of 'technical regulations,'" which are defined in Annex 1.1 of the TBT Agreement. There is nothing in the TBT Agreement that *a priori* excludes measures regulating the use of a trademark from the scope of Article 2.2. Japan is of the view that the tobacco plain packaging measure is in fact a "technical regulation," as defined under Annex 1.1 of the TBT Agreement.

17. Finally, Australia refers to certain statement by the Appellate Body in *EC – Bananas III* to support its position[14]. However, the Appellate Body's findings there related to the order of analysis and do not stand for the proposition that a provision of one covered agreement which "deals specifically, and in detail" with the particular subject matter applies to the exclusion of a provision on another agreement which also deal with the same matter.

IV. ARTICLE 2.2 OF THE TBT AGREEMENT – TRADE RESTRICTIVENESS

18. Australia considers it "axiomatic that, in order to make a *prima facie* case under this standard [of Article 2.2], a complainant must establish, as a threshold matter, that the technical regulation at issue is 'trade-restrictive'."[15] Trade-restrictiveness was not characterized by the Appellate Body as a threshold issue in *US – Tuna II (Mexico)*, or subsequently in *US – COOL*. Rather, the trade-restrictiveness of the measure is one of the factors of the relational, multi-factor test developed by the Appellate Body to determine whether a measure is consistent with Article 2.2 of the TBT Agreement.[16]

V. ARTICLE 2.2 OF THE TBT AGREEMENT – IDENTIFICATION OF LEGITIMATE OBJECTIVE AND THE MEASURE'S CONTRIBUTION

19. Japan considers that, in order to conduct an objective analysis on the legitimacy of the objective and the relational and comparative analyses of the necessity of the measure (especially with regard to the degree of contribution and the risks of non-fulfilment) under Article 2.2 of the TBT Agreement, it is essential to identify the objective or the policy rationale of the challenged measure as precisely as possible at the outset. As the Appellate Body explained, "the relevant objective is the benchmark against which a panel must assess the degree of contribution made by a challenged technical regulation, as well as by proposed alternative measures." [17]

---

[14] Australia's first written submission, para. 511.
[15] Australia's first written submission, para. 522 (referring to Appellate Body Report, *US – Tuna II (Mexico)*, footnote 647 to para. 322).
[16] Appellate Body Report, *US – Tuna II (Mexico)*, para. 322. *See also* Appellate Body Report, *US – COOL*, para. 374.
[17] Appellate Body Report, *US – COOL*, para. 387.

20.   Accordingly, Japan invites the Panel to examine the objectives of the plain package measure in the same manner as described by Japan with regard to Article 20 of the TRIPs Agreement (i.e., to examine whether the objective is to prevent consumers from misunderstanding the health risk of tobacco products or to cause consumers not to smoke even if they fully and accurately understand such risk, what aspects of trademarks give rise to the consumers' misunderstanding, and the consistency with the generally recognized function of trademarks of distinguishing goods or services).

VI.   ARTICLE 2.2 OF THE TBT AGREEMENT – BURDEN OF PROOF

21.   Japan recognizes that, as the Appellate Body has established, the complainant has the burden of proof for its claim under Article 2.2 that the challenged measure creates an unnecessary obstacle to international trade. After the complainant has presented its *prima facie* case, it is then for the respondent to rebut the complainant's *prima facie* case. Japan notes that, considering that the respondent country is in the best position to have the relevant facts and evidence about its own measures or the regulatory context of the measures, complainants should not be required to bear too heavy a burden to establish its *prima facie* case under Article 2.2 of the TBT Agreement. In other words, complainants should not be required to provide a full analysis of the trade-restrictiveness of the alternative measure, before the burden shifts to the respondent to rebut the complainant's *prima facie* case.

VII.   ARTICLE 2.5 OF THE TBT AGREEMENT

22.   Japan observes that Article 2.5 establishes a rebuttable presumption that a technical regulation does not create an unnecessary obstacle to international trade when certain conditions are met. Such legal presumptions, while capable of being rebutted, are by definition not easily overcome, as new evidence and argumentation would be needed to shift the burden once again. In Japan's view, the difficulty in rebutting a presumption under Article 2.5 may depend on the *level of precision* in the international standards at issue. If the international standard is quite prescriptive and is followed closely by the relevant Member, such a presumption would arguably be more difficult to rebut. If, on the other hand, the reliance on the international standard is loosely based, or the international standard is too broad, the presumption would be easier to rebut. Such determinations should, in Japan's assessment, be made on a case-by-case basis.

ANNEX C-8

EXECUTIVE SUMMARY OF THE ARGUMENTS
OF THE REPUBLIC OF KOREA[*]

Mr. Chairman and Members of the Panel,

1.   Korea appreciates this opportunity to present its views in this dispute, in which Korea has systemic interest with respect to the interpretation of the TBT and TRIPS Agreements. Korea also has systemic interest in how the WTO decides on the relationship between WTO rules and other international agreements. Today, Korea would like to briefly comment on a couple of key issues on which we request the Panel's clear guidance.

2.   Korea believes that WTO Members have the right to pursue legitimate domestic regulatory and public policy objectives, such as public health. This right to regulate should be protected as a sovereign right of all Member countries, and is sufficiently reflected in the GATT 1994, as well as the TBT and SPS agreements.

3.   At the same time, Korea is mindful of a main function of the WTO, that is ensuring that "trade flows as smoothly, predictably, and freely as possible." Striking the right balance between pursuing public health objectives, and securing free trade is particularly important in this dispute. In this regard, Korea would like to submit the following observations.

4.   First, this Panel should provide clear guidance on the relationship between WTO rules and rules established by other international organizations. In this dispute, the WHO is the other international organization. But the Panel should also consider provisions of the TRIPS Agreement. Since protecting intellectual property rights is essential for creating value through trade, trade-restrictive measures that violate the TRIPS Agreement should not be allowed.

5.   Second, Korea requests the Panel to provide guidance on the relationship between WTO rules and WHO rules. While in principle the object and purpose of other international agreements should not be allowed to undermine the interpretation or application of WTO Agreement provisions, the value of the Framework Convention on Tobacco Control ("FCTC") should be sufficiently respected. The FCTC is currently ratified by 180 countries, making it the most widely ratified convention among UN Member states. In particular, Korea notes that Article 46 of the guidelines for Article 11 of the FCTC recommends the adoption of plain packaging. Korea believes that the Panel's decision with

---

[*]   Korea requested that its oral statement serve as its executive summary.

respect to the relationship between this specific FCTC recommendation and relevant provisions of the WTO Agreements will be crucial in resolving the key issues of this dispute.

6.   Third, Korea requests the Panel to give clear guidelines on the scope of the rights under the TRIPS Agreement. The complainants claim that the plain packaging measure improperly restricts the use of trademarks, and is thus inconsistent with the TRIPS Agreement. Australia argues that the TRIPS Agreement provides negative rights of exclusion; therefore, it is argued that Australia's measure is TRIPS-consistent. The Panel's interpretation of the scope of trademark rights will have a significant impact on the policies of WTO Members. In Korea's view, a narrow interpretation of Article 20 of the TRIPS Agreement would lead to severe restrictions on trademark rights.

7.   In this regard, Korea notes the panel's interpretation of Article 17 of the TRIPS Agreement in *EC – Trademarks and Geographical Indications*. The panel in that dispute found that a "legitimate interest" includes the trademark owner's interest in using its own trademark. In interpreting Article 20 of the TRIPS Agreement, this legitimate interest of the trademark owner should be considered.

8.   Finally, Korea respectfully requests this Panel to give guidance on the interpretation of Article 8.1 of the TRIPS Agreement. Article 8.1 reaffirms the right to adopt measures necessary to protect public health in formulating laws and regulations. It is noted, however, that such legitimate policy goals are permissible only if consistent with provisions of the TRIPS Agreement.

9.   This concludes Korea's oral statement. Thank you.

ANNEX C-9

EXECUTIVE SUMMARY OF THE ARGUMENTS
OF MALAWI

I. INTRODUCTION

1.   Malawi presented its views to the Panel in *Australia - Certain Measures Concerning Trademarks, Geographical Indications And Other Plain Packaging Requirements Applicable To Tobacco Products And Packaging (DS435, DS441, DS458, DS467)* in a written submission dated 10 April 2015 and in a third party oral statement on 3 June 2015. Malawi is pleased to provide the Panel with a summary of the views it expressed in these dispute settlement proceedings.

2.   For Malawi, the strict packaging requirements imposed by Australia under the Tobacco Plain Packaging Act 2011, Tobacco Plain Packaging Regulations 2011 and 2012 and the Trade Marks Amendment (Tobacco Plain Packaging) Act 2011 (the "plain packaging measures") raise systemic questions about international trade and intellectual property law. These measures also have the potential to greatly and negatively impact the economic and trade interests of Malawi, as a small, landlocked least-developed country, which depends on tobacco farming for a substantial portion of its economic output and its economic development.

3.   Malawi is the world's largest producer of Burley tobacco and the sixth largest grower of unmanufactured tobacco. Tobacco is the third largest export product by volume (after maize and sugar), but the value of the tobacco is more than double the value exports of maize and sugar combined. Agriculture accounts for about 33 percent of Malawi's GDP and 90 percent of export revenues. Tobacco accounts for over 60 percent of the value of Malawi's exports and it contributes to 15 percent of its GDP. Malawi's share in world total exports is a mere 0.01 percent.

4.   Over two families in Malawi or about seventy percent of the population directly rely on tobacco and related industries for their livelihood. All of Malawi's tobacco production is used for the production of cigarettes sold internationally.

5.   Given the predominant role for tobacco in Malawi's international trade portfolio, it is essential for Malawi to ensure that measures directly or indirectly affecting the trade of tobacco and tobacco products are consistent with the WTO Agreements. Plain packaging measures are highly trade distortive and will have a substantial and disproportionate effect on Malawi's economy by driving down legitimate demand for high-quality tobacco leaf and supporting illicit trade in low-quality products outside of the legitimate international trade in this important export product.

6.   Malawi considers that the balancing requirement of Article 2.2 of the Agreement on Technical Barriers to Trade ("TBT Agreement"), which provides that any technical regulation must not be more trade-restrictive than necessary, is a fundamental and central principle of the WTO system. A careful assessment of the contribution, if any, of the plain packaging measures to its legitimate objective must thus be performed on the basis of the evidence before the Panel to undertake the weighing and balancing exercise of Article 2.2.

7.   Malawi does not question the health objective pursued by Australia but considers that a WTO Member cannot simply invoke health-related grounds to justify highly trade restrictive measures particularly in the absence of evidence that these measures will contribute to the stated objective.

8.   Based on the review of the facts before the Panel, Malawi submits that no convincing evidence exists regarding the contribution of plain packaging to the reduction of smoking. Australia has not engaged on the assessment of the actual effectiveness of its measure by reference to actual smoking behaviour and has instead relied on theories of behavioral sciences to explain a convoluted chain reaction of affecting perceptions and attitudes that should first take place in order to, at some later stage, affect smoking behavior. Malawi takes note of the arguments regarding the lack of predictive validity of behavioral sciences. This seems to be confirmed by the most recent market data from Australia and, in particular, the analysis of the data collected by Australia in its National Plain Packaging Tracking-Survey that demonstrate the ineffectiveness of plain packaging to change smoking behavior or even have an impact on individuals' perceptions, intentions and attitudes about smoking.

9.   Malawi also submits that plain packaging is not at all necessary because less trade restrictive alternatives, such as an increase in taxes, were available to Australia and would have had a contribution to the stated objective. Experience in other Members evidences that smoking can be more effectively combated without plain packaging.

10.   Malawi is of the view that the provisions of Article 2.2 of the TBT Agreement must be strictly applied in the present disputes. Absent sufficient evident of an actual effective contribution of technical regulations to the stated objective and the absence of less trade-restrictive alternatives, highly trade-restrictive technical regulations such as plain packaging measures cannot be confirmed. A lowering of the standards set in previous disputes would lead to increase risks of the imposition of unnecessary and restrictive technical regulations not supported by sufficient justifications. In addition to having a direct impact on the products they regulate, technical regulations affect the inputs in such products. It is essential for Malawi that the impact of Australia's plain packaging measures on the trade of tobacco be considered by the Panel as it directly affects economic development and the livelihood of most of its population.

11.   As regards arguments under the TRIPS Agreement, Malawi understands that Australia's view is effectively that for certain products that pose a health

risk, including but certainly not limited to tobacco products, trademarks are necessarily misleading and their use may be restricted, without any indication that the affected signs provide misleading information. Under Australia's approach, substantive trademark rights would depend on the policy choices by each Member whether products or category of products are to be considered as harmful or not. Given that a great variety of products pose certain health or other risks, accepting Australia's position would effectively mean that any Member could ban the use of trademarks for any product category. Because of the crucial role of trademarks in a global economy as a means of entering new markets and competing over market share, this would have devastating consequences for the export strategy of Malawi in the tobacco sector.

12.   By significantly restricting the forms of signs that may constitute a trademark with the imposition of plain packaging, Australia violates Article 15.1 of the TRIPS Agreement.

13.   The plain packaging measures imposed by Australia fail to take into consideration the purpose and benefit of trademarks for consumers and producers alike. Trademarks are used with the view of differentiating products and services and are thus essential to competition. They are recognized as one of the essential tools to penetrate new markets. If they cannot be affixed on products and their packaging, trademarks cannot pursue their distinguishing function.

14.   The prohibition of the use of trademark on plain packaging coupled with the imposition of strict packaging requirements results in the adoption of a generic form of packaging that will lead to the commoditization of tobacco products. The reduction in the ability of consumers to distinguish between products will have a negative impact on the prices of tobacco products and, in turn, affect prices of tobacco as manufacturers of tobacco products will have to be more competitive. This will be highly detrimental to Malawi as it is a least-developed country whose economy is dependent tobacco.

15.   Australia's plain packaging measures also constitute an unjustifiable encumbrance on the use of trademarks that is inconsistent with Article 20 of the TRIPS Agreement because they prohibit trademark owners from using their trademarks, as registered, tobacco products. Australia has prohibited the use of registered trademarks without examining whether registered trademarks previously used were one of the reasons that led people to smoke or prevented them from smoking. Given the constant decline in smoking and prevalence in Australia over the decade that preceded the introduction of plain packaging, trademarks are unlikely to have had any significant effects on smoking rates.

16.   Malawi further considers that the restrictions imposed on the use of geographical indications is contrary to Articles 24.3 and 22.2(b) of the TRIPS Agreement. Plain packaging measures diminish the protection that existed in Australia before the entry into force of the WTO Agreement and do not provide any means to prevent the use of geographical indications. Geographical indications are particularly important for developing and least-developed

Members as it may allow their products to gain market recognition because of the characteristics or quality that is attributable to their origin.

17.   The livelihood of the majority of Malawi's population is dependent on tobacco growing and trade for its livelihood. The ever-increasing regulatory requirements imposed on tobacco products significantly impair the economic development of Malawi as they have negative effects on the volume and value of tobacco traded. The negative consequences of plain packaging measures on least-developed country Members that are dependent on tobacco must be considered together with the legal arguments presented by all the Parties. The economic and social consequences of plain packaging on the most vulnerable Members that have no other option but to continue to rely on tobacco growing for their economic development cannot be ignored.

18.   For Malawi, the plain packaging measures adopted by Malawi are inconsistent with its obligations under the TBT and TRIPS Agreements. Malawi does not question the objective pursued by Australia but is of the view that it has sufficient policy space to such objective and could have adopted effective and less trade-restrictive measures consistent with the WTO Agreements.

ANNEX C-10

EXECUTIVE SUMMARY OF THE ARGUMENTS
OF NEW ZEALAND

I. INTRODUCTION

1. This case raises important systemic issues concerning the right of WTO Members to regulate the marketing of a product in order to protect their legitimate public health objectives. New Zealand is concerned to ensure that the balance of rights and obligations that Members negotiated in the WTO Agreement is maintained, and that the *Agreement on Trade-Related Aspects of Intellectual Property Rights* ("TRIPS Agreement") and the *Agreement on Technical Barriers to Trade* ("TBT Agreement") are properly interpreted and applied. This is particularly important when dealing with a product that is the single largest cause of preventable death and disease in New Zealand, Australia and many other countries.

2. The complainants in this dispute allege that Australia's tobacco plain packaging measure is inconsistent with a large number of provisions in the TRIPS Agreement and the TBT Agreement. The complainants have proposed interpretations of the provisions they rely on that do not have any basis within the text of the agreements at issue, and ignore customary rules of treaty interpretation. This raises serious concerns for New Zealand.

II. THE "NATURE OF THE GOODS" DOES NOT FORM AN OBSTACLE TO THE REGISTRATION OF A TOBACCO TRADEMARK UNDER ARTICLE 15.4

3. Article 15 of the TRIPS Agreement sets out what is the "Protectable Subject Matter" with respect to trademarks. Article 15.1 addresses what may constitute a trademark, and Article 15.4 addresses what obstacles to registration of a trademark are not permitted. Section 28 of Australia's *Tobacco Plain Packaging Act* 2011 means that even if a person is prevented by the tobacco plain packaging measure from using a trademark on retail packaging of tobacco products, the ability to register the trademark in Australia is not affected. The nature of the tobacco products to which a trademark is applied therefore *cannot* form an obstacle to the registration of the trademark. The complainants argue that by preventing the use of certain "signs" the tobacco plain packaging measure is an "obstacle to registration" as it prevents those signs from acquiring distinctiveness and therefore becoming a trademark. However this seeks to conflate Article 15.1 with Article 15.4 and goes well beyond the ordinary meaning of Article 15.4. Australia is not in violation of Article 15.4, properly interpreted.

III. THE TOBACCO PLAIN PACKAGING MEASURE DOES NOT REDUCE THE RIGHTS CONFERRED ON THE OWNER OF A REGISTERED TRADEMARK UNDER ARTICLE 16.1 OR ARTICLE 16.3

4.   Article 16 of the TRIPS Agreement sets out the "Rights Conferred" on the owners of registered trademarks. Article 16.1 provides an "exclusive right to prevent" the use of certain signs where such use would result in the likelihood of confusion. Article 16.3 confers on owners of well-known registered trademarks the right to prevent third parties from using the trademark. The "right to prevent" is a negative right that enables the trademark owner to seek relief where a third party uses its trademark in certain circumstances. The rights of the trademark owner are rights vis-à-vis other traders. They are not positive rights vis-à-vis a WTO Member to *use* the trademark. Members are required, however, to provide the opportunity for trademark owners to register the trademark so that the rights of the trademark owner can be protected. Australia has complied with its obligations in this regard and has not violated Articles 16.1 or 16.3 of the TRIPS Agreement.

IV. THE TOBACCO PLAIN PACKAGING MEASURE DOES NOT VIOLATE ARTICLE 20 OF TRIPS

5.   In order to demonstrate a violation of Article 20 of the TRIPS Agreement, a complainant must establish that:

(i)   the measure at issue imposes *special requirements* on the use of trademarks;

(ii)   the special requirements *encumber* the *use* of a trademark *in the course of trade*; and

(iii)   the measure at issue imposes the encumbrance *unjustifiably*.

6.   Article 20 of the TRIPS Agreement sets out that the use of a trademark in the course of trade shall not be unjustifiably encumbered by special requirements, a non-exhaustive list of which are set out in Article 20, each of which deal with the *use* of a trademark. If it is established that the tobacco plain packaging measure imposes special requirements, which encumber the use of a trademark in the course of trade, it must further be established that the use is not "unjustifiably" encumbered. Drawing on the views of the WTO Appellate Body expressed in *Brazil - Retreaded Tyres*[1] and *EC – Seal Products*,[2] the ordinary meaning of "unjustifiably", in its context and in light of its object and purpose, is clear that the use of a trademark is justifiably encumbered by special requirements only if there is no rational connection between the imposition of the special requirements and a legitimate objective.

---

[1]   Appellate Body Report, paras. 226-227.
[2]   Appellate Body Report, para. 5.306.

7.   New Zealand acknowledges that the wording, and object and purpose, of Article XX of the GATT are different to Article 20 of the TRIPS Agreement and that Article 20 does not include the notion of discrimination. Notwithstanding those differences, New Zealand considers that the Appellate Body's reasoning in *Brazil – Retreaded Tyres* and *EC – Seal Products* provides useful guidance on, and is consistent with, the ordinary meaning of the term "unjustifiably" in the context of Article 20 of the TRIPS Agreement.

8.   This interpretation of the term "unjustifiably" is consistent with the context provided by other provisions of the TRIPS Agreement and the object and purpose of the TRIPS Agreement. Article 8.1 and the 2001 Doha Ministerial *Declaration on the TRIPS Agreement and Public Health* confirm that the TRIPS Agreement should be interpreted in a manner supportive of WTO Members' right to protect public health, and signal that protecting public health is of particular importance to Members.

9.   The complainants appear to interpret Article 20 as importing a "necessity" test or a "least trade-restrictive" test. Such an approach reads words into the text of Article 20 which are absent. Given that the notions of "necessity" and "least trade-restrictive" were not included in Article 20, it is reasonable to draw the inference that the drafters of Article 20 did not intend to incorporate those notions. The fact that these notions are nowhere evident on the face of Article 20 means that the ordinary meaning of the terms must be given their interpretative effect. New Zealand also notes that it is important to not bring a necessity or least trade-restrictive test in through the back door by developing a test which is, in all intents and purposes, equivalent to a "necessity" or "least trade restrictive" test.

V.   THE TOBACCO PLAIN PACKAGING MEASURE IS NOT TRADE-RESTRICTIVE UNDER ARTICLE 2.2

10.   The complainants have alleged that Australia's tobacco plain packaging measure contravenes Article 2.2 of the Technical Barriers to Trade (TBT) Agreement. The protection of human health is clearly one of the "legitimate objectives" covered by Article 2.2 of the TBT Agreement and the risks of non-fulfilment are grave. Article 2.2 protects the expectations of WTO Members that technical regulations will not limit trade to a greater extent than is necessary to fulfil a legitimate objective, taking into account the risks non-fulfilment would create. It has not been established that the tobacco plain packaging measure is trade-restrictive or that there are any changes in market conditions resulting from the tobacco plain packaging measure which have a limiting effect on trade in imported tobacco products. In any case, the evidence adduced by Australia demonstrates that the tobacco plain packaging measure contributes to its public health objectives by reducing the appeal of tobacco products and contributing to the broader objectives of discouraging uptake, encouraging quitting and thereby reducing exposure to smoke. The complainants have failed to discharge their burden of making a *prima facie* case of violation of Article 2.2 of the TBT

Agreement. Furthermore, the Guidelines for the implementation of Articles 11 and 13 of the Framework Convention on Tobacco Control (FCTC) recommend that Parties consider the adoption of plain packaging of tobacco products. As such, the measures fall under Article 2.5 of the TBT Agreement.

VI. ANALYSIS OF THE COMPLAINANTS' EVIDENCE COMPARING SMOKING PREVALENCE IN AUSTRALIA AND NEW ZEALAND

11.   New Zealand also comments on the complainants' evidence which seeks to compare smoking prevalence in Australia and New Zealand. The "Expert Report of J. Klick" on the Effect of Australia's Plain Packaging Law on Smoking, submitted by Ukraine,[3] contains numerous shortcomings, flawed analysis and draws invalid conclusions. This is of particular concern to New Zealand because of the comparison the Report makes with data from New Zealand. In particular, Klick's study sets up a false and virtually impossible evaluation test by looking for a marked short-term reduction in population smoking prevalence and tobacco consumption. Furthermore, the use of New Zealand as a comparison case is superficial and misleading, the data sets used by Professor Klick cannot be relied upon, and the presentation of the survey results in the Report is also misleading.

12.   New Zealand notes that the Panel is entitled to rely on empirical evidence available at the time of the implementation of a measure, and post-implementation evidence which assists in assessing the rational connection between the measure and the legitimate objective, and the degree to which the measure contributes to the legitimate public policy objectives of a WTO Member. To discard such evidence would fail to fulfil the standard of review of a Panel set out in Article 11 of the DSU: to make an objective assessment of the facts of the case. In assessing such empirical evidence, however, a Panel should examine any evidence objectively with an inquiring mind. Where there are fatal flaws in the evidence, such as Professor Klick's Report, the Panel should not give that evidence any weight.

13.   Furthermore, the fact that Australia's measures have been implemented relatively recently is an important factor that the Panel should bear in mind when assessing the complainants' evidence and Australia's evidence concerning the post-implementation period. When determining the significance of each piece of evidence, and what weight the Panel should give to that evidence, the Panel should keep in mind that the impact of tobacco plain packaging on smoking rates as part of a comprehensive suite of measures will be felt most significantly in the longer-term. Where an objective is to change behaviour over the long-term, evidence of impact in the immediate post-implementation period will clearly be

---

[3]   Expert Report by J. Klick, "The Effect of Australia's Plain Packaging Law on Smoking: Evidence from Survey and Market Data" (Exhibit UKR-5).

less persuasive. This is especially the case where, as in this case, the complainants seek to draw definitive conclusions on the success of tobacco plain packaging solely on the basis of rates of smoking prevalence soon after the measure's implementation.

VII. CONCLUSION

14. In New Zealand's view that the complainants have failed to demonstrate that Australia's measure is inconsistent with the WTO agreements at issue in this dispute.

ANNEX C-11

EXECUTIVE SUMMARY OF THE ARGUMENTS
OF NICARAGUA

1.   This Executive Summary of the arguments of Nicaragua in this dispute reflects the written and oral submissions of Nicaragua to the Panel.[1] The Government of Nicaragua is grateful for this opportunity to summarize its views and sincerely hopes that the Panel will take into account its concerns in respect of Australia's *Tobacco Plain Packaging Act of 2011*.

2.   Nicaragua is a developing country and a party to the World Health Organization's Framework Convention on Tobacco Control. Nicaragua shares therefore the objective of implementing effective tobacco-control measures to protect public health while, at the same time, facilitating and promoting trade and economic growth.

3.   Nicaragua is very concerned with the imposition of tobacco-control measures that have not proven to be effective and that negatively impact its trade and economic interests. In this respect, Nicaragua notes that it has an important domestic tobacco sector involved in growing tobacco leaf and manufacturing tobacco products. More than 30,000 workers are directly employed by the tobacco sector and an additional 180,000 individuals are indirectly employed. Thus, Nicaragua is concerned with this trade-restrictive technical regulation that lacks a sound scientific basis and is not consistent with the covered Agreements of the World Trade Organization ("WTO").

4.   Nicaragua is not questioning Australia's right to seek to regulate the sale of tobacco products. It is seriously concerned about the fact that plain packaging has failed to contribute to its public health objective. Plain packaging limits the ability to use trademarks on lawfully available products and is having the effect of severely restricting international trade.

5.   In the course of this dispute, Nicaragua has highlighted some of the WTO obligations Australia violates by enforcing an unnecessary measure restricting the ability to use trademarks to distinguish lawful products, and the effects this has on a developing country like Nicaragua. In this regard, Nicaragua notes its support of the claims and arguments developed by Cuba, the Dominican Republic, Honduras, Indonesia and Ukraine under the WTO Agreements.

6.   Before considering its concerns with the Australian measure under the Agreement on Trade-Related Aspects of Intellectual Property Rights ("TRIPS

---

[1]   Nicaragua's third party written submission of 10 April 2015, oral statement at the third party session of the first Panel hearing of 3 June 2015, and replies to the questions to the third parties of the Panel of 6 July 2015.

Agreement") and the Agreement on Technical Barriers to Trade ("TBT Agreement"), Nicaragua wishes to point out that it sees no "systemic concerns" with the application of both Agreements to the same measure. Indeed, applying all relevant and applicable WTO disciplines to a Members' challenged measure is a common feature of WTO disputes and is required of Panels by Articles 7.2 and 11 of the Understanding on Rules and Procedures Governing the Settlement of Disputes ("DSU").

7.   Considering its impact on intellectual property rights issues protected by the TRIPS Agreement, Australia's plain packaging measure is a unique regulation. It is the first of its kind to deny the essential functions of trademarks to a specific group of products. No longer can trademarks perform their essential function of source identification and distinguishing products between competitors. Thus, rather than to "protect" trademark rights under the TRIPS Agreement and the Paris Convention for the Protection of Industrial Property ("Paris Convention"), Australia, through the implementation of the plain packaging measure, prevents trademark protection.

8.   Nicaragua considers that the plain packaging measure violates Articles 15.1 and 15.4 of the TRIPS Agreement by prohibiting the use of all non-word marks without individually assessing them. The figurative and non-inherently distinctive signs resulting from the plain packaging requirements imposed by Australia cannot constitute a "trademark" as defined in the TRIPS Agreement. Australia's plain packaging measure is product-specific because the prohibition to use registered trademarks only applies to a distinct category of products.

9.   Nicaragua is not convinced by Australia's formalistic argument that plain packaging does not affect the substantive rights set forth in Article 16 of the TRIPS Agreement because trademarks that can no longer be used remain registered in Australia. The text of Article 16 establishes an important link between the use of a trademark, its strength, and the ability for a trademark owner to protect its mark against infringement. Thus, by preventing the ability to use trademarks, Australia reduces the level of protection below the minimum level guaranteed by Articles 16.1 and 16.3 of the TRIPS Agreement.

10.   In relation to Article 20 of the TRIPS Agreement, Nicaragua is of the view that the requirement it imposes is very clear. This article establishes that a regulatory measure that encumbers the use of trademarks is subject to the disciplines of the TRIPS Agreement. Thus, the argument that trademarks only provide "negative" rights is disproved by the text of Article 20, which clearly protects the use of a trademark from unjustifiable encumbrances. In other words, trademarks must, in principle, be permitted to be used without undue government encumbrances.

11.   Further, Nicaragua notes that the plain packaging measure is a "special requirement" subject to Article 20 of the TRIPS Agreement, but that general advertising restrictions are not "specific" to trademark use and thus not within the purview of Article 20. This distinction is important because Nicaragua submits that Members retain a wide degree of latitude for effective regulation of

private conduct which may impact on trademark use in an incidental way. The great degree of policy space afforded to Members to regulate in this area also provides context to understand the broad scope of the term "unjustifiably."

12.   Nicaragua considers that the term "unjustifiably" must not be interpreted in a narrow manner to allow any encumbrance that is merely related to a legitimate policy objective. In this respect, Australia's reading of the term as only requiring "a rational connection" with the policy objective is clearly not sustainable. Most Members appear to agree that Australia's reading of "unjustifiable" is unduly narrow. In the view of Nicaragua, "unjustifiably" denotes a standard of proportionality and suitability and the term was included in Article 20 to allow limited and proportionate encumbrances only. Nicaragua notes that Article XX of the General Agreement on Tariffs and Trade of 1994 ("GATT 1994") provides relevant context to interpreting Article 20 of the TRIPS Agreement but would remind the Panel that a number of differences between those provisions must be taken into account, as set out in our replies to the Panel's questions. The same is true for the terms of Article 8.1 of the TRIPS Agreement, as also set out in our replies to the Panel's questions.

13.   Nicaragua submits that Australia violates its obligations under Article 20 because a special requirement that prohibits the use of a trademark and has, as its main goal the destruction of its origin and distinguishing functions, is not a "proportionate" encumbrance and is thus necessarily "unjustifiable." In addition, a measure that does not individually assess the trademarks in question but instead bluntly prohibits the use of these trademarks violates Article 20. In other words, Australia's plain packaging measure is a disproportionate regulatory measure that impairs the very substance of the rights afforded to trademarks under the TRIPS Agreement.0

14.   Finally, Nicaragua has reviewed the evidence submitted in this dispute concerning the contribution of the plain packaging measure to its public health objective. It is persuaded by the evidence of the Complainants showing that plain packaging has not had any positive effect either on overall numbers of smokers or on consumption in the two years following its implementation. Nicaragua notes that Australia has not been able to adequately respond and provide information to counter the evidence submitted by the Complainants. Australia's reliance on behavioral sciences and theories of marketing is not persuasive when there are facts to the contrary on the record. Thus, plain packaging is an unjustifiable encumbrance because it is not "necessary" for the protection of public health as it does not contribute to reducing smoking, as confirmed by the data before the Panel.

15.   In sum with respect to the TRIPS issues in this dispute, Nicaragua considers that the prohibition on the use of trademarks and the requirement to use brand names in a standardized form are unjustifiable encumbrances imposed on the use of a trademark. Plain packaging therefore the obligations of Australia under the TRIPS Agreement.

16.   As regards the consistency of the Australian measure with the TBT Agreement, Nicaragua finds that the measure – which is contained in a document that lays down product or production-related requirements for marking and labeling – is clearly a technical regulation subject to the disciplines of that Agreement. Regarding the claim of violation of Article 2.2 of the TBT Agreement, Nicaragua considers that plain packaging is more trade-restrictive than necessary to fulfill the stated objective of reducing the use of tobacco products.

17.   The legal standard to be applied has been developed over time in disputes relating to Article 2.2 of the TBT Agreement and Article XX of the GATT 1994, both of which set forth a "necessity" test. Nicaragua notes that a measure which is trade-restrictive and which does not effectively contribute at all to the fulfillment of the legitimate objective can never be considered to be "necessary." All such measures constitute "unnecessary" obstacles to trade and need not be analyzed with respect to less trade-restrictive alternative measures.

18.   First, the very strict packaging and product requirements imposed by Australia necessarily restrict competitive opportunities in the Australian market, despite the irrelevant fact that origin-based discrimination may not be a part of the measure. In fact, plain packaging is a strong disincentive for Nicaragua and other Members to export their products to Australia as it makes it extremely difficult, if not impossible, for any manufacturer of tobacco products not currently present in the Australian market to enter that market.

19.   Second, as presented by the Complainants, the facts show the lack of contribution of the plain packaging measure to its public health objective. Nothing in the evidence submitted by Australia convincingly contradicts these conclusions. Plain packaging has had a detrimental effect as it has, in particular, resulted in a development of illicit trade. Less trade restrictive alternatives were available to Australia to pursue its stated health objectives. Thus, to Nicaragua it is clear that Australia is in violation of Article 2.2 of the TBT Agreement.

20.   In conclusion, Nicaragua supports effective tobacco control policies that genuinely contribute to reducing smoking and protecting health. However, Australia's tobacco plain packaging measure that was adopted with a health protection objective in mind fails to comply with the international obligations imposed by the TRIPS Agreement in respect of trademarks and violates Australia's obligations under Article 2.2 of the TBT Agreement.

21.   The protection of trademarks and the enforcement of rules governing the imposition of technical regulations are important, especially so for developing countries where tobacco is grown and where tobacco products are manufactured. Nicaragua therefore respectfully requests the Panel to take its comments into consideration when resolving these disputes which have important systemic implications for all WTO Members.

ANNEX C-12

EXECUTIVE SUMMARY OF THE ARGUMENTS
OF NIGERIA*

INTRODUCTION

1.   Nigeria appreciates the opportunity to present its views to the Panel in disputes DS434, DS435, DS441, DS458 and DS467. The measure in this dispute relates to the Australia Tobacco Plain Packaging Act 2011 ("TPP Act"), which: (1) prohibits the use of logos, brand imagery, colours and promotional text on the retail packaging of tobacco products; (2) permits the use of brand, business or company name and any variant names on retail packaging, as long as these names appear in a standardised form; (3) imposes certain restrictions upon the shape and finish of retail packaging for tobacco products; and (4) imposes other requirements pertaining to the appearance of tobacco products. In addition, the measure also imposed the use of large pictorial health warnings covering 75% of the front of the package and 90% of the back of a package of cigarettes.

2.   This submission would focus on: (i) economic importance of Tobacco in Nigeria; (ii) the protection of trademarks under the Agreement on Trade Related Aspects of Intellectual Property Rights (TRIPS Agreement); and (iii) regulatory requirements under the Agreement on Technical Barriers to Trade (TBT Agreement).

ECONOMIC IMPORTANCE OF TOBACCO IN NIGERIA

3.   Nigeria has manufacturing facilities that generates substantial economic activity, tax revenue and employment. Therefore, tobacco provides employment and income to many Nigerian farmers. Given the importance of tobacco to Nigeria's economic development, we believe that the health concerns related to tobacco use do not lead to the adoption of unnecessary trade restrictiion and unlawful regulatory measures which harm producers without benefiting the general public interest.

4.   Nigeria is a party to the World Health Organization's Framework Convention on Tobacco Control ("FCTC") to which TPP Act refers. Nigeria considers that the FCTC does not mandate plain packaging and does not permit Members to violate their international obligations. In fact, no provision of the FCTC refers to plain packaging and it is thus not part of any of the minimum obligations of the FCTC. Article 2.1 of the FCTC suggests that the parties may

---

*   Nigeria's written submission is used as its executive summary.

go beyond their FCTC obligations as long as they act in accordance with international law, including WTO law. When the non-binding Guidelines on Articles 11 and 13 dealing with packaging and advertising were adopted, it was recommended that plain packaging should be considered, it is clear that this was neither an obligation to adopt plain packaging nor a suggestion to ignore domestic constitutional principles nor international legal obligations. The adoption suggested by the FCTC Guidelines was simply to review if plain packaging would be an effective means and whether it was a measure that could be consistent with Member's international legal obligations under the TRIPS Agreement.

PROTECTION OF TRADEMARKS UNDER THE TRIPS AGREEMENT

6.   Nigeria considers that it is well-established that trademarks play an important role in a competitive market by allowing producers to differentiate their products. This function of distinguishing products is the essence of trademarks and it fulfils an important role in ensuring fair and effective competition in the market. A global market without trademarks is unimaginable.

7.   The evidence presented by Ukraine, Honduras, Dominican Republic, Indonesia and Cuba (hereinafter "the Complainants") confirms the essential role that trademarks play in competition and trade. The function of distinguishing products is what creates competitive opportunities, domestically and in international trade. The WIPO report on "Global Brands" that some of the Complainants have referred to adequately summarises the vital role of trademarks in the marketplace.[1] In addition, the expert report of Professor Neven, submitted by Ukraine, offers further useful insights into the different functions that trademarks perform and their important role for entering new markets through their communication function.[2]

8.   The important role of trademarks in competition and trade does not seem to be disputed between the Parties. Clearly, only when permitted to be used on products can trademarks perform this function and not when they simply sit on a register. One of the issues in dispute is whether these economic functions of trademarks are translated into binding legal obligations in the TRIPS Agreement.

9.   In this respect, Nigeria has carefully considered the legal arguments presented by both sides on the interpretation of the relevant provisions of the TRIPS Agreement. The Complainants[3] argue that the trademark ban imposed by Australia's plain packaging measure contradicts a number of principles

---

[1]   See World Intellectual Property Organization, "World Intellectual Property Report: Brands – Reputation and Image in the Global Market Place" – Exhibit UKR-20.

[2]   Expert Report by D. Neven, et al., "The Effects of Plain Packaging Regulation on Competition and Tobacco Consumption: An Economic Assessment" – Exhibit UKR-3, p. 39.

[3]   Although there are some differences between the specific arguments of the Complainants and some develop certain arguments that others do not, as a third party to all five disputes, we refer to the arguments of the Complainants as a whole.

embodied in the various provisions of the TRIPS Agreement. They point out that the measure does not address specific concerns related to particular trademarks in contradiction with the trademark-specific approach of the TRIPS Agreement. They also highlight that the measure bans all non-word marks thus creating a differentiation between different types of marks based on their form, in violation of the principle enshrined in Article 15.1. Furthermore, it is argued that it is the nature of the product rather than the nature of the trademark that is driving Australia's ban on trademarks in violation of the rule laid down in Article 15.4 of the TRIPS Agreement.

10.   According to the Complainants, the rights that are to be conferred to trademark owners as a result of registration are based on and determined by the possibility of using the trademark in commerce (i.e. in relation with consumers). The essence of their argument under Article 16 of the TRIPS Agreement is that there is a direct and inseparable link between the use of the mark, the strength of the mark, and its scope of protection guaranteed under Article 16 of the TRIPS Agreement. Furthermore, they argue that the ability of a trademark owner to prevent unauthorized use by third parties, is a means to an end; the end being the use of the trademark as a distinctive sign by the trademark owner.

13.   In view for the importance of trademarks, Nigeria is of the view that the arguments presented by Australia are not convincing. Nigeria agrees with the Complainants that prohibiting the use of validly registered trademarks for reasons unrelated to the specific trademark is inconsistent with the TRIPS Agreement's requirement to "protect" trademarks. The TRIPS Agreement, therefore, seeks to protect intellectual property rights for the value they bring to trade as sources for ensuring effective competition and providing competitive opportunities. In Nigeria's view, if this measure that prohibits the use of otherwise valid trademarks had been applied to a different product, the violation would have been obvious, therefore, trademarks are not protected and the rights conferred on trademark owners are not guaranteed if the trademarks cannot be used since they are distinguishing marks that differentiate products.

14.   Nigeria considers that the expert report of Professor Dinwoodie that was submitted by Ukraine as exhibit UKR-1 convincingly explains how the opportunity to use a trademark is inseparable from and determinative of the scope of protection of the trademark. It is almost a matter of common sense that if genuine use of the trademark is a requirement for maintaining trademark protection - as foreseen in Article 19 of the TRIPS Agreement and as reflected in Australian law - then a minimum opportunity of use must be considered to form part of the framework of trademark protection. This we understand to be reflected also in Article 20 of the TRIPS Agreement which prevents Members from encumbering the use of trademarks with unjustifiable regulatory requirements.

15.   The text of the TRIPS Agreement thus reflects the economic logic that trademarks are worth protecting in international agreements because of their distinguishing function and their related beneficial role in the economy. A trademark can only play this role when it is used. That is the reason why the

TRIPS Agreement focuses on distinctiveness as the only criterion for finding a sign to constitute a 'trademark'; that is why use may be required to maintain registration; and that is why Article 20 exists (i.e. to protect the use of trademarks in commerce from unjustifiable regulatory requirements). The registration and the possibility of preventing unauthorized third parties from using similar signs on similar products, or even on dissimilar products in the case of well-known marks, is effectively meaningless if the trademark is not allowed to perform its main function. To read the entire chapter of the TRIPS Agreement on the "protection" of trademarks without taking into consideration the rationale of such protection does not give effective meaning to the provisions of the TRIPS Agreement.

16.   Use is thus an essential element of the rights conferred by the TRIPS Agreement to owners of trademarks. The opposite approach that the fundamental, minimum rights conferred on trademark owners is simply to have their marks registered but without an opportunity to use them. It is not a convincing interpretation of the TRIPS Agreement. This we understand also to be the view expressed by another leading expert on public international law, Judge Schwebel, in his expert report submitted as exhibit UKR-2[4].

17.   In sum, we agree with the Complainants that Australia's plain packaging measure is inconsistent with key provisions of the TRIPS Agreement dealing with the definition of trademarks, the rights conferred and the limitations imposed on governmental requirements encumbering the use of trademarks. This is not to say that Australia cannot deal with trademarks that are misleading or deceptive or that are of such a nature to violate public morals; those are all well-established reasons for invalidating the registration and protection of a trademark and can be the basis for preventing its use. However, that requires an analysis of the specific sign in question and its allegedly misleading nature. Australia's blunt plain packaging measure does not examine the trademark against a general criterion of deception but simply bans all trademarks. That is not permissible under the TRIPS Agreement.

18.   Although trademark rights may be "negative rights", these rights are dependent on, determined by and ultimately conferred for the purpose of the trademark owner's use of the trademark. Nigeria agrees with Professor Dinwoodie's characterization of "use" as the "lifeblood" of the trademark.[5]

19.   Nigeria is of the view that Australia's plain packaging measure prevents owners from enjoying the benefits of their trademarks' value and goodwill and makes it impossible for trademark owners to differentiate their brands from those of their competitors. A measure that commoditizes the product and its packaging will encourage the influx of counterfeit and pirated products in the market. From

---

[4]   Expert Report by S.M. Schwebel, "On Whether the Owner of a Registered Trademark Has the Right To Use that Trademark". Exhibit UKR-2.
[5]   Expert Report by G.B. Dinwoodie, "Compatibility of Restrictions on the Use of Trade Marks within the TRIPS Agreement", p. 1. Exhibit UKR-1.

a trade perspective, Nigeria considers that trademarks play an important role in penetrating new markets. Plain packaging thus frustrates manufacturers who are not presently active on the Australia market to launch their products in that market.

20.   This does not mean that Nigeria considers that trade or intellectual property rights are more important than health; clearly not. But, based on the arguments presented by the Parties that does not seem to be the question under consideration in these disputes. The TRIPS Agreement allows for health-based exceptions as is clear in the context of patent protection where the TRIPS Agreement expressly allows for compulsory licensing. This flexibility has been further clarified in the 2001 Doha Declaration on TRIPS and Public Health and the 2003 Decision on implementation of paragraph 6 of the Doha Declaration on the TRIPS Agreement and public health that related to access to medicines. Trademarks were never the subject of such debate.

21.   The conditions imposed for permitting compulsory licensing however reveal a balanced approach in a very dramatic context where access to medicines can have a direct and demonstrably life-saving effect. There is no similar provision in the TRIPS section on trademarks permitting direct or indirect trademark expropriation and imposing conditions safeguarding respect for different interests. This is probably a reflection of the different nature of trademarks compared with patents. A patent owner claims exclusivity over a potentially life-saving product and can dictate the conditions for making this product available to the public. A health exception therefore seems obvious. In contrast, a trademark owner merely claims ownership over a sign that it wants to use to distinguish the product from that of competitors. Given that it is clear from the text of the TRIPS Agreement that a sign that is misleading for example, about the product's positive health characteristics must not be registered and may be refused from being used, no other health exception seems to be necessary.

22.   Finally, Nigeria considers that the result of adopting Australia's interpretation would have negative effects on trademark owners as well as the consumers and would not be a correct approach to balancing trade and health interests at the WTO.

REGULATORY REQUIREMENTS UNDER THE TBT AGREEMENT

23.   Nigeria recalls that in 2011 Australia's proposed plain packaging measure was notified in the WTO as a technical regulation that may significantly affect trade with other Members. Many Members, including Nigeria, expressed their concern over this proposal in the TBT Committee. Nigeria referred to the manufacturing facilities in the tobacco sector which generated substantial economic activity, tax revenue and employment in Nigeria. Tobacco provided employment and income to many Nigerian farmers, and there was therefore a concern about the systemic implications of the Australian measure, and its direct and indirect commercial consequences for Nigeria's national economy. Nigeria expressed the view that the proposed plain packaging measure was more trade

restrictive than necessary to fulfil legitimate health objectives, and was contrary to Article 2.2 of the TBT Agreement.[6]

24.   Nigeria subsequently explained that it was concerned that the measure would remove all distinguishing designs, logos, colours and other similar marks from the packaging of branded tobacco making it virtually impossible to identify any specific branded product. This would make it difficult for foreign manufacturers to enter the Australian market. Nigeria thus requested scientific and technical information demonstrating that plain packaging would reduce the number of smokers in Australia and how the measure would comply with Articles 2.2 and 2.4 of the TBT Agreement and urged Australia to take into account Members' views and concerns and to produce an alternative measure that would ensure compliance with Australia's WTO obligations.[7]

25.   More recently, Nigeria also raised concern over a similar plain packaging proposal of Ireland. At the TBT Committee meeting of March 2014, Nigeria expressed concern over the precedent that plain packaging measures could set, particularly regarding the imposition of similar restrictions on heavily regulated products such as alcoholic beverages, snack foods and carbonated drinks. At the meeting, Nigeria did not object to the objective of protecting human health, but considered that it was uncertain whether plain packaging measures could contribute to the achievement of such objective. Nigeria stated that these measures appeared to be more trade restrictive than necessary to fulfil their objective.[8] Nigeria was therefore particularly interested in examining the Parties' legal and factual arguments relating to Australia's plain packaging measure.

26.   Nigeria notes that the Complainants have challenged Australia's plain packaging measure for being inconsistent with Article 2.2 of the TBT Agreement. The Complainants argue that Article 2.2 requires a weighing and balancing of the trade restrictiveness of the measure, the degree of contribution to the fulfilment of the objective and the availability of less restrictive but equally effective alternative measures.

27.   Nigeria considers that the TBT Agreement disciplines Members' application of technical regulations that are unnecessarily trade restrictive. The Agreement requires WTO Members to weigh and balance approaches to legitimate public policy objectives, like the reduction of the level of smoking, with the interests of WTO trading partners. At a minimum, the costs and market access difficulties that a regulation imposes must actually contribute to the fulfilment of the objective. Furthermore, the trade restriction that results from the regulation should be proportionate to the contribution to the fulfilment of the objective. Also, if an alternative measure exists that constitutes less of a market impediment and is as effective or more effective as the measure actually

---

[6]   G/TBT/M/55, paras. 185 – 186.
[7]   G/TBT/M/56, para. 166.
[8]   G/TBT/M/62, para. 2.182.

imposed, the less restrictive alternative measure should be applied. That legal standard is well-established and should not be different dependent on the nature of the product.

28.   Nigeria carefully reviewed the many facts and evidence included in the numerous exhibits submitted by the Parties on the actual or likely effectiveness of the measure. Based on this review, Nigeria considers that the evidence presented by the Complainants demonstrates that the plain packaging measure has failed to contribute to the reduction of smoking and is not likely to reduce smoking in the future either.

29.   The plain packaging measure is a technical regulation that contains a number of strict packaging and labelling requirements that apply to tobacco products. The objective of Australia when adopting the plain packaging measure was to reduce smoking prevalence levels for the Australian population as a whole and for Aboriginals and Torres Straight Islanders in particular. The public health objective that is also reflected in the text of the TPP Act is thus to improve public health by reducing initiation and increasing cessation. Nigeria fully supports this objective. However, the legitimate nature of the objective does not justify the means chosen to pursue this objective.

30.   Economic expert evidence that the Complainants submitted to the Panel highlights the detrimental effect on access to the Australian market and the distortion of competitive opportunities that result from the mandated lack of opportunity to differentiate products through trademarks and packaging designs.[9] Thus, the plain packaging measure imposes a very significant restriction on competition and trade. However, the evidence submitted also shows that Australia's trade-restrictive plain packaging measure is not at all necessary to fulfil the stated objective of health protection. The facts show that two years after the implementation of plain packaging, the measure has not contributed to the reduction of smoking or the changing of smoking behaviour more generally. It has therefore not contributed to the protection of public health. The study by Professor Klick comparing the situation in Australia (with plain packaging) with that in New Zealand (without plain packaging) over the same period of time, confirms that plain packaging has not changed people's smoking behaviour and there is therefore no evidence that it has reduced smoking.[10] The study confirms the market data and other objective evidence from Australia that the Complainants submitted.

31.   It seems speculative to argue, as Australia does, that the measure is likely to contribute in the future if in the first two years it has not produced any effects. In fact, Nigeria considers persuasive the evidence presented by the Complainants on the reasons why people take up smoking and why they find it difficult to quit.

---

[9]   Expert Report by D. Neven, et al., "The Effects of Plain Packaging Regulation on Competition and Tobacco Consumption: An Economic Assessment.", pp. 37-40. Exhibit UKR-5.
[10]   Expert Report by J. Klick, "The Effect of Australia's Plain Packaging Law on Smoking: Evidence from Survey and Market Data", p. 2. Exhibit UKR-5.

The experts consider that packaging and trademarks do not play a role in these behaviours. If that is the case, then it is difficult to see on what basis one would expect the removal of trademarks and the standardization of packaging to have any effect. In so far as the measure is supposed to deal with consumer information, Nigeria notes that plain packaging does not provide any information. In fact, there is general awareness that smoking is very dangerous to consumers' health so it is not clear to Nigeria what and the consumer information objective plain packaging would serve. In any case, Nigeria notes that the large health warnings imposed by Australia under a different set of rules and regulations have not been challenged by the Complainants.

32.   The economic analysis of supply and demand presented by Professor Neven in his expert report confirms the unlikely nature of any positive contribution of plain packaging. In fact, his conclusion is that it is highly likely that plain packaging will have the opposite effect.[11] This suggests that the "risk of non-compliance" with the objective is higher *with* plain packaging than it is *without* plain packaging. The trends analysis submitted by the Dominican Republic shows the down-trading effect of plain packaging and also confirms the adverse consequences of plain packaging.[12]

33.   All of the evidence points in the same direction. Australia's plain packaging measure has not changed smoking behaviour thus far and will not do so in the future because it is simply not apt to do so. Rather, the evidence confirms that the measure risks undercutting Australia's health objective by promoting price-based competition that increases consumption and by stimulating illicit trade.

Under such circumstances, the debate about alternatives becomes meaningless. In any case, Nigeria wishes to make two observations on the alternatives that were presented and on Australia's rejection of these alternatives. First, the fact that a measure already exists does not mean that there cannot be an "alternative". Indeed, it is well established that taxation is the single most effective tobacco control instrument. That being the case, then for sure a proposed increase of the relevant Australian taxes to meet the recommendation of the World Health Organization would constitute an alternative measure. Nigeria understands this to have been the view of the WTO in the past as well.[13] Second, Nigeria considers that if an institution exists for dealing with consumer protection issues related to packaging, as is the case in Australia, then a better use of this

---

[11]   Expert Report by D. Neven, et al., "The Effects of Plain Packaging Regulation on Competition and Tobacco Consumption: An Economic Assessment.", Exhibit UKR-3, pp 32 -35, p. 44.

[12]   Empirical Assessment of Australia's Plain Packaging Regime, prepared by the Institute for Policy Evaluation (Dr. David Afshartous, Ph.D; Professor Marcus Hagedorn; Professor Ashok Kaul; and Professor Michael Wolf) (7 October 2014), p. 2. Exhibit DR-100.

[13]   See, for example, Panel Reports, *China – Measures Related to the Exportation of Rare Earths, Tungsten, and Molybdenum*, WT/DS431/R / WT/DS432/R / WT/DS433/R / and Add.1, adopted 29 August 2014, upheld by Appellate Body Reports WT/DS431/AB/R / WT/DS432/AB/R / WT/DS433/AB/R, para. 7.186.

institution seems to be an alternative that merits further consideration before imposing novel measures like plain packaging.

34.   Nigeria is of the view that ample policy space should be given to Members to pursue legitimate objectives like the protection of public health. Australia has one of the strictest tobacco control regimes in the world and we commend Australia for its effective fight against smoking. However, precisely in such circumstances, care should be taken to maintain a balanced approach and to ensure that further restrictions on trade and intellectual property rights are lawful and necessary. Nigeria considers that the legal arguments presented by the Complainants in respect of the violation of intellectual property rights and the evidence submitted to demonstrate the lack of contribution of the plain packaging measure confirm that Australia's plain packaging measure is an unnecessary and unlawful means to a legitimate end. Nigeria is of the view that, if the product is legally available on the market and if there are no indications that the specific trademark is misleading or deceptive, and if it is not otherwise offensive or violating public morals in Australia, then trademarks should in principle be allowed to be used on a product to fulfil their important economic functions.

CONCLUSION

Nigeria continue to support the right of Members to take measures to protect public health in accordance with the WTO agreements and we commend Australia for its fight against smoking. However, care should be taken to maintain a balanced approach that would ensure consistency with the WTO law. Nigeria considers that the legal arguments presented by the complainants in respect of the violation of WTO law and the evidence confirms that the measure at issue is inconsistent with the WTO law. It is therefore, our view that if a product is legally available in the market and if there is no indications that the specific trademark is misleading or deceptive, then trademarks should in principle be allowed to be used on a product to fulfil their important economic function.

ANNEX C-13

EXECUTIVE SUMMARY OF THE ARGUMENTS
OF NORWAY

I   ISSUES RELATED TO THE TRIPS AGREEMENT

A.   The TRIPS Agreement and the protection of public health

1.   The TRIPS Agreement recognizes a right for Members to protect public health. Of particular relevance in this regard are Articles 7 and 8.1, as well as the *Declaration on the TRIPS Agreement and Public Health* (Doha Declaration on Public Health). *The Doha Declaration on Public Health* gives express interpretative guidance, affirming that "the Agreement can and should be interpreted and implemented in a manner supportive of WTO members' right to protect public health". While the Declaration does not qualify as an authoritative interpretation under the Marrakesh Agreement, paragraph 4 of the Declaration must be considered a "subsequent agreement" within the meaning of Article 31(3)(a) of the Vienna Convention. In light of this, the relevant TRIPS provisions should be interpreted in a manner supportive of Members' rights to protect public health.

B.   The TRIPS Agreement does not provide for a "right to use" a trademark

2.   The complainants' legal claims under the TRIPS Agreement are based on a contention that the Agreement provides for a positive right to use a registered trademark.[1] Norway strongly disagrees with this contention, and submits that the complainants' assertion of a "right to use" does not have any support in the relevant provisions of the Agreement, when properly interpreted. Rather, the TRIPS Agreement confers negative rights to prevent certain uses by third parties.

C.   Legal issues related to Article 20 of the TRIPS Agreement

3.   The parties disagree on whether it is the complainants or the respondent that has the burden of proof under Article 20. According to the Appellate Body, "the burden of proof rests upon the party, whether complaining or defending, who asserts the affirmative of a particular claim of defence".[2] Who has the burden of proof depends on the legal character of the provision at issue. Norway

---

[1]   See, for instance, Australia's First Written Submission para. 227-229, 235.
[2]   Appellate Body Report, *United States – Wool Shirts and Blouses*, p. 14.

holds that Article 20 is best characterized as "a single affirmative obligation".[3] Based on this, the burden of proof under Article 20 rests on the complainants. To establish a violation of Article 20, the complainants must show that the use of a trademark "in the course of trade" has been "unjustifiably" "encumbered by special requirements". In the following, Norway will set out its view on the interpretation of these different elements.

4. Firstly, regarding the term "in the course of trade", Norway agrees with most of the parties in this dispute that it refers to the process of buying and selling goods and services, and that any encumbrance after this point of time is outside the scope of Article 20.[4] Secondly, Norway submits that the term "special requirement" must be understood as referring to requirements regarding how a trademark may be used, and not to requirements prohibiting the use of a trademark. Reference is made to Australia's arguments in this regard.[5]

5. Thirdly, when it comes to the test to be applied in assessing the "unjustifiability" of an encumbrance on use, Norway agrees with Australia that the term "unjustifiably" must be interpreted to be referring to an inquiry of whether there is a "rational connection" between the "special requirements" and the policy directive behind those requirements.[6] In Norway's view, the complainants' argument that the term "unjustifiably" refers to a similar standard to that of "necessity", is not compatible with a proper interpretation in accordance with the ordinary meaning to be given to this term in its context and in light of the object and purpose of the TRIPS Agreement.

6. "Unjustifiably" is defined to mean "not capable of being justified".[7] This does not encompass notions of "necessity" and "least restrictiveness". The term "unjustifiable" is used several places in the WTO Agreements, as part of the phrase "arbitrary and unjustifiable discrimination". In that context, the Appellate Body has set out that one of "the most important factors" in the assessment of "unjustifiable" is "the question of whether the discrimination can be reconciled with, or is rationally related to, the policy objective with respect to which it has been provisionally justified".[8] The ordinary meaning of the word "unjustifiable", as it is interpreted in these reports, supports the understanding that "unjustifiably" in Article 20 must be referring to an inquiry of whether there is a "rational connection" between the "special requirements" and the policy directive behind those requirements.

---

[3]   Australia's First Written Submission, paras. 428-430.
[4]   See Australia's First Written Submission para. 349, fn. 539. Only Honduras seems to have a divergent view, see Honduras' First Written Submission, para. 224. See also Australia's First Written Submission, fn. 350.
[5]   Australia's First Written Submission, part IV, D, 2.
[6]   See Australia's First Written Submission, paras. 362-363.
[7]   *Collins English Dictionary*, 9th ed. HarperCollins Publishers, 2007.
[8]   Appellate Body Report, *EC – Seal Products*, para. 5.306.

7.   The context of the term "unjustifiable" further substantiates this understanding. In this regard, Norway would in particular refer to the fact that the drafters of the TRIPS Agreement included the term "necessary" several places in the Agreement, but chose *not* to use it in Article 20. This choice must be given effect. Thus, the complainants cannot be heard with their argument that the term "unjustifiably" should be interpreted as to encompass notions of "necessity", "least restrictiveness" and "reasonable available alternatives".

8.   The "object and purpose of the Agreement, as expressed, in particular," in Article 8.1 supports an interpretation of the word "unjustifiably" that preserves the scope of Members' right to pursue legitimate policy objectives through measures that are in conformity with the provisions of the Agreement. Norway submits that an interpretation in line with the ordinary meaning of the term, as set out above, best serves the principle in Article 8.1

9.   Based on the above, it is clear that the scope of Article 20 does not include the prohibitive elements of the plain packaging measure. Furthermore, it follows from a proper interpretation of the word "unjustifiably" that it does not refer to notions such as "necessity" or least trade-restrictiveness", but rather to an inquiry of whether there is a "rational connection" between the "special requirements" and the policy directive behind those requirements.

II   ISSUES RELATED TO THE TBT AGREEMENT

A.   Introduction

10.   The TBT Agreement Article 2.2 contains rules applicable to measures that meet the definition of a "technical regulation" in paragraph 1 of Annex 1 of the TBT Agreement.[9] Norway finds that the requirements relating to packaging, marking or labelling must be considered to be "technical regulations" in accordance with this definition, and does not find it necessary to distinguish between the restriction on the use of a trademark and the physical requirements in the assessment of Article 2.2.

B.   The FCTC Guidelines are relevant international standards in accordance with Article 2.5 of the TBT Agreement

11.   Article 2.5 provides that technical regulations that are prepared, adopted or applied for a legitimate objective mentioned in Article 2.2, and is "in accordance with relevant international standards" are rebuttably presumed not to constitute "unnecessary obstacles to international trade" within the meaning of Article 2.2.

12.   Norway is of the view that, firstly, the technical regulation at issue has been adopted in order to protect human health, which is a legitimate objective

---

[9]   See *e.g.* Appellate Body Reports, *EC – Sardines*, para. 175; and *EC - Asbestos*, para. 59.

under Article 2.2. Secondly, the plain packaging measure was adopted *inter alia* to give effect to Australia's obligations under the FCTC, in particular the Guidelines for the implementation of FCTC Articles 11 and 13. Thirdly, Norway agrees with Australia's reasoning and conclusion in its first written submission that the FCTC Guidelines for the implementation of Articles 11 and 13 can be considered to be "relevant international standards" under Article 2.5, in line with the definition in the TBT Agreement Annex 1 and the ISO/IEC Guide 2: 1991. Finally, the plain packaging measure must be considered to be "in accordance" with these guidelines.

13.   Consequently, the measure shall be "rebuttably presumed not to create an unnecessary obstacle to international trade". The presumption seems to imply that a higher standard of proof is required in relation to the question of whether a measure is an unnecessary international trade obstacle under Article 2.2, as compared to the cases where the presumption in Article 2.5 is not applicable.

C.   The assessment of whether the measure can be considered to be more trade restrictive than necessary under Article 2.2 of the TBT Agreement

14.   According to Article 2.2, it must be assessed whether a measure is "more trade-restrictive than necessary to fulfil a legitimate objective". Norway is of the view that the complainants as a threshold matter must demonstrate that the technical regulation at issue is "trade-restrictive".

15.   If the Panel deems that the complainants have made a *prima facie* case that the measure is trade-restrictive, the Panel must assess whether the measure is more trade-restrictive than necessary to fulfil a legitimate objective, taking into account the risks non-fulfilment would create. The Appellate Body has explained that the assessment of "necessity" requires an identification of the objective pursued with the measure[10] an evaluation of the objectives' legitimacy[11] as well as a relational analysis.[12]

16.   In this regard, Norway firstly recalls that the plain packaging measure aims at protecting human health, a legitimate objective under Article 2.2. This objective is "both vital and important in the highest degree"[13] a consideration that must be taken into account in the assessment of whether the measure is necessary.

---

[10]   Appellate Body Report, *US – Tuna II (Mexico)*, paras. 313-314; and Appellate Body Report, *US – COOL*, para. 371.

[11]   Appellate Body Report, *US – Tuna II (Mexico)*, para. 313; and Appellate Body Report, *US – COOL*, paras. 370 and 372.

[12]   Appellate Body Report, *US – Tuna II (Mexico)*, paras. 315, 318- 319 and 321. See also Appellate Body Report, *US – COOL*, para. 373-375, 377 and 390.

[13]   In the context of Article XX(b) of the GATT 1994, see Panel Report, *EC – Asbestos*, para. 172 (citing Appellate Body Report, *Korea – Various Measures on Beef*, para. 162);Appellate Body Report, *Brazil – Retreaded Tyres*, para. 144.

17.   Secondly, if the Panel were to conclude that the measure is trade-restrictive, it must assess the degree of trade-restrictiveness. In case the restrictiveness is considered to be minimal, even a small degree of contribution by the measure to the legitimate objective would in Norway's view be sufficient to conclude that the measure does not exceed what is necessary.

18.   Thirdly, when assessing the measure's degree of contribution to the legitimate objective, the Panel should view complex health problems, such as the one at issue, in the broader context of the comprehensive strategies implemented to fight such problems.[14] The Panel should in particular take into account the difficulties in measuring the effects of an instrument working in synergy with other measures, the overarching objective of promoting public health, as well the expectation that the effects of the measure may manifest themselves gradually over several years.

19.   Fourthly, Norway is of the view that both the nature and gravity of the risks that non-fulfilment would create, supports a conclusion that the plain packaging measure is not more restrictive to trade than what is necessary. The nature of the risks to human health is both vital and important in the highest degree, and the gravity of the consequences that would arise from non-fulfilment of the objective is also unquestionably severe.

20   Lastly, Norway agrees with Australia that equally efficient alternative measures do not appear to exist.[15] *Inter alia*, some of the proposed alternatives measures must rather be considered *supplements* to the plain packaging measure. Norway also questions whether some of the alternative measures in fact would be less trade restrictive. Further, it must be noted that one of the intended effects of the plain packaging measure is to close the last gap in the ban on tobacco advertising. In Norway's view, none of the proposed alternative measures can close this gap and thereby reinforce the effect of existing measures.

---

[14]   Appellate Body Report, *Brazil – Retreaded Tyres*, para. 154.
[15]   The complainants submit that the objective of the measure could equally well be attained through other measures, such as excise increases, youth access to tobacco products, the Australian consumer law, social marketing campaigns and pre-vetting schemes.

ANNEX C-14

EXECUTIVE SUMMARY OF THE ARGUMENTS
OF OMAN

1.   Oman views tobacco use as one of the greatest threats to public health the world has ever faced. According to the WHO, tobacco consumption currently kills nearly six million people a year through direct use and the deadly effects of second-hand smoke that averages to one person dying every six seconds. Tobacco is without doubt the single most preventable cause of death in the world today. It is the only legal consumer product that kills up to half of those who use it as intended and recommended by the manufacturer.

2.   Oman is of the view that the challenged Australian Plain Packaging Legislation aims to prevent tobacco advertising and promotion. It achieves its stated goals of: reducing the attractiveness and appeal of tobacco products to consumers, particularly young people; increasing the noticeability and effectiveness of mandated health warnings; and reducing the ability of the tobacco product packaging to mislead consumers about the harms of smoking.

3.   Oman considers that the relevant provisions of the Covered Agreements raised in this dispute achieve a balance that respects WTO Members' sovereign regulatory autonomy, particularly in relation to public health.

4.   Oman notes that Article 2.2 of the TBT was designed to provide policy space for Members to implement various national policies, including on human health or life in the form of technical regulations. Article 2.2 recognises Members' right to implement such technical regulations upon the understanding that such measures should not create unnecessary obstacles to trade. In other words, the text recognises the existence of legitimate concerns that may result in the application of measures that may restrict or inhibit trade, and permits such measures provided that they are "...not more trade-restrictive than necessary to fulfil a legitimate objective, taking account of the risks non-fulfilment would create".

5.   Accordingly, an assessment of Article 2.2 is not about whether the measure at issue restricts trade, but rather whether it satisfies the requirements enunciated in Article 2.2 that bear upon its contribution to achieving a legitimate objective on the one hand and the necessity of the measure on the other.

6.   In respect of the issue of "necessity" in the context of TBT Article 2.2, Oman recalls that in *US-Tuna II*,[1] the Appellate Body drew on its reasoning in

---

[1]   Appellate Body Report, *United States – Measures Concerning the Importation, Marketing and Sale of Tuna and Tuna Products*, WT/DS381/AB/R, para. 318.

Korea – Various Measures on Beef,[2] noting that: "[a]t one end of this continuum lies 'necessary' understood as 'indispensible'; at the other end, is 'necessary' taken to mean as 'making a contribution to.'" Oman considers that this assessment is of instructive value to the Panel and should inform its Article 2.2 analysis for the determination of what is to be considered "necessary".

7.   Oman subscribes to the relevant argumentation and factual evidence articulated in Australia's Submission that clearly demonstrate that plain packaging contributes to a reduction in smoking rates and tobacco consumption.

8.   Protecting public health is a legitimate objective of the utmost importance to each WTO member individually and to the global community as a whole. The objective or target of protecting human health by reducing tobacco use is not achieved by any one measure, but rather by a host of measures working collectively to achieve the legitimate objective at the levels sought by the Member implementing the measure. Plain packaging is one such measure.

9.   Moreover, Paragraph 4 of the preamble of the TBT Agreement expressly acknowledges a Member's right to implement measures for the protection of human life or health "...at the levels it considers appropriate", subject to the requirement that they do not discriminate between members or act as a disguised restriction on trade. Plain packaging is aimed at protecting human health through reducing tobacco use, which is a legitimate objective. The measure treats all tobacco products on an equal footing and is therefore not discriminatory. And the WHO FCTC Guidelines expressly acknowledges plain packaging as a legitimate measure to curb smoking[3], it can therefore hardly be deemed a disguised restriction on trade.

10.   Oman considers the language used in the preamble as expressly affording discretion for Members to determine the level of aspiration of their technical regulations.

11.   The Panel in *US-Clove Cigarettes*[4] established that the burden of proof rests upon the party alleging a violation of Article 2.2. This means that in order for a complainant to successfully argue an Article 2.2 claim they would be required to present a prima facie case demonstrating inconsistency with said Article.

12.   Moreover, Article 2.5 provides that where a technical regulation is in accordance with relevant international standards there shall be a rebuttable presumption that it does not create unnecessary obstacles to international trade. In other words, where the measure at issue meets the conditions set out in Article 2.5, the Panel's Article 2.2 analysis must begin from a rebuttable presumption

---

[2]   Appellate Body Report, *Korea – Measures Affecting Import of Fresh, Chilled and Frozen Beef*, WT/DS161/AB/R, para. 161.
[3]   See Part II.F of the WHO Framework Convention on Tobacco Control Guidelines.
[4]   Panel Report, *United States – Measures Affecting the Production and Sale of Clove Cigarettes*, WT/DS406/R, para. 7.331.

that the measure is not an unnecessary obstacle to trade. Oman regards that such a rebuttable presumption should have the effect of placing a heavier burden on the complainant alleging an Article 2.2 violation to substantiate its claims.

13.   In this respect, Oman considers that the WHO Framework Convention on Tobacco Control ("FCTC") constitutes "relevant international standards". We are mindful that there does not exist an explicit definition for international standards in the WTO covered agreements, but we consider that the TBT Agreement provides sufficient guidance in this regard for a finding that the FCTC constitutes "relevant international standards".

14.   In respect of the claims made under the TRIPS Agreement, Oman considers that nothing in the TRIPS Agreement confers on owners of trade marks a positive right to use their trade marks. Moreover, Article 8.1 of the TRIPS Agreement contemplates Members' right to formulate and amend their regulations for the protection of public health as long as they are consistent with the TRIPS Agreement.

15.   Furthermore, the Doha Declaration on the TRIPS Agreement and Public Health, adopted by the WTO Ministerial Conference on 14 November 2001, explicitly recognises "WTO Members' right to protect public health" and confirms WTO Members' agreement that TRIPS "can and should be interpreted and implemented in a manner supportive of" that right.

16.   In addition to the WTO Agreements, WHO FCTC also provides the international legal basis for the implementation of the Plain Packaging of tobacco products. Australia's measure reflects multilateral consensus on tobacco control. The Guidelines for the implementation of Articles 11 and 13 of the WHO FCTC specifically recommend that all Parties to this convention (180 parties thus far) consider adopting tobacco plain packaging to "increase the ... effectiveness of health warnings" and "eliminate the effects of advertising ... on packaging".

17.   Oman considers that the matters before this Panel must be considered in the broader context of international efforts to curb the global consumption of tobacco products, an aspiration which is grounded in the indisputable scientific evidence connecting tobacco consumption to various diseases.

ANNEX C-15

EXECUTIVE SUMMARY OF THE ARGUMENTS
OF PERU*

1.   Peru welcomes this opportunity to participate in these disputes as a third party. As we indicated when we asked to be joined as a third party, our interest is mainly systemic, inasmuch as we are interested in the interpretation given to the relevant provisions of the TRIPS Agreement, the TBT Agreement and the GATT 1994, in relation to the public health measures adopted by a WTO Member regarding tobacco products and products derived from tobacco. At the same time, this case is of interest to us because the Panel's decision will also have an impact on the commitments made under the WTO agreements with regard to the implementation of other international instruments, such as the WHO Framework Convention on Tobacco Control, among others.

2.   A plain packaging measure on a particular product, of the kind implemented by Australia, could be considered a limitation of the use of a trademark granted to tobacco products or products derived from tobacco. In particular, Article 20 of the TRIPS Agreement provides that the use of a trademark in the course of trade shall not be unjustifiably encumbered by special requirements, such as use in a manner detrimental to its capability to distinguish the goods or services of one undertaking from those of other undertakings. However, the key term in this provision is "unjustifiably", since it recognizes that the right to use the trademark is not absolute and that there could be justified grounds for its limitation. In this connection, the TRIPS Agreement itself recognizes the principle that Members have the capacity to adopt measures necessary to protect public health, including tobacco control measures.

3.   On the other hand, the WTO commitments are not isolated from the international commitments assumed by Members in other areas. In particular, the WHO Framework Convention on Tobacco Control has been in force since 2005. There are currently 180 Parties to the Convention, including Australia, Ukraine, Honduras and Peru.

4.   Australia has indicated that the measure at issue is in line with the "Guidelines for implementation of Article 11 (Packaging and labelling of tobacco products) of the WHO Framework Convention on Tobacco Control" and that the document in question constitutes a relevant international standard, within the meaning of Article 2.4 of the TBT Agreement. In this connection, paragraph 46 of the Guidelines calls on the Parties to consider adopting measures to restrict or prohibit the use of logos, colours, brand images or

---

*   Original Spanish. Peru's oral statement is used as its executive summary.

promotional information on packaging other than brand names and product names displayed in a standard colour and font style, i.e. plain packaging.

5.	In this regard, in addition to the analysis of the provisions of the TRIPS Agreement, it is necessary to resolve the dispute by analysing the provisions of the TBT Agreement, in order to determine whether it is possible to consider the Conference of the Parties (COP) to the WHO Framework Convention on Tobacco Control as a standard-setting institution and, if so, whether the above-mentioned Guidelines constitute a relevant international standard.

6.	In the present case, Peru considers it necessary for the Panel to rule on both aspects, given the impossibility of applying the principle of judicial economy, since the measure at issue covers both intellectual property aspects (use of the trademark) and provisions relating to technical regulations (labelling of tobacco products and by-products).

7.	Peru thanks the Panel, the parties and the other third parties for their attention and, having concluded its statement at this hearing, remains at the disposal of the Panel to provide any further clarification required.

Thank you.

ANNEX C-16

EXECUTIVE SUMMARY OF THE ARGUMENTS
OF THE PHILIPPINES[*]

1. Mr. Chairman, members of the Panel, staff of the Secretariat, the Philippines appreciates the opportunity to appear before you today as a third party in these disputes.

2. As we had articulated in the 1 May 2012 consultations in DS435, the Philippines has multi-dimensional interests in the dispute. We noted our substantial trade interest in the matter, having started cigarette exports to Australia in 2010 and experiencing significant export growth with a promising upside.

3. On the other hand, the Philippines also noted that it is a party to the Framework Convention on Tobacco Control (FCTC), and is interested in understanding the relevance of the measure to the effective implementation of the FCTC, and the nexus of the measure and its avowed public health policy objective. We give importance to public health policy objectives, as espoused in Article 8 of the TRIPS Agreement and the Doha Ministerial Declaration on Public Health.

4. Equally important, the Philippines takes note of the importance of the dispute. We are keen on further understanding the nexus between the measure at issue on one hand, and the Trade-Related Aspects of Intellectual Property Rights (TRIPS) Agreement and the Technical Barriers to Trade (TBT) Agreement on the other hand, in the context of the public health policy objectives. This nexus, we believe, is possible to define in the least trade distortive or restrictive manner.

5. The measure at issue is Australia's Tobacco Plain Packaging Act 2011 and related legal instruments, which mandates the use of uniform plain packaging on retail packs and the tobacco products themselves. The measure is in furtherance of the public health policy objective of regulating tobacco consumption. It distinguishes the products mainly by the brand name, which is itself printed in uniform font and size.

6. The Philippines is aware of the unprecedented attention placed by various Members and stakeholders in these consolidated disputes, having joined the five complainants, the respondent, and forty-one other third parties in the panel proceedings.

7. Given the comprehensive written submissions and statements by the parties and third parties before this esteemed Panel, we trust that a fair and

---

[*] The Philippines' oral statement is used as its executive summary.

enlightened outcome that upholds the WTO agreements and legitimate interests of Members within the multilateral trading system will be achieved.

8.	Even as we closely monitor the proceedings in order to determine how best to protect and promote the interests of thousands of our tobacco farmers and employment-generating enterprises, as well as the health and well-being of our citizens, the Philippines understands that a legal determination of the consistency of the measure with the TRIPS Agreement and the TBT Agreement would have to be made.

9.	On the intellectual property side, the findings of these disputes would touch upon the scope, nature (i.e., a positive or negative right), and allowable special requirements on the use of a trademark and a geographical indication. The findings may also delve into the extent of the public health policy space vis-à-vis the rights provided in the TRIPS Agreement. On the technical regulation aspect, evidence will show whether or not the measure is an unnecessary obstacle to trade, and whether it is more trade-restrictive than necessary.

10.	We are cognizant, furthermore, that in the bigger picture, trade in the 21st century is imbued with multi-dimensional aspects. Intellectual property, public health policy, environmental concerns, and information technology are but some areas that affect trading between economies. Even domestically, balancing the immediate concerns of farmers and manufacturers with long-term health imperatives is necessary to fully protect and project national interest. We do not conduct trade in a vacuum, and the other dimensions affecting trade are often politically significant. These other dimensions may also have to be considered in any positive resolution to the disputes.

11.	The Philippines is also interested in knowing whether the measure and the findings in these disputes would have any implications on the conduct of international trade in other goods and services. Will tobacco products, given their public health effects, be considered *sui generis*, or will they be a gateway towards a more prevalent use of plain packaging to deter the use of other products?

12.	Mr. Chairman, as we listen intently to our discussions today and analyze carefully developments in the months ahead, we are still left to wonder how a plain pack of cigarettes aimed at reducing attractiveness has generated an unprecedented amount of global attention.

13.	This serves to remind us that the rules and decisions we undertake abstractly in this esteemed organization have concrete, real-life impact on our peoples – from the farmers that painstakingly plant and harvest tobacco for a living, to manufacturers that produce and package high-quality goods, and to consumers and citizens whose well-being this organization has vowed to uphold. We trust that the decisions we undertake in these disputes will ultimately redound to the benefit of our peoples.

14.   This dispute has put forward novel arguments and interpretations of the relevant covered agreements, and the Philippines as a 3rd party has assessed the implications of these proceedings taking into account national objectives. The Philippines reserves its rights under Article X.4 of the DSU for a recourse to normal dispute settlement proceedings under the DSU.

15.   Thank you, Mr. Chairman.

ANNEX C-17

EXECUTIVE SUMMARY OF THE ARGUMENTS
OF SINGAPORE

I.   INTRODUCTION

1.   This dispute is about whether the measure at issue ("Plain Packaging Measure") is permitted under the covered agreements. It is not about whether public health or trade should prevail. It is also not about whether or not intellectual property rights (IPR) are important and should be protected. There is no question that the covered agreements can and should be read harmoniously, in a manner that strikes a proper balance between respect for IPR and the right to protect public health.

2.   Singapore has grave concerns that in seeking to challenge the Plain Packaging Measure, the complainants have sought to stretch the meaning of the provisions beyond the terms of the covered agreements and created obligations where there are none. Such interpretation will inject considerable uncertainty into the multilateral trading system and must be rejected.

II.   ANALYSIS AND COMMENTS

A.   Claims under the TRIPS Agreement

Horizontal Remarks

3.   The complainants claim that they do not assert that the TRIPS Agreement establishes a positive right of use of a trademark. Nonetheless, they argue that trademarks must be allowed to be used or granted an opportunity to be used. In substance, this is no different from asserting a positive right of use. However, trademark rights, as accorded by the TRIPS Agreement, are negative rights. They are a right to exclude others from using certain signs. They do not encompass a right to use a trademark. Any claim of a right of use of a trademark under the TRIPS Agreement is neither supported by the relevant text, context, or objective and purpose of the TRIPS Agreement, nor by WTO jurisprudence. Although the panel in *EC – Protection of Trademarks and Geographical Indications (US)* suggested that owners of trademarks have a legitimate interest to preserve the distinctiveness of their trademarks, the panel also made clear that legitimate interest is *not* synonymous with rights conferred under the TRIPS Agreement. Hence, it would be erroneous to conflate the two when interpreting the TRIPS Agreement.

TRIPS Articles 2.1, 15.4, 16.1, 16.3, 22.2(b) and 24.3

4. In Singapore's view, the claims in respect of Articles 2.1, 15.4, 16.1, 16.3, 22.2(b) and 24.3 must fail. The correct interpretation and application of the provisions are as follows:

a) Article 6*quinquies* of the Paris Convention (incorporated by Article 2.1 of the TRIPS Agreement) obliges a Member to accept for filing and protection "as is" trademarks that are duly registered in another country. The provision does not address the nature of the protection that flows from registration, or obligate Members to grant trademark owners a "right of use" in respect of their trademarks. This reading is consistent with WIPO's view that Article 6*quinquies* A(1) does not address the question of use;

b) Article 10*bis* of the Paris Convention (incorporated by Article 2.1 of the TRIPS Agreement) addresses "acts of unfair competition" which are acts of commercial dishonesty in the sense of misrepresentation. The provision is not directed at market conditions. The ability to use brand, business or company names with variant names on tobacco packaging (which themselves may be trademarks or elements of trademarks) enables consumers to clearly distinguish the tobacco products of one undertaking from another;

c) Article 15.4 addresses the registration of a trademark by providing that the nature of the goods to which a trademark is to be applied shall not form an obstacle to registration. The provision deals with registration and not use. Contrary to what the complainants claim, tobacco-related signs that are non-inherently distinctive and have not acquired distinctiveness are not capable of constituting trademarks; they are non-registrable *per se* and therefore *a fortiori*, there cannot be any "obstacle to registration" because of the nature of the goods or services involved. Furthermore, Members are under no obligation to enable a sign to acquire distinctiveness;

d) Article 16.1 accords the protection that follows from registration which is the exclusive right to prevent unauthorised use of identical or similar signs on identical or similar goods where such use would result in a likelihood of confusion. It creates a negative right to exclude and *not* a positive right of use. Even if it is argued that trademark owners have a legitimate interest to preserve the distinctiveness of their trademarks, such interest is not a "right" under Article 16.1, much less a right to use a trademark. The erosion of any legitimate interest to preserve distinctiveness through use is not a violation of Article 16.1;

e) Article 16.3 protects registered well-known trademarks by preventing the registration or use of those trademarks on dissimilar goods. The provision creates a negative right to prevent registration or use and *not* a positive right of use. Article 16.3 does not impose on Members an obligation to enable an owner to maintain the well-known status of a trademark. Likewise, Article 16.3 does not oblige Members to permit the use of a trademark in order to enable it to acquire well-known status;

f) Article 22.2(b) obliges a Member to provide, in respect of geographical indications ("GI"), the legal means for interested parties to *prevent any use* that constitutes an act of unfair competition. This is not the same as a positive right of use;

g) Article 24.3 prohibits a Member from diminishing the protection of GI that existed in the Member immediately prior to the date of entry into force of the WTO Agreement. The complainants have not demonstrated a relevant GI that existed in Australia prior to 1 January 1995. In any event, the protection of GI in Australia has not been diminished by the Plain Packaging Measure because no positive right of use of GI ever existed under Australian law.

TRIPS Article 20

5. Article 20 provides that the use of a trademark in the course of trade shall not be unjustifiably encumbered by special requirements. In Singapore's view, Article 20 addresses the use of trademarks on goods that are lawfully placed on the market and is not concerned with measures that regulate the availability of the goods themselves on the market. However, this does not mean that all measures that address the use of trademarks on goods that may be lawfully placed on a market fall within the scope of Article 20. We submit that aspects of the Plain Packaging Measure that prohibit the use of "non-word" trademarks are outside the scope of Article 20.

6. We also submit that the Plain Packaging Measure is not unjustifiable as it bears a rational connection with a legitimate public health objective and does not go against that objective. Accordingly, the measure does not contravene Article 20.

Encumbered by special requirements

7. For the reasons that follow, aspects of the Plain Packaging Measure that prohibit the use of trademarks fall outside the scope of Article 20. First, having regard to the *ejusdem generis* canon of construction, we note that a prohibition on the use of trademarks is not of the same type as the situations illustrating the term "encumbered by special requirements".

8. Second, this reading is confirmed by the negotiating history of Article 20. Commentators have explained that Article 20 was directed at certain practices during the Uruguay Round, such as requiring foreign trademarks to be used with the trademark or trade name of the local licensee. We note that in the records of the Uruguay Round negotiations, the practices discussed did not include prohibitions on the use of trademarks.

9.   Third, the objection that this reading creates a "loophole" which would allow Article 20 to be circumvented by prohibiting the use of trademarks altogether is entirely beside the point. Article 20 clearly does not contemplate or deal with the prohibition of use of trademarks and we must be cautious when tenuous policy arguments are being made to over-ride the clear ambit of a carefully negotiated provision.

Unjustifiably

10.   In Singapore's view, the test of "unjustifiably" is not that as found in Article 17, which governs exceptions to rights conferred by a trademark, because the ability to use a trademark is not a right conferred by Article 16. Therefore, a test that involves the sort of balancing exercise envisaged in Article 17 should be rejected as Article 17 is not applicable in this context.

11.   Secondly, the test is also not that of necessity, whether as understood under Article XX of GATT 1994 or Article 2.2 of the TBT Agreement. Singapore notes that the term "necessary" is used in other parts of the TRIPS Agreement, such as Articles 8.1, 27.2 and 39.3, and can have a range of meanings depending on the context in which it is used. The adoption of different terms in separate provisions of the same agreement – "unjustifiably" in Article 20 and "necessary" in Articles 8.1, 27.2 and 39.3 *etc.* – indicates that the drafters intended "unjustifiably" in Article 20 to have a meaning other than "necessary".

12.   Thirdly, contrary to the complainants' view, the test does not require individualized assessment of trademarks. Singapore submits that if no such requirement exists in the assessment of exceptions to "rights" conferred by a trademark, *a fortiori* the same does not apply in the present context as the ability to use a trademark is not a "right" conferred by a trademark. Furthermore, the Plain Packaging requirements should be assessed holistically rather than individually to determine if they are unjustifiable under Article 20 as the requirements reinforce one another to, among others, reduce the appeal of tobacco products to consumers.

13.   In our view, consistent with past decisions by the Appellate Body, a measure is not unjustifiable if it bears a rational connection to a legitimate objective and does not go against that objective. The assessment of whether a measure bears a rational connection to a legitimate objective involves the assessment of the following factors:

- The importance of the interest sought to be protected;
- The extent of the encumbrance; and
- The degree of contribution of the measure to the policy objective.

14.   We submit that this reading is consistent with the ordinary meaning of the term "unjustifiably", in its context, and in light of the object and purpose of the TRIPS Agreement. Pursuant to Article 8.1, which recognizes and affirms the sovereign right of Members to adopt public health measures, and paragraph 4 of the *Doha Declaration on the TRIPS Agreement and Public Health*, which

constitutes a subsequent agreement within the meaning of Article 31(3)(a) of the *Vienna Convention on the Law of Treaties*, the term "unjustifiably" *should be* interpreted in a manner which supports WTO Members' right to protect public health.

15.   Finally, the Plain Packaging Measure is not unjustifiable as it bears a rational connection with legitimate public health objectives and does not go against those objectives. In this connection, we note that the body of evidence supports the conclusion that Plain Packaging is effective in reducing the appeal of tobacco products.

B. Claim under the TBT Agreement

TBT Article 2.2

16.   Singapore submits that the Plain Packaging Measure is not more trade-restrictive than necessary to fulfil its public health objectives.

17.   As a preliminary matter, we consider that both the trademark requirements and format requirements should be considered together, in assessing the consistency of the Plain Packaging Measure with Article 2.2 of the TBT Agreement. In our view, both trademark requirements and format requirements are "technical regulations" within the meaning of Annex 1.1 of the TBT Agreement and are subject as a whole to the TBT Agreement.

Trade-restrictiveness

18.   We submit that trade-restrictiveness should be seen as an absolute standard, rather than as a relative standard, and suggest that the Panel assess trade-restrictiveness by comparing the effect on an imported product before and after the introduction of the measure, solely by assessing the effect on *that product alone*. To have to delve into a "like product" analysis will be inappropriately veering towards an Article 2.1 analysis. The test of trade-restrictiveness should accommodate a scenario where a respondent Member imposes a technical regulation that adversely affects an imported product, where such product stands alone and has *no other competition in the market*. Furthermore, contrary to Australia's and EU's position, we take the view that affected trade can be between the complaining Member and the defending Member alone.

19.   Based on the object and purpose of the TBT Agreement, we suggest that the heart of the Article 2.2 obligation lies in the necessity test. We see the attractiveness of the Dominican Republic's argument that "Article 2.2 *assumes* that technical regulations are restrictive" (emphasis added). The TBT Agreement is about technical *barriers* to trade. We submit that even if technical regulations should not be considered to be inherently trade-restrictive, the threshold for "trade-restrictiveness" in this context should not be unduly onerous.

Legitimate objective

20.   The Panel should reject the complainants' narrow focus on smoking prevalence as the primary basis for assessing the degree of the Plain Packaging Measure's contribution to its objectives. The objectives of the Plain Packaging Measure are set out in section 3 of the Tobacco Plain Packaging Act, and further elaborated on in Part II.H of Australia's first written submission. Singapore supports Australia's submission on the causal pathway through which the Plain Packaging Measure will ultimately contribute to the achievement of its broader objectives by discouraging uptake, encouraging quitting, discouraging relapse and reducing exposure to smoke.

Suite of tobacco control measures

21.   The contribution of the Plain Packaging Measure to its public health objectives has to be understood and evaluated in the context of the comprehensive suite of tobacco control measures in Australia. The adoption of a comprehensive suite of tobacco control measures leads to greater reductions in tobacco use than would result from the separate effects of individual tobacco control policies.

Contribution to public health objectives

22.   The scientific and expert evidence submitted by Australia demonstrates the contribution of the Plain Packaging Measure to its public health objectives. Singapore notes that no single study forms an evidence base by itself, but multiple well-conducted studies that point towards the same conclusions and provide a strong evidence base for public policy. On the other hand, the expert reports relied on by the complainants to challenge the evidence base for plain packaging are flawed for the reasons set forth in paragraphs 3 to 10 of Annexure E to Australia's first written submission.

23.   Finally, we agree that each of the alternative measures proposed by the complainants cannot substitute for the contribution of the Plain Packaging Measure to its objectives as the Plain Packaging Measure plays a distinct and complementary role within the suite of tobacco control measures.

III.   CONCLUSION

24.   For the reasons stated above, Singapore's view is that the Plain Packaging Measure does not contravene: (i) Articles 2.1, 15.4, 16.1, 16.3, 20, 22.2(b) and 24.3 of the TRIPS Agreement; and (ii) Article 2.2 of the TBT Agreement.

ANNEX C-18

EXECUTIVE SUMMARY OF THE ARGUMENTS
OF SOUTH AFRICA

I.   INTERPRETATION OF THE TRIPS AGREEMENT

1.   Paragraph 5(a) of the Doha Declaration on the TRIPS Agreement and Public Health recognises that: "In applying the customary rules of interpretation of public international law, each provision of the TRIPS Agreement shall be read in the light of the object and purpose of the Agreement as expressed, in particular, in its objectives and principles."

2.   Article 31(1) of the Vienna Convention on the Law of Treaties sets out the general rule on interpretation in the following manner: "A treaty shall be interpreted in good faith in accordance with the ordinary meaning to be given to the terms of the treaty in their context and in the light of its object and purpose."

3.   In EC — Trademarks and Geographical Indications[1], the Panel referred to the principles of the TRIPS Agreement set out in Article 8.1: "These principles reflect the fact that the TRIPS Agreement does not generally provide for the grant of positive rights to exploit or use certain subject matter, but rather provides for the grant of negative rights to prevent certain acts.

4.   It is evident that the only "rights conferred" with respect to trademark owners under the TRIPS Agreement are negative rights of exclusion provided for in Article 16 which protect the position of trademark owners in relation to other traders in the market. These negative rights do not delimit the public regulatory relationship between owners of trademarks and sovereign governments and does not prohibit legitimate public policy measures in respect of the use of such trademarks or geographical indications.

5.   The Panel is hereby reminded that the "right of use" theory as advanced by the complainants under Articles 2.1, 15, 16, 20, 22, and 24 of the TRIPS Agreement are unsupported by the ordinary meaning of these provisions.

II.   ARTICLES 2.1, 15.4 & 16.1 OF THE TRIPS AGREEMENT

A.   Article 2.1 of the TRIPS Agreement

6.   Article 2.1 of the TRIPS Agreement provides that WTO 'Members shall comply with Articles 1 through 12, and Article 19, of the Paris Convention (1967)' in respect of Parts II, III and IV of the TRIPS Agreement. Article

---

[1]   (Panel Reports, EC — Trademarks and Geographical Indications (US), para. 7.210 (Australia), para. 7.246.)

6quinquies A(1) of the Paris Convention, which provision is incorporated into the TRIPS Agreement pursuant to TRIPS Article 2.1. *It provides that a Member may not deny the registration of a trademark that is registered in the territory of another Member based on its form.* Article 6quinquies A(1) is not directed towards the "use" of trademarks but towards their registration and validity and does not *grant the trademark owners a positive "right of use" in respect of their trademarks.*

7.   A trademark registered under Article 6quinquies can be the subject of a limitation or prohibition for other grounds contained in laws outside of trademark law.

B.   Article 15.4 of the TRIPS Agreement

8.   Article 15.4 of the TRIPS Agreement makes clear that a Member can regulate a product in a way that may restrict or prohibit the use of a trademark in its territory, as long as a Member does not refuse to register a trademark based on the nature of a product.

9.   No positive right of use is accorded by Article 15.4 of the TRIPS Agreement to any holder and cannot be interpreted as preventing a Member from limiting or prohibiting the use of trademarks for the commercialization of goods or services based on public health, security, or other reasons.

10.   Hence it should be noted that tobacco plain packaging measures should be considered consistent with Article 15.4 because they do not prevent the registration of trademarks based on the nature of the underlying product (i.e. tobacco).

C.   Article 16.1 of the TRIPS Agreement

11.   On the basis of the ordinary meaning of the terms contained in Article 16.1, the right accorded to the owners of registered trademarks is a negative right, i.e. the right to exclude use by others.

12.   Consequently plain packaging measures should be adjudged not to prevent owners of registered trademarks from exercising their right to seek forms of relief in the event that a third party uses an identical or similar sign in the course of trade where such use creates a likelihood of confusion based on the nature of the right conferred under Article 16.1.

III.   ARTICLE 20 OF THE TRIPS AGREEMENT

13.   A proper interpretation of the term "unjustifiably" in Article 20 dictates that no "necessity" or "least trade-restrictive" standard is present in Article 20. The term "unjustifiably" does not have the same meaning as "necessary" and should not be interpreted to impose a standard similar to the analysis required under Article 2.2 of the TBT Agreement, including its notions of "least restrictiveness" and "reasonably available alternatives".

14.   Since previous interpretations of the word "unjustifiable" have been made in context of the phrase "arbitrary or unjustifiable discrimination", as it appears in Article XXof the GATT 1994 and Article XIV of the GATS, the Panel is invited to note that Article 20 of the TRIPS Agreement is fundamentally different to Article XX of the GATT 1994 and Article XIV of the GATS. The latter articles operate as exceptions to a violation of another provision of the covered agreements whereas Article 20 of the TRIPS Agreement is not of such a nature. The physical text of Article 20 of the TRIPS Agreement simply does not support such a reading. If the drafters of the agreement intended such an outcome they would have explicitly provided for this.

IV.   ARTICLE 2.2 OF THE TBT AGREEMENT

15.   Since South Africa is a signatory to the Framework Convention on Tobacco Control (FCTC), it would be appropriate to direct the Panel's attention to the "Guidelines" for the implementation of Articles 11 and 13 of the FCTC which recommend that parties consider the adoption of plain packaging of tobacco products.[2] If plain packaging measures are to be seen as technical regulations, the FCTC Guidelines are "relevant international standards" within the meaning of Article 2.5.

16.   Accordingly, and to the extent that the definition of a "technical regulation" encompasses measures affecting the use of a trademark, any tobacco plain packaging measure is presumed not to create an unnecessary obstacle to international trade under the second sentence of Article 2.5.

V.   CONCLUSION

17.   Any "plain packaging" measures that are undertaken by any Member should be adjudged to be legitimate policy measures to achieve public health objectives insofar as they comply with the requirements of the TRIPS Agreement or insofar as they may be adjudged technical measures, that they do not violate provisions of the TBT Agreement.

18.   The Panel is reminded of the provisions of Article 3(2) of the Understanding on Rules and Procedures Governing the Settlement of Disputes (Annex 2).

---

[2]   At the third session of the Conference of the Parties (COP) to the Framework Convention adopted Guidelines for implementation of Article 13' and Guidelines for implementation of Article 11 on packaging and labelling of tobacco products in November 2008.

ANNEX C-19

EXECUTIVE SUMMARY OF THE ARGUMENTS OF THE SEPARATE CUSTOMS TERRITORY OF TAIWAN, PENGHU, KINMEN AND MATSU[*]

1. In May 2003, the World Health Organization (WHO) adopted the Framework Convention on Tobacco Control (FCTC) – a treaty with public health objectives that required signatories to enact a set of universal tobacco control policies to limit the use of tobacco in all forms worldwide.

2. Article 11 of the FCTC stipulates that each Party shall adopt and implement effective packaging and labelling measures to ensure that "tobacco product packaging and labelling do not promote a tobacco product by any means that are false, misleading, deceptive or likely to create an erroneous impression about its characteristics, health effects, hazards or emissions. . ." Guidelines for implementation of Article 11 of the WHO FCTC suggest Parties should consider adopting plain packaging measures that we believe will lower the consumer's affinity for and consumption of tobacco products.

3. Our accession to the FCTC was approved by the Legislative Yuan on January 18, 2005, and promulgated by the President on March 30, 2005. We are committed to abide by the FCTC obligations. We are also in full support of the direction to adopt measures restricting the packaging and labelling of tobacco products pursuant to the FCTC Guidelines, which is universally proposed and overwhelmingly supported by governments, experts, and NGOs alike.

4. Even though our Government has not enacted any plain packaging-related legislation to date, we will continue to monitor international trends, including the outcome of this case, and solicit comments from all interested parties, taking into account the balance between national health and free trade, scientific evidence, and prior implementation experiences, as bases for our future tobacco policy.

---

[*] Chinese Taipei's written submission is used as its executive summary.

ANNEX C-20

EXECUTIVE SUMMARY OF THE ARGUMENTS
OF THAILAND[*]

I.   INTRODUCTION

1.   The health risks and negative effects of smoking are well-recognized around the world. Several countries have been actively taking a variety of measures to combat tobacco consumption and reduce smoking prevalence. The necessity of measures adopted in pursuit of public health interests is explicitly recognized under the WTO framework itself. Under certain conditions, WTO Members are allowed to take actions in order to regulate and control tobacco products so as to address public health concerns. Indeed, while states have to exercise their regulatory powers within the boundaries of their accepted commitments, a proper balance needs to be struck to ensure that the WTO's rules-based trading system is compatible with and supportive of public health interests.

2.   Thailand joins the *Australia - Tobacco Plain Packaging* dispute because of our systemic interest in the interpretation of the WTO's rights and obligations when the measures at issue are adopted for public health objectives. Needless to say, the rulings of this dispute will have important implications on how WTO Members could adopt and implement tobacco regulation measures, especially in the manner that may affect intellectual property rights holders. Several WTO Members are awaiting the result of this dispute in order to decide whether or not they are able to take measures similar to Australia's plain packaging requirements consistently with the WTO obligations. In this regard, Thailand hopes that the Panel's decision on the legal issues raised in this dispute will provide a clear guidance for WTO Members in an attempt to regulate tobacco products in a WTO-consistent manner.

3.   Thailand acknowledges that the complainants have made several claims against Australia's plain packaging requirements under the *Agreement on Trade-Related Aspects of Intellectual Property Rights* ("TRIPS Agreement"), the *Agreement on Technical Barrier to Trade* ("TBT Agreement"), and the *General Agreement on Tariffs and Trade 1994* ("GATT 1994"). In this written submission, Thailand would like to focus on the issue as to how the TRIPS Agreement should be interpreted in general, but reserve the right to make any further comment on other legal issues at the later stage in the proceedings.

---

[*]   Thailand's written submission is used as its executive summary.

II. THE INTERPRETATION OF THE TRIPS AGREEMENT

4.   One of the important tasks of the Panel in this dispute is to clarify and interpret the TRIPS Agreement with respect to the use of tobacco control measures allegedly affecting trademarks and geographical indications rights holders. Thailand believes that any interpretation of the TRIPS provisions should be carried out in accordance with the well-established rules of treaty interpretation under public international law, with particular attention given to the objective and purpose agreed upon by the parties of the treaty at issue. In addition, any subsequent agreement between the parties relevant to the interpretation of the concerned subject matters also needs to be considered. This submission will examine each of these elements in the following sections.

A.   Customary rules of interpretation of public international law

5.   At the outset, *the Understanding on Rules and Procedures Governing the Settlement of Disputes* ("DSU") provides a mandate that the dispute settlement system of the WTO serves to clarify the existing provisions of the covered agreements "in accordance with customary rules of interpretation of public international law".[1] These customary rules of treaty interpretation are codified under Article 31 of *the Vienna Convention of the Law of Treaties* ("VCLT") which provides in relevant part that:

> 1.   A treaty shall be interpreted in good faith in accordance with the ordinary meaning to be given to the terms of the treaty in their context and in the light of its object and purpose.
>
> ...
>
> 3.   There shall be taken into account, together with the context:
>
> (a)   any subsequent agreement between the parties regarding the interpretation of the treaty or the application of its provisions;

6.   Article 31 of the VCLT has been recognized by the Appellate Body in various disputes as customary rules for the interpretation of the covered agreements.[2] Accordingly, Thailand is of the view that the customary rules of treaty interpretation set forth in the VCLT need to be strictly followed by the Panel for its interpretation of the TRIPS Agreement. In particular, any unclear TRIPS provision must be interpreted in good faith according to the ordinary meaning of the words in their context and in the light of the object and purpose of the TRIPS Agreement. Moreover, any subsequent agreement among WTO

---

[1]   Article 3.2 of the DSU; The "covered agreements" refers to the agreements listed in Appendix to the DSU. See also Article 1.1 of the DSU.

[2]   See, for example, Appellate Body Report, *US – Gasoline*, p. 17; Appellate Body Report, *India – Patents (US)*, para. 46; Appellate Body Report, *US – Hot-Rolled Steel*, para. 60.

Members relevant to the TRIPS Agreement also needs to be taken into account by the Panel in forming the interpretation.

B.   The objective and purpose of the TRIPS Agreement

7.   Pursuant to the customary rules of treaty interpretation of public international law set out above, Thailand wishes to draw the Panel's attention to the objective and purpose of the TRIPS Agreement, which is indispensable for the interpretation of controversial issues in this dispute. The provisions relating to the objective and purpose of the TRIPS Agreement are set forth under Articles 7 and 8, which provide in relevant part as follows:

Article 7

Objectives

The protection and enforcement of intellectual property rights should contribute to the promotion of technological innovation and to the transfer and dissemination of technology, to the mutual advantage of producers and users of technological knowledge and *in a manner conducive to social and economic welfare, and to a balance of rights and obligations.* (emphasis added)

Article 8

Principles

1.   *Members may, in formulating or amending their laws and regulations, adopt measures necessary to protect public health* and nutrition, and to promote the public interest in sectors of vital importance to their socio-economic and technological development, *provided that such measures are consistent with the provisions of this Agreement.* (emphasis added)

1.   Article 7 of the TRIPS Agreement

8.   TRIPS Article 7 makes clear that, in implementing the TRIPS Agreement, the protection and enforcement of intellectual property rights should promote social and economic welfare in the society. As such, it is evident that the TRIPS Agreement does not intend only to protect the interests of "private rights", but also to safeguard other important socio-economic interests of WTO Members.[3]

---

[3]   See the fourth recital of the Preamble of the TRIPS Agreement, which reads "[r]ecognizing that intellectual property rights are private rights".

9.   Moreover, Article 7 establishes that the TRIPS Agreement needs to strike a balance between rights and obligations. In *US — Section 211 Appropriations Act*, the panel observed that this objective constitutes an expression of "good faith" which "prohibits the abusive exercise of a state's rights".[4] Although Thailand agrees that WTO Members must exercise their rights *reasonably* in accordance with the obligations prescribed under the TRIPS Agreement, the legitimate rights of WTO Member governments, on the other hand, cannot be *unreasonably* undermined by the TRIPS obligations.[5] In this regard, Thailand considers that the TRIPS Agreement must be interpreted, in the light of the objectives of the TRIPS Agreement, so as to enable WTO Members to implement the TRIPS obligations in a manner that could maintain the overall balance between the protection of private rights and the sovereign rights to pursue socio-economic interests for public in general.

2.   Article 8 of the TRIPS Agreement

10.   Article 8 is regarded as one of the TRIPS provisions providing for the object and purpose of the TRIPS Agreement.[6] In particular, Article 8.1 explicitly recognizes WTO Members' right to adopt measures necessary to protect public health, among other public policy objectives, on condition that such measures are consistent with the terms of the TRIPS Agreement. As the importance and necessity of public health protection cannot be overemphasized, the following points should be borne in mind while reading the TRIPS principles for the Agreement's interpretation purposes.

11.   First, previous case law has confirmed that meaning and effect must be given to all terms of the treaty. According to the Appellate Body in *US - Gasoline*, "[a]n interpreter is not free to adopt a reading that would result in reducing whole clauses or paragraphs of a treaty to redundancy or inutility".[7] Accordingly, Thailand considers that the whole Article 8.1 should be read by the Panel in a way that harmoniously gives meaning and effect to each and every parts of the said Article, which includes not only the TRIPS-consistency requirement but also the affirmation of WTO Members' rights to act in pursuit of public health interests.

---

[4]   Panel Report, *US — Section 211 Appropriations Act*, para. 8.57; Appellate Body, *US - Shrimp*, para. 158.

[5]   The Appellate Body in *US - Shrimp* stated that the good faith principle "controls the exercise of rights by states. One application of this principle, the application widely known as the doctrine of *abus de droit*, prohibits the abusive exercise of a state's rights and enjoins that whenever the assertion of a right "impinges on the field covered by [a] treaty obligation, it must be exercised bona fide, that is to say *reasonably*"" (emphasis added) (footnote omitted). See Appellate Body Report, *US - Shrimp*, para. 158.

[6]   See Doha Ministerial Conference, Declaration on the TRIPS Agreement and Public Health, Adopted on 14 November 2001, WT/MIN(01)/DEC/2, 20 November 2001, paragraph 5(a).

[7]   Appellate Body Report, *US - Gasoline*, p. 23.

12.   Secondly, it should be noted that the TRIPS Agreement only establishes *minimum* levels of protection that must be extended by WTO Members to specific types of intellectual property and requires WTO Members to implement certain enforcement obligations to ensure that those levels of protection are observed within their respective territories. According to TRIPS Article 1.1, "Members may, but shall not be obliged to, implement in their law more extensive protection than is required by this Agreement". As such, in assessing the TRIPS-consistency, it is essential for the Panel to determine what the *minimum* standards relating to the protection of intellectual property rights at issue are. In Thailand's view, the *minimum* standards that WTO Members are obliged to give effect to are those expressed by the text of the TRIPS Agreement. Any additional requirement resulting in higher standards of protection should not be implied or read into the Agreement unless the text itself says so.

13.   Moreover, while WTO law provides for general exceptions to the GATT obligations under certain conditions, an exception to the TRIPS obligations does not clearly exist. That is to say, whereas a measure necessarily adopted to protect public health is justifiable pursuant to GATT Article XX(b), the very same measure may not be excused from the violations of the TRIPS obligations if it does not meet the minimum standards of protection set forth under the TRIPS Agreement.[8] Given the absence of TRIPS general exceptions, Thailand is of the view that the interpretation of obligations under the TRIPS Agreement should be treated with greater care and supportive of public interests that are of vital importance to the society as a whole. This position is reinforced by the Preamble of the TRIPS Agreement which desires to establish a mutually supportive relationship between the WTO and relevant international organizations, which presumably includes the World Health Organization in terms of public health issues.[9]

14.   In the light of the discussion above, Thailand considers that, for the purposes of the TRIPS Agreement's interpretation, Article 8.1 is an interpretative guidance which affirms that WTO Members may exercise their rights to adopt measures necessary to address public health concerns. Such measures are presumed to be TRIPS-consistent unless the complainants discharge a burden of proving otherwise. In deciding so, the Panel needs to be cautious not to assert higher standards of protection than those explicitly required by the TRIPS Agreement. Any interpretation made out of any unclear TRIPS provision should be supportive of public health so as to avoid possible conflicts between intellectual property rights and public interests to the greatest extent possible.

---

[8]   See paragraph 12 of this written submission for the discussion of the *minimum* standards of protection as required by the TRIPS Agreement.

[9]   See the Preamble of the TRIPS Agreement, which reads "[d]esiring to establish a mutually supportive relationship between the WTO and the World Intellectual Property Organization (referred to in this Agreement as "WIPO") as well as other relevant international organizations".

C.   The Declaration on the TRIPS Agreement and Public Health

15.   On 14 November 2001, WTO Ministers adopted by consensus *the Declaration on the TRIPS Agreement and Public Health* (the "Doha Declaration"), stressing the significant role of the objectives and principles contained in the TRIPS Agreement.[10] In particular, paragraphs 4 and 5(a) of the Doha Declaration read:

> 4.   We agree that the TRIPS Agreement does not and should not prevent Members from taking measures to protect public health. Accordingly, while reiterating our commitment to the TRIPS Agreement, we affirm that the Agreement can and should be interpreted and implemented in a manner supportive of WTO Members' right to protect public health and, in particular, to promote access to medicines for all.

> In this connection, we reaffirm the right of WTO Members to use, to the full, the provisions in the TRIPS Agreement, which provide flexibility for this purpose.

> 5.   Accordingly and in the light of paragraph 4 above, while maintaining our commitments in the TRIPS Agreement, we recognize that these flexibilities include:

> (a)   In applying the customary rules of interpretation of public international law, each provision of the TRIPS Agreement shall be read in the light of the object and purpose of the Agreement as expressed, in particular, in its objectives and principles.

16.   Thailand is of the view that, for the purposes of this dispute, the Doha Declaration is relevant to the interpretation of the TRIPS provisions at issue. In this section we will first examine the legal status of the Doha Declaration and then its implications on the TRIPS Agreement and public health.

1.   The Legal status of the Doha Declaration

17.   At the beginning, Thailand acknowledges that the Doha Declaration may fall short of being characterized as an authoritative interpretation within the meaning of Article IX:2 of the *Marrakesh Agreement Establishing the WTO* (the "WTO Agreement"), which provides that the Ministerial Conference and the General Council of the WTO possess the "exclusive authority to adopt interpretations of [the WTO Agreement] and of the Multilateral Trade Agreements".[11] Since the Doha Declaration was not adopted based on a recommendation of the TRIPS Council, one of the "two specific requirements"

---

[10]   Doha Ministerial Conference, Declaration on the TRIPS Agreement and Public Health, Adopted on 14 November 2001, WT/MIN(01)/DEC/2, 20 November 2001.
[11]   The "Multilateral Trade Agreements" refers to the agreements and associated legal instruments included in Annexes 1, 2, and 3 of the WTO Agreement. See Article II of the WTO Agreement.

prescribed under Article IX:2 of the WTO Agreement, it may not strictly constitute an authoritative interpretation which has a "pervasive legal effect" and is generally "binding on all Members".[12]

18.   Nevertheless, given the way it was adopted, Thailand considers that the Doha Declaration should have the interpretative effects indifferent from the formal authoritative interpretation. In particular, the Doha Declaration was agreed at the WTO Ministerial Conference, the highest decision-making body of the WTO. The Doha Declaration, therefore, arguably constitutes a "Ministerial Decision" within the meaning of Article IX:1 of the WTO Agreement, establishing an interpretative guidance of the TRIPS Agreement in the area of public health.[13] As a result, the Doha Declaration is an indispensable instrument complement to the reading and interpreting of the TRIPS provisions in this dispute.

19.   In addition, Thailand believes that the Doha Declaration also reflects a "subsequent agreement" within the meaning of Article 31.3(a) of the VCLT. In *US - Clove Cigarettes*, the Appellate Body found that paragraph 5.12 of the Doha Ministerial Decision is a subsequent agreement among Members on the interpretation of Article 2.12 of the TBT Agreement on the basis that "it clearly expresses a common understanding, and an acceptance of that understanding among Members".[14] Since the Doha Declaration expresses an agreed understanding of WTO Members and was adopted by consensus, it should be regarded as a subsequent agreement among WTO Members relevant to the TRIPS Agreement's interpretation. This subsequent agreement states a common understanding regarding the right of WTO Members to address public health concerns, while reaffirming that the TRIPS Agreement are meant to be interpreted in a manner supportive of such right. Pursuant to Article 31.3(a) of the VCLT, therefore, the Panel has to take the Doha Declaration into account for the purposes of the treaty interpretation.

---

[12]   According to the Appellate Body in *US - Clove Cigarette*, "two specific requirements" under Article IX:2 of the WTO Agreement are (i) a decision by the Ministerial Conference or the General Council to adopt such interpretations shall be taken by a three-fourths majority of Members; and (ii) such interpretations shall be taken on the basis of a recommendation by the Council overseeing the functioning of the relevant Agreement. See Appellate Body Report, *US - Clove Cigarette*, paras. 250-251.

[13]   Article IX:1 of the WTO Agreement provides that "The WTO shall continue the practice of decision making by consensus followed under GATT 1947. Except as otherwise provided, where a decision cannot be arrived at by consensus, the matter at issue shall be decided by voting. At meetings of the Ministerial Conference and the General Council, each Member of the WTO shall have one vote. Where the European Communities exercise their right to vote, they shall have a number of votes equal to the number of their member States which are Members of the WTO. Decisions of the Ministerial Conference and the General Council shall be taken by a majority of the votes cast, unless otherwise provided in this Agreement or in the relevant Multilateral Trade Agreement" (footnote omitted).

[14]   Appellate Body Report, *US - Clove Cigarette*, para. 267.

2. The Implications of the Doha Declaration

20. The Doha Declaration recognizes WTO Members' right to adopt measures for public health objectives and emphasizes that "the TRIPS Agreement does not and should not prevent members from taking measures to protect public health".[15] Following this principle, all WTO Members agreed that the TRIPS Agreement "can and should be interpreted and implemented in a manner supportive of WTO members' right to protect public health".[16]

21. The first part of paragraph 4 of the Doha Declaration makes clear that the interpretation of the TRIPS Agreement should not diminish WTO Members' right to address public health concerns for the sake of society as a whole. Indeed, when the relevant provisions are clear and explicit, it goes without saying that WTO Members should adopt any necessary measure in accordance with such provisions of the TRIPS Agreement. But in cases of ambiguity or where more than one interpretation is possible, Thailand considers that the Panel should attach a greater importance to the interpretation that causes the least interferences with the exercise of WTO Members' right to protect public health. Pursuant to the Doha Declaration, the interpretation of the TRIPS provisions should demonstrate the supportive role of the trade-related intellectual property rights to protect public health interests.

22. The second part of paragraph 4 of the Doha Declaration reaffirms the right of WTO Members to use flexibilities contained in the TRIPS Agreement for the purposes of public health protection. One of the available TRIPS flexibilities is spelled out under paragraph 5(a) of the Doha Declaration, reiterating that the TRIPS Agreement must be read in the light of the objective and purpose, particularly those expressed in TRIPS Articles 7 and 8. Thailand considers that this statement goes beyond merely affirming the relevance of objectives and principles of the TRIPS Agreement for the purposes of treaty interpretation. In particular, it suggests that the interpretation of the TRIPS Agreement in the light of the object and purpose set out in Articles 7 and 8 is one of the *flexibilities* that may be used by WTO Members "to the full".[17] As a result, in discharging the duty of legal interpretation, the Panel should read the TRIPS Agreement in a manner that gives sufficient flexibility to accommodate the public health needs of WTO members, in accordance with objectives and principles of the TRIPS Agreement.

---

[15] The Doha Declaration, para. 4.
[16] *Ibid.*
[17] *Ibid.*

III.   CONCLUSION

23.   In reaching a conclusion whether or not Australia's plain packaging requirements fall foul of the TRIPS obligations, the Panel needs to conduct an interpretation of several TRIPS provisions. In Thailand's view, the TRIPS Agreement should be read and interpreted through a strict application of the customary rules of interpretation of public international law. The objective and purpose of the TRIPS Agreement, as well as the Doha Declaration, are particularly relevant to the case at hand. They explicitly affirm that WTO Members have the right to adopt measures necessary to protect public health. The burden is on the complainants to prove that Australia's plain packaging requirements do not meet the *minimum* standards explicitly required by the terms of the TRIPS Agreement. For the interpretation of any unclear provision, the Panel should exercise its discretion in a manner that gives necessary flexibility to WTO Members to address public health concerns, and ensures that the spirit of the TRIPS Agreement is supportive of and compatible with public interests.

24.   Thailand hopes that our submission are of assistance to the Panel.

ANNEX C-21

EXECUTIVE SUMMARY OF THE ARGUMENTS
OF TURKEY[*]

I. INTRODUCTION

1. Turkey thanks the Panel for giving the opportunity to present its views in the proceedings of this important Panel. At the outset, we would like to underline that Turkey fully respects members' rights to seek for methods of enhancing the protection of public health. In this regard, like all the parties to the dispute, Turkey has the understanding that measures addressed to the control of consumption of tobacco and particularly those aiming at preventing tobacco products from becoming appealing to under-aged consumers, encompass legitimate public health objectives within the World Trade Organization (WTO) context. This is an objective to which Turkey, as well, is strongly committed.

2. Within this understanding, Turkey wishes to contribute by expressing its views on some systemic issues regarding the interpretation of the provisions of the Agreement on Trade-Related Aspects of Intellectual Property Rights (the TRIPS Agreement).

3. Therefore, with this submission, Turkey aims to contribute to the Panel's analysis by assessing two elements, which, in Turkey's view, have systemic implications. These issues are; i) Whether there exists a "right of use" in the TRIPS Agreement for the trademark owners, and ii) burden of proof under Article 20 of the TRIPS Agreement.

II. WHETHER THERE EXISTS "A RIGHT OF USE" IN THE TRIPS AGREEMENT FOR THE TRADEMARK OWNERS

4. One of the core issues lying at the heart of the legal claims related to the TRIPS Agreement in this dispute is whether there is a positive "right of use" for the trademark owners implied in the provisions of the Agreement. In other words, the parties to the dispute disagree on whether there is an obligation on Members, stemming from the TRIPS Agreement, to recognise trademark owners' right to use their trademarks during the course of trade.

5. The respondent, Australia, argues that the provisions of the TRIPS Agreement do not include any explicit right to use for trademark owners.[1] After a provision by provision analysis, Australia concludes that in none of the

---

[*] Turkey requested that its third party submission serve as its executive summary.
[1] Australia's First Written Submission, para. 243.

provisions related to trademarks, the right to use is mentioned except in Article 20. In its view, even Article 20 of the TRIPS Agreement, which provides that "the use of a trademark in the course of trade shall not be unjustifiably encumbered by special requirements", does not confirm the existence of such a right as the Article "governs the relationship between a government as a regulator and all traders and trademark owners rather than the relationship between competing traders"[2] Accordingly, for Australia, Article 20 does not provide, explicitly or implicitly, that "WTO Members are obliged to recognize the right to use trademarks, even if the commercialization of the goods is permitted."[3]

6.   In Australia's view, the text of the TRIPS Agreement confirms that trademark rights conferred under the Agreement are negative in nature rather than positive. This means that rights conferred in the Agreement are the rights of trademark owners to exclude or prevent other parties from using the same or similar marks whereas positive rights would refer to rights to actually use the trademark.[4] Therefore, Members are free to pursue legitimate policy objectives, and the negative rights granted under the Agreement do not limit regulations adopted by Members which may or may not restrain the use of trademarks.

7.   Australia's position with regard to right to use of a trademark is significant since, if this position holds true, then, as Australia argues, most of the claims under the TRIPS Agreement would lose their legal grounds as they assume an implicit right to use in the relevant provisions. If there is no right to use for trademark owners, the complainants will have very little legal grounds to challenge a restriction of the use of trademark in the course of trade.

8.   On the other hand, the complainants argue that, contrary to Australia's view, the right to use a trademark for a trademark owner is inherent in the provisions of the TRIPS Agreement. In complainants' view, first, use is a fundamental component of trademark regimes. For instance, Dominican Republic makes an extensive argumentation on why use is essential for the trademark owner. For Dominican Republic, the function of a trademark – creating distinctiveness or differentiation of the goods or services from others- cannot be fulfilled without the use in commerce.[5] Without the use, a registered trademark would be unable to differentiate a product, and expectation for economic benefit cannot be realized.[6] It is indeed for this purpose that business invests money and resources to develop a brand: to earn more profits through its use.[7]

---

[2]   Australia's First Written Submission, para. 254.
[3]   *Ibid.*
[4]   Australia's First Written Submission, paras. 255-258.
[5]   Dominican Republic's First Written Submission, para. 236.
[6]   Dominican Republic's First Written Submission, paras. 239-240.
[7]   Honduras' First Written Submission, para. 167.

9.   Second, the complainants argue that the provisions of the TRIPS Agreement support their position. For example, Dominican Republic pursues an article by article legal analysis and reaches the conclusion that the text of Articles 15.4, 16.1, 16.3 and 20 of the TRIPS Agreement implies a right to use for the trademark owners.[8] Hence, for the complainants, Australia's argument that TRIPS provisions do not include any positive right to use is baseless and should be rejected.[9]

10.   Turkey is of the view that when considering whether the TRIPS Agreement comprises of a right to use for trademark owners or not, all relevant factors, including the context of the trademark chapter in the TRIPS Agreement, should be taken into account. It is a matter of fact that "use" is an inseparable part of trademark regimes. Without use, the ultimate function of a trademark – to distinguish a product from others with an expectation for economic benefit- cannot be realized.[10] In this context, it is no surprise that many WTO Members, including Turkey, have an actual use requirement in order to be eligible for the rights attached to trademark registration. Indeed, registration without use creates an unnecessary barrier for new registrations and without use, money and other resources spent on the registration and promotion of a trademark become meaningless.

11.   This has been highlighted in the Intellectual Property Handbook prepared by World Intellectual Property Organization (WIPO):

> "Trademark protection is not an end in itself. Even though trademark laws generally do not require use as a condition for the application for trademark registration, or even the actual registration, the ultimate reason for trademark protection is the function of distinguishing the goods on which the trademark is used from others. It makes no economic sense, therefore, to protect trademarks by registration without imposing the obligation to use them. Unused trademarks are an artificial barrier to the registration of new marks. There is an absolute need to provide for a use obligation in trademark law."[11]

12.   In the light of the above, for Turkey, there are strong grounds to believe that the right to use for a trademark owner is a right inherent in the registration of a trademark. Turkey is of the view that the provisions of the TRIPS Agreement are in line with this understanding.

---

[8]   Dominican Republic's First Written Submission, paras. 248-260.
[9]   Honduras' First Written Submission, paras. 165-175; Cuba's First Written Submission, paras. 317-320; Indonesia'a First Written Submission, paras. 137-146.
[10]   See WIPO (2013) *World Intellectual Property Report 2013*, p 81-87 for a detailed discussion on the effects of use of trademarks in the course of trade.
[11]   WIPO, *WIPO Intellectual Property Handbook*, 2nd edition (World Intellectual Property Organization, 2008) ("WIPO IP Handbook"), para. 2.390.

13.   The right to use of a trademark for a trademark owner is assumed and implicitly recognized in trademark-related provisions of the TRIPS Agreement. Particularly, the very existence of Article 20 indicates that trademark owners have an inherent right to use their trademarks attached to their registration. Article 20 of the TRIPS Agreement mandates that "the use of a trademark in the course of trade shall not be unjustifiably encumbered by special requirements".

14.   Thus, in Turkey's view, the general practice regarding trademark regimes as well as the provisions of the TRIPS Agreement sufficiently allow us to conclude that the use of trademark is a right of the trademark owner inherent in the registration of a trademark. This, however, does not mean that the use of a trademark by a trademark owner is an absolute right. WTO Members have the right to regulate markets, and use trademark in the course of trade for fulfilling various legitimate policy objectives.[12]

15.   Indeed, Article 8.1 of the TRIPS Agreement clearly recognizes Members' right to regulate. The Article provides:

> Members may, in formulating or amending their laws and regulations, adopt measures necessary to protect *public health* and nutrition, and to promote the public interest in sectors of vital importance to their socio-economic and technological development, provided that such measures are consistent with the provisions of this Agreement. (emphasis added)

16.   Accordingly, Article 8.1 recognizes protection of public health and nutrition and promotion of public interest in sectors of vital importance to Members' socio-economic and technological development as the two legitimate public policy objectives. Nevertheless, the Article also requires that any measure to fulfill those objectives should be consistent with the provisions of the Agreement.

17.   Article 20 of the TRIPS Agreement, read together with Article 8.1 mentioned above, lays down a clear picture. As mentioned above, Article 20 mandates that "the use of a trademark in the course of trade shall not be unjustifiably encumbered by special requirements" and gives examples to those unjustifiable encumbrances. From this wording, it is self-evident that there are instances where the use of a trademark in the course of trade can be restricted "justifiably". For Turkey, a justifiable restriction can only arise as a result of a regulation to fulfill a legitimate policy objective of a Member. One of the natural candidates for such legitimate policy objectives is to protect public health and nutrition, as explicitly mentioned in Article 8.

18.   In other words, some of the measures taken by Members which have some level of restrictive effects on the use of a trademark in the course of trade

---

[12]   COTTIER, Thomas " The Agreement on Trade-Related Aspects of Intellectual Property Rights" in MACRORY, Patrick F.J.; APPLETON, Arthur; PLUMMER, Micheal G. (eds.)*The World Trade Organization: Legal, Economic and Political Analysis Vol 1,* 2005, pp. 1046-1047.

can be justified within the meaning of Article 20 while some of them cannot. In Turkey's view, the policy objective connected to a measure has an important role in order to determine which measures can be justified and which of them cannot be justified.

19.   However, for Turkey, a deeper analysis of the case is necessary in order to maintain a delicate balance with legitimate policy concerns of Members such as the protection of public health versus effective protection of intellectual property rights. Turkey believes that this will be a key task before the Panel to resolve the current dispute.

II.   BURDEN OF PROOF UNDER ARTICLE 20 OF THE TRIPS AGREEMENT

20.   In their submissions while the complainants argue that the burden of proof that a measure unjustifiably encumbers the use of a trademark rests upon the respondent[13], the respondent, Australia, contends that it rests upon the complainants.[14]

21.   Article 20 of the TRIPS Agreement provides as follows:

> The use of a trademark in the course of trade shall not be *unjustifiably encumbered* by special requirements, such as use with another trademark, use in a special form or use in a manner detrimental to its capability to distinguish the goods or services of one undertaking from those of other undertakings....(emphasis added)

22.   It is well established by the Appellate Body in US-Wool Shirts and Blouses that

> ...the burden of proof rests upon the party, whether complaining or defending, *who asserts the affirmative of a particular claim or defence*. If that party adduces evidence sufficient to raise a presumption that what is claimed is true, the burden then shifts to the other party, who will fail unless it adduces sufficient evidence to rebut the presumption[15]. (emphasis added)

23.   Since then this approach has been followed in many Panel and Appellate Body reports.[16] Thus, consistent with this approach, depending on the provision,

---

[13]   Dominican Republic's First Written Submission, paras. 369-375.

[14]   Australia's First Written Submission, para. 430.

[15]   Appellate Body Report, *United States – Measure Affecting Imports of Woven Wool Shirts and Blouses from India*, WT/DS33/AB/R, adopted 23 May 1997, and Corr.1, DSR 1997:I, 323, (*US – Wool Shirts and Blouses*), p 14 Australia's First Written Submission, paras. 427-440.

[16]   For instance, Appellate Body Reports, United States – Certain Country of Origin Labelling (COOL) Requirements, WT/DS384/AB/R / WT/DS386/AB/R, adopted 23 July 2012, para. 379, Appellate Body Report, United States – Countervailing Duties on Certain Corrosion-Resistant Carbon Steel Flat Products from Germany, WT/DS213/AB/R and Corr.1, adopted 19 December

---

whether it sets a positive obligation or defence, the burden rests upon a party or the other. Furthermore, it is also important to look at the party who sets forth a provision either by asserting a particular violation of a provision or defending against an allegation of a violation. Therefore, the key question before the Panel is first to determine whether Article 20 of the TRIPS Agreement is an affirmative obligation or an exception. Second, the Panel should also take into account the Party who asserts the provision.

24.   Concerning the first question, Turkey considers that the obligation in Article 20 is of an affirmative nature rather than exceptional one. The fact that the word "unjustifiably" exists in Article 20 does not change the affirmative nature of the obligation. Turkey believes that the logic in Article 2.2 of the Agreement on Technical Barriers to Trade (TBT) can similarly apply to Article 20 of the TRIPS Agreement. TBT Agreement in general and the preamble of the Agreement in particular recognize that WTO Members may take measures for the protection of the human, animal or plant life or health, which are among the legitimate policy objectives that the Agreement identifies. Nevertheless, Article 2.2 of the TBT Agreement provides that technical regulations shall not be applied more trade restrictive than necessary to fulfil such legitimate objectives.

25.   With regard to the burden of proof issue, the Panel in US-Clove Cigarettes established that the burden of proof rests upon the Party alleging violation of Article 2.2 of the TBT Agreement[17]. Turkey believes that this approach would shed light on the determination of the burden of proof under Article 20 of the TRIPS Agreement. As highlighted before in this submission, Article 8.1 of the TRIPS Agreement allows Members to take measures for fulfilling various legitimate policy objectives, provided that such measures are consistent with the provisions of the Agreement. Similar to the situation under 2.2 of the TBT Agreement, Members' right to take measures under Article 20 of the TRIPS Agreement in regard to the use of a trademark is not an absolute right. Such measures shall not unjustifiably encumber the use of a trademark. If a party sets forth an allegation that such an unjustifiable encumbrance occurs, in Turkey's view, that Party has the burden of proof of its allegations.

26.   As regards the second question, in US-Wool Shirts and Blouses the Appellate Body emphasized that "...the burden of proof rests upon the party, whether complaining or defending, who asserts the affirmative of a particular claim or defence..."[18] (emphasis added.) Turkey understands from this wording

---

2002, DSR 2002:IX, 3779, paras. 4.484-496 or Panel Report, China – Measures Affecting Trading Rights and Distribution Services for Certain Publications and Audiovisual Entertainment Products, WT/DS363/R and Corr.1, adopted 19 January 2010, as modified by Appellate Body Report WT/DS363/AB/R, DSR 2010:II, 261, para. 174.

[17]   Panel Report, United States – Measures Affecting the Production and Sale of Clove Cigarettes, WT/DS406/R, adopted 24 April 2012, as modified by Appellate Body Report WT/DS406/AB/R, para. 7.381.

[18]   Appellate Body Report, *US – Wool Shirts and Blouses*, p. 14.

that not only the nature of the provision but also the owner of the particular claim or the defense is also an important factor in deciding who bears the burden of proof.

27. Having said that, as noted by the Panel in Argentina - Import Measures, Turkey would also like to underline that "[c]ollaboration from parties to a dispute is essential for a panel to be able to discharge its function of making "an objective assessment of the matter before it".[19]

III. CONCLUSION

28. Turkey appreciates this opportunity to present its views to the Panel. Turkey requests that this Panel review the comments stated in this submission, in interpreting the TRIPS Agreement.

---

[19] Panel Report in Argentina – Measures Affecting the Importation of Goods, WT/DS438/RWT/DS444/RWT/DS445/R, adopted 26 January 2015, para. 6.31.

ANNEX C-22

EXECUTIVE SUMMARY OF THE ARGUMENTS
OF URUGUAY[*]

1.   This dispute relates basically to the regulatory capacity of the State in pursuit of a public policy objective and the limits to that capacity in the light of the international obligations assumed by the State. Another focus of the dispute concerns the scope and the type of right generated for the use of a trademark in the light of the terms of the World Trade Organization (WTO) agreements.

2.   One outstanding feature of this case is the low level of trade involved, since of the four complaining Members, only one, Indonesia, has a high volume of exports to the Australian market. In fact, in the recent period and according to the statistics consulted by Uruguay, exports of tobacco products from three of the complainants to Australia have been negligible since well before Australia brought the measure into force.

3.   Taking into account the state of bilateral trade in these products between Australia and the four complainants in recent years, it cannot be assumed that there is a case of nullification or impairment as described in Article 3.8 of the Dispute Settlement Understanding (DSU). There could be a negative trade impact of negligible scale or there could be an indirect effect in third markets where the Australian measures are not applied and where Australia has no jurisdiction. The specific trade effects in Australia and possibly in third markets are a matter on which the complaints remain silent or say very little, but they implicitly underpin some of the arguments presented.

4.   The plain packaging measure contained in the legislation known as the "TPP Act and TPP Regulations" forms part of a coherent set of measures that have been applied by Australia for some time, together with a policy to curb the tobacco epidemic. Uruguay has followed a very similar path which is described in the presentation made before the Panel. It is noteworthy that the plain packaging measure is the only one that is challenged, there being no challenge to any of the previous measures introduced by Australia. Moreover, as can be seen in the submission to the Panel from the World Health Organization (WHO) and the WHO Framework Convention on Tobacco Control (FCTC), tobacco consumption is a global epidemic that has serious effects on human health, and the plain packaging measure is an FCTC guideline.

5.   The lengthy arguments of the complainants concerning the provisions of Article 20 of the Agreement on Trade-Related Aspects of Intellectual Property Rights (TRIPS) cannot have various readings. A Member's right and obligation

---

[*]   Original Spanish.

to protect public health through different instruments cannot be completely limited by the obligation to protect intellectual property rights. These are different obligations, and although they may be connected, they cannot and must not be mutually conflicting. The goods they protect are different and of a different type. One is a public policy objective which covers the whole of society, and it may even take some time until the measure begins to produce effects. The other is the use of a commercial-type instrument such as a trademark which has exclusive use protection in relation to other commercial users.

6.   Moreover, for Uruguay the direct effect should be quantifiable or measurable, and there is no question of an indirect effect in third markets, since Australia, of course, exercises neither control nor jurisdiction outside its territory.

7.   The measures limit the use of the mark and have a practical impact on consumption; moreover, there are no measurable alternatives with the same efficacy. The alternatives proposed by some of the complainants suggest a tax increase, a measure that Australia has already applied; they also suggest a lack of familiarity with the market situation and the anti-tobacco programme that Australia has been applying for some time, and they are mutually contradictory.

8.   The measure is justified on the basis of TRIPS Article 20. The complainants themselves, such as Honduras and the Dominican Republic, do not dispute a Member's right and - we would add - obligation to adopt measures for the protection of public health. The type of right protected for the owners of the mark is its exclusive use against third parties, which is typically the protection of a right with commercial value in the private sphere; the scope is delimited in Article 17 of the TRIPS Agreement.

9.   In Uruguay's opinion, no violation of the rules is proved in the documents submitted by the complainants. An argument is made for a distorting effect caused by the Australian measure in the Australian market, which generates a shift in consumption towards products in the lower-end and lower-cost segment. However, the complaints hardly refer to the price segmentation of products in the Australian market. What the complainants describe is a specific prejudice to the Australian market caused by this trend in consumption towards the lower-end segment (in terms of price and quality), but this cannot be assessed or estimated since, as was mentioned previously, there is very little trade. This argument, which is an economic one, seeks to present a commercial prejudice which is indemonstrable on the part of the complainants, although in any case Australia hopes that trade and imports will grow in the coming years.

10.   According to the complainants, the measures generate a disadvantage for premium brands which are differentiated by their better quality in the case of both cigarettes and cigars (including geographical indications in the latter category). However, the concept of quality or premium products is hardly elaborated upon and price appears to be the sole determinant in establishing a distinction between products of higher and lower quality.

11.   It is important to emphasize that from the public health standpoint there are no cigarettes of higher or lower quality, since they all cause sickness and death because of the carcinogenic and toxic substances they contain.

12.   Of the four complainants, only Cuba and the Dominican Republic have geographical indications for cigars and therefore this issue is not raised in respect of cigarettes. The arguments are similar to those used for restrictions on the use of the mark and are based on the adverse effects on competition in the Australian market, the effect of the shift in consumption towards lower priced products and the alternative of less restrictive measures on the use of the trademark, which would allegedly be more effective, although this is hypothetical.

13.   The legal arguments focus on the provisions of the TRIPS Agreement and the Agreement on Technical Barriers to Trade (TBT), but are limited to restrictions on the use of the trademark and to characterizing the plain packaging measure as a technical regulation, the objective of which is not challenged, although it is affirmed that there are alternatives to the measure that could have less effect on trade. At no point is there any mention of the fact that the WHO Framework Convention recommended plain packaging measures, for good reasons, as an effective instrument under a broader policy and a battery of measures to reduce consumption.

14.   However, the connection between the obligations laid down in the agreements means that the measure in force must contribute to the defined objective which, in this case, is to protect public health, and must do so with the least possible impact on the rights of other Members. In the relevant documentation, Australia has demonstrated the reduction in consumption and an increase in the understanding of tobacco impacts on health, and the consequent correlation and causal link between the measures and tobacco consumption.

15.   For various reasons, Uruguay has a substantial interest in this proceeding in accordance with the provisions of Article 10.2 of the Dispute Settlement Understanding. It is important to point out that Uruguay has for some time been conducting a programme to combat the tobacco epidemic which has become a serious public health problem in our country and which generates an enormous cost in terms of medical treatment and premature deaths.

16.   Above all, Uruguay wishes to reaffirm that the protection of public health is a responsibility and power under the sovereign authority of States, and each Member has the right and obligation to legislate and regulate in the public interest with a view to protecting a legitimate public health objective. Within the WTO system, this right is recognized in the TRIPS Agreement, the TBT Agreement and the GATT 1994. It is also recognized by other bodies of international law, such as the WHO Framework Convention on Tobacco Control (FCTC); moreover, and no less importantly, it is provided for in the national legislation and regulations of numerous States that are Members of the WTO and the WHO.

ANNEX C-23

EXECUTIVE SUMMARY OF THE ARGUMENTS
OF ZAMBIA

1.   Zambia hereby submits its Executive Summary of its written submission in the dispute over Australia's tobacco plain packaging measure.

2.   The Tobacco Plain Packaging Act 2011, Tobacco Plain Packaging Regulations 2011 and 2012 and the Trade Marks Amendment (Tobacco Plain Packaging) Act 2011, which prohibit the use of registered trademarks and impose strict packaging, labelling and product requirements, raise serious concerns for Zambia under the World Trade Organization ("WTO") Agreement on Technical Barriers to Trade ("TBT Agreement") and the WTO Agreement on Trade-Related Aspects of Intellectual Property Rights ("TRIPS Agreement"). The resolution of these issues is critical to ensure that Members comply with their obligations and do not impose measures that unduly restrict trade with a particular impact on developing and least-developed country Members.

3.   Zambia emphasizes at the beginning the importance of tobacco in its economic development and wishes to place this dispute in context by briefly describing the importance of tobacco growing and trade in Zambia as well as Zambian policies to limit tobacco consumption and prevalence. Zambia is a land-locked southern African country endowed with ample land and abundant water resources. The agricultural sector is the backbone of the Zambian economy, contributing to economic growth and export diversification. Primary agriculture contributes to about 35 percent of the country's non-traditional exports (i.e., exports other than copper and cobalt), and it comprises around 10 percent of export earnings. The vital agricultural sector provides for about 70 percent of total employment and is a government priority to ensure food security and income generation, create employment and reduce poverty.

4.   Tobacco is a strategic agricultural crop in Zambia, which is 7.5 times more profitable per hectare than maize production and 14 times more profitable than cotton. Over 26,000 Zambian farmers grow tobacco, and 40,000 workers are employed in the sector. The majority works on small farms of less than 5 hectares. Tobacco production – largely unaffected by important price fluctuations that have impacted other crops – is essential to guarantee a minimum income to farmers, given that 70 percent of the rural population lives below the poverty line. The full tobacco value chain provides direct and indirect employment to close to 450,000 people.

5.   Tobacco also significantly contributes to Zambian export earnings as it was the fifth most exported commodity in 2013, amounting to USD 180 million. Zambia has begun leaf processing and cigarette manufacturing with USD 20 million of cigarette exports in 2013. Zambian tobacco is recognized to be of high quality. The Australian plain packaging measures will certainly have a negative

impact on the value of tobacco produced and exported by Zambia as manufacturers will no longer be willing to pay a premium price for quality leaf. Since price is the main distinguishing factor for tobacco, manufacturers will have to reduce their selling prices or opt to use lower quality and lower-priced leaf to remain competitive.

6.   Zambia is also committed to tobacco control policies. It implemented the Public Health Regulations in 2002 and became a party to the World Health Organization ("WHO") Framework Convention on Tobacco Control ("FCTC") in 2008. Zambia submits that WTO Members that are party to the FCTC can fully comply with their WTO and FCTC obligations at the same time. Contrary to Australia's assertion, the Guidelines for FCTC Articles 11 and 13 do not constitute international standards within the meaning of Article 2.5 of the TBT Agreement, nor do they mandate FCTC parties to impose plain packaging.

7.   Turning to the TBT Agreement, Zambia recalls that it expressed its serious concerns about the consistency with Article 2.2 of the TBT Agreement of Australia's measure in the TBT Committee in November 2011. Zambia noted that the TBT Agreement forbids unnecessary obstacles to trade, which are more trade-restrictive than necessary to fulfil a legitimate objective. Zambia considered that plain packaging was a disproportionate response to the health objectives and was not supported by credible evidence that it would achieve Australia's legitimate objective. Almost four years after its initial exchanges with Australia and over two years after the implementation of Australia's plain packaging measures, Zambia's concerns are confirmed.

8.   The packaging, labelling and product requirements Australia imposes are highly trade-restrictive. These stringent product, packaging and labelling requirements render the production of tobacco products for the Australian market more onerous and costly and have a detrimental impact on the competitive opportunities of imports.

9.   Zambia does not question the objective stated by Australia; indeed this legitimate public health objective is shared. Zambia, however, fails to see the contribution of the plain packaging measures and their objective. After two years of plain packaging, no evidence shows that it reduces smoking prevalence or changes in smoking behavior, other that which indicates the measure is not working such as a commoditization of the market and consumers down-trading to cheaper products. The qualitative and quantitative evidence placed before the Panel shows the absence of contribution to the fulfilment of Australia's stated objective and thus that there is no reason to expect any effect of the measure in the future. Consequently, the plain packaging measures cannot be found to contribute to Australia's stated objective.

10.   Zambia further believes that alternative and WTO-consistent regulatory solutions as discussed by the Complainants could better achieve the stated objective. Thus, Zambia considers that plain packaging constitutes a clear violation of Article 2.2 of the TBT Agreement that harms the rights of all tobacco producing Members.

11.   Zambia has also previously raised its concerns on the intellectual property aspects of the measures in the Council for TRIPS. Zambia recognizes the importance to trade and competition of trademarks and geographical indications, which allow producers to differentiate their goods in the market and which allow consumers to make informed choices about those goods.

12.   In light of the role that intellectual property rights play in the commercial process, Zambia considers that Australia's measures are an unjustifiable encumbrance under Article 20 of the TRIPS Agreement. Plain packaging imposes drastic "special requirements" on the few remaining word marks and prohibits all other trademark use entirely. They thus impose the "ultimate encumbrance" on the use of trademarks.

13.   Zambia fails to see any justification for plain packaging, in light of the evidence mentioned above and the failure of the measure to consider each trademark individually. The application to all trademarks based on the nature of the goods is an unreasonable and disproportionate requirement that is "detrimental to [a trademark's] capability to distinguish the goods or services of one undertaking from those of other undertakings." This is the case under the "necessity" test of Article 20. Australia's argument that justifiability under Article 20 is based on a "rational connection" is not supported by the text of the TRIPS Agreement and would effectively remove any discipline on trademark restrictions under Article 20 of the TRIPS Agreement as any measure with some tenuous connection to a legitimate objective would meet this low threshold no matter how restrictive it may be on trademark use.

14.   Zambia believes that the object and purpose of the TRIPS Agreement is based on the legitimate expectation of owners to exercise their ability to make use of trademarks in the course of trade, which must be considered in the analysis of Complainants' claims of violation of Articles 15 and 16 of the TRIPS Agreement.

15.   This dispute raises a number of important systemic issues on the role of trademarks in a global economy and the balance between policy considerations and trade-restrictive measures. A measure that goes against the essence of the intellectual property rights and that has disproportionate trade effects and is not proven to contribute to the stated objective cannot be found to be consistent with the provisions of the TBT and TRIPS Agreement.

16.   Zambia invites the Panel to consider these remarks which taken into account the importance of this product for many developing and least-developed Members in its analysis of the claims in this dispute.

ANNEX C-24

EXECUTIVE SUMMARY OF THE ARGUMENTS
OF ZIMBABWE

1.   This Executive Summary of Zimbabwe reviews the arguments in this dispute made in Zimbabwe's Third Party Written Submission of 10 April 2015 and its Oral Statement at the Third Party Session of the First Panel Hearing of 3 June 2015. Zimbabwe appreciates the opportunity to make known its views on the WTO-inconsistency of the Australian tobacco plain packaging measure.

2.   The Australian measure prohibits the use of registered trademarks and imposes strict requirements on packaging and labelling and as such raises serious concerns under the World Trade Organization's ("WTO") Agreements on Trade-Related Aspects of Intellectual Property Rights ("TRIPS Agreement") and on Technical Barriers to Trade ("TBT Agreement"), as well as causing great detrimental impact on Zimbabwe's economic opportunities and development.

3.   Zimbabwe recently acceded to the World Health Organization's Framework Convention on Tobacco Control and thus supports the legitimate public health objective of Australia. Zimbabwe desires that such goals be pursued through well-designed measures that actually contribute to the objective and are within the bounds of Members' WTO obligations.

4.   Zimbabwe is a small, landlocked and low-income developing country with an economy dependent on a few agricultural commodities. Tobacco is the largest agricultural product produced in Zimbabwe after corn and cotton, and it has a much greater yield than those crops, providing greater financial stability for farmers. Zimbabwean Virginia leaf is of high quality and is exported to customers around the world, making tobacco Zimbabwe's largest agricultural export by volume and value and its third largest overall export by value. Tobacco accounted for about 15% of Zimbabwe's GDP in 2013, with substantial increases in 2014 and further projected increases for 2015.

5.   The tobacco sector directly provides an estimated 350,000 jobs and indirectly supports up to five million people. Tobacco is expected to be the major contributor to the growth and recovery projected for the Zimbabwean agricultural sector, as well as for the country at large as it leads to investments in infrastructure and jobs.

6.   Since the tobacco sector is increasing its focus on sourcing high-quality Virginia tobacco leaf, which Zimbabwe is well-placed to provide, the imposition of a generic form of packaging, which limits the means consumers have to make informed choices regarding the product quality, will devalue superior Zimbabwe-produced Virginia tobacco. Such a devaluation would directly threaten the livelihood of 120,000 farmers and their families who depend on tobacco production; of millions Zimbabweans who indirectly depend on tobacco

and tobacco production for jobs and income; and of the prospects for the overall economic development of the country.

7.   Under Article 2.2 of the TBT Agreement, a technical regulation must not be more trade-restrictive than necessary to fulfil a legitimate objective, and equally effective but less trade-restrictive alternative measures should be preferred. A trade restriction that is not contributing to the fulfilment of a legitimate objective or that goes beyond what is necessary to achieve the objective cannot be justified. These basic obligations are an expression of the principle of good faith implementation of a Member's WTO obligations in the international trading system, which require that they avoid ineffective, disproportionate and unnecessarily restrictive regulations.

8.   Zimbabwe notes that it is uncontested that the form or physical requirements of the measure fall within the definition of a "technical regulation," though Australia contends that the trademark requirements are not covered by the definition of a technical regulation. Zimbabwe is of the view that all of the measure's aspects provide for "mandatory" requirements "which lay down product characteristics" with respect to "symbols, packaging, marking or labelling requirements" and apply to an identifiable group of products. Thus, the attempt to distinguish the types of requirements is not meaningful as all aspects of the challenged measure are covered by the disciplines of the TBT Agreement.

9.   The plain packaging measure is also highly trade-restrictive. The adaptation and compliance costs associated with the plain packaging requirements constitute a major disincentive to export, particularly for developing countries such as Zimbabwe.

10.   Further, the possible imposition of plain packaging by Members other than Australia which are very important export markets for Zimbabwe, would further restrict trading opportunities. In recent years, using its quality Virginia tobacco leaf, Zimbabwe has developed the manufacturing of tobacco products. Exports of tobacco products, however, have been declining since 2012. This trend could continue if Members were granted the right to impose plain packaging and other trade-restrictive measures.

11.   Regarding Australia's objective to reduce smoking prevalence among its populations, Zimbabwe agrees that it is legitimate. However, Zimbabwe is not convinced that the measure can actually contribute to that objective. In this regard, Zimbabwe points to the expert reports by Professor Klick and the Institute for Policy Evaluation ("IPE"), which find that Australia's measure is not having its intended effect by analyzing Australia's post-implementation circumstances in relation to a counterfactual jurisdiction (New Zealand in Prof. Klick's report) and in relation to trends in Australia over time (in the IPE report). These reports support the other reports and arguments regarding the measure's design, architecture, and structure and reveal that plain packaging is not likely to reduce and in fact is not reducing smoking prevalence. The data from the Australian market confirms that the measure may have the opposite of its intended effect.

12.   The removal of trademarks and standardization of packaging will have the effect of greatly restricting the possibility to differentiate between products on the basis of quality. This results in the "commoditization" of these products and a downward pressure on prices. By preventing quality-based distinctions, the plain packaging measures will undoubtedly negatively impact trade of high-quality Virginia tobacco leaf such as that produced by Zimbabwe. Increased price competition will have a downward effect on prices of tobacco leaf as manufacturers of tobacco products will be attempting to safeguard their profit margins by sourcing cheaper raw materials. A decline in prices of tobacco leaf would have devastating consequences for the economy of Zimbabwe as a whole because of the importance of tobacco as well as for small farmers and their families who are subsisting by growing tobacco. Zimbabwe cannot afford a decline in prices of tobacco leaf and has no viable alternatives to continuing to grow tobacco.

13.   The Panel is invited to strictly enforce the provisions of Article 2.2 of the TBT Agreement in the present disputes. These regulatory requirements are detrimental to Zimbabwe as its economic development is dependent on increasingly regulated products, including tobacco products, and the livelihood of most of its population remains directly or indirectly reliant on the tobacco sector. The trade and economic effects of plain packaging on tobacco products as well as on tobacco leaf and other raw materials concerned by the measures adopted by Australia must be taken into account by the Panel.

14.   Zimbabwe considers that the plain packaging measure significantly weakens intellectual property rights by prohibiting all trademarks from appearing on tobacco products, but for certain brand names and origin marks. Plain packaging also diminishes the protection that geographical indications enjoyed in Australia.

15.   Trademarks are key to differentiating products and ensuring fair competition in the marketplace. They are recognized as essential to open up new markets, thereby supporting competition and the international trade of products. From the perspective of consumers, trademarks provide information about the quality of and differences between products and allow them to distinguish products available on the market. Trademarks fulfill these functions by their use on products and their packaging. A prohibition on the use of trademarks on lawful products gives no consideration to the purpose and benefit of marks to consumers and manufacturers in developing countries to build strong and well-known brands. The absence of distinction that results from the imposition of plain packaging will undoubtedly have a negative impact on the price of tobacco and significantly affect producers of superior quality leaf.

16.   Zimbabwe, like many WTO Members, provides for protection of the right to use trademarks in its national law. Zimbabwe considers that the use of trademarks is protected under international law, in particular in Articles 16 and 20 of the TRIPS Agreement as explained in the expert report by Professor Dinwoodie. Therefore, Zimbabwe considers that Australia violates its

obligations under the TRIPS Agreement by prohibiting the legitimate commercial use of trademarks on tobacco products.

17.   Additionally, geographical indications are important indicators of the geographical origin of goods and the quality, reputation or characteristics essentially attributable to their origin. Yet Australia's measure prevents the use of a word geographical indications other than the name of the country at the expense of producers and consumers. Thus, the restrictions that the plain packaging measure imposes on geographical indications diminish the protection of geographical indications that existed in Australia before the entry into force of the WTO Agreement and do not provide any means to prevent the use of geographical indications, in violation of Articles 24.3 and 22.2(b) of the TRIPS Agreement.

18.   In light of the foregoing, Zimbabwe considers that Australia's plain packaging measures violate its obligations under the TRIPS Agreement, including Articles 2.1, 15, 16, 20, 24.3 and 22.2(b).

19.   Tobacco leaf and tobacco products are vital for the economic and social development of Zimbabwe. As millions of Zimbabweans depend on tobacco for their livelihood, the Panel should in addition to considering the arguments put forward by the Parties fully take into account the actual and potential negative effects of the plain packaging measures adopted by Australia on developing and least-developed country Members.

20.   Given the lack of scientific evidence to show that the plain packaging measure at issue contributes to the stated public health objective, the extreme and unjustifiable restrictions on trademark rights, and the existence of alternative measures that would be more effective and less restrictive of trade and trademarks, Zimbabwe submits that the Panel find that the measure is inconsistent with Australia's obligations under the TBT and TRIPS Agreements.

AUSTRALIA - CERTAIN MEASURES CONCERNING TRADEMARKS, GEOGRAPHICAL INDICATIONS AND OTHER PLAIN PACKAGING REQUIREMENTS APPLICABLE TO TOBACCO PRODUCTS AND PACKAGING

Reports of the Panels[*][a]
WT/DS458/R, WT/DS467/R
and Add.1 and Supp.1[b]

SCI redacted, as indicated [[***]]

*Adopted by the Dispute Settlement Body
on 27 August 2018*

Report of the Panel[*][a]
WT/DS435/R
and Add.1 and Supp.1[b]

SCI redacted, as indicated [[***]]

Appealed on 19 July 2018

Report of the Panel[*][a]
WT/DS441/R
and Add.1 and Supp.1[b]

SCI redacted, as indicated [[***]]

Appealed on 23 August 2018

---

[*] These Panel Reports are in the form of a single document constituting four separate Panel Reports: WT/DS435/R, WT/DS441/R, WT/DS458/R and WT/DS467/R. The cover page, preliminary pages, sections 1 through 7, appendices, and annexes are common to all four Panel Reports. Section 8 on page HND-5225 of Volume IX contains the Panel's conclusions and recommendations in the Panel Report WT/DS435/R; section 8 on page DOM-5226 of Volume IX contains the Panel's conclusions and recommendations in the Panel Report WT/DS441/R; section 8 on pages CUB-5228 of Volume IX contains the Panel's conclusions and recommendations in the Panel Report WT/DS458/R; and section 8 on page IDN-5230 of Volume IX contains the Panel's conclusions and recommendations in the Panel Report WT/DS467/R.

[a] The Panel's findings on the Trips Agreement can be found in DSR 2018:IX, starting at section 7.3.

[b] Annexes A to C and Suppl.1 can be found in this volume.

APPENDICES

TABLE OF CONTENTS

LIST OF FIGURES

APPENDIX A

POST-IMPLEMENTATION EVIDENCE ON NON-BEHAVIOURAL OUTCOMES OF THE TPP MEASURES

1.   In these proceedings, the parties submitted as exhibits a number of peer-reviewed studies investigating the post-implementation impact of the TPP measures and enlarged GHWs on non-behavioural proximal outcomes, namely: (i) reduction in the appeal of tobacco products; (ii) increased effectiveness of GHWs; and (iii) reduction in the ability of the pack to mislead consumers about smoking harms.[1] This Appendix reviews and discusses this evidence, in the light of the relevant expert reports submitted by the parties.

2.   Australia submits that the available post-implementation empirical studies on non-behavioural outcomes confirm that TPP and enlarged GHWs have (i) reduced appeal, (ii) increased the effectiveness of GHWs, and (iii) reduced the ability of packaging to mislead consumers about the harmful effects of tobacco products.[2]

3.   Based on the review of these peer-reviewed papers, and in some cases the re-analysis of the data used in these papers, the Dominican Republic, Honduras and Indonesia argue that the TPP measures have not had the expected effects on the antecedents of behaviour posited in Australia's conceptual framework of the TPP measures.[3] In particular, they contend that beyond the obvious findings that the pack is less visually appealing and people more often notice the larger GHWs first, empirical evidence shows little or no effects of the policies on the antecedents of behaviour. They further claim that the variables relating to beliefs, attitudes and intentions towards smoking were almost entirely unaffected by the TPP measures.[4]

4.   In addition, the experts of the Dominican Republic and Indonesia argue that some of the published empirical studies on Australia's TPP measures provide an inaccurate picture of the empirical evidence. They state that some of these papers failed to report the results for more than half of all the variables available in the survey dataset, which were overwhelmingly not statistically

---

[1]   Some of these papers also analyse more distant variables, such as beliefs, attitudes and intentions towards smoking and quitting as well as quitting attempts. These papers are also discussed in Appendix B.

[2]   See Australia's first written submission, paras. 201-205; and comments on the complainants' responses to Panel question No. 146, para. 7.

[3]   See Ajzen et al. Data Report, (Exhibit DOM/IDN-2); Ajzen et al. Second Data Report, (Exhibit DOM/IDN-4); Ajzen et al. Data Rebuttal Report, (Exhibit DOM/IDN-6); Ajzen et al. Second Data Rebuttal Report, (Exhibit DOM/IDN-8); Klick Supplemental Rebuttal Report, (Exhibit HND-122); and Klick Second Supplemental Rebuttal Report, (Exhibit HND-165).

[4]   See Ajzen et al. Data Report, (Exhibit DOM/IDN-2), paras. 10-22.

significant, suggesting no impact by plain packaging on these variables. The Dominican Republic and Indonesia contend that the authors of some of these published studies also failed to explain that a number of the reported statistically significant effects had vanished by the end of the first year of Australia's implementation of the TPP measures as a result of wear-out effects. The Dominican Republic and Indonesia further criticize these papers for failing to report the magnitude of the statistically significant effects. According to their experts, most of the reported statistically significant effects are small, suggesting that the TPP measures have little importance in shifting behaviour.[5]

5.   Each peer-reviewed empirical paper discussed by the parties either addresses different questions or is based on specific survey data, or both. We discuss, for each proximal outcome, each survey data and corresponding paper separately, before turning to an overall assessment. We approach this assessment on the basis that our task is not to conduct our own econometric assessment of the TPP measures' impact on the proximal outcomes identified above but rather to examine, on the basis of the evidence before us, the overall robustness of the econometric evidence submitted by the parties in this respect.[6]

1.   EVIDENCE RELATING TO THE APPEAL OF TOBACCO PRODUCTS SINCE THE ENTRY INTO FORCE OF THE TPP MEASURES

6.   Four peer-reviewed papers have analysed empirically the impact of Australia's TPP measures on the appeal of tobacco products: (i) Wakefield et al. 2015; (ii) Dunlop et al. 2014; (iii) White et al. 2015a; and (iv) Miller et al. 2015.[7]

7.   Different survey data were used by several of these published papers. Most survey data cover adult smokers, with the exception of a survey of students attending secondary schools.[8] Most of these peer-reviewed papers analyse only cigarette smokers, although some of these survey datasets also include information on cigar smokers. Only one peer-reviewed study analyses appeal-related outcomes in relation to cigar and cigarillo smokers.[9]

---

[5]   See Ajzen et al. Data Report, (Exhibit DOM/IDN-2), paras. 23-27.
[6]   For a similar approach, see Panel Reports, *US – COOL (Article 21.5 – Canada and Mexico)*, para. 7.183 (citing Panel Reports, *US – COOL*, para. 7.539).
[7]   See Wakefield et al. 2015, (Exhibits AUS-206, DOM-306); Dunlop et al. 2014, (Exhibits AUS-207, HND-132, DOM-199); White et al. 2015a, (Exhibits AUS-186, DOM-235); Miller et al. 2015, (Exhibits AUS-102, DOM-315).
[8]   See White et al. 2015a, (Exhibits AUS-186, DOM-235); and White et al. 2015b, (Exhibits HND-135, DOM-236, DOM-288).
[9]   See Miller et al. 2015, (Exhibits AUS-102, DOM-315).

1.1   Datasets and related studies

1.1.1   National Tobacco Plain Packaging Tracking Survey

8.   In order to track the effect of the TPP measures, Australia's Department of Health and Ageing funded the National Tobacco Plain Packaging Tracking Survey (NTPPTS), a nationwide tracking survey conducted by the Cancer Council Victoria (CCV). The NTPPTS is a continuous cross-sectional baseline survey of about 100 interviews per week of current smokers and recent quitters aged 18 to 69 years, conducted from 9 April 2012 to 30 March 2014. A follow-up survey of baseline participants then took place approximately four weeks after the initial survey, with follow-up surveys conducted from 7 May 2012 to 4 May 2014.[10] The NTPPTS data have been used in several peer-reviewed papers published in the supplement to the *Tobacco Control* journal in 2015.[11]

9.   Wakefield et al. 2015 use the NTPPTS data to investigate among adult smokers the impact of Australia's TPP measures on its three specific mechanisms, namely (i) the appeal of tobacco products, (ii) the effectiveness of GHWs, and (iii) the ability of packaging to mislead about smoking harms.[12] The authors estimate a logistic model, using baseline survey weights and controlling for individual characteristics, such as sex, age, highest educational attainment, nicotine dependence and socio-economic status.

10.   Overall, Wakefield et al. 2015 conclude that Australia's TPP measures have statistically reduced the appeal of tobacco products for adult cigarette smokers. This statistically significant effect was sustained up to 12 months after implementation. In particular, the authors report a statistically significant increase in the proportion of adult smokers that disliked their pack, perceived lower pack appeal, lower cigarette quality, lower satisfaction and lower value, and disagreed that brands differed in prestige. However, the authors find that there was no statistically significant change in the proportion of adult smokers that perceived differences in the taste of different brands.

11.   The Dominican Republic and Indonesia submitted an expert report by Ajzen et al.[13], also relied upon by Honduras[14], which reviews the accuracy and completeness of the findings reported in Wakefield et al. 2015. They reconsider the NTPPTS dataset and present the results of a logistic model for dichotomized outcome variables, a linear model for continuous outcome variables, and an

---

[10]   See Dominican Republic's second written submission, paras. 380-429.

[11]   See Ajzen et al. Data Report, (Exhibit DOM/IDN-2), para. 6.

[12]   See Wakefield et al. 2015, (Exhibits AUS-206, DOM-306).

[13]   Ajzen et al. Data Report, (Exhibit DOM/IDN-2).

[14]   See Honduras's second written submission, paras. 171-185. We note that Cuba states, "Cuba did not submit [this] expert report prepared by Professor Ajzen, and therefore no assumptions can be made as to Cuba's position concerning the effectiveness of plain packaging on the basis of that report." Cuba's response to Panel question No. 146.

ordered logit model for categorical outcome variables, using baseline survey weights and controlling for individual characteristics.

12.   The Dominican Republic argues that the published studies greatly underreport the results of the NTPPTS survey, with a pattern of underreporting unfavourable results.[15] Ajzen et al. argue that Wakefield et al. 2015 failed to report the results of three other appeal-related outcome variables that were not statistically significant. According to Ajzen et al., the authors also failed to address the small magnitude of the observed statistically significant effects.[16] More generally, the Dominican Republic considered Australia's argument that the NTPPTS was much broader in scope than Wakefield et al. 2015 to be surprising, as this message was not expressed in Wakefield et al. 2015 or in the journal's editorial and the papers were presented as the first comprehensive evaluation of the TPP measures.[17]

13.   Ajzen et al. conclude that the TPP measures have had very little impact on the mechanisms posited to underlie change in smoking behaviours because the most notable changes were only in pack appeal, with the effect on pack dislike moderate to strong, but the impact on product dislike, brand loyalty and identification was much smaller or statistically not significant. In particular, the authors find that the increase in the proportion of adult smokers that perceived lower pack appeal was statistically moderate to large but with partial evidence of wear-out effect. Ajzen et al. also report that the effects on perceived lower cigarette quality and satisfaction were statistically positive but small and without any wear-out effect. Similarly, they find that the effects on perceived lower value and brands' prestige were statistically very small but without any wear-out effect. They further confirm Wakefield et al.'s 2015 finding that there was no statistically significant change in the proportion of adult smokers that perceived differences in the taste of different brands. They reach a similar conclusion for three other variables, not reported by Wakefield et al. 2015, namely whether the smoker would stay loyal to a regular brand if the store ran out of it; agreed that they felt connected to others smoking their regular brand, and (very) often noticed others with their regular brand in the past month.[18]

14.   Honduras submitted an expert report by Professor Klick, which examines the NTPPTS data on the effect of the TPP measures on the appeal of smoking.[19] Professor Klick submits that there are a host of items relating to the appeal of

---

[15]   Dominican Republic's comments on Australia's response to Panel question No. 198, paras. 700-709.

[16]   See Ajzen et al. Data Report, (Exhibit DOM/IDN-2), paras. 98-101.

[17]   Dominican Republic's comments on Australia's response to Panel question No. 198, para. 705.

[18]   See Ajzen et al. Data Report, (Exhibit DOM/IDN-2), paras. 89-97, 148-150, Appendix A, pp. 78-80.

[19]   See Klick Supplemental Rebuttal Report, (Exhibit HND-122), paras. 54-73.

smoking that appear to have worsened following the introduction of the TPP measures, but which have been ignored by Wakefield et al. 2015.[20]

15.   Professor Klick presents the results of an ordered probit model, which controls for the TPP measures (early TPP period and formal TPP period), gender, age, education, socio-economic status and a linear time trend.[21] He finds that the TPP measures are not associated with a decrease in the reported frequency of thoughts about enjoying smoking.[22]

16.   According to Australia, the survey data are most suited to assessing changes in the specific mechanisms of the TPP measures. In that context, Australia contends that the positive findings reported by Ajzen et al. are completely consistent with Wakefield et al. 2015's findings, i.e. that Australia's TPP measures reduce the appeal of tobacco products.[23] Australia further argues that because the scope of the NTPPTS was much broader than the specific and limited focus of Wakefield et al. 2015, the results of the study in question were reported appropriately and consistently. Australia also contends that the complainants' implication that unfavourable results were not reported is directly contradicted by the facts.[24]

1.1.2   Cancer Institute New South Wales Tracking Survey

17.   The Cancer Institute New South Wales Tobacco Tracking Survey (CITTS) is a weekly tracking telephone survey of smokers and recent quitters (who quit in the past 12 months) involving approximately 50 interviews conducted per week throughout the year. The survey monitors smoking-related thoughts and behaviours among adult smokers and recent quitters in New South Wales.

18.   Dunlop et al. 2014 uses the CITTS data to investigate the impact of Australia's TPP measures on two of the specific mechanisms: (1) decreasing the promotional appeal of packaging and (2) increasing the impact of health warnings.[25] The analysis covers 15,375 randomly selected adult smokers between April 2006 and May 2013 (i.e. six months after the introduction of the TPP measures). Adjusting for background trends, seasonality, antismoking

---

[20]   See Klick Supplemental Rebuttal Report, (Exhibit HND-122), paras. 61-63.

[21]   Professor Klick explains that, unlike Wakefield et al. 2015, he omits the measure of exposure to mass media anti-smoking messages, cigarette costliness and heaviness of smoking index, because these variables are endogenous. He further explains that the inclusion of these variables does not change the results he presents. See Klick Supplemental Rebuttal Report, (Exhibit HND-122), fn 35.

[22]   See Klick Supplemental Rebuttal Report, (Exhibit HND-122), paras. 66-68. We note that Professor Klick considers the questions "how important is quitting to the person" and "how frequently people think about quitting" relevant to the appeal of tobacco. The results of these questions are discussed in Appendix B.

[23]   Australia's comments on the complainants' responses to Panel question No. 146, para. 7.

[24]   Australia's response to Panel question No. 198, paras. 298-303.

[25]   See Dunlop et al. 2014, (Exhibits AUS-207, HND-132, DOM-199).

advertising activity and cigarette costliness, the authors estimate autoregressive integrated moving average (ARIMA) models.

19.   Overall, Dunlop et al. 2014 conclude that Australia's TPP measures have had an early statistically significant effect in reducing the promotional appeal of the packaging among adult smokers.[26] In particular, the authors find a significant increase in the proportion of adult smokers strongly disagreeing that the look of their cigarette pack is attractive, says something good about them, influences the brand they buy, makes their pack stand out, is fashionable and matches their style. According to Dunlop et al. 2014, changes in these appeal-related outcomes were maintained six months following the TPP measures' implementation.

1.1.3 Australian Secondary Students Alcohol Smoking and Drug Survey

20.   The 2013 Australian Secondary Students Alcohol Smoking and Drug (ASSAD) survey extension is a follow-up survey of students attending secondary schools that participated in the 2011 ASSAD survey in Victoria and Queensland. In total 82 schools across both states participated. The 2013 survey extension was designed to compare attitudes to cigarette packaging before and after the introduction of Australia's TPP measures, and included questions about beliefs and attitudes about cigarette packaging, ratings of popular cigarette brands, noticing health warnings on cigarette packs, awareness of the specific harms of tobacco use, and perceptions of the prevalence of smoking and intention to smoke.[27]

21.   White et al. 2015a use the responses from the ASSAD survey extension to analyse, among other things, the impact of plain packaging on the appeal of cigarette packs and brands among students aged 12-17 years.[28] The authors estimate generalized linear regression models and multinomial logistic regression models controlling for smoking status, age, sex, school education sector and state.

22.   Overall, White et al. 2015a conclude that the TPP measures have reduced the appeal of cigarette packs among adolescents. In particular, they found a statistically significant decrease in the proportion of students, who had seen a cigarette pack in the previous six months, that rated positively the brand character and cigarette pack. The authors note that the effect on brand character and cigarette pack was even larger among younger smokers. White et al. 2015a also report a statistically significant increase in the proportion of students, who had seen a cigarette pack in the previous six months, rating negatively cigarette packs.[29]

---

[26]   See Tobacco Plain Packaging PIR, (Exhibit AUS-624), paras. 77-80.
[27]   See, e.g. Dominican Republic's second written submission, paras. 443-456.
[28]   See White et al. 2015a, (Exhibits AUS-186, DOM-235).
[29]   *Ibid.*

23.   The Dominican Republic and Honduras argue that, in the absence of full access to the ASSAD survey data it requested, it is impossible to make an objective assessment of the findings in White et al. 2015a. The Dominican Republic submits that as its analysis of the NTPPTS data showed, the published results in White et al. 2015a may provide an unduly positive and inaccurate impression of the full dataset. The Dominican Republic argues that although the study concludes that there is a change in the visual appeal of packs, that reduced appeal does not have any meaningful impact on perceptions of the harmfulness of smoking, quit intentions and secondary indicators of quitting.[30] Professor Ajzen, in an expert report submitted by the Dominican Republic, Honduras and Indonesia, submits that the impact of Australia's TPP measures on visual appeal of tobacco products reported in White et al. 2015a and defined as "modest" by their authors makes it difficult for the change in appeal to carry all the way through the posited chain of effects to behaviour.[31]

1.1.4   Cigar and cigarillo smokers surveys

24.   Miller et al. 2015 conducted individual interviews with ten regular premium cigar smokers, as well as two focus groups with premium cigarillo smokers and occasional premium cigar smokers (with a total of 14 smokers), and four focus groups with non-premium cigarillo smokers (with a total of 28 smokers), in February and March 2014, 15 months after the TPP measures became mandatory. In addition, in February and March 2014 the authors conducted an online survey of current cigar and cigarillo smokers. Of the original 56,589 people contacted, only 268 met all inclusion criteria, one of these criteria being current smokers of these products.[32] Rather than undertaking an econometric analysis, the authors present descriptive statistics of the results of these interviews, focus groups and the online survey.

25.   According to Miller et al. 2015, there was incomplete exposure to the TPP measures on cigar and cigarillo smokers during the first 15 months following their implementation, with many premium cigar smokers purchasing fully branded cigars in boxes duty free or online and singles in non-compliant packaging. Reported exposure was seemingly highest among non-premium cigarillo smokers. However, the authors note that when exposure occurred, the TPP measures reduced perceived packaging appeal. In particular, they find that although changes in perceived taste, harm and value were minimal for experienced premium cigar smokers, they indicated some fear of being equated with cigarette smokers. Miller et al. 2015 also find that occasional premium cigar and premium cigarillo smokers with higher plain packaging exposure (gained by purchasing boxes rather than singles cigars) perceived that

---

[30]   See Dominican Republic's second written submission, paras. 443-456; and comments on Australia's response to Panel question No. 196, para. 390.
[31]   See Ajzen Report, (Exhibit DOM/HND/IDN-3), paras. 174-178.
[32]   See Miller et al. 2015, (Exhibits AUS-102, DOM-315).

cigar/package appeal and value had declined. Similarly, they report that more non-premium cigarillo smokers affirmed that the perceived appeal, quality, taste, enjoyment and value had decreased. They also find that online survey participants stated that packaging appeal had diminished since the implementation of the TPP measures.[33]

26.   Ajzen et al., in their expert report submitted by the Dominican Republic and Indonesia, contend that the results reported by Miller et al. 2015 suffers from several methodological shortcomings, such as the non-representativeness of survey participants, unsuitability of focus groups and interviews to draw causal inferences, failure to control for exposure to anti-smoking campaigns and changes in tobacco prices, and absence of "baseline" information collected before the implementation of the TPP measures. According to Ajzen et al., these methodological shortcomings severely limit any conclusions that can be drawn from the results.[34]

27.   Ajzen et al. claim that even if Miller et al.'s 2015 results were taken at face value, the study revealed a few notable effects of the TPP measures that were clearly to be expected and unlikely to influence actual smoking behaviour, namely the changes in the appeal of the package, increased noticeability of the health warnings, and perceived less value for money. However, according to Ajzen et al., the fact that tobacco products were seen as less value for money may have been due to the rise in their cost as a result of the December 2013 tax increase and other factors. In addition, they argue that Miller et al. 2015 failed to mention that the participants also reported no change with respect to smoking enjoyment. More generally, Ajzen et al. contend that smoking cigarettes and smoking cigars (or cigarillos) are different behaviours, and their determinants are also likely to differ. They conclude that consequently whatever effects the TPP measures are, or are not, found to have on cigarette-related cognitions and behaviours, such findings cannot be generalized to cigars.[35]

1.2   Analysis by the Panel

28.   We note that among the peer-reviewed papers discussed by the parties, four studies analyse the impact of the TPP measures, as applied together with enlarged GHWs, on the appeal of tobacco products.

29.   A careful review of Wakefield et al. 2015 and Dunlop et al. 2014 and the econometric evidence submitted by the Dominican Republic, Honduras and Indonesia leads us to conclude that there is some empirical evidence suggesting that the TPP measures have reduced the appeal of tobacco products among adult cigarette smokers, in terms of pack dislike, product dislike, perceived lower

---

[33] *Ibid.*

[34] See Dominican Republic's second written submission, paras. 457-462. See Ajzen et al. Data Report, (Exhibit DOM/IDN-2), paras. 251-262.

[35] See Ajzen et al. Data Report, (Exhibit DOM/IDN-2), paras. 251-262.

quality, satisfaction and value, lower brands' prestige, and connection and identification.[36]

30.   We further note that the Dominican Republic and Indonesia qualify the findings reported in Wakefield et al. 2015 by highlighting that for most of the appeal-related outcomes, although statistically significant, the impact is small, or very small in the case of perceived lower value and brand prestige, but without any evidence of wear-out effects. Only the impact on perceived lower pack appeal, which is found to be statistically moderate, shows some partial evidence of wear-out effect.[37] We also note that Ajzen et al.'s claim that Wakefield et al. 2015 did not report the results of three other outcome variables[38], which were not statistically significant, is actually only valid for the variable related to brand loyalty[39] and to a lesser extent to the variable related to brand connection. In fact, Ajzen et al. also find in the ordered logistic regression of the variable on brand connection a statistically significant increase in the proportion of adult smokers that disagree they feel connected to others smoking their regular brand. Similarly, Ajzen et al. report a decrease, albeit small, in the proportion of adult smokers that (very) often noticed others with their regular brand in the past month, which is statistically significant at 10% level in the logistic regression or 5% level in the linear regression and ordered logistic regression.[40]

31.   We note that the empirical evidence available to us on the impact of the TPP measures on the perception of tobacco appeal among adolescents is limited to one peer-reviewed study by White et al. 2015a. In particular, White et al. 2015a suggest that the reduction in the appeal of cigarette packs and brands to adolescents, though modest, was statistically significant seven to 12 months after the introduction of the TPP measures. This result is consistent with the findings reported in Wakefield et al. 2015 and Dunlop et al. 2014.

32.   Similarly, we note that specific empirical evidence before us on the impact of the TPP measures on appeal of cigars and cigarillos is limited to the

---

[36]   See Wakefield et al. 2015, (Exhibits AUS-206, DOM-306); Dunlop et al. 2014, (Exhibits AUS-207, HND-132, DOM-199); and Ajzen et al. Data Report, (Exhibit DOM/IDN-2), paras. 89-97, 148-150, Appendix A, pp. 78-80. We note that in his review of Dunlop et al.'s 2014 analysis, Professor Klick did not discuss and re-analyse the questions of the CITTS related to appeal. We also note that Professor Klick did not mention in his reports whether the commissioned Roy Morgan Research Survey also asked questions related to the appeal of tobacco products.

[37]   See Ajzen et al. Data Report, (Exhibit DOM/IDN-2), paras. 89-97, 148-150, Appendix A, pp. 78-80.

[38]   We are also not persuaded that the variable "thought about enjoying smoking" referred to by Professor Klick is directly relevant to assess the impact of the appeal of tobacco products. See para. 15 above. In fact, we note that this variable was discussed by Ajzen et al. Data Report, (Exhibit DOM/IDN-2) in the context of the balance between smoking enjoyment and concern. See Appendix B.

[39]   We note that Ajzen et al. did not discuss the fact that in some specifications, such as the logistic regression of the brand loyalty variable, only three explanatory variables are statistically significant (besides the constant). See Ajzen et al. Data Report, (Exhibit DOM/IDN-2), back-up material.

[40]   See Ajzen et al. Data Report, (Exhibit DOM/IDN-2), Appendix A, pp. 78-80.

peer-reviewed paper by Miller et al. 2015, in which a descriptive statistics analysis finds that occasional premium cigar and premium cigarillo smokers with higher TPP exposure, non-premium cigarillo smokers, and online survey participants reported reduced perceived appeal since the implementation of the TPP measures.[41] We note that many of the criticisms raised by Ajzen et al. are actually acknowledged by Miller et al. 2015. Specifically, the authors recognize that the primary limitations of the study are the representativeness of the samples and the accuracy of self-report measures, most notably recall. In the absence of other relevant data or study on cigars, it is however unclear to what extent the results would have changed if Miller et al. 2015 had explicitly accounted for exposure to anti-smoking campaigns and changes in tobacco prices or applied a different methodology. In that context, we note that although Ajzen et al. submit that the conclusions about the impact of the TPP measures on cigarettes cannot be generalized to cigars, they also recognize themselves that the impact of the TPP measures on appeal reported in Miller et al. 2015 was to be expected. In fact, we note that Miller et al.'s findings are consistent with the findings published in the peer-reviewed studies on adult cigarette smokers and adolescents reviewed above. We therefore see no basis to reject in its entirety Miller et al.'s study on the basis of Ajzen et al.'s criticism of it.[42]

2. EVIDENCE RELATING TO THE EFFECTIVENESS OF GHWS SINCE THE ENTRY INTO FORCE OF THE TPP MEASURES

33.   Based on different datasets, five peer-reviewed papers have empirically investigated the impact of Australia's TPP measures on the effectiveness of GHWs: (i) Wakefield et al. 2015; (ii) Yong et al. 2015; (iii) Dunlop et al. 2014; (iv) White et al. 2015b; and (v) Miller et al. 2015.[43] An expert report prepared by Professor Klick and submitted by Ukraine also contains an analysis of the impact of the TPP measures on the effectiveness of GHWs.[44]

2.1   Datasets and related studies

2.1.1   National Tobacco Plain Packaging Tracking Survey

34.   In addition to analysing the impact on tobacco products appeal, Wakefield et al. 2015 use the NTPPTS data to investigate the impact of Australia's TPP measures on GHW effectiveness among adult smokers.[45] The

---

[41]   See Miller et al. 2015, (Exhibits AUS-102, DOM-315).

[42]   See Ajzen et al. Data Report, (Exhibit DOM/IDN-2), paras. 255-256.

[43]   See Wakefield et al. 2015, (Exhibits AUS-206, DOM-306); Yong et al. 2015, (Exhibit DOM-382); Dunlop et al. 2014, (Exhibits AUS-207, HND-132, DOM-199); White et al. 2015b, (Exhibits HND-135, DOM-236, DOM-288); Miller et al. 2015, (Exhibits AUS-102, DOM-315).

[44]   See section 1.6.6 in the main body of these Reports for a description of Ukraine's participation in these proceedings.

[45]   See para. 8 above for a description of the NTPPTS data. See Wakefield et al. 2015, (Exhibits AUS-206, DOM-306).

authors estimate a logistic model, using baseline survey weights and controlling for individual characteristics.

35.   Overall, Wakefield et al. 2015 conclude that Australia's TPP measures have had a statistically significant effect among adult cigarette smokers, generally sustained for up to 12 months after implementation, on increasing health warning effectiveness. In particular, the authors report a statistically significant increase in the proportion of adult smokers who noticed GHWs, attributed more motivation to quitting to GHWs, avoided specific GHWs when purchasing and covered their pack. However, they find that there was no statistically significant change in the proportion of adult smokers who perceived exaggeration of harms.[46]

36.   Ajzen et al., in their expert report submitted by the Dominican Republic and Indonesia, argue that Wakefield et al. 2015's conclusion that the TPP measures are associated with consistent improvement in health warning effectiveness outcomes cannot withstand careful examination. According to Ajzen et al., Wakefield et al. 2015 underreported the results of seven questions related to knowledge about diseases that were not statistically significant, did not pay attention to the magnitude of the statistically significant effects and failed to mention vanishing effects of some of these small effects.[47] The Dominican Republic considered Australia's claim that the NTPPTS was much broader in scope than Wakefield et al. 2015 to be surprising, as this message was not expressed in Wakefield et al. 2015 or in the journal's editorial in which the study was published.[48] Ajzen et al. reconsider the NTPPTS data and present the results of a logistic model for dichotomized outcome variables, linear model for continuous outcome variables and ordered logit model for categorical outcome variables, using baseline survey weights and controlling for individual characteristics.

37.   Ajzen et al. conclude that the TPP measures have had a statistically moderate effect on the attention paid to the enlarged GHWs, but the impact of the TPP measures on concealing packs and requesting packs with different GHWs was statistically small. They also find that the increase in the proportion of adult smokers that attributed more motivation to quitting to GHWs was statistically small and subject to a wear-out effect. However, Ajzen et al. find that the TPP measures had no impact on most beliefs about the health risks of smoking, many of which were not published in Wakefield et al. 2015. In particular, Ajzen et al. report a statistically significant small increase in the proportion of adult smokers that freely recalled a disease on a current GHW and

---

[46]   As discussed in Appendix B, we also note that Durkin et al. 2015 use the NTPPTS data to analyse the impact of the TPP measures on quitting-related variables and report greater increases in pack concealment and stubbing out cigarettes because of thoughts about the harm of smoking. See Appendix B and Durkin et al. 2015, (Exhibits AUS-215 (revised), DOM-305).

[47]   See Ajzen et al. Data Report, (Exhibit DOM/IDN-2), paras. 115-122.

[48]   Dominican Republic's comments on Australia's response to Panel question No. 198, para. 705.

agreed that smoking causes blindness. For the remaining outcome variables related to beliefs about the health risks of smoking, Ajzen et al. find that there is no statistically significant change in the proportion of adult smokers that perceived exaggeration of harms and that agreed that there are diseases caused by smoking, that smoking causes harm to unborn babies, that lung cancer is an old age disease, and that smoking causes stroke, mouth cancer, bladder cancer, and gangrene.[49]

38.   Similarly, Ajzen et al. argue that Wakefield et al. 2015 failed to report the results on the balance between smoking enjoyment and concern. In their view, this is all the more surprising given that, in Brennan et al. 2015, the same six authors use the NTPPTS data and hypothesize that the balance between smoking enjoyment and concern is "influenced by cigarette appeal, graphic health warning [GHW] effectiveness and perceived harm".[50] Ajzen et al. find no statistically significant change in the proportion of adult smokers that thought about enjoyment of smoking several/many times in the past month, were very/extremely concerned that smoking may affect health, and experienced more concern than enjoyment from/of smoking.[51] Overall, Ajzen et al. contend that the weakening of the policy across the chain of effects does not reflect a limitation of the NTPPTS dataset, as argued by Professor Chaloupka, but the theoretically expected decline in the impact of TPP across the chain of effects from pack appeal to behaviour.[52]

39.   Professor Klick, in his expert report submitted by Honduras, reviews the NTPPTS data relating to the effect of the TPP measures on the effectiveness of GHWs.[53] Professor Klick contends that a large number of outcomes in the NTPPTS data, not reported by Wakefield et al. 2015, show that the TPP measures have not improved the effectiveness of GHWs.[54]

40.   Professor Klick presents the results of an ordered probit model and a logistic model, which control for the TPP measures (early TPP period and formal TPP period), gender, age, education, socio-economic status and a linear time trend.[55] He finds that the TPP measures had no statistically significant impact on the concerns about the effect of smoking on health but had a negative

---

[49]   See Ajzen et al. Data Report, (Exhibit DOM/IDN-2), paras. 102-114, 151-155, Appendix A, pp. 81-83.
[50]   See para. 8 above for a description of the NTPPTS data. Ajzen et al. Data Report, (Exhibit DOM/IDN-2), paras. 138-142.
[51]   See Ajzen et al. Data Report, (Exhibit DOM/IDN-2), paras. 132-137, 159-162, Appendix A, pp. 87-89.
[52]   Ajzen et al. Data Rebuttal Report, (Exhibit DOM/IDN-6), para. 11 and Table 1.
[53]   See Klick Supplemental Rebuttal Report, (Exhibit HND-122), paras. 74-81.
[54]   See Klick Supplemental Rebuttal Report, (Exhibit HND-122), paras. 74-75.
[55]   Professor Klick explains that unlike Wakefield et al. 2015 he omits the measure of exposure to mass media anti-smoking messages, cigarette costliness and heaviness of smoking index, because these variables are endogenous. He further explains that the inclusion of these variables does not change the results he presented. See Klick Supplemental Rebuttal Report, (Exhibit HND-122), fn 35.

and statistically significant in respondents' awareness of the causal relationship between smoking and mouth cancer.[56]

41.   Professor Chaloupka, in an expert report submitted by Australia, contends that the pattern of results reported by Ajzen et al. is consistent with the strengths and limitations of the NTPPTS data. Australia further claims that the results of Wakefield et al. 2015, whose focus is more specific and limited than the much broader scope of the NTPPTS data, were reported appropriately and consistently. According to Australia the complainants' implication that unfavourable results were not reported is directly contradicted by the facts.[57] In particular, Professor Chaloupka argues that, as expected, Ajzen et al. found consistent and statistically significant effects for the impact of the TPP measures on the most proximal outcomes, such as noticing and avoiding health warnings, but the impact is smaller, less statistically significant and less consistent as the focus shifts to less proximal outcomes, such as health knowledge and perceptions of the health risks, when looking at the impact in the overall sample of smokers and recent quitters.[58] Professor Chaloupka further contends that the NTPPTS data cannot be used to assess the impact of TPP on the population most likely to be influenced by the measure, namely, never users who might have taken up tobacco use in the absence of TPP. According to Professor Chaloupka, the NTPPTS data can also not measure the impact of TPP on relapse among former smokers who are not categorised as "recent quitters".[59]

2.1.2   International Tobacco Control Policy Evaluation Project

42.   The International Tobacco Control (ITC) Policy Evaluation Project (ITC Project) is a longitudinal cohort survey to assess the impact, and identify the determinants of, effective tobacco control policies in more than 20 countries, including Australia. The ITC Project covers a number of issues related to GHWs, including attention to health warnings, salience of health warnings and the effect of health warnings on consumers' thoughts, behaviours and intentions to quitting. The wave survey prior to the implementation of the TPP measures was conducted between September 2011 and February 2012, while the wave after the implementation was conducted between February and May 2013.

43.   Yong et al. 2015 use data from the Australian component of the ITC Project to assess the impact of the TPP measures' GHW effectiveness. The authors estimate various generalised estimating equation (GEE) models

---

[56]   See Klick Supplemental Rebuttal Report, (Exhibit HND-122), paras. 74-78 and 80-81. We note that Professor Klick considers the question "how often the person stub out due to thoughts about the harm of smoking" to be relevant to the effectiveness of GHWs. The results of this question are discussed in Appendix B.
[57]   Australia's response to Panel question No. 198, paras. 298-303.
[58]   See Chaloupka Rebuttal Report, (Exhibit AUS-582), para. 9; and Chaloupka Third Rebuttal Report, (Exhibit AUS-604), paras. 2-7.
[59]   Chaloupka Rebuttal Report, (Exhibit AUS-582), para. 3.

controlling for age, sex, income, education, cigarettes per day, past year quit attempts, survey mode (phone vs. web) and wave of recruitment.[60]

44.   Yong et al. 2015 find a statistically significant increase in the proportion of adult smokers who increased their attentional orientation towards health warning labels, noticed them more, experienced cognitive reactions with respect to health warning labels and avoided health warning labels. However, the authors report no statistically significant change in the proportion of adult smokers who read health warning labels and forego cigarettes. Yong et al. 2015 further find that the subgroup of respondents that switched from initially focusing away to focusing on the health warning labels following the introduction of the TPP measures, noticed and read the health warning labels more, thought more about the harmful effects of smoking and avoided health warning labels, but did not forego cigarettes. Conversely, Yong et al. 2015 show that the subgroup of respondents who chose to focus away from the health warning labels, noticed them less, experienced less cognitive reactions, and avoided the health warning labels less.[61]

45.   Ajzen et al., in their expert report submitted by the Dominican Republic and Indonesia, claim that they were unable to present a comprehensive assessment of the ITC dataset, including correcting for the possibility of false positive findings due to multiple hypothesis testing (i.e. statistically significant results might have occurred by chance), controlling for anti-smoking advertising in mass media and testing for wear-out effects, because they only had access to a small subset of the data.[62] Similarly, Ajzen et al. criticise Yong et al. 2015 for failing to justify their selection of outcome variables available in the ITC dataset and having chosen not to report the results of downstream variables and actual smoking behaviour and other questions related to warning labels. According to Ajzen et al., Yong et al. 2015 also failed to report effect sizes, explore wear-out effects and correct for multiple hypothesis testing.[63] Ajzen et al. replicate the analysis of Yong et al. 2015 by re-estimating GEE models controlling for the survey mode (phone vs. web) and wave of recruitment, as well as respondents' age, sex, income, education, cigarettes per day consumed and past year quit attempts.

46.   Overall, Ajzen et al. conclude that the results based on the ITC data are similar to those based on the NTPPTS dataset, namely that the TPP measures have had a mixed and overall weak impact on GHW effectiveness. In particular, Ajzen et al. find that, although the TPP measures have had a moderate positive and statistically significant effect on increasing smokers' attentional orientation

[60]   See Yong et al. 2015, (Exhibit DOM-382).

[61]   Yong et al. 2015 (Exhibit DOM-382) note that the mechanism for this apparent reactance, i.e. the minority of smokers stimulated to shift from initially focusing on to focusing away from the warnings and reporting a reduction in avoidance, is not clear.

[62]   See Dominican Republic's comments on Australia's response to Panel question No. 196, paras. 409-414; and Ajzen et al. Second Data Report, (Exhibit DOM/IDN-4), paras. 12-19.

[63]   See Ajzen et al. Second Data Report, (Exhibit DOM/IDN-4), paras. 30-37 and 53-58.

towards health warning labels and a statistically significant small positive effect on the noticeability of the enlarged GHWs, smokers did not actually read the GHWs more. Similarly, they report that the TPP measures have had a statistically significant small positive impact on cognitive reactions and a statistically significant moderate positive impact on avoiding health warning labels.[64]

47.   Australia contends that Ajzen et al. correctly conclude that the TPP measures have significantly increased attention paid to GHWs, noticeability of GHWs, cognitive reactions to GHWs, and avoidance of GHWs.[65] Professor Chaloupka further submits that Ajzen et al. fail to recognize that the impact of plain packaging should be smaller for the less proximal outcomes, such as knowledge about the health consequences of tobacco use, when one looks at the impact in the overall sample of smokers and recent quitters, because one would not expect that a smoker whose likelihood of noticing health warnings did not increase following plain packaging would show any change in his/her knowledge about the health consequences of smoking.[66]

48.   Ajzen et al. argue that Australia and its experts do not contest the accuracy of the analytical approach they adopted or the results they obtained and do not challenge their serious criticisms of Yong et al. 2015.[67] They further contend that Professor Chaloupka's assertion that the more distal outcomes will be less affected by the policy than the most proximal outcomes is unfounded. In their view, this weakening of the policy across the chain of effect does not reflect a limitation of the data, but the theoretically expected decline in the impact of plain packaging across the chain of effect from pack appeal to behaviour.[68]

2.1.3   Cancer Institute New South Wales Tobacco Tracking Survey

49.   As well as analysing the impact of the TPP measures on the appeal of tobacco products, Dunlop et al. 2014 use the CITTS data to investigate their impact on GHW effectiveness among a large group of randomly selected adult smokers between April 2006 and May 2013.[69] The authors present the results of ARIMA models controlling for background trends, seasonality, anti-smoking advertising activity and cigarette costliness.

---

[64]   See Ajzen et al. Second Data Report, (Exhibit DOM/IDN-4), paras. 22-27. We note that Ajzen et al. use the terms "intermediate", "moderate", and "medium" interchangeably to interpret effect sizes of their estimates. See, e.g. Ajzen et al. Data Report, (Exhibit DOM/IDN-2), paras. 90 and 119, and Appendix B, pp. 100-102.

[65]   See Australia's response to Panel question No. 196, paras. 225 and 237.

[66]   See Chaloupka Rebuttal Report, (Exhibit AUS-582), para. 4.

[67]   See Ajzen et al. Second Data Rebuttal Report, (Exhibit DOM/IDN-8), paras. 13-16.

[68]   See Ajzen et al. Data Rebuttal Report, (Exhibit DOM/IDN-6), paras. 39-45.

[69]   See para. 17 above for a description of the CITTS data. See Dunlop et al. 2014, (Exhibits AUS-207, HND-132, DOM-199).

50.   Overall, Dunlop et al. 2014 conclude that Australia's TPP measures have had an early statistically significant effect on increasing effectiveness of health warnings among adult smokers.[70] In particular, the authors report that two to three months following the introduction of the TPP measures, the absolute proportion of adult smokers having strong cognitive ("graphic warnings encourage me to stop smoking"), emotional ("with the graphic warnings, each time I get a cigarette out I worry that I should not be smoking") and avoidant ("they make me feel that I should hide or cover my packet from the view of others") responses to on-pack GHWs has increased. They find, however, that the impact of the TPP measures on smokers' responses to the salience of GHWs ("the only thing I notice on my cigarette pack is the graphic warnings") was positive but statistically not significant.

51.   Professor Klick, in an expert report submitted by Honduras, re-examines the impact of the TPP measures on GHW effectiveness using more recent CITTS data. Unlike Dunlop et al. 2014, Professor Klick restricts the sample to be more evenly spread between the pre- and post-implementation periods, namely from January 2009 to December 2014. In addition, rather than looking only at "strong agreement" with a statement, as Dunlop et al. 2014 did, Professor Klick also analyses "strong disagreement" with a statement. Professor Klick presents the results of a logistic regression controlling for annual time trend, week of survey and individual characteristics, and submits that comparable results may be found using the ARIMA models.

52.   Professor Klick finds that the TPP measures have had a positive and statistically significant impact on adult smokers' cognitive, emotional, avoidant and salience responses when the outcome variables are defined as "strong agreement" with a given statement. However, when the outcome variables are defined as "strong disagreement" with a given statement, the results are reversed and the impact of the TPP measures on adult smokers' cognitive, emotional, avoidant and salience responses is found to be negative and statistically significant. Professor Klick submits that this situation of contradictory outcomes likely results from consumer perceptions and intentions being ill-conceived, in a context where there is no cost to providing inaccurate or even inconsistent answers.[71]

53.   Professor Klick further submits that Dunlop et al. 2014 have cherry-picked questions to analyse GHW effectiveness and failed to examine other equally relevant questions, whose results contradict the authors' conclusions. In particular, Professor Klick finds that the TPP measures had a positive and statistically significant impact on the probability that the respondent strongly agrees with the statements "I do not look at the warnings each time the smoker gets a cigarette out" and "the graphic warnings are exaggerated". In addition, Professor Klick finds a negative but not statistically significant impact

---

[70]   See Tobacco Plain Packaging PIR, (Exhibit AUS-624), paras. 77-80.
[71]   See Klick Second Supplemental Rebuttal Report, (Exhibit HND-165), paras. 35-58.

of the TPP measures on the probability that the respondent strongly agrees with the statement "I have read the detailed information on the warning labels".

54.   Australia's expert Professor Chaloupka submits that the CITTS dataset has features, including many of the same features of the NTPPTS data, which limit its utility in fully assessing the impact of plain packaging on the proximal and distal outcomes that are likely to be affected by the TPP measures.[72] Professor Chaloupka claims that the CITTS dataset does not include young people and never smokers and, therefore, cannot assess the impact of the TPP measures on the population most likely to be influenced by the measure. Professor Chaloupka further submits that any analysis that uses responses to questions, which are only asked of smokers, is likely to be considerably understating the effects of the TPP measures because recent quitters, who seem most likely to have responded positively to these questions and to have already been influenced by the TPP measures, are not included in the analysis. Professor Chaloupka contends also that Professor Klick's analyses fail to appropriately account for significant changes in the CITTS's sampling methods implemented in 2013, resulting in an increase in the share of the sample accounted for by younger people and by men.

2.1.4   Australian Secondary Students Alcohol Smoking and Drug Survey[73]

55.   In another paper, White et al. 2015b use the 2013 ASSAD survey dataset to examine the impact of Australia's TPP measures on the effectiveness of GHWs among students aged 12-17 years in Victoria and Queensland.[74] The authors estimate linear and logistic regression models controlling for individual characteristics, such as age, sex, school type, state and smoking status.

56.   Overall, White et al. 2015b conclude that Australia's TPP measures have increased awareness among adolescents of bladder cancer, blindness and smoking as leading cause of death. However, the authors find that the TPP measures had no impact on adolescents' other health beliefs and cognitive processing of warning information. In particular, they find no change over time in responses to the statements that smoking is addictive, is toxic (from tobacco smoke), clogs arteries, harms unborn babies, increases the risk of having a heart attack, doubles the risk of stroke, and causes mouth cancer, diseases of the gums, kidney disease, lung cancer, emphysema, and diseases in toes and fingers (gangrene).[75] Similarly, the authors report that there is no statistically significant

---

[72]   See Chaloupka Second Rebuttal Report, (Exhibit AUS-590), paras. 24-30.
[73]   See Dominican Republic's second written submission, paras. 443-456.
[74]   See White et al. 2015b, (Exhibits HND-135, DOM-236, DOM-288). See para. 20 above for a description of the ASSAD survey.
[75]   We note that White et al. 2015b report a statistically significant at 10% level increase in responses to the statement that smoking causes mouth cancer.

change in the proportion of adolescents that read GHWs, paid close attention to GHWs, thought about GHWs, and talked about GHWs.[76]

57.   The Dominican Republic argues that without having full access to the data, it is impossible to make an objective assessment of the findings reported in White et al. 2015b. The Dominican Republic submits that, as the analysis of the NTPPTS data showed, the published results in White et al. 2015b may provide an unduly positive and inaccurate impression of the full dataset.[77] Professor Ajzen, in an expert report submitted by the Dominican Republic, Honduras and Indonesia, further submits that the change in knowledge about bladder cancer could very well be attributable to a confounding factor, namely new information contained in new health warnings.[78] More generally, the Dominican Republic notes that White et al. 2015b conclude that a period of one year following the implementation of the TPP measures was not too short to detect effects on adolescents. The Dominican Republic also submit that White et al. 2015b recognize that a "process of habituation" means that these initially weak effects are likely to weaken further over time.[79]

2.1.5   Cigar and cigarillo smokers surveys

58.   As part of their analysis of cigar and cigarillo smokers, Miller et al. 2015 review the responses to questions related to GHW effectiveness obtained from individual interviews, focus groups and an online survey conducted 15 months after the introduction of the TPP measures.[80]

59.   Miller et al. 2015 find that exposure of cigar and cigarillo smokers to the TPP measures was incomplete during the first 15 months following the implementation of the TPP measures because they purchased fully branded cigars in boxes duty free or online and singles in non-compliant packaging. They note, however, that when exposure occurred, the TPP measures increased the noticeability of health warnings. In particular, the authors report that premium cigar smokers who were exposed had noticed and were concerned by the health warnings, tried to avoid them and felt more like "dirty smokers". Similarly, they find that occasional premium cigar and premium cigarillo smokers with higher plain packaging exposure (gained by purchasing boxes rather than singles) and online survey participants reported having noticed GHWs more. They also note that non-premium cigarillo smokers reported high plain packaging exposure, somewhat increased perceived harm, as well as greater noticeability of GHWs and concealment of packs.

---

[76]   See White et al. 2015b, (Exhibits HND-135, DOM-236, DOM-288).
[77]   See Dominican Republic's second written submission, paras. 443-456; and comments on Australia's response to Panel question No. 196, para. 390.
[78]   See Ajzen Report, (Exhibit DOM/HND/IDN-3), para. 178.
[79]   See Dominican Republic's second written submission, paras. 451-455.
[80]   See para. 24 above for a description of the cigar and cigarillo smokers surveys data. See Miller et al. 2015, (Exhibits AUS-102, DOM-315).

60.   Ajzen et al., in their expert report submitted by the Dominican Republic and Indonesia, claim that the results reported by Miller et al. 2015 suffer from several serious methodological shortcomings, including the non-representativeness of survey participants, impossibility of drawing causal inferences, failure to control for confounding factors, and absence of information collected during the pre-implementation period of the TPP measures, which severely limits any conclusions that can be drawn from the analysis.[81]

61.   According to Ajzen et al., even if the results published by Miller et al. 2015 are taken at face value, the few notable effects of the TPP measures revealed in the paper, including the increased noticeability of health warnings, are clearly to be expected and unlikely to influence actual smoking behaviour. Ajzen et al. further claim that Miller et al. 2015 did not mention that the participants also reported no change with respect to concerns that smoking may damage health, stubbing out cigars or cigarillos and stopping smoking. More generally, Ajzen et al. contend that whatever effects the TPP measures are, or are not, found to have on cigarette-related cognitions and behaviours, such findings cannot be generalized to cigars. This, they submit, is because smoking cigarettes and cigars (or cigarillos) are different behaviours, and their determinants are also likely to differ.[82]

2.1.6   Commissioned Roy Morgan Research Survey (Australia and New Zealand)

62.   Roy Morgan Research dataset, commissioned by Professor Klick, is a survey of individuals who were current or former (in the past 12 months) smokers in both Australia and New Zealand undertaken using random digit dialling sampling techniques. The first wave of the survey was completed prior to the implementation of Australia's TPP measures between 2 November 2012 and 26 November 2012 in Australia and between 8 November 2012 and 1 December 2012 in New Zealand. Subsequent waves were carried out at three-month intervals up until February 2014. The survey probed the respondents' experience with attempts to quit and their intention to do so in the future as well as other attempts to change some aspect of their smoking behaviour.[83]

63.   Professor Klick uses the Roy Morgan Research data to estimate a difference-in-difference logit model that explains non-behavioural outcomes related to GHWs in Australia and New Zealand, controlling for the TPP measures, an Australian baseline variable, a common baseline variable and a post-TPP implementation time-period.

---

[81]   See Dominican Republic's second written submission, paras. 457-462; and Ajzen et al. Data Report, (Exhibit DOM/IDN-2), paras. 251-262.

[82]   See Ajzen et al. Data Report, (Exhibit DOM/IDN-2), paras. 251-262.

[83]   See Klick Report, (Exhibit UKR-5), pp. 6-8. See section 1.6.6 in the main body of these Reports for a description of Ukraine's participation in these proceedings.

64.   Overall, Professor Klick concludes that the TPP measures have had no statistically significant effect on smokers' beliefs about the health effects of smoking and the degree to which they notice warnings on their cigarette packages in Australia relative to New Zealand.[84] In particular, Professor Klick finds there was no statistically significant TPP impact in Australia relative to New Zealand on the likelihood that the respondent answered positively on whether smoking is a major issue, a minor or major issue, and harmful to the heart, stomach, mouth, bladder, throat, sight, skin, or teeth. In addition, Professor Klick finds that the TPP measures have had no statistically significant impact in Australia relative to New Zealand on placing a cover over the cigarettes, placing the cigarettes in a different container and keeping the pack out of sight.[85]

65.   Although Australia's expert, Dr Chipty, does not address directly Professor Klick's analysis of non-behavioural outcomes based on the Roy Morgan Research data, a number of criticisms raised by Dr Chipty regarding Professor Klick's difference-in-difference analysis of smoking incidence also apply to the analysis of non-behavioural outcomes. Dr Chipty argues that Professor Klick's analysis of the Roy Morgan Research data is invalid because Professor Klick's commissioned Roy Morgan survey does not contain a pre-period and is incapable of distinguishing which respondents had noticed plain packaging. Furthermore, Dr Chipty considers that New Zealand is an invalid counterfactual for the purposes of studying the effects of plain packaging, because of New Zealand's January 2013 excise tax increase, one month after the introduction of TPP measures.[86]

2.2   Analysis by the Panel

66.   We note that a slightly larger number of peer-reviewed studies before us (six in total) analyse the impact of the TPP measures and enlarged GHWs on outcome variables related to GHW effectiveness, compared to the number of studies before us addressing the impact on appeal of tobacco products.

67.   A careful review of Wakefield et al. 2015 and Yong et al. 2015 and the econometric evidence submitted by the Dominican Republic, Honduras and Indonesia leads us to conclude that there is some empirical evidence that suggests that the TPP measures have improved the GHW effectiveness among adult cigarette smokers by increasing the noticeability of GHWs, attention towards them, avoidance of health warnings labels, pack concealment, request for a pack with a different GHW and attribution to the motivation to quit to GHWs (cognitive responses).[87] We note that although Ajzen et al. qualify these

---

[84]   See Klick Report, (Exhibit UKR-5), pp. 18, 47-54.
[85]   See Klick Report, (Exhibit UKR-5), pp. 18, 54-56.
[86]   See Chipty Rebuttal Report, (Exhibit AUS-535) (SCI), paras. 54-71.
[87]   See Wakefield et al. 2015, (Exhibits AUS-206, DOM-306); Dunlop et al. 2014, (Exhibits AUS-207, HND-132, DOM-199); Yong et al. 2015, (Exhibit DOM-382); and Ajzen et al. Data Report, (Exhibit DOM/IDN-2), paras. 89-97, 148-150, Appendix A, pp. 78-80. We also note that in

impacts as small or moderate in the case of attention and avoidant responses, they are still statistically significant, with no evidence of wear-out effects, except in the case of the cognitive responses.[88]

68.   However, we note that the empirical evidence on the impact of the TPP measures on knowledge about health risks is more nuanced and statistically not significant as regards the balance between smoking enjoyment and concern. Ajzen et al. and Professor Klick contend that the impact of the TPP measures on GHW effectiveness is mixed because the impacts on reading the GHW, perceived exaggeration of harms and knowledge about specific risks are not statistically significant.[89] We note in this respect that while the analysis suggests that the TPP measures seem to have a limited impact on recalling specific smoking risks, the results also suggest that the TPP measures have had a small but positive and statistically significant impact on recalling a disease on a current GHW and on believing that smoking causes blindness without evidence of a wear-out effect.[90] In that context, we find that Ajzen et al.'s claim that Wakefield et al. 2015 underreported non-statistically significant results should be qualified.[91] First, we note that Wakefield et al. 2015 did not report some results. However, following their own analysis of the unreported results with respect to questions assessing whether the TPP measures and enlarged GHWs increased knowledge about diseases caused by smoking, Ajzen et al. acknowledge that the TPP measures had a "very small effect" on respondents' ability to freely recall a disease on a current GHW and their belief that smoking causes blindness.[92] Second, Ajzen et al. also find an increase, albeit very small, in the proportion of adult smokers who believe smoking causes bladder cancer, which is statistically significant at the 10% level in the logistic regression. Similarly, Ajzen et al. report in the linear regression and ordered logistic regression a very small but statistically significant (at the 10% level) increase in the proportion of adult smokers who disagree that lung cancer is a disease smokers only get in old age.[93] Third, and more generally, we agree with Professor Chaloupka that the impact of the TPP measures is likely to be smaller for the less proximal outcomes, when

---

his review of Dunlop et al. 2014's analysis, Professor Klick did not discuss and re-analyse the questions of the CITTS related to appeal. We also note that Professor Klick did not mention in his reports whether the commissioned Roy Morgan Research survey also asked questions related to the appeal of tobacco products.

[88]   See Ajzen et al. Data Report, (Exhibit DOM/IDN-2), paras. 102-114, 151-155, Appendix A, pp. 81-83; and Ajzen et al. Second Data Report, (Exhibit DOM/IDN-4), paras. 22-27.

[89]   See Ajzen et al. Data Report, (Exhibit DOM/IDN-2), paras. 102-114, 151-155, Appendix A, pp. 81-83. See also Ajzen et al. Second Data Report, (Exhibit DOM/IDN 4), para. 22.

[90]   See Ajzen et al. Data Report, (Exhibit DOM/IDN-2), Appendix A, pp. 81-83.

[91]   See Ajzen et al. Data Report, (Exhibit DOM/IDN-2), para. 116.

[92]   See Ajzen et al. Data Report, (Exhibit DOM/IDN-2), paras. 112 and 116-117.

[93]   See Ajzen et al. Data Report, (Exhibit DOM/IDN-2), pp. 81-83. We also note that Ajzen et al. report in the logistic regression results table a very small but statistically significant at the 10% level decrease in the proportion of adult smokers that agree that smoking causes mouth cancer.

looking at the impact in an overall survey sample composed of smokers and recent quitters.[94]

69.   A careful review of the analysis of the CITTS data reported by Dunlop et al. 2014 and Professor Klick confirms the findings reported in Wakefield et al. 2015 and Yong et al. 2015 that the TPP measures had, in the two to three months following their introduction, a positive and statistically significant impact on adult smokers' cognitive, emotional and avoidant reactions to GHWs.[95] We are not persuaded that the econometric results presented by Professor Klick can be taken at face value and provide sufficient basis to dismiss Dunlop et al.'s results. A comparison between Professor Klick's re-analysis with Dunlop et al. 2014 is not straightforward, not only because the sample period is different but more importantly because the estimation method is different. Professor Klick submits that using Dunlop et al. 2014 would yield similar results.[96] Yet, Professor Klick reports a statistically significant impact of the TPP measures on smokers' responses to GHW salience, while in Dunlop et al. 2015 the impact is found to be not significant.[97] It is therefore unclear to what extent Professor Klick's findings are the result of his model specification (i.e. not controlling for exposure to advertising and tobacco costliness) or a different sample period or both. It is also unclear why Professor Klick decided to discard data from April 2006 to December 2008. Likewise, it is unclear if Professor Klick's findings are affected by the changes in the survey's sampling methods. Professor Klick also did not provide an explanation as to why the TPP measures would decrease GHW effectiveness, as suggested by some of his counter-intuitive results.

70.   As noted above in our review of the post-implementation studies before us on appeal, only one peer-reviewed study by White et al. 2015b reports empirical evidence of the impact of the TPP measures on adolescents. In the context of GHW effectiveness, we note that White et al. 2015b suggest that one year after their implementation, the TPP measures have had a limited impact on adolescents' beliefs about the health risks of smoking and no impact on their cognitive processing of the GHW information.[98] The authors report that acknowledgement of negative health effects of smoking among Australian adolescents remains high. This could explain why the TPP measures did not increase adolescents' health beliefs, except as regards bladder cancer, mouth cancer, blindness and smoking as a leading cause of death.

71.   Post-implementation empirical evidence on cigar and cigarillo smokers is also limited to a single peer-reviewed paper, by Miller et al. 2015, who present a

---

[94]   See Chaloupka Rebuttal Report, (Exhibit AUS-582), para. 9.
[95]   See para. 17 above for a description of the CITTS data. See Dunlop et al. 2014, (Exhibits AUS-207, HND-132, DOM-199).
[96]   See Klick Second Supplemental Rebuttal Report, (Exhibit HND-165), para. 42.
[97]   See Klick Second Supplemental Rebuttal Report, (Exhibit HND-165), pp. 18 and 21-23.
[98]   See White et al. 2015b, (Exhibits HND-135, DOM-236, DOM-288).

descriptive statistics analysis of various personal interviews, focus groups and an online survey. The authors find that 15 months after the introduction of the TPP measures, cigar and cigarillo smokers exposed to plain packaging reported greater noticeability of the GHWs and in a few cases greater concerns about the health warnings, avoidance of graphic health labels and pack concealment.[99] As pointed out by Ajzen et al., the evidence on cigar and cigarillo smokers' health beliefs and cognitive responses are more mixed. As explained in our review of the post-implementation studies on appeal, many of the criticisms raised by Ajzen et al. regarding Miller et al.'s methodology, such as the representativeness of the samples and accuracy of self-report measures, have been identified as limitations by the authors themselves. It is however unclear to what extent the results would have changed if Miller et al. 2015 had explicitly accounted for confounding factors or applied a different methodology, noting that no other relevant data on cigars have been provided by the parties. That being said, we note that although Ajzen et al. submit that conclusions about the impact of the TPP measures on cigarettes cannot be generalized to cigars, they also recognize that the impact of the TPP measures on increased noticeability of the health warnings on cigars was to be expected.[100] Therefore, we see no basis to reject in its entirety Miller et al.'s study on the basis of Ajzen et al.'s. criticism of it, noting that the overall findings reported in Miller et al. 2015 are to some extent in line with the results reported in the other peer-reviewed papers analysing the impact of GHW effectiveness on adult cigarette smokers reviewed above.

72.   Finally, after a careful review, we question the robustness of Professor Klick's analysis of the commissioned Roy Morgan Research data. We note that unlike in the context of his empirical analysis of smoking incidence based on the Roy Morgan Research data, Professor Klick did not re-estimate his model specification to address some of the criticisms raised by Dr Chipty.[101] We also question the validity of Professor Klick's difference-in-difference analysis, for two main reasons. First, the structure of the commissioned data prevents Professor Klick from accurately identifying the respondents who had noticed plain packs in the pre-period. This is because the question about noticing changes in the packaging was not asked to all respondents, making the pre-period covered by the commissioned data, in our view, very questionable.[102] Second, it is unclear how controlling for the excise tax increase that took place in New Zealand between Waves 1 and 2 and Waves 5 and 6 of the commissioned survey would have changed the results.

---

[99]   See Miller et al. 2015, (Exhibits AUS-102, DOM-315).
[100]   See, Ajzen et al. Data Report, (Exhibit DOM/IDN-2), paras. 255-256.
[101]   We are aware that most of Dr Chipty's critics referred to Professor Klick's analysis of smoking prevalence, but some of these critics apply to the difference-in-difference methodology in general.
[102]   See Chipty Rebuttal Report, (Exhibit AUS-535) (SCI), paras. 54-62.

3. **EVIDENCE RELATING TO THE ABILITY OF TOBACCO PACKAGING TO MISLEAD CONSUMERS ABOUT THE HARMFUL EFFECTS OF SMOKING SINCE THE ENTRY INTO FORCE OF THE TPP MEASURES**

73. Two peer-reviewed papers analyse empirically the impact of Australia's TPP measures on the ability of the pack of tobacco products to mislead consumers among adult cigarette smokers and adolescents, respectively: (i) Wakefield et al. 2015; and (ii) White et al. 2015a.[103]

3.1 Datasets and related studies

3.1.1 National Tobacco Plain Packaging Tracking Survey

74. In addition to analysing the impact of the TPP measures on appeal and GHWs effectiveness, Wakefield et al. 2015 uses the NTPPTS data to investigate their impact among adult smokers on tobacco packaging's ability to mislead consumers about smoking harms.[104] The authors present the results of a logistic model, using baseline survey weights and controlling for individual characteristics.[105]

75. Wakefield et al. 2015 find that, 12 months after their implementation, the TPP measures have had a positive and statistically significant effect on the proportion of adult smokers who believed that brands do not differ in harmfulness. However, the authors report no statistically significant change in the proportion of adult smokers who rated their current cigarette or tobacco as more harmful compared to a year ago and who believed brand variants do not differ in strength.[106]

76. Ajzen et al. in their expert report submitted by the Dominican Republic and Indonesia, submit that although Wakefield et al. 2015 acknowledges that the impact of the TPP measures on reducing the ability of packaging to mislead was mixed, the picture they presented must be considered incomplete because they failed to mention an important wear-out effect and to report statistically not significant results.[107] In particular, Ajzen et al. find that the increase in the proportion of adult smokers who believed that brands did not differ in harmfulness was very small and showed a wear-out effect. In addition, Ajzen et al. report no statistically significant change in the proportion of adult smokers that perceived their cigarettes are more harmful compared to a year ago, believed that brand variants do not differ in strength and agreed they had trouble

---

[103] See Wakefield et al. 2015, (Exhibits AUS-206, DOM-306); and White et al. 2015a, (Exhibits AUS-186, DOM-235).
[104] See para. 8 above for a description of the NTPPTS data. See Wakefield et al. 2015, (Exhibits AUS-206, DOM-306).
[105] See para. 8 above for a description of the NTPPTS data.
[106] See para. 8 above for a description of the NTPPTS data. See Wakefield et al. 2015, (Exhibits AUS-206, DOM-306).
[107] See Ajzen et al. Data Report, (Exhibit DOM/IDN-2), paras. 128-132.

believing that their regular brand of cigarettes is harmful.[108] More generally, the Dominican Republic considered Australia's claim that the NTPPTS was much broader in scope than Wakefield et al. 2015 to be surprising, as this message was not expressed in Wakefield et al. 2015 or in the journal's editorial in which the study was published.[109]

77.   Professor Klick, in his expert report submitted by Honduras, reviews the NTPPTS data relating to the effect of the TPP measures on the ability of packaging to mislead consumers about the harm of smoking.[110] Professor Klick contends that there are other outcomes in the NTPPTS data, not reported by Wakefield et al. 2015, which go against their conclusion that the TPP measures are achieving their goal regarding the ability of packaging to mislead consumers about smoking harms.[111]

78.   Professor Klick presents the results of an ordered probit model, which controls for the TPP measures (early TPP period and formal TPP period), gender, age, education, socio-economic status and a linear time trend.[112] He finds that the TPP measures had no statistically significant impact on the respondents' belief about the harmfulness of the regular brand.[113]

79.   Australia contends that the findings reported by Ajzen et al. are completely consistent with the findings of Wakefield et al. 2015 regarding the impact of the TPP measures on reducing the ability of packaging to mislead consumers about the harmful effects of smoking.[114] More generally, Australia argues that the results of Wakefield et al. 2015 were reported appropriately since the scope of the NTPPTS was much broader than the specific and limited focus of Wakefield et al. 2015. Australia further claims that the complainants' implication that unfavourable results were not reported is directly contradicted by the facts.[115]

---

[108]   See Ajzen et al. Data Report, (Exhibit DOM/IDN-2), paras. 123-127 and 156-158, Appendix A, pp. 84-86.

[109]   Dominican Republic's comments on Australia's response to Panel question No. 198, para. 705.

[110]   See Klick Supplemental Rebuttal Report, (Exhibit HND-122), paras. 82-86.

[111]   See Klick Supplemental Rebuttal Report, (Exhibit HND-122), para. 84.

[112]   Professor Klick explains that, unlike Wakefield et al. 2015, he omits the measure of exposure to mass media anti-smoking messages, cigarette costliness and heaviness of smoking index, because these variables are endogenous. He further explains that the inclusion of these variables does not change the results he presented. See Klick Supplemental Rebuttal Report, (Exhibit HND-122), fn 35.

[113]   See Klick Supplemental Rebuttal Report, (Exhibit HND-122), paras. 85-86. We note that in Professor Klick's model specification with an early TPP period and a formal TPP period, the impact of the early TPP period variable is positive and statistically significant, suggesting that the respondents are not more convinced that their regular brand is harmful.

[114]   Australia's comments on the complainants' responses to Panel question No. 146, para. 7.

[115]   Australia's response to Panel question No. 198, paras. 298-303.

3.1.2 Australian Secondary Students Alcohol Smoking and Drug Survey

80.   In addition to assessing the impact of Australia's TPP measures on the appeal of tobacco products, White et al. 2015a employ the 2013 ASSAD survey extension to examine the impact of the TPP measures on the ability of tobacco product packaging to mislead about smoking harms among students aged 12-17 years.[116] The authors present the results of several generalized linear regression models and multinomial logistic regression models controlling for individual characteristics.

81.   Overall, White et al. 2015a conclude that the impact of Australia's TPP measures on reducing the ability of cigarette packaging to mislead young smokers regarding the harmful effects of smoking is mixed. In particular, the authors report a statistically significant increase in the proportion of students who had seen a cigarette pack in the previous six months and disagreed that some brands are more addictive than others and that some cigarette brands contain more harmful substances than others. However, the authors find that the number of students agreeing that some cigarette brands are easier to smoke than others has increased, while there was no change over time in responses to the statement "some cigarette brands are easier to quit than others". White et al. 2015a conclude that further research is needed to determine whether continued exposure to standardized packs leads adolescents to develop more uncertainty or disagreement regarding brand differences in ease of smoking and quitting, perceived addictiveness and harms.[117]

82.   As explained previously, the Dominican Republic argues that in the absence of full access to the dataset, it is impossible to make an objective assessment of the findings in White et al. 2015a. According to the Dominican Republic, the published results in White et al. 2015a may provide an unduly positive and inaccurate impression of the full dataset.[118] The Dominican Republic notes that White et al. 2015a acknowledge that the impact of plain packaging and enlarged GHWs on deception are "mixed" and that the authors refrain from concluding that the pack changes have reduced deception.[119]

3.2   Analysis by the Panel

83.   Among the various peer-reviewed studies discussed by the parties, two assess the impact of the TPP measures and enlarged GHWs on the ability of the

---

[116]   See para. 20 above for a description of the ASSAD survey dataset. See also White et al. 2015a, (Exhibits AUS-186, DOM-235).

[117]   See White et al. 2015a, (Exhibits AUS-186, DOM-235).

[118]   See Dominican Republic's second written submission, paras. 443-456; and comments on Australia's response to Panel question No. 196, para. 390.

[119]   See Dominican Republic's comments on Australia's response to Panel question No. 200, paras. 793-794; and Ajzen Report, (Exhibit DOM/HND/IDN-3), paras. 174-178.

packaging of tobacco products to mislead consumers about the harmfulness of smoking among adult cigarette smokers and adolescents.

84.   A careful review of Wakefield et al. 2015 paper and the econometric evidence submitted by the Dominican Republic and Indonesia suggests that the impact of the TPP measures on the ability of the pack to mislead is much more mixed. Wakefield et al. 2015 only find a statistically significant impact of the TPP measures in reducing the belief that brands differ in harmfulness, but no impact on the belief that there is no difference in strength level across brands and that the current tobacco product is perceived as more harmful than a year ago.[120] While Ajzen et al. confirm these results, they also qualify the impact on the belief about difference in harmfulness across brands as being small and subject of wear-out.[121] Ajzen et al. and Professor Klick further claim that Wakefield et al. 2015 failed to report the result associated with the question on the harmfulness of their own brand, which according to them is statistically not significant. We note, however, that the results of the linear regression and ordered logistic regression suggest a small decrease in the proportion of adult smokers who do not have trouble believing that their brand is harmful, which is statistically significant at the 10% level.[122]

85.   We note that the empirical evidence reported in Wakefield et al. 2015 regarding the mixed impact of the TPP measures on the packaging ability to mislead among adult smokers is supported by White et al. 2015b in the case of adolescents. A review of White et al. 2015b suggests that, one year after their implementation, the TPP measures have had some impact in reducing adolescents' beliefs in difference in addiction and harmfulness across brands. However, the authors find that the TPP measures have had no impact on adolescents' belief that some brands are easier to quit than others and, surprisingly, a positive impact on the belief that some cigarette brands are easier to smoke than others.[123]

4.   OVERALL CONCLUSION ON POST-IMPLEMENTATION EVIDENCE ON NON-BEHAVIOURAL OUTCOMES

86.   Overall, based on the studies and expert reports before us and discussed above, the empirical evidence available to us regarding the impact of the TPP measures, together with enlarged GHWs, since their entry into force, on the proximal outcomes of interest suggests that:

---

[120]   See Wakefield et al. 2015, (Exhibits AUS-206, DOM-306).
[121]   See Ajzen et al. Data Report, (Exhibit DOM/IDN-2), paras. 123-127, 156-158, Appendix A, pp. 84-86.
[122]   See Ajzen et al. Data Report, (Exhibit DOM/IDN-2), Appendix A, pp. 85-86.
[123]   See White et al. 2015b, (Exhibits HND-135, DOM-236, DOM-288).

a. The TPP measures and enlarged GHWs have statistically significantly reduced the appeal of cigarettes among adult smokers.

b. The TPP measures and enlarged GHWs have statistically significantly increased GHWs' effectiveness on the noticeability of health warnings, avoidance of graphic health labels and pack concealment among adult cigarette smoker, albeit modestly for some outcomes, while the impact of the TPP measures and enlarged GHWs on adult cigarette smokers' health beliefs is relatively more limited and nuanced.

c. The TPP measures and enlarged GHWs have had a more mixed and limited impact on the ability of the pack to mislead adult cigarette smokers about the harmful effects of smoking.

d. While the TPP measures (together with enlarged GHWs) have contributed statistically significantly in reducing the appeal of cigarettes among adolescents, the impact of the TPP measures (with enlarged GHWs) on adolescents' health beliefs and cognitive processing of warning information on cigarettes packs is much more limited. Similarly, the impact of the TPP measures (with enlarged GHWs) on the ability of the pack to mislead adolescents about the harmful effects of smoking is more mixed and limited.

e. There has been a decrease in perceived packaging appeal when cigar and cigarillo smokers were exposed to the TPP measures (and enlarged GHWs). In addition, there has been an increase in the noticeability of health warnings and pack concealment among cigar and cigarillo smokers but the evidence is mixed regarding health beliefs.

87. No post-implementation empirical evidence has been presented to us on the impact of the TPP measures on the ability of the pack to mislead cigarillo and cigar smokers about smoking harms.

APPENDIX B

EVIDENCE ON QUITTING-RELATED OUTCOMES AND OTHER DISTAL OUTCOMES SINCE THE ENTRY INTO FORCE OF THE TPP MEASURES

1.   Earlier in these Reports, we referred to behaviours such as calling a Quitline and concealing a pack in public as "smoking-related behaviours". Australia's experts have referred to changes in quit intentions and quit attempts as "distal" outcomes of the TPP measures.[1] The Dominican Republic and Indonesia have similarly referred to quit intentions, secondary quit indicators, and quit attempts as "distal" outcomes and "antecedents of smoking behaviour".[2] We focus our discussion in this Appendix on the post-implementation evidence submitted by the parties with respect to these variables.

2.   Australia submits that several peer-reviewed studies, which focus on quitting-related cognitions, pack concealment, and quit attempts, confirm that the TPP measures have resulted in increased calls to Quitline and the number of quit attempts.[3] Australia further submits that the features of certain survey data are most suited to detecting changes in proximal outcomes (i.e. tobacco products appeal, GHW effectiveness, and ability of packaging to mislead) than in more distal variables, such as intentions and quitting-related behaviours.[4]

3.   The Dominican Republic and Indonesia submit that the TPP measures have not had the expected effects on the antecedents of behaviour posited by Australia's conceptual framework of the TPP measures. In particular, the Dominican Republic and Indonesia contend that beyond the obvious findings that the pack is less visually appealing and people more often notice the larger GHW first, empirical evidence shows little or no effects of the policies on the antecedents of behaviour. The Dominican Republic's, Honduras's and Indonesia's experts further argue that the empirical evidence shows that the TPP measures have had no impact on variables relating to quitting and relapse.[5] The Dominican Republic and Indonesia submitted expert reports dedicated to reviewing a series of peer-reviewed papers assessing the impact of the TPP measures on quitting-related outcomes. In some cases, the experts of the

---

[1]   See Chaloupka Rebuttal Report, (Exhibit AUS-582), para. 2; and NTPPTS Technical Report, (Exhibits AUS-570, HND-124, DOM-307), pp. 6 and 21.

[2]   Ajzen et al. Data Rebuttal Report, (Exhibit DOM/IDN-6), paras. 27 and 35.

[3]   Australia's second written submission, para. 464.

[4]   Australia's comments on the complainants' responses to Panel question No. 197, paras. 371-375.

[5]   See Ajzen et al. Data Report, (Exhibit DOM/IDN-2), paras. 10-22.

Dominican Republic, Honduras and Indonesia also re-analysed the data used in the studies.[6]

4.   In addition, the experts of the Dominican Republic and Indonesia contend that some of the published empirical studies relied upon by Australia provide an inaccurate picture of the empirical evidence. According to them, some of these papers failed to report the results for more than half of all variables available in the survey dataset, which were overwhelmingly not statistically significant, suggesting no impact of plain packaging on these variables. The Dominican Republic and Indonesia contend that the authors of some of these studies failed also to explain that a number of the reported statistically significant effects had "vanished" by the end of the first year of the TPP measures' implementation as a result of wear-out effects. The Dominican Republic and Indonesia further criticize these papers for failing to report the effects size of the statistically significant effects. According to their experts, most of the reported statistically significant effects are small, suggesting that they have little importance in shifting behaviour. The Dominican Republic and Indonesia also criticize the authors of one of the studies for having removed the effects of a non-existent daily trend in survey responses, which has distorted the analysis by finding wrongly statistically significant effects.[7]

5.   For each main type of outcome, namely quit intention, pack concealment and quit attempt, we discuss the survey data and corresponding papers separately, before turning to an overall assessment of the evidence before us. As in respect of the evidence relating to proximal outcomes addressed in Appendix A, we approach this assessment on the basis that our task is not to conduct our own econometric assessment of the impact of the TPP measures on the relevant outcomes but rather to examine, on the basis of the evidence before us, the overall robustness of the econometric evidence submitted by the parties in this respect.[8]

1.   EVIDENCE RELATING TO QUITTING-RELATED COGNITIONS SINCE THE ENTRY INTO FORCE OF THE TPP MEASURES

6.   Four peer-reviewed papers empirically analyse the impact of Australia's TPP measures on quitting-related cognitions: (i) Durkin et al. 2015; (ii) Yong

---

[6]   See Ajzen et al. Data Report, (Exhibit DOM/IDN-2); Ajzen et al. Second Data Report, (Exhibit DOM/IDN-4); Ajzen et al. Data Rebuttal Report, (Exhibit DOM/IDN-6); Ajzen et al. Second Data Rebuttal Report, (Exhibit DOM/IDN-8); and Klick Report, (Exhibit UKR-5).

[7]   See Ajzen et al. Data Report, (Exhibit DOM/IDN-2), paras. 23-27.

[8]   For a similar approach, see Panel Reports, *US – COOL (Article 21.5 – Canada and Mexico)*, para. 7.183 (citing Panel Reports, *US – COOL*, para. 7.539).

et al. 2015; (iii) White et al. 2015b; and (iv) Miller et al. 2015.[9] An expert report prepared by Professor Klick, submitted by Ukraine, also contains a study analysing the impact on quitting-related cognitions.[10]

1.1 Datasets and related studies

1.1.1 National Tobacco Plain Packaging Tracking Survey

7.   As described in Appendix A, the NTPPTS, funded by Australia's Department of Health and Ageing, is a nationwide tracking survey conducted from 9 April 2012 to 30 March 2014 with a follow-up survey of baseline participants from 7 May 2012 to 4 May 2014.[11] Durkin et al. 2015 employ the NTPPTS data to examine the effects of the TPP measures on short-term changes in quit intentions. The authors estimate various logistic models based on the respondents' experiences regarding quit intentions over the one-month follow-up period for the cohorts surveyed before the implementation of the TPP measures, over the transition period to TPP, and during the first year of implementation. The authors adjusted the models for baseline levels of the outcome and controlled for the date of the follow-up survey, number of days between baseline and follow-up surveys, anti-smoking television advertising in the three months prior to the follow-up survey, change in cigarette costliness, sex, age, education, socio-economic status, and addiction level.[12] Durkin et al. 2015 also present the results of unadjusted models, where the only control variable is the baseline response.

8.   Durkin et al. 2015 find that the TPP measures were associated with increased rates of quitting cognitions among adult cigarette smokers. In particular, compared to the referent group of smokers having completed their follow-up survey in the pre-TPP period, smokers who were followed-up with in the late transition period reported greater increases in their intentions to quit in the next month. However, the authors find that there was no statistically significant change in the proportion of adult smokers who were followed-up with in the first year of implementation of the TPP measures who thought daily about quitting in the past week, intended to quit in the next month or set a firm date to quit in the next month compared with the pre-TPP period.

9.   Ajzen et al., in their expert report submitted by the Dominican Republic and Indonesia, use the NTPPTS data to review the findings reported in Durkin et al. 2015. They argue that Durkin et al.'s 2015 conclusions are unwarranted and contradicted by the data. According to Ajzen et al., Durkin et al. 2015 overstate

---

[9]   See Durkin et al. 2015, (Exhibits AUS-215 (revised), DOM-305); Yong et al. 2015, (Exhibit DOM-382); White et al. 2015b, (Exhibits HND-135, DOM-236, DOM-288); and Miller et al. 2015, (Exhibits AUS-102, DOM-315).

[10]   See section 1.6.6 in the main body of these Reports for a description of Ukraine's participation in these proceedings.

[11]   Dominican Republic's second written submission, paras. 380-429.

[12]   See Durkin et al. 2015, (Exhibits AUS-215 (revised), DOM-305).

their findings because the TPP measures have had no impact on the majority of the quitting-related measures.[13] More generally, Ajzen et al. contend that Durkin et al. 2015 have adopted a very different and unorthodox comparison methodology compared to Wakefield et al. 2015, despite being the same six authors using the same dataset.

10.   Ajzen et al. submit that Durkin et al.'s analytical approach suffers from three serious methodological shortcomings. First, unlike Wakefield et al. 2015, Durkin et al. 2015 control for a non-existent daily trend that distorts the estimates of the impact of the TPP measures by conflating the contribution to behavioural change due to the daily trend on the one hand, and the TPP measures on the other. When the daily trend is removed from Durkin's own analysis, each of the significant results reported in Durkin et al. 2015 disappears.[14] Second, Durkin et al. 2015 failed to show that the statistically significant results experienced wear-out effects, with none of the results still significant in the final quarter of the first year following the introduction of the TPP measures.[15] Third, Durkin et al. 2015 did not correct for multiple significances tests that would have shown that none of the effects reported as being statistically significant by Durkin et al. 2015 remain statistically significant.[16] Ajzen et al. further argue that Durkin et al.'s claim that relying on changes in participants' responses from month to month minimizes the influence of sampling variation and increase the power of the statistical tests has been mathematically proven to be wrong.[17]

11.   Ajzen et al. present the results of a logistic model for dichotomized outcome variables, linear model for continuous outcome variables and ordered logit model for categorical outcome variables, controlling for the same covariates as Durkin et al. 2015 except for the date of the follow-up interview. They find no statistically significant change in the proportion of adult smokers who were followed-up in the first year of the TPP measures who thought daily about quitting in the past week, intended to quit in the next month or set a firm date to quit in the next month.[18] In addition, Ajzen et al. claim that Durkin et al. 2015 failed to report the result showing that the TPP measures did not bring about any increase in respondents' ability to perceive the importance of staying quit.[19]

12.   Professor Klick, in his expert report submitted by Honduras, looks at the NTPPTS data on the effect of the TPP measures on quitting-related cognitions and intentions.[20] Professor Klick claims that Wakefield et al. 2015 did not

---

[13]   See Ajzen et al. Data Report, (Exhibit DOM/IDN-2), paras. 174-179.
[14]   See Ajzen et al. Data Report, (Exhibit DOM/IDN-2), paras. 188-192.
[15]   See Ajzen et al. Data Report, (Exhibit DOM/IDN-2), paras. 193-195.
[16]   See Ajzen et al. Data Report, (Exhibit DOM/IDN-2), paras. 196-198.
[17]   See Ajzen et al. Data Report, (Exhibit DOM/IDN-2), paras. 184-185.
[18]   See Ajzen et al. Data Report, (Exhibit DOM/IDN-2), paras. 165-173, Appendix A, pp. 90-92.
[19]   See Ajzen et al. Data Report, (Exhibit DOM/IDN-2), para. 179.
[20]   See Klick Supplemental Rebuttal Report, (Exhibit HND-122), paras. 69-73, 88-100.

present the results of some variables related to quitting that did not improve or might have even gotten worse with the TPP measures.[21]

13.   Professor Klick presents the results of an ordered probit model, which controls for the TPP measures (early TPP period and formal TPP period), gender, age, education, socio-economic status and a linear time trend.[22] He finds that there is no evidence that the TPP measures increased the importance of quitting in respondents' mind. He reports, however, a negative and statistically significant impact of the TPP measures on the respondents' thoughts about quitting.[23]

14.   Professor Klick further contends that Durkin et al.'s 2015 results of the unadjusted models, which show that none of the quitting-related cognition variables are statistically distinguishable from the pre-TPP period, must be given appropriate weight and considered as at least equally valid compared with the results of the adjusted models, for various reasons.[24] First, Professor Klick claims that accounting for the respondent's characteristics does not seem necessary, because they should be captured by the individual's baseline response. Second, he argues that the variables for the individual's heaviness of smoking and cigarette price are likely to be endogenous, which could bias the estimates of the TPP measures. Third, he claims that the variable for the exposure to mass media anti-smoking messages, which is computed over a fixed three-month time-period, measures different things for different respondents and controlling for days between interviews does not address this problem. Finally, Professor Klick argues that Durkin et al. 2015 do not explain what adjusting the models for the date of the follow-up survey means.[25]

15.   Professor Chaloupka, Australia's expert, contends that Ajzen et al.'s analysis suffers from several limitations, in part resulting from the particular features of the NTPPTS data. As a result, this analysis creates more confusion than it provides help in understanding whether Australia is achieving the specific and broad objectives of the TPP measures.[26] In his view, the fact that there are inherent limitations to any data and analysis is the primary reason for considering the overall weight of the evidence based on a variety of data and

---

[21]   See Klick Supplemental Rebuttal Report, (Exhibit HND-122), paras. 61-63.
[22]   Professor Klick explains that unlike Wakefield et al. 2015 he omits the measure of exposure to mass media anti-smoking messages, cigarette costliness and heaviness of smoking index, because these variables are endogenous. He further explains that the inclusion of these variables does not change the results presented. See Klick Supplemental Rebuttal Report, (Exhibit HND-122), fn 35.
[23]   See Klick Supplemental Rebuttal Report, (Exhibit HND-122), paras. 69-73. We note that Professor Klick considers these two questions to be relevant to the appeal of tobacco.
[24]   Klick Supplemental Rebuttal Report, (Exhibit HND-122), paras. 91-100.
[25]   Klick Supplemental Rebuttal Report, (Exhibit HND-122), paras. 96-99.
[26]   See Australia's response to Panel question No. 196, para. 236; and Australia's comments on the complainants' responses to Panel question No. 197, paras. 369-376.

methods, rather than relying on any one set of data or analysis.[27] Professor Chaloupka argues that the NTPPTS data cannot be used to assess the impact of the TPP measures on the population most likely to be influenced by TPP, namely individuals who might have taken up tobacco use in the absence of the TPP. Professor Chaloupka further submits that because of its cross-sectional nature, the NTPPTS data limit the ability of analysts to follow the impact of the TPP measures through the pathway from its impact on the most proximal outcomes, like perceived appeal and noticing of the labels, through less proximal outcomes, such as increased interest in quitting, to the most distal outcomes, such as actual tobacco use behaviour. Professor Chaloupka is of the view that a true longitudinal survey tracking the impact of the TPP measures over a number of years on the same sample of current tobacco users and recent quitters would allow for the type of sequential analysis that would be more helpful in fully understanding how the TPP measures affect the more and less proximal outcomes they are expected to influence, as well as to more fully understand their impact on actual tobacco use behaviour.[28]

16.   According to Professor Chaloupka, Ajzen et al. fail to recognize that the power to detect statistically significant changes will fall for outcomes that are increasingly distal. The analysis of distal outcomes requires relatively large sample sizes to detect these increasingly smaller effects when it is based on all current tobacco users and recent quitters, and not just the subsample of users for whom more proximal outcomes were influenced by the TPP measures.[29] Professor Chaloupka further submits that given that the questions about quitting-related behaviours were only asked of smokers, any analysis that uses these as outcomes are likely to considerably understate the effects of the TPP measures on quitting⬚related intentions and behaviour. This is especially so given that the recent quitters whose intentions and behaviour are likely to have already been influenced by the TPP measures are not included in the analysis. Instead, analyses that employ these outcomes focus on the sample of smokers that are least likely to have been influenced by the TPP measures, making it less than surprising that the findings on the impact of the TPP measures on quitting-related behaviour variables are relatively weak.[30]

17.   Overall, Professor Chaloupka contends that the pattern of results reported by Ajzen et al. is consistent with the strengths and limitations of the NTPPTS data. As expected, Ajzen et al. found consistent and statistically significant effects for the impact of the TPP measures on the most proximal outcomes. The

[27]   See Chaloupka Rebuttal Report, (Exhibit AUS-582), paras. 2 and 10; Chaloupka Second Rebuttal Report, (Exhibit AUS-590), para. 12; and Chaloupka Third Rebuttal Report, (Exhibit AUS-604), para. 7.
[28]   See Chaloupka Rebuttal Report, (Exhibit AUS-582), paras. 2-5.
[29]   See Chaloupka Rebuttal Report, (Exhibit AUS-582), para. 6; and Chaloupka Third Rebuttal Report, (Exhibit AUS-604), paras. 4-5.
[30]   See Chaloupka Rebuttal Report, (Exhibit AUS-582), para. 7; Chaloupka Second Rebuttal Report, (Exhibit AUS-590), para. 20; and Chaloupka Third Rebuttal Report, (Exhibit AUS-604), para. 6.

impact is smaller, less statistically significant and less consistent as the focus shifts to less proximal outcomes, such as health knowledge and perceptions of the health risks. Likewise, the impact is smaller, less significant and less consistent as the focus shifts to more distal outcomes, including intentions and other quit⬜related measures.31

18.   Ajzen et al. respond that Professor Chaloupka's assertion that the more distal outcomes will be less affected by the policy than the more proximal outcomes is unfounded. In their view, this weakening of the policy across the chain of effect does not reflect a limitation of the NTPPTS data, but the theoretically expected decline in the impact of the TPP measures across the chain of effect from pack appeal to behaviour.[32] Ajzen et al. further contend that Professor Chaloupka's assertion that the NTPPTS data cannot reveal longer-term effects of the TPP measures because of its cross-sectional nature is unfounded. According to them, a cross-sectional design is widely used and accepted. In addition, the results found in the NTPPTS data are confirmed by the findings based on the longitudinal International Tobacco Control (ITC) Policy Evaluation Project (ITC Project).[33] Likewise, Ajzen et al. argue that Professor Chaloupka's assertion that the NTPPTS dataset has enough statistical power to detect small changes in the most proximal outcomes but not in more distal outcomes is unfounded. Ajzen et al. claim that the statistical power of the NTPPTS data to detect small changes in proximal and distal outcomes is very similar.[34] Similarly, Ajzen et al. contend that Professor Chaloupka's assertion that the NTPPTS data underestimate changes in some measures of intention because recent quitters who gave up smoking because of the TPP measures have not been asked is unfounded because the TPP measures did not increase quitting behaviours in the short term.[35]

1.1.2   International Tobacco Control Policy Evaluation Project

19.   As described in Appendix A, the ITC Project is a longitudinal cohort survey on the determinants of tobacco control policies in more than 20 countries, including Australia. The ITC Project covers a number of questions related to GHWs, including on consumers' thoughts, behaviours and intentions towards quitting.

20.   The Australian component of the ITC Project used by Yong et al. 2015 was conducted between September 2011 and February 2012 for the pre-implementation period and between February and May 2013 for the post-implementation period.

---

[31]   See Chaloupka Rebuttal Report, (Exhibit AUS-582), para. 9; and Chaloupka Third Rebuttal Report, (Exhibit AUS-604), paras. 2-7.
[32]   See Ajzen et al. Data Rebuttal Report, (Exhibit DOM/IDN-6), paras. 39-45.
[33]   See Ajzen et al. Data Rebuttal Report, (Exhibit DOM/IDN-6), paras. 46-49, Appendix I.
[34]   See Ajzen et al. Data Rebuttal Report, (Exhibit DOM/IDN-6), paras. 50-54, Appendix II.
[35]   See Ajzen et al. Data Rebuttal Report, (Exhibit DOM/IDN-6), paras. 55-62, Appendix III.

21.   Yong et al. 2015 analyse the relationship between health warning label reactions and quit intentions. The authors present the results of various GEE models controlling for age, sex, income, education, cigarettes per day, past year quit attempts, survey mode (phone vs. web) and wave of recruitment.[36]

22.   Yong et al. 2015 find that the TPP measures have led to a statistically significant increase in the proportion of adult smokers thinking more about smoking health risks and quitting as a result of the GHWs. In particular, they report a statistically significant increase in the proportion of respondents who did not focus on health warning labels first, but who now focus on them first, and thought more about quitting as a result of the health warning labels. Conversely, the subgroup of respondents who chose not to focus on the health warning labels experienced less cognitive reactions and thought less about quitting. In addition, Yong et al. 2015 find that adult smokers, who had been stimulated by health warning labels to think about the harm caused by smoking and about quitting, were more motivated to quit smoking in the future. In that context, the authors argue that the cognitive reactions serve as an important pathway through which the effects of more upstream reactions to the health warning labels exert their influence on quit intentions. Yong et al. 2015 explain, however, that given that the prediction of quit intentions was based on cross-sectional data, caution needs to be exercised in interpreting the finding as causal. The authors note that while intentions are logically subsequent to reported past reactions, it is possible that the person's intentional state may affect their recall of past reactions.[37]

23.   Ajzen et al., in their expert report submitted by the Dominican Republic and Indonesia, review Yong et al.'s analysis and submit that given that they only had access to a small subset of the ITC dataset, they were unable to present a comprehensive assessment of data, including correcting for the possibility of false positive findings due to multiple hypothesis testing (i.e. statistically significant results might have occurred by chance), controlling for anti-smoking advertising in mass media and testing for wear-out effects.[38] Ajzen et al. further contend that Yong et al. 2015 failed to report effect sizes, explore wear-out effects, correct for multiple hypothesis testing and justify their selection of outcome variables available in the ITC dataset. In particular, they criticise Yong et al. 2015 for not reporting the statistically significant or non-significant impact of the TPP measures on certain downstream variables.[39]

24.   Ajzen et al. find that although the TPP measures have had a small positive and statistically significant impact on thinking about quitting as a result of the GHWs, there was also a small but statistically significant decrease in the proportion of adult smokers that reported interest in quitting and intentions to

---

[36]   See Yong et al. 2015, (Exhibit DOM-382).
[37]   *Ibid.*
[38]   See Dominican Republic's comments on Australia's response to Panel question No. 196, paras. 409-414. See also Ajzen et al. Second Data Report, (Exhibit DOM/IDN-4), paras. 12-19.
[39]   See Ajzen et al. Second Data Report, (Exhibit DOM/IDN-4), paras. 30-37 and 53-58.

quit. According to Ajzen et al., Yong et al. 2015 did not report these two last results, which are in the "wrong direction" for the TPP measures.[40]

25.   Australia contends that Ajzen et al. correctly conclude that the TPP measures have significantly increased cognitive reactions to GHWs.[41] However, Australia is of the view that Ajzen et al., when concluding that interest in and intentions to quit decreased post-plain packaging, do not acknowledge or appear to appreciate that questions relating to quit intentions were not asked of recent quitters – the cohort whose intentions and behaviours were most likely to have been influenced by the TPP measures.[42] Australia concludes that consequently the sample Ajzen et al. used to analyse quit intentions was negatively biased. According to Ajzen et al., Australia and its experts do not contest the accuracy of their analytical approach or their results, and do not challenge their "serious criticisms" of Yong et al. 2015.[43] They submit that Australia's sole criticism regarding the ITC analysis seeks to denigrate the quality of the ITC dataset itself, claiming that it provides a "biased" sample to measure the impact on quit intentions and quit interests. According to Ajzen et al., Australia's argument assumes that the TPP measures led smokers to quit shortly after their introduction, and that these "recent quitters" were subsequently excluded from responding to questions on quit intentions and quit interests in the ITC survey. However, Ajzen et al. submit that the data show that no additional quit attempts were made post-implementation, which contradict Australia's argument. Further, Ajzen et al. consider it surprising to hear (for the first time) from Australia that the ITC dataset is "biased" in this regard because it was developed by the tobacco control community to measure the real-world impact of tobacco control measures, such as plain packaging, on smoking-related outcomes, including the impact of the TPP measures on quit intentions.[44] Ajzen et al. argue that it is only after having demonstrated that quit intentions have not increased post-implementation that Australia claims that the ITC sample is biased in relation to this particular measure.[45]

1.1.3   Australian Secondary Students Alcohol Smoking and Drug Survey

26.   As described in Appendix A, the 2013 ASSAD survey extension is a survey of students in 82 secondary schools in Victoria and Queensland tracking their beliefs and attitudes about cigarette packaging, ratings of popular cigarette brands, noticing health warnings on cigarette packs, awareness of the specific

---

[40]   See Ajzen et al. Second Data Report, (Exhibit DOM/IDN-4), paras. 24 and 28.

[41]   See Australia's response to Panel question No. 196, paras. 225 and 237.

[42]   Australia's response to Panel question No. 196, para. 237.

[43]   See Dominican Republic's comments on Australia's response to Panel question No. 196, paras. 409-414. See also Ajzen et al. Second Data Rebuttal Report, (Exhibit DOM/IDN-8), paras. 13-16.

[44]   See Ajzen et al. Second Data Rebuttal Report, (Exhibit DOM/IDN-8), paras. 15-16.

[45]   See Ajzen et al. Second Data Rebuttal Report, (Exhibit DOM/IDN-8), para. 14.

harms of tobacco use, and perceptions of the prevalence of smoking and intention to smoke.[46]

27.   White et al. 2015b employ the ASSAD survey data to examine the impact of the TPP measures on students aged 12-17 years. The authors estimate a logistic regression model of youth smokers' experience with quit intentions controlling for age, sex, school type, state and smoking status.[47]

28.   White et al. 2015b find that the TPP measures have had no impact in the proportion of students who, having seen a cigarette pack in the previous six months, thought about quitting smoking. The authors conclude that the data suggest that the introduction of the TPP measures did not induce adolescent to attend to and process warnings on cigarette packs to a greater extent than when GHWs covered 30% of the front of a fully branded pack.[48]

29.   According to the Dominican Republic, the results published in White et al. 2015b may provide an unduly positive and inaccurate impression of the full dataset, but without full access to the ASSAD survey data, it cannot make an objective assessment of White et al.'s findings.[49] The Dominican Republic further contends that although in another study White et al. 2015a conclude that there is a change in the visual appeal of packs among adolescents[50], that reduced appeal does not have any meaningful impact on quit intentions.[51]

1.1.4   Cigar and cigarillo smokers surveys

30.   Miller et al. 2015 conducted, in February and March 2014, individual interviews with regular premium cigar smokers, as well as two focus groups with premium cigarillo smokers and occasional premium cigar smokers, four focus groups with non-premium cigarillo smokers, and an online survey of current cigar and cigarillo smokers.[52] The interviews took place 15 months after the TPP measures became mandatory. The authors present descriptive statistics of the responses of these interviews, focus groups and the online survey.

31.   Miller et al. 2015 find that non-premium cigarillo smokers reported high plain packaging exposure and more contemplation of quitting.

32.   Ajzen et al., in their expert report submitted by the Dominican Republic and Indonesia, argue that the conclusions that can be drawn from the results reported by Miller et al. 2015 are limited by several methodological shortcomings, such as the non-representativeness of survey participants, the unsuitability of focus groups to draw causal inferences, failure to control for

---

[46]   See Dominican Republic's second written submission, paras. 443-456.
[47]   See White et al. 2015b, (Exhibits HND-135, DOM-236, DOM-288).
[48]   See White et al. 2015b, (Exhibits HND-135, DOM-236, DOM-288), p. ii56.
[49]   See Dominican Republic's second written submission, para. 445.
[50]   See White et al. 2015a, (Exhibits AUS-186, DOM-235).
[51]   See Dominican Republic's second written submission, paras. 443-456; and Dominican Republic's comments on Australia's response to Panel question No. 196, para. 390.
[52]   See Miller et al. 2015, (Exhibits AUS-102, DOM-315).

exposure to anti-smoking campaigns and changes in tobacco prices, and absence of "baseline" information collected before the implementation of the TPP measures.[53] They further claim that Miller et al. 2015 did not mention that the cigar and cigarillo smokers participating in the online survey reported no change in thinking about quitting. According to Ajzen et al., the TPP measures have had no impact on reported changes in thoughts about quitting among cigar and cigarillo smokers, because the TPP measures did not affect their ratings of the appeal, taste or quality of the products they currently smoked, their enjoyment of smoking or its perceived health risks. More generally, Ajzen et al. contend that smoking cigarettes and smoking cigars (or cigarillos) are different behaviours, with potentially different determinants, which implies that the findings about the TPP measures on cigarette-related cognitions and behaviours cannot be generalized to cigars.[54]

1.1.5 Commissioned Roy Morgan Research Survey (Australia and New Zealand)

33.   Roy Morgan Research dataset, commissioned by Professor Klick, is a survey of current or former (in the past 12 months) smokers in both Australia and New Zealand. The first wave of the survey was completed prior to the implementation of Australia's TPP measures between 2 November 2012 and 26 November 2012 in Australia and between 8 November 2012 and 1 December 2012 in New Zealand. Subsequent waves were carried out at three-month intervals up until February 2014.[55] Professor Klick employs the Roy Morgan Research data to estimate a difference-in-difference logit model that explains the respondents' experience with their intention to quit in Australia and New Zealand, controlling for the TPP measures, an Australian baseline variable, a common baseline variable and a post-TPP implementation time-period.

34.   Professor Klick finds that the TPP measures have had no statistically significant effect on smokers' quit intentions and expectations about future smoking in Australia relative to New Zealand. In particular, he reports no statistically significant impact of the TPP measures in Australia relative to New Zealand on the likelihood that the respondents seriously considered quitting smoking, had the desire, even slightly, to give up smoking, or had the intention to try to quit smoking in the next six months.[56] Similarly, Professor Klick's finds no statistically significant impact of the TPP measures on the likelihood that the respondents were thinking about increasing future smoking, smoking just as

---

[53] See Dominican Republic's second written submission, paras. 457-462. See also Ajzen et al. Data Report, (Exhibit DOM/IDN-2), paras. 251-262.
[54] See Ajzen et al. Data Report, (Exhibit DOM/IDN-2), paras. 251-262.
[55] See Klick Report, (Exhibit UKR-5), pp. 6-8. See section 1.6.6 in the main body of these Reports for a description of Ukraine's participation in these proceedings.
[56] See Klick Report, (Exhibit UKR-5), pp. 18 and 37-44.

much, trying and easing up future smoking, changing to a low tar brand or making a definitive attempt to quit.[57]

35.   As explained in Appendix A, Australia's expert, Dr Chipty, does not refer directly to Professor Klick's analysis of quitting-related cognitions outcomes based on the Roy Morgan Research data. However, a number of general criticisms formulated by Dr Chipty regarding Professor Klick's difference-in-difference analysis of smoking incidence are also relevant to the analysis of quitting-related cognitions outcomes. Dr Chipty submits that Professor Klick's analysis of the Roy Morgan Research data is invalid because the commissioned Roy Morgan survey does not include a pre-period and does not allow for distinguishing which respondents had noticed in plain packaging. Dr Chipty contends also that New Zealand is an invalid counterfactual for the purposes of studying the effects of plain packaging, because New Zealand increased the excise tax on cigarettes in January 2013 one month after the introduction of the TPP measures.[58]

1.2   Analysis by the Panel

36.   We note that only four peer-reviewed studies papers assess the impact of Australia's TPP measures and enlarged GHWs on quitting-related cognitions among adult cigarette smokers, cigar and cigarillo smokers and adolescents.

37.   A careful review of the Durkin et al. 2015 and Yong et al. 2015 papers and the econometric evidence submitted by the Dominican Republic, Honduras and Indonesia suggests that the impact of the TPP measures on quitting intentions among adult smokers is limited and mixed.

38.   We note that Durkin et al. 2015 only find some evidence that the TPP measures have had a positive and statistically significant impact on the intention to quit during the late transition period of the TPP. They report no statistically significant impact of the TPP measures on daily thoughts about quitting, intention to quit and setting a firm date to quit among adult smokers in the first year of the TPP.[59] We note that Ajzen et al., applying an alternative estimation methodology, which consists of re-estimating the model without the daily trend, confirm most of Durkin et al.'s results. We note, however, that the results of the logistic model reported by Ajzen et al. suggest that the TPP measures have had a positive and statistically significant (at the 10% level) impact on the likelihood of adult smokers reporting having set a firm date to quit in the next month. The results of the linear regression also suggest that the TPP measures have had a negative and statistically significant (at the 10% level) impact on quitting importance.[60] More generally, we note that Australia did not rebut Ajzen et al.'s and Professor Klick's alternative estimation methodology and

---

[57]   See Klick Report, (Exhibit UKR-5), pp. 18 and 37-47.
[58]   See Chipty Rebuttal Report, (Exhibit AUS-535) (SCI), paras. 54-71.
[59]   See Durkin et al. 2015, (Exhibits AUS-215 (revised), DOM-305).
[60]   See Ajzen et al. Data Report, (Exhibit DOM/IDN-2), paras. 165-173, Appendix A, pp. 90-92.

associated results. We are, however, not persuaded by Professor Klick's claim that unadjusted models, which do not control for individual characteristics, addiction level and other tobacco control policies (exposure to anti-smoking television advertising and cigarette costliness), should be considered at least equally valid compared with adjusted models that do control for these variables. We note that Ajzen et al. focused their analysis on the adjusted models. We further note that the econometric results for quitting-related variables (i.e. quitting importance, thoughts about quitting) reported by Professor Klick are also based on adjusted models that control for the respondent's individual characteristics. Professor Klick further acknowledges that the results he reported do not change when the variables for addiction level, exposure to anti-smoking television advertising and cigarette costliness are included in the model specification, which would suggest that the risk of endogenous bias might be limited.

39.   Unlike Durkin et al. 2015, Yong et al. 2015 find relatively more evidence of a positive impact of the TPP measures on quitting-related cognitions. In particular, Yong et al. 2015 report a statistically significant impact of the TPP measures on thinking more about quitting as a result of health warnings among adult smokers who switched from initially focusing away to focusing on health warning labels. They further find that adult smokers, having been stimulated by health warning labels to think about the harms of smoking and about quitting, reported being more motivated to quit smoking in the future.[61] We note that Ajzen et al. confirm that the TPP measures have had a positive and statistically significant impact on thinking about quitting but qualify it as small.[62] Ajzen et al. further report a small and statistically significant decrease in the proportion of adult smokers reporting their interest in quitting and intention to quit.[63] We note that Ajzen et al. do not offer an explanation as to why the TPP measures would have *decreased* smokers' interest in quitting and intention to quit. We note that it is conceivable that these findings could partly result from the fact that, as observed by Australia, questions on quitting intention were not asked of recent quitters, contrary to Ajzen et al.'s claim that the question was asked to both smokers and recent quitters, although it is not clear, in the absence of specific evidence relating to the number of recent quitters, to what extent this circumstance may account for the results.

40.   We observe that the conclusion that the impact of the TPP measures on quitting intentions is limited and mixed is confirmed by the two other peer-reviewed studies on adolescent and cigar and cigarillo smokers. White et al. 2015b suggest that the TPP measures have had no impact on thinking about

---

[61]   See Yong et al. 2015, (Exhibit DOM-382).
[62]   We note that Ajzen et al. only replicate one part of the analysis of Yong et al. 2015 and do not analyse the relationship of changes in attentional orientation response pattern with changes in GHW reactions and the association of GHWs with quit intentions.
[63]   See Ajzen et al. Second Data Report, (Exhibit DOM/IDN-4), paras. 24 and 28.

quitting smoking among adolescents, which is consistent with the findings reported in Durkin et al. 2015. Conversely, the descriptive statistics analysis of Miller et al. 2015 suggests that the share of non-premium cigarillo smokers contemplating quitting increased.[64] As explained in our review of the post-implementation studies before us on proximal outcomes[65], we see no basis to reject Miller et al.'s findings on the basis of Ajzen et al.'s criticism, noting that the result on quitting intentions reported in Miller et al. 2015 is in line with the results reported in Durkin et al. 2015. We note, however, that Miller et al. 2015 provide no empirical evidence on quitting intentions among (premium or non-premium) cigar smokers.

41.   Finally, as explained in our review of Professor Klick's analysis of GHW effectiveness and smoking incidence based on the commissioned Roy Morgan Research data, we question the robustness of his results. We question the validity of the pre-period of the commissioned data, because it corresponds to the TPP measures transition period, during which plain packs could already be sold on the Australian market. In addition, Professor Klick's analysis does not control for New Zealand's excise tax increase one month after the introduction of the TPP measures, which leads us to question the use of New Zealand as a counterfactual.[66]

2.   EVIDENCE RELATING TO PACK CONCEALMENT AND MICRO-INDICATORS OF CONCERN SINCE THE ENTRY INTO FORCE OF THE TPP MEASURES

42.   Six peer-reviewed papers analyse empirically the impact of Australia's TPP measures on distal outcomes related to quitting: (i) Durkin et al. 2015; (ii) Yong et al. 2015; (iii) Zacher et al. 2014; (iv) Zacher et al. 2015; (v) White et al. 2015b; and (vi) Miller et al. 2015.[67] Professor Klick, in his expert report submitted by Ukraine, also assesses the impact of the TPP measures on pack concealment and related variables.[68]

---

[64]   See Miller et al. 2015, (Exhibits AUS-102, DOM-315).
[65]   See Appendix A, paras. 32 and 71 above.
[66]   See Appendix A, para. 72 above.
[67]   See Durkin et al. 2015, (Exhibits AUS-215 (revised), DOM-305); Yong et al. 2015, (Exhibit DOM-382); Zacher et al. 2014, (Exhibits AUS-222 (revised), JE-24(68), DOM-286); Zacher et al. 2015, (Exhibits AUS-223 (revised), DOM-287); White et al. 2015b, (Exhibits HND-135, DOM-236, DOM-288); and Miller et al. 2015, (Exhibits AUS-102, DOM-315).
[68]   See section 1.6.6 in the main body of these Reports for a description of Ukraine's participation in these proceedings.

2.1   Datasets and related studies

2.1.1   National Tobacco Plain Packaging Tracking Survey

43.   Durkin et al. 2015 use the NTPPTS data to analyse the impact of the TPP measures on pack concealment and micro-indicators of concern.[69] The NTPPTS Technical Report measured two micro-indicators of concern about smoking, namely stubbing out a tobacco product before finishing due to thoughts about the harms of smoking, and stopping oneself from smoking despite an urge to smoke.[70] The authors estimate logistic models of the respondents' experiences regarding pack concealment and other related behaviours by adjusting for baseline levels and controlling for the date of the follow-up survey, number of days between baseline and follow-up survey, anti-smoking television advertising in the three months prior to the follow-up survey, change in cigarette costliness, addiction level and other individual characteristics.[71] Durkin et al. 2015 also present the results of unadjusted models, where the baseline response is the only control variable.

44.   Durkin et al. 2015 find that the TPP measures were associated with increased rates of pack concealment and micro-indicators of smoking concern among adult cigarette smokers.[72] In particular, they find that compared to the referent group of smokers having completed their follow-up survey in the pre-TPP period, smokers who were followed-up in the late transition period showed greater increases in pack concealment, amounting to several or many times in the previous month. Similarly, they find that smokers who were followed-up in the first year of the TPP measures reported greater increases in pack concealment and stubbing out their cigarettes before finishing them because they thought about the harm of smoking.[73]

45.   Ajzen et al., in their expert report submitted by the Dominican Republic and Indonesia, claim that Durkin et al.'s conclusions are unwarranted and contradicted by the data, because the TPP measures have had no impact on the majority of the quitting-related measures.[74] They further contend that Durkin et al. 2015 have adopted a very different and unorthodox comparison methodology compared to Wakefield et al. 2015, despite being the same six authors using the same dataset, including analysing the same variable on pack concealment. According to Ajzen et al., Durkin et al.'s 2015 analytical approach suffers from serious methodological shortcomings, including controlling for a non-existent daily trend, failing to investigate wear-out effects and not correcting

---

[69]   See Appendix A, para. 8 for a description of the NTPPTS data.

[70]   NTPPTS Technical Report, (Exhibits AUS-570, HND-124, DOM-307), p. 52.

[71]   See Durkin et al. 2015, (Exhibits AUS-215 (revised), DOM-305).

[72]   As discussed in Appendix A, Wakefield et al. 2015 used the NTPPTS data and concluded also that there was a statistically significant increase in smokers covering their packs. See Wakefield et al. 2015, (Exhibits AUS-206, DOM-306).

[73]   See Durkin et al. 2015, (Exhibits AUS-215 (revised), DOM-305).

[74]   See Ajzen et al. Data Report, (Exhibit DOM/IDN-2), paras. 174-179.

for multiple significances tests.[75] According to Ajzen et al., Durkin et al.'s 2015 assertion that analysing changes in the participants' responses from month to month minimizes the influence of sampling variation and increase the power of the statistical tests has been mathematically proven to be wrong.[76]

46.   Based on the NTPPTS data, Ajzen et al. estimate a logistic model for dichotomized outcome variables, linear model for continuous outcome variables and ordered logit model for categorical outcome variables with the same specification considered by Durkin et al. 2015 but without the variable for date of the follow-up interview. They find a statistically significant increase in the proportion of adult smokers, who were followed-up in the first year of TPP, who concealed their pack several or many times. However, they report no statistically significant change in the proportion of adult smokers who were followed-up in the first year of TPP, that stubbed out and foregone cigarettes several or many times.[77] Ajzen et al. further argue that Durkin et al. 2015 failed to report the result showing that the TPP measures has had no impact on respondents' ability to limit their consumption of cigarettes.[78]

47.   Professor Klick, in his expert report submitted by Honduras, analyses the NTPPTS data on the effect of the TPP measures on quitting-related variables.[79] Professor Klick claims that Wakefield et al. 2015 did not present the results of some variables related to quitting that did not improve or might have even gotten worse with the TPP measures.[80]

48.   Professor Klick presents the results of an ordered probit model controlling for the TPP measures (early TPP period and formal TPP period), gender, age, education, socio-economic status and a linear time trend.[81] He finds that the TPP measures had no statistically significant impact on stubbing out cigarettes because of thoughts about smoking harms.[82]

49.   Professor Klick further contends that Durkin et al.'s 2015 results of the unadjusted models, which show that none of the variables related to pack concealment and micro-indicators of concerns are statistically distinguishable from the pre-TPP period, must be given appropriate weight and considered as at

---

[75]   See Ajzen et al. Data Report, (Exhibit DOM/IDN-2), paras. 188-198.
[76]   See Ajzen et al. Data Report, (Exhibit DOM/IDN-2), paras. 184-185.
[77]   See Ajzen et al. Data Report, (Exhibit DOM/IDN-2), paras. 165-173, Appendix A, pp. 90-92.
[78]   See Ajzen et al. Data Report, (Exhibit DOM/IDN-2), para. 180.
[79]   See Klick Supplemental Rebuttal Report, (Exhibit HND-122), paras. 69-73 and 88-100.
[80]   See Klick Supplemental Rebuttal Report, (Exhibit HND-122), paras. 61-63.
[81]   Professor Klick explains that, unlike Wakefield et al. 2015, he omits the measure of exposure to mass media anti-smoking messages, cigarette costliness and heaviness of smoking index, because these variables are endogenous. He further explains that the inclusion of these variables do not change the results he presented. See Klick Supplemental Rebuttal Report, (Exhibit HND-122), fn 35.
[82]   See Klick Supplemental Rebuttal Report, (Exhibit HND-122), paras. 74-78 and 80-81. We note that in one of Professor Klick's specification, the impact of the early TPP period variable on stubbing out is negative and statistically significant.

least equally valid compared with the results of the adjusted models for various reasons.[83]

50.   As explained above, Australia's expert Professor Chaloupka argues that Ajzen et al.'s analysis suffer from several limitations, in part due to the fact that the NTPPTS data do not track non-smokers who might have taken up tobacco use in the absence of the TPP measures and are cross-sectional.[84] In that context, Professor Chaloupka submits that Ajzen et al. fail to recognize that given the analysis considers all current tobacco users and recent quitters, and not just the users for whom the TPP measures have influenced their more proximal outcomes, relatively large sample sizes are required to detect the increasingly smaller effects of more distal outcomes. According to Professor Chaloupka, it is therefore not surprising that by focusing on the sample of smokers least likely to have been influenced by the TPP measures, the findings on the impact of the TPP measures on quitting-related behaviour variables are relatively weak.[85]

51.   Ajzen et al. contend that, contrary to what Professor Chaloupka submits, the weakening of the TPP measures across the chain of effect from pack appeal to behaviour is not explained by the NTPPTS data's limitation, but by the theoretically expected decline in the impact of the TPP measures.[86] They further argue that the findings based on the NTPPTS, whose cross-sectional nature is widely used and accepted, are supported by those based on the longitudinal ITC survey data.[87] Ajzen et al. also claim that the NTPPTS dataset has enough statistical power to detect proximal and distal outcomes.[88] Likewise, Ajzen et al. disagree with Professor Chaloupka and argue that the NTPPTS data do not underestimate changes in some measures of secondary indicators because the TPP measures have had no impact on quitting behaviours in the short term.[89]

2.1.2   International Tobacco Control Policy Evaluation Project

52.   Yong et al. 2015 also use the ITC data to investigate the impact of the TPP measures on pack concealment and foregoing smoking behaviours. The authors present the results of a GEE model controlling for age, sex, income, education, cigarettes per day, past year quit attempts, survey mode (phone vs. web) and wave of recruitment.[90]

53.   Yong et al. 2015 find a statistically significant increase in the proportion of adult cigarette smokers that avoided health warning labels but no statistically

---

[83]   See para. 14 above for a full summary of Professor Klick's argument and Klick Supplemental Rebuttal Report, (Exhibit HND-122), paras. 91-100.
[84]   See para. 16 above for a full summary of Professor Chaloupka's arguments; and Chaloupka Rebuttal Report, (Exhibit AUS-582), paras. 2-5 and 10.
[85]   See Chaloupka Rebuttal Report, (Exhibit AUS-582), paras. 6-7 and 9.
[86]   See Ajzen et al. Data Rebuttal Report, (Exhibit DOM/IDN-6), paras. 39-45.
[87]   See Ajzen et al. Data Rebuttal Report, (Exhibit DOM/IDN-6), paras. 46-49, Appendix I.
[88]   See Ajzen et al. Data Rebuttal Report, (Exhibit DOM/IDN-6), paras. 50-54, Appendix II.
[89]   See Ajzen et al. Data Rebuttal Report, (Exhibit DOM/IDN-6), paras. 55-62, Appendix III.
[90]   See Yong et al. 2015, (Exhibit DOM-382).

significant change in the proportion of those foregoing cigarettes. Similarly, Yong et al. 2015 find that the subgroup of respondents that switched from initially focusing away to focusing on the health warning labels following the TPP measures' introduction avoided health warning labels, but did not forego cigarettes. Conversely, the subgroup of respondents, which chose to focus away from the health warning labels, avoided fewer health warning labels, but did not forego cigarettes.[91]

54.   As explained in the review of post-implementation studies on quit intentions, Ajzen et al., in their expert report submitted by the Dominican Republic and Indonesia, argue that they could not undertake a comprehensive assessment of the ITC dataset, because they only had access to a small subset of the data.[92] They further claim that Yong et al. 2015 did not discuss effect sizes, analyse wear out effects and account for multiple hypothesis testing. They also criticise Yong et al. 2015 for failing to justify the outcome variables available in the ITC dataset they selected for their analysis and to report the results of some variables. Ajzen et al. replicate the analysis of Yong et al. 2015 by re-estimating GEE models controlling for the survey mode (phone vs. web) and wave of recruitment, as well as respondents' age, sex, income, education, cigarettes per day consumed and past year quit attempts.[93]

55.   Ajzen et al. find that although the TPP measures have had a moderate positive and statistically significant impact on avoiding health warning labels, the TPP measures did not prompt smokers to forego cigarettes.[94]

56.   Australia contends that Ajzen et al. correctly conclude that the TPP measures have significantly increased avoidance of GHWs.[95] However, Australia argues that when Ajzen et al., conclude that interest in and intentions to quit decreased post-plain packaging, they do not acknowledge or appear to appreciate that questions relating to quit intentions were not asked of recent quitters, which are the cohort whose intentions and behaviours were most likely to have been influenced by the TPP measures.[96] Australia concludes that consequently the sample Ajzen et al. used to analyse quit intentions was negatively biased. The Dominican Republic disagrees with Australia's argument. According to Ajzen et al., the exclusion of recent quitters could not have produced a biased sample because the ITC data show that the number of quitters was about the same before and after implementation of the TPP measures, implying that Australia's argument is contradicted by the data.[97] Further, Ajzen et al. consider it surprising to hear (for the first time) from Australia that the ITC

---

[91]   *Ibid.*
[92]   See Dominican Republic's comments on Australia's response to Panel question No. 196, paras. 409-414. See also Ajzen et al. Second Data Report, (Exhibit DOM/IDN-4), paras. 12-19.
[93]   See Ajzen et al. Second Data Report, (Exhibit DOM/IDN-4), paras. 30-37 and 53-58.
[94]   See Ajzen et al. Second Data Report, (Exhibit DOM/IDN-4), paras. 22-27.
[95]   See Australia's response to Panel question No. 196, paras. 225 and 237.
[96]   Australia's response to Panel question No. 196, para. 237.
[97]   See Ajzen et al. Second Data Rebuttal Report, (Exhibit DOM/IDN-8), paras. 15-16.

dataset is "biased" in this regard because it was developed by the tobacco control community to measure the real-world impact of tobacco control measures, such as plain packaging, on smoking-related outcomes, including quit intentions.[98]

2.1.3   Personal pack display dataset

57.   CCV undertook an observational survey of the prevalence of cigarette pack display and smoking in outdoor venues in Victoria and South Australia between October 2011 and April 2012, and again between October 2012 and April 2013 and between January and April 2014. The survey provides information on active smoking rates and personal display of cigarette packs on tables observed among patrons of public venues with outdoor seating (visible from the footpath) before and after the introduction of Australia TPP measures. Two peer-reviewed papers employed the personal pack display data.

58.   Zacher et al. published two papers assessing empirically the impact of the TPP measures on pack display, smoking and pack orientation. Zacher et al. 2014 use the personal pack display dataset to analyse the rates of pack display, smoking and pack orientation between October and April 2011-2012 (pre-TPP period) and 2012-2013 (post-TPP).[99] The authors report the results of a multi-level Poisson regression analysis. Zacher et al. 2014 find that the TPP measures reduced active smoking in outdoor areas of cafés, restaurants and bars, reduced personal pack display on tables, and increased steps taken by smokers to conceal packs that would otherwise be visible. In particular, the authors find that the decrease of pack display was stronger in venues with children present and limited to mid- and high- socio-economic status areas. Conversely, the decrease in packs orientated face-up was found to be stronger in low socio-economic status areas.

59.   Zacher et al. 2015 re-analyse the rates of pack display, smoking and pack orientation   by   extending   the   period   of   analysis   with   a   longer post-implementation period, between January and April 2012 (pre-TPP period), 2013 (early post-TPP period) and 2014 (one year post-TPP period).[100] The authors conclude that after one year Australia's TPP measures have reduced visibility of tobacco products and active smoking in public venues, particularly in the presence of children. In particular, the authors report a statistically significant decrease in pack display from pre-TPP to early post-TPP that remained low after one year following the introduction of the TPP measures. That being said, Zacher et al. 2015 find that the statistically significant change from pre-TPP to early post-TPP was not sustained one year post-TPP for packs orientated face-up, packs concealed by telephones, wallets or other items and for the use of external case.

---

[98]   See Ajzen et al. Second Data Rebuttal Report, (Exhibit DOM/IDN-8), para. 6.
[99]   See Zacher et al. 2014, (Exhibits AUS-222 (revised), JE-24(68), DOM-286).
[100]   See Zacher et al. 2015, (Exhibits AUS-223 (revised), DOM-287).

60.   Ajzen et al., in their expert report submitted by the Dominican Republic and Indonesia, reviewed the accuracy and completeness of the findings reported in Zacher et al. 2015. According to Ajzen et al., Zacher et al. 2015 failed to report or discuss effect sizes.[101] Ajzen et al. further argue that Zacher et al.'s explanation that pack changes may have made smokers less inclined to smoke in public is hard to reconcile with the finding that pack display did not decline among smokers, who continued to smoke at outdoor venues, and that smokers' pack avoidant behaviours vanished within a year. Ajzen et al. contend that Zacher et al.'s alternative explanation, according to which the small decline observed in outdoor smoking could reflect the overall declining trend in smoking in Australia, seems more consistent with the data. According to Ajzen et al., Zacher et al. 2015 acknowledge that the Personal Pack Display dataset is unable to establish whether the small decline observed in outdoor smoking was caused by the implementation of the TPP measures.[102] Ajzen et al. replicated Zacher et al's 2015 analytical approach and conclude that although there was a small decrease in packs displayed and active smoking at outdoor venues, pack-avoidant behaviours such as packs orientated face-up, packs concealed and use of external case, "had entirely vanished" one-year after the implementation of the TPP measures.[103]

61.   Australia submits that there is no evidence before the Panel to support a finding that the impact of the TPP measures will wear out. Australia argues that Professor Ajzen relies on the two studies by Zacher et al. 2014, 2015 to support the claim of wear out, although Ajzen et al. concede that Zacher et al. 2014, 2015 demonstrate that there was a statistically significant decline in active smoking at outdoor venues after the introduction of tobacco plain packaging, an effect which was enhanced over time. Similarly, Australia argues that while the Dominican Republic and Indonesia contend that changes in the way packs are displayed at outdoor venues wore out over the course of the study, Ajzen et al. concede that there was a statistically significant and lasting decline in the total number of packs displayed.[104]

62.   The Dominican Republic disagrees with Australia's claim that a statistically significant decline in outdoor smoking was enhanced over time and that the TPP measures have already been successful in reducing smoking prevalence. The Dominican Republic argues that outdoor smoking initially declined and then increased again, although it did not return to its earlier level. The Dominican Republic further submits that Zacher et al. 2015 themselves acknowledge that the finding on the level of outdoor smoking cannot be

---

[101]   See Dominican Republic's second written submission, para. 487; response to Panel question No. 126, paras. 294-297; and comments on Australia's response to Panel question No. 196, paras. 416 and 419-423.
[102]   See Ajzen et al. Second Data Report, (Exhibit DOM/IDN-4), paras. 42 and 45-47.
[103]   See Ajzen et al. Second Data Report, (Exhibit DOM-IDN-4), paras. 38-47 and 59-60.
[104]   See Australia's response to Panel question No. 196, paras. 246-247.

attributed to the TPP measures, because they did not control for a host of unrelated factors that could explain the decline in outdoor smoking levels.[105]

2.1.4 Australian Secondary Students Alcohol Smoking and Drug Survey

63. White et al. 2015b use the ASSAD survey data to examine the impact of the TPP measures on foregoing behaviours by students aged 12-17 years. The authors estimate a logistic regression model controlling for age, sex, school type, state and smoking status.[106]

64. White et al. 2015b find that the TPP measures have had no impact on the proportion of students, who had seen a cigarette pack in the previous six months, and that did not have a cigarette because of the health warnings. The authors conclude that the data suggest that the introduction of the TPP measures did not induce adolescents to attend to and process warnings on cigarette packs to a greater extent than when GHWs covered 30% of the front of a fully branded pack.[107]

65. The Dominican Republic submits that it could not make an objective assessment of White et al.'s findings without full access to the ASSAD survey data. The Dominican Republic further argues that although in a different study White et al. 2015a conclude that the TPP measures have reduced the visual appeal of packs among adolescents[108], that reduced appeal does not have any meaningful impact on quit intentions and secondary indicators of quitting.[109]

2.1.5 Cigar and cigarillo smokers surveys

66. Miller et al. 2015 use the responses from a series of interviews, focus groups and an online survey of current cigar and cigarillo smokers and find that premium cigar and cigarillo smokers, who were exposed to the TPP measures, tried to avoid the health warning labels by decanting the individual cigars and cigarillos from the box to a humidor or an unbranded tin. Similarly, they report an increase in pack concealment among non-premium cigarillo smokers.[110]

67. Ajzen et al., in their expert report submitted by the Dominican Republic and Indonesia, consider that the conclusions that can be drawn from Miller et al.'s results are limited by several methodological shortcomings, such as the

---

[105] See Ajzen et al. Second Data Rebuttal Report, (Exhibit DOM/IDN-8), paras. 17-21; Dominican Republic's second written submission, para. 487; Dominican Republic's response to Panel question No. 126, paras. 294-297; and Dominican Republic's comments on Australia's response to Panel question No. 196, paras. 416 and 419-423.
[106] See White et al. 2015b, (Exhibits HND-135, DOM-236, DOM-288).
[107] See White et al. 2015b, (Exhibits HND-135, DOM-236, DOM-288), p. ii56.
[108] See Appendix A, paras. 20-22 and 80-81 (reviewing White et al. 2015a, (Exhibits AUS-186, DOM-235)).
[109] See Dominican Republic's second written submission, paras. 443-456; and comments on Australia's response to Panel question No. 196, para. 390.
[110] See Miller et al. 2015, (Exhibits AUS-102, DOM-315).

non-representativeness of survey participants, unsuitability to draw causal inferences from focus groups and interviews, failure to control for confounding factors, and absence of "baseline" information collected before the TPP measures' implementation. They further argue that Miller et al. 2015 failed to report that the online survey participants in the online survey reported no change in stubbing out cigars or cigarillos and in stopping smoking. More generally, Ajzen et al. submit that any findings about the TPP measures on cigarette-related cognitions and behaviours cannot be generalized to cigars because smoking cigarettes and smoking cigars are different behaviours, with potentially different determinants.[111]

2.1.6 Commissioned Roy Morgan Research Survey (Australia and New Zealand)

68.   Professor Klick uses the Roy Morgan Research data to estimate a difference-in-difference logit model that explains the respondents' experiences concealing their packs in Australia and New Zealand, controlling for the TPP measures, an Australian baseline variable, a common baseline variable and a post-TPP implementation time-period.[112]

69.   Professor Klick concludes that the TPP measures have had no statistically significant effect on smokers' preferences or feelings about being seen with a plain pack in Australia relative to a non-plain pack in New Zealand.[113] In particular, Professor Klick finds no statistically significant impact of the TPP measures in Australia relative to "regular" packs in New Zealand on the likelihood of respondents reporting they had placed a cover over the cigarettes, placed the cigarettes in a different container or kept the pack out of sight.[114] Professor Klick further reports no statistically significant impact of the TPP measures in Australia relative to New Zealand on the likelihood the respondents successfully giving up smoking for more than a month, switching to a brand with lower tar or nicotine, reducing the number of cigarettes smoked in a day, or recently stopping smoking for 24 hours at least once during the last three months. In addition, he reports no statistically significant impact on the likelihood of the respondents increasing the number of cigarettes smoked, unsuccessfully trying to switch to a brand with lower tar or nicotine or unsuccessfully trying to reduce the number of cigarettes smoked in a day.[115]

70.   Although Australia's expert Dr Chipty does not address directly Professor Klick's analysis of pack concealment behaviours based on the Roy Morgan Research data, she raises several criticisms of Professor Klick's

---

[111]   See Dominican Republic's second written submission, paras. 457-462. See also Ajzen et al. Data Report, (Exhibit DOM/IDN-2), paras. 251-262.

[112]   See Appendix A, paras. 62-63 and Appendix B, para. 33 for a description of the Roy Morgan Research data.

[113]   See Klick Report, (Exhibit UKR-5), pp. 18 and 54-56.

[114]   Ibid.

[115]   See Klick Report, (Exhibit UKR-5), pp. 18 and 37-44.

difference-in-difference analysis of smoking incidence, which also apply to his analysis of pack concealment behaviours. Dr Chipty contends that Professor Klick's analysis of the Roy Morgan Research data is invalid because the Roy Morgan survey does not contain a pre-period and is unable to distinguish which respondents had noticed plain packaging. Dr Chipty further argues that New Zealand is an invalid counterfactual for the purposes of studying the effects of plain packaging, because New Zealand increased its excise tax in January 2013, one month after the introduction of the TPP measures.[116]

2.2   Analysis by the Panel

71.   The parties submitted five peer-reviewed papers that investigate empirically the impact of the TPP measures and enlarged GHWs on pack concealment and micro-indicators of concern. While four of these studies use responses of survey data on adult smokers, cigar and cigarillo smokers or adolescents, the two papers by Zacher et al. 2014, 2015 analyse actual observed behaviours of pack concealment among adult smokers. In addition, an expert report prepared by Professor Klick, submitted by Ukraine, contains a study assessing the impact of the TPP measures on pack concealment.[117]

72.   A careful assessment of Durkin et al. 2015, Yong et al. 2015 and Zacher et al. 2014, 2015 and the econometric evidence submitted by the Dominican Republic, Honduras and Indonesia suggests that the TPP measures have increased pack concealment among adult cigarette smokers. However, empirical evidence of the impact of the TPP measures on stubbing out cigarettes before finishing them due to thoughts about the harms caused by smoking and stopping smoking among adult cigarette smokers is much more limited and mixed.

73.   We note that Durkin et al. 2015 find some evidence that the TPP measures have had a positive and statistically significant impact on pack concealment and stubbing out cigarettes but no impact on stopping smoking among adult cigarette smokers in the first year of implementation of the TPP measures.[118] Ajzen et al., applying an alternative estimation methodology and correcting for multiple testing bias, reverse the results reported in Durkin et al. 2015 and find that the TPP measures have had no impact on pack concealment, stubbing out or stopping smoking.[119] Similarly, Professor Klick, using a different model specification, finds that the TPP measures had no impact

---

[116]   See Chipty Rebuttal Report, (Exhibit AUS-535) (SCI), paras. 54-71.
[117]   See section 1.6.6 in the main body of these Reports for a description of Ukraine's participation in these proceedings.
[118]   See Durkin et al. 2015, (Exhibits AUS-215 (revised), DOM-305).
[119]   See Ajzen et al. Data Report, (Exhibit DOM/IDN-2), paras. 188-198. We note that a comparison of the results with and without the trend variable shows that the coefficient of the constant variable is very large when the trend variable is included in the model specification. The coefficient value of the other variables is usually marginally affected by removing the trend variable.

on stubbing out. We note that Australia did not challenge Ajzen et al.'s and Professor Klick's alternative estimation methodology and results, but generally considers that the structure of the NTPPTS is likely to be more suited to detecting changes in proximal outcomes than in more distal variables, such as quitting-related behaviours.[120] As explained in our review of the evidence on quitting-related cognition, we are not persuaded by Professor Klick's claim that unadjusted models, which do not control for individual characteristics and tobacco control policies, should be considered at least equally valid compared to adjusted models, noting that Ajzen et al. focused their analysis on adjusted models and Professor Klick presented econometric results for stubbing out based on an adjusted model that controls for the respondent's individual characteristics.[121]

74.   We observe that the results presented in Yong et al. 2015 are partially in line with those in Durkin et al. 2015. Yong et al. 2015 report a positive and statistically significant impact of the TPP measures on avoiding the health warning labels and a statistically non-significant impact on foregoing among adult smokers.[122] We note that Ajzen et al. confirm that the TPP measures have had a positive and statistically significant impact on avoiding GHWs and that they qualify it as a medium effect.[123]

75.   The empirical evidence regarding the positive impact of the TPP measures on smokers' avoidant responses published in Durkin et al. 2015 and Yong et al. 2015 is to some extent corroborated by Zacher et al.'s 2014, 2015 papers, who suggest that one year after the introduction of the TPP measures, the display of personal pack in outdoor areas of cafés, restaurants and bars has decreased, particularly in the presence of children.[124] Zacher et al. 2015 find, however, that the reduction in the proportion of packs oriented face-up and the increase in concealed packs by telephones, wallets or other items and in the use of external cases was not sustained one year after the introduction of the TPP measures. We note that Ajzen et al.'s analysis of the Personal Pack Display dataset confirms all the findings reported in Zacher et al. 2015 but that they qualify the impact for both packs displayed and active smoking at outdoor venues as small.[125]

---

[120]   See Australia's comments on the complainants' responses to Panel question No. 197, paras. 371-375.
[121]   Professor Klick further acknowledges that the results he reported do not change when the variables for addiction level, exposure to anti-smoking television advertising and cigarette costliness are included in the model specification, which would suggest that the risk of endogenous bias might be limited.
[122]   See Yong et al. 2015, (Exhibit DOM-382).
[123]   See Ajzen et al. Second Data Report, (Exhibit DOM/IDN-4), paras. 22-27.
[124]   See Zacher et al. 2014, (Exhibits AUS-222 (revised), JE-24(68), DOM-286); and Zacher et al. 2015, (Exhibit AUS-223 (revised), DOM-287).
[125]   See Ajzen et al. Second Data Report, (Exhibit DOM/IDN-4), para. 44.

76. Similarly, the limited available evidence on adolescents and cigar and cigarillo smokers corroborates part of the findings reviewed above. Although White et al. 2015b provide no empirical evidence on pack concealment among young smokers, they find that the TPP measures have had no statistically significant impact on the frequency of not having a cigarette because of the health warnings[126], which is in line with the findings on foregoing smoking reported in Durkin et al. 2015 and Yong et al. 2015. The descriptive statistics analysis by Miller et al. 2015 suggests that the share of premium cigar and cigarillo smokers and of non-premium cigarillo smokers reporting decanting the cigar from the boxed to a humidor or concealing their pack have increased[127], which is partially in line with the results reported in Durkin et al. 2015, Yong et al. 2015 and Zacher et al. 2014, 2015. As explained in more detail in Appendix A, we see no basis to reject entirely Miller et al.'s findings on the basis of Ajzen et al.'s criticism.[128]

77. Finally, as explained above and in our review of Professor Klick's analysis of GHWs effectiveness and smoking incidence based on the commissioned Roy Morgan Research data, we question the validity of the pre-period of the commissioned data and the use of New Zealand as a counterfactual, and therefore the overall robustness of Professor Klick's results based on these data.[129]

3. EVIDENCE RELATING TO QUIT ATTEMPTS SINCE THE ENTRY INTO FORCE OF THE TPP MEASURES

78. Two peer-reviewed papers investigate empirically the impact of Australia's TPP measures on quit attempts: (i) Durkin et al. 2015 and Young et al. 2014.[130] The expert report by Professor Klick, submitted by Ukraine, also contains an analysis of the impact of the TPP measures on quitting.[131]

3.1 Datasets and related studies

3.1.1 National Tobacco Plain Packaging Tracking Survey

79. Durkin et al. 2015 use the NTPPTS data to assess the impact of the TPP measures on short-term changes in quitting-related behaviours. The authors estimate various logistic models of respondents' experiences with quit attempts by adjusting for baseline levels and controlling for the date of the follow-up survey, number of days between baseline and follow-up survey, anti-smoking

---

[126] See White et al. 2015b, (Exhibits HND-135, DOM-236, DOM-288).
[127] See Miller et al. 2015, (Exhibits AUS-102, DOM-315).
[128] See Appendix A, paras. 32 and 71 above.
[129] See Appendix A, para. 72 above.
[130] See Durkin et al. 2015, (Exhibits AUS-215 (revised), DOM-305); Young et al. 2014, (Exhibits AUS-214, JE-24(67), DOM-285).
[131] See section 1.6.6 in the main body of these Reports for a description of Ukraine's participation in these proceedings.

television advertising in the three months prior to the follow-up survey, change in cigarette costliness, addiction level and demographic characteristics.[132] Durkin et al. 2015 also present the results of unadjusted models, where the only control variable is the baseline response.

80.   Durkin et al. 2015 find that the TPP measures were associated with increased rates of quit attempts among adult cigarette smokers. In particular, the authors report that compared to the referent group of smokers who completed their follow-up survey in the pre-TPP period, smokers who were followed-up in the early transition period showed significantly greater increases in quit attempt in the past month. Similarly, smokers who were followed-up in the first year of TPP showed greater increases in quit attempt in the past month.[133]

81.   Ajzen et al., in their expert report submitted by the Dominican Republic and Indonesia, claim that Durkin et al.'s conclusions are unwarranted and contradicted by the data. According to Ajzen et al., Durkin et al. 2015 overstate their findings because they failed to report the results showing that the TPP measures did not bring about any increase in respondents' attempts to ever quit, to quit more than once, and to quit for more than one week between baseline and follow-up.[134] More generally, Ajzen et al. criticize Durkin et al. 2015 for having adopted a very different and unorthodox methodology than in Wakefield et al. 2015, despite being the same six authors using the same dataset. In their view, Durkin et al.'s analytical approach suffers from three serious methodological shortcomings, namely controlling for a non-existent daily trend, not investigating wear-out effects and not correcting for multiple significances tests.[135] Ajzen et al. further argue that, contrary to Durkin et al.'s claim, relying on changes in the responses of participants from month to month does not minimize the influence of sampling variation and increase the power of the statistical tests.[136]

82.   Ajzen et al. estimate a logistic model for dichotomized outcome variables, a linear model for continuous outcome variables and an ordered logit model for categorical outcome variables, which include the same covariates considered by Durkin et al. 2015 except for the dates of the follow-up interviews. They find that the TPP measures have had virtually no significant effect on quit attempts among adult cigarette smokers. In particular, they find no statistically significant change in the proportion of adult smokers who were followed-up in the first year of TPP that attempted to ever quit, attempted more than once to quit, and attempted to quit for more than one week, which Durkin et al. 2015 failed to report. The only exception is a positive and statistically significant but short-lived effect of the TPP measures on calls to Quitline to help with the last

---

[132]   See Durkin et al. 2015, (Exhibits AUS-215 (revised), DOM-305).
[133]   *Ibid.*
[134]   See Ajzen et al. Data Report, (Exhibit DOM/IDN-2), paras. 174-180.
[135]   See Ajzen et al. Data Report, (Exhibit DOM/IDN-2), paras. 188-198.
[136]   See Ajzen et al. Data Report, (Exhibit DOM/IDN-2), paras. 184-185.

quit attempt, which was also not published in Durkin et al. 2015. Ajzen et al. further find that for the quit-related variables considered in Durkin et al. 2015, the TPP measures have statistically increased the proportion of adult smokers who attempted to quit in past month in the linear and ordered logistic regressions, but in the logistic regression the TPP measures have reduced their attempts to quit in past month.[137]

83.   Professor Klick submits that the results of the unadjusted models, which show that none of the variables related to quit attempts are statistically distinguishable from the pre-TPP period, must be given appropriate weight and considered as at least equally valid compared with the results of the adjusted models for various reasons.[138]

84.   As mentioned in the review of quitting-related cognitions and pack concealment, Professor Chaloupka, Australia's expert, submits that Ajzen et al.'s analysis suffers from several limitations that are partly related to the structure of the NTPPTS data, which do not include non-smokers who might have taken up tobacco use in the absence of the TPP measures and are cross-sectional.[139] In that context, Professor Chaloupka argues that Ajzen et al. do not recognize that relatively large sample sizes are required to detect the increasingly smaller effects of more distal outcomes, because the sample includes all current tobacco users and recent quitters, and not just the users influenced by the TPP measures in terms of more proximal outcomes. Professor Chaloupka is of the view that it is not surprising that the findings on the impact of the TPP measures on quitting-related behaviour variables are relatively weak when one considers the sample of smokers, who are least likely to have been influenced by the TPP measures.[140]

85.   Ajzen et al. disagree with Professor Chaloupka and claim that the declining impact of the TPP measures across the chain of effect is not due to the NTPPTS data's limitation but to the theoretically expected decline in the impact of the TPP measures.[141] They further contend that the findings based on the NTPPTS, whose cross-sectional nature is widely used and accepted, are corroborated by those obtained using the longitudinal ITC survey data.[142] Ajzen et al. are also of the view that the NTPPTS dataset has enough statistical power to detect proximal and distal outcomes.[143] Ajzen et al. claim that given the

---

[137] See Ajzen et al. Data Report, (Exhibit DOM/IDN-2), paras. 165-173, Appendix A, pp. 90-92.

[138] See para. 14 above for a full summary of Professor Klick's argument and Klick Supplemental Rebuttal Report, (Exhibit HND-122), paras. 91-100.

[139] See para. 15 above for a full summary of Professor Chaloupka's arguments; and Chaloupka Rebuttal Report, (Exhibit AUS-582), paras. 2-5 and 10.

[140] See Chaloupka Rebuttal Report, (Exhibit AUS-582), paras. 6-7 and 9; and Chaloupka Third Rebuttal Report, (Exhibit AUS-604), paras. 2-7.

[141] See Ajzen et al. Data Rebuttal Report, (Exhibit DOM/IDN-6), paras. 39-45.

[142] See Ajzen et al. Data Rebuttal Report, (Exhibit DOM/IDN-6), paras. 46-49, Appendix I.

[143] See Ajzen et al. Data Rebuttal Report, (Exhibit DOM/IDN-6), paras. 50-54, Appendix II.

TPP measures have had no impact on quitting behaviours in the short term, the NTPPTS data do not underestimate changes in quit attempts.[144]

3.1.2 International Tobacco Control Policy Evaluation Project

86.   In their review of Yong et al. 2015, who use the ITC data to analyse whether the TPP measures are associated with increased desirable reactions towards the health warning labels, Ajzen et al., in their expert report submitted by the Dominican Republic and Indonesia, criticise the authors for not reporting the results of actual smoking behaviour. They reconsider the ITC data and estimate a GEE model of the decision to attempt to quit in the last 12 months controlling for the survey mode (phone vs. web) and wave of recruitment, as well as the respondents' ages, sex, income, education, cigarettes per day consumed and past year quit attempts.[145]

87.   Ajzen et al. find no statistically significant change in the proportion of adult smokers that attempted to quit in the last 12 months. They note that this result was not reported in Yong et al. 2015.[146]

88.   Professor Chaloupka is of the view that Ajzen et al. do not recognize that the impact of the TPP measures should be smaller for more distal outcomes, when one looks at the impact in the overall sample of smokers and recent quitters, because a smoker, whose likelihood of noticing health warnings did not increase following the introduction of the TPP measures, would not be expected to show any change in his/her tobacco use behaviour.[147]

89.   Ajzen et al. argue that Professor Chaloupka does not contest the accuracy of their analytical approach and results, and does not question their serious criticisms of Yong et al. 2015.[148] They state that Professor Chaloupka's sole criticism regarding the ITC analysis seeks to denigrate the quality of the ITC dataset itself, claiming that it provides a "biased" sample to measure the impact on quit intentions and quit interests. According to Ajzen et al., Professor Chaloupka's argument assumes that the TPP measures led smokers to quit shortly after their introduction, and that these "recent quitters" were subsequently excluded from responding to questions on quit intentions and quit interests in the ITC survey. However, they state that the question on "quit attempt in the last 12 months" was asked of smokers and recent quitters, and, moreover, the data show that no additional quit attempts were made post-implementation.[149]

---

[144]   See Ajzen et al. Data Rebuttal Report, (Exhibit DOM/IDN-6), paras. 55-62, Appendix III.

[145]   See Ajzen et al. Second Data Report, (Exhibit DOM/IDN-4), paras. 30-37 and 53-58.

[146]   See Ajzen et al. Second Data Report, (Exhibit DOM/IDN-4), paras. 24 and 28.

[147]   See Chaloupka Rebuttal Report, (Exhibit AUS-582), para. 4.

[148]   See Dominican Republic's comments on Australia's response to Panel question No. 196, paras. 409-414; and Ajzen et al. Second Data Rebuttal Report, (Exhibit DOM/IDN-8), paras. 13-16.

[149]   See Ajzen et al. Second Data Rebuttal Report, (Exhibit DOM/IDN-8), paras. 15-16.

3.1.3 Quitline calls

90.   The Quitline calls dataset reports the weekly number of calls to the quit smoking hotline Quitline in New South Wales and the Australian Capital Territory between 1 March 2005 and 7 April 2013.[150] Young et al. 2014 use the Quitline calls data to investigate the impact of the introduction of the TPP measures on Quitline calls by comparing this number to the nationwide introduction of GHWs on cigarette packaging in 2006. The authors estimate an autoregressive integrated moving average (ARIMA) model controlling for seasonal variation, anti-smoking advertising activity, number of smokers in the population and cigarette costliness.[151]

91.   Young et al. 2014 find a sustained increase in calls to the Quitline, which occurred four weeks after the introduction of the TPP measures and lasted for 43 weeks. The authors further report that the positive impact of the TPP measures on calls to the Quitline has continued for a longer period than for the 2006 GHWs.

92.   Ajzen et al. re-analyse the Quitline Calls data by applying a different methodology from the one used by Young et al. 2014. They present the results of a graphical analysis as well as an "event study" analysis comparing the "actual" volume of calls to the Quitline with the "forecast" volume of calls in the pre-implementation period obtained by estimating a model controlling for seasonal variation, anti-smoking advertising, number of smokers and cigarette costliness.

93.   Ajzen et al. find that, as reported in Figure B.1, there was a statistically significant increase in the number of calls to the Quitline after the introduction of the TPP measures, which occurred approximately three weeks before the sale of plain packs with enlarged GHWs became mandatory. However, they report that the increase in the number of calls was only significant in the first 13 week period following the introduction of the TPP measures. In the second 13 week period, the level of calls dropped quickly to that of the calls level prevailing in the pre-implementation period. Ajzen et al. argue that Young et al. 2014 came to qualitatively similar conclusions using an alternative empirical strategy and controlling for the same confounding factors. They posit that, based on Young et al.'s findings, by the week of mandatory implementation (1 December 2012), the level of calls had dropped by more than 36%; by the end of 2012, the level of calls had dropped 65% compared with the peak week; and by the end of July 2013, there was no longer one extra call per week left compared to the pre-implementation period.[152]

---

[150]   See Dominican Republic's second written submission, paras. 434-442.
[151]   See Young et al. 2014, (Exhibits AUS-214, JE-24(67), DOM-285).
[152]   See Ajzen et al. Data Report, (Exhibit DOM/IDN-2), paras. 237-245.

Figure B.1: Event Study of Calls to the Quitline[153]

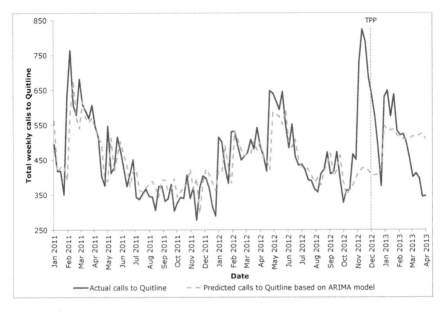

Note: The vertical dashed line indicates the introduction of TPP and enlarged GHWs.

Source: Ajzen et al. Data Report, (Exhibit DOM/IDN-2), p. 62.

94. Professor Chaloupka argues that Ajzen et al.'s conclusion that calls to the Quitline rose sharply following the implementation of the TPP measures, and then eventually returned to pre-implementation levels, does not mean that the effect of the TPP measures has "worn out". Referring to two recent econometric analyses that report strong statistically significant effects of tobacco tax increases in driving increased calls volume in the United States, Professor Chaloupka submits that the decline in call volume in the months following a tax increase does not imply that the effects of tax and price increases on tobacco use "wear out" over time. According to Professor Chaloupka, the extensive economic research that has looked at the short- and long☐run effects of tax and prices on tobacco use concludes that estimates for the long☐run impact of tax and price increases exceed estimates for the short☐run impact, implying that the effects grow over time. Professor Chaloupka is of the view that rather than "wearing out" over time, the effects of the TPP measures are likely to

---

[153] We note that Figure 8 in Ajzen et al. Data Report, (Exhibit DOM/IDN-2, p. 62) includes the vertical line representing the TPP measures is set to 1 October 2012.

grow over time as new cohorts of young people are less likely to take up tobacco use in the absence of branded packaging.[154]

95.   Ajzen et al. counter that Professor Chaloupka draws a faulty analogy with the effect of a tax increase on smoking. Ajzen et al. submit that for a change in smoking behaviour to persist after Quitline calls have receded to prior levels, the intervention must reduce smoking behaviour in the first place. In the case of the TPP measures, Ajzen et al. contend that given that the TPP measures have had no impact on consumption, quitting, relapse, or prevalence, there is no change in behaviour that could persist over time, after the increase in calls to the Quitline has vanished.[155]

3.1.4   Commissioned Roy Morgan Research Survey (Australia and New Zealand)

96.   Professor Klick uses the Roy Morgan Research data to estimate a difference-in-difference logit model of quit-related behaviours in Australia and New Zealand, controlling for plain packaging, an Australian baseline, a common baseline and a post plain packaging implementation time-period.

97.   Professor Klick reports no statistically significant impact of the TPP measures in Australia relative to New Zealand on the likelihood that the respondents recently attempted to quit smoking.[156]

98.   According to Dr Chipty, Professor Klick's analysis of the Roy Morgan Research data is invalid because the Roy Morgan survey does not include a pre-period and does not make it possible to distinguish which respondents noticed plain packaging. Dr Chipty further submits that New Zealand is an invalid counterfactual for the purposes of studying the effects of the TPP measures, because of New Zealand's excise tax increase implemented one month after the introduction of the TPP measures.[157]

3.2   *Analysis by the Panel*

99.   We note that only three peer-reviewed studies analyse empirically the impact of the TPP measures and enlarged GHWs on quit attempts among adult smokers. In addition, the expert report prepared by Professor Klick, submitted by Ukraine, investigates the impact on quit attempts.[158] We note that none of the

---

[154]   See Australia's response to Panel question No. 196, paras. 238 and 245; Australia's comments on the complainants' responses to Panel question No. 197; and Chaloupka Rebuttal Report, (Exhibit AUS-582), para. 15.

[155]   See Dominican Republic's response to Panel question No. 126, para. 293; Dominican Republic's second written submission, paras. 411, 434-442 and 447; Dominican Republic's comments on Australia's response to Panel question No. 196, paras. 424-425; and Ajzen et al. Data Rebuttal Report, (Exhibit DOM/IDN-6), paras. 73-74.

[156]   See Klick Report, (Exhibit UKR-5), pp. 18 and 37-44.

[157]   See Chipty Rebuttal Report, (Exhibit AUS-535) (SCI), paras. 54-71.

[158]   See section 1.6.6 in the main body of these Reports for a description of Ukraine's participation in these proceedings.

peer-reviewed papers that focus on adolescents or cigar and cigarillo smokers provide post-implementation evidence on quit attempts.

100.   A careful review of Durkin et al. 2015, Yong et al. 2015 and Young et al. 2014 studies and the econometric evidence submitted by the Dominican Republic and Indonesia suggests that although the TPP measures have increased calls to the Quitline, empirical evidence of the impact on quit attempts is very limited and mixed.[159]

101.   We note that, based on the NTPPTS data, Durkin et al. 2015 report evidence that the TPP measures have had a positive and statistically significant impact on quit attempts among adult smokers in the first year of the TPP.[160] Ajzen et al., applying an alternative estimation methodology and correcting for multiple testing bias, reverse the results reported in Durkin et al. 2015 and find that the TPP measures have had no impact on attempting to ever quit, attempting to quit more than once and attempting to quit for more than a week.[161] We note, however, that very few explanatory variables, and sometimes only two variables, are statistically significant at 5% and 10% in some of the model specifications for the variables quitting more than once and quitting for more than a week. We further note that Ajzen et al.'s own results of the linear and ordered logistic regressions confirm Durkin et al.'s finding of a positive and statistically significant impact on quit attempts. Ajzen et al. qualify this impact as small without evidence of any wear-out effect. Conversely, Ajzen et al.'s results of the linear regression suggest that the TPP measures have reduced quit attempts. We note that Ajzen et al. did not provide any rationale that would explain why the TPP measures would lead to reduced quit attempts.[162] Using the ITC dataset, Ajzen et al. also report a non-statistically significant impact of the TPP measures on quit attempts. A review of this result shows, however, that very few explanatory variables in that specification are statistically significant at 5% and 10%.[163] As noted previously, Australia did not challenge Ajzen et al.'s

---

[159]   See Ajzen et al. Second Data Report, (Exhibit DOM/IDN-4), paras. 24 and 28.

[160]   See Durkin et al. 2015, (Exhibits AUS-215 (revised), DOM-305).

[161]   See Ajzen et al. Data Report, (Exhibit DOM/IDN-2), paras. 165-173, Appendix A, pp. 90-92.

[162]   As explained in paras. 38 and 73 we are not persuaded by Professor Klick's claim that unadjusted models, which do not control for individual characteristics and tobacco control policies, should be considered at least equally valid compared with adjusted models.

[163]   We note that in their review of Scollo et al. 2015b (Exhibit CUB-80), Ajzen et al. also present the results of several logistic, linear, and ordered logit models for various measures related to quitting and relapse. They find that there was no statistically significant change in the proportion of adult smokers that quitted for more than one month or successfully quitted between baseline and follow-up. Similarly, they find that there was no statistically significant change in the proportion of adult ex-smokers who relapsed, still abstained from smoking at follow-up or stayed quit for more than one week at follow-up. We note that in several of these results, only a few explanatory variables in the model specification are statistically significant. In some cases, such as the linear and ordered logistic models for the relapse variable, none of the explanatory variables are statistically significant, which suggests that the model might be misspecified given the low coefficient of determination. The results of the logistic model also suggest that the TPP measures have had a negative and statistically significant change at 10% in the proportion of adult smokers that quit for more than one month, did

alternative estimation methodology and results based on the NTPPTS and ITC data.[164] Australia generally submits, however, that the structure of both NTPPTS and ITC data are likely to be less suited to detecting changes in more distal variables, such as quitting-related behaviours.[165]

102. As explained previously in our review of Professor Klick's analysis of GHW effectiveness and smoking incidence based on the commissioned Roy Morgan Research data, it is unclear how robust Professor Klick's results are given the issues regarding the validity of the pre-period of the commissioned data and the use of New Zealand as a counterfactual.[166]

103. We note that, unlike the impact on quit attempts, the empirical evidence on the impact of the TPP measures on calls to the Quitline is unambiguous. Both Young et al. 2014 and Ajzen et al. find that there was a statistically significant increase in calls to the Quitline after the introduction of the TPP measures.[167] The only main difference between the results reported in Young et al. 2014 and Ajzen et al. is that in Young et al. 2014 the estimated TPP impact on calls to the Quitline lasted 43 weeks and was considered by "sustained" by the authors, while in Ajzen et al. the estimated TPP impact was found to last 13 weeks and qualified as "short-lived". We note that none of the explanatory variables in Ajzen et al.'s ARIMA model specification are statistically significant at 5% or 10%, except the New Year variable and the first-order autoregressive term.[168] We further note that in the pre-implementation period most of the predicted Quitline calls obtained from the ARIMA model are not close to the actual level of Quitline calls and tend to lag behind the observed level of calls. This could explain why Ajzen et al. find that the increase in Quitline calls occurred three weeks before the mandatory implementation of the TPP measures. In any event, we are not persuaded that a decline in the volume of Quitline calls following an increase in calls immediately after the introduction of the TPP measures would necessarily imply that the impact of the TPP measures on tobacco use would wear out, since such Quitline calls reflect effects of the TPP measures on *existing* smokers, and would not inform their effect on those would-be smokers who abstain from tobacco use as a result of the TPP measures.

---

not relapse and still remained quit. See Ajzen et al. Data Report, (Exhibit DOM/IDN-2), paras. 221-224, Appendix A pp. 95-97 and backup material.
[164] A comparison of the results with and without the trend variable shows that the coefficient of the constant variable is very large when the trend variable is included in the model specification. The coefficient value of the other variables is usually marginally affected by removing the trend variable.
[165] See Australia's response to Panel question No. 196, para. 237; and Australia's comments on the complainants' responses to Panel question No. 197, paras. 371-375.
[166] See Appendix A, para. 72 above.
[167] See Young et al. 2014, (Exhibit AUS-214, JE-24(67), DOM-285); and Ajzen et al. Data Report, (Exhibit DOM/IDN-2), paras. 237-245.
[168] See Ajzen et al. Data Report, (Exhibit DOM/IDN-2), backup material.

4.   **EVIDENCE RELATING TO THE PREDICTIVE RELATIONSHIPS BETWEEN PROXIMAL OUTCOMES AND DISTAL OUTCOMES SINCE THE ENTRY INTO FORCE OF THE TPP MEASURES (NATIONAL TOBACCO PLAIN PACKAGING TRACKING SURVEY)**

4.1   Datasets and related studies

104.   Brennan et al. 2015 use the NTPPTS data to examine the predictive relationships between proximal outcomes (i.e. tobacco appeal, GHW effectiveness and pack misleading) and distal outcomes (i.e. quitting-related thinking and behaviours).[169] The authors present the results of a logistic regression analysis testing whether baseline measures of cigarette appeal, GHW effectiveness, perceived harm and concern/enjoyment predicted each of seven follow-up measures of quitting-related cognitions and behaviours, adjusting for baseline levels of the outcome and controlling for the date of the follow-up survey, number of days between the baseline and follow-up survey, anti-smoking television advertising, change in cigarette costliness, sex, age, education, socio-economic status and addiction level.

105.   Brennan et al. 2015 find that some of the appeal-related variables, namely pack dislike and lower satisfaction, are prospectively associated with thoughts about quitting. Similarly, the authors find that several indicators of GHW effectiveness, such as noticing GHWs first, believing dangers of smoking are not exaggerated, and attributing much more motivation to quit to GHWs, have positively and significantly predicted the likelihood that smokers reported thinking daily about quitting, intending to quit and setting a firm date to quite. Similarly, they report a statistically significant association between concealing packs and daily thought about quitting as well as between feeling more smoking-related concern than enjoyment and daily thoughts about quitting and intention to quit. However, the authors find no statistically significant association between lower pack appeal, lower quality and lower value for money, on the one hand, and quitting-related cognition variables, on the other hand. They also report no statistically significant association between brand perception variables and quitting-related cognition variables.

106.   Turning to pack concealment and micro-indicators of concern, Brennan et al. 2015 find that among all the appeal-related variables, only lower satisfaction is statistically associated with stubbing out and stopping smoking. The authors further find that several measures of GHWs effectiveness, namely noting the GHW first, attributing much more motivation to quit to graph health warning, concealing packs and requesting different GHWs, positively and significantly have predicted the likelihood that smokers at the following-up reported stubbing out. Similarly, they find a statistically significant association between not believing dangers of smoking are exaggerated and attribution of

---

[169]   See Brennan et al. 2015, (Exhibits AUS-224, DOM-304).

much more motivation to quit to GHW, on the one hand, and stopping oneself from smoking on the other hand. They also report that stubbing out and stopping smoking are predicted by feeling more smoking-related concern than enjoyment. However, the authors find that none of the proximal outcomes variables, such as disliking packs, lower pack appeal, lower quality, lower value for money, believing brands do not differ in prestige, not believing dangers of smoking are exaggerated, and attributing much more motivation to quit to GHWs, have predicted pack concealment.

107. Finally, Brennan et al. 2015 report that only two measures of GHW effectiveness, namely attributing much more motivation to quit to GHWs and requesting different GHWs, have positively and significantly predicted that smokers reported having attempted to quit. The authors find that the other proximal outcomes related to appeal, perceived harm and balance between smoking enjoyment and concern have not predicted quit attempts.

108. Ajzen et al. argue that Brennan et al.'s conclusion that quitting-related cognitions and behaviours are prospectively predicted by the more proximal beliefs and perceptions and that, among adults, GHWs are likely to be particularly influential in driving quitting behaviour is unfounded, reflecting a basic misconception of the logic inherent in correlation analysis. They consider that Brennan et al.'s analysis is unable to establish that the TPP measures have changed quit intentions/secondary indicators. According to Ajzen et al., if there is no evidence that the intervention had an effect on the outcome (quit intentions/secondary indicators), a mediation analysis cannot be used to establish that the intervention did have such an effect. They contend that contrary to the requirements for a mediation analysis, Brennan et al. 2015 mostly explored correlations between assumed mediators (e.g. appeal-related variables) and outcome measures (quit intentions and secondary indicators), for which at least one, and often both of the variables involved in the correlation analysis had not been found to have changed in a statistically significant way as a result of the TPP measures. For instance, Ajzen et al. argue that not believing that dangers of smoking are exaggerated, smoking enjoyment, smoking concern and balance between smoking enjoyment and concern are mechanism (mediator) variables for which there are no statistically significant changes reported in Wakefield et al. 2015. Similarly, they claim that daily thoughts about quitting, intending to quit, setting a firm date to quit and refraining from smoking are quit intention/secondary indicator variables for which there is no statistically significant change reported in Durkin et al. 2015.[170]

109. Professor Chaloupka argues that limiting the analysis of more distal measures to continuing smokers effectively forces the estimates to suggest that the effects of the TPP measures are wearing out over time, when the opposite may actually be the case. Professor Chaloupka submits that while there is

---

[170] See Ajzen et al. Data Report, (Exhibit DOM/IDN-2), paras. 200-213.

relatively little evidence of wear out for the most proximal outcomes, such as appeal and noticing/avoiding GHWs, most wear out evidence is obtained for the more distal outcomes, such as quitting-related measures. According to Professor Chaloupka rather than wearing out over time, the impact of the TPP measures on overall population attitudes, beliefs, and behaviours are likely to grow over time as young people, who might otherwise have taken up tobacco use, are discouraged from doing so, while younger current users are encouraged to quit.[171]

110.   Professor Chaloupka further contends that neither Brennan et al. 2015 nor Ajzen et al. use the NTPPTS data to assess directly the impact of the TPP measures on proximal intermediate and/or distal tobacco-related outcomes. Professor Chaloupka argues that several measures on appeal, not included in Brennan et al. 2015 but analysed by Ajzen et al., are questionable, at best, measures of appeal. Similarly, several quit-related measures, not analysed in Brennan et al. 2015, are questionable measures of quitting. According to Professor Chaloupka, Ajzen et al. do not asses the relationship between other proximal outcomes and quitting-related outcomes, or between intermediate outcomes, which are found to have stronger associations. Professor Chaloupka argues that Ajzen et al. do not report other quitting-related measures (e.g. having daily thoughts about quitting in the past). Professor Chaloupka further submits that Ajzen et al. are using a much more stringent criterion for defining statistical significance than that used by Brennan et al. 2015.[172]

111.   Ajzen et al. respond that the NTPPTS data provide no empirical basis for the assertion that there is a strong correlation between the appeal of tobacco production and smoking behaviour. Using the NTPPTS data, they replicate Brennan et al.'s analysis for appeal-related variables and correct for multiple hypothesis testing. They find that of the 130 potential correlations between appeal variable and downstream variables relating to quit intentions, quit attempts, secondary quit indicators and smoking behaviours, 129 showed no significant correlation.[173]

112.   Ajzen et al. further contend that Professor Chaloupka formulates a series of unsubstantiated and unfounded criticisms regarding the NTPPTS data and their correlational analysis. In particular, they argue that the correlational analysis measures the association among variables but does not assess the impact of the TPP measures on proximal, or distal outcomes by using the longitudinal component of the NTPPTS. They further claim that the NTPPTS technical report underscores the importance of the appeal and downstream variables, considered as inappropriate or questionable by Professor Chaloupka. They submit that Professor Chaloupka fails to understand that the correlation analysis only focuses on the appeal mechanism and not on GHW effectiveness and pack

---

[171]   See Chaloupka Rebuttal Report, (Exhibit AUS-582), paras. 12-14.
[172]   See Chaloupka Second Rebuttal Report, (Exhibit AUS-590), paras. 16-23.
[173]   See Ajzen Rebuttal Report, (Exhibit DOM/HND/IDN-5), paras. 128-130 and 207-212, p. 44.

ability to deceive in order to address Professor Fong's and Australia's core argument that the appeal of tobacco products is "very highly" correlated with smoking behaviour. According to Ajzen et al., Professor Chaloupka's comment regarding the criterion for defining statistical significance shows his failure to understand the importance of correcting for multiple hypothesis testing. They also argue that Professor Chaloupka's assertion that the NTPPTS data underestimate changes in some measures of intention and secondary indicators by not asking these questions to recent quitters is unfounded because the TPP measures did not increase quitting behaviour. They further disagree with Professor Chaloupka's assertion that some appeal variables do not measure change over time, because the NTPPTS data do measure change over time for these variables. According to the authors, the NTPPTS data show that although the TPP measures did increase pack dislike there were no changes in quit-related outcomes. Finally, Ajzen et al. argue that Professor Chaloupka's assertion that the NTPPTS data do not measure the impact of initiation by mirror is unwarranted because Australia and CCV have been unwilling to share the results of the 2013 schools-based survey.[174]

4.2   Analysis by the Panel

113.   We note that Brennan et al. 2015 is the only peer-reviewed study analysing the association between proximal outcomes and distal outcomes based on the NTPPTS data.

114.   A careful review of Brennan et al. 2015 suggests that there is a positive and statistically significant association between several outcomes related to GHW effectiveness and quitting cognitions and behaviour among adult smokers. The empirical evidence of the association between appeal variables and quitting-related thinking and behaviour outcomes is much more mixed and limited. Similarly, Brennan et al. 2015 report no statistically significant association between the perceived harm variable and any of the quitting-related thinking and behaviour outcomes.[175]

115.   We note that Ajzen et al. did not replicate completely Brennan et al.'s 2015 analysis of the predictive relationships between proximal outcomes and quitting-related cognitions and behaviours. Ajzen et al. only replicate the analysis for appeal-related variables. They find that there was no significant correlation between the appeal of tobacco products and quit intention, secondary indicators and actual quitting behaviours, except between lower values and making more than one quit attempt. More generally, Ajzen et al. submit that Brennan et al.'s (2015) analysis is unable to establish that the TPP measures have changed quit intentions and secondary indicators, because Brennan et al. 2015 mostly explore correlations between assumed mediators and outcome measures, for which at least one, and often both of the variables involved in the correlation

---

[174]   See Ajzen et al. Second Data Rebuttal Report, (Exhibit DOM/IDN-8), paras. 22-59.
[175]   See Brennan et al. 2015, (Exhibits AUS-224, DOM-304).

analysis have not been found to have changed in a statistically significant way as a result of the TPP measures.[176]

116.   We note that Ajzen et al.'s results confirm to a large extent the findings of Brennan et al.'s findings related to appeal-related variables. Brennan et al. find no statistically significant association between most of the appeal variable and quitting-related cognitions and behaviours, while noting that further studies would be needed to explore this relationship. However, in many estimation results obtained with the resampled data based on the multiple testing procedure, Ajzen et al. find that none or only one or two explanatory variables (besides the variable of interest) are statistically significant, which could suggest that the resample data are subject to multicollinearity. Multicollinearity arises when two (or more) explanatory variables convey the same information. As a result, the coefficient estimates may become very sensitive to minor changes in the model specification or data and their confidence interval may increase. We further note that, as mentioned above, Ajzen et al. did not replicate the analysis for the variables related to GHW effectiveness, perceived harm and balance between enjoyment and concern. Brennan et al. themselves acknowledge that further mediation analyses and controlled experimental studies are required to establish if appeal, GHW effectiveness, perceived harm and enjoyment/concern variables are causally responsible for the observed changes in quitting-related outcomes.[177]

5.   OVERALL CONCLUSION ON POST-IMPLEMENTATION EVIDENCE ON QUITTING-RELATED OUTCOMES AND OTHER DISTAL OUTCOMES

117.   As discussed above, the parties have referred to several peer-reviewed studies analysing empirically the impact of the TPP measures and enlarged GHWs on quitting-related cognitions, pack concealment and quit attempts. The Dominican Republic, Indonesia and Honduras also provided several expert reports reviewing, and in some cases replicating, the results reported in these published papers. In response, Australia discussed the features of some of the survey datasets used in these peer-reviewed papers, but did not provide its own econometric analysis, unlike in the discussion on smoking prevalence and cigarette consumption.

118.   At the outset, we note that the survey data used in these studies, may, as suggested by Australia, be more suited to analysing the impact of the TPP measures and enlarged GHWs on proximal outcomes, such as appeal, GHWs and ability of the pack to mislead than more distal outcomes, such as quitting intentions and quit attempts. Questions on quit intentions and quit interests were not asked to "recent quitters". In addition, none of the survey

---

[176]   See Ajzen et al. Data Report, (Exhibit DOM/IDN-2), paras. 200-213.
[177]   Brennan et al. 2015, (Exhibits AUS-224, DOM-304).

datasets discussed above track non-smokers who might have taken up smoking in the absence of the TPP measures and enlarged GHWs.

119.   We also note that the parties disagree on the extent to which the variables related to appeal, GHW effectiveness, perceived harm and enjoyment/concern variables may be considered to be predictive of smoking and quitting behaviours. The authors of the peer-reviewed study analysing the predictive relationships between proximal outcomes and quitting-related outcomes acknowledge that further empirical analyses and experimental studies are required to establish causality.

120.   With this in mind, and based on the studies and expert reports before us and discussed above, the empirical evidence available to us regarding quitting-related outcomes and other distal outcomes, which is sometimes scarce, suggests that:

    a.   The impact of the TPP measures and enlarged GHWs on adult cigarette smokers' quitting intention and quitting-related cognition reactions is limited and mixed.

    b.   The TPP measures and enlarged GHWs have had a statistically significant positive impact on avoidant behaviours, such as pack concealment, among adult cigarette smokers, while their impact on stubbing out and stopping smoking is much more limited and mixed.

    c.   Although the TPP measures and enlarged GHWs have statistically significantly increased calls to the Quitline, the observed impact of the TPP measures and enlarged GHWs on quit attempts is very limited and mixed.

    d.   The empirical evidence of the impact of the TPP measures and enlarged GHWs on adolescents' quitting-related outcomes is limited. This evidence suggests that the impact of the TPP measures and enlarged GHWs on adolescents' refraining from smoking cigarettes and thoughts about quitting is statistically not significant. No empirical evidence has been submitted to us on pack concealment among adolescent smokers.

    e.   The empirical evidence of the impact of the TPP measures and enlarged GHWs on cigar and cigarillo smokers' quitting-related outcomes is limited. This evidence suggests that the shares of premium cigar and cigarillo smokers and of non-premium cigarillo smokers reporting having decanted the cigars and cigarillos from their boxes to a humidor or an unbranded tin or concealed their pack have increased and there has been an increase in the share of non-premium cigarillo smokers contemplating quitting.

121.   No post-implementation empirical evidence has been presented to us on the impact of the TPP measures on quit attempts among adolescent smokers and cigar and cigarillo smokers.

APPENDIX C

EVIDENCE ON SMOKING PREVALENCE FOLLOWING THE ENTRY INTO FORCE OF THE TPP MEASURES

1.   A number of expert reports submitted by the parties are dedicated in part or in whole to an assessment of the contribution of the TPP measures to reducing smoking prevalence.[1] These expert reports rely on different databases, statistical analysis and econometric methods to determine whether TPP and enlarged GHWs have contributed to a reduction in smoking prevalence.

2.   One of the only points of agreement among the parties in the discussion on the impact of the TPP measures on smoking prevalence is that the empirical econometric studies they submitted do not assess separately the impact of TPP and the impact of the enlarged GHWs, because both measures were implemented at the same time.[2] Unless specified otherwise, in this Appendix, references to the impact of the TPP measures therefore refer to the impact of the TPP measures *and* the enlarged GHWs implemented simultaneously.

3.   The complainants argue that the overall empirical statistical and econometric studies carried out by their experts conclude that the TPP measures have failed to reduce cigarette and cigar smoking prevalence.[3] The complainants also initially suggested that the TPP measures "backfired" by increasing youth

---

[1]   See Chipty Report, (Exhibit AUS-17); Chipty Supplementary Report, (Exhibit AUS-511); Chipty Rebuttal Report, (Exhibit AUS-535) (SCI); Chipty Surrebuttal Report, (Exhibit AUS-586); Chipty Second Rebuttal Report, (Exhibit AUS-591); Chipty Third Rebuttal Report, (Exhibit AUS-605); Chaloupka Rebuttal Report, (Exhibit AUS-582); Chaloupka Third Rebuttal Report, (Exhibit AUS-604); List Report, (Exhibit DOM/IDN-1); List Rebuttal Report, (Exhibit DOM/IDN-3); List Second Supplemental Report, (Exhibit DOM/IDN-5); List Third Supplemental Report, (Exhibit DOM/IDN-7); List Summary Report, (Exhibit DOM/IDN-9); IPE Report, (Exhibit DOM-100); IPE Updated Report, (Exhibit DOM-303); IPE Second Updated Report, (Exhibit DOM-361); IPE Third Updated Report, (Exhibit DOM-375); IPE Summary Report, (Exhibit DOM-379); Klick Report, (Exhibit UKR-5); Klick Rebuttal Report, (Exhibit HND-118); Klick Supplemental Rebuttal Report, (Exhibit HND-122); Klick Second Supplemental Rebuttal Report, (Exhibit HND-165); Klick Third Supplemental Rebuttal Report, (Exhibit HND-166); and Klick Fourth Supplemental Rebuttal Report, (Exhibit HND-169).

[2]   See Australia's first written submission, para. 518; Honduras's response to Panel question No. 8; Dominican Republic's response to Panel question No. 8, para. 61; and Indonesia's response to Panel question No. 8, para. 8.

[3]   See Honduras's second written submission, paras. 56-60; Dominican Republic's comments on responses to Panel questions following the second substantive meeting, paras. 681-682; Cuba's second written submission, paras. 276-277; and Indonesia's second written submission, para. 192.

smoking prevalence[4], although they did not pursue this argument in later stages of the proceedings.

4.   Notwithstanding its position that, in the early stages of introduction of the measures, the most appropriate way to discern their effects is to rely on experiments and surveys which consider drivers of choice, attitudes, and ultimately, the elicitation of behavioural intentions[5], Australia engaged in estimating econometrically the impact of the TPP measures on smoking prevalence, in response to the submissions of the Dominican Republic, Honduras and Indonesia. Australia argues that using the most appropriate dataset available and correcting for flaws in the econometric models put forward by the experts of the Dominican Republic, Honduras and Indonesia, the results show that the TPP measures have already contributed to reducing cigarette and cigar smoking prevalence.[6]

5.   Overall, we note that the approaches proposed by the parties to analyse the trends in smoking prevalence evolved over the course of the proceedings. They address the following three main aspects, that we will review in turn:

- First, the parties have submitted economic figures and descriptive statistics analyses aimed at determining whether smoking prevalence has decreased following the implementation of the TPP measures;

- Second, Australia, the Dominican Republic, Honduras and Indonesia have submitted statistical analyses to determine whether there was a break in the trend in smoking prevalence following the implementation of the TPP measures, and in particular, whether the reduction of smoking prevalence has accelerated following the implementation of the TPP measures;

- Finally, Australia, the Dominican Republic, Honduras and Indonesia have submitted econometric analysis to determine whether the TPP measures have contributed to a reduction in smoking prevalence by isolating and quantifying the different factors that can explain the evolution of smoking prevalence.

---

[4]   See Honduras's first written submission, para. 395; Dominican Republic's first written submission, para. 523; Cuba's first written submission, para. 163; and Indonesia's first written submission, para. 412.

[5]   See Australia's first written submission, paras. 147 and 670. See also the discussion reflected at section 7.2.5.3.3. in the main body of these Reports.

[6]   See Australia's comments on complainants' response to Panel question No. 197, para. 214.

1. WHETHER SMOKING PREVALENCE DECREASED FOLLOWING THE IMPLEMENTATION OF THE TPP MEASURES

6.   The parties have submitted different data sources tracking smoking prevalence in Australia. Each dataset is presented separately. We consider each in turn before turning to an overall assessment.

1.1   Datasets and related analyses

1.1.1   Roy Morgan Single Source

7.   The Roy Morgan Single Source (RMSS), submitted first by the Dominican Republic, is a large survey dataset based on more than 50,000 interviews conducted each year with randomly selected individuals across Australia. The dataset is based on a representative survey of the Australian population and solicits responses from respondents regarding socio-economic and demographic characteristics, as well as consumer behaviour such as smoking status and brand choices. The same individuals are however not surveyed over time. Monthly data are available for the period January 2001 through September 2015.

8.   As shown in **Figure C.1**, the RMSS data reveal a downward trend in smoking prevalence that has accelerated since July 2006. In 2001, the smoking prevalence was around 24%. In 2006, smoking prevalence was slightly lower at 23%. In 2015, the level of smoking prevalence was 18%.

Figure C.1: Smoking Prevalence Based on RMSS Data

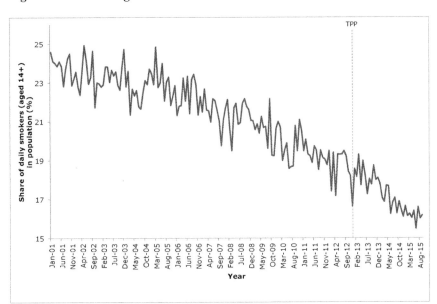

Note: The vertical dashed line indicates the introduction of TPP and enlarged GHWs.

Source: RMSS data (January 2001 – September 2015).

1.1.2   Organisation for Economic Co-operation and Development Dataset on Non-Medical Determinants

9.   The Organisation for Economic Co-operation and Development (OECD) Dataset on Non-Medical Determinants is a panel dataset on various smoking behaviours, including yearly smoking prevalence rates covering all 34 OECD countries from 1960 through 2014 (2013 in the case of Australia).

10.   The IPE Report submitted by the Dominican Republic contends that there is a secular downward trend in smoking prevalence in Australia and other high income countries, which are presumably, at least in part due to a combination of demographic shifts (change in the composition of population, education, etc.) as well as other factors entirely unrelated to tobacco control interventions (such as a general trend towards a healthier lifestyle and away from smoking).[7]

---

[7]   See IPE Updated Report, (Exhibit DOM-303), paras. 43-46; and IPE Third Updated Report, (Exhibit DOM-375), paras. 193-201.

Figure C.2: **Smoking Prevalence Based on OECD Dataset on Non-Medical Determinants in Australia and Selected OECD Countries**

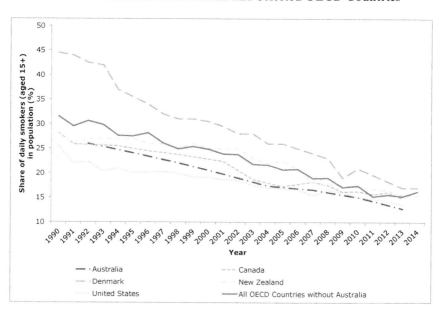

Source: IPE Updated Report, (Exhibit DOM-303), p. 24

11.   Professor Chaloupka, in an expert report submitted by Australia, disagrees that (1) tobacco use has been falling consistently in all OECD countries, (2) this decline has been largely linear over time and (3) these downward trends are expected to continue into the future regardless of what happens in these countries. According to Professor Chaloupka trends in tobacco use differ considerably across OECD countries and that assuming a linear downward trend over time is overly simplistic and fails to fully capture the role of tobacco control policies (or lack thereof) in accelerating (decelerating) any downward trend in tobacco use.[8] He further argues that the differences in trends in smoking prevalence between Australia and other OECD countries are more pronounced when one looks at countries, such as Germany or Italy, that have not been included in the figures shown in the IPE Report, such as in **Figure C.2**.[9] According to Australia and as shown in **Figure C.3**, the assertion that there is a secular downward trend in smoking across all OECD countries is belied by the rising trend in prevalence in Greece, which is largely attributable to the weak

---

[8]   See Chaloupka Rebuttal Report, (Exhibit AUS-582), paras. 37-44; and Chaloupka Third Rebuttal Report, (Exhibit AUS-604), paras. 20-28.
[9]   See IPE Updated Report, (Exhibit DOM-303), p. 24.

tobacco control policies the country has implemented (29th out of 34 European countries in the 2013 tobacco control scale).[10]

Figure C.3: Smoking Prevalence Based on OECD Dataset on Non-Medical Determinants in Australia and Selected European Countries

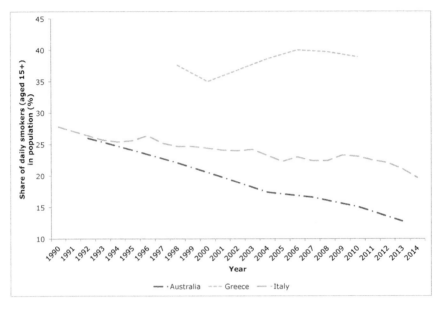

Source: Chaloupka Rebuttal Report, (Exhibit AUS-582), pp. 37-38.

1.1.3   National Drug Strategy Household Survey

12.   The National Drug Strategy Household Survey (NDSHS) is a nationally representative survey run by the Australian Government approximately every two or three years. At the time of these proceedings, the most recent wave of the NDSHS had been undertaken in 2013, and was the only wave of the NDSHS to have been undertaken since the introduction of the TPP measures.

13.   The Dominican Republic note that the last eight NDSHS reports indicate, as shown in **Figure C.4**, that smoking prevalence (both overall smoking prevalence and daily smoking) has decreased along a roughly linear trend since 1993. The most recent NDSHS survey reveals that smoking rates in 2013, the first year after the implementation of TPP, have evolved according to this trend without "break", "shift" or "kink" in the trend line that could be attributable to the TPP measures.[11]

---

[10]   Chaloupka Rebuttal Report, (Exhibit AUS-582), para. 44.
[11]   Dominican Republic's first written submission, para. 523.

Figure C.4:   Smoking Prevalence Based on NDSHS Data

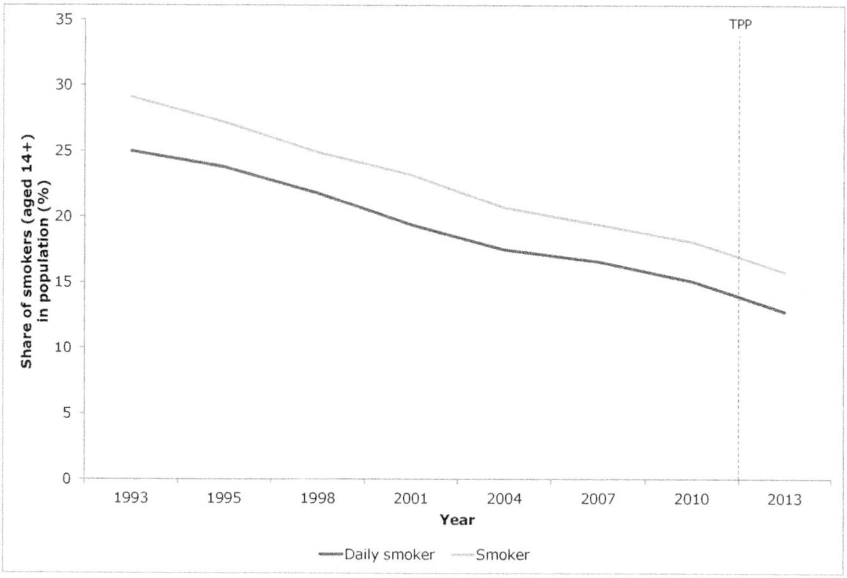

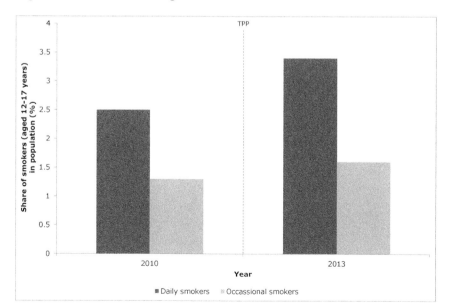

Note: The vertical dashed line indicates the introduction of TPP and enlarged GHWs.

Source: Dominican Republic's first written submission, p. 157.

Figure C.5:   Youth Smoking Prevalence Based on NDSHS Data

Note: The vertical dashed line indicates the introduction of TPP and enlarged GHWs.

Source: Gibson Report, (Exhibit DOM-92), p. 22.

14.   According to the Dominican Republic, Honduras and Indonesia the most recent NDSHS data show an increase in smoking prevalence in certain segments of the Australian population. For instance, as shown in **Figure C.5**, prevalence of daily smoking in the 12–17 year old group has increased from 2.5% in 2010 to 3.4% in 2013, marking the first increase in prevalence rates after years of decline for this category, from 5.2% in 2004 to 3.2% in 2007 to 2.5% in 2010.[12]

15.   According to Australia and its expert Dr Chipty, there were significant reductions in daily and overall smoking prevalence reported in the most recent wave of the NDSHS data. In particular, between 2010 and 2013, rates of daily smoking among people aged 18 years or older dropped from 15.9% to 13.3%. In 2013, 12.8% of people in Australia aged 14 or older were daily smokers, declining from 15.1% in 2010.[13]

16.   Australia, however, notes that given the small sample sizes, particularly for certain subgroups, like adolescents or residents of specific Australian states, trend lines can be difficult to interpret. Australia argues that, for example, one cannot conclude from these data that daily smoking increased in the youth population following TPP. This is because actual youth daily smoking prevalence among the underlying population may, in reality, be flat or decreasing given the small sampling error associated with these estimates, as shown in **Figure C.6**.[14] Australia's Post-Implementation Review Tobacco Plain Packaging 2016 further explains that the NDSHS report states that this rise in the number of 12-17 year olds smoking in the 2010-2013 reporting period is not statistically significant and should be interpreted with caution.[15]

---

[12]   Honduras's first written submission, paras. 395-396; Dominican Republic's first written submission, para. 523; Indonesia's first written submission, para. 412; and Gibson Report, (Exhibit DOM-92), p. 22.

[13]   See Australia's first written submission, para. 36; and Chipty Report, (Exhibit AUS-17), paras. 77-84.

[14]   See Chipty Report, (Exhibit AUS-17), paras. 77-84; and Australia's comments on the complainants' responses to Panel question No. 197, para. 387.

[15]   See Australia's first written submission, Annexure E, para. 77; and Tobacco Plain Packaging PIR, (Exhibit AUS-624), para. 119.

Figure C.6: Youth Smoking Prevalence with Confidence Interval Based on NDSHS Data

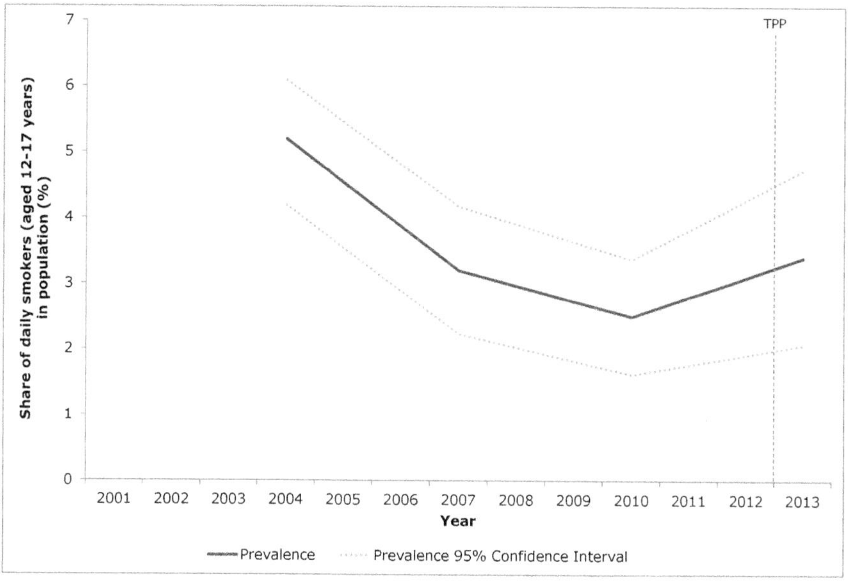

Note: The vertical dashed line indicates the introduction of TPP and enlarged GHWs.

Source: Chipty Report, (Exhibit AUS-17), p. 46.

1.1.4   National Health Survey

17.   The National Health Survey (NHS) is a nationally representative survey, released by the Australian Bureau of Statistics (ABS). The latest NHS covered the period 2014-2015 and surveyed approximately 19,000 respondents. Previous surveys releases covered the period 1995, 2001, 2004-2005, 2007-2008 and 2011-2012.

18.   Australia notes that according to the first results of the 2014-2015 NHS, daily smoking among Australians aged 18 and over was 14.5% in 2014-2015, down from 16.1 % in 2011-2012, as shown in **Figure C.7**.[16] Australia further recognizes that the specific results of the NDSHS and NHS are not directly comparable due to differences in methodology, age cohorts, timing and sample sizes (including across age cohorts).

---

[16]   See Australia's comments on the complainants' responses to Panel question No. 197, para. 389; NHS Results, (Exhibit AUS-622), p. 30; and Tobacco Plain Packaging PIR, (Exhibit AUS-624), para. 126.

Figure C.7: Smoking Prevalence Based on NHS Data

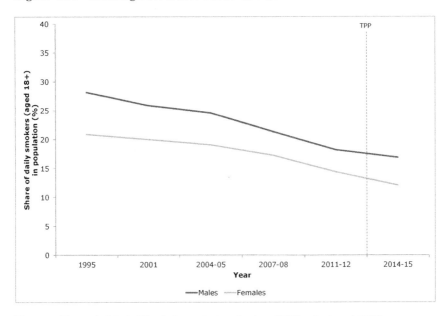

Note: The vertical dashed line indicates the introduction of TPP and enlarged GHWs.

Source: NHS Results, (Exhibit AUS-622), p. 30.

1.1.5   Australia Secondary Students' Alcohol and Drug survey

19.   The Australian Secondary Students' Alcohol and Drug (ASSAD) survey is a triennial national survey of secondary school students' use of licit and illicit substances. This survey assesses, among others, their use of alcohol and tobacco and was conducted collaboratively by Cancer Councils across Australia, commencing in 1984.

20.   According to Australia and in contrast to assertions of the Dominican Republic, Honduras and Indonesia with respect to the youth smoking findings in the NDSHS, more recent data from the ASSAD survey shows statistically significant declines in current smoking prevalence between 2011 and 2014 for students aged 12 to 17 years, as depicted in Figure C.8.[17]

---

[17]   See Australia's comments on the complainants' responses to Panel question No. 197, para. 390; CCV 2014 Survey, (Exhibit AUS-621), Table 6.1; Tobacco Plain Packaging PIR, (Exhibit AUS-624), para. 126; and Dessaix et al. 2016, (Exhibit AUS-623), p. 1.

Figure C.8: Youth Smoking Prevalence Based on ASSAD Data

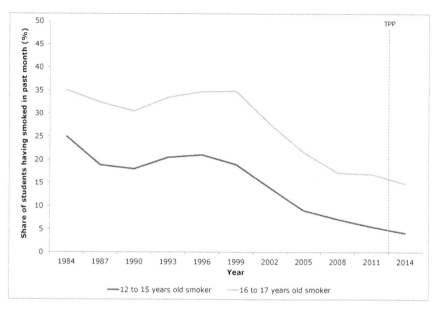

Note: The vertical dashed line indicates the introduction of TPP and enlarged GHWs.

Source: CCV 2014 Survey, (Exhibit AUS-621), pp. 33 and 37.

1.1.6 Commissioned Roy Morgan Research Survey (Australia and New Zealand)

21. Roy Morgan Research data, commissioned by Honduras's expert Professor Klick, is a survey of individuals who were current or former (in the past 12 months) smokers in both Australia and New Zealand undertaken using random digit dialling sampling techniques. The first wave of the survey was completed prior to the introduction of the TPP measures in December 2012 between 2 November 2012 and 26 November 2012 in Australia and between 8 November 2012 and 1 December 2012 in New Zealand. Subsequent waves have been carried out at three-month intervals: Wave 2 between 28 February 2013 and 19 March 2013; Wave 3 between 30 May 2013 and 20 June 2013; Wave 4 between 8 August 2013 and 26 August 2013; Wave 5 between 8 November 2013 and 24 November 2013 and Wave 6 between 7 February 2014 and 28 February 2014.

22. Professor Klick notes, as shown in **Figure C.9**, that the change in Australian respondents reporting a daily smoking status from before the TPP measures (72.0%) to after the TPP measures (69.6%) was 2.4% points (averaged across the post-TPP waves), while for New Zealand, the decline was 3.6% points (before 70.5% vs. after 66.9%). Similarly, the decline in occasional

smoking status in Australia was 6.2% and 7.1% point decline observed in New Zealand.[18]

Figure C.9: Smoking Behaviour Based on Roy Morgan Research Data

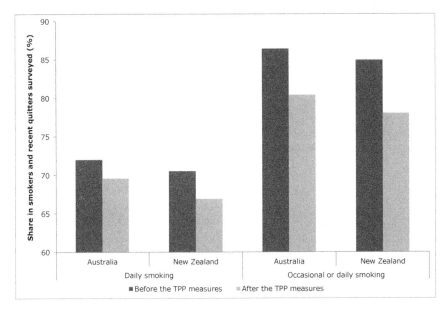

Source: Klick Report, (Exhibit UKR-5), pp. 8-10.

23. Australia's expert, Dr Chipty, notes that the "smoking incidence", defined by Professor Klick as the share of current smokers and individuals who have been smokers at some point during the past 12 months, is different from "smoking prevalence", which is the share of the entire population that is smoking.[19] Dr Chipty further submits that daily smoking incidence fell more in Australia after the introduction of the TPP measures (5% between Wave 1 and 6, 5% between Wave 2 and 6) than in New Zealand (3% between Wave 1 and 6, 0% between Wave 2 and 6). In addition, a higher proportion of New Zealand respondents cited costs as the primary reason for quitting as compared to Australian respondents, while a higher proportion of Australian respondents cited health as the primary reason for quitting, as compared to New Zealand respondents.[20]

---

[18] See Klick Report, (Exhibit UKR-5), pp. 8-10.
[19] See Chipty Report, (Exhibit AUS-17), fn 13.
[20] See Chipty Report, (Exhibit AUS-17), paras. 25-31, Appendix C.

1.1.7   State-level smoking prevalence datasets

24.   In their first written submissions, the complainants presented data for four Australian States, namely New South Wales (NSW), South Australia, Queensland, and Victoria, suggesting that smoking prevalence had increased after the implementation of the TPP measures.[21] Most of these datasets were not discussed by the complainants in later submissions, except Honduras and Cuba for some datasets.[22] Each state-level dataset is reviewed next.

1.1.7.1   Cancer Institute New South Wales Tobacco Tracking Survey

25.   The Cancer Institute New South Wales Tobacco Tracking Survey (CITTS) is a weekly tracking telephone survey of smokers and recent quitters (in the past 12 months) based in NSW. The data discussed by the Dominican Republic, Honduras and Indonesia cover the years 2012, 2013 and 2014.

26.   The Dominican Republic, Honduras and Indonesia refer to the Gibson Report, which was prepared at the request of British American Tobacco UK and submitted to a UK government consultation process on the introduction of the TPP measures. As shown in Figure C.10, the Gibson Report presents the CITTS data showing that the proportion of smokers surveyed, who smoke on a daily basis, actually increased from 70% in 2012, the year before the implementation of the TPP measures, to 77% in 2013 and remained above the 2012 levels in 2014. Similarly, the proportion of people smoking over 11 cigarettes a day increased from 62% in 2012 to 64% in 2014.[23]

---

[21]   See Honduras's first written submission, para. 396; Dominican Republic's first written submission, paras. 525-527; Indonesia's first written submission, para. 23; and Cuba's first written submission, paras. 164, 251.

[22]   See Honduras's response to Panel question No. 199, pp. 46-47 (referring to previous analysis of the CITTS and NDSHS data); and Cuba's response to Panel question No. 199, pp. 20-21 (referring to previous analysis of the NDSHS, RMSS and CITTS data, among others).

[23]   Honduras's first written submission, para. 396; Dominican Republic's first written submission, para. 525; Indonesia's first written submission, para. 23; and Gibson Report, (Exhibit DOM-92), p. 22.

Figure C.10: New South Wales Consumer Smoking Behaviour Based on CITTS Data

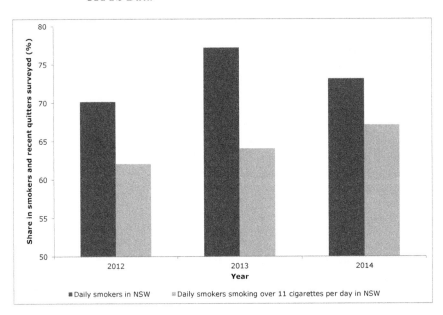

Source: Gibson Report, (Exhibit DOM-92), p. 20.

27.   Australia considers that the Gibson Report's analysis is fundamentally flawed because the figures reported are incorrectly labelled as representing the "proportion of smokers" smoking on a daily basis, while they represent the proportion of the entire sample (including both smokers and recent quitters), who are, or in the case of recent quitters were, daily smokers. Accordingly, Australia submits that since the CITTS is a survey of smokers and recent quitters, and not a population survey, it is not designed to measure (and indeed is not capable of measuring) changes in smoking prevalence in the entire population.[24]

28.   Australia further considers that the RMSS data, collected monthly, is better suited to comparing more accurately, including by states, smoking rates immediately prior to and following the introduction of the TPP measures. According to RMSS data, overall smoking prevalence in New South Wales has fallen significantly in the 12 months following the introduction of the TPP measures.[25] Australia's Post-Implementation Review Tobacco Plain

---

[24]   See Australia's first written submission, Annexure E, paras. 60-61; and CINSW Rebuttal of BATA Analysis of CITTS Data, (Exhibit AUS-504).
[25]   See Australia's first written submission, Annexure E, paras. 82-86. See also Chipty Report, (Exhibit AUS-17), paras. 80-81.

Packaging 2016 also reports a reduction in daily smoking prevalence in New South Wales based on the NSW survey data (data up to 2014) for individuals aged 16 years and over, as shown in Figure C.11, and the NDSHS (data up to 2013) for individuals aged 14 years and over.[26]

Figure C.11: Smoking Prevalence in New South Wales Based on CINSW Survey Data

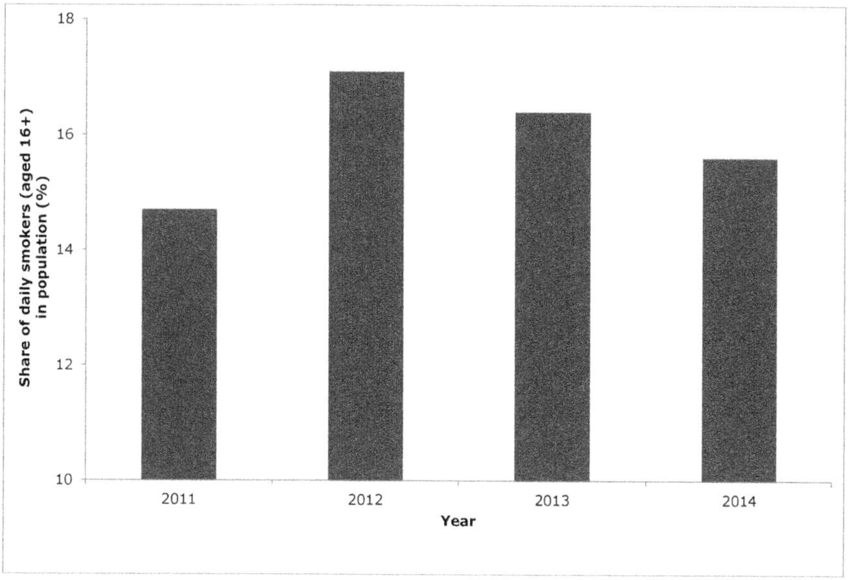

Source: Tobacco Plain Packaging PIR, (Exhibit AUS-624), p. 42.

1.1.7.2   New South Wales School Students Health Behaviours Survey

29.   The New South Wales School Students Health Behaviours Survey (SSHBS) asked students aged 12–17 years a range of questions on alcohol, demographics, height and weight (including perception of body mass), injury, nutrition, physical activity, psychological distress, sedentary behaviour, substance use, sun protection (including sunburn experience and solarium use), and tobacco.

30.   Australia submitted a recent study by Dessaix et al. 2016 based on SSHBS data showing, as highlighted in Figure C.12, the proportion of

---

[26]   See Tobacco Plain Packaging PIR, (Exhibit AUS-624), para. 128.

adolescents reporting current smoking as 6.7% in 2014, down from 23.5% in 1996.[27]

Figure C.12: Smoking Prevalence Among Youth in New South Wales Based on SSHBS Data

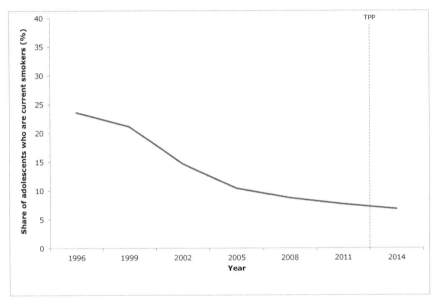

Note: The vertical dashed line indicates the introduction of TPP and enlarged GHWs.

Source: Dessaix et al. 2016, (Exhibit AUS-623), p. 1.

1.1.7.3   South Australian Health Omnibus Survey

31.   The South Australian Health Omnibus Survey (SAHOS) is a representative, cross-sectional survey that has been in operation since 1990. The data discussed by the Dominican Republic cover the years 2004 to 2013.

32.   According to the Dominican Republic, the SAHOS data show, as depicted in **Figure C.13**, that smoking prevalence of the responding population has increased, rather than decreased, in South Australia between 2012, the year prior to the implementation of the TPP measures, and 2013.[28]

---

[27]   See Australia's comments on the complainants' responses to Panel question No. 197, para. 390; and Dessaix et al. 2016, (Exhibit AUS-623), p. 1.
[28]   See Dominican Republic's first written submission, para. 526.

33.   Australia considers that the RMSS data allow a more accurate
comparison of smoking rates immediately prior to and following the introduction
of the TPP measures. Based on the RMSS data, overall smoking prevalence in
South Australia reduced significantly in the 12 months following the
introduction of the TPP measures.[29] Australia's Post-Implementation Review
Tobacco Plain Packaging 2016 also reports a reduction in daily smoking
prevalence in South Australia based on SAHOS (data up to 2014) for individuals
aged 15 years and over, as shown in **Figure C.14**, and the NDSHS (data up to
2013) for individuals aged 14 years and over.[30]

**Figure C.13: Smoking Prevalence in South Australia Based on SAHOS
               Data**

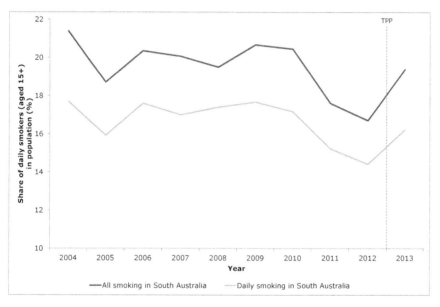

Note: The vertical dashed line indicates the introduction of TPP and enlarged GHWs.

Source: SAHOS data, (Exhibit DOM-93), p. 1.

---

[29]   See Australia's first written submission, Annexure E, paras. 82-86; and Chipty Report, (Exhibit
AUS-17), paras. 80-81.
[30]   See Tobacco Plain Packaging PIR, (Exhibit AUS-624), para. 128.

Figure C.14: Smoking Prevalence in South Australia Based on South Australia Survey Data

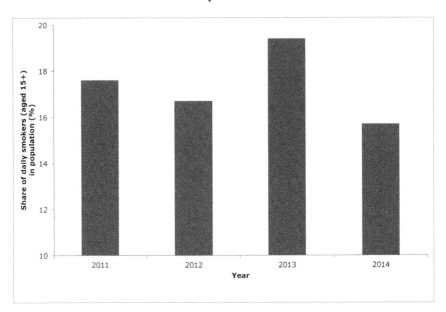

Source: Tobacco Plain Packaging PIR, (Exhibit AUS-624), p. 42.

1.1.7.4   Victorian Smoking and Health Survey

34.   The Victorian Smoking and Health Surveys (VSHS) are cross-sectional telephone surveys undertaken with representative samples of adults aged 18 years and over and residing in the general population of the Australian state of Victoria. The surveys were undertaken from 2 November to 5 December 2011 (inclusive), from 1 November to 3 December 2012, and from 7 November to 11 December 2013.[31]

35.   According to the Dominican Republic, the VSHS data demonstrate, as depicted in **Figure C.15**, that smoking prevalence of the responding population has increased, rather than decreased, in Victoria between 2012, the year prior to the implementation of the TPP measures, and subsequent periods.[32]

36.   Australia claims that the VSHS data does not allow for a proper before/after analysis with respect to the introduction of the TPP measures because the 2012 survey was run from 1 November to 3 December 2012 when a majority of smokers were already using plain packaged products.[33] Australia

---

[31]   See Scollo et al. 2014, (Exhibits AUS-507, JE-24(57)).
[32]   See Dominican Republic's first written submission, para. 526.
[33]   See Australia's first written submission, Annexure E, para. 84.

further argues that, based on the RMSS data, overall smoking prevalence in Victoria reduced significantly in the 12 months following the introduction of the TPP measures.[34] Australia's Post-Implementation Review Tobacco Plain Packaging 2016 also reports a reduction in daily smoking prevalence in Victoria based on the NDSHS (data up to 2013) for individuals aged 14 years, as shown in **Figure C.16**.[35]

Figure C.15: Smoking Prevalence in Victoria Based on VSHS Data

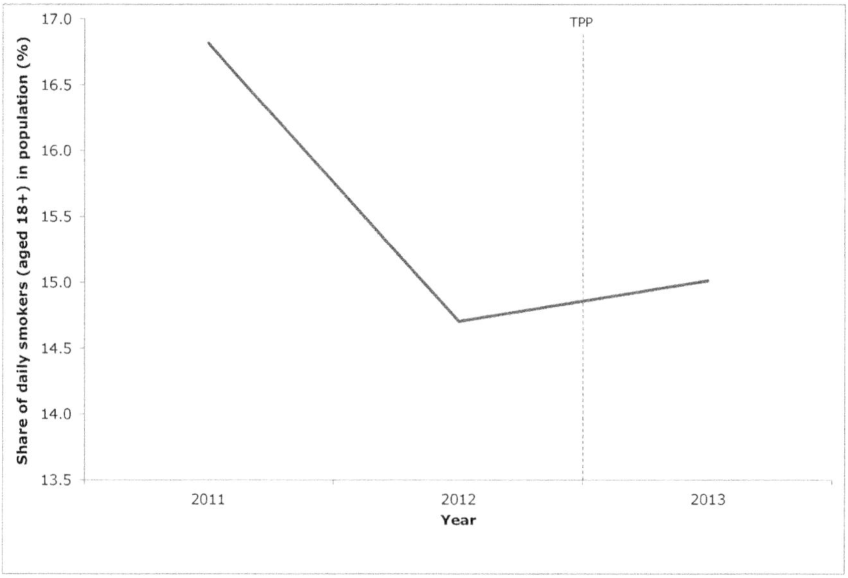

Note: The VSHS are conducted annually from November to December. The vertical dashed line indicates the introduction of TPP and enlarged GHWs.

Source: Dominican Republic's first written submission, p. 159.

---

[34]   See Australia's first written submission, Annexure E, paras. 82-86; and Chipty Report, (Exhibit AUS-17), paras. 80-81.
[35]   See Tobacco Plain Packaging PIR, (Exhibit AUS-624), para. 128.

Figure C.16: Smoking Prevalence in Victoria Based on NDSHS Data

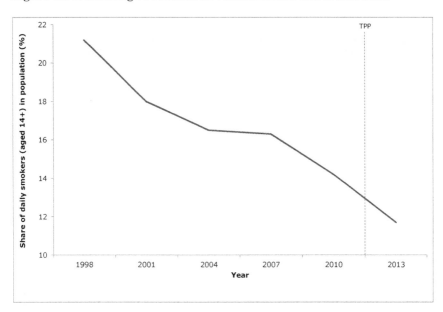

Note: The vertical dashed line indicates the introduction of TPP and enlarged GHWs.

Source: Tobacco Plain Packaging PIR, (Exhibit AUS-624), p. 43.

1.1.7.5 Cancer Council Queensland Survey

37.   Referring to a news item published in an Australian website, the Dominican Republic noted that while prevalence levels decreased for some subsets of the population, there had been a sharp increase in prevalence among Queenslanders aged between 25 and 34 after the implementation of the TPP measures.[36]

38.   Australia submits that according to the RMSS data, overall smoking prevalence in Queensland decreased significantly in the 12 months following the introduction of the TPP measures.[37] More recently, Australia's Post-Implementation Review Tobacco Plain Packaging 2016 reports a reduction in daily smoking prevalence in Queensland based on Queensland survey (data up to 2014) for individuals aged 18 years and over and the NDSHS (data up to 2013) for individuals aged 14 years and over.[38]

---

[36] See Dominican Republic's first written submission, para. 527; and ABC News 2014, (Exhibit DOM-96).
[37] See Australia's first written submission, Annexure E, paras. 82-86; and Chipty Report, (Exhibit AUS-17), paras. 80-81.
[38] See Tobacco Plain Packaging PIR, (Exhibit AUS-624), para. 128.

1.2 Analysis by the Panel

39.   We note at the outset the usefulness of relying on the most recent available (i.e. 2014 and early 2015) and comparable data to analyse trends in smoking prevalence. This is particularly important because the different datasets before us and presented above do not always cover the same period. For instance, the RMSS data continuously cover the period January 2001-September 2015, while the NDSHS covers the period 1993-2013 with data available every two or three years. We also note the importance of distinguishing between smoking prevalence, which measures the proportion of smokers in the population, and smoking incidence, which measures the proportion of smokers in a population of smokers and recent quitters. Unless specified otherwise, we focus on smoking prevalence because, unlike smoking incidence, which ignores individuals who never smoked, smoking prevalence is based on the entire population (i.e. smokers, recent quitters and non-smokers).

40.   After a careful review of the datasets described above, we observe that smoking prevalence fluctuates, even more when the unit of measure is disaggregated (monthly vs. yearly or state-level vs. country-level observations). We agree with Australia that in the presence of small sample sizes, in particular for subgroups such as youth and specific Australian states, it can be particularly difficult to interpret trends. That being said, we see, as depicted in **Figure C.17**, that despite different estimates and fluctuations of smoking prevalence, most of the datasets described above, including the RMSS data, OECD Dataset on Non-Medical Determinants, and NHS, show continuing declines in smoking prevalence at the national level in the period following the introduction of the TPP measures.[39]

41.   While the most recent available data on smoking prevalence confirm that smoking prevalence in Australia continued to decrease following the introduction of the TPP measures, simply observing the existence of the trend does not inform, however, whether this downward trend in smoking prevalence has accelerated. This question is reviewed next.

---

[39]   We note that the smoking prevalence rates reported by the RMSS data are higher than the ones reported by the NHS and OECD data. These differences could be due to different methodology, timing and sample sizes. See Chipty Third Rebuttal Report, (Exhibit AUS-605); NHS Results, (Exhibit AUS-622); Tobacco Plain Packaging PIR, (Exhibit AUS-624); CCV 2014 Survey, (Exhibit AUS-621); and IPE Updated Report, (Exhibit DOM-303).

Figure C.17: Smoking Prevalence in Australia

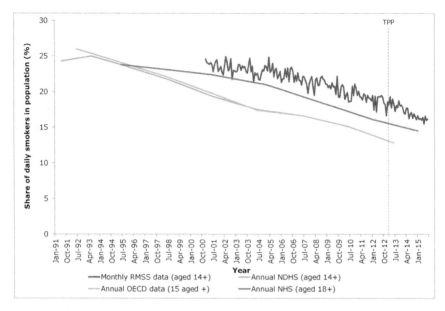

Note: The vertical dashed line indicates the introduction of TPP and enlarged GHWs.

Source: RMSS, NHS, NDHS and OECD data based on Chipty Third Rebuttal Report, (Exhibit
           AUS-605); Tobacco Plain Packaging PIR, (Exhibit AUS-624); NHS Results, (Exhibit
           AUS-622); and IPE Updated Report, (Exhibit DOM-303).

2.   WHETHER THE REDUCTION OF SMOKING PREVALENCE ACCELERATED FOLLOWING THE IMPLEMENTATION OF THE TPP MEASURES (ROY MORGAN SINGLE SOURCE)

42.   As discussed above, the majority of the most recent datasets presented to us show continuing declines in smoking prevalence in Australia in the period following the introduction of the TPP measures. Rather than assessing directly the TPP measures' impact on smoking prevalence, which will be discussed in detail next, the Dominican Republic's experts initially investigated whether there was a shift in smoking prevalence in the post-TPP implementation period. In other words they assessed whether the reduction of smoking prevalence accelerated or slowed down following the implementation of the TPP measures. According to them, if the reduction in smoking prevalence follows the same pre-existing downward trend after the introduction of the TPP measures, this implies that the TPP measures have not reduced smoking prevalence.

2.1   Datasets and related studies

43.   The Dominican Republic first submitted, through IPE, a statistical trend analysis of smoking prevalence using the RMSS dataset. The trend analysis consists of (1) estimating the time trend of smoking prevalence for the pre-TPP

implementation period (before December 2012); (2) predicting the prevalence rate that would have been obtain in any given month following the implementation of the TPP measures on 1 December 2012, in the absence of the TPP measures using the pre-TPP implementation trend; and (3) determining whether the difference between the observed prevalence and the estimated counterfactual prevalence is different from zero by computing confidence intervals.[40]

44.   The trend analysis is undertaken by estimating either a quadratic time trend for the January 2001-March 2014 period or a linear trend model for the January 2006-March 2014 period. In both cases, IPE concludes that there is no statistical difference between observed smoking prevalence of the full population and the estimated counterfactual prevalence of the full population with the exception of the month of December 2012, implying overall that the post-implementation trend did not shift. Similar results are found when the analysis focuses only on minor population and young adult population.[41]

Figure C.18: Smoking Prevalence and Linear Trend

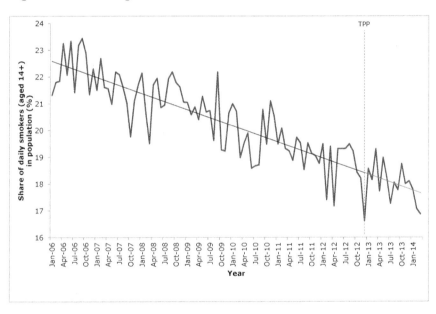

Note: The vertical dashed line indicates the introduction of TPP and enlarged GHWs. The black and red lines represent the linear trends.

Source: RMSS data, based on IPE Report, (Exhibit DOM-100), p. 28.

---

[40]   See IPE Report, (Exhibit DOM-100), pp. 26-27.
[41]   See IPE Report, (Exhibit DOM-100), pp. 28-35, 105-116, 119-156, and 181-199.

45.   Australia's expert, Dr Chipty, rejects the IPE Report's results on the grounds, *inter alia*, that (1) IPE asserts without support that historical trends will continue into the future in the absence of new regulatory measures; (2) IPE does not attempt to evaluate the extent to which past policies contributed to the trend in prevalence; and (3) IPE's model design makes it less likely, and sometimes impossible, to find a policy effect.[42] Australia posits that trends in available data show that overall prevalence in Australia is declining over time, including following the TPP measures. However, given the small sample sizes for certain subgroups, like adolescents or residents of specific Australian states, trends in prevalence can be difficult to interpret.

46.   Australia also submits another expert report by Professor Scharfstein, who further argues that (1) IPE's assumption that smoking prevalence would have continued to decline at the same rate after December 2012, even if the TPP measures had never been introduced, is entirely unsupported without assumptions or a valid natural experiment; (2) IPE's date restriction (i.e. January 2006) in the linear trend model is derived by simply looking at the data; (3) IPE's statistical trend analysis lacks statistical rigor by not specifying a null hypothesis to evaluate whether there is a TPP measures' effect; and most importantly (4) IPE's statistical trend analysis has low statistical power and is inadequate to detect important declines in smoking prevalence after the introduction of the TPP measures.[43]

47.   Professor Scharfstein submits that IPE's methodology applied to the excise tax increase introduced by Australia in April 2010 does not identify a reduction in smoking prevalence after the tax increase, although the complainants have argued that excise taxes, in general, are an effective tool to discourage smoking. Professor Scharfstein further argues that monthly data from the RMSS data cannot reasonably rule out important declines in smoking prevalence in the post-TPP period.[44]

48.   The Dominican Republic's and Indonesia's expert, Professor List, disagrees with Professor Scharfstein and argues that according to Borland (2010) the RMSS data have power to detect small effects. Professor List further argues that the justification for Scharfstein's linear and quadratic time trends starting in 2001 and 2006, respectively, are unsubstantiated. Given the nature of the data, especially the seasonality, the start date chosen will affect the estimate of the downward trend absent of the TPP measures, and therefore change the null hypothesis used. According to Professor List, Professor Scharfstein should have simultaneously considered a gradual descent and a step down of smoking prevalence. Since the only significant decrease in prevalence is December 2012 when the TPP measures were introduced, it is possible that there is a large initial

---

[42] See Chipty Report, (Exhibit AUS-17), paras. 40-43.
[43] See Scharfstein Report, (Exhibit AUS-20), paras. 11-12, 35, and 37-64.
[44] See Scharfstein Report, (Exhibit AUS-20), paras. 12, 51-55, and 65-68.

deviation in smoking prevalence followed by a return to the pre-implementation trend (mean regression).[45]

49.   More generally, Professor List submits that abstracting from the general downward trend in smoking prevalence, there is no sustained change in the previously existing rate of prevalence following the vertical dashed line, depicted in a figure similar to Figure C.18, that denotes the start of the TPP measures in Australia.[46]

50.   Australia's expert, Dr Chipty, contests Professor List's claim that the RMSS data have "power to detect small effects". In Dr Chipty's view, using the classification system in Borland (2010), IPE's methodology does not have sufficient power to detect "small" (less than 0.5 standard deviations of trend), "medium" (between 0.5 and 1), or even most "large" (greater than 1) effects.[47]

51.   Dr Chipty further contends that, unlike Professor List's claim of no sustained change in the smoking prevalence trend following the introduction of the TPP measures, allowing the trend line to be different before and after the TPP measures shows, as depicted in Figure C.19, a break in the trend of smoking prevalence after the TPP measures' implementation, about one percentage point lower relative to where it would have been by June 2015.[48, 49]

---

[45]   See List Report, (Exhibit DOM/IDN-1), paras. 109-112.

[46]   See List Report, (Exhibit DOM/IDN-1), paras. 22-23.

[47]   See Chipty Rebuttal Report, (Exhibit AUS-535) (SCI), paras. 4 and 8.

[48]   See Australia's comments on the complainants' responses to Panel question No. 146, para. 15; and Chipty Second Rebuttal Report, (Exhibit AUS-591), paras. 8-12. A similar graphic for the period January 2001-September 2015 is included in the Tobacco Plain Packaging PIR (Exhibit AUS-624), p. 35.

[49]   See Australia's comments on the complainants' responses to Panel question No. 146, para. 15.

Figure C.19: Smoking Prevalence and Pre- and Post-TPP Trends

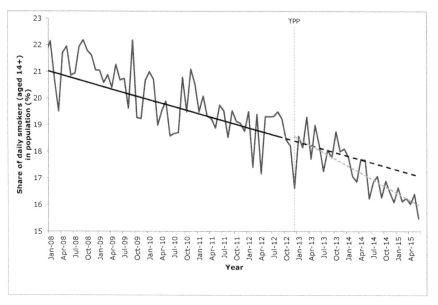

Note: The vertical dashed line indicates the introduction of TPP and enlarged GHWs. The dashed line and the dotted line denote, respectively, the pre-TPP linear trend and the post-TPP linear trend.

Source: RMSS data, based on Chipty Second Rebuttal Report, (Exhibit AUS-591), p. 10.

52.   A similar figure for the period January 2001-September 2015 is included in the Post-Implementation Review Tobacco Plain Packaging 2016, with which the Dominican Republic took issue. According to the Dominican Republic, the figure is misleading, for at least three reasons: (1) it glosses over the clear break in trend that occurred in June 2006, as demonstrated by IPE[50]; (2) October, November, and December 2012 are omitted in the construction of the pre-TPP trend, thus artificially making the pre-implementation trend line less steep; (3) the post-implementation trend is inconsistent with previous visualizations adduced by Dr Chipty during the WTO proceedings. The Dominican Republic submits that given Dr Chipty's failure to provide back-up material for her analysis, this inconsistency is difficult to explain.[51]

---

[50]   See IPE Report, (Exhibit DOM-100), p. 109; and IPE Third Updated Report, (Exhibit DOM-375), paras. 32-49.
[51]   See Dominican Republic's comments on Australia's Post-Implementation Review, paras. 69-70 and fn 85.

2.2   Analysis by the Panel

53.   We note at the outset that the parties have discussed extensively whether there is a secular and long-term downward trend in smoking prevalence in Australia and how to specify the smoking prevalence trend (e.g. linear or quadratic) in different contexts related to the contribution of the TPP measures. This will be discussed more extensively in the next subsection, which reviews the econometric studies aimed at assessing the impact of the TPP measures on smoking prevalence and smoking incidence.

54.   We further note that, although more recent data were available over the course of the proceedings, IPE did not update the results of its statistical trend analysis. Instead, in reply to some of the criticism raised by Australia's experts, IPE proposed a "modified trend analysis", which acknowledges that the original statistical trend analysis does not control for other relevant variables explaining the evolution of smoking prevalence beyond the trend. The "modified trend analysis" is based on an entirely different methodology discussed in the next subsection.

55.   In this context, we consider that the results of the original trend analysis provided by the IPE Report are not informative, not only because it fails to control for other relevant variables affecting smoking prevalence but also because it is unclear if the results of the trend analysis would have changed with the more recent data made available to us.

56.   Overall, based on the most recent available RMSS data, we note that smoking prevalence in Australia has not only continued to decrease following the introduction of the TPP measures, but that the downward trend in smoking prevalence has accelerated with a steeper slope of the smoking prevalence trend between December 2012 and September 2015 (latest available observations submitted by the parties) compared to the pre-TPP periods.

57.   That being said, this change in the smoking prevalence trend following the introduction of the TPP measures does not necessarily imply that the TPP measures are having a statistically significant impact, to the extent that other factors could explain such evolution, including other tobacco control policies. Indeed, most of the discussion among the parties' experts focused on assessing econometrically the impact of the TPP measures on smoking prevalence by controlling for other factors. This is reviewed next.

3.   WHETHER THE TPP MEASURES CONTRIBUTED TO THE REDUCTION IN SMOKING PREVALENCE

58.   The parties disagree on whether the TPP measures contributed to reducing smoking prevalence, i.e. had a negative impact on smoking prevalence. This issue gave rise to detailed technical exchanges between IPE for the Dominican Republic, Professor List for the Dominican Republic and Indonesia, Professor Klick for Honduras, and Dr Chipty for Australia, who each proposed different econometric methods to estimate the TPP measures' impact on smoking

prevalence or smoking incidence. As mentioned above, all parties, however, recognize that the empirical econometric evidence on smoking prevalence submitted does not distinguish between the impact of TPP and the impact of enlarged GHWs, because both measures were implemented at the exact same time.[52]

59.   Australia has argued that the impacts of the TPP measures on prevalence may not fully manifest in short term datasets[53] and that it is inappropriate to seek to judge the efficacy of the TPP measures on the basis of limited short term datasets.[54] First, reducing smoking prevalence is a long-term objective.[55] Second, large changes in the root behaviours (i.e. initiation, cessation, and relapse) stemming from the TPP measures are likely masked in smoking prevalence because of the stock of current smokers whose behaviours may not be as affected by the TPP measures.[56] Notwithstanding this position, Australia re-estimated the impact of the TPP measures on smoking prevalence, in response to the submissions of the Dominican Republic, Honduras and Indonesia. During the course of the proceedings and as more prevalence-related data became available, Australia argued that using the most appropriate dataset available and correcting for flaws in the econometric models put forward by the experts of the Dominican Republic, Honduras, and Indonesia, the results show that the TPP measures have already contributed to the reduction of cigarette and cigar smoking prevalence.[57]

60.   A particular feature of the exchange between the parties on this issue is that, on several occasions, the experts of the Dominican Republic, Honduras and Indonesia proposed in their rebuttal reports new models or methodologies, or both, that sometimes contradict some of the approaches taken in their earlier reports and invalidate the results reported in those reports.[58] For this reason, the

---

[52]   See List Report, (Exhibit DOM/IDN-1), para. 113.

[53]   See Australia's response to Panel questions No. 126 and 200 and Australia's first written submission, para. 670.

[54]   See Australia's first written submission, para. 17.

[55]   See Australia's first written submission, para. 670. Instead Australia claimed that the TPP measures' impact should be investigated through its mechanisms by looking at its impact on non-behavioural outcomes, that is, (1) reduction in the appeal of tobacco products, (2) increased effectiveness of health warnings, and (3) reduction of the ability of the pack to mislead. The evidence on these non-behavioural outcomes is considered in Appendix A.

[56]   See Chipty Report, (Exhibit AUS-17), paras. 32-39; Scharfstein Report, (Exhibit AUS-20), para. 68.

[57]   See Australia's opening statement at the second hearing of the Panel, paras. 110-111; and comments on the complainants' responses to Panel question No. 197, para. 214.

[58]   For instance, as discussed in detail below, IPE initially proposed to control for excise tax increases by including (dummy) indicator variables for each excise tax increase (IPE Updated Report, (Exhibit DOM-303)), but subsequently contended that a more appropriate measure to capture the excise tax increases is the weighted average price per cigarette in Australia (IPE Second Updated Report, (Exhibit DOM-361)). Similarly, Professor List and IPE initially applied the STATA software command ivreg2 in order to calculate standard errors that are robust to heteroscedasticity and serial correlation using the automatic bandwidth selection procedure by Newey and West 1994. IPE

description of the approaches and results below is based primarily on the most recent expert reports submitted by the parties.[59]

3.1 Datasets and related studies

3.1.1 Roy Morgan Single Source

61. The RMSS data were used by the experts of the Dominican Republic, Honduras, Indonesia, and Australia to assess whether the TPP measures have contributed to the reduction in smoking prevalence.

62. Australia and its expert Professor Scharfstein consider that the RMSS data covering 15 post-implementation months (December 2012 to March 2014) cannot rule out important declines in smoking prevalence in the post-policy period.[60] Australia's expert Dr Chipty nonetheless considers the RMSS data, which is a nationally representative dataset available from January 2001 to September 2015, to be her "preferred data source" for the analysis of smoking prevalence.[61]

3.1.1.1 IPE Reports

63. The Dominican Republic submitted five reports prepared by IPE aimed at estimating econometrically the TPP measures' impact on, among other things, smoking prevalence using the RMSS data. Throughout these IPE Reports, different econometric approaches have been proposed: (1) statistical trend analysis[62]; (2) two-stage micro-econometric analysis; (3) modified trend analysis; (4) autoregressive integrated moving average with explanatory variable (ARIMAX) model; and (5) one-stage micro-econometric analysis.[63] The first two approaches were only presented in the first IPE Report.[64] The second and

---

Updated Report, (Exhibit DOM-303); and List Report, (Exhibit DOM/IDN-1). Subsequently, both Professor List and IPE applied an alternative way of calculating standard errors, that, according to them, is adjusted to reflect more accurately the original suggestion by Newey and West (1994). IPE Second Updated Report, (Exhibit DOM-361); and List Rebuttal Report, (Exhibit DOM/IDN-3).

[59] We note that we have nonetheless considered all the relevant evidence before us, including all the expert reports, including the methodologies and models contained therein.

[60] Australia's first written submission, Annexure E, para. 45; and Scharfstein Report, (Exhibit AUS-20), para. 68.

[61] See Chipty Third Rebuttal Report, (Exhibit AUS-605), para. 70.

[62] As described above, given that the statistical trend analysis does not specify explicitly the impact of the TPP measures, we consider it to be different from the remaining approaches, which explicitly control for the TPP measures and other relevant variables beyond the trend.

[63] See IPE Report, (Exhibit DOM-100); IPE Updated Report, (Exhibit DOM-303); IPE Second Updated Report, (Exhibit DOM-361); IPE Third Updated Report, (Exhibit DOM-375); and IPE Summary Report, (Exhibit DOM-379).

[64] The two-stage micro-econometric analysis initially proposed but then set aside by IPE was the object of several critiques raised by Australia's expert, Professor Scharfstein. Professor Scharfstein argues that the analysis misinterprets the constant terms in the first-stage model by considering the estimated likelihood of smoking for a specific nonsensical subgroup of individuals: males, age zero, with zero years of education, who are positioned at the very top of the income distribution. In Professor Scharfstein's view, this misinterpretation is important because these constant terms serve as

---

subsequent IPE Reports only focused on the last three approaches, which to some extent have been adopted to address some of the criticisms raised by Australia's experts, Dr Chipty and Professor Scharfstein. As well as using different estimation techniques, these approaches differ also in terms of model specifications, that is the set of explanatory variables used to explain the evolution of smoking prevalence and that are included explicitly in the model, such as tobacco policies and demographic variables. The only variable common to all econometric approaches is a variable capturing the smoking prevalence trend, although the trend is assumed to be linear in some cases and quadratic (i.e. curved) in others depending on the sample period covered. The most recent econometric analysis presented in the IPE Report covers the period July 2006 to September 2015.

64.   Overall, IPE concludes that the TPP measures had no statistically significant effect on general smoking prevalence and on cigar smoking prevalence.[65] Other factors explain the reduction in smoking prevalence, such as the overall declining trend. According to IPE, these results are robust across different specifications (e.g. different TPP measures' starting date: October, November and December; controlling for the weighted average price of cigarettes and/or tax policy change, population sample weighting changes by Roy Morgan Research, extending the sample period back to January 2001-September 2015).

65.   Australia's expert, Dr Chipty, rejects the econometric results of the IPE Reports on various technical grounds. First, according to Dr Chipty, there is no

---

the critical input to IPE's second-stage analysis and are the basis of IPE's conclusions about the effects of the TPP measures. Professor Scharfstein submits that the results of IPE's two-stage micro-econometric analysis would show evidence of a TPP effect if different demographic subgroups were considered by redefining ("centering") the variables in the first-stage model. See Scharfstein Report, (Exhibit AUS-20), paras. 73-84.

IPE argues in its report that Professor Scharfstein's analysis is misspecified, and that his findings are entirely driven by this misspecification, which attributes the effects of the secular downward trend to the TPP measures. See IPE Updated Report, (Exhibit DOM-303), paras. 69-74.

Professor List criticises the fact that Professor Scharfstein's analysis suffers from the same issues Professor Scharfstein argues affect the constructed constant term in the IPE Report by constructing the constant term for individuals that do not exist in the data and failing to construct the constant term for some individuals. Professor List further argues that Professor Scharfstein's reanalysis overstates the importance of the TPP measures' impact for two reasons. First, the statistical analysis does not account for the fact that this is a case of multiple hypothesis testing, which increases the probability of at least one incorrect rejection. Second, the statistical analysis does not account in the second stage analysis for all background changes not related to the policy, such as tax increases and macroeconomic factors. See List Report, (Exhibit DOM/IDN-1), paras. 113-122.

Professor Scharfstein contends that both IPE and Professor List have misinterpreted his critiques of the two-stage micro-econometric analysis, confusing his demonstration of its flaws with an affirmative opinion about the effect of the TPP measures. In his view, the two-stage micro-econometric analysis, even after the modification he made to it, remains flawed and should not be used to assess the impact of the TPP measures. See Scharfstein rebuttal report, (Exhibit AUS-587), paras. 12-19.

[65]   See IPE Summary Report, (Exhibit DOM-379), paras. 11-24, Appendix 6.

credible justification for excluding data prior to July 2006 and the analysis should cover the 2001-2015 period.[66] Second, Dr Chipty rejects IPE's assertion that the STATA software command, ivreg2, used to estimate standard errors robust to "heteroscedasticity"[67] and "autocorrelation"[68] (Newey-West standard errors) is wrong, noting that IPE used the same STATA command, before Professor List claimed he found an error in the STATA programming code.[69] Third, Dr Chipty argues that controlling for prices inclusive of tax while attempting to measure the effects of a tax hike ignores the TPP measures' effect on price, leading the TPP indicator variable to capture only a partial effect of the TPP measures, and the price variable capturing the rest of its effect. Dr Chipty further notes that IPE initially controlled for excise tax increase with indicator variables in its model specification but then decided to replace it with a price variable.[70] Fourth, and similarly, Dr Chipty submits that the use of single tax level variable, as proposed by IPE, is only valid under the proportionality assumption (i.e. the effect of tax changes on prevalence is proportional to the size of the tax change), which may only be satisfied in some specifications (for instance, the model of cigar smoking prevalence does not satisfy this assumption).[71] Finally, Dr Chipty argues that the inability of IPE to measure a negative and statistically significant effect of the TPP measures on prevalence stems from challenges associated with the inclusion of a time trend: (a) the inclusion of a linear trend (for the July 2006-September 2015 sample); or (b) allowing the trend line to both shift and change slope at July 2006 (for the January 2001-September 2015). In each case, Dr Chipty notes that the time trend absorbs all policy effects, noting that in most specifications the impact of excise tax (or tobacco price), considered by all complainants as one of the most effective tobacco control measures, is not statistically significant.[72]

3.1.1.2 Professor List's reports

66. The Dominican Republic and Indonesia's expert Professor List reconsiders the RMSS data and estimates a two-stage micro-econometric model. The first stage estimates the likelihood of a representative person being a smoker for each month controlling for demographic characteristics (e.g. age, fourth order polynomials[73] of gender, education, and income). The second stage conducts a before and after analysis on the likelihood for each month computed

---

[66] See Chipty Surrebuttal Report, (Exhibit AUS-586), para. 9; and Chipty Third Rebuttal Report, (Exhibit AUS-605), paras. 34-35.
[67] Heteroscedasticity arises when the regression errors variances are not constant across observations. W. H. Green, *Econometric Analysis*, 5th edn (Prentice Hall, 2002).
[68] Autocorrelation or serial correlation of the disturbances arises when the disturbances are correlated across periods. W. H. Green, *Econometric Analysis*, 5th edn (Prentice Hall, 2002).
[69] See Chipty Second Rebuttal Report, (Exhibit AUS-591), paras. 13-31.
[70] See Chipty Surrebuttal Report, (Exhibit AUS-586), para. 12.
[71] See Chipty Third Rebuttal Report, (Exhibit AUS-605), paras. 22-26 and 29-32.
[72] See Chipty Third Rebuttal Report, (Exhibit AUS-605), paras. 36-42.
[73] A fourth order polynomial of a given variable x corresponds to x^1, x^2, x^3 and x^4.

in the first stage by estimating a linear probability model controlling for the TPP measures, price and/or linear trend, and weighting changes by Roy Morgan Research. The most recent econometric analysis presented in Professor List's report covers the period from July 2006 to September 2015.

67. Overall, Professor List concludes that the TPP measures had no statistically significant effect on the likelihood of a representative Australian smoker or of a representative Australian minor and young adult smoking.[74] According to Professor List, these results are robust across different specifications (e.g. different TPP starting date: October, November and December). The results are also robust to an alternative way of calculating the explanatory variables' standard errors that are robust to heteroscedasticity and autocorrelation and correct compared to the STATA software package ivreg2 used by Dr Chipty. The standard error of the explanatory variables, including the TPP measures, is important to determine whether the respective variable is statistically different from zero or not. According to Professor List, his new procedure to compute standards errors follows exactly the procedure described in the seminal article of Newey and West (1994) in order to select the maximum amount of time that the data can be correlated over time (maximum lag selection). The same method was also used in the latest IPE Reports.

68. Australia's expert, Dr Chipty, submits that the econometric results on smoking prevalence of Professor List are flawed for many of the same reasons formulated with respect to IPE Reports. In particular, Dr Chipty contests restricting the sample to the period 2006-2015; using a price variable without correcting for the TPP measures' effect on price; including a trend variable that absorbs all policy effects, and the assertion that the STATA software command ivreg2, used to estimate robust standard errors, is wrong. In addition, Dr Chipty considers Professor List's attempts to correct for the sample re-weighting contained in the RMSS data to be unsound, noting that this was an entirely new concern about the RMSS data that had not been raised before in any of the expert debate.[75]

3.1.1.3 Professor Klick's reports

69. Honduras's expert Professor Klick also reconsiders the RMSS data and estimates a two-stage micro-econometric model. The first stage estimates the TPP measures' impact on tobacco price controlling for excise tax indicators. The second stage estimates the TPP measures' impact on the likelihood a respondent is a smoker by estimating a linear probability model controlling for the TPP measures, the logarithm of tobacco price instrumented by excise tax indicators in the first stage, quadratic trend, 2006 GHW and demographic characteristics (e.g. sex, married status, urban status, age, income, education, territory and job category). The TPP measures' impact corresponds to the sum of

---

[74] See List Third Supplemental Report, (Exhibit DOM/IDN-7), paras. 78-80.
[75] See Chipty Second Rebuttal Report, (Exhibit AUS-591), paras. 32-38.

the direct effect of TPP measures on the probability a respondent is a smoker and the indirect effect of the TPP measures defined as the product of the TPP measures' effect on price and the effect of price change on the probability a respondent is a smoker.[76] The most recent econometric analysis presented in Professor Klick's Report covers the period from January 2001 to June 2015.

70.   Overall, Professor Klick concludes that the TPP measures had no statistically significant effect on the likelihood that a respondent is a smoker.[77] Professor Klick further re-estimates his model focusing on young people (14-24 years old). While the TPP measures' impact is not statistically significant for the age groups 14-17 and 18-19, the TPP measures' impact is positive and statistically significant for the age group 20-24.[78] According to Professor Klick, these results are robust across different specifications (e.g. different TPP starting date: October, November and December).

71.   Dr Chipty rejects Professor Klick's use of a quadratic time trend variable, because it absorbs virtually all of the variation in smoking prevalence and leaves no room for any other explanatory variables, including price, to have a measurable effect on smoking prevalence.[79] In addition, Dr Chipty argues that Professor Klick's two-steps instrument variables approach does not yield reliable estimates for the standard error and confidence interval of the TPP measures' total effect.[80]

3.1.1.4 Dr Chipty's reports

72.   Dr Chipty considers the RMSS data to be her preferred data for assessing the TPP measures' impact on smoking prevalence because of its large sample size, sufficient pre-period, and national representativeness. However, as explained above, Dr Chipty rejects the econometric results of the reports by IPE, Professor List and Professor Klick on various technical grounds. Dr Chipty addresses these critics by re-estimating the models of smoking prevalence developed by IPE (one-stage micro-econometric analysis and modified trend analysis) by extending the period of analysis from January 2001 to September 2015, controlling for a linear trend, a 2006 GHW dummy, a set of excise tax indicators and a set of socio-demographic characteristics, and correcting for robust standard errors (when necessary). Dr Chipty also re-estimates the model of smoking prevalence developed by Professor List (two-stage micro-econometric analysis) by correcting for robust standard errors. Similarly, Dr Chipty re-estimates Professor Klick's two-stage instrument variables micro-econometric analysis by replacing the quadratic linear variable with a linear trend.

---

[76]   See Klick Third Supplemental Rebuttal Report, (Exhibit HND-166), para. 21.
[77]   See Klick Third Supplemental Rebuttal Report, (Exhibit HND-166), paras. 11-23.
[78]   See Klick Third Supplemental Rebuttal Report, (Exhibit HND-166), paras. 54-55.
[79]   See Chipty Third Rebuttal Report, (Exhibit AUS-605), paras. 49-53.
[80]   See Chipty Third Rebuttal Report, (Exhibit AUS-605), paras. 54-60.

73.   Overall, Dr Chipty concludes that the TPP measures had a negative and statistically significant effect on smoking prevalence.[81] Most of the results show statistically significant declines in smoking prevalence even when using Professor List's own standard error calculation procedure. The negative and statistically significant impact of the TPP measures on smoking prevalence is also robust to controlling for the reweighting of the RMSS data. Similarly, replacing the tax indicator variables with a single tax level variable produces similar point estimates of the TPP measures' effect.

74.   IPE, Professor List and Professor Klick raise a number of criticisms of Dr Chipty's econometric approaches. According to IPE, Dr Chipty's model specifications covering the January 2001-September 2015 period fail to account for two different linear downward trends in smoking prevalence: one for the January 2001-June 2006 period and another for the July 2006-September 2015 period. As a result, Dr Chipty overestimates the downward trend in smoking prior to June 2006, while underestimating it afterwards.[82]

75.   IPE further contends that the use of tax hike dummies, as proposed by Dr Chipty, are inferior control variables compared to cigarette prices and tax levels for three reasons: (i) consumers base their choices on what cigarettes cost; (ii) it is important to control for, by how much a certain price increase affects prevalence, and not only whether it affects prevalence; and (iii) tax hike dummies (or tax levels) do not control for changes in tobacco affordability other than the price changes resulting from the tax hikes themselves.[83]

76.   Professor List submits that Dr Chipty's opposition to using control variables for reweighting events of the population sample in the RMSS data may stem from the fact that an adjustment for reweighting would reverse Dr Chipty's estimates of the TPP measures' effect.[84] Failure to correct for reweighting changes may thus lead to misspecification.[85]

77.   Professor List, IPE and Professor Klick argue that Dr Chipty computed incorrect standards errors by applying the STATA command ivreg2, which substantially deviates from the seminal article by Newey and West (1994). Professor List further submits that Dr Chipty's method to compute standards errors assigns statistical significance nearly 400% more frequently than it should. Applying the exact procedure proposed by Newey and West (1994),

[81]   See Chipty Third Rebuttal Report, (Exhibit AUS-605), paras. 29-32, 52-53 and 70-73; and Chipty Second Rebuttal Report, (Exhibit AUS-591), paras. 28-38, 53-54, Appendix D.
[82]   See IPE Summary Report, (Exhibit DOM-379), paras. 50-52.
[83]   See IPE Third Updated Report, (Exhibit DOM-375), para. 139; and IPE Summary Report, (Exhibit DOM-379), paras. 56-60.
[84]   See List Third Supplemental Report, (Exhibit DOM/IDN-7), paras. 51-55.
[85]   See IPE Summary Report, (Exhibit DOM-379), paras. 53-54.

Professor List and IPE conclude that most of Dr Chipty's specifications no longer exhibit a statistically significant TPP effect.[86]

3.1.2 Commissioned Roy Morgan Research Survey (Australia and New Zealand)

78.   Honduras's expert Professor Klick proposes comparing Australia's smoking behaviour before and after the introduction of the TPP measures with another jurisdiction that has not implemented plain packaging during the same period. Professor Klick posits that although Australia is unique in many ways, it is reasonable to use New Zealand as a reliable counterfactual jurisdiction, because (i) both countries share many similarities culturally, historically, and demographically; (ii) both countries are in the same region and share the same seasonality (useful when dealing with subannual measures); (iii) the governments of both countries themselves also recognize that they are especially comparable along dimensions such as health behaviour and socio-economic issues; (iv) tobacco prices, including taxes, are comparable between both countries; and (v) smoking rates in both countries are highly correlated (0.95 for the period 1964-2012 based on OECD data on the fraction of residents ages 15 years and older who are daily smokers).[87] Professor Klick's analysis, defined as a difference-in-difference estimation, covers the period from November 2012 to February 2014.

79.   Overall, Professor Klick concludes that the TPP measures' impact on daily or occasional smoking in Australia relative to New Zealand is not statistically significant.[88] Similar findings are obtained by using different estimators (linear probability model and logit model and fixed effects), restricting the sample to only individuals who answered the survey in the 6 waves (to mitigate attrition), restricting the sample to only individuals who answered the survey at least in one post-PP waves (to mitigate attrition), restricting the sample to Wave 1 and Wave 6 (to not overweight immediate responses), restricting the sample to smokers planning to quit during Wave 1, and controlling for individual characteristics (income, unemployed, male, age).

80.   Dr Chipty argues that Professor Klick's difference-in-differences analysis of smoking incidence is invalid because Professor Klick's commissioned Roy Morgan survey does not contain a pre-period and is incapable of distinguishing which respondents had noticed plain packaging. Furthermore, Dr Chipty is of the view that New Zealand is an invalid counterfactual for the purposes of studying

---

[86]   See List Third Supplemental Report, (Exhibit DOM/IDN-7), paras. 42-50; List Summary Report, (Exhibit DOM/IDN-9), paras. 83-98; IPE Summary Report, (Exhibit DOM-379), paras. 61-65; and Klick Fourth Supplemental Rebuttal Report, (Exhibit HND-169), paras. 16-20.

[87]   See Klick Report, (Exhibit UKR-5), pp. 3-6.

[88]   See Klick Report, (Exhibit UKR-5), pp. 23-32; and Klick Rebuttal Report, (Exhibit HND-118), paras. 19-38.

the effects of the TPP measures, because of New Zealand's January 2013 excise tax increase, a month after the TPP measures' introduction.[89]

81.   Dr Chipty submits that Professor Klick's data show that Australia has experienced both a bigger absolute decline and faster rate of decline in daily smoking incidence than New Zealand, although there is no measurable decline in overall smoking, which is consistent with the possibility that the TPP measures are having its intended effect.[90]

3.1.3   New South Wales Population Health Survey

82.   The New South Wales Population Health Survey (NSWPHS) reports yearly observation of daily smoking prevalence and smoking in general prevalence among men and women in NSW, the most populated state in Australia.

83.   Professor Klick estimates a model of (daily or overall) smoking prevalence in NSW controlling for the TPP measures and a linear time trend. The econometric analysis covers the period from 2002 to 2014. Because the NSWPHS data are only available on an annual basis, the TPP variable is coded in different ways for the year 2012: (i) using the value of 0.25 (representing three months out of the year if an October start date is assumed); (ii) using the value of 0.08 (representing a single month if a December start date is assumed), or (iii) using the value of zero (if it is assumed that the vast majority of survey respondents would have answered the survey pre-TPP).

84.   Overall, Professor Klick concludes that the TPP measures either had no statistically significant effect on daily smoking prevalence in NSW or had a positive and statistically significant impact on smoking prevalence in general in NSW.[91] An analysis across age groups and/or by gender yields relatively similar results.

85.   Dr   Chipty   considers   that   Professor Klick's   analysis   of   smoking prevalence in NSW should be disregarded in its entirety because of three basic problems. First, Dr Chipty argues that Professor Klick is incorrect to assert that Australia-wide   data   are   not   granular   enough   to   credibly   examine   the TPP measures' effects on smoking prevalence. Second, Dr Chipty is of the view that the NSWPHS data are incapable of providing a basis to study the TPP measures' effects in NSW, because the estimate of the TPP effect is

---

[89]   See Chipty Rebuttal Report, (Exhibit AUS-535) (SCI), paras. 54-71. In its third-party submission, New Zealand similarly argues that Professor Klick's study sets up a false and virtually impossible evaluation test by looking for a marked short-term reduction in population smoking prevalence. New Zealand also submits that the use of New Zealand as a comparison case is superficial and misleading, because Professor Klick does not separately analyse the declining trends in smoking prevalence in each country by taking into account the range and variety of tobacco control interventions taken in each country, including the 10% excise tax increase implemented in New Zealand in January 2013, which was unique to New Zealand during the relevant time period.
[90]   See Chipty Report, (Exhibit AUS-17), paras. 25-31, Appendix C.
[91]   See Klick Supplemental Rebuttal Report, (Exhibit HND-122), paras. 33-43.

calculated from two to three data points and cannot be distinguished from the two excise tax increases in 2013 and 2014. Finally, Dr Chipty asserts that there have been changes in the NSW survey methodology that led to a greater number of younger people and males in the survey sample; both of these groups have relatively higher smoking rates, leading to a higher overall reported rate of current smoking.[92]

3.1.4 Cancer Institute New South Wales Tobacco Tracking Survey

86.   Professor Klick estimates a logit model of the likelihood that the respondent is a smoker, an ordered logit model of the smoking status, and a negative binomial model of the number of adults who are smokers in the household controlling for the TPP measures, annual time trend, gender, individual age fixed effects, week of survey fixed effects and location fixed effects. The econometric analysis covers the period from January 2009 to December 2014.

87.   Overall, Professor Klick concludes that the TPP measures either had no statistically significant effect on the likelihood of being a smoker in NSW and on the number of adult smokers in household or had a positive and statistically significant impact on the likelihood of being a daily smoker in NSW and on the smoking status.[93]

88.   Australia posits that although Honduras has presented analyses based on a range of other datasets, such as the CITTS data, these are not sources of smoking prevalence data.[94] Australia's expert, Professor Chaloupka, is further of the view that using these data to assess the TPP measures' impact on the likelihood of being a smoker, as Professor Klick does, is inappropriate. Professor Chaloupka further argues that Professor Klick's conclusion of no evidence of a decline in smoking associated with the TPP measures is highly misleading, because the nature of the NSW Tracking Survey data does not allow one to use these data to assess the TPP measures' impact on adult smoking prevalence given that the sample is not a representative sample of the NSW adult population. In addition, Professor Chaloupka contends that Professor Klick failed to appropriately account for the changes in the CITTS methodology that led to a greater number of younger people and males in the survey sample; both of these groups have relatively higher smoking rates, leading almost certainly to biased estimates towards showing an increase in smoking following the change in method.[95]

---

[92]   See Chipty Surrebuttal Report, (Exhibit AUS-586), paras. 78-86.
[93]   See Klick Second Supplemental Rebuttal Report, (Exhibit HND-165), paras. 15-24.
[94]   See Australia's response to Panel question No. 196, para. 252.
[95]   See Chaloupka Second Rebuttal Report, (Exhibit AUS-590), paras. 26-27.

3.1.5   National Tobacco Plain Packaging Tracking Survey

89.   As described in Appendix A, Australia funded the National Tobacco Plain Packaging Tracking Survey (NTPPTS), a nationwide cross-sectional baseline tracking survey conducted by CCV, to track the effects of the TPP measures. The results from the NTPPTS were published in April 2015 in the supplement to the *Tobacco Control* journal dedicated to investigating the effects of Australia's implementation of the TPP measures.

3.1.5.1   Ajzen et al.'s reports

90.   Ajzen et al. re-analysed part of Scollo et al. 2015a[96], applying the approach in Wakefield et al. 2015.[97] Ajzen et al. estimated logistic, ordered logistic and linear regressions of the proportion of daily or weekly smokers, while controlling for age group, gender, education group, socio-economic status group, potential exposure to televised anti-smoking advertising campaigns in the past three months and cigarette costliness.[98]

91.   Overall, Ajzen et al. conclude that the TPP measures had no statistically significant impact on the proportion of daily or weekly smokers.[99] A similar finding is found with quarterly data.[100] Ajzen et al. argue that, unlike Professor Chaloupka's assertion that the NTPPTS dataset has less power for detecting statistically significant changes in the more distal outcomes, such as actual tobacco use behaviour, the statistical power of the NTPPTS data to detect small changes in proximal and distal outcomes is very similar.[101]

92.   Australia's expert, Professor Chaloupka, argues that Ajzen et al.'s analyses of the NTPPTS data fail to recognize that the TPP measures' impact should be smaller for the less proximal outcomes when one looks at the impact in the overall sample of smokers and recent quitters, given that smokers and

---

[96]   Ajzen et al. argue that Scollo et al. 2015a's conclusion that the TPP measures had no significant effect on the average number of cigarettes consumed per day underreports additional results that were not statistically significant. According to Ajzen et al., Scollo et al. 2015a reported on only one of the seven measures on smoking behaviours and the TPP measures' impact on each of the six unreported variables, dealing with the percentage of daily or weekly smokers, quitting, and relapse was not statistically significant. See Ajzen et al. Data Report, (Exhibit DOM/IDN-2), paras. 225-227. We note, however, that Ajzen et al. do not reassess the analysis by Scollo et al. 2015a of the TPP measures' impact and tax increase on type of tobacco products and price.

[97]   Wakefield et al. 2015, (Exhibits AUS-206, DOM-306).

[98]   We note that Ajzen et al. also re-estimate their models by replacing the TPP measures dummies with a monthly time trend.

[99]   Ajzen et al. reach the same conclusion with respect to measures related to quitting and relapse, which were unreported by Scollo et al. 2015a. In particular, on quitting, Ajzen et al. conclude that there was no statistical change in the proportion of adult smokers that quit for more than one month or had successfully quit between baseline and follow-up. On relapse, Ajzen et al. conclude that there was no statistical change in the proportion of adult ex-smokers that relapsed, still abstained from smoking at follow-up or had stayed quit for more than one week at follow-up. See Ajzen et al. Data Report, (Exhibit DOM/IDN-2), paras. 221-224, Appendix A, pp. 95-97.

[100]   See Ajzen et al. Data Rebuttal Report, (Exhibit DOM/IDN-6), para. 90.

[101]   See Ajzen et al. Data Rebuttal Report, (Exhibit DOM/IDN-6), paras. 50-54, Appendix II.

recent quitters for whom the most proximal outcomes were unaffected would not be expected to show any change in the less proximal outcomes.[102]

3.1.5.2   Professor Klick's report

93.   Professor Klick estimates a logistic regression of the likelihood the respondent is a daily smoker or a smoker in general or an ordered logit model of the smoking status, controlling for the TPP measures, gender, age, education, socio-economic status and a linear time trend. The econometric analysis covers the period from 9 April 2012 to 4 May 2014.[103]

94.   Overall, Professor Klick concludes that the TPP measures had no statistically significant effect on the likelihood of being a smoker and on the smoking status during their first year of implementation.[104]

95.   Australia posits that the NTPPTS data are not a source of smoking prevalence data.[105] Although Australia's experts do not specifically address Professor Klick's results on smoking status based on the NTPPTS data, Professor Chaloupka generally argues that the NTPPTS is particularly useful in assessing the TPP measures' impact on proximal outcomes (appeal, noticeability of health warnings and misleading) but the largely cross☐sectional nature of the survey does not allow one to track the TPP measures' effects on more distal outcomes (e.g. interest in quitting) and on tobacco use behaviour (prevalence and consumption).[106] Professor Chaloupka further claims that the impact of the TPP measures on more distal outcomes should be smaller when the analysis is based on the overall sample of smokers and recent quitters, given that smokers and recent quitters for whom the most proximal outcomes were unaffected by the TPP measures would not be expected to show any change in more distal outcomes.

3.2   Analysis by the Panel

96.   As discussed above, there is some evidence of an acceleration of the reduction in smoking prevalence since the entry into force of the TPP measures. The question before us at this stage of our analysis is whether this acceleration may, in part or in whole, be attributed to the TPP measures.

97.   We note that the evidence relied on by the parties in this part of the discussion is based on an econometric analysis of the evolution of smoking prevalence or smoking incidence aimed at distinguishing and assessing the impact of the TPP measures and other determinants on the level of smoking prevalence or smoking incidence. In particular, the "dependent" variable, smoking prevalence or smoking incidence, is modelled as a function of a number

---

[102]   See Chaloupka Rebuttal Report, (Exhibit AUS-582), para. 4.
[103]   See Klick Supplemental Rebuttal Report, (Exhibit HND-122), paras. 15-32.
[104]   See Klick Supplemental Rebuttal Report, (Exhibit HND-122), paras. 21-32.
[105]   See Australia's response to Panel question No. 196, para. 252; and Chaloupka Second Rebuttal Report, (Exhibit AUS-590), para. 26.
[106]   See Chaloupka Third Rebuttal Report, (Exhibit AUS-604), paras. 8-13.

of "explanatory" variables, including the TPP measures.[107] The parties use different econometric estimators (namely the ordinary least square (OLS) estimator, the maximum likelihood estimator, the linear probability estimator, and the logistic estimator) to estimate the parameters of the explanatory variables that best fit the relevant data. Each estimated parameter is assigned a standard error, which enables the evaluation of whether this estimated value of the parameter is statistically different from zero, i.e. statistically significant, at a given level of significance typically 1%, 5% or 10%. The standard error provides information on the degree of confidence and reliability of the estimated value of each parameter considered in the model. As described above, the Dominican Republic, Honduras and Indonesia submit that the TPP measures' impact on smoking prevalence or smoking incidence is statistically not different from zero, while Australia submits that the impact of the TPP measures on smoking prevalence is negative and statistically different from zero.

98.   At the outset, we note that we approach this assessment on the basis that our task is not to conduct our own econometric assessment of the impact of the TPP measures on smoking prevalence, but rather to review the robustness of the econometric evidence submitted by the parties in this respect.

99.   While we acknowledge that no data are perfect, we agree with Australia that the RMSS data is the most suited available data submitted by the parties to analyse the impact of the TPP measures on smoking prevalence, for two main reasons. First, the RMSS data provide an actual measure of smoking prevalence (based on a population of smokers, recent quitters and non-smokers). Second, the data are available monthly for a long period of time before and after the introduction of the TPP measures. The parties disagree with respect to the selection sample period. We concur with Australia that a larger number of observations is likely to increase the precision of the estimates. In addition, we note that Professor List, in his report submitted by the Dominican Republic and Indonesia, suggests limiting the sample period to analyse smoking prevalence,

---

[107] Explanatory variables ideally represent the full set of factors that have an impact on the dependent variable, and therefore contribute in "explaining" the behaviour of the dependent variable. In general, explanatory variables are assumed to be independent with respect to the dependent variables. In other words, the dependent variable is assumed to have no (direct or indirect) impact on the explanatory variables that, in turn, have an impact on the dependent variable. For this reason, explanatory variables are often referred to as independent variables. A specific parameter is attached to each explanatory variable included in the econometric model, which represents the impact that the associated explanatory variable might have on the dependent variable. Thus, when the econometric model is well specified with all the relevant explanatory variables, each parameter isolates the impact of the associated explanatory variable on the dependent variable. In addition to the explanatory variables, the econometric model includes an error term, also known as the "residual" term, to capture the facts that no matter how well the model is specified (i) it is often impossible to account for every factor that has an impact on the dependent variable, (ii) the actual relationship between the dependent variable and (some of) the explanatory variables may not be necessarily linear, (iii) data may suffer from measurement errors, and (iv) unpredicted – stochastic – effects can affect the dependent variable. Ultimately, econometric analysis consists of estimating each parameter of the explanatory variables specified in the model.

but does not propose the same restriction in the analysis of cigarette consumption.[108]

100.   The other data sources considered by Professor Klick suffer, in our view, from a number of drawbacks in comparison with the RMSS data. In particular, the commissioned Roy Morgan Research Survey data collected in Australia and New Zealand cover a short period prior to the introduction of the TPP measures in December 2012, during which plain packs were already authorized for sale in the market. In comparison, the pre-TPP period of the RMSS data are available starting January 2001. In addition, the commissioned Roy Morgan Research Survey data, just like the CITTS and NTPPTS datasets, do not actually measure smoking prevalence, because the sample is based only on smokers and recent quitters. Finally, although the NSWPHS data provide information on smoking prevalence in NSW, the fact that they are only available yearly imply that the post-TPP period used to assess the impact of TPP measures covers only two to three observations. This is extremely short in comparison with the RMSS data encompassing up to 34 post-TPP observations (December 2012-September 2015).

101.   Turning to the econometric results based on the RMSS data, we note at the outset that the different conclusions reached by the parties regarding the impact of the TPP measures on smoking prevalence stem from the fact that the parties' experts use different model specification (i.e. different explanatory variables included in the model), estimation approaches and in some cases sample periods. Even among the experts of the Dominican Republic, Honduras and Indonesia, different model specifications are used.[109]

102.   On a number of occasions, the rebuttal reports of the Dominican Republic's, Honduras's and Indonesia' experts proposed new model specifications or methodologies or both, to address some of Australia's criticisms but also to take into account issues that their experts themselves highlighted. For instance, IPE initially proposed (in its analysis of cigarette sales volumes) controlling for excise tax increases by including indicator variables for each excise tax increase in the sample period.[110] However, it subsequently contended that a more appropriate measure to capture the excise tax increases was the

---

[108]   See List Third Supplemental Report, (Exhibit DOM/IDN-7), pp. 4-8.
[109]   For instance, IPE initially (see IPE Updated Report, (Exhibit DOM-303)) and Professor Klick (see Klick Third Supplemental Rebuttal Report, (Exhibit HND-166)) control for excise tax increases by specifying dummy variables for each excise tax hike implemented during the sample period, while IPE later in the proceedings (see, e.g. IPE Second Updated Report, (Exhibit DOM-361)) and Professor List (see, e.g. List Report, (Exhibit DOM/IDN-1)) consider the variable of cigarette price to be a better proxy for excise tax increases. Similarly, Professor Klick applies the instrument variables estimator to address the potential endogeneity of the price variable, while IPE and Professor List do not. Another difference among the experts of the Dominican Republic, Honduras, and Indonesia is the fact that IPE and Professor Klick use monthly sample sizes as weights in the estimation, while Professor List does not, except in the first stage of his micro-econometric analysis.
[110]   See IPE Report, (Exhibit DOM-100), pp. 67-69.

average price per cigarette in Australia.[111] Although the experts of the Dominican Republic, Honduras and Indonesia ultimately reach the same conclusion when the changes they proposed are taken into account, they explicitly or in some cases implicitly suggest ignoring or giving less weight to their previous results affected by the issues their experts themselves recognized or highlighted. As explained above, it is not our task to present a unified econometric analysis but rather assess the robustness of each report.

3.2.1   IPE's and Professor List's econometric results

103.   After a careful review of the econometric reports on smoking prevalence based on the RMSS data submitted by the Dominican Republic's and Indonesia's experts[112], we are not persuaded that these econometric results can be taken at face value, mainly because most of their model specifications are unable to detect the impact of tobacco costliness (including excise tax increases) on smoking prevalence. Yet, all parties consider tobacco excise tax to be one of the most effective tobacco control policies.[113] To some extent, the Dominican Republic, Honduras and Indonesia are asking the Panel to conclude that the TPP measures had no impact on smoking prevalence, because its effect is statistically not significant, but to disregard the fact that the same econometric results suggest that excise tax or price increase have also had no impact on smoking prevalence.

104.   The manner in which the smoking prevalence trend is modelled with respect to the sample period considered (i.e. January 2001-September 2015 or July 2006-September 2015) has an important consequence on whether the econometric analysis is able to identify the impact of other variables. These variables can contribute, along with demographic shifts and other factors unrelated to tobacco control policies, to creating the smoking prevalence trend.[114] This problem is defined as overfitting. For instance, the issue of overfitting associated with the trend variable is so severe in the ARIMAX

---

[111]   See IPE Second Updated Report, (Exhibit DOM-361).

[112]   Although the methodologies proposed by IPE and Professor List differ, they share a number of similarities, including the sample period, the choice of the variable to control for tobacco price control policies and the procedure to estimate the standard errors. That is why both experts' results are discussed together. See List Report, (Exhibit DOM/IDN-1); List Rebuttal Report, (Exhibit DOM/IDN-3); List Second Supplemental Report, (Exhibit DOM/IDN-5); List Third Supplemental Report, (Exhibit DOM/IDN-7); List Summary Report, (Exhibit DOM/IDN-9); IPE Report, (Exhibit DOM-100); IPE Updated Report, (Exhibit DOM-303); IPE Second Updated Report, (Exhibit DOM-361); IPE Third Updated Report, (Exhibit DOM-375); and IPE Summary Report, (Exhibit DOM-379).

[113]   See Australia's first written submission, para. 719; Honduras's first written submission, para. 589; Dominican Republic's first written submission, paras. 758 and 1027; Cuba's first written submission, para. 276; and Indonesia's first written submission, para. 63.

[114]   IPE considers a linear trend for the sample period July 2006-September 2015 and a quadratic trend for the sample period January 2001-September 2015. Similarly, Professor List specifies a linear trend for the sample period July 2006-September 2015. Professor Kick specifies a quadratic trend for the sample period January 2001-September 2015.

models reported in the IPE Reports that even the lagged dependent variable is not statistically significant, suggesting that the level of smoking prevalence does not depend on the level of smoking prevalence in the previous month, which is in complete contradiction with the fact that smoking prevalence follows a downward trend, as agreed by all parties.[115] Similarly, the results of Professor List's two-stage micro-econometric shows how the inclusion of the secular (long-term) trend[116] captures most of the explaining power making the price variable no longer significant in most of the specifications, while the price variable is always statistically significant when the trend variable is not included.[117]

105.   In our view, it is important that the trend variable specified in the model avoids overfitting the data, to allow an identification of the impact of other variables of interest, such as individual tobacco control policies. Otherwise, one cannot rule out the possibility that the smoking prevalence trend included in the model accounts not only for the trend itself but potentially also reflects any tobacco control policies that contributed to its trend. We note that while the experts of the Dominican Republic, Honduras and Indonesia discussed extensively the importance of accounting properly for the secular downward trend in smoking prevalence, they do not address the fact that in the vast majority of their results, the price variable was not statistically significant.

106.   In this context, we also consider it important to specify the tobacco price control policy in the most appropriate manner. We note that the Dominican Republic's experts' view on this issue has evolved throughout the proceedings. IPE was the first party to propose controlling for tobacco tax excise increases with indicator variables (in its analysis of cigarette sales discussed in Appendix D), but later changed its view when Professor List used a price variable in his own analysis.[118] IPE referred to the tobacco price variable as a measure for costliness of tobacco products (reflecting also the effect of tax increases). IPE also proposed the level of tax as an alternative to the price variable. In our view, the three types of variables (dummy variables, tax level variable and price variable) are in theory complementary, each with advantages and disadvantages. The dummy variables are, by construction, exogenous and specific to each excise tax increase but do not specify the actual level of the tax increase. The tax level variable is also, by definition, exogenous and accounts

---

[115]   See, e.g. IPE Third Updated Report, (Exhibit DOM-375), pp. 34 and 106-108.

[116]   See para. 11 above for a discussion on the secular trend.

[117]   See, e.g. List Rebuttal Report, (Exhibit DOM/IDN-3), pp. 15 and 24; List Second Supplemental Report, (Exhibit DOM/IDN-5), pp. 32-33; and List Third Supplemental Report, (Exhibit DOM/IDN-7), pp. 18-19 and 29-30. In addition, we also question the validity of some of the results obtained by Professor List in the first stage, where none of the explanatory variables are statistically significant (at 10%), not even the constant. Such results suggest that the associated model specification might be misspecified or affected by another econometric issue that Professor List failed to address.

[118]   See IPE Updated Report, (Exhibit DOM-303), para. 150; and IPE Second Updated Report, (Exhibit DOM-361), para. 29.

for the actual level of the tax increase. However, as explained by Australia, it relies on the assumption that the effect of the tax increase on prevalence is proportional to the size of the tax increase. The price variable is a broader variable and accounts implicitly for all the factors that affect tobacco price, including the excise tax increases but not only that. The TPP measures can also affect the price variable, as pointed by Dr Chipty and addressed by Professor Klick.

107. In addition, we observe after a careful review, that there is, as shown in **Figure C.20**, evidence of multicollinearity between the price variable and the linear trend variable, in particular when the sample period is restricted to July 2006 to September 2015.[119] Multicollinearity arises when two (or more) explanatory variables convey the same information. In the presence of multicollinearity, the predictive power of the model remains unchanged, but the confidence interval of the coefficient estimates may increase. Moreover, the coefficient estimates may become very sensitive to minor changes in the model specification or data. One way to mitigate multicollinearity is to increase the sample period. We note, however, that including a second linear trend specific to the July 2006-September 2015 period, as suggested by IPE, would not resolve this issue. We also note that unlike Professor Klick, IPE and Professor List does not address the fact that the TPP measures might affect the price variable. IPE and Professor List's model specifications are unable to distinguish between the impact specific to the price variable and the TPP measures. Overall, given that neither IPE nor Professor List address the issue of multicollinearity, and the potential impact of the TPP measures on prices, we call into question the econometric results based on the price variable. We also note that the expert reports submitted by the Dominican Republic, Honduras and Indonesia (and Australia) failed to mention that standard unit root tests suggest that the tax level and the price variables are not stationary.[120] Yet, econometric theory recommends not estimating a model when the dependent variable (i.e. smoking prevalence) is stationary and one of the explanatory variables (i.e. tax level or price) is not stationary in order to avoid spurious and biased results.

108. The parties' experts also disagree with the manner in which the population sampling correction is addressed in the RMSS data. We first note, as pointed out by Australia, that Professor List did not consider the sample reweighting in the RMSS data to be an issue in his first two reports. Similarly, IPE did not address the issue of reweighting in its first three reports.[121] We recognize the importance of attempting to control for sample re-weighting events in the RMSS data. We note, however, that the inclusion of the three indicator

---

[119] Evidence of multicollinearity is confirmed by the variance inflation factors statistic.

[120] A variable is said to be stationary, when its statistical properties, such as mean and variance are all constant over time.

[121] We note that, unlike Professor List and IPE, Professor Klick does not address the sample reweighting corrections in the RMSS data in his analysis.

variables to control for the reweighting correction in April 2009, July 2010, and April 2014, as suggested by Professor List, increases the issue of multicollinearity, in particular when the price (or tax level) and trend variables are included in the specification.[122] This problem is accentuated when a fully flexible reweighting correction is adopted. For instance, none of the explanatory variables is statistically significant at 5% when the linear trend and price variables and the fully flexible reweighting correction are included in Professor List's model specification for smoking prevalence among minor and young adult.[123] Similar findings apply to IPE's modified trend analysis of overall smoking prevalence, where the only significant variable is the dummy for the trend shift in July 2006.[124] Some results of IPE's modified trend analysis even suggest that the TPP measures have led to a statistically significant increase in cigar smoking prevalence.[125] The idea that the TPP measures "backfired" is rejected not only by Australia, but also by the Dominican Republic's and Indonesia's experts. Professor List has explicitly questioned the possibility that the TPP measures "backfired".[126] IPE explains also that it does not interpret the statistically significant and positive impact of the TPP measures on cigar smoking prevalence as evidence that the TPP measures led to an increase in cigar smoking prevalence, but rather as strong evidence to reject the claim of the intended negative TPP measures' effect on cigar smoking prevalence.[127] Yet, the Dominican Republic's and Indonesia's experts do not explain why such finding should be interpreted differently, without questioning the validity of the model specification that yields such result, especially when it relates to the main variable of interest of the econometric analysis. In fact, none of the Dominican Republic's and Indonesia's experts sought to explain why the TPP measures would lead to an increase in the number of smokers. Overall, and based on the above, we have doubts about the reliability of the results obtained

---

[122] For instance, the results reported in columns (3) and (4) of Table 8 in List Second Supplemental Report, (Exhibit DOM/IDN-5), p. 43 suggest that the TPP measures' effect on smoking prevalence of minors and young adults is positive and statistically significant at 10%. In other more recent results on smoking prevalence among minor and young adult, presented in column 3 of Table 13 in List Third Supplemental Report, (Exhibit DOM/IDN-7), p. 32, the only variable, besides the constant, that is statistically significant is the trend when the price and time trend variables as well as reweighting correction dummies are included. We note, however, that the issue of multicollinearity is less severe when excise tax increase dummies or the real tax level variable are used.

[123] For instance, in the results on overall smoking prevalence presented in column 3 of Table 14 in List Third Supplemental Report, (Exhibit DOM/IDN-7), p. 33, the only variable, besides the constant, that is statistically significant is the trend when the price and time trend variables as well as fully flexible reweighting correction dummies are included.

[124] Similar findings also apply to IPE's micro-econometric analysis, where the only significant variable is the dummy for the trend shift in July 2006, besides the constant and the socio-demographic variables. See IPE Third Updated Report, (Exhibit DOM-375), p. 38. We also note that IPE decided not to update the results of the ARIMAX model with the reweighting correction dummies.

[125] See the IPE Third Updated Report, (Exhibit DOM-375), pp. 48-50.

[126] See List Report, (Exhibit DOM/IDN-1), para. 106.

[127] See IPE Summary Report, (Exhibit DOM-379), fn 124.

when the price variable, time trend and sample reweighting dummies are included in the model specifications.

Figure C.20: Tobacco Price and Linear Trend

[[***]]

Note: Weighted average price per stick (in AUD) of factory-made cigarettes and roll-your-own tobacco (based on a 0.8 grams conversion rate of roll-your-own tobacco to cigarette sticks). The vertical dashed line indicates the introduction of TPP and enlarged GHWs. The dashed and dotted linear time trends correspond, respectively, to the sequence 1, 2, 3 ... up to 177 or the sequence 1, 2, 3, up to 111.

Source: In-Market-Sales data and Coles and Woolworths data, based on data update and computer code and calculations supporting the IPE Updated Report, (Exhibit DOM-373) (SCI); and List Second Supplemental Report, (Exhibit DOM/IDN-5).

109.   Another technical issue that has been the object of extensive discussions among the parties is the choice of the procedure used to compute the standard error of each of the estimated coefficients associated with the variables specified in the econometric model.[128] As explained earlier, statistical significance is essential because, as well as being the variable's estimated coefficient, it is also important to determine whether the coefficient's variable is statistically different from zero. Yet, a standard error is required to determine the estimated coefficient's level of statistical significance. We therefore recognize, like the parties, the importance of computing standard errors that are robust to heteroscedasticity and autocorrelation.

110.   We note, however, that the treatment of standard errors evolved over the course of the proceedings. Initially, Professor List and IPE chose to apply the STATA software command ivreg2 to calculate standard errors that are robust to heteroscedasticity and serial correlation using the automatic bandwidth selection procedure by Newey and West (1994).[129] Subsequently, Professor List, and later on IPE, applied an alternative way of calculating standard errors, that, according to Professor List, is adjusted to reflect more accurately the original suggestion by Newey and West (1994).[130] Technically speaking, the disagreement between

---

[128]   Heteroscedasticity and autocorrelation consistent standard errors are computed for the following models on smoking prevalence: IPE's modified trend analysis and ARIMAX models, and Professor List two-stage micro-econometric analysis. Similarly, robust standard errors are computed for the following models on cigarette consumption: IPE's modified trend analysis and ARIMAX models, and Professor List's event study analysis.

[129]   See IPE Report (Exhibit DOM-100); IPE Updated Report, (Exhibit DOM-303); List Report (Exhibit DOM/IDN-1); and List Rebuttal Report, (Exhibit DOM/IDN-3).

[130]   See Second IPE updated report, (Exhibit DOM-361); IPE Third Updated Report, (Exhibit DOM-375); and IPE Summary Report, (Exhibit DOM-379); List Second Supplemental Report,

Professor List (as well as IPE and Professor Klick) and Dr Chipty concerns the procedure to correct for autocorrelation, in particular the choice of the maximum amount of time, defined as the maximum lag, that the data can be correlated over time. Professor List proposes to set a smaller parameter value, resulting also in a smaller maximum lag than the one specified in the ivreg2 command. A careful review of the evidence and discussions shows that the choice of the maximum lag is not well established in the statistics and econometric literature, as pointed out by in an email exchange with STATA developers.[131] As a result, it is unclear whether the results associated with Professor List's procedure would have changed for a range of parameter values, taking into consideration the fact that the maximum lag should be able to take into account all lags until the serial correlation in the data vanishes.[132]

111.   In sum, and based on the elements discussed above, we have reservations regarding IPE and Professor List's methodologies[133] and therefore question their results, based on these methodologies, that suggest that the TPP measures had no statistically significant impact on smoking prevalence.[134]

(Exhibit DOM/IDN-5); List Third Supplemental Report, (Exhibit DOM/IDN-7); and List Summary Report, (Exhibit DOM/IDN-9).

[131]   See the correspondence between the parties and STATA developers in the IPE Summary Report, (Exhibit DOM-379), p. 70; and Chipty Second Rebuttal Report, (Exhibit AUS-591), pp. B1-B2. In the email exchange, the STATA software developers also explain that the automatic choice of the maximum lag in the command ivreg2 is in line with the criteria necessary for asymptotic optimality.

[132]   Professor List presents the results of simulations to compare the frequency of so-called false positives using Professor List's procedure and the ivreg2's automatic selection procedure. Professor List concludes that the STATA ivreg2's automatic selection procedure leads to a wrong finding of a statistically significant result 16% of the time, instead of 5% (see List Summary Report, (Exhibit DOM/IDN-9), paras. 95-98). We note that the results are based on the sample size of 111 observations (July 2006-September 2015), while Dr Chipty considers a larger sample period of 177 observations (January 2001-September 2015). It is therefore unclear to what extent Professor List's results would change if the sample size increases, taking into account the fact that according to the STATA developers the formulae used in ivreg2 meet the criteria necessary for asymptotic optimality.

[133]   We note that Gibson Report (Exhibit DOM-92) presents the main results of an econometric analysis of smoking prevalence of adolescents based on the RMSS data. The results suggest that the TPP measures and enlarged GHWs had no statistically significant impact on the smoking prevalence of 14-17 year-old smokers of manufacturing cigarettes, RYO cigarettes, pipes and cigars, respectively. We question however the validity of these results for some of the same reasons that apply to the econometric analysis of adult smoking prevalence reported by IPE, namely the use of the price variable and (quadratic) time trend.

[134]   Professor List proposes a framework to synthesize the diverse analyses, submitted by all the parties, on the TPP measures' impact on smoking prevalence and cigarette consumption (see for instance List Second Supplemental Report, (Exhibit DOM/IDN-5), paras. 30-71). According to Professor List, the probability that the TPP measures are working as intended is nearly zero whether just the studies of the experts of the Dominican Republic, Honduras and Indonesia or the universe of the work of all the experts are considered. List Summary Report, (Exhibit DOM/IDN-9), paras. 167-173. Dr Chipty argues that Professor List's framework for reweighing the evidence is both misleading and misguided because it amounts to nothing but a counting exercise that does not account for the interdependence of studies or the biases they may contain. Chipty Third Rebuttal Report, (Exhibit AUS-605), paras. 6-8. We acknowledge the usefulness of having a single number (Post-Study Probability) determining the likelihood that the TPP measures have caused a reduction in

3.2.2 Professor Klick's econometric results

112. Similarly, a review of the econometric results based on the RMSS data reported by Professor Klick leads us to question their robustness.[135] In particular, as demonstrated by Dr Chipty, the use of a quadratic trend to capture the downward trend in smoking prevalence leads the predicted tobacco price variable to be not significant. As explained above, specifying an excessively flexible smoking prevalence trend (i.e. quadratic trend) is likely to overfit the data on smoking prevalence and make redundant any other variables, such as individual tobacco control policies, that can potentially have also an impact on smoking prevalence. Finally, it is also unclear how the standard error and confidence interval of the total effect of the TPP measures, composed of the direct estimated impact of the TPP measures on smoking prevalence obtained in the second stage of the procedure and the indirect estimated impact of the TPP measures on cigarette price obtained in the first stage of the procedure through the impact of cigarette price on smoking prevalence, were calculated.

113. Our review of Professor Klick's econometric analyses of the TPP measures' impact on smoking prevalence and incidence based on the other datasets leads us also to question his results. With the exception of the NSWPHS data, the other datasets used smoking incidence, instead of smoking prevalence, by focusing only on smokers and recent quitters. As a result, data on smoking incidence is, by definition, unable to measure the impact of TPP measures on non-smokers. Therefore, the studies on smoking incidence are in our view less relevant than the studies focusing on smoking prevalence.

114. We question the validity of Professor Klick's difference-in-difference analysis on smoking incidence based on the commissioned Roy Morgan Research Survey, because Professor Klick is unable to accurately identify the respondents, who had noticed plain packs in the pre-period given that the question about noticing changes in the packaging was not asked of all respondents. As a result, the pre-period is, in our view, not valid. In addition, when Professor Klick attempts to address some of Dr Chipty's critics regarding the pre-period, several results find a positive and statistically significant TPP measures' effect on the likelihood an individual reports being a smoker. Professor Klick explains that he does not view these results as suggesting that smoking has surely increased under the TPP measures, because of the "multiple comparison problem", which implies that when "very many outcomes" are examined, there is a relatively high likelihood that one will find statistically

---

smoking prevalence based on all available econometric studies. We note, however, that Professor List assigns the same weight to all the results prepared by the experts of the Dominican Republic, Honduras and Indonesia, even when Professor List, himself, questions the validity of some of these results. For instance, Professor List is not persuaded that the TPP measures "backfired" as suggested by Professor Klick's difference-in-difference analysis. We are of the view that a methodology that is unable to make a distinction between robust results and biased results is not informative.

[135] See Klick Third Supplemental Rebuttal Report, (Exhibit HND-166), paras. 11-23.

significant results even by mere chance.[136] Yet, Professor Klick does not explain how ten different alternative specifications should be viewed as "very many outcomes".[137] Furthermore, Professor Klick fails to account for the excise tax increase that took place in New Zealand between Waves 1 and 2 and Waves 5 and 6 of the commissioned survey, making any inference about the reduction in smoking incidence in Australia compared to New Zealand questionable.

115.   We are also not persuaded by Professor Klick's results based on an analysis of the NSWPHS data on the ground that the nature of the data (i.e. yearly observations) limits the number of observations to two post-packaging observations (2013 and 2014), which prevents distinguishing between the TPP measures and tobacco excise tax increases in 2013 and 2014.

116.   We question also Professor Klick's results of the CITTS data, which, as explained above, do not analyse smoking prevalence, but smoking status. Unlike Dunlop et al. 2014, who also analyse the CITTS data but for a shorter period[138], Professor Klick does not explicitly account for other tobacco control policies (besides the TPP measures), such as the respondents' level of exposure to anti-smoking advertising prior to their interview and changes in cigarette costliness. Professor Klick includes an annual time trend, but the variable is actually never statistically significant. This result is at odds with the view shared by all the experts of the Dominican Republic, Honduras and Indonesia, including Professor Klick, that smoking prevalence is characterized by a downward trend. Similarly, several results suggest that the TPP measures "backfired" and led to an increase in the likelihood of a respondent reporting smoking daily and in general. It is unclear what such results can be attributed to, and for that reason we cannot consider these results as relevant.

117.   We also question the validity of Professor Klick's results on smoking incidence and self-reported frequency of smoking based on the NTPPTS data. Professor Klick chose not to control for the exposure to tobacco-related media activity and tobacco costliness, on the grounds that the results do not change and both omitted variables are likely to be endogenous.[139] We note that, unlike in his analysis of the RMSS data, Professor Klick did not attempt to address the potential endogeneity of cigarette costliness. Yet, failing to account for other tobacco control policies, in particular the December 2013 excise tax hike, might lead to biased results. We further note that although Professor Klick refers to Durkin et al. 2015 and other articles in *Tobacco Control*, the explanatory variables considered by Professor Klick are different to those in Durkin et al. 2015. For instance, Professor Klick uses a single variable for age, while Durkin

---

[136]   See Klick Rebuttal Report, (Exhibit HND-118), fn 24.
[137]   The ten specifications for daily smoker are reported in Tables 3 to 10 in Klick Rebuttal Report, (Exhibit HND-118). The ten specifications for overall smokers are reported in Tables 3 to 9 and Table 11 in Klick Rebuttal Report, (Exhibit HND-118).
[138]   Dunlop et al. 2014, (Exhibits AUS-207, HND-132, DOM-199).
[139]   See Klick Supplemental Rebuttal Report, (Exhibit HND-122), fn 10.

et al. 2015 considers a dummy variable for each age group. The same difference applies to the variable education. In addition, unlike the vast majority of the micro-econometric results submitted by the parties, Professor Klick's econometric results suggest that being a male has no statistically significant effect on the probability an individual reported being a (daily or in general) smoker and on the self-reported frequency of smoking. This finding contradicts econometric evidence submitted by the parties, including Professor Klick, according to which men are more likely to smoke (daily) than women.[140] This puzzling result raises questions about the validity of Professor Klick's model specification.[141]

118.   In sum, and based on the elements discussed above, we have reservations regarding Professor Klick's methodologies and therefore question his contradictory results suggesting that the TPP measures either had no statistically significant impact on smoking prevalence and/or smoking incidence or a positive and statistically significant impact on smoking prevalence and/or smoking incidence.

3.2.3   Ajzen et al.'s econometric results

119.   A careful review of Ajzen et al.'s analysis of the proportion of daily or weekly smokers reported in the NTPPTS data leads us to conclude that Ajzen et al.'s finding is in line with Scollo et al. 2015a, who find that daily cigarette consumption did not change during the first year of implementation of the TPP measures.[142] Like the results submitted by Professor Klick, we note, however, that Ajzen et al. surprisingly find that gender has no statistically significant effect on the probability that an individual reported being a (daily or weekly) smoker.

3.2.4   Dr Chipty's econometric results

120.   Turning to the econometric results analysing smoking prevalence based on the RMSS data submitted by Australia's expert, Dr Chipty, we note that a number of concerns that we raised while reviewing the complainants' approaches and results have been addressed by Dr Chipty. In particular, Dr Chipty acknowledges and addresses the issue of overfitting associated with a too flexible trend. Dr Chipty's model specification also includes the excise tax

---

[140]   See NHS Results, (Exhibit AUS-622), p. 30; and Klick Supplemental Rebuttal Report, (Exhibit HND-122).
[141]   We also note that only three out of the 54 variables are statistically significant in the model for the number of adults who are smokers in household. See Klick Supplemental Rebuttal Report, (Exhibit HND-122), backup material.
[142]   We note that the model specification considered by Ajzen et al. is different from the one developed by Professor Klick. For instance, Ajzen et al. include dummies variables for two age groups, while Professor Klick includes a single age variable. Ajzen et al. include also dummies variables for different groups of education and socio-economic status, respectively, while Professor Klick includes a single variable for education and another variable for socio-economic status.

increases dummy variables and thus avoids the problems of multicollinearity and endogeneity associated with the inclusion of the price variable (in combination with a quadratic trend variable). In addition, the use of the tax dummies avoids the issue of non-stationarity of the price or tax level variables.

121.   A careful review of Dr Chipty's econometric results further shows that the negative and statistically significant impact of the TPP measures on overall smoking prevalence is robust to alternative specifications, including different TPP starting date (October, November and December 2012), the use of an excise tax level variable (instead of the excise tax increase dummies) and sample reweighting dummies.[143] In addition, the impact of the TPP measures on overall smoking prevalence remains negative and statistically significant in most specifications when Professor List's procedure to compute standard errors is implemented.[144]

122.   Overall, based on the most recent econometric evidence submitted by Australia, there is econometric evidence suggesting that TPP and enlarged GHWs contributed to the reduction in overall smoking prevalence in Australia.[145] A similar conclusion applies also to cigar smoking prevalence in Australia.

4.   OVERALL CONCLUSION ON POST-IMPLEMENTATION EVIDENCE ON SMOKING PREVALENCE

123.   Overall, based on the most recent data available and econometric evidence submitted by the parties, we find that:

a.   There is evidence that overall smoking prevalence in Australia continued to decrease following the introduction of the TPP measures.

b.   The downward trend in overall smoking prevalence in Australia appears to have accelerated in the post-TPP period.

c.   Although it is impossible to distinguish between the impact of TPP and the impact of enlarged GHWs, there is some econometric evidence suggesting that the TPP measures, together with the enlarged GHWs implemented at the same time, contributed to the reduction in overall smoking prevalence as well as in cigar smoking prevalence observed after their entry into force.

---

[143]   See Chipty Third Rebuttal Report, (Exhibit AUS-605), p. 22; and Chipty Second Rebuttal Report, (Exhibit AUS-591), p. D2.
[144]   See Chipty Second Rebuttal Report, (Exhibit AUS-591), p. 33.
[145]   See Chipty Third Rebuttal Report, (Exhibit AUS-605), pp. 22 and 51; and Chipty Second Rebuttal Report, (Exhibit AUS-591), pp. 33, D1 and D2.

124.   We note, however, that no post-implementation empirical evidence has been presented to us on the impact of the TPP measures on cigarillos smoking prevalence.

APPENDIX D

EVIDENCE RELATING TO TOBACCO PRODUCT SALES AND CONSUMPTION FOLLOWING THE ENTRY INTO FORCE OF THE TPP MEASURES

1.   Similar to smoking prevalence, the contribution of the TPP measures to reducing tobacco consumption has been the object of extensive discussion between the parties. A number of expert reports are dedicated in part or in whole to this discussion.[1] Different databases, statistical analysis and econometric methods have been proposed to determine whether TPP and enlarged GHWs have contributed to the reduction in cigarette consumption.

2.   Most studies use cigarette sales volumes as a measure of cigarette consumption, with the exception of a few other studies[2], which use reported cigarettes consumption. Cigarette sales volumes are taken from market data, while data on cigarette consumption are reported in various surveys. The underlying assumption is that cigarette consumption (i.e. cigarette demand) can be proxied by cigarette sales (i.e. supply of cigarettes). We note that none of the parties questioned this assumption. Where relevant, this Appendix will distinguish between cigarette consumption and cigarette sales.

3.   As in respect of the analysis of smoking prevalence, one of the only points of agreement among the parties is that the empirical econometric evidence on cigarette consumption submitted does not distinguish between the impact of TPP and the impact of enlarged GHWs on cigarette sales or consumption, because both measures were implemented at the exact same time.[3] Unless

---

[1]   See Chipty Report, (Exhibit AUS-17); Chipty Supplementary Report, (Exhibit AUS-511); Chipty Rebuttal Report, (Exhibit AUS-535) (SCI); Chipty Surrebuttal Report, (Exhibit AUS-586); Chipty Second Rebuttal Report, (Exhibit AUS-591); Chipty Third Rebuttal Report, (Exhibit AUS-605); List Report, (Exhibit DOM/IDN-1); List Rebuttal Report, (Exhibit DOM/IDN-3); List Second Supplemental Report, (Exhibit DOM/IDN-5); List Third Supplemental Report, (Exhibit DOM/IDN-7); List Summary Report, (Exhibit DOM/IDN-9); IPE Report, (Exhibit DOM-100); IPE Updated Report, (Exhibit DOM-303); IPE Second Updated Report, (Exhibit DOM-361); IPE Third Updated Report, (Exhibit DOM-375); IPE Summary Report, (Exhibit DOM-379); Klick Report, (Exhibit UKR-5); Klick Rebuttal Report, (Exhibit HND-118); Klick Supplemental Rebuttal Report, (Exhibit HND-122); Klick Second Supplemental Rebuttal Report, (Exhibit HND-165); Klick Third Supplemental Rebuttal Report, (Exhibit HND-166); Klick Fourth Supplemental Rebuttal Report, (Exhibit HND-169); Ajzen et al. Data Report, (Exhibit DOM/IDN-2); and Ajzen et al. Second Data Report, (Exhibit DOM/IDN-4).

[2]   See Klick Report, (Exhibit UKR-5); Klick Supplemental Rebuttal Report, (Exhibit HND-122); Klick Second Supplemental Rebuttal Report, (Exhibit HND-165), Ajzen et al. Data Report, (Exhibit DOM/IDN-2); and Ajzen et al. Second Data Report, (Exhibit DOM/IDN-4).

[3]   See Australia's first written submission, para. 518; Dominican Republic's response to Panel question No. 8, para. 61; Honduras's responses to Panel question No. 8; and Indonesia's response to Panel question No. 8, para. 8.

---

specified otherwise, the impact of TPP in this Appendix therefore refers to the impact of TPP *and* enlarged GHWs.

4.   The Dominican Republic, Honduras and Indonesia argue that all their experts' empirical statistical and econometric studies show that the TPP measures failed to reduce cigarette sales volumes or consumption.[4] The complainants even suggested initially that TPP measures "backfired" by increasing tobacco sales.[5] This argument was however not developed later in the proceedings.

5.   Notwithstanding its contention that it is too early to investigate the impact of TPP on tobacco consumption[6], Australia submitted expert reports estimating the TPP measures' impact on cigarette sales, in response to the submissions of the Dominican Republic, Honduras and Indonesia. Australia contends that once the most appropriate dataset available (i.e. In-Market-Sales data) are used and the flaws of the econometric models put forward by the experts of the Dominican Republic, Honduras and Indonesia are corrected, the econometric results show that TPP measures have already contributed to their objectives by reducing cigarette sales volumes.[7]

6.   Similarly to the discussion on smoking prevalence, we note that the approaches presented by the parties to analyse cigarette sales volumes and consumption evolved over the course of the proceedings. Overall, these address three main aspects, reviewed below in sections 1 to 3:

- First, the parties have submitted economic figures and descriptive statistics analyses aimed at determining whether cigarette sales or consumption have decreased following the implementation of the TPP measures;[8]

- Second, Australia, the Dominican Republic and Indonesia have submitted statistical analyses to determine whether there was a break in the trend in cigarette sales following the implementation

---

[4]   See Dominican Republic's comments on Australia's response to Panel question No. 196, paras. 681-682; Honduras's second written submission, paras. 56-60; Indonesia's second written submission, para. 192; and Cuba's second written submission, paras. 276-277.

[5]   See Indonesia's first written submission, para. 412; Cuba's first written submission, para. 163; Dominican Republic's first written submission, para. 523; and Honduras's first written submission, para. 395.

[6]   See Australia's first written submission, para. 670. Australia considers that, in the early stages of introduction of the measures, the most appropriate way to discern their effects was to rely on experiments and surveys which concern drivers of choice, attitudes and, ultimately, the elicitation of behavioural intentions. Australia's first written submission, para. 147.

[7]   See Australia's response to Panel question No. 196, para. 214.

[8]   We note that the parties also submitted data on the value and volume of Australian imports of tobacco, including cigars and cigarillos. See HoustonKemp Report, (Exhibit AUS-19) (SCI); Dominican Republic's response to Panel question No. 5.; Honduras's response to Panel question No. 5; Cuba's response to Panel question No. 5; and Indonesia's response to Panel question No. 5. These data are not reviewed here because they were not used in any of the econometric reports submitted by the parties.

of the TPP measures, and in particular, whether the reduction of cigarette volumes sales has accelerated in the post-TPP period;

- Finally, Australia, the Dominican Republic, Honduras and Indonesia have submitted econometric analysis to determine whether the TPP measures have contributed to a reduction of cigarette sales or consumption by isolating and quantifying the different factors that can explain the evolution of cigarette sales or consumption.

7.   The parties also presented and discussed a graphical and descriptive analysis of cigar trade data. This is addressed below in Section 4.

1.   WHETHER CIGARETTE SALES VOLUMES DECREASED FOLLOWING THE IMPLEMENTATION OF THE TPP MEASURES

8.   Different market data sources tracking cigarette sales volumes in Australia have been submitted by Australia, the Dominican Republic, Honduras and Indonesia. We first present these datasets, before providing an overall analysis on the basis of these data.

1.1   Main datasets and arguments

1.1.1   In-Market-Sales/Exchange of Sales

9.   Managed by InfoView Technologies, In-Market-Sales (IMS), also known as Exchange of Sales (EOS), is a dataset comprising monthly sales volume data at the Stock-Keeping Unit-level for factory-made cigarettes (FMC) and fine-cut tobacco covering the period from January 2000 through September 2015. The data comprise monthly sales from manufacturers to wholesalers and retailers, as reported by the three largest tobacco companies in Australia - British American Tobacco Australia (BATA), Philip Morris Limited, and Imperial Tobacco Australia Limited (ITA) - which collectively account for 99% of sales in the Australian market. The total tobacco sales volumes include FMC and fine-cut tobacco converted to cigarette stick equivalents (CSE).

10.   IPE notes, as depicted in Figure D.1, that cigarette sales volumes based on the IMS/EOS data, as a proxy for cigarette consumption, are marked by strong seasonal patterns, with sales spikes at the end of each quarter (especially in December and June), followed by a trough immediately thereafter. IPE further argues that there is an observable overall downward trend in the total volume of cigarette sticks (FMC and CSE) sold in Australia over the period 2000-2013, as depicted in Figure D.2.[9] IPE contends that the downward trend accelerated after

---

[9]   See IPE Report, (Exhibit DOM-100), pp. 65-68.

the introduction of the 2010 excise tax increase. IPE further submits that the data reveal an increase in the total volume of cigarette sticks sold in 2013.

Figure D.1: Monthly Cigarette Sales Volumes Based on IMS/EOS Data

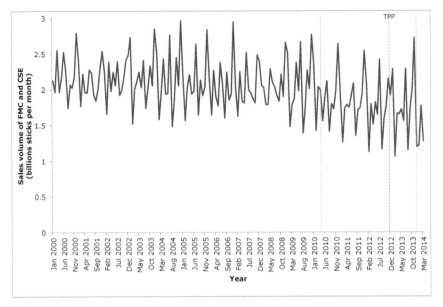

Note: Conversion rate of 0.8 grams of fine-cut tobacco per stick. The vertical dotted lines indicate excise tax increases. The vertical dashed line indicates the introduction of TPP and enlarged GHWs.

Source: IPE Report, (Exhibit DOM-100), p. 67.

Figure D.2: Annual Cigarette Sales Volumes Based on IMS/EOS Data

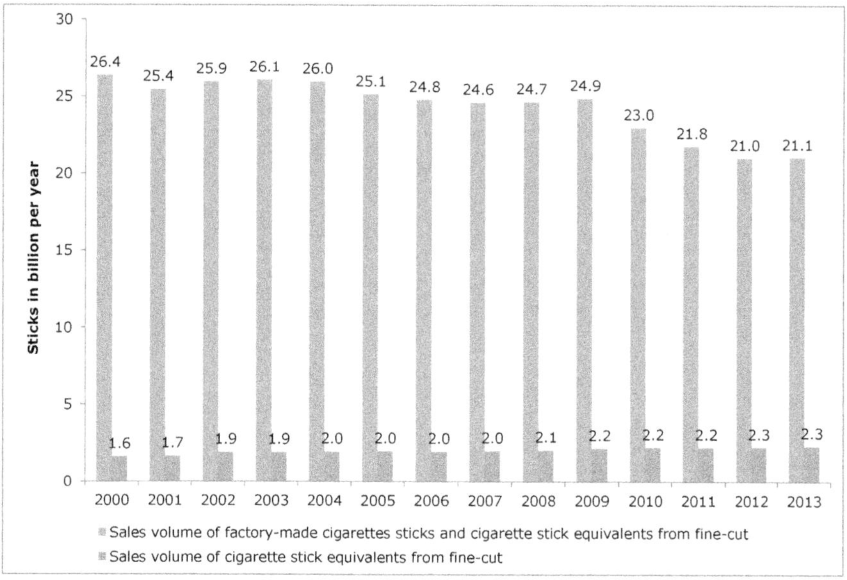

Note: Conversion rate of 0.8 grams of fine-cut tobacco per stick.

Source: IPE Report, (Exhibit DOM-100), p. 66.

11.   Professor Klick argues that while sales data are not equivalent to smoking incidence, market data are valuable because they do not suffer from the potential inaccuracies associated with self-reported survey responses, and captures even those smokers who would not be included in the survey sample such as underage smokers.[10] Professor Klick further submits that there is some doubt regarding whether the TPP measures are associated with a decline in cigarette flows given that despite the steady decline in cigarette sales flows observed in the pre-TPP period, cigarette flows increased by 0.3% between 2012 and 2013, as depicted in Figure D.3. In comparison, Professor Klick argues that although the pre-December 2012 decline in average monthly cigarette sales was just as striking in New Zealand as in Australia, the decline in cigarette sales continued into 2013 in New Zealand, unlike in Australia.[11] In addition, Professor Klick contends that, unlike Dr Chipty's claim of positive strategic inventory effects on sales in anticipation of the December 2013 tax increase in Australia , the decline

---

[10]   See Klick Report, (Exhibit UKR-5), p. 12.
[11]   See Klick Report, (Exhibit UKR-5), p. 16.

in cigarette wholesale sales in Australia appears to have diminished with the introduction of the TPP measures unlike in New Zealand.[12]

Figure D.3:   Average Monthly Cigarette Sales Volumes Based on IMS/EOS Data

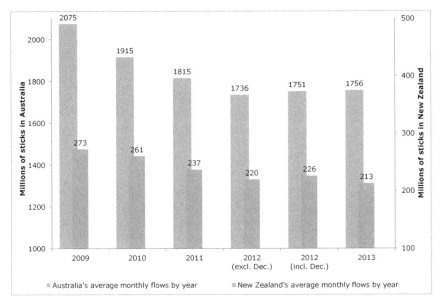

Note: Conversion rate of 0.8 grams of fine-cut tobacco per stick.

Source: Klick Report, (Exhibit UKR-5), pp. 17-18.

12.   Unlike IPE and Professor Klick, Professor List considers the evolution of cigarette sales per capita, as shown in **Figure D.4**, and argues that smoking consumption is characterized by a general downward trend in smoking consumption.[13]

---

[12]   See Klick Rebuttal Report, (Exhibit HND-118), paras. 66-68.
[13]   See List Report, (Exhibit DOM/IDN-1), p. 27; List Rebuttal Report, (Exhibit DOM/IDN-3), p. 12; List Second Supplemental Report, (Exhibit DOM/IDN-5), p. 8; and List Third Supplemental Report, (Exhibit DOM/IDN-7), p. 35. We note that IPE presents also a graphical analysis of cigarette sales per capita in its second report, without updating it in its subsequent reports. IPE Updated Report, (Exhibit DOM-303), p. 57.

Figure D.4: Per Capita Monthly Cigarette Sales Volumes Based on IMS/EOS Data

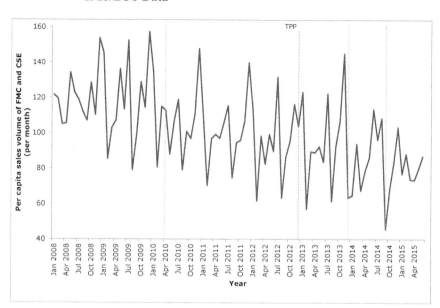

Note: Conversion rate of 0.8 grams of fine-cut tobacco per stick. The vertical dotted lines indicate excise tax hikes. The vertical dashed line indicates the introduction of TPP and enlarged GHWs.

Source: List Rebuttal Report, (Exhibit DOM/IDN-3), p. 12; and List Third Supplemental Report, (Exhibit DOM/IDN-7), p. 35.

13.   Australia's expert Dr Chipty argues that IPE's and Professor Klick's graphical analysis is misleading and fails to account for strategic inventory management that likely took place on the eve of the December 2013 tax increase in the post-TPP period. Dr Chipty is of the view that the presence of the anticipated tax response at the end of December 2013 coupled with the fact that the TPP measures went into effect in October 2012 makes the comparison of sales volume between 2012 and 2013 not meaningful. Dr Chipty contends that a comparison of the year beginning October before and after TPP is analytically sounder and shows a reduction in cigarettes sales volumes.[14]

1.1.2   Nielsen Retail Sales (Australia and New Zealand)

14.   The Nielsen data reports actual sales of cigarettes, including "roll your own" equivalents, through all retailers in Australia and New Zealand's markets except specialty tobacconist shops in Australia from February 2011 through

---

[14]   See Chipty Report, (Exhibit AUS-17), paras. 62-66.

December 2013. Professor Klick also included in his analysis Nielsen processed data on the specialty tobacconist channel, which is collected by BATA and not available from any other source. According to Professor Klick, the inclusion of this channel is preferred as the specialty tobacconist channel in Australia accounts for about 25% of the Australian market. The Nielsen data for Australia are available at monthly intervals, while they are available for New Zealand on a four week rolling basis.[15]

15.   Professor Klick argues that there was a decline in sales post-TPP in Australia. Specifically, average monthly sales in Australia before TPP (1,720 million) fell to 1,719 million for a reduction of 0.07%. However this reduction in cigarette sales is lower after the introduction of the TPP measures than the drop of almost 6% in New Zealand during the same period and without any TPP, as shown in **Figure D.5**.[16]

Figure D.5:   Cigarette Sales Volumes Based on Nielsen Data

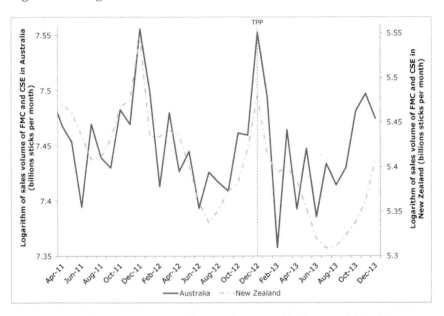

Note: Conversion rate of 0.8 grams of fine-cut tobacco per stick. The vertical dashed line indicates the introduction of TPP and enlarged GHWs.

Source: Klick Report, (Exhibit UKR-5), pp. 6 and 15.

---

[15]   The four-week interval of the Nielsen data for New Zealand does not align with months. Professor Klick notes that: "[t]o align the periods between the two countries, I allocated the New Zealand 4 week periods to the months in which they were collected, using linear interpolation to account for periods that spanned two months". See Klick Report, (Exhibit UKR-5), fn 35.
[16]   Klick Report, (Exhibit UKR-5), p. 15.

16.   Australia's expert Dr Chipty is of the view that Professor Klick's analysis is uninformative. She argues that even in the pre-TPP period, cigarette sales volume is trending down faster than in Australia. In her view, New Zealand appears to be trending differently from Australia before and after the introduction of the TPP measures.[17]

1.1.3   Aztec Scanner Retail Sales

17.   The Aztec scanner data tracks sales on a weekly basis at the store- and stock-keeping unit-level, recording detailed product information on brand and variant, quantity, and price per package for factory-made cigarettes and fine-cut tobacco sold across Australia. The Aztec scanner dataset covers the period 27 July 2008 through 27 September 2015.[18]

18.   The experts of the Dominican Republic, Honduras and Indonesia do not present a graphical analysis using the Aztec data. Instead, they use the Aztec scanner data to estimate econometrically the TPP measures' impact on (per capita) cigarette sales volumes, which will be reviewed in detail below. In that context, Professor List reports the evolution of per capita sales based on the Aztec data, as depicted in Figure D.6.[19]

---

[17]   See Chipty Report, (Exhibit AUS-17), paras. 45-48.
[18]   As discussed below, Professor Klick combines the Nielsen and Aztec data without the Convenience Independent sample when Nielsen data are missing.
[19]   See List Rebuttal Report, (Exhibit DOM/IDN-3), p. 18. We note, however, that unlike IPE, Professor List does not include the sales of RYO tobacco in his analysis of the Aztec data.

Figure D.6: Per Capita Monthly Cigarette Sales Volumes Based on Aztec Scanner Data

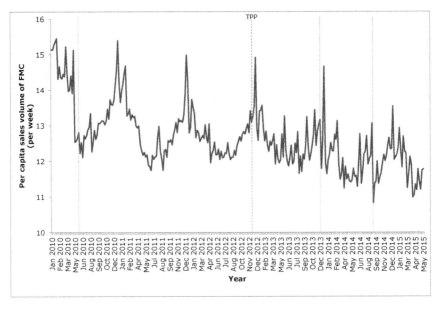

Note: Conversion rate of 0.8 grams of fine-cut tobacco per stick. The vertical dotted lines indicate excise tax hikes. The vertical dashed line indicates the introduction of TPP and enlarged GHWs.

Source: List Rebuttal Report, (Exhibit DOM/IDN-3), p. 18.

19.   Australia's expert, Dr Chipty, notes that the Aztec scanner data covers only a portion of total retail sales in Australia, as evident in a side-by-side comparison of the Aztec, Nielsen and IMS/EOS data, as depicted in **Figure D.7**. Dr Chipty further argues that the (econometric) analysis of the Aztec scanner data is misleading because the share of total cigarette sales covered by the Aztec data has grown over time. Dr Chipty submits that these changes in the underlying data interfere with the ability to use them meaningfully to study changes in cigarette sales before and after the introduction of the TPP measures.[20]

20.   Professor Klick disagrees with Dr Chipty and submits that the Aztec dataset coverage of the retail market has stayed substantially the same over the sample period, while noting that there are changes as some retail outlets close and others open (including within the convenience independent market segment). Professor Klick argues that Dr Chipty did not present direct evidence

---

[20]   See Chipty Report, (Exhibit AUS-17), paras. 55-61.

demonstrating that the coverage of the Aztec sales data relative to total sales is growing over time. Professor Klick further rejects Dr Chipty's indirect evidence of such a change, which can, according to Professor Klick, be explained by the strategic inventory management that Dr Chipty identified.[21]

Figure D.7: Quarterly Cigarette Sales Volume based on IMS/EOS, Nielsen and Aztec Data

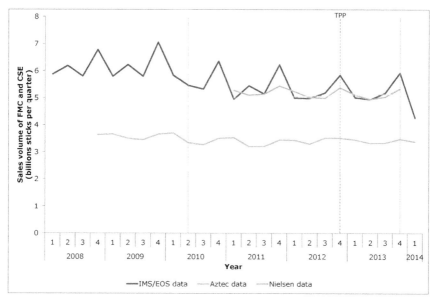

Note: Conversion rate of 0.8 grams of fine-cut tobacco per stick. The vertical dotted lines indicate excise tax hikes. The vertical dashed line indicates the introduction of TPP and enlarged GHWs.

Source: Chipty Report, (Exhibit AUS-17), p. 33.

1.1.4   Australian Bureau of Statistics Household Expenditure

21.   Australia's Post-Implementation Review Tobacco Plain Packaging 2016 reports the evolution of estimated household expenditure on tobacco and cigarettes released by the Australian Bureau of Statistics (ABS), as shown in Figure D.8. According to the ABS, although there was a rise in estimated consumption expenditure in the June 2013 and September 2013 quarters compared with the previous quarters, estimated consumption expenditure on

---

[21]   See Klick Third Supplemental Rebuttal Report, (Exhibit HND-166), paras. 33-34; and Klick Fourth Supplemental Rebuttal Report, (Exhibit HND-169), paras. 6-8 fn 4.

tobacco and cigarettes has been declining in the March 2013 quarter and in all other quarters since implementation.[22]

Figure D.8: Household Expenditure on Tobacco and Cigarettes based on ABS Data

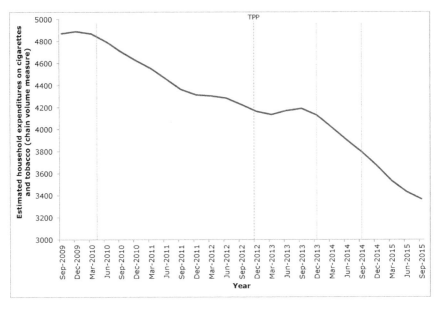

Note: The vertical dotted lines indicate excise tax hikes. The vertical dashed line indicates the introduction of TPP and enlarged GHWs.

Source: Tobacco Plain Packaging PIR, (Exhibit AUS-624), p. 45.

1.2   Analysis by the Panel

22.   As with smoking prevalence, we acknowledge the importance of analysing the trends in cigarette sales with the most recent available data. We further recognize, as pointed out by IPE, that there is no perfect dataset for a sales analysis in terms of market coverage, frequency (weekly, monthly or annually) and period covered.[23]

---

[22]   See Tobacco Plain Packaging PIR, (Exhibit AUS-624), paras. 132-134. The Tobacco Plain Packaging PIR also refers to a 2014 Euromonitor Report on Tobacco, which shows a continued decline in tobacco sales, although limited information about the sources of the data and methodological processes used is provided in the report. *Ibid.*, para. 135. Similarly, the Tobacco Plain Packaging PIR refers to the Australian Taxation Office and Customs clearance data showing a reduction in tobacco clearances in stick equivalent terms (including excise and customs duty) between calendar year 2012 and calendar year 2014.
[23]   See IPE Updated Report, (Exhibit DOM-303), para. 137.

23.   The IMS/EOS data cover sales from manufacturers to wholesalers and retailers, while both Aztec and Nielsen data cover sales from retailers to consumers. Similarly, both Aztec and Nielsen data are only available for February 2011 to December 2013, and 27 July 2008 to 27 September 2015, respectively, while the IMS/EOS data cover the larger sample period, from January 2000 to September 2015. The Nielsen data and the IMS/EOS data cover, respectively, almost 100% and 99% of the Australian market, while the Aztec data cover 67% of the Australian market.[24] We also note that the experts of the Dominican Republic, Honduras and Indonesia used different definitions of cigarette sales, namely level of cigarette sales and per capita cigarette sales. We further note that survey datasets on cigarette consumption have been used by some of the experts of the Dominican Republic, Honduras and Indonesia to analyse the impact of the TPP measures. These will be reviewed in detail when discussing the econometric analysis.

Figure D.9:   Monthly Cigarette Sales Volumes Based on IMS/EOS, Nielsen and Aztec Data

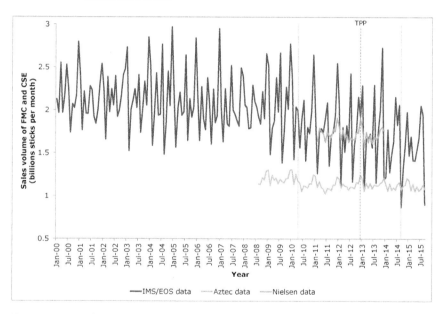

Note: Conversion rate of 0.8 grams of fine-cut tobacco per stick. The vertical dotted lines indicate excise tax hikes. The vertical dashed line indicates the introduction of TPP and enlarged GHWs.

Source: IPE Summary Report, (Exhibit DOM-379), back-up material.

---

[24]   See IPE Summary Report, (Exhibit DOM-379), paras. 131-133.

24.   We note, at the outset, that neither IPE nor Professor Klick updated their graphical analysis of cigarette sales volume with more recent data in the course of the proceedings. The Dominican Republic, Honduras and Indonesia no longer referred to their initial assertion that cigarette sales volumes increased in the post-TPP period. After a careful review of the most recent available IMS/EOS and Aztec datasets, we note that despite fluctuating, cigarette sales volumes follow a downward trend in the period following the introduction of the TPP measures, as depicted in **Figure D.9**.[25] However, the downward trend is more pronounced in the IMS/EOS data than in the Aztec scanner data. As pointed out by Australia and acknowledged by Professor List and IPE[26], the share of total cigarette sales covered by the Aztec data has grown over time, which would explain, at least partially, why the downward trend is less pronounced in the Aztec data.[27]

25.   We will review in the next subsections all the econometric evidence submitted to us based on the IMS/EOS, Nielsen and Aztec data. However, we consider the IMS/EOS data to be the most appropriate available market data for analysing the impact of the TPP measures on cigarette sales, for a number of reasons. First, the IMS/EOS data are available for the longest period, which is more likely to yield more accurate estimates. Second, although the IMS/EOS data do not cover sales from retailers to consumers, the correlation between the IMS/EOS data and the Nielsen data, which do cover sales from retailers to consumers, is relatively high, with a correlation coefficient of 0.58, as shown in

---

[25]   The weekly Aztec data were aggregated to monthly data by assuming that each weekly cigarette quantity can be evenly split for each day of the week.

[26]   See List Rebuttal Report, (Exhibit DOM/IDN-3), fn 15; and IPE Third Updated Report, (Exhibit DOM-375), para. 171.

[27]   We note that Professor Klick is the only one of the complainants' experts to reject the claim that the Aztec dataset's market coverage has increased. Professor Klick argues that the upward trend of the ratio between the retail and wholesale data is the result of strategic inventory management. See Klick Fourth Supplemental Rebuttal Report, (Exhibit HND- 169), paras. 33-34. Dr Chipty disagrees with Professor Klick's claim and argues that strategic inventory management cannot explain the upward trend of the ratio beyond the 2012 and 2014 excise tax increase. See Chipty Third Rebuttal Report, (Exhibit AUS-605), fn 148. We note that Professor Klick does not provide in his reports any evidence that would suggest that the retail market coverage has stayed substantially the same over the sample period. In fact, a review of the underlying Aztec data reporting the associated store count for each sales channel shows that the number of stores covered by the data increased from 6,605 in January 2012 to 9,437 covered stores in September 2015. See Klick Fourth Supplemental Rebuttal Report, (Exhibit HND-169), back up material. We also note that a comparison of the Aztec data to tax statistics suggests that the market share covered by the Aztec has increased over time. The same conclusion applies with a comparison of the Aztec data to the IMS/EOS data. See IPE Report, (Exhibit DOM-100), pp. 101-103.

Figure D.10.[28] The correlation coefficient is even higher when the unit of analysis is quarterly sales, with a correlation coefficient equal to 0.85.[29]

Figure D.10: Indexes of Cigarette Sales Volumes Based on IMS/EOS, Nielsen and Aztec Data

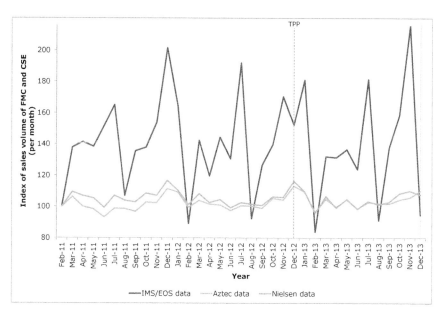

---

[28] According to the English Oxford Dictionary, the correlation coefficient is a number between -1 and 1 calculated so as to represent the linear interdependence of two variables. *Shorter Oxford English Dictionary*, 5th edn, W.R. Trumble and A. Stevenson (eds.) (Oxford University Press, 2002), Vol. 1, p. 524.

[29] We note that Professor Klick submits that for the March 2012-December 2013 period the correlation coefficient between the Nielsen data and the Aztec data is 0.985 if the Convenience Independent sample is included in the Nielsen data, and 0.999 if the Convenience Independent sample is omitted. See Klick Supplemental Rebuttal Report, (Exhibit HND-122), para. 123. We note, however, that the monthly Aztec data considered by Professor Klick differs significantly from the monthly cigarette sales constructed from the weekly Aztec data considered by IPE, Professor List, and Dr Chipty. This explains why the correlation coefficient between the Nielsen data (including the Convenience Independent sample) and the Aztec data we obtained for the March 2012-December 2013 period is different and equal to 0.929. In addition, we note that the correlation coefficient between the Nielsen data and the Aztec data for the February 2011-December 2013 period is smaller and equal to 0.84. In other words, the Nielsen data and the Aztec data are less correlated for the February 2011-February 2012 period than for the March 2012-December 2013 period, which is in line with the Aztec data's growing market coverage (given that the Nielsen data's market coverage is close to 100%). The correlation coefficient is also smaller (0.756) when the data are aggregated at the quarter level for the February 2011-December 2013 period.

Note: Conversion rate of 0.8 grams of fine-cut tobacco per stick. The vertical dotted lines
         indicate excise tax hikes. The vertical dashed line indicates the introduction of TPP and
         enlarged GHWs. Each data are normalized to its respective cigarette sales in
         January 2011.

Source: IPE Summary Report, (Exhibit DOM-379), back-up material.

26.   Although the Nielsen data cover sales from retailers to consumers, which
represent a closer measure to cigarette consumption than the IMS/EOs data, they
are only available for a short period, with only 13 post-implementation
observations, which could make it more difficult to estimate accurately any
impact on sales volumes. Similarly, although the Aztec data have the advantage
of covering sales from retailers to consumers, the share of total cigarette sales
covered by the Aztec data has grown over time, unlike the general downward
trend of cigarette sales in the Australian market, which could make it more
difficult to identify the impact of any factors from the increasing market
coverage.

27.   The evolution of per capita cigarette sales volumes, as depicted in Figure
D.11, leads us to the same conclusion, namely that the evidence before us
suggests that per capita cigarette sales have, on average, continued to decrease
after the introduction of the TPP measures. This finding is in line with the
evolution of house expenditure on tobacco and cigarettes. Evidence before us on
the extent to which the downward trend in cigarette sales has accelerated or not
in the post-TPP period is reviewed next.

Figure D.11: Per Capita Cigarette Sales Volumes Based on IMS/EOS, Nielsen and Aztec Data

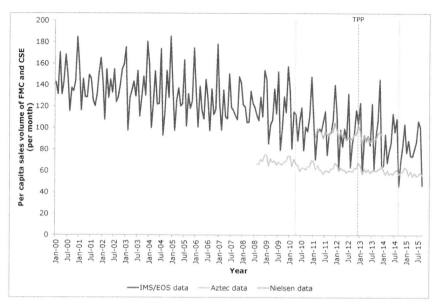

Note: Conversion rate of 0.8 grams of fine-cut tobacco per stick. The vertical dotted lines indicate excise tax hikes. The vertical dashed line indicates the introduction of TPP and enlarged GHWs.

Source: IPE Summary Report, (Exhibit DOM-379), back-up material.

2.   WHETHER THE REDUCTION OF CIGARETTE SALES VOLUMES ACCELERATED AFTER THE ENTRY INTO FORCE OF THE TPP MEASURES

28.   Having determined that the most recent market data show continuing declines in cigarette sales volumes in the period following the introduction of the TPP measures, we turn to whether there was a shift in cigarette sales volumes in the post-TPP implementation period. Instead of assessing directly the impact of the TPP measures on cigarette sales, which we review next, the Dominican Republic's and Indonesia's expert Professor List investigated whether there was a change in cigarette sales in the post-TPP implementation period. The underlying assumption is that if cigarette sales follow the same pre-existing pattern after the introduction of the TPP measures, then it follows that the TPP measures failed to reduce cigarette sales.

29.   Professor List investigates this question using two distinct datasets: the IMS/EOS data and the Aztec scanner data.[30] We describe Professor List's results and Australia's criticisms before presenting our analysis of this evidence.

2.1   Main datasets and arguments

2.1.1   In-Market-Sales/Exchange of Sales

30.   Professor List presents an event study analysing whether there has been a shift in the evolution of per capita cigarette sales following the introduction of TPP and enlarged GHWs. Specifically, a seasonally adjusted Autoregressive Integrated Moving Average (ARIMA) model and a dynamic model of per capita cigarette wholesales volumes are estimated controlling for per capita cigarette wholesales during the previous month, price during the previous month, a linear time trend and the 2006 GHWs.[31] The most recent analysis covers the period from February 2002 to June 2015.

31.   Overall, Professor List concludes that according to both models, there is no statistical difference between the observed per capita cigarette sales volumes and the estimated counterfactual per capita cigarette sales volumes, implying that the post-implementation downward trend in cigarette sales did not shift.[32]

32.   In response, Australia's expert, Dr Chipty, argues that Professor List's event study is fundamentally flawed. Dr Chipty contends that the estimates of Professor List's first-stage consumption model are highly imprecise and many of the explanatory variables are statistically insignificant, sometimes with the wrong estimated coefficient sign, making the post-TPP projections unreliable. In her view, the estimated moving average parameters of the seasonal ARIMA model indicate that the model is not specified correctly and most likely over-differenced. According to Dr Chipty, this over-differencing would likely lead to large forecasting errors when the model parameters are used to predict consumption levels during the post-period. Dr Chipty further argues that Professor List's analysis of the 2010 excise tax increase does not bolster

---

[30]   We note that Professor List's event study is a trend-projection analysis that does not estimate directly the impact of the TPP measures, but rather assesses whether there is a difference between the counterfactual per capita cigarette sales in the absence of the TPP measures and the actual per capita cigarette sales. That is why we have decided to discuss Professor List's event study under the subsection addressing whether there was a change in (per capita) cigarette sales trend in the post-implementation period.

[31]   An event analysis consists of (1) estimating the model of per capita cigarette sales during the pre-TPP period; (2) forecasting the per capita cigarette sales that would have been prevailed in the absence of the TPP measures using the estimated model's parameters in the post-implementation period; and (3) determining whether the difference between the observed per capital cigarette sales volumes and the estimated counterfactual cigarette sales volumes is statistically different from zero. See List Report, (Exhibit DOM/IDN-1), paras. 123-132.

[32]   See List Report, (Exhibit DOM/IDN-1), paras. 133-134; List Rebuttal Report, (Exhibit DOM/IDN-3), paras. 65-68; List Second Supplemental Report, (Exhibit DOM/IDN-5), paras. 26, 72, 74 and 144-154; and List Third Supplemental Report, (Exhibit DOM/IDN-7), paras. 26-28 and 56-61.

confidence in Professor List's conclusion that there is no shift in the downward trend in cigarette sales, because the result of the ordinary least square (OLS) model, intended to corroborate the result for the TPP measures, predicts higher consumption with taxes than without.[33]

33.   Dr Chipty also submits that by controlling for prices in the pre-period model and using actual prices in the post-period forecasting, Professor List's event study fails to account for the effect of tobacco control policies that work through price.[34] According to Dr Chipty, failure to control for the 2010 excise tax increase has the effect of crediting the trend with the effect of the tax increase. In her view, Professor List implicitly assumes that the effect of the 2010 tax increase will continue in perpetuity.[35] Dr Chipty reconsiders the dynamic model by controlling for the 2010 excise tax increase and finds a statistically significant shift in the post-implementation downward trend in cigarette sales. However, controlling for other problems, namely correcting the definition of the GHWs variable (from March 2006 onwards instead of between March 2006 and November 2012), accounting for all excise tax changes, and strategic inventory management associated with the tax changes, Dr Chipty concludes that the shift of the post-implementation downward trend in cigarette sales is economically significant (similar in magnitude to the estimates obtained in the preferred before-after consumption model) but not statistically significant. More generally, Dr Chipty contends that Professor List's conclusions regarding the statistical significance of the TPP measures' effect are unreliable because Professor List does not calculate any standard error associated with the estimated policy effect in the first stage. Dr Chipty submits that a before-after analysis, as discussed below, is preferable to Professor List's event study analysis for determining statistical significance.[36]

34.   Professor List counters that Dr Chipty does very little to engage with the event study as it pertains to TPP nor with the results reported but tears down an analysis of Australia's 2010 tax policy he never conducted. Professor List submits that when properly done, an event study identifies a negative and statistically significant effect on cigarette consumption of Australia's 2010 tax increase. According to Professor List, Dr Chipty confuses the interpretation of variables in a predictive model with the interpretation of explanatory variables in a causal model. Unlike Dr Chipty's claim that the over-differencing in the ARIMA model would likely lead to large forecasting errors, Professor List contends that the OLS model of cigarette sales does not suffer from this

---

[33] See Chipty Rebuttal Report, (Exhibit AUS-535) (SCI), paras. 37-44; and Chipty Surrebuttal Report, (Exhibit AUS-586), paras. 30-33.

[34] See Chipty Rebuttal Report, (Exhibit AUS-535) (SCI), paras. 33-44; and Chipty Surrebuttal Report, (Exhibit AUS-586), paras. 30-33.

[35] Chipty Third Rebuttal Report, (Exhibit AUS-605), paras. 61—67.

[36] See Chipty Rebuttal Report, (Exhibit AUS-535) (SCI), paras. 33-44; Chipty Surrebuttal Report, (Exhibit AUS-586), paras. 30-33; Chipty Second Rebuttal Report, (Exhibit AUS-591), paras. 39-42, Appendix C; and Chipty Third Rebuttal Report, (Exhibit AUS-605), paras. 61-68.

over-differencing problem. Professor List submits that although the predicted values are treated as if they were true, the hypothesis testing would actually be much wider if the uncertainty related to the predictors were taken into account. Professor List concludes that when an event study on the TPP measures finds no effect on cigarette sales, it is not because the data are too underpowered to detect changes induced by effective tobacco control policies, or because specific control variables have been chosen, but because the TPP measures are not working.[37]

2.1.2 Aztec Scanner Retail Sales

35.   Professor List performs the same event study using the Aztec scanner data. A seasonally adjusted ARIMA model and a dynamic model of per capita cigarette sales volumes are estimated controlling for per capita cigarette consumption during the previous month, price during the previous month, a linear time trend and the 2006 GHWs. The analysis covers the period from July 2008 to May 2015.

36.   Professor List concludes that there is no statistical difference between observed per capita cigarette sales volumes and the estimated counterfactual per capita cigarette sales volumes, implying that the post-implementation downward trend in cigarette sales did not shift. However, one of Professor List's specifications finds an upward and statistically significant trend in per capita cigarette sales, suggesting that per capital cigarette sales have increased in the post-TPP period. Professor List explains that this result is reported for the sake of comprehensiveness but he does not place much emphasis on the finding, given that the Aztec market share is increasing over the relevant time period.[38]

37.   Australia's expert Dr Chipty submits that the Aztec data should be disregarded because they are confounded by the growing coverage of the retail outlets included in the data. Dr Chipty submits that given this problem with the Aztec data, the analyses built on these data are also problematic.[39]

38.   Professor List counters that Dr Chipty favours discarding the Aztec dataset altogether without making any attempt to apply simple empirical tools available to deal with the alleged problem.[40] In particular, Professor List referred to IPE's proposal to benchmark quarterly Aztec data to IMS/EOS data in order to adjust for a growing market coverage of Aztec data.[41]

2.2   Analysis by the Panel

39.   As explained in our analysis of the contribution of the TPP measures on smoking prevalence, we assess the evidence before us on the basis that our task

---

[37]   See List Second Supplemental Report, (Exhibit DOM/IDN-5), paras. 151-154; and List Third Supplemental Report, (Exhibit DOM/IDN-7), paras. 26-28 and 56-61.
[38]   See List Third Supplemental Report, (Exhibit DOM/IDN-7), paras. 56-61 and 80.
[39]   See Chipty Surrebuttal Report, (Exhibit AUS-586), para. 31.
[40]   See List Summary Report, (Exhibit DOM/IDN-9), para. 107.
[41]   See IPE Third Updated Report, (Exhibit DOM-375), paras. 169-176.

is not to present a unified econometric analysis of this question but to assess the robustness of the results submitted by the parties. In addition, our conclusions in this respect relate exclusively to the data (including the sample period) and econometric results submitted by the parties in these proceedings, and are not intended to be generalized to other datasets or econometric studies.

2.2.1 Professor List's reports

40. After a careful review of the results of Professor List's event study of the TPP measures' impact on per capita cigarette sales, we question the validity of his results for a number of reasons, some of which are specific to one of the models considered by Professor List.

41. We note that in most estimations of the ARIMA model for the pre-TPP period based on the IMS/EOS data that are used to forecast the value of per capita cigarette sale in the post-implementation period, none of the explanatory variables, including the constant, is statistically significant, besides the moving averages parameters.[42] In our view, the lack of statistically significant variables is surprising, given the relatively small number of explanatory variables included in the ARIMA model. We further note that, as pointed out by Dr Chipty, the estimated moving average parameters are not statistically different from -1, which would likely lead to large forecasting errors. This is, in our view, problematic because Professor List's approach relies on the post-implementation forecasting errors to determine whether there was a statistically significant change in the downward trend in per capita cigarette sales. We note that Professor List recognized the issue of over-differencing but failed to address it or propose a solution. Instead, Professor List suggests considering the dynamic model, which, according to him, does not suffer from this over-differencing problem.[43]

42. Yet, a visual inspection of the results of the ARIMA model and the dynamic model based on the IMS/EOS data shows, as depicted in Figure D.12, that most of the estimated per capita cigarette sales associated with the dynamic model are not close at all to the actual values of the per capita sales in the pre-implementation period. In other words, the dynamic model does not fit well the per capita cigarette sales in the pre-TPP period. For instance, the predicted value of per capita sales in December 2010 given by the dynamic model is equal to 100.6, while the actual value of per capita sales amounts to 147.7. Similarly, the dynamic model predicts a value of 95.6 in February 2012, while the observed value is 61.8. We therefore question how the dynamic model specification can be used to accurately forecast the per capita cigarette sales that would have

---

[42] We note that the same issue applies to Professor List's event study of the 2010 tax change on cigarette sales, where most explanatory variables are not statistically significant, except for some of the moving average parameters. List Second Supplemental Report, (Exhibit DOM/IDN-5), backup material.

[43] See List Second Supplemental Report, (Exhibit DOM/IDN-5), para. 49.

prevailed in the absence of the TPP measures in the post-implementation period, when it already performs relatively poorly in the pre-implementation period.

Figure D.12: Event Study of Per Capita Cigarette Sales Volumes Based on IMS/EOS Data

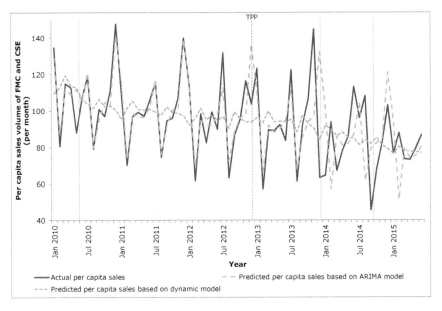

Note: Conversion rate of 0.8 grams of fine-cut tobacco per stick. The vertical dotted lines indicate excise tax hikes. The vertical dashed line indicates the introduction of TPP and enlarged GHWs.

Source: List Rebuttal Report, (Exhibit DOM/IDN-3), p. 16.

43.   We further note that, similar to the ARIMA model, most explanatory variables in the estimated dynamic models using the IMS/EOS data are not statistically significant (except the constant) at 5%. In particular, the results of the benchmark specification, which includes the price variable in the previous month, suggest that per capita cigarette sales are not explained by the value of per capita sales in the previous month or the linear time trend. This result contradicts the fact that per capita sales follow a dynamic process and a downward trend, as acknowledged by Professor List.[44] While Professor List explains that the predictive models he employs are not designed to precisely describe every causal dynamic in Australia's cigarette market, we note that he does not explain how this justifies the lack of statistically significant explanatory

---

[44]   See List Second Supplemental Report, (Exhibit DOM/IDN-5), para. 23.

variables.[45] In fact, the only explanatory variable (besides the constant) that is statistically significant is the time trend variable when the price variable is omitted or replaced by a tax level variable. This finding, as explained in the analysis of smoking prevalence, suggests that the price variable and the time trend might be collinear, that is both variables might convey the same information and one of them then becomes redundant. As with the technical exchange between the experts of the Dominican Republic, Honduras, Indonesia and Australia regarding smoking prevalence, they disagree on the use of the price variable. As explained in our review of the econometric studies assessing the impact of the TPP measures on smoking prevalence in Appendix C, we question the results of the dynamic model specification with the price variable based on the IMS/EOS data.[46] Finally, we note that, as pointed out by Dr Chipty, Professor List did not correctly define the March 2006 GHW variable and implicitly assumes that the GHW policy no longer had an effect on consumption as of the beginning December 2012, when the TPP measures were fully implemented. It is also unclear to what extent defining correctly the dummy variable for the GHW policy would have changed the results.

44.   Some of the issues we raised above also apply to the results of Professor List's event study based on the Aztec data. In particular, both the ARIMA model and the dynamic model include the price variable in the previous month, which as explained above, appears to be non-stationary and do not account for the potential impact of the TPP measures on prices.[47] In addition, the results of the dynamic model find a statistically significant upward trend in per capita cigarette sales. As acknowledged by Professor List, Aztec's market share has been increasing over the relevant time period.[48] Yet, Professor List does not control for this feature of the data, so it is unclear to what extent the results of an upward trend shift would prevail, if the increasing market share was accounted for. In any event, we are not persuaded that we can simply ignore or down-weigh this contradictory result, as Professor List suggests, without questioning the model specification and data. Overall, in this context, we consider the results of Professor List's event study to be of limited use in

[45]   See List Second Supplemental Report, (Exhibit DOM/IDN-5), para. 149.

[46]   We note that the price variable is also included in the ARIMA model but it is expressed in difference (i.e. the difference in price with respect to the previous year). Differentiating the data is often used to address the non-stationary (unit root) of the data. In fact, standard unit root tests suggest that price differential variable is stationary. Therefore, the issue of non-stationary price variable does not apply to the results of Professor List's ARIMA model.

[47]   We note that Professor List decided to remove the observation associated with 3 August 2008 in his analysis without providing any explanation. We also note that the results of the ARIMA model show that the STATA software is unable to compute the standard error of the second lagged moving average coefficient. In addition, unlike the specification of the ARIMA model based on the IMS/EOS data, Professor List removed the constant term, supposedly as a result of the procedure implemented by Professor List to select the model specification by optimizing the information criteria of the model. See List Rebuttal Report, (Exhibit DOM/IDN-3), fn 14.

[48]   See List Rebuttal Report, (Exhibit DOM/IDN-3), fn 15.

informing whether the TPP measures led to a change in the downward trend of per capita cigarette sales.

2.2.2 Dr Chipty's reports

45. We note that Dr Chipty re-estimated Professor List's dynamic model based on the IMS/EOS data by addressing some of the issues we raised above. In particular, replacing the price variable with an excise tax increase dummy reverses Professor List's conclusions and suggests that there was a statistically significant shift in the post-implementation downward trend in per capita cigarette sales. We note, however, that the shift is still negative but no longer statistically significant when the excise tax changes, and strategic inventory management associated with these tax changes are taken into account in the post-implementation estimation. As shown in **Figure D.13**, a visual inspection of the results of Dr Chipty's dynamic model specification based on the IMS/EOS data shows that, although Dr Chipty's specification, with a higher adjusted coefficient of determination, predicts slightly more accurately the values of per capita sales in the pre-implementation period than Professor List, the dynamic model continues to perform relatively poorly in the pre-implementation period.[49] As explained above, we continue to have doubts about how the dynamic model specification can be used to accurately forecast the per capita cigarette sales that would have prevailed in the absence of the TPP measures in the post-implementation period, when it already performs relatively poorly in the pre-implementation period.

---

[49] The (adjusted) coefficient of determination measures the share of the variance in the dependent variable (e.g. per capita cigarette sales) is predictable from the independent variables included in the model (e.g. price, trend, …). W. H. Green, *Econometric Analysis*, 5th edn (Prentice Hall, 2002).

Figure D.13: Alternative Event Study of Per Capita Cigarette Sales Volumes Based on IMS/EOS Data

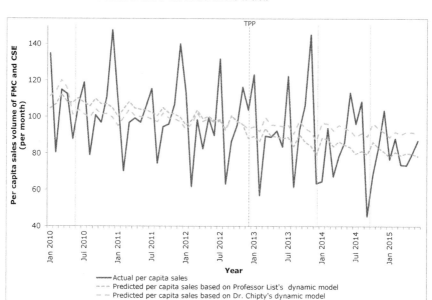

Note: Conversion rate of 0.8 grams of fine-cut tobacco per stick. The vertical dotted lines indicate excise tax hikes. The vertical dashed line indicates the introduction of TPP and enlarged GHWs.

Source: Chipty Third Rebuttal Report, (Exhibit AUS-605), para. 67.

46.   That being said, we find that, according to a standard mean-comparison test, the average cigarette sales volumes based on the IMS/EOS data in the post-implementation period are statistically significantly lower than in the pre-implementation period.[50] This is confirmed by the fact that, as described in **Figure D.14**, the cigarette sales trend in the post-implementation period has become steeper compared to the pre-implementation trend, implying that the fall in cigarette sales has accelerated in the post-implementation period. The same conclusion can be drawn based on the Aztec data. In any case, as for prevalence, the fact that the downward trend in sales from manufacturers to wholesalers and

---

[50]   For completeness sake, we note that the mean-comparison test applied to the Nielsen data concludes that there is no difference between the pre- and post-implementation period trends. However, the Nielsen data are only available for the February 2011-December 2013 period. When the mean-comparison test is applied to the IMS/EOS data for the same February 2011-December 2013 period, the test result suggests also that there is no shift in the pre- and post-trend, while the conclusion is reversed when the sample period is extended to September 2015. We, therefore, do not consider the result of the mean-comparison test applied to the Nielsen data to be relevant given that other more recent datasets are available and yield a different conclusion.

retailers has accelerated in the post-implementation period does not necessarily mean that the TPP measures are having a statistically significant impact, given that other factors, unrelated to the TPP measures, could explain the trend shift. Evidence relating to the extent to which the TPP measures have an impact on cigarette sales or in some reports on cigarette consumption is reviewed next.

Figure D.14: Cigarette Sales Volumes Pre- and Post-TPP Trends

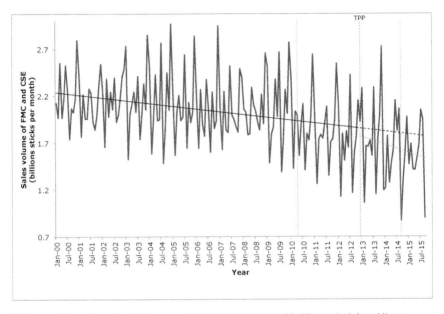

Note: Conversion rate of 0.8 grams of fine-cut tobacco per stick. The vertical dotted lines indicate excise tax hikes. The vertical dashed line indicates the introduction of TPP and enlarged GHWs.

Source: IPE Summary Report, (Exhibit DOM-379), back-up material.

3.   WHETHER THE TPP MEASURES CONTRIBUTED TO THE REDUCTION IN CIGARETTE SALES VOLUMES AND CONSUMPTION

47.   As explained above, we have determined that the evidence presented to us shows that cigarette sales volumes in Australia have continued to experience a decline, which has accelerated in the post-TPP period. To the extent that there has been a greater reduction in cigarette sales volumes after the entry into force of the TPP measures, the question arises whether, and if so, to what extent, the TPP measures contributed to reducing cigarette consumption.

48.   As for smoking prevalence, IPE (for the Dominican Republic), Professor List (for the Dominican Republic and Indonesia), Professor Klick (for

Honduras) and Dr Chipty (for Australia) proposed different econometric methods to estimate the TPP measures' impact on cigarette sales or reported cigarette consumption. As mentioned above, all parties recognize, however, that the empirical econometric results submitted do not distinguish between the impact of TPP *and* the impact of enlarged GHWs on cigarette sales and consumption, because both measures were implemented at the exact same time.[51]

49.   Australia submits that, with regard to prevalence, it is too early to look at cigarette consumption to assess the contribution of the TPP measures, for two main reasons. First, reduction in cigarette consumption through smoking prevalence is a long-term objective.[52] Second, significant changes in the root behaviours (i.e. initiation, cessation, and relapse) stemming from TPP are likely masked in cigarette consumption because of the stock of current smokers whose behaviours may not be as affected by TPP.[53] Instead Australia considered that the impact of TPP should be investigated through its three mechanisms, i.e. appeal, GHW effectiveness, and the packs' ability to mislead. Australia referred to a series of peer-reviewed studies published in the *Tobacco Control* journal. Notwithstanding this position, Australia engaged in estimating the TPP measures' impact on cigarette sales in response to the Dominican Republic's, Honduras's and Indonesia's submissions, and found on that basis that the TPP measures have already contributed to the reduction of cigarette sales volumes.[54]

50.   Just as with the empirical results submitted in the context of prevalence, new methodologies or new model specifications or both were proposed by the experts of the Dominican Republic, Honduras and Indonesia in the course of the proceedings in response to the exchange of arguments between the parties. In some cases, the new models proposed invalidate some of the previous estimations (even though they yielded the same conclusion).[55] For this reason,

---

[51]   See Australia's first written submission, para. 518; Dominican Republic's response to Panel question No. 8, para. 61; List Report, (Exhibit DOM/IDN-1), para. 113; Honduras's response to Panel question No. 8; and Indonesia's response to Panel question No. 8, para. 8.

[52]   See Australia's first written submission, para. 670. Australia considers that in the early stages of introduction of the measures, the most appropriate way to discern their effects is to rely on experiments and surveys which consider drivers of choice, attitudes, and ultimately, the elicitation of behavioural intentions (Australia's first written submission, para. 147).

[53]   See Chipty Report, (Exhibit AUS-17), paras. 32-39.

[54]   See Australia's response to Panel question No. 196, para. 214.

[55]   For instance, as in the review of the econometric studies on smoking prevalence, IPE initially proposed to control for excise tax increases by including (dummy) indicator variables for each excise tax increase (IPE Updated Report, (Exhibit DOM-303)), but subsequently contended that a more appropriate measure to capture the excise tax increases is the weighted average price per cigarette in Australia. IPE Second Updated Report, (Exhibit DOM-361). Similarly, Professor List and IPE initially applied the STATA software command ivreg2 in order to calculate standard errors that are robust to heteroscedasticity and serial correlation using the automatic bandwidth selection procedure by Newey and West (1994). IPE Updated Report, (Exhibit DOM-303); and List Report, (Exhibit DOM/IDN-1). Subsequently, both Professor List and IPE applied an alternative way of calculating standard errors, that, according to them, is adjusted to reflect more accurately the original suggestion

the approaches and results discussed below are drawn mostly from the most recent expert reports submitted by the parties.[56] Similar to the review of the econometric studies on smoking prevalence, we first describe the relevant results and related discussions by dataset, before presenting our analysis.

3.1 Datasets and related studies

3.1.1 In-Market-Sales/Exchange of Sales

51.   The IMS/EOS data were used by several of the Dominican Republic's and Honduras's experts to estimate econometrically the impact of the TPP measures on cigarette wholesale volumes.

3.1.1.1 IPE Reports

52.   The Dominican Republic submitted several reports prepared by IPE, estimating econometrically the TPP measures' impact on the logarithm of cigarette sales using the IMS/EOS data. Throughout the IPE Reports submitted, different econometric approaches and model specifications have been proposed: (1) time series regression analysis of cigarette sales; (2) modified trend analysis of per capita cigarette sales; and (3) ARIMAX model of per capita cigarette sales.[57] The first approach was only presented in the first IPE Report and is based on a model specification of the logarithm of cigarette sales that includes at least a dummy variable for the TPP measures, dummy variables for the 2010 and 2013 excise tax increase, month fixed effects and a trend (in some specifications). The second and subsequent IPE Reports only focused on the last two approaches, which to some extent were adopted to address some of the critiques raised by Australia's expert, Dr Chipty. Under these two approaches, the model specification was modified to focus on the logarithm of per capita cigarette sales and to include at least a TPP measures dummy variable, a tobacco price variable, a 2006 GHW dummy, dummy variables for strategic inventory and a linear trend. The most recent econometric analysis reported in the IPE Report covers the period January 2001 through August 2015 (for the model specifications without the price variable) or February 2002 through August 2015 (for the model specifications with the price variable).[58]

53.   Overall, IPE concludes that the TPP measures had no statistically significant effect on cigarette sales and per capita cigarette sales. According to IPE, these results are robust across different specifications (e.g. different TPP starting date: October, November and December; excluding the October and

---

by Newey and West (1994). IPE Second Updated Report (Exhibit DOM-361); and List Rebuttal Report, (Exhibit DOM/IDN-3).

[56]   We note that we nonetheless considered all the relevant evidence before us, including all the expert reports, including the methodologies and models contained therein.

[57]   See IPE Report, (Exhibit DOM-100), pp. 67-73 and 201-210; and IPE Updated Report, (Exhibit DOM-303), paras. 135-175 and 290-326.

[58]   The difference between the two sample periods stem from the fact that the price variable is not available prior to February 2002.

November 2012 observations; controlling for the weighted average price of tobacco, tax levels or tax policy change; and strategic inventory management). The results are also robust to Professor List's procedure to compute the explanatory variables' robust standard errors, which is different from the STATA software package ivreg2 used by Dr Chipty.[59] However, when excise tax dummy variables are included in the model specification, some of the results of the modified trend analysis suggest that the TPP measures had a negative and statistically significant impact on cigarette wholesales and per capita cigarette wholesales.[60]

54.   Australia's expert, Dr Chipty, rejects the econometric results of the IPE Reports on various technical grounds. Dr Chipty is of the view that the analysis should be extended to the 2000-2015 period, instead of restricting the sample to the period 2001-2015 or 2002-2015, noting that there is no reason for ignoring available data.[61] For similar reasons as for the IPE Reports and Professor List's econometric studies on smoking prevalence, Dr Chipty disagrees with Professor List and IPE's claim that the Stata command, ivreg2, used to estimate standard errors robust to "heteroscedasticity" and "autocorrelation" (Newey-West standard errors) is wrong, noting that both IPE and Professor List used the same Stata command, before Professor List argued he found an error in the Stata programming code.[62] Similarly, Dr Chipty submits that controlling for tobacco prices inclusive of tax while attempting to measure the effects of a tax hike ignores the effect of the TPP measures on price, leading the TPP measures indicator variable to capture only a partial effect of the TPP measures, and the price variable capturing the rest of its effect. Dr Chipty further notes that IPE initially controlled for excise tax increase with indicator variables in their model specification.[63] Dr Chipty further submits that the use of a single tax level variable, as proposed by IPE, is only valid under the proportionality assumption (i.e. the effect of tax changes is proportional to the size of the tax change), which may only be satisfied in some specifications, and is inappropriate in models of consumption/sales.[64] Dr Chipty argues that IPE's consumption analyses rely heavily on the use of time trends by assuming trends in consumption exist in a vacuum without addressing the issue of whether any of the changes in consumption with the time trends around the TPP measures should themselves be interpreted as the TPP measures' effects.[65]

---

[59]   IPE Report, (Exhibit DOM-100), pp. 67-73 and 201-210; IPE Updated Report, (Exhibit DOM-303), paras. 143-155, 290-295; IPE Second Updated Report, (Exhibit DOM-361), paras. 26-31; IPE Third Updated Report, (Exhibit DOM-375), paras. 117-145; and IPE Summary Report, (Exhibit DOM-379), paras. 123-150.

[60]   See IPE Summary Report, (Exhibit DOM-379), paras. 144-145 and backup material.

[61]   See Chipty Surrebuttal Report, (Exhibit AUS-586), para. 9; and Chipty Third Rebuttal Report, (Exhibit AUS-605), paras. 34-35.

[62]   See Chipty Second Rebuttal Report, (Exhibit AUS-591), paras. 13-31.

[63]   See Chipty Surrebuttal Report, (Exhibit AUS-586), paras. 12, 45 and 65.

[64]   See Chipty Third Rebuttal Report, (Exhibit AUS-605), paras. 22-26 and 29-32.

[65]   See Chipty Surrebuttal Report, (Exhibit AUS-586), paras. 68-70.

3.1.1.2 Professor Klick's reports

55. Like his analysis of smoking prevalence, Honduras's expert, Professor Klick, proposes comparing Australia's cigarette sales before and after the introduction of the TPP measures relative with another jurisdiction that has not implemented TPP during the same period. Professor Klick posits that although Australia is unique in many ways, it is, notwithstanding Dr Chipty's criticisms, reasonable to use New Zealand as a reliable counterfactual jurisdiction, because (i) both countries share many similarities culturally, historically, and demographically; (ii) both countries are in the same region and share the same seasonality (useful when dealing with sub-annual measures); (iii) the governments of both countries acknowledge that they are comparable in areas such as health behaviour and socio-economic issues; (iv) tobacco prices, including taxes, are comparable between both countries; and (v) smoking rates in both countries are highly correlated (0.95 for the period 1964-2012 based on the OECD data on the fraction of residents ages 15 years and older who are daily smokers).[66]

56. Professor Klick reconsidered the IMS/EOS data for Australia and New Zealand and estimated a difference-in-difference model that explains the logarithm of cigarette sales in Australia relative to New Zealand controlling for a TPP measures dummy variable, the logarithm of tobacco price, country fixed effects, time-period fixed effects and country-specific trends. In Professor Klick's first submission, the model only controlled for a TPP measures dummy variable, time-period fixed effects and differential intercept term for New Zealand. Professor Klick subsequently modified his model specification to address some of Dr Chipty's criticisms. In Professor Klick's first report, a differential trends model was also estimated controlling for a TPP measures dummy variable, an Australia monthly trend, and a New Zealand monthly trend. The most recent econometric analysis covers the period February 2011 to September 2015.[67]

57. Professor Klick considers it unlikely that prices may be endogenous to cigarette sales, in other words prices may be determined by cigarette sales, a concern raised by Dr Chipty. This is because tobacco taxes make up the bulk of tobacco prices, and are, theoretically, less likely to be determined endogenously to cigarette sales, at least on a month-to-month basis, since taxes are the result of political decisions that take significant time to reach and implement. Nevertheless, Professor Klick implements an instrument variable (IV) estimation procedure to address the theoretical possibility of an endogeneity bias of the tobacco price variable. The IV estimation procedure involves (1) estimating a model of tobacco price that includes a TPP measures dummy variable, an excise

---

[66] See Klick Report, (Exhibit UKR-5), pp. 3-6; and Klick Third Supplemental Rebuttal Report, (Exhibit HND-166), paras. 30-31.

[67] See Klick Report, (Exhibit UKR-5), pp. 35-36; Klick Rebuttal Report, (Exhibit HND-118), paras. 66-68; and Klick Supplemental Rebuttal Report, (Exhibit HND-122), paras. 107-121.

tax dummy variable, country fixed effects and time fixed effects (and country-specific trends in some specifications); and (2) reconstructing the tobacco price variable using the estimated parameters of the model obtained in the first stage. This constructed (instrumented) price variable replaces the original price variable in the model of cigarette sales.[68] The overall impact of the TPP measures corresponds to the sum of the impact of the TPP measures on cigarette sales and the impact of the TPP measures on cigarette price multiplied by the impact of cigarette price on cigarette sales. In addition, Professor Klick contends that New Zealand's 2013 excise tax increase does not invalidate it as a comparator to Australia, because taxes influence behaviour through prices and the model specification controls for price and accounts for its potential endogeneity through the instrumental variables technique.[69]

58.   Overall, Professor Klick concludes that the TPP measures have not resulted in a decline in cigarette sales in Australia relative to sales in New Zealand.[70] However, Professor Klick's most recent estimations find a positive and statistically significant impact of the TPP measures on cigarette sales, suggesting that the TPP measures led to an increase in cigarette sales in Australia relative to New Zealand.[71]

59.   Dr Chipty contends that Professor Klick's analysis is flawed on various technical grounds. As in the case of Professor Klick's econometric analysis on smoking prevalence, Dr Chipty is of the view that New Zealand is an invalid counterfactual for the purposes of studying the TPP measures' effects, because of New Zealand's January 2013 excise tax increase, a month after the introduction of the TPP measures.[72] In particular, Dr Chipty submits that there is no reliable way to correct for the failure to account for differential country-specific tax policies introduced at different times in Australia and New Zealand because there is only a single month of data in New Zealand between implementation of the TPP measures in Australia and the January 2013 New Zealand excise tax increase.[73] Dr Chipty also questions the use of a highly flexible time trend that makes it difficult to estimate the effects of the very policies that likely created the trend.[74]

---

[68]   See Klick Rebuttal Report, (Exhibit HND-118), paras. 52-60.
[69]   See Klick Third Supplemental Rebuttal Report, (Exhibit HND-166), para. 32.
[70]   See Klick Supplemental Rebuttal Report, (Exhibit HND-122), paras. 117-119; and Klick Third Supplemental Rebuttal Report, (Exhibit HND-166), paras. 44-45.
[71]   See Klick Third Supplemental Rebuttal Report, (Exhibit HND-166), paras. 44-45.
[72]   See Chipty Supplementary Report, (Exhibit AUS-511), paras. 16-19; and Chipty Rebuttal Report, (Exhibit AUS-535) (SCI), paras. 67-71.
[73]   See Chipty Supplementary Report, (Exhibit AUS-511), paras. 3 and 12-19. Dr Chipty also argued that Professor Klick failed to account for the strategic inventory management associated with excise tax hikes but acknowledged that the failure to account for the buy up problem did not affect the estimates in Professor Klick's analysis. *Ibid.* paras. 22-24.
[74]   See Chipty Supplementary Report, (Exhibit AUS-511), para. 25.

3.1.1.3 Dr Chipty's reports

60.   Australia's expert, Dr Chipty, considers the IMS/EOS data to be the only appropriate data to assess the TPP measures' impact on cigarette sales volumes, because the IMS/EOS data capture virtually all sales in Australian market, given that the big three manufacturers account for all but 1% of total sales. In addition, the IMS/EOS data are available for a longer period.[75]

61.   Dr Chipty re-estimated the model of cigarette sales developed by IPE in its first report (time series regression analysis) by extending the period of analysis from January 2000 to September 2015 and controlling for a TPP measures dummy variables, tax increases dummy variables (for May 2010, December 2013 and September 2014), a 2006 GHW dummy variable, a linear trend and month fixed effects.[76]

62.   Overall, Dr Chipty concludes that the TPP measures had a negative and statistically significant effect on cigarette sales.[77] Most of the results show statistically significant declines in cigarette sales even when using Professor List's own standard error calculation.[78] However, Dr Chipty notes that the results are sensitive to the decision whether to use a tobacco price variable or the tax levels variable instead of the tax indicators, and that specification testing suggests the use of tax levels are not appropriate.[79]

63.   IPE counters that Dr Chipty "cherry-picked" a small subset of IPE's analyses for the purposes of undertaking adaptations or "corrections". According to IPE, Dr Chipty engaged in further "cherry-picking", reporting results from only a small subset of specifications, for example by using only one specific measure of tobacco affordability (tax dummies) and simply ignoring the two superior alternatives (tax levels and tobacco prices, respectively). IPE submits that Dr Chipty never even discussed any of the ARIMAX models, thus completely ignoring an entire class of models.[80]

3.1.2 Nielsen Retail Sales

64.   Similar to the IMS/EOS data, the Nielsen retail sales data were used by the Dominican Republic's and Honduras's experts to estimate econometrically the impact of the TPP measures on cigarette retail volumes.

---

[75]   See Chipty Third Rebuttal Report, (Exhibit 605), para. 70.
[76]   See Chipty Second Rebuttal Report, (Exhibit AUS-591), paras. 28-31.
[77]   See Chipty Surrebuttal Report, (Exhibit AUS-586), paras. 65-66; Chipty Second Rebuttal Report, (Exhibit AUS-591), paras. 29-31, 53-54, Appendix D; and Chipty Third Rebuttal Report, (Exhibit AUS-605), paras. 74-75.
[78]   See Chipty Second Rebuttal Report, (Exhibit AUS-591), paras. 28-31.
[79]   See Chipty Third Rebuttal Report, (Exhibit 605), paras. 15-28 and 75.
[80]   See IPE Summary Report, (Exhibit DOM-379), paras. 156-161.

3.1.2.1 IPE Reports

65.   IPE argues that Dr Chipty's decision to dismiss the Nielsen data due to its short sample period is unscientific. According to IPE, despite the relatively shorter period for which the Nielsen data are available, the dataset has two important advantages as compared to the IMS/EOS data and the Aztec data: (1) compared to the IMS/EOS data, the Nielsen dataset provides actual sales to customers and is not affected by wholesalers' strategic inventory management behaviour; and (2) compared to the Aztec data, which are also at the retail level, the Nielsen data cover virtually the whole market.[81]

66.   Similar to the analysis of the IMS/EOS and the Aztec data, IPE presents the results of the (1) modified trend analysis and (2) ARIMAX model of tobacco retail sales per capita controlling for at least a TPP measures dummy variable, a cigarette price variable and a linear trend.[82] The econometric analysis based on the Nielsen data covers the period February 2011 to December 2013.[83]

67.   Overall, IPE concludes that the TPP measures had no statistically significant effect on retail sales of cigarettes per capita.[84] According to IPE, these results are robust across different specifications (e.g. different TPP starting date: October, November and December; controlling for the weighted average price of cigarettes, tax levels or tax policy change; and adjusting for seasonality in order to reduce the number of parameters to be estimated). In reality, some of IPE's results of the modified trend analysis (when the TPP measures dummy variable starts in December 2012) suggest that the TPP measures led to an increase in retail sales of cigarettes per capita.[85]

68.   Dr Chipty agrees with IPE that the Nielsen data cover "virtually the whole market" and as such are superior to the Aztec data in this respect. However, Dr Chipty contends that the sample size of the Nielsen data is a serious problem for IPE, which attempts to estimate at least 15 different coefficients, including 12-month indicators for seasonality, using 35 monthly observations. Dr Chipty argues that in IPE's Nielsen analysis, the monthly effects are identified off of variation from three data points each, with only two for the January effect. Dr Chipty submits that unlike the IMS/EOS data, which are affected by the issue of strategic inventory management, but can be corrected for it, there is no workaround for the insufficient data issue.[86]

---

[81] See IPE Updated Report, (Exhibit DOM-303), para. 157; and IPE Third Updated Report, (Exhibit DOM-375), paras. 158-168.
[82] See IPE Report, (Exhibit DOM-100), pp. 67-73 and 201-210; and IPE Updated Report, (Exhibit DOM-303), paras. 135-175 and 290-326.
[83] See IPE Updated Report, (Exhibit DOM-303), para. 156.
[84] See IPE Updated Report, (Exhibit DOM-303), paras. 156-162; IPE Second Updated Report, (Exhibit DOM-361), paras. 32-35; IPE Third Updated Report, (Exhibit DOM-375), paras. 158-168; and IPE Summary Report, (Exhibit DOM-379), paras. 146-147.
[85] See IPE Third Updated Report, (Exhibit DOM-375), paras. 146-147 and 158-168.
[86] See Chipty Surrebuttal Report, (Exhibit AUS-586), para. 77.

3.1.2.2 Professor Klick's reports

69.   Professor Klick also used the Nielsen retail sales data for Australia and New Zealand to estimate a difference-in-difference model of the logarithm of cigarette retail sales per capita controlling for a TPP measures dummy variable, the logarithm of tobacco price, country fixed effects, time-period fixed effects and country-specific trends. In Professor Klick's first submission, the analysis focused on cigarette retail sales and not cigarette retail sales per capita. Professor Klick's first difference-in-difference model also only controlled for a TPP measures dummy variable, time-period fixed effects and differential intercept term for New Zealand. In addition, a differential trends model was also estimated controlling for a TPP measures dummy variable, an Australia monthly trend, and a New Zealand monthly trend. The econometric analysis covers the period February 2011 to December 2013.[87]

70.   Overall, Professor Klick concludes that the TPP measures are not associated with a statistically significant reduction in cigarette retail sales and cigarette retail sales per capita in Australia relative to New Zealand.[88] However, two initial specifications, which do not control for price, find a positive and statistically significant TPP effect, suggesting that the TPP measures led to an increase in cigarette sales in Australia relative to New Zealand.[89]

71.   Professor Klick also presents the results of a "crossfold validation" analysis to test various predictive models using the Nielsen data in terms of predictive accuracy. Professor Klick concludes that the January 2013 tax increase in New Zealand does not disqualify New Zealand as a proper comparator because the best performing model is the one that includes New Zealand's natural log per capita sales and monthly fixed effects and for which the TPP measures' impact on per capita cigarette sales in Australia (relative to New Zealand) is statistically not significant.[90]

72.   As described above, Dr Chipty is of the view that New Zealand is an invalid counterfactual for the purposes of studying the TPP measures' effects, because of New Zealand's January 2013 excise tax increase, a month after the introduction of the TPP measures.[91] Dr Chipty further submits that the predictive

---

[87]   See Klick Report, (Exhibit UKR-5), pp. 12-16; and Klick Rebuttal Report, (Exhibit HND-118), paras. 10, 39-42, 44-48 and 49-51.
[88]   See Klick Report, (Exhibit UKR-5), pp. 32-34; and Klick Rebuttal Report, (Exhibit HND-118), paras. 54-64.
[89]   However, Dr Chipty notes that Professor Klick made a transcription error and erroneously reported a statistically significant increase in sale in Professor Klick's two specifications controlling for price. See Chipty Report, (Exhibit AUS-17), para. 53.
[90]   See Klick Rebuttal Report, (Exhibit HND-118), paras. 44-51; and Klick Third Supplemental Rebuttal Report, (Exhibit HND-166), para. 32.
[91]   See Chipty Rebuttal Report, (Exhibit AUS-535) (SCI), paras. 67-71.

ability measured by the "crossfold validation" is insufficient to validate a control group given New Zealand's January 2013 tax increase.[92]

3.1.3   Aztec Scanner Retail Sales

73.   Similar to the analysis of the IMS/EOS data, IPE used the Aztec data and applied different econometric approaches and model specification throughout their reports: (1) time series regression analysis of cigarette retail sales; (2) modified trend analysis of cigarette retail sales per capita; and (3) ARIMAX model of cigarette retail sales per capita.[93] The first approach was only presented in the first IPE Report and is based on a model specification of the logarithm of retail sales of cigarettes that includes at least a TPP measures dummy variable, dummies for the 2010 and 2013 excise tax increase, month fixed effects and a trend. The second and subsequent IPE Reports only focused on the last two approaches, which to some extent were adopted to address some of the criticisms raised by Australia's expert, Dr Chipty. In those two approaches, the model specification was modified to focus on the logarithm of retail sales of cigarettes *per capita* and to include at least a TPP measures dummy variable, a cigarette price variable and a linear trend. IPE argues that Dr Chipty's decision to dismiss the Aztec dataset due to its growing market coverage is unscientific because the use of linear time trends means it is possible to take into account changes in market coverage.[94] The most recent econometric analysis reported in the IPE Report covers the period from 27 July 2008 through 27 September 2015.[95]

74.   Overall, IPE concludes that the TPP measures had no statistically significant effect on retail sales of cigarettes per capita.[96] According to IPE, these results are robust across different specifications (e.g. different TPP starting date: October, November and December; controlling for the weighted average price of cigarettes, tax levels or tax policy change; and adjusting for the increasing market share by benchmarking quarterly Aztec data to IMS/EOS data). In reality, when IPE's modified trend analysis specification controls for tax levels (instead of cigarette price or tax dummies), the results suggests that the TPP measures led to an increase in retail sales of cigarettes. Similarly, in a few ARIMAX specifications, the TPP measures' impact on retail sales of cigarettes is positive and statistically significant.

75.   As explained above, Dr Chipty argues that not all data are worth studying. She notes that the Aztec scanner data in particular has a growing coverage of retail sales over time, either through the growth of the sales outlets it

---

[92]   See Chipty Rebuttal Report, (Exhibit AUS-535) (SCI), paras. 70-71.
[93]   See IPE Report, (Exhibit DOM-100), pp. 67-73 and 201-210; and IPE Updated Report, (Exhibit DOM-303), paras. 135-175 and 290-326.
[94]   See IPE Third Updated Report, (Exhibit DOM-375), paras. 146-147, 156-157 and 169-170.
[95]   See IPE Third Updated Report, (Exhibit DOM-375), paras. 240-242.
[96]   See IPE Updated Report, (Exhibit DOM-303), paras. 163-172; IPE Second Updated Report, (Exhibit DOM-361), paras. 26-31, 36-38; IPE Third Updated Report, (Exhibit DOM-375), paras. 169-175, 240-242; and IPE Summary Report, (Exhibit DOM-379), paras. 148-150.

covers or through the inclusion of additional sales outlets, which could lead to the wrong conclusion that the TPP measures increased cigarette sales even when it did not.[97] Dr Chipty contends that, contrary to IPE's claim that the inclusion of a time trend mitigates the risk of bias, the inclusion of a time trend does not eliminate the risk of bias for at least two reasons: (1) the inclusion of a simple time trend in IPE's model may mitigate some of the problem, but there is no reason to expect that it will eliminate it, because the trend is likely not flexible enough to adequately capture the variety of different business explanations that result in the Aztec data's growing footprint; and (2) more importantly, the simple time trend in IPE's model cannot resolve the fact that the Aztec data are missing information on total sales because they only contain information from 12 retail chains and do not contain information on certain retail channels of tobacco distribution.[98]

3.1.4   Nielsen Retail Sales-Aztec Scanner

76.   Professor Klick considers that, contrary to Dr Chipty's claim, the Aztec scanner data are valid because there is no evidence that the market share covered by the Aztec data has been growing over time.[99] In that context, Professor Klick combines the Nielsen and Aztec data presented above by omitting the Convenience Independent sample from the Nielsen data, and for the months where the data sources overlap, using the Aztec data.[100] Professor Klick re-estimated the difference-in-difference model of retail sales of cigarettes in Australia relative to New Zealand. In addition to the difference-in-difference analysis of Australia and New Zealand, Professor Klick also estimated a model without New Zealand as a counterfactual control. The model specification controls for a TPP measures dummy variable, the logarithm of tobacco price, the logarithm of the number of stores covered by the Aztec data and a linear trend. The tobacco price variable is instrumented to address any endogeneity bias.[101] In addition, to control for the Aztec data's alleged growing market coverage, a variable reporting the number of stores covered by the Aztec data is included in Professor Klick's most recent model specification. The econometric analysis covers the period February 2011 to September 2015 or is restricted to the January 2012-September 2015 period because the data relating to the number of stores are only available beginning January 2012.

---

[97]   See Chipty Report, (Exhibit AUS-17), paras. 55-60; and Chipty Surrebuttal Report, (Exhibit AUS-586), para. 10.

[98]   See Chipty Surrebuttal Report, (Exhibit AUS-586), paras. 75-76.

[99]   See Klick Fourth Supplemental Rebuttal Report, (Exhibit HND-169), paras. 6-8.

[100]   Professor Klick explains that beginning in February 2014, the scanner data are no longer provided by the Nielsen Company. The Nielsen Company also did not continue its Convenience Independent sample from January 2014 onward. However, scanner data, without the Convenience Independent sample, is available from Aztec beginning in March 2012 and continuing through June 2015. See Klick Supplemental Rebuttal Report, (Exhibit HND-122), paras. 122-126.

[101]   See Klick Fourth Supplemental Rebuttal Report, (Exhibit HND-169), paras. 9-11.

77.   Overall, Professor Klick concludes that the TPP measures had no statistically significant effect on the retail sales of cigarettes.[102] However, one of Professor Klick's two difference-in-difference estimations finds a positive and statistically significant TPP effect suggesting that the TPP measures led to an increase in retail sales of cigarettes. Similarly, the results of the model specification without New Zealand as a counterfactual and without a trend variable suggest that the TPP measures led to an increase in the retail sales of cigarettes. Professor Klick explains that he does not view these results as suggesting that smoking has increased under the TPP measures, because of the "multiple comparison problem", which implies that when very many outcomes are examined, there is a relatively high likelihood that one will find statistically significant results even by mere chance.[103]

78.   Dr Chipty argues that Professor Klick's analysis based on the Nielsen-Aztec data is flawed because the Nielsen-Aztec data appear to be covering a greater share of total market sales over time. According to Dr Chipty, one reason for the growing share of Professor Klick's Nielsen-Aztec data over time in Australia is the exclusion of downward-trending sales from the Convenience Independent channel. Dr Chipty submits that the IMS/EOS data are decreasing much faster than Professor Klick's constructed Nielsen-Aztec data, suggesting that the Nielsen-Aztec data are not an adequate proxy for total cigarette sales in Australia. In addition, Dr Chipty contends that Professor Klick's Nielsen-Aztec model does not allow for the possibility of estimating the net effect of the TPP measures because the regression model controls for price, which itself embodies some of the policy effect.[104]

3.1.5   Commissioned Roy Morgan Research Survey (Australia and New Zealand)

79.   As explained in the section discussing smoking prevalence and smoking incidence, the Roy Morgan Research dataset is a survey of individuals who were current or former (in the past 12 months) smokers in both Australia and New Zealand undertaken using random digit dialling sampling techniques. The first wave of the survey was completed prior to the December 2012 implementation of the TPP measures between 2 November 2012 and 26 November 2012 in Australia and between 8 November 2012 and 1 December 2012 in New Zealand. Subsequent waves have been carried out at three-month intervals.

80.   Professor Klick used the Roy Morgan Research data and estimated a difference-in-difference linear regression model and negative binomial models

---

[102]   See Klick Supplemental Rebuttal Report, (Exhibit HND-122), paras. 129-130; Klick Third Supplemental Rebuttal Report, (Exhibit HND-166), paras. 11-23; and Klick Fourth Supplemental Rebuttal Report, (Exhibit HND-169), paras. 12-14.

[103]   See Klick Fourth Supplemental Rebuttal Report, (Exhibit HND-169), fn 10.

[104]   See Chipty Surrebuttal Report, (Exhibit AUS-586), paras. 92-96.

that explain the reported number of cigarettes consumed controlling for a TPP measures dummy variable, a dummy variable for an Australian baseline and a dummy variable for a post-TPP implementation time-period. The difference-in-difference analysis covers the period from November 2012 to February 2014.[105]

81.   Overall, Professor Klick concludes that the TPP measures had no statistically significant effect on the cigarette consumption in Australia relative to New Zealand.[106] According to Professor Klick, this finding is robust to specifying the number of cigarettes smoked in logarithm (to mitigate outliers), applying different estimators (linear regression, negative binomial regression, robust regression), restricting the sample to only individuals who answered the survey in the 6 waves (to mitigate attrition), restricting the sample to only individuals who answered the survey at least in one post-TPP waves, restricting sample to Wave 1 and Wave 6, restricting sample to smokers planning to quit during Wave 1, and computing robust standard errors or standard errors clustered by individuals.[107] However, some of the results (when respondents who had noticed plain packs in Wave 1 or a pack change of any kind in Wave 1 are discarded) suggest that the TPP measures led to an increase in cigarettes consumption. Professor Klick explains that he does not view these results as suggesting that smoking has increased under the TPP measures, because of the "multiple comparison problem", which implies that when very many outcomes are examined, there is a relatively high likelihood that one will find statistically significant results even by mere chance.[108]

82.   Dr Chipty submits that Professor Klick's difference-in-difference study does not provide a reliable estimate of the TPP measures' effect in Australia, because one cannot reliably implement a difference-in-difference estimation strategy without: (1) a pre-period data, yet a majority of smokers were likely smoking plain packs during the survey's first wave; (2) a control group that resembles the treatment group (i.e. Australia) in important dimensions other than the treatment, yet New Zealand had a unique and significant tax change between Waves 1 and 2.[109] Dr Chipty further contends that Professor Klick invalidated his own commissioned survey data analysis by arguing that (1) it makes little sense to talk about trends in very short time spans; (2) examining differential trends with five or six data points is demanding more from the data than is reasonable; (3) wave-to-wave variability is quite large in the data; (4) Dr

---

[105]   See Klick Report, (Exhibit UKR-5), pp. 20-21 and 30-32.
[106]   See Klick Report, (Exhibit UKR-5), pp. 30-32.
[107]   See Klick Rebuttal Report, (Exhibit HND-118), paras. 25-28, 31-33 and 37-38.
[108]   See Klick Rebuttal Report, (Exhibit HND-118), fn 24.
[109]   See Chipty Report, (Exhibit AUS-17), para. 24; and Chipty Rebuttal Report, (Exhibit AUS-535) (SCI), paras. 54-71. Dr Chipty initially contended that Professor Klick did not use clustered standard errors except in his fixed-effects models. Dr Chipty further argued that Professor Klick did not allow for heteroscedasticity in the error structure and account for the longitudinal nature of the data by clustering at the respondent level. *Ibid.* Appendix C.

Chipty's analysis is inappropriate because it involves estimating a trend using data from a single calendar year; and (5) no meaningful analysis can be conducted by seeking a time trend between Waves 2 and 6.[110]

3.1.6   International Tobacco Control Policy Evaluation Project

83.   The International Tobacco Control (ITC) Policy Evaluation Project (ITC Project) is a longitudinal cohort survey to assess the impact, and identify the determinants of, effective tobacco control policies in more than 20 countries, including Australia. The ITC Project covers a number of questions related to GHWs, including attention towards the health warnings, salience of the health warnings and the effect of health warnings on consumers' thoughts, behaviours and intentions towards quitting.

84.   Ajzen et al., in their expert report submitted by the Dominican Republic and Indonesia, used the ITC dataset to estimate a generalized estimating equation model of the reported number of cigarettes smoked per day controlling for the survey mode (phone vs. web) and wave of recruitment, as well as respondents' age, sex, income, education and past year quit attempts.[111] The econometric analysis covers the period from September 2011 to May 2013.[112]

85.   Overall, Ajzen et al. conclude that TPP and enlarged GHWs had no impact on the average number of cigarettes smoked per day in the first five months following the introduction of the TPP measures.[113] The same result is found when the sample is restricted to the participants involved in the surveys pre- and post-implementation.[114]

86.   Australia responds that Ajzen et al. have misunderstood certain features of the ITC data and that their claim that there have been no changes in smoking behaviour post-TPP is without foundation.[115]

3.1.7   National Tobacco Plain Packaging Tracking Survey

87.   To track the effect of the TPP measures, Australia funded the National Tobacco Plain Packaging Tracking Survey (NTPPTS), a nationwide tracking survey that was conducted by CCV. The NTPPTS is a continuous cross-sectional baseline survey of about 100 interviews per week conducted from 9 April 2012 to 30 March 2014. A follow-up survey of baseline participants then took place approximately four weeks after the initial survey, with the follow-up surveys conducted from 7 May 2012 to 4 May 2014.

---

[110]   See Chipty Rebuttal Report, (Exhibit AUS-535) (SCI), paras. 50-53.
[111]   We note that Ajzen et al. used the ITC dataset to replicate part of the analysis of Yong et al. 2015, who did not analyse cigarettes consumption. Ajzen et al. argue that Yong et al. 2015 failed to explain why they did not report the impact of the pack changes on cigarette consumption. Ajzen et al. Second Data Report, (Exhibit DOM/IDN-4), para. 34.
[112]   See Ajzen et al. Second Data Report, (Exhibit DOM/IDN-4), paras. 21-29 and 48-58.
[113]   See Ajzen et al. Second Data Report, (Exhibit DOM/IDN-4), para. 28.
[114]   See Ajzen et al. Data Rebuttal Report, (Exhibit DOM/IDN-6), para. 83.
[115]   See Australia's response to Panel question No. 196, paras. 225 and 235.

88.   The NTPPTS were used by scholars as well as several of the experts of the Dominican Republic, Honduras and Indonesia to estimate econometrically the impact of the TPP measures on reported cigarette consumption.

3.1.7.1   Scollo et al. 2015a peer-reviewed study

89.   Scollo et al. 2015a[116] used the NTPPTS data to assess changes in reported price paid and changes in reported numbers of cigarettes consumed following the introduction of TPP and enlarged GHWs in the period up to and after the large increase in excise duty on 1 December 2013. The authors estimated logistic and linear models to assess changes between the pre-TPP period (April to September 2012) and three subsequent time periods: the transition phase during which plain packages were being introduced into the Australian market (October and   November 2012);   TPP   year   1   (December 2012   to November 2013); and TPP post-tax (December 2013 to March 2014). All regression models control for sex, age, area socio-economic status, education, past three-month exposure to antismoking campaigns (for cigarette consumption analysis).

90.   Overall, Scollo et al. 2015a conclude, among others things, that the introduction of TPP and enlarged GHWs were not associated with a change in consumption among daily, regular or current smokers or among smokers of brands in any market segment during the first year of implementation of the TPP measures. However, the authors find that reported consumption among regular smokers declined significantly following the December 2013 tax increase.[117]

3.1.7.2   Ajzen et al.'s reports

91.   Ajzen et al. re-analysed part of Scollo et al. 2015a[118], applying the approach in Wakefield et al. 2015.[119] Ajzen et al. estimated logistic, ordered logistic and linear regressions of the reported number of cigarettes smoked daily and the proportion of smokers consuming a given number of cigarettes or more per day. The model specification includes a set of variables controlling for age group, gender, education group, socio-economic status group, potential exposure

---

[116]   Scollo et al. 2015a, (Exhibits HND-133, DOM-237, DOM-311).

[117]   Scollo et al. 2015a also find that the introduction of TPP and enlarged GHWs was associated with an increase in use of value brands and smaller increases in prices for value relative to premium brands.

[118]   Ajzen et al. argue that Scollo et al.'s conclusion that TPP and enlarged GHWs had no significant effect on the average number of cigarettes consumed per day underreports additional results that were not statistically significant. According to Ajzen et al., Scollo et al. 2015a reported on only one of the seven measures on smoking behaviours and the impact of TPP and enlarged GHWs on each of the six unreported variables, dealing with the percentage of daily or weekly smokers, quitting, and relapse was not statistically significant. See Ajzen et al. Data Report, (Exhibit DOM/IDN-2), paras. 225-227. We note, however, that Ajzen et al. do not reassess the analysis by Scollo et al. 2015a of the impact of TPP and enlarged GHWs and tax increase on type of tobacco products and price.

[119]   Wakefield et al. 2015, (Exhibits AUS-206, DOM-306).

to televised antismoking advertising campaigns in the past three months and cigarette costliness.[120]

92.   Overall, Ajzen et al. conclude that the TPP measures had no statistically significant impact on any measure of actual cigarette consumption.[121] Ajzen et al. argue that, unlike Professor Chaloupka's assertion, using a threshold of 20 or more cigarettes per day is not inappropriate because the results continue to find no change in cigarette consumption when thresholds of 5, 10, and 15 cigarettes per day are used.[122] In addition, Ajzen et al. present the quarterly results of the logit model, which suggests that there was an immediate increase in the probability of smoking 20 or more cigarettes per day in the first quarter following the implementation of the TPP measures but no impact in the following quarters.[123] More generally, Ajzen et al. disagree with Professor Chaloupka's assertion that the NTPPTS dataset has less power for detecting statistically significant changes in the more distal outcomes, such as actual tobacco use behaviour. According to Ajzen et al., a power analysis of the NTPPTS data concludes that the statistical power of the NTPPTS data to detect small changes in proximal and distal outcomes is very similar.[124]

93.   Australia's expert, Professor Chaloupka, argues that Ajzen et al.'s analyses of the NTPPTS data fail to recognize that the TPP measures' impact should be smaller for the less proximal outcomes when one looks at the impact in the overall sample of smokers and recent quitters, given that smokers and recent quitters for whom the most proximal outcomes were unaffected would not be expected to show any change in the less proximal outcomes.[125] Professor Chaloupka further contends that using an insensitive measure of consumption, whether or not the smoker reports consuming 20 or more cigarettes per day, appears to be an inappropriate threshold given that the average daily consumption of smokers in Australia is well below this level. According to Professor Chaloupka, based on the 2013 Australian National Drug Strategy Household Survey, average daily consumption of Australian smokers was 13.7 cigarettes per day.[126]

---

[120]   We note that Ajzen et al. also re-estimate their models by replacing the TPP measures dummies with a monthly time trend.

[121]   Ajzen et al. reach the same conclusion with respect to measures related to quitting and relapse, which were unreported by Scollo et al. 2015a. In particular, on quitting, Ajzen et al. conclude that there was no statistical change in the proportion of adult smokers that quit for more than one month or had successfully quit between baseline and follow-up. On relapse, Ajzen et al. conclude that there was no statistical change in the proportion of adult ex-smokers that relapsed, still abstained from smoking at follow-up or had stayed quit for more than one week at follow-up. See Ajzen et al. Data Report, (Exhibit DOM/IDN-2), paras. 221-224, Appendix A, pp. 95-97).

[122]   See Ajzen et al. Data Rebuttal Report, (Exhibit DOM/IDN-6), paras. 63-65, Appendix IV.

[123]   See Ajzen et al. Data Rebuttal Report, (Exhibit DOM/IDN-6), para. 90.

[124]   See Ajzen et al. Data Rebuttal Report, (Exhibit DOM/IDN-6), paras. 50-54, Appendix II.

[125]   See Chaloupka Rebuttal Report, (Exhibit AUS-582), para. 4.

[126]   See Chaloupka Rebuttal Report, (Exhibit AUS-582), para. 8.

3.1.7.3 Professor Klick's report

94.   Professor Klick also reconsiders the NTPPTS data and estimated a negative binomial model of the average cigarettes consumption per day for daily smokers, smokers in general, or all participants, controlling for a TPP measures dummy variable, gender, age, education, socio-economic status and linear trend. The econometric analysis covers the period from 9 April 2012 to 4 May 2014.[127]

95.   Overall, Professor Klick concludes that the TPP measures did not reduce consumption levels. In some of Professor Klick's specifications, the TPP measures' impact on average cigarettes per day for daily smokers and smokers in general is positive and statistically significant. According to Professor Klick, these results are consistent with his findings based on the Roy Morgan longitudinal survey data as well as with Scollo et al. 2015a's findings, which note that the NTPPTS data show no decline in self-reported smoking consumption associated with the TPP measures.[128]

96.   As explained above, although Australia's expert, Professor Chaloupka, does not address specifically Professor Klick's analysis of cigarette consumption based on the NTPPTS data, Professor Chaloupka generally contends that because of its cross-sectional nature, the NTPPTS data limits the ability to follow the impact of the TPP measures through the pathway from its impact on the most proximal outcomes, like perceived appeal and noticing of the labels, through less proximal outcomes, such as increased interest in quitting, to the most distal outcomes, such as actual tobacco use behaviour.[129] Professor Chaloupka further argues that the impact of the TPP measures on more distal outcomes should be smaller when the analysis is based on the overall sample of smokers and recent quitters because smokers and recent quitters for whom the most proximal outcomes were unaffected by the TPP measures would not be expected to exhibit any change in more distal outcomes.

3.1.8 Cancer Institute New South Wales Tobacco Tracking Survey

97.   The Cancer Institute New South Wales Tobacco Tracking Survey (CITTS) is a weekly tracking telephone survey of smokers and recent quitters (who quit in the past 12 months).

98.   Professor Klick used the CITTS data to estimate a negative binomial model of the average number of reported tobacco units smoked per week controlling for the TPP measures, annual time trend, gender, individual age fixed effect, week of survey fixed effects and location fixed effects. The econometric analysis covers the period from January 2009 to December 2014.[130]

---

[127]   See Klick Supplemental Rebuttal Report, (Exhibit HND-122), paras. 44-51.
[128]   See Klick Supplemental Rebuttal Report, (Exhibit HND-122), paras. 47-51.
[129]   See Chaloupka Rebuttal Report, (Exhibit AUS-582), paras. 2-5.
[130]   See Klick Second Supplemental Rebuttal Report, (Exhibit HND-165), paras. 25-26.

99.   Overall, Professor Klick concludes that the TPP measures led to an increase in cigarette consumption, irrespective of whether the TPP period is taken to start in December 2012 or October 2012.[131] Professor Klick argues that these results are consistent with the finding from his study of the Roy Morgan Research Survey, Nielsen, Aztec, IMS/EOS and NTPPTS data.

100.   Although Professor Chaloupka does not address directly Professor Klick's analysis of cigarette consumption based on the CITTS data, Professor Chaloupka contends that Professor Klick failed to appropriately account for the changes in the CITTS methodology that led to a greater number of younger people and males in the survey sample, both of which have relatively higher smoking rates, leading almost certainly to biased estimates towards showing an increase in smoking following the change in method.[132]

3.2   Analysis by the Panel

101.   Having determined above that the wholesale market data presented to us suggests an acceleration of the reduction in cigarette sales following the entry into force of the TPP measures, the question before us at this stage of our analysis is whether this acceleration may, in part or in whole, be attributed to the TPP measures.[133]

102.   As explained above, while we acknowledge that no data are perfect, we agree with Australia that the IMS/EOS data is the most suitable available market data submitted by the parties to analyse the TPP measures' impact on cigarette sales because the data are available monthly for a long period of time before and after the introduction of the TPP measures. In addition, the IMS/EOS data display a relatively high correlation coefficient with respect to the Nielsen retail cigarette sales data.

103.   We consider that the other market data sources considered by the experts of the Dominican Republic, Honduras and Indonesia suffer from a number of drawbacks in comparison with the IMS/EOS data. In particular, the Nielsen and Aztec data are both only available for a shorter sample period. In addition, the Aztec data are characterized by an increasing market coverage making it difficult to distinguish the impact of other factors.

104.   At the outset, we note that for a given market dataset, the different conclusions reached by the parties regarding the impact of the TPP measures on cigarette sales stem from the fact that their experts use different model specification (i.e. different independent variables (e.g. cigarette sales or per capita cigarette sales) and different explanatory variables included in the model), estimation approaches and in some cases sample period. Even among the experts

---

[131]   See Klick Second Supplemental Rebuttal Report, (Exhibit HND-165), paras. 25-32.

[132]   See Chaloupka Second Rebuttal Report, (Exhibit AUS-590), paras. 26-27.

[133]   We note that the parties did not present any graphical analysis of reported cigarette consumption based on survey data. That is why the conclusions we reached so far only apply to cigarette sales used as a proxy of cigarette consumption.

of the Dominican Republic and Honduras, different model specifications are used.[134]

105.   As explained in our review of the econometric study on smoking prevalence in Appendix C, we consider that our task is not to conduct our own econometric assessment of the contribution of the TPP measures on cigarette sales or cigarette consumption, but rather to review the robustness of the econometric evidence submitted by the parties.

3.2.1   IPE's econometric results

106.   A careful review of the econometric results based on the IMS/EOS data reported by IPE leads us to question their robustness on various grounds, many of which are similar to those considered in our review of IPE's analysis of smoking prevalence in Appendix C. In particular, we note that IPE's preferred specification of the modified trend analysis and the ARIMAX model includes both a price variable and a time trend variable, which happen to be highly collinear with each other. Multicollinearity appears to be even more marked when the model specification of the ARIMAX model includes five lags of the logarithm of per capita sales variables and of the price variable.[135] Furthermore, we note that IPE fails to take into account the potential impact of the TPP measures on tobacco prices. Similarly, IPE ignores the fact that the proportionality assumption underlying the use of the tax level in the analysis of the IMS/EOS data is rejected. Moreover, IPE does not address the fact that the price variable and the tax level variable appear to be non-stationary. We note, however, that when the model includes the excise tax dummy variables, which were initially proposed by IPE itself in its first report but later rejected as inferior control variables, most results suggest the TPP measures had a negative and statistically significant impact on wholesales cigarette sales.

107.   We also question the validity of IPE's results based on the Nielsen data for the same reasons mentioned above, namely the use of the price variable. In particular, we note that in some specifications of the modified trend analysis, which include a trend variable and the price variable in the past month, only a

---

[134]   For instance, IPE initially analysed the impact of the TPP measures on (the logarithm of) cigarette sales (see IPE Report, (Exhibit DOM-100)) but subsequently analysed the impact on (the logarithm of) per capita cigarette sales. See, e.g. IPE Updated Report, (Exhibit DOM-303). Similarly, IPE initially (see IPE Report, (Exhibit DOM-100)) control for excise tax increases by specifying dummy variables for each excise tax hike implemented during the sample period, while IPE later in the proceedings (see, e.g. IPE Second Updated Report, (Exhibit DOM-361)) consider the variable of tobacco price to be a better proxy for excise tax increases. Professor Klick applies an IV estimation procedure to take into account the potential endogeneity of the price variable with respect to cigarette sales while IPE and Professor List do not address the potential endogeneity of the price variable. See Klick Rebuttal Report, (Exhibit HND-118), paras. 52-60.

[135]   See IPE Second Updated Report, (Exhibit DOM-361), pp. 38-40; and IPE Third Updated Report, (Exhibit DOM-375), pp. 120-122.

couple of month dummies are statistically significant.[136] The same issue arises in several specifications of the ARIMAX model, where the time trend variable and the logarithm of cigarette sales per capita in the previous month are both not statistically significant, which would suggest that cigarette sales do not follow a dynamic pattern, despite graphical evidence attesting to the contrary.[137] We also note that some of the results of the modified analysis based on the procedure to compute the standard errors applied initially, but that were later rejected by the IPE, find a positive and statistically significant impact of the TPP measures on cigarette sales.[138] As explained in the review of the econometric studies on smoking prevalence, the choice of the maximum lag required to compute robust standard error is not well established in the statistics and econometric literature and it is therefore unclear to what extent these results would have changed for a range of different parameter values.[139] We note also that in some specifications of the ARIMAX model based on the deseasonalized Nielsen data the estimated coefficient of the lagged dependent variable is negative and statistically significant, which is in contradiction with the results of the same model based on the Aztec data.[140] In addition, as explained earlier, the sample period of the Nielsen data is limited with only 35 observations available. Yet, a smaller sample size (i.e. number of observations) makes it, all else being equal, more difficult to estimate more accurately any impacts on cigarette sales.

108.   We also question the IPE's results based on the Aztec data.[141] As explained above, the Aztec data are characterized by a growing market coverage, which, in our view, makes it more difficult to distinguish the impact of the explanatory variables, including the TPP measures dummy variable, from the growing market coverage. We note that the IPE proposed as a robustness check to adjust the Aztec data for the increasing market coverage. Yet, we note that the IPE did not provide any evidence that would justify why the transformed Aztec

---

[136]   We also note that the estimated coefficients of the modified trend analysis based on the Nielsen data are different between IPE Second Updated Report (Exhibit DOM-361), pp. 41-42 and IPE Summary Report (Exhibit DOM-379), p. 54 and backup material, although this is the same model specification and sample period. We also note that the model specification with tax dummies based on the Nielsen data reported in Table 4.2-2 in IPE Summary Report (Exhibit DOM-379) actually do not include the December 2013 tax dummy variable. See IPE Summary Report, (Exhibit DOM-379), backup material.

[137]   See IPE Second Updated Report, (Exhibit DOM-361), pp. 45-46.

[138]   See IPE Second Updated Report, (Exhibit DOM-361), backup material.

[139]   See the email exchange between the parties and STATA developers in the IPE Summary Report, (Exhibit DOM-379), p. 70; and Chipty Second Rebuttal Report, (Exhibit AUS-591), pp. B1-B2.

[140]   See IPE Third Updated Report, (Exhibit DOM-375), pp. 76-77. In addition, we note that in some specifications of the modified trend analysis based on the deseasonalized Nielsen data the estimated coefficient of the TPP measures is positive and statistically significant.

[141]   We note that in a couple of specifications, which include, for instance, the tax level variable, the results find a positive and statistically significant TPP measures' effect. See IPE Summary Report, (Exhibit DOM-379), p. 54; and IPE Third Updated Report, (Exhibit DOM-375), pp. 124 and 127. Similar findings are sometimes found when the standard errors are computed applying the initial procedure proposed by IPE, namely the IVREG2 command, for the July 2008-May 2015 sample period. See IPE Second Updated Report, (Exhibit DOM-361), backup material.

data would reflect more accurately the actual fluctuation of the cigarette retail sales. In fact, we note that the correlation coefficient between the adjusted Aztec data and the Nielsen data or the IMS/EOS data is lower than with respect to the original Aztec data.[142]

3.2.2   Professor Klick's econometric results

109.   Similarly, a review of the econometric results reported by Professor Klick leads us to question their robustness. In particular, we note that in the first stage of the IV estimation of Professor Klick's difference-in-difference analysis based on the IMS/EOS data, surprisingly none of the 54 time-fixed effects are statistically significant. We further note that the second stage of the IV estimation is affected by the multicollinearity between the instrumented price variable and the linear trend variable.[143] In addition, it is unclear how the standard error and confidence interval of the total effect of the TPP measures, composed of the direct estimated TPP measures' impact on cigarette sales obtained in the second stage of the procedure and the indirect estimated TPP measures' impact on cigarette price obtained in the first stage of the procedure through the impact of cigarette price on cigarette sales, were calculated. We also question the results of the difference-in-difference analysis based on the Nielsen-Aztec data because of the use of the price variable as well as the growing market coverage of the data.[144] In particular, we note that in the first stage of the IV estimation procedure, multicollinearity appears to be high between the change in excise tax variable, the country-specific trend variable and the TPP measures dummy variable. Similarly, the multicollinearity between the instrumented price variable, the country-specific trends and several time-fixed effects is particularly high in the second stage of the IV estimation procedure.[145] In addition, we note that surprisingly most of the time-fixed effects in both first and second stages of the IV estimation procedure are not statistically significant. We also question the results of the model specification without New Zealand counterfactual control, because the specification without a time trend finds a positive and statistically significant TPP measures' effect and the

---

[142]   The weekly adjusted Aztec data were aggregated to monthly data by assuming that each weekly cigarette quantity can be evenly split for each day of the week. The correlation coefficient between the Nielsen data and the original Aztec data is equal to 0.84, while the correlation between the Nielsen data and the adjusted Aztec data is equal to 0.71. The correlation between the original Aztec data and the IMS/EOS data is 0.38, while the correlation between the adjusted Aztec data and the IMS/EOS data is 0.32.

[143]   Evidence of multicollinearity is confirmed by the variance inflation factors statistic.

[144]   We note that the Aztec data used by Professor Klick is available monthly, while IPE and Professor List used the Aztec data reported at the weekly level.

[145]   We also note that without the country-specific trend variable, the change in excise tax variable continues to display a high variance inflation factor statistics, when the country-specific trend variable is removed (see Klick Fourth Supplemental Rebuttal Report, (Exhibit HND-169), backup material).

specifications with (linear or quadratic) trend find that none of the explanatory variables, except the constant, are statistically significant.[146]

110. Similar to our conclusion regarding Professor Klick's difference-in-difference analysis of smoking incidence based on the Roy Morgan Research Survey data, we question the validity of the results on the reported number of cigarettes consumed on the same grounds, namely the pre-period of the analysis is not valid because Professor Klick is unable to accurately identify the respondents, who had noticed plain packs in the pre-period. Furthermore, we note that the instrumented tax used in the second stage of the IV estimation procedure displays signs of multicollinearity with respect to the TPP measures dummy and several time fixed effects.[147]

111. We also question Professor Klick's results on the average reported number of cigarettes smoked per day based on the NTPPTS data because the majority of the results suggest that the TPP measures' effect is positive and statistically significant.[148] It is unclear to what extent this finding is the result of the model not being specified correctly given that Scollo et al. 2015a using the same NTPPTS data but applying a different model specification find that cigarette consumption did not change during the first year of the implementation of the TPP measures.[149] For instance, we note that unlike Scollo et al. 2015a, Professor Klick does not control for the past three-month exposure to anti-smoking campaigns that aired on television during the survey period.

112. Similarly, we question the validity of Professor Klick's results on the reported number of tobacco units consumed per week based on the CITTS data. We note that most of the 49 fixed effects associated with the week of survey are surprisingly not statistically significant in most specifications.[150] In addition, as noted in Appendix B, the survey data, such as the CITTS data, may, as suggested by Australia, be more suited to analysing the impact of the TPP measures on proximal outcomes, such as appeal, GHWs and ability of the pack to mislead than more distal outcomes, such as smoking behaviours.

---

[146] See Klick Third Supplemental Rebuttal Report, (Exhibit HND-166), backup material; and Klick Fourth Supplemental Rebuttal Report, (Exhibit HND-169), backup material. We also note that according to standard unit root tests, the variable reporting the number of stores covered by the Aztec data is not stationary.

[147] We also note that in the first stage of the IV estimation procedure, surprisingly the majority of the time fixed effects are not statistically significant. The same issues arise in a couple of specifications considered in Professor Klick's "crossfold validation". In one specification, the only variable statistically significant is the constant term or the level of cigarette sales in New Zealand (see Klick Rebuttal Report, (Exhibit HND-118), backup material).

[148] See Klick Supplemental Rebuttal Report, (Exhibit HND-122), pp. 19-21.

[149] See Scollo et al. 2015a, (Exhibits HND-133 DOM-237, DOM-311), p. ii73.

[150] See Klick Second Supplemental Rebuttal Report, (Exhibit HND-165), pp. 11-12. We also note that most of the results suggest that the TPP measures' effect on reported tobacco units consumed per week is positive and statistically significant.

3.2.3 Ajzen et al.'s econometric results

113. A careful review of Ajzen et al.'s analysis of the reported number of cigarettes smoked daily and the proportion of smokers consuming at least a given number of cigarettes per day reported in the NTPPTS data leads us to conclude that Ajzen et al. corroborate Scollo et al.'s (2015a) findings that there were no changes in daily cigarette consumption during the first year of implementation of the TPP measures.[151] We note, however, that in several specifications, Ajzen et al. do not analyse directly the quantity of cigarettes smoked reported by the respondent, but, instead, focus on the probability the respondent consumes a given number of cigarettes or more per day. We further note that Ajzen et al.'s quarterly results find that the probability of reporting smoking 20 cigarettes or more per day increased in the first quarter following the introduction of the TPP measures.[152] Yet, Ajzen et al. do not provide any explanation that would explain such a result.

114. The review of Ajzen et al.'s analysis of the number of cigarettes smoked per day reported in the ITC dataset also raises a number of questions. At the outset, we note that Ajzen et al. do not analyse directly the number of cigarettes smoked per day, but a categorical variable distinguishing between 0-10, 11-20, 21-30 and more than 30 cigarettes per day. We further note that the model specification does not control for anti-smoking advertising in mass media, as acknowledged by Ajzen et al.[153], and for cigarette costliness. It is therefore unclear if the results would be similar if these explanatory variables had been taken into account. In addition, we note that the results of the weighted prevalence estimates are based in a specification in which only a few variables, namely the variables for high education level, quit attempt and survey mode, are statistically significant, besides the constant.[154] It is therefore unclear why most explanatory variables in the model considered by Ajzen et al. are not statistically significant.

3.2.4 Dr Chipty's econometric results

115. Turning to the econometric results analysing wholesale cigarette sales based on the IMS/EOS data submitted by Australia's expert, Dr Chipty, we note

---

[151] We note that the model specification considered by Ajzen et al. is different from the one developed by Professor Klick. For instance, Ajzen et al. include dummy variables for two age groups, while Professor Klick includes a single age variable. Ajzen et al. also includes dummy variables for different groups of education and socio-economic status, respectively, while Professor Klick includes a single variable for education and another variable for socio-economic status.

[152] See Ajzen et al. Data Rebuttal Report, (Exhibit DOM/IDN-6), p. 22.

[153] See Ajzen et al. Second Data Report, (Exhibit DOM/IDN-4), para. 18.

[154] See Ajzen et al. Second Data Report, (Exhibit DOM/IDN-4), backup material. When the sample is restricted to participants involved in the pre- and post-implementation surveys, the only statistically significant variables are two age categories, quitting attempt and the constant. In the weighted prevalence estimates results, the only statistically significant variables are two age group categories. Ajzen et al. Data Rebuttal Report, (Exhibit DOM/IDN-6), backup material.

that some concerns that we raised regarding the experts of the Dominican Republic's, Honduras's and Indonesia's approaches and results of the market data have been to some extent addressed by Dr Chipty. In particular, Dr Chipty specifies excise tax increases dummy variables and thus avoids the problems of endogeneity associated with the inclusion of the price variable as well as the unit root problem of the price or tax level variables. We further note that part of Dr Chipty's model specification is based on the first specification proposed by the IPE but modified to account for strategic inventory management and the 2006 GHWs regulation.

116.   A careful review of Dr Chipty's econometric results further shows that the negative and statistically significant impact of the TPP measures on wholesale cigarette sales is robust to alternative specifications, including different TPP starting date (October, November and December 2012), and to Professor List's procedure to compute standard errors.[155] We note however that the TPP measures' effects are no longer statistically significant when the set of tax hikes dummies are replaced by a tax levels variable. Yet, we note as explained earlier that specification testing suggests tax levels are not appropriate in the model specification.[156] Furthermore, the tax levels variable is likely to be non-stationary.

117.   Overall, based on the most recent econometric evidence submitted by Australia, there is some econometric evidence suggesting that TPP and enlarged GHWs contributed to the reduction in wholesale cigarette sales in Australia.[157]

4.   EVIDENCE RELATING TO THE EVOLUTION OF IMPORTS OF CIGARS

118.   The parties did not present an econometric analysis of the post-implementation impact of the TPP measures on cigar consumption. Rather, the parties addressed a graphical and descriptive analysis of trade data.

119.   According to data analysed by Australia[158], the value and volume of Australian cigar and cigarillo imports shows fluctuations within a set range throughout the period between March 2005 and March 2015.[159] Australia notes,

---

[155]   See Chipty Surrebuttal Report, (Exhibit AUS-586), p. 40; and Chipty Second Rebuttal Report, (Exhibit AUS-591), pp. 19-20, 33, and D1.
[156]   See Chipty Third Rebuttal Report, (Exhibit AUS-605), paras. 27-29.
[157]   See Chipty Third Rebuttal Report, (Exhibit AUS-605), pp. 22 and 51; and Chipty Second Rebuttal Report, (Exhibit AUS-591), pp. 33, D1, and D2.
[158]   Supplementary Graphs, Import Volumes, Value and Share of the Market, (Exhibit AUS-512).
[159]   Supplementary Graphs, Import Volumes, Value and Share of the Market, (Exhibit AUS-512), Figures 7, 8, 13, and 14.

in any event, that the values represented in this dataset are "customs values", and may not represent the actual value of the products.[160]

120.   Australia also submits the HoustonKemp Report[161], which notes that all cigars and cigarillos sold in Australia are currently imported.[162] The HoustonKemp Report concludes that imports of cigars and cigarillos have fluctuated over time and have fallen significantly since 20[[***]]: annual imports of cigars and cigarillos fell by [[***]]% from 20[[***]] to 20[[***]], following the introduction of the TPP measures in December 2012, whereas annual import volumes fell at a faster rate prior to the TPP measures being introduced, by [[***]]% from 20[[***]] to 20[[***]].[163] As regards monthly cigar and cigarillo imports to Australia, the HoustonKemp Report finds that the level of monthly imports varies substantially, although, on average, these have been falling since the TPP measures came fully into force. The HoustonKemp Report adds that some of the increases in imports for a particular month coincide with the introduction of the TPP measures and increases in excise tax rates.[164]

121.   Based on data from the International Trade Centre's trade statistics database, the complainants argue that cigar imports to Australia have remained relatively stable over the period 2010-2014, and point out that the difference between the evolution of cigarette and cigar imports to Australia can be explained by the fact that the reduced-fire risk requirements did not apply to cigars.[165]

122.   As regards large cigars (i.e. excluding cigarillos and little cigars), the HoustonKemp Report adds that total imports into Australia from all countries have varied within the range of [[***]],000 kg to [[***]],000 kg from 20[[***]] to 20[[***]], and the level of imports fell from 20[[***]] to 20[[***]], immediately before the TPP measures came into force, but have risen in 20[[***]].[166] The HoustonKemp Report concludes that "[i]t follows that there is no evidence of the TPP measure[s] causing a fall in the imports of large cigars".[167]

123.   We have difficulty drawing conclusions from the above evidence on the evolution of Australian cigar, large handmade (LHM) cigar, or cigarillo consumption and imports. Based on the above evidence, we conclude that, despite fluctuations, overall imports of cigars and cigarillos have experienced a

---

[160]   Supplementary Graphs, Import Volumes, Value and Share of the Market, (Exhibit AUS-512), Figures 7, 8, 13, and 14.
[161]   HoustonKemp Report, (Exhibit AUS-19) (SCI).
[162]   HoustonKemp Report, (Exhibit AUS-19) (SCI), p. 45.
[163]   Ibid.
[164]   Ibid.
[165]   Dominican Republic's response to Panel question No. 5. See also Honduras's response to Panel question No. 5; Cuba's response to Panel question No. 5 (annexed to its response to Panel question No. 138); and Indonesia's response to Panel question No. 5.
[166]   HoustonKemp Report, (Exhibit AUS-19) (SCI), p. 47.
[167]   Ibid.

downward trend in recent years. However, it is unclear whether and to what extent this is attributable to the TPP measures.

124.   Some of the evidence submitted by the parties relates to cigar imports per complainant. In particular, the HoustonKemp Report submitted by Australia explains that the complainants have accounted for a small proportion of Australia's annual imports of cigars and cigarillos in general. From 19[[***]] to 20[[***]], Cuba accounted for between [[***]]% and [[***]]% of total annual imports, the Dominican Republic accounted for between [[***]]% and [[***]]% of imports, and the other complainants collectively accounted for less than [[***]]% of imports.[168]

125.   Furthermore, the Panel explored with Cuba, Honduras, and the Dominican Republic whether they had data on cigar sales to Australia and how these were affected by the TPP measures. Cuba does not provide a direct answer to the Panel's question concerning how volumes and values of sales of Cuban cigars in Australia, including Cuban LHM cigars, and Cuban LHM cigars carrying the Habanos GI and/or the Cuban Government Warranty Seal might have changed as a result of the TPP measures, and whether the price of cigars in the above product categories has changed as a result of the TPP measures.[169] Cuba states that a reply to this question would require access to the data on retail sales of Cuban LHM cigars in Australia as well as other markets for purposes of comparison, and these data would have to be analysed and compared so as to take account of the specific features of each market (such as the level of taxes) in order to draw reasonable conclusions; however, "[a]t present, Cuba does not have access to such data".[170] Australia points out that Cuba's response does not provide the Panel with any information or evidence about the volume and value of sales of Cuban cigars in Australia following the introduction of tobacco plain packaging.[171]

126.   Nonetheless, Cuba provides data as regards sales volumes of Cuban LHM cigars in Australia, namely data relating to wholesale sales of LHM cigars in Australia between January 2009 and July 2014 by Pacific Cigar Company (PCC).[172] Cuba considers such data as a relevant measure of consumption of LHM cigars as it is estimated that PCC have held a market share of approximately 70% of total LHM cigar sales in Australia over the relevant period.[173] According to Cuba, these data show that monthly sales of LHM cigars in Australia largely fluctuated within a set range of sticks per month for the majority of the relevant period, rising to the upper end of this range from 2013 onwards.[174] Cuba adds that there does not appear to have been any decrease in

---

[168]   HoustonKemp Report, (Exhibit AUS-19) (SCI), pp. 46-47.
[169]   Cuba's response to Panel question No. 193.
[170]   *Ibid.*
[171]   Australia's comments on Cuba's response to Panel question No. 193.
[172]   Cuba's first written submission, paras. 159-161.
[173]   Cuba's first written submission, para. 159.
[174]   Cuba's first written submission, para. 160.

monthly sales of LHM cigars after December 2012 when the TPP measures were introduced, not least when the post-implementation sales volumes are compared to monthly sales in the two years immediately prior to the introduction of the TPP measures.[175] According to Cuba, indeed, it appears that sales of LHM cigars in Australia have marginally increased since December 2012.[176] Cuba draws similar conclusions from the same sales information in half-yearly, rather than monthly, format. According to Cuba, the same sales data in half-yearly format illustrate the consistency of sales volumes over time and the apparent increase in sales of LHM cigars in the post-implementation period.[177]

127.   Australia points out that the HoustonKemp Report demonstrates that although overall volumes of cigar and cigarillo imports into Australia have been declining since the introduction of tobacco plain packaging, in 20[[***]] imports of Cuban cigars into Australia "rose to their highest level since 19[[***]], after the TPP measure was introduced".[178] Indeed, the HoustonKemp Report finds that approximately [[***]],000 kg of cigars and cigarillos were imported from Cuba each year from 20[[***]] to 20[[***]]; however, in 20[[***]], Cuba's imports into Australia rose to the highest level since 19[[***]], after the TPP measures were implemented.[179] As regards large cigar imports into Australia (i.e. excluding cigarillos and other cigars), the HoustonKemp Report finds that Cuba's share has increased from 19[[***]] to 20[[***]].[180]

128.   Based on the data concerning PCC and the data available in the HoustonKemp Report, we conclude that there has been an increase in the volume of Cuban LHM cigar and cigar/cigarillo sales in Australia. Of note, the underlying data is limited and indirect in that it does not provide any information on the factors driving the evolution of sales of Cuban cigars in Australia or address the role of the TPP measures in that regard.

129.   As regards sales of Dominican Republic cigars in Australia, the Dominican Republic notes, as a preliminary matter, that general international trade statistics that capture trade reported by domestic customs authorities, such as the UN Comtrade Database, do not provide a reliable source of information. In particular, for the purposes of tracking Dominican Republic cigar sales in Australia, this data is not helpful for a number of reasons, not least because it can mis-specify the true country of origin if a company is domiciled in a third country and because Dominican Republic cigars may be mis-classified if the

---

[175]   *Ibid.*
[176]   *Ibid.*
[177]   Cuba's first written submission, para. 161.
[178]   Australia's comments on Cuba's responses to Panel question Nos. 192, 194, and 195 (citing HoustonKemp Report, (Exhibit AUS-19) (SCI), p. 47).
[179]   HoustonKemp Report, (Exhibit AUS-19) (SCI), p. 47.
[180]   *Ibid.*

product is imported into, and then re-exported by, a third country (e.g. Belgium, the Netherlands, Singapore or Hong Kong).[181]

130. Rather, the Dominican Republic submits data from the Dominican Republic's cigar industry for sales of Dominican Republic cigars in Australia.[182] According to the Dominican Republic, this data shows that following the implementation of the TPP measures, there has been a decline in sales of Dominican Republic cigars, which are predominantly premium hand-rolled products.[183] The Dominican Republic notes that it has not been able to obtain data regarding the price and value of Dominican Republic cigar sales in Australia following the imposition of the TPP measures.[184]

131. Australia responds that the Dominican Republic's data show that the volume of sales of Dominican Republic cigars in Australia has declined in the period following the introduction of tobacco plain packaging; however, the Dominican Republic provides no evidence of the impact of the TPP measures on the value and prices of sales of Dominican Republic cigars in Australia.[185] Further, Australia notes, although requested by the Panel, the Dominican Republic has not provided any information on the impact of the measure on the subset of cigars that were permitted to use the GI "Cigarro Dominicano" prior to the implementation of tobacco plain packaging."[186]

132. We agree with the Dominican Republic that the UN Comtrade Database has limitations, for establishing export patterns from an individual exporter. We also concur with the limitations of the Dominican Republic's sales data highlighted by Australia. Importantly, none of the data explains the role of the TPP measures in any changes to sales of Dominican Republic cigars in Australia.

133. Based on data from the UN Comtrade Database, Honduras argues that the volumes and values of Honduran cigars imported into Australia have "drastically decreased".[187] According to Honduras, "at face value", the value and volume of trade in Honduran cigars to Australia has "drastically decreased" as there has been "a drop by 98%" between 2010 and 2014.[188] Honduras adds that, in terms of the combined value and quantity of imports of Honduran cigars into Australia, if one compares 2010 and 2011 to 2013 and 2014 (i.e. discounting the year of 2012 as the year when plain packaging was introduced), import values have decreased by 91% and import volume by 97%.[189] Honduras points out that in the

---

[181] Dominican Republic's response to Panel question No. 194.
[182] *Ibid.*
[183] *Ibid.*
[184] *Ibid.*
[185] Australia's comments on Cuba's response to Panel question No. 194.
[186] *Ibid.*
[187] Honduras's response to Panel question No. 195.
[188] *Ibid.*
[189] *Ibid.*

same period, its exports of cigars to the world substantially increased, which confirms that there was not a general downward trend of Honduran cigar exports in the period 2010 to 2014 but that the drastic decline is specific to the Australian market with tobacco plain packaging.[190]

134. Australia notes that Honduras relies on the UN Comtrade Database, which the Dominican Republic has qualified as "unreliable" and "not helpful"[191], and does not provide any data on the prices of its cigars in the Australian market.[192] Australia adds that notwithstanding the disagreement among Honduras and the Dominican Republic as to the reliability of the UN Comtrade Database, the data presented by Honduras appears to show a rapid decline in sales of Honduras cigars in Australia beginning in 2012 (the year that the TPP measures were introduced), and such decline in imports is consistent with Australia's argument that the packaging changes introduced in late 2012 led to a decline in cigar smoking prevalence.[193]

135. As noted, we agree with Australia and the Dominican Republic concerning the serious limitations of the UN Comtrade Database highlighted by the Dominican Republic for establishing total imports (direct and indirect) from an individual exporting country. Accordingly, we have difficulty drawing conclusions from such data specifically for all imports (direct and indirect) of Honduran cigars to Australia.

136. In the light of the above, we conclude that the evidence before us on cigars, cigarillos and LHM cigars allows us to draw limited conclusions on the evolution of certain consumption trends. We note that despite fluctuations, overall imports of cigars and cigarillos to Australia have followed a downward trend in recent years. However, we have no evidence to link these conclusions to the TPP measures that would allow us to draw conclusions on the basis of this evidence on the effect of the TPP measures on cigar consumption in Australia.

5. OVERALL CONCLUSION ON POST-IMPLEMENTATION EVIDENCE ON TOBACCO PRODUCT SALES VOLUMES

137. Overall, based on the most recent data available and evidence submitted by the parties, we find that:

a. There is some evidence that cigarette sales in Australia continued to decrease following the introduction of the TPP measures.

b. The downward trend in cigarette sales in Australia appears to have accelerated in the post-TPP period.

---

[190] *Ibid.*

[191] Australia's comments on Cuba's response to Panel question No. 195 (referencing Dominican Republic's response to Panel question No. 194).

[192] Australia's comments on Cuba's response to Panel question No. 195.

[193] *Ibid.*

c.   Although it is impossible to distinguish between the impact of TPP and enlarged GHWs, there is some econometric evidence suggesting that the TPP measures, in combination with the enlarged GHWs implemented at the same time, contributed to the reduction in wholesale cigarette sales, and therefore cigarette consumption, after their entry into force.

d.   The evidence before us on the evolution of consumption of cigars in the post-TPP period is more limited and does not allow us to draw clear conclusions on the effect of the TPP measures on cigar consumption in Australia.

138.   We note, however, that no post-implementation empirical evidence has been presented to us on the impact of the TPP measures on cigars and cigarillos consumption.

APPENDIX E

POST-IMPLEMENTATION EVIDENCE ON DOWNWARD SUBSTITUTIONIN THE CIGARETTE MARKET

1.   The Dominican Republic and Indonesia submitted empirical statistical and econometric studies analysing the impact of the TPP measures (and enlarged GHWs) on the change in consumption patterns from premium to lower-priced brands.[1] Different terms have been used to refer to this phenomenon: downward substitution[2] or downtrading.[3]

2.   One of the only points of agreement among the parties is that it is not possible, on the basis of the available data, to distinguish between the impact of plain packaging and the impact of the enlarged GHWs on cigarette sales or consumption, because both measures were implemented at exactly the same time.[4] Unless specified otherwise, the impact of plain packaging in this section therefore refers to the impact of plain packaging *and* enlarged GHWs.

3.   The Dominican Republic and Indonesia argue that all the empirical statistical and econometric studies undertaken by their experts, the IPE (for the Dominican Republic), and Professor List (for the Dominican Republic and Indonesia), point to the fact that the TPP measures led consumers to replace higher-priced cigarettes with low-priced cigarettes and to shift their preferences from higher-priced to low-priced cigarettes.[5]

4.   Similar to the discussion on smoking prevalence and cigarette consumption, we note that the evidence presented to us to analyse substitution can be grouped in three main approaches, that are reviewed separately next:

- First, the Dominican Republic and Indonesia have submitted descriptive statistics analysis aimed at determining whether the shares of higher- to low-priced cigarettes sales and smokers have increased following the implementation of the TPP measures;

---

[1]   See IPE Report, (Exhibit DOM-100); IPE Updated Report, (Exhibit DOM-303); IPE Second Updated Report, (Exhibit DOM-361); IPE Third Updated Report, (Exhibit DOM-375); IPE Summary Report, (Exhibit DOM-379); and List Rebuttal Report, (Exhibit DOM/IDN-3).

[2]   See IPE Report, (Exhibit DOM-100), pp. 16-17.

[3]   See IPE Updated Report, (Exhibit DOM-303), paras. 212 and 228-235; and List Rebuttal Report, (Exhibit DOM/IDN-3), paras. 104 and 111.

[4]   See Australia's first written submission, para. 518; Dominican Republic's response to Panel question No. 8, para. 61; Honduras's response to Panel question No. 8; and Indonesia's response to Panel question No. 8, para. 8.

[5]   See IPE Report, (Exhibit DOM-100), paras. 4 and 61-67; IPE Updated Report, (Exhibit DOM-303), paras. 176-180; IPE Second Updated Report, (Exhibit DOM-361), paras. 43-59; IPE Third Updated Report, (Exhibit DOM-375), paras. 23 and 245-258; IPE Summary Report, (Exhibit DOM-379), paras. 43-45; and List Rebuttal Report, (Exhibit DOM/IDN-3), paras. 104-111.

- Second, the Dominican Republic and Indonesia have submitted statistical analysis to determine whether there was a break in the trend in downward substitution following the implementation of the TPP measures, and in particular, whether the reduction in the shares of higher- to low-priced cigarette sales and smokers have accelerated following the implementation of the TPP measures;

- Finally, some of the parties have submitted econometric analyses to determine whether the TPP measures have contributed to the downward trend of the relative quantities and preferences by isolating and quantifying the different factors that can explain the evolution of the share of sales volume of higher- to low-priced cigarettes as well as the evolution of the share of higher-priced cigarette smokers relative to smokers of low-priced cigarettes.

5.   Unlike the discussion on smoking prevalence and cigarette consumption, however, Australia did not engage in estimating the impact of plain packaging on downward substitution in cigarettes. Australia argues that the Dominican Republic and Indonesia have failed to demonstrate that any downward substitution effects that have occurred in the Australian market are attributable to the TPP measures and not to other factors.[6]

1.   WHETHER DOWNWARD SUBSTITUTION IN CIGARETTES INCREASED FOLLOWING THE IMPLEMENTATION OF THE TPP MEASURES

6.   Two market data sources tracking cigarette sales volumes in Australia were used by the experts of the Dominican Republic, Honduras and Indonesia to compute the share of sales volume of higher- to low-priced cigarettes: (1) In-Market-Sales/Exchange of Sales (IMS/EOS) data and (2) Aztec data. In addition, the experts of the Dominican Republic and Indonesia used the Roy Morgan Single Source (RMSS) survey data to compute the difference between the share of higher-priced cigarette smokers and the share of low-priced cigarette smokers.

1.1   Datasets and related studies

1.1.1   In-Market-Sales/Exchange of Sales

7.   The IPE classifies monthly tobacco product sales from manufacturers to wholesalers and retailers reported in the IMS/EOS data by classifying the cigarette market into two distinct price segments, derived from information provided from the Aztec data: (1) higher-priced cigarettes comprising "premium" and "mid-price" factory-made cigarettes, and (2) low-priced

---

[6]   Australia's first written submission, paras. 542-546.

cigarettes comprising "low-price" and "deep discount" factory-made cigarettes and cigarette stick equivalents (CSE) from fine-cut tobacco.[7]

Figure E.1:   Monthly Sales Volumes of Higher- and Low-Priced Sticks Based on IMS/EOS Data

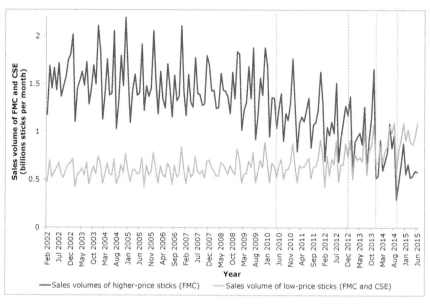

Note: Conversion rate of 0.8 grams of fine-cut tobacco per stick. The vertical dotted lines indicate excise tax hikes. The vertical dashed line indicates the introduction of plain packaging and enlarged GHWs.

Source: IPE Updated Report, (Exhibit DOM-303), p. 73.

8.   The IPE notes, as depicted in **Figure E.1**, that sales volumes of both higher- and low-priced cigarettes are marked by strong seasonal patterns. According to the IPE the overall relationship between sales of higher-priced and low-priced cigarettes changes over time and is not linear.[8] In particular, between 2002 and up to 2008, sales volumes for higher-priced cigarettes and low-priced cigarettes remained relatively stable, with volumes of higher-priced products being more than twice as large as those for low-priced products. From mid-2007 on, sales volumes of higher-priced cigarettes started to decline, but volumes of low-priced goods remained largely stable. From late 2012 onwards and following the entry into force of the TPP measures, volumes of low-prices sticks

---

[7]   See IPE Report, (Exhibit DOM-100), p. 76.
[8]   See IPE Report, (Exhibit DOM-100), p. 80.

began to increase, and from late 2013 on, more low-priced cigarettes were sold than higher-priced cigarettes.

9.   The IPE further compares the evolution of the ratio of higher- to low-priced cigarettes with respect to the ratio of cigarettes' average high prices to low prices, as shown in **Figure E.2**.[9] The IPE notes that the relative sales volumes were quite stable up to mid-2007, with a weak linear downward trend. During the same period, relative prices increased only slightly. From mid-2007 onwards, relative prices started to increase much faster than before, meaning that higher-priced cigarettes became more and more expensive relative to low-priced alternatives. Coinciding with the relative price increase (from mid-2007 onwards), relative quantities (quantities of higher-priced sticks relative to low-priced sticks sold) started to decrease from mid-2007. Since the introduction of the TPP measures, the sales ratio of higher- to low-priced cigarettes continued to decrease, while the relative prices continued to increase.[10]

---

[9]   We note that Professor List reports also the evolution of the ratio of higher- to low-priced cigarettes based on the IMS/EOS data. List Rebuttal Report, (Exhibit DOM/IDN-3), pp. 27-28. We note, however, that unlike IPE, Professor List does not include the sales of RYO tobacco in his analysis of the Aztec data.
[10]   See IPE Updated Report, (Exhibit DOM-303), pp. 192-194.

Figure E.2:   Monthly Sales Volumes Ratio of Higher-to Low-Priced Sticks and Ratio of Average Higher to Low Prices Based on IMS/EOS Data

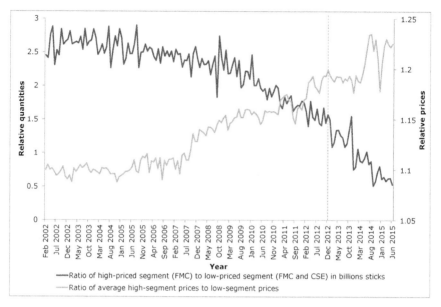

Note: Conversion rate of 0.8 grams of fine-cut tobacco per stick. The vertical dashed line indicates the introduction of plain packaging and enlarged GHWs.

Source: IPE Updated Report, (Exhibit DOM-303), p. 75.

1.1.2   Aztec Scanner

10.   The experts of the Dominican Republic and Indonesia do not present a graphical analysis of downward substitution using the Aztec data. Instead, the IPE and Professor List use the Aztec scanner data in the context of econometric studies, which will be reviewed in detail next. But in that context, Professor List presents the evolution of the ratio of higher- to low-priced cigarettes based on the Aztec data, which, as shown in Figure E.3, displays a downward trend and continues to decrease in the post-TPP period.[11]

---

[11]   See List Rebuttal Report, (Exhibit DOM/IDN-3), pp. 28-29. We note, however, that unlike IPE, Professor List does not include the sales of RYO tobacco in his analysis of the Aztec data.

Figure E.3: Weekly Sales Volumes Ratio of Higher-to Low-Priced Sticks Based on Aztec Data

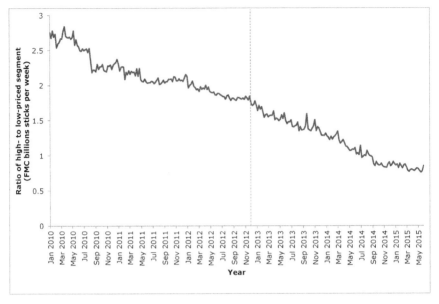

Note: Conversion rate of 0.8 grams of fine-cut tobacco per stick. The vertical dashed line indicates the introduction of plain packaging and enlarged GHWs.

Source: List Rebuttal Report, (Exhibit DOM/IDN-3), p. 29.

1.1.3   Roy Morgan Single Source

11.   In addition to market data, the IPE considers the RMSS survey data and presents, as shown in **Figure E.4**, the evolution of the difference between the share of smokers preferring brands from the higher-priced segment and the share of smokers preferring brands from the low-priced segment.[12] According to the IPE, the share of higher-priced cigarette smokers relative to smokers of low-priced cigarettes has been declining, with very little development in relative brand preferences and relative prices between 2002 up to mid-2007. Thereafter, relative prices rose and relative brand preference declined, implying an inverse relationship between relative brand preferences and relative prices between

---

[12]   See IPE Report, (Exhibit DOM-100), p. 90; and IPE Updated Report, (Exhibit DOM-303), para. 89.

mid-2007 and late 2012. In the post-TPP period, relative brand preference has continued to decline.[13]

Figure E.4: **Monthly Brand Preference for Higher-Priced versus Low-Priced Brands and Ratio of Average Higher to Low Prices Based on RMSS Data**

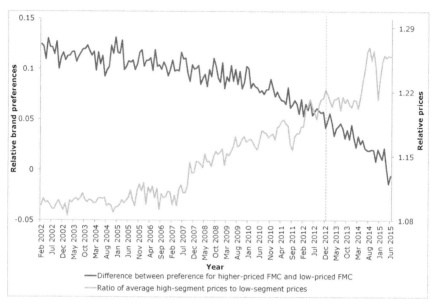

Note: The vertical dashed line indicates the introduction of plain packaging and enlarged GHWs.

Source: IPE Updated Report, (Exhibit DOM-303), p. 89.

1.2 Analysis by the Panel

12. As in the case of analysing smoking prevalence and cigarette consumption, we acknowledge the importance of analysing the trends of the ratio of higher- to low-priced cigarettes and the difference in share of higher-priced cigarette smokers relative to smokers of low-priced cigarettes with the most recent available data. As explained in the analysis of cigarette consumption, we recognize that there is no perfect market sales data in terms of market coverage, frequency (weekly, monthly or annually) and period covered.[14]

---

[13] See IPE Report, (Exhibit DOM-100), pp. 87-90; and IPE Updated Report, (Exhibit DOM-303), paras. 217-221.
[14] See IPE Updated Report, (Exhibit DOM-303), para. 137; and IPE Summary Report, (Exhibit DOM-379), paras. 131-133. In particular, the IMS/EOS data cover sales from manufacturers to

We also note, at the outset, that neither the IPE nor Professor List subsequently updated their graphical analysis of the ratio of higher- to low-priced cigarettes with more recent data.

13.   After a careful review of the most recent available IMS/EOS and Aztec datasets, we notice that despite fluctuations, the ratio of higher- to low-priced cigarettes sales has experienced a downward trend in the period following the introduction of plain packaging, as depicted in **Figure E.5**.[15] Conversely, we note that the ratio of the average higher-segment prices to low-segment prices has on average increased over the same period. Furthermore, we note that the co-relation between the ratio of higher- to low-priced cigarettes sales and the ratio of the average higher-segment prices to low-segment prices is strong and negative.

---

wholesalers and retailers, while the Aztec data cover sales from retailers to consumers. Similarly, the Aztec dataset is only available from 27 July 2008 to 27 September 2015, while the IMS/EOS data cover a larger sample period, from January 2000 to September 2015. Likewise, the IMS/EOS data cover almost 99% of the Australian market, while the Aztec data cover 67% of the Australian market.
[15]   The weekly Aztec data were aggregated to monthly data by assuming that each weekly cigarette quantity can be evenly split for each day of the week.

Figure E.5: **Graphical Assessment of Monthly Sales Volumes Ratio of Higher- to Low-Priced Sticks Based on IMS/EOS and Aztec Data**

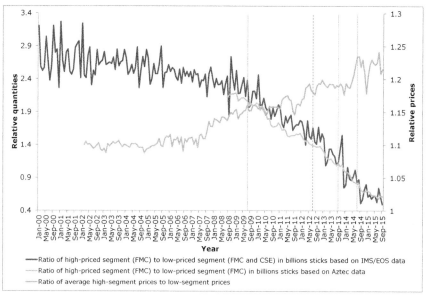

——Ratio of high-priced segment (FMC) to low-priced segment (FMC and CSE) in billions sticks based on IMS/EOS data
‑‑‑‑Ratio of high-priced segment (FMC) to low-priced segment (FMC) in billions sticks based on Aztec data
——Ratio of average high-segment prices to low-segment prices

Note: Conversion rate of 0.8 grams of fine-cut tobacco per stick. The vertical dotted lines indicate excise tax hikes. The vertical dashed line indicates the introduction of plain packaging and enlarged GHWs.

Source: IPE Third Updated Report, (Exhibit DOM-375), backup material.

14.   The evolution of the shares of smokers preferring higher-priced brands and those preferring low-priced brands, as depicted in Figure E.6, leads us to qualify our previous conclusion. In particular, we note that the share of smokers preferring higher-priced brands has decreased, while the share of smokers preferring low-priced brands has experienced a small but positive increase. In addition, the share of smokers preferring higher-priced brands has, on average, decreased at a much faster rate than the share of smokers preferring low-priced brands has increased, confirming the decrease in smoking prevalence.[16] This explains why, as shown in Figure E.7, the difference between the shares of smokers preferring higher-priced brands and low-priced brands has, on average, continued to decrease after the introduction of the TPP measures, such that in

---

[16]   The growth rate differential between the shares of smokers preferring higher-priced brands and those preferring low-priced brands is equal to 2.7 for the period from June 2001 to September 2015. The growth rate differential is equal to 2.3 for the period from June 2007 to September 2015. See IPE Third Updated Report, (Exhibit DOM-375), back-up material.

May, June and September 2015, the share of smokers preferring low-priced brands is higher than the share of smokers preferring higher-priced brands.

15.   We further note that the downward trend of relative preferences based on the RMSS data is slightly more pronounced that the downward trend of relative quantities based on the IMS/EOS and Aztec data. We next review whether the downward trend of the ratio of higher- to low-priced cigarettes sales and the difference between the shares of smokers preferring higher-priced brands and those preferring low-priced brands have accelerated in the post-TPP period.

Figure E.6:   Graphical Assessment of Brand Preference Based on RMSS Data

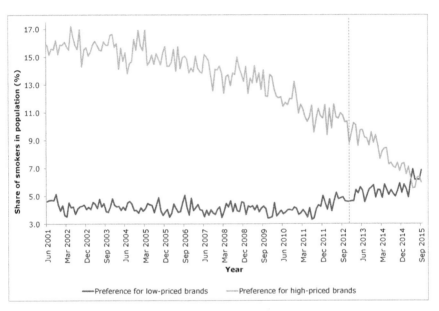

Note: The vertical dashed line indicates the introduction of plain packaging and enlarged GHWs.

Source: IPE Third Updated Report, (Exhibit DOM-375), back-up material.

Figure E.7: **Graphical Assessment of Difference in Brand Preference Based on RMSS Data**

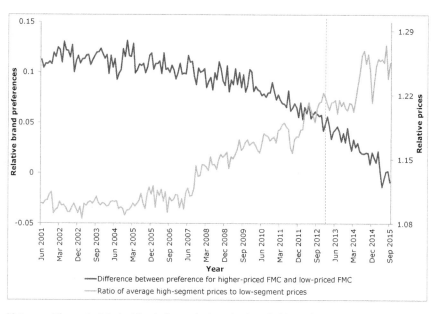

Note: The vertical dashed line indicates the introduction of plain packaging and enlarged GHWs.

Source: IPE Third Updated Report, (Exhibit DOM-375), back-up material.

2.   WHETHER DOWNWARD SUBSTITUTION IN CIGARETTES ACCELERATED AFTER THE ENTRY INTO FORCE OF THE TPP MEASURES

16.   We determined that, in the period following the introduction of the TPP measures, the most recent market and survey data show two trends. First, there is a continuing decrease of the ratio of higher- to low-priced cigarettes sales. Second, there is a decrease in the share of smokers preferring higher-priced brands to those preferring low-priced brands. We now turn to consider whether there was a shift in these trends in the post-TPP implementation period. The Dominican Republic's and Indonesia's experts examine this issue by applying different methodologies, which are described next. We then present our analysis.

2.1 Datasets and related studies

2.1.1 In-Market-Sales/Exchange of Sales

2.1.1.1 IPE Reports

17. Based on the graphical assessment discussed above[17], the IPE submits that since the implementation of the TPP measures in December 2012, relative quantities of higher- to low-priced cigarettes sales have been significantly lower than the interpolated pre-plain packaging trend, as depicted in **Figure E.8**.[18]

Figure E.8: Trend Assessment of Monthly Sales Volumes Ratio of Higher- to Low-Priced Sticks and Ratio of Average Higher to Low Prices Based on IMS/EOS Data

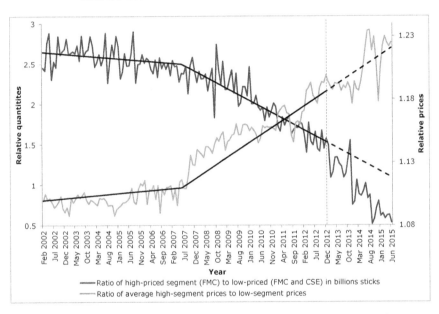

Note: Conversion rate of 0.8 grams of fine-cut tobacco per stick. The vertical dashed line indicates the introduction of plain packaging and enlarged GHWs.

Source: IPE Updated Report, (Exhibit DOM-303), p. 75.

2.1.1.2 Professor List's report

18. Professor List presents the results of an event study analysing whether there has been a shift in the evolution of the ratio of higher- to low-priced

---

[17]   See paras. 8 and 9 above.
[18]   See IPE Updated Report, (Exhibit DOM-303), para. 194.

cigarettes sales following the introduction of plain packaging and enlarged GHWs.[19] Specifically, a seasonally adjusted Autoregressive Integrated Moving Average (ARIMA) model is estimated controlling for the change in the ratio of higher- to low-priced cigarettes sales during the previous month and the change in the 2006 GHWs. A dynamic model of the ratio of higher- to low-priced cigarettes sales is also estimated controlling for the quantity ratio of higher- to low-priced cigarettes sales during the previous month, the price ratio of higher-to low priced cigarettes in the previous month, a linear time trend, and the 2006 GHWs.[20] The most recent analysis covers the period from February 2002 to June 2015.

Figure E.9: Event Study on Sales Volumes Ratio of Higher- to Low-Priced Sticks Based on IMS/EOS Data

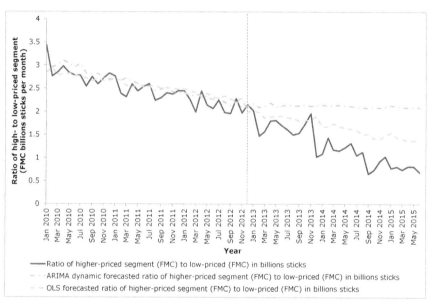

---

[19] We note that Professor List's event study is a trend-projection analysis that does not estimate directly the impact of the TPP measures, but rather assesses whether there is a difference between the counterfactual ratio of higher- to low-priced cigarettes sales in the absence of the TPP measures and the actual ratio of higher- to low-priced cigarettes sales. That is why we have decided to discuss Professor List's event study under the subsection addressing whether there was a change in downward substitution in cigarettes in the post-implementation period.

[20] An event analysis consists of (1) estimating the model of the ratio of higher- to low-priced cigarettes sales during the pre-plain packaging period; (2) forecasting the ratio of higher- to low-priced cigarettes sales that would have been prevailed in the absence of the TPP measures using the estimated model's parameters in the post-implementation period; and (3) determining whether the difference between the observed ratio of higher- to low-priced cigarettes sales volumes and the estimated counterfactual ratio of higher- to low-priced cigarettes volumes is statistically different from zero. See List Rebuttal Report, (Exhibit DOM/IDN-3), para. 109.

Note: Conversion rate of 0.8 grams of fine-cut tobacco per stick. The vertical dashed line
         indicates the introduction of plain packaging and enlarged GHWs.

Source: List Rebuttal Report, (Exhibit DOM/IDN-3), p. 28.

19.   Professor List concludes that according to both models, there is a
negative and statistically significant difference between the observed ratio of
higher- to low-priced cigarettes sales and the estimated counterfactual ratio of
higher- to low-priced cigarettes sales, as depicted in **Figure E.9**. According to
Professor List, the fact that the ratio of higher- to low-priced cigarettes sales did
decrease faster in the post-implementation period provides evidence that the
TPP measures have led to important changes to the composition of sales in the
Australian market, which is consistent with Australian consumers "downtrading"
when making their cigarette choices.[21]

2.1.2   Aztec Scanner

20.   Professor List carried out the same event study using the Aztec scanner
data. A seasonally adjusted ARIMA model and a dynamic model of the ratio of
higher- to low-priced cigarettes sales volumes are estimated controlling for
change in the quantity ratio of higher- to low-priced cigarettes sales during the
previous month as well as the price ratio of the higher- to low-priced cigarettes
during the previous month and the linear time trend variable for the dynamic
model. The analysis covers the period from July 2008 to May 2015.

21.   Professor List reaches the same conclusion that there is a statistically
significant decrease in the ratio of higher-priced to low-priced cigarettes sales in
the post-implementation period relative to the predicted ratio, as shown in
Figure E.10, which is consistent with downward substitution from higher-priced
to low-priced cigarettes.[22]

---

[21] See List Rebuttal Report, (Exhibit DOM/IDN-3), paras. 110-111.
[22] See List Third Supplemental Report, (Exhibit DOM/IDN-7), paras. 56-61 and 80.

Figure E.10: Event Study on Sales Volumes Ratio of Higher-to Low-Priced Sticks Based on Aztec Data

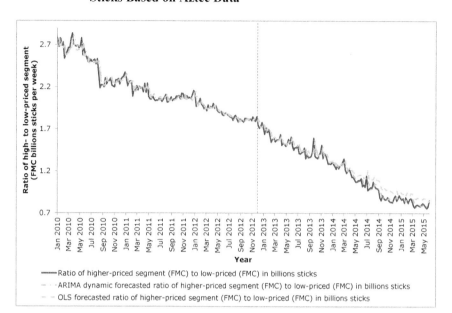

Note: The vertical dashed line indicates the introduction of plain packaging and enlarged GHWs.

Source: List Rebuttal Report, (Exhibit DOM/IDN-3), p. 29.

22.   Although Professor List acknowledges that it is impossible to separate the GHW effect from the plain packaging effect without making an assumption on the size of one of the effects, he proposes to examine the effect of Canada's GHW policy on the composition of higher- and low-priced cigarette sales. In September 2011, Canada mandated an increase in the GHW to 75% of the front and back of the pack, which is, according to Professor List, similar to the GHW increase that coincided with Australia's implementation of its TPP measures in December 2012. Professor List presents the econometric results of an event study of the ratio of higher- to low-tier cigarettes in Canada controlling for the sales composition in the previous month, the price ratio in the previous month, a linear time trend and a dummy variable for the 2011 GHW change. Professor List concludes that the 2011 GHW change in Canada had no impact in the decrease in the ratio of higher- to low-priced cigarette sales. Professor List argues that the evidence of no impact of the GHW on cigarettes sales composition in Canada is consistent with the plain packaging element and not the enlarged GHWs having an important role on the change in the composition

of higher- and low-priced cigarette sales observed after the introduction of the TPP measures in Australia.[23]

2.1.3 Roy Morgan Single Source

23.   Based on the graphical assessment of the RMSS data presented above[24], the IPE submits that shortly after the introduction of the TPP measures, relative brand preferences started to shift downwards to a much greater extent, and at a much greater rate, compared to the pre-plain packaging trend, as depicted in Figure E.11.[25]

Figure E.11: Monthly Preference for Higher-Priced versus Low-Priced Brands and Ratio of Average Higher to Low Prices Based on RMSS Data

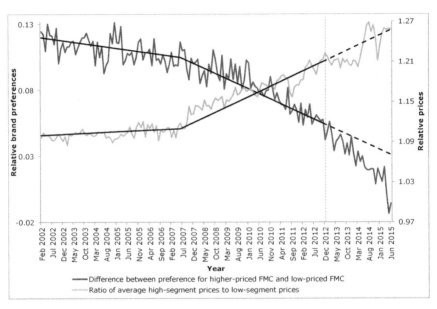

Note: The vertical dashed line indicates the introduction of plain packaging and enlarged GHWs.

Source: IPE Updated Report, (Exhibit DOM-303), p. 89.

---

[23]   See List Rebuttal Report, (Exhibit DOM/IDN-3), paras. 112-118.
[24]   See para. 11 above.
[25]   See IPE Updated Report, (Exhibit DOM-303), para. 194.

2.2 Analysis by the Panel

24.   As explained in our analysis of the TPP measures' impact on smoking prevalence and cigarette consumption[26], we are not required to present a unified econometric analysis but to assess the robustness of the results submitted by the parties. In addition, our conclusions apply exclusively to the data (including the sample period), and econometric results submitted by the parties, and cannot in any way be generalized to other datasets and econometric studies.

2.2.1 IPE Reports

25.   A careful review of the IPE's graphical analysis of the ratio of higher- to low-priced cigarettes sales leads us to the same conclusion reached by the IPE. In particular, extending the analysis to the most recent available data provided by the parties, we find that, according to a standard mean-comparison test, the ratio of higher- to low-priced cigarettes sales based on the IMS/EOS data in the post-implementation period is statistically significantly lower than in the pre-implementation period. This is confirmed by Figure E.12, which shows that the trend of relative quantities in the post-implementation has become steeper compared to the pre-implementation trend, implying that the fall in the ratio of higher- to low-priced cigarettes sales has accelerated in the post-implementation period. The same conclusion can be drawn with the Aztec data.

---

[26]   See Appendices C and D.

**Figure E.12: Preference for Higher-Priced versus Low-Priced Brands Pre-
and Post-TPP Trends Based on RMSS Data**

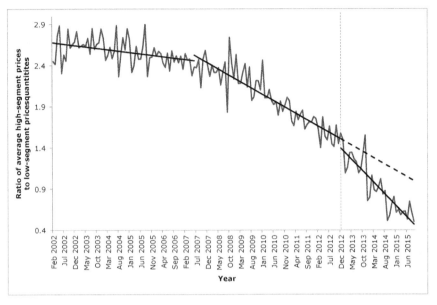

Note: Conversion rate of 0.8 grams of fine-cut tobacco per stick. The vertical dotted lines
indicate excise tax hikes. The vertical dashed line indicates the introduction of plain
packaging and enlarged GHWs.

Source: IPE Third Updated Report, (Exhibit DOM-375), backup material.

26.   We reach a similar conclusion with respect to the difference between the
share of smokers preferring higher-priced brands and those preferring
low-priced brands. We note that the downward trend of the difference between
smokers preferring higher-priced brands and those preferring low-priced brands
has accelerated in the post-implementation period, as shown in **Figure E.13**.

Figure E.13: Sales Volumes Ratio of Higher-to Low-Priced Sticks Pre- and Post-TPP Trends Based on IMS/EOS Data

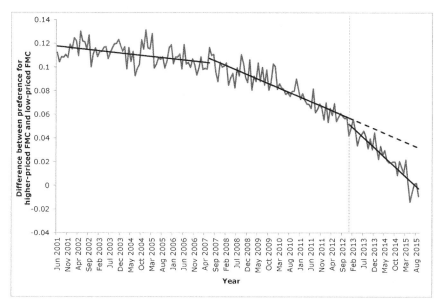

Note: Vertical dashed line indicates the introduction of plain packaging (and enlarged graphic warnings).

Source: IPE Updated Report, (Exhibit DOM-303), p. 89.

2.2.2   Professor List's report

27.   After a careful review of the results of Professor List's event study of the impact of the TPP measures on the ratio of higher-priced to low-priced cigarettes sales, we question the validity of Professor List's results for a number of reasons, some of which are specific to one model considered by Professor List.

28.   We note that in most estimations of the ARIMA model for the pre-plain packaging period based on the IMS/EOS and Aztec data that are used to forecast the value of the ratio of higher-priced to low-priced cigarettes sales in the post-implementation period, none of the explanatory variables is statistically significant, besides the moving averages parameters. The lack of statistically significant variables is surprising to us given that the ARIMA model only includes one or two explanatory variables. We further note, as in the ARIMA model analysing smoking prevalence, that the estimated lagged moving average parameter of the ARIMA model based on the IMS/EOS data is not statistically different from -1, which would likely lead to large forecasting errors. This is, in our view, problematic because Professor List's approach relies on the post-implementation forecasting errors to determine whether there was a

statistically significant change in the downward trend in the ratio of higher-priced to low-priced cigarettes sales.

Figure E.14: Ratio of Average Higher to Low Prices and Linear Time Variable Based on RMSS Data

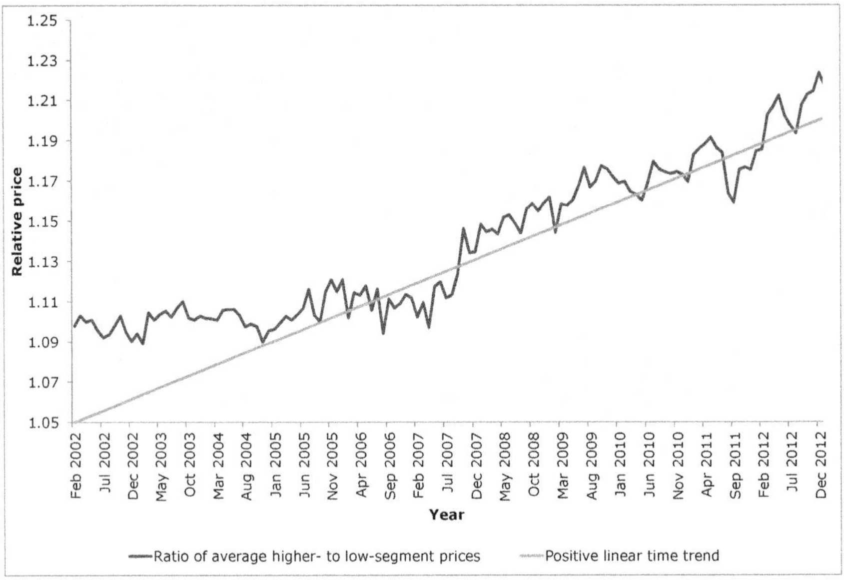

Source: List Rebuttal Report, (Exhibit DOM/IDN-3), backup material.

29.   We also note that the dynamic model faces multicollinearity problems between the time trend variable and the price ratio variable when using the IMS/EOS data and between the time trend variable and the ratio of higher-priced to low-priced cigarettes sales during the previous month when using the Aztec data.[27] In other words, the price ratio variable and the time trend variable seem to convey the same information, as shown in **Figure E.14**, and as a result one of them becomes redundant in the model specification with the IMS/EOS data. A similar conclusion applies to the time trend variable and the ratio of higher-priced to low-priced cigarettes sales during the previous month with the Aztec data. In both cases, this multicollinearity problem could explain why the dynamic model finds that the lagged price ratio variable is not statistically significant. This is particularly surprising given that one of the Dominican Republic's experts, the IPE, considers relative prices to be one of the factors leading to downward substitution from higher-priced to low-priced

---

[27]   Evidence of multicollinearity is confirmed by the variance inflation factors statistic.

cigarettes.[28] We also question why Professor List implicitly assumes in the models based on the IMS/EOS data that the effect of the 2006 GHW disappears following the introduction of the TPP measures. More generally, Professor List did not take into account the impact of the excise tax hikes in the pre- and post-plain packaging periods. Yet, according to Australia, tobacco manufacturers operating in Australia have attributed downtrading effects to increases in excise taxes.[29]

30.   We also question the relevance of using Canada's GHW policy change to infer that plain packaging and not the enlarged GHWs had an impact on the ratio of higher- to low-tier cigarettes in Australia. Professor List did not provide evidence that would justify making such an inference, although he acknowledges that the empirical estimates for Canada rest on strong assumptions.[30]

31.   Overall, and in this context, we consider the results of Professor List's event study to be of limited use in helping to answer the question whether the TPP measures led to a change in the downward trend of the ratio of higher-priced to low-priced cigarettes sales. That being said, and as explained above, we find that, according to a standard mean-comparison test, the average cigarette sales volumes based on the IMS/EOS data and the Aztec data in the post-implementation period are statistically significantly lower than in the pre-implementation period. Similarly, the downward trend of the difference between the shares of smokers preferring higher-priced brands and those preferring low-priced brands based on the RMSS data has accelerated in the post-plain packaging period.

32.   In any event, as in respect of smoking prevalence and smoking consumption, the fact that the downward trends of the ratio of higher- to low-priced cigarettes sales and the difference between the share of smokers preferring higher-priced brands and those preferring low-priced brands have accelerated in the post-implementation period does not necessarily imply that the TPP measures are having a statistically significant impact, given that other factors, unrelated to the TPP measures, could explain the respective trend shift. The extent to which the TPP measures have an impact on the ratio of higher-priced to low-priced cigarettes sales and on the difference between the shares of smokers preferring higher-priced brands and low-priced brands is reviewed next.

---

[28]   See IPE Updated Report, (Exhibit DOM-303), para. 194.
[29]   See Australia's first written submission, paras. 544-545; Australia's second written submission, paras. 418-419; BATA Media Release, (Exhibit AUS-255); and BAT, Half-Year Results 2015, (Exhibit AUS-556).
[30]   List Rebuttal Report, (Exhibit DOM/IDN-3), para. 118.

3.   WHETHER THE TPP MEASURES CONTRIBUTED TO DOWNWARD SUBSTITUTION IN CIGARETTES

33.   As explained above, we have determined that the ratio of higher-priced to low-priced cigarettes sales and the difference between the shares of smokers preferring higher-priced brands and those preferring low-priced brands in Australia have continued to experience a decline, which has accelerated in the post-plain packaging period. To the extent that there has been a greater reduction in these metrics after the entry into force of the TPP measures, the question arises whether, and if so, to what extent, plain packaging contributed to reducing these metrics.

34.   As for the analyses of smoking prevalence and cigarette sales and consumption, the Dominican Republic's and Indonesia's experts proposed different econometric methods to estimate the impact of the TPP measures on relative quantities and preferences of higher-priced cigarettes with respect to low-priced cigarettes. As mentioned above, the Dominican Republic's and Indonesia's experts recognize, however, that it is impossible to technically distinguish between the impact of plain packaging *and* the impact of the enlarged GHWs on relative quantities and preferences of higher-priced cigarettes with respect to low-priced cigarettes, because both measures were implemented at the exact same time.[31]

3.1   Datasets and related studies

3.1.1   In-Market-Sales/Exchange of Sales

35.   Several reports by the IPE have been submitted, estimating econometrically the impact of the TPP measures on the logarithm of the ratio of higher- to low-priced cigarette wholesale sales using the IMS/EOS data. Throughout these reports, different econometric approaches and model specifications have been proposed: (1) time series regression analysis; (2) modified trend analysis; and (3) Autoregressive Integrated Moving Average with Explanatory Variable (ARIMAX) model.[32]

36.   The first approach was only presented in the first IPE Report and is based on a model specification of the logarithm of the ratio of higher- to low-priced cigarette sales that includes a TPP measures dummy variable, dummy variables for the 2010 and 2013 excise tax increases, a 2006 GHW dummy, the logarithm of the higher- to low-priced cigarettes price ratio, month fixed effects and a time trend variable. The second and subsequent IPE reports only focused on the last two approaches. The modified trend analysis estimates a standard time series

---

[31]   See Dominican Republic's response to Panel question No. 8, para. 61; List Report, (Exhibit DOM/IDN-1), para. 113; Honduras's response to Panel question No. 8; and Indonesia's response to Panel question No. 8, para. 8.

[32]   See IPE Report, (Exhibit DOM-100), pp. 67-73 and 201-210; and IPE Updated Report, (Exhibit DOM-303), paras. 135-175 and 290-326.

regression model of the logarithm of the ratio of higher-to lower-priced cigarette sales using (heteroscedastic) autocorrelation-robust standards errors and controlling for a TPP measures dummy variable, dummy variables for the 2010, 2013 and 2014 excise tax increases, a 2006 GHW dummy, the (current or lagged) logarithm of the higher- to low-priced cigarettes price ratio, month fixed effects and a time trend variable. The ARIMA model includes the same set of explanatory variables as well as the (one up to four) lagged logarithm of the ratio of higher-to lower-priced cigarette sales and the (one up to four) lagged logarithm of the price ratio. The most recent econometric analysis covers the period February 2002 through August 2015.

37.   Overall, the IPE concludes that the TPP measures had a negative and statistically significant effect on the logarithm of the ratio of higher- to low-priced cigarette sales. According to the IPE, these results are robust across different specifications (e.g. different plain packaging starting date: October, November and December; alternative time trend specification: linear, quadratic and cubic; and alternative methods of calculating standard errors of the modified trend analysis).[33]

38.   Although the IPE acknowledges that there is no perfect way to separate the plain packaging and enlarged GHW effects, it argues that there are indirect ways to study any effect of the enlarged GHW requirement on downtrading in Australia, such as estimating the downtrading effect of another tobacco control policy introduced in isolation in Australia, without the simultaneous introduction of a confound. The IPE proposes using the introduction of GHWs in Australia in 2006 as a proxy for the implementation of the enlarged GHW requirement in December 2012. Given that the econometric results of the analysis of the logarithm of the ratio of higher- to low-priced cigarette wholesale sales find that the impact of the 2006 GHW is negative but not statistically significant, the IPE argues that the plain packaging component is likely responsible for the vast majority of the downtrading effect found from the December 2012 policy change.[34]

3.1.2   Aztec Scanner

39.   The IPE performed the same (1) time series regression analysis; (2) modified trend analysis; and (3) ARIMAX model analysis using the Aztec scanner data.[35] The exact same set of explanatory variables is included, except

---

[33]   See IPE Report, (Exhibit DOM-100), pp. 83-86 and 223-233; IPE Updated Report, (Exhibit DOM-303), paras. 195-201; IPE Second Updated Report, (Exhibit DOM-361), paras. 45-48; and IPE Third Updated Report, (Exhibit DOM-375), paras. 249-251.

[34]   See IPE Updated Report, (Exhibit DOM-303), paras. 228-234. IPE also presented a graphic analysis of the relative quantities with respect to the introduction of GHWs in 2006 and plain packaging in 2012.

[35]   See IPE Report, (Exhibit DOM-100), pp. 80-83; and IPE Updated Report, (Exhibit DOM-303), paras. 205-206.

the 2006 GHW dummy. The analysis covers the period from July 2008 to May 2015.

40.   Overall, the IPE finds the same conclusion as the analysis based on the IMS/EOS data, namely the impact of the TPP measures on the logarithm of the ratio of higher- to low-priced cigarette retail sales is negative and statistically significant. According to the IPE, these results are robust across different specifications (e.g. different plain packaging starting date: October, November and December; alternative time trend specification: linear, quadratic and cubic; and alternative methods of calculating standard errors of the modified trend analysis).[36] In reality, the estimated coefficient of the TPP measures dummy variable is not statistically significant in a couple of specifications.[37]

3.1.3   Roy Morgan Single Source

41.   The RMSS data were used by the Dominican Republic's and Indonesia's experts to estimate econometrically the impact of the TPP measures on the relative preferences of higher-priced cigarettes with respect to low-priced cigarettes.

3.1.3.1   IPE Reports

42.   The IPE presented in various reports the results of a standard probit model of the probability of an individual cigarette smoker consuming higher-priced cigarettes. The model controls for a TPP measures dummy variable, (current or lagged) relative price of higher-priced versus low-priced cigarettes, gender dummy, polynomial of degree 4 of the age variable, polynomial of degree 4 of the education variable, polynomial of degree 4 of the income group variable, dummy variables for the 2010, 2013, 2014 and 2015 excise tax increases, and a trend variable.[38] In its first report, the IPE also estimated a linear probability model, whose model specification included the same demographic variables as well as a social class variable but without any of the tax hike dummy variables and the trend variable.[39] The analysis covers the period from July 2006 through September 2015.

43.   Overall, the IPE concludes that the impact of the TPP measures on the probability that an individual smoker prefers higher-priced brands is negative and statistically significant.[40] According to the IPE, this finding is robust to

---

[36]   See IPE Report, (Exhibit DOM-100), pp. 234-244; IPE Updated Report, (Exhibit DOM-303), paras. 202-208; IPE Second Updated Report, (Exhibit DOM-361), paras. 49-52; and IPE Third Updated Report, (Exhibit DOM-375), paras. 252-254.

[37]   This is the case when the starting date of the TPP measures dummy variable is set to October 2012. See IPE Third Updated Report, (Exhibit DOM-375), p. 140.

[38]   See IPE Updated Report, (Exhibit DOM-303), paras. 245-250.

[39]   See IPE Report, (Exhibit DOM-100), pp. 245-250.

[40]   See IPE Report, (Exhibit DOM-100), pp. 90-94; IPE Updated Report, (Exhibit DOM-303), paras. 223-227, p. 134; IPE Second Updated Report, (Exhibit DOM-361), paras. 53-55; and IPE Third Updated Report, (Exhibit DOM-375), paras. 255-256.

different model specifications (e.g. different plain packaging starting date: October, November and December, inclusion of the first lagged of the price ratio, and excise tax increases dummies).

44.   The IPE further submits that plain packaging and not the enlarged GHWs is likely responsible for the vast majority of the downtrading effect from the introduction of the TPP measures because a modification of the model specification enabling to extend the sample period from February 2002 to September 2015 and controlling for the 2006 GHW finds a negative but not statistically significant impact of the 2006 GHWs on the probability of smoking cigarettes from the higher-priced segment.[41]

3.1.3.2   Professor List's Report

45.   Professor List presented econometric results of a two-stage micro-econometric model based on the RMSS data. The first stage estimates the likelihood of a representative person smoking a high or medium-priced segment brand of cigarettes, conditional on being a smoker, in a given month and controlling for demographic characteristics (e.g. age, fourth order polynomials of gender, education, and income position). The second stage conducts a before and after analysis on the likelihood for each month computed in the first stage by estimating a linear probability model controlling for the TPP measures, higher- to low-priced cigarettes price ratio and/or linear trend, and weighting changes by Roy Morgan Research. Professor List re-estimated the same model for a representative person smoking a low-priced segment brand of cigarettes. The econometric analysis covers the period from July 2006 to June 2015.

46.   Overall, Professor List concludes that the TPP measures had a statistically significant negative effect on the likelihood of consuming higher-priced cigarettes but a positive and statistically significant effect on the likelihood of consuming lower-priced cigarettes.[42]

3.2   Analysis by the Panel

47.   Having determined above that the decrease in the ratio of higher- to low-priced cigarette sales and in the difference between the share of smokers preferring higher-priced brands and the share of those preferring low-priced brands has accelerated following the entry into force of the TPP measures, the question before us at this stage of our analysis is whether this acceleration may, in part or in whole, be attributed to the TPP measures.

48.   At the outset, we note, as explained above, that Australia did not provide any econometric evidence on downward substitution. We also note that

---

[41]   See IPE Updated Report, (Exhibit DOM-303), paras. 231-235, p. 134.
[42]   See List Rebuttal Report, (Exhibit DOM/IDN-3), paras. 106-107.

Dominican Republic's and Indonesia's experts use the same data sources but consider different model specifications and approaches.[43]

49.   As explained in our review of the econometric study on smoking prevalence and cigarette sales and consumption, it is not our task to conduct our own econometric assessment but rather review the robustness of the econometric evidence submitted by each party.

3.2.1   IPE's econometric results

50.   A careful review of the econometric results based on the IMS/EOS data provided in the IPE reports leads us to conclude that there is some evidence, albeit limited, that the TPP measures, together with the englarged GHWs introduced on the same date, appear to have had a negative impact on the ratio of higher- to low-priced cigarette wholesale sales. We note, however, that the price ratio has a much larger impact on the ratio of higher- to low-priced cigarette wholesale sales. This finding is in line with the strong negative correlation between price ratio and quantity ratio, as well as the evidence submitted by Australia regarding the impact of the tobacco industry's own marketing and pricing strategies on downtrading in the Australian market.[44] Similarly, the econometric results show that the overall impact of the excise tax hikes on the ratio of higher- to low-priced cigarette wholesale sales is larger the TPP measures.

51.   That being said, we note that some specifications of the modified trend analysis are characterized by multicollinearity between the quadratic or cubic trend variables and the current and/or lagged price ratio. We note that the issue of multicollinearity is even more severe in all of the specifications of the ARIMAX model based on the IMS/EOS data. The multicollinearity is particularly high between the quadratic or cubic time trend variables, the lagged price ratio and lagged quantity ratio.[45] We also question the results of most ARIMAX models, because the results find that the higher- to low-priced cigarettes price ratio has either no impact or a statistically positive impact. It is unclear what drives such results, although we note that the price ratio is negative and statistically significant in the specifications, which are less affected by multicollinearity by including only a linear time variable. The results of some specifications also suggest that the trend variable has a positive and statistically significant impact, which is in contradiction with other econometric results and the graphical analysis discussed above. We therefore reject the results of the ARIMAX model based on the IMS/EOS data.

---

[43]   For instance, Professor List does not include dummy variables for the excise tax increases unlike IPE. Similarly, Professor List presents the results of a two-stage econometric model applied to the RMSS data, while IPE presents the results of one-stage micro-econometric analysis.
[44]   See Australia's second written submission, paras. 418-419.
[45]   Evidence of multicollinearity is confirmed by the variance inflation factors statistic.

52.   We also question the validity of the econometric results based on the Aztec retail data on the same grounds. We note that the results of the modified trend analysis are affected by high collinearity between the linear trend variable and the current price ratio as well as the price ratio in the previous month. The collinearity problem also arises in the ARIMAX model between the logarithm of the ratio of higher- to low-priced cigarette retail sales in the previous month, the trend variable(s) and the price ratio in the previous (second to fourth) months. The collinearity is even more severe when the current price ratio is included in the model specification. We also note that all the results of the ARIMAX model find that the impact of the logarithm of the ratio of higher- to low-priced cigarette wholesale sales in the previous month is positive and statistically significant, which is in contradiction with the negative and statistically significant impact found in the econometric analysis based on the IMS/EOS data.

53.   Our review of the IPE's micro analysis of the effect of the TPP measures on smokers' relative preference for higher-priced versus low-priced cigarettes based on the RMSS data leads to question the validity of some of its results. Besides the issue of collinearity between the price ratio and the time trend variable, we note that the impact of the relative price of higher-priced cigarettes with respect to low-priced cigarettes in the current or previous month on the probability of choosing higher-priced cigarettes is never statistically significant. This finding is, in our view, rather surprising given that as acknowledged by the IPE itself, the individual choice of higher-priced versus low-priced cigarettes is likely to be influenced by the relative price of the two product groups.[46] Yet, the IPE did not provide any explanations that would justify such surprising results.

3.2.2   Professor List's econometric results

54.   We also question the validity of Professor List's two-stage econometric model of the probability of a representative person smoking a high or medium price segment brand of cigarettes based on the RMSS data on various grounds. First, we note that, in the first stage of the model of the representative smoker, more than 60% of the individual monthly estimations report that either none or only one or two of the explanatory variables are statistically significant.[47] Similarly, there is only up to two explanatory variables that are statistically significant in more than 43% of the individual monthly estimations in the first stage of the model of the representative smoker of low-tier cigarettes. It is therefore unclear to what extent the results of the second stage of the analysis are reliable given the lack of statistical significance in the first stage. Second, as explained above, issues of multicollinearity arise between the ratio of higher- to low-priced cigarettes prices and the time trend. Third, several estimation results

---

[46]   See IPE Updated Report, (Exhibit DOM-303), paras. 231-235 and 218.
[47]   12 demographic characteristics and the constant term are included in the first-stage model specification.

find surprisingly that the price ratio is statistically not significant. Finally, we note that Professor List does not, unlike the IPE, take into account the impact of the excise tax hikes on the probability of smoking, which is considered by the parties to be one of the most efficient tobacco control policies.

55.   Although we question the validity of Professor List two-stage econometric model analysis, we cannot rule out that plain packaging and enlarged GHWs contributed to the reduction in the ratio of higher- to low-priced cigarette wholesale sales in Australia based on the most recent econometric evidence on wholesale data submitted by the IPE. That being said, the extent to which this reduction in the ratio of higher- to low-priced cigarette wholesale sales in Australia that could be attributed to the TPP measures, represents only downtrading is unclear to our eyes. As highlighted in the graphical analysis presented above, the reduction in higher-priced segment wholesale sales has decreased at a much faster rate than the sales of low-priced cigarettes, which implies that at least part of the reduction in the ratio of higher- to low-priced cigarette wholesale sales is due to the overall reduction in the total wholesale sales volume following and due to the introduction of the TPP measures, as we concluded earlier.

4.   OVERALL CONCLUSION ON POST-IMPLEMENTATION EVIDENCE ON DOWNWARD SUBSTITUTION IN CIGARETTES

56.   Overall, based on the most recent data available and econometric evidence submitted by the parties, we find that:

a.   There is evidence that the ratio of higher- to low-priced cigarette wholesale and retail sales and the difference between the share of smokers preferring higher-priced cigarettes and the share of those preferring low-priced cigarettes in Australia continued to decrease following the introduction of the TPP measures.

b.   The downward trend in the ratio of higher- to low-priced cigarette wholesale and retail sales and the difference between the share of smokers preferring higher-priced cigarettes and the share of those preferring low-priced cigarettes in Australia appears to have accelerated in the post-plain packaging period.

c.   Although it is impossible to distinguish between the impact of plain packaging and GHWs, there is some econometric evidence suggesting that the TPP measures contributed to the reduction in the ratio of higher- to low-priced cigarette wholesale sales. That said, it is unclear to what extent this reduction in the quantity ratio attributable to the TPP measures represents only downward substitution. In fact, given that the reduction in higher-priced segment wholesale sales has decreased at a much faster rate than the increase in sales of low-priced cigarettes, at least part of the reduction in the quantity ratio is due to the overall reduction in the total wholesale sales volume following and due to the introduction of the TPP measures and enlarged GHWs, as we have concluded in our previous analysis on cigarette consumption. In addition, the econometric results show that the increase in relative cigarette price and excise tax hikes have had a negative and greater impact on the the ratio of higher- to low-priced cigarette wholesale sales than the TPP measures.

57.   We note, however, that no post-implementation empirical evidence has been presented to us on the impact of the TPP measures on the ratio of higher- to low-priced cigars and cigarillos.

UNITED STATES - CERTAIN METHODOLOGIES AND THEIR APPLICATION TO ANTI-DUMPING PROCEEDINGS INVOLVING CHINA - ARBITRATION UNDER ARTICLE 21.3(C) OF THE DSU

Award of the Arbitrator
WT/DS471/RPT[*]

Circulated
on 19 January 2018

Parties:

China

United States

Arbitrator:

Simon Farbenbloom

TABLE OF CONTENTS

---

[*] Note concerning document symbol: As of 13 April 2017, for ease of reference, awards of arbitrators under Article 21.3(c) of the DSU bear the symbol WT/DS[number]/RPT.

ABBREVIATIONS USED IN THIS AWARD

Abbreviation	Description
Anti-Dumping Agreement	Agreement on Implementation of Article VI of the General Agreement on Tariffs and Trade 1994
Appellate Body Report	Appellate Body Report, *United States – Certain Methodologies and Their Application to Anti-Dumping Proceedings Involving China, WT/DS471/AB/R*
DSB	Dispute Settlement Body
DSU	Understanding on Rules and Procedures Governing the Settlement of Disputes
GATT 1994	General Agreement on Tariffs and Trade 1994
NME	non-market economy
Panel Report	Panel Report, *United States – Certain Methodologies and Their Application to Anti-Dumping Proceedings Involving China, WT/DS471/R*
Section 123 of the URAA	Uruguay Round Agreements Act, Public Law No. 103-465, 108 Stat. 4838, codified as *United States Code*, Title 19, Section 3533 (Exhibit USA-1)
Section 129 of the URAA	Uruguay Round Agreements Act, Public Law No. 103-465, 108 Stat. 4838, codified as *United States Code*, Title 19, Section 3538 (Exhibit USA-2)
SRP	Single Rate Presumption
USDOC	United States Department of Commerce
USTR	United States Trade Representative
W-T	weighted average-to-transaction
WTO	World Trade Organization
URAA	Uruguay Round Agreements Act

CASES CITED IN THIS AWARD

Short title	Full case title and citation
Brazil – Retreaded Tyres (Article 21.3(c))	Award of the Arbitrator, *Brazil – Measures Affecting Imports of Retreaded Tyres – Arbitration under Article 21.3(c) of the DSU*, WT/DS332/16, 29 August 2008, DSR 2008:XX, p. 8581
Canada – Pharmaceutical Patents (Article 21.3(c))	Award of the Arbitrator, *Canada – Patent Protection of Pharmaceutical Products – Arbitration under Article 21.3(c) of the DSU*, WT/DS114/13, 18 August 2000, DSR 2002:I, p. 3
Chile – Price Band System (Article 21.3(c))	Award of the Arbitrator, *Chile – Price Band System and Safeguard Measures Relating to Certain Agricultural Products – Arbitration under Article 21.3(c) of the DSU*, WT/DS207/13, 17 March 2003, DSR 2003:III, p. 1237
China – GOES (Article 21.3(c))	Award of the Arbitrator, *China – Countervailing and Anti-Dumping Duties on Grain Oriented Flat-Rolled Electrical Steel from the United States – Arbitration under Article 21.3(c) of the DSU*, WT/DS414/12, 3 May 2013, DSR 2013:IV, p. 1495
Colombia – Ports of Entry (Article 21.3(c))	Award of the Arbitrator, *Colombia – Indicative Prices and Restrictions on Ports of Entry – Arbitration under Article 21.3(c) of the DSU*, WT/DS366/13, 2 October 2009, DSR 2009:IX, p. 3819
Colombia – Textiles (Article 21.3(c))	Award of the Arbitrator, *Colombia – Measures Relating to the Importation of Textiles, Apparel and Footwear – Arbitration under Article 21.3(c) of the DSU*, WT/DS461/13, 15 November 2016
EC – Bananas III (Article 21.3(c))	Award of the Arbitrator, *European Communities – Regime for the Importation, Sale and Distribution of Bananas – Arbitration under Article 21.3(c) of the DSU*, WT/DS27/15, 7 January 1998, DSR 1998:I, p. 3
EC – Chicken Cuts (Article 21.3(c))	Award of the Arbitrator, *European Communities – Customs Classification of Frozen Boneless Chicken Cuts – Arbitration under Article 21.3(c) of the DSU*, WT/DS269/13, WT/DS286/15, 20 February 2006
EC – Fasteners (China)	Appellate Body Report, *European Communities – Definitive Anti-Dumping Measures on Certain Iron or Steel Fasteners from China*, WT/DS397/AB/R, adopted 28 July 2011, DSR 2011:VII, p. 3995
EC – Hormones (Article 21.3(c))	Award of the Arbitrator, *EC Measures Concerning Meat and Meat Products (Hormones) – Arbitration under Article 21.3(c) of the DSU*, WT/DS26/15, WT/DS48/13, 29 May 1998, DSR 1998:V, p. 1833
EC – Tariff Preferences (Article 21.3(c))	Award of the Arbitrator, *European Communities – Conditions for the Granting of Tariff Preferences to Developing Countries – Arbitration under Article 21.3(c) of the DSU*, WT/DS246/14, 20 September 2004, DSR 2004:IX, p. 4313
Japan – DRAMs (Korea) (Article 21.3(c))	Award of the Arbitrator, *Japan – Countervailing Duties on Dynamic Random Access Memories from Korea – Arbitration under Article 21.3(c) of the DSU*, WT/DS336/16, 5 May 2008, DSR 2008:XX, p. 8553

Short title	Full case title and citation
Peru – Agricultural Products (Article 21.3(c))	Award of the Arbitrator, *Peru – Additional Duty on Imports of Certain Agricultural Products – Arbitration under Article 21.3(c) of the DSU, WT/DS457/15*, 16 December 2015
US – 1916 Act (Article 21.3(c))	Award of the Arbitrator, *United States – Anti-Dumping Act of 1916 – Arbitration under Article 21.3(c) of the DSU, WT/DS136/11, WT/DS162/14*, 28 February 2001, DSR 2001:V, p. 2017
US – COOL (Article 21.3(c))	Award of the Arbitrator, *United States – Certain Country of Origin Labelling (COOL) Requirements – Arbitration under Article 21.3(c) of the DSU, WT/DS384/24, WT/DS386/23*, 4 December 2012, DSR 2012:XIII, p. 7173
US – Countervailing Measures (China) (Article 21.3(c))	Award of the Arbitrator, *United States – Countervailing Duty Measures on Certain Products from China – Arbitration under Article 21.3(c) of the DSU, WT/DS437/16*, 9 October 2015
US – Offset Act (Byrd Amendment) (Article 21.3(c))	Award of the Arbitrator, *United States – Continued Dumping and Subsidy Offset Act of 2000 – Arbitration under Article 21.3(c) of the DSU, WT/DS217/14, WT/DS234/22*, 13 June 2003, DSR 2003:III, p. 1163
US – Oil Country Tubular Goods Sunset Reviews (Article 21.3(c))	Award of the Arbitrator, *United States – Sunset Reviews of Anti-Dumping Measures on Oil Country Tubular Goods from Argentina – Arbitration under Article 21.3(c) of the DSU, WT/DS268/12*, 7 June 2005, DSR 2005:XXIII, p. 11619
US – Anti-Dumping Methodologies (China)	Appellate Body Report, *United States – Certain Methodologies and Their Application to Anti-Dumping Proceedings Involving China, WT/DS471/AB/R and Add.1*, adopted 22 May 2017
US – Anti-Dumping Methodologies (China)	Panel Report, *United States – Certain Methodologies and Their Application to Anti-Dumping Proceedings Involving China, WT/DS471/R and Add.1*, adopted 22 May 2017, as modified by Appellate Body Report WT/DS471/AB/R
US – Shrimp II (Viet Nam)	Panel Report, *United States – Anti-Dumping Measures on Certain Shrimp from Viet Nam, WT/DS429/R and Add.1*, adopted 22 April 2015, upheld by Appellate Body Report WT/DS429/AB/R
US – Shrimp II (Viet Nam) (Article 21.3(c))	Award of the Arbitrator, *United States – Anti-Dumping Measures on Certain Shrimp from Viet Nam – Arbitration under Article 21.3(c) of the DSU, WT/DS429/12*, 15 December 2015
US – Shrimp and Sawblades	Panel Report, *United States – Anti-Dumping Measures on Certain Shrimp and Diamond Sawblades from China, WT/DS422/R and Add.1*, adopted 23 July 2012, DSR 2012:XIII, p. 7109
US – Stainless Steel (Mexico) (Article 21.3(c))	Award of the Arbitrator, *United States – Final Anti-Dumping Measures on Stainless Steel from Mexico – Arbitration under Article 21.3(c) of the DSU, WT/DS344/15*, 31 October 2008, DSR 2008:XX, p. 8619
US – Washing Machines (Article 21.3(c))	Award of the Arbitrator, *United States – Anti-Dumping and Countervailing Measures on Large Residential Washers from Korea – Arbitration under Article 21.3(c) of the DSU, WT/DS464/RPT*, 13 April 2017

1. INTRODUCTION

1.1   On 22 May 2017, the Dispute Settlement Body (DSB) adopted the Appellate Body Report[1] and the Panel Report[2] in *United States – Certain Methodologies and Their Application to Anti-Dumping Proceedings Involving China*. This dispute concerns China's challenge of certain methodologies used by the United States in anti-dumping investigations. The Panel found certain of the United States' measures at issue to be inconsistent "as such" or "as applied" with various provisions of the Agreement on Implementation of Article VI of the General Agreement on Tariffs and Trade 1994 (Anti-Dumping Agreement) and the General Agreement on Tariffs and Trade 1994 (GATT 1994). These Panel findings were not appealed by the United States and, in ruling on China's appeal, the Appellate Body did not make any additional findings of inconsistency with the covered agreements.

1.2   At the meeting of the DSB held on 19 June 2017, the United States indicated its intention to implement the DSB's recommendations and rulings in this dispute, and stated that it would need a reasonable period of time in which to do so.[3] On 11 July 2017, the United States and China sent a joint letter to the Chairman of the DSB. In their letter, the United States and China indicated that, in order to allow sufficient time to discuss a mutually agreed period of time for implementation, they had agreed that, in the event that an arbitration was requested under Article 21.3(c) of the Understanding on Rules and Procedures Governing the Settlement of Disputes (DSU), it should be completed no later than 60 days after the date of the appointment of an arbitrator, unless the arbitrator, following consultation with the parties, were to consider that additional time was required. In the same letter, the parties also confirmed that any award of the arbitrator, including an award not made within 90 days after the date of the DSB's recommendations and rulings in this dispute, would be deemed to be an award of the arbitrator for purposes of Article 21.3(c) of the DSU in determining the reasonable period of time for the United States to implement the recommendations and rulings of the DSB.[4]

1.3   By letter dated 17 October 2017, China informed the DSB that it had engaged in consultations with the United States on the reasonable period of time for implementation pursuant to Article 21.3(b) of the DSU, but that those consultations had not resulted in an agreement. China therefore requested that the reasonable period of time be determined through binding arbitration pursuant to Article 21.3(c) of the DSU. China expressed its intention to begin discussions with the United States with a view to reaching agreement on an arbitrator.[5]

---

[1]   WT/DS471/AB/R.
[2]   WT/DS471/R.
[3]   WT/DSB/M/398, para. 2.7.
[4]   WT/DS471/13.
[5]   WT/DS471/14.

1.4   By letter dated 30 October 2017, China informed the Director-General of the World Trade Organization (WTO) that it had engaged in consultations with the United States but that those consultations had not led to mutual agreement on an arbitrator. China therefore requested the Director-General to appoint an arbitrator pursuant to footnote 12 to Article 21.3(c) of the DSU.

1.5   After consulting with the parties, the Director-General appointed me as the Arbitrator on 7 November 2017.[6] On the same day, I informed the parties of my acceptance of the appointment as Arbitrator and transmitted to them a Working Schedule identifying the dates for the filing of the parties' written submissions and the date for the hearing.[7]

1.6   On 9 November 2017, the United States sent a letter requesting that the due date for its written submission be extended by one week, in light of pre-existing scheduling constraints affecting key members of its litigation team, as well as the need for cooperation between two federal agencies, namely, the United States Trade Representative (USTR) and the United States Department of Commerce (USDOC). On the same day, I invited China to comment on the United States' letter. On 10 November 2017, China sent a letter objecting to the United States' request. China argued that the reasons given by the United States did not justify the requested extension and that such extension would cause undue delay in this arbitration. However, in the event that an extension of the due date was granted for the United States' written submission, China requested that a similar extension be granted for its written submission.

1.7   Having taken account of the United States' request and China's comments, and in view of a number of meetings and other activities taking place in early December 2017, on 10 November 2017, I sent a revised Working Schedule to the parties. In accordance with the revised Working Schedule, the United States filed its written submission on 17 November 2017, and China filed its written submission on 27 November 2017. The parties elaborated on their positions and answered my questions at the hearing held on 8 December 2017. At the hearing, I indicated that every effort would be made to issue the Award in January 2018. The parties expressed no objection.

2.   ARGUMENTS OF THE PARTIES

2.1   Annexes A and B to this Award contain the executive summaries of the parties' submissions. Certain details of the parties' arguments are further described below, insofar as they are relevant to my analysis.

---

[6]   WT/DS471/15.

[7]   The Working Schedule of 7 November 2017 indicated that the written submission of the United States should be filed on 14 November 2017; the written submission of China should be filed on 21 November 2017; and the hearing would be held on 27 November 2017.

3.   REASONABLE PERIOD OF TIME

3.1   Introduction

3.1   I have been appointed by the Director-General, at the request of China, to determine the reasonable period of time for the United States to implement the recommendations and rulings of the DSB in *United States – Certain Methodologies and Their Application to Anti-Dumping Proceedings Involving China*.

3.2   The United States considers that I should determine that 24 months is a reasonable period of time for the United States to implement the DSB's recommendations and rulings in this dispute.[8] In China's view, the United States' proposal for 24 months "far exceeds what is reasonable under the circumstances" of this dispute[9], and submits that a period of 6 months is a reasonable period of time for implementation.[10]

3.3   In this section, I begin by setting out the mandate of an arbitrator under Article 21.3(c) of the DSU. I then identify the specific measures to be brought into conformity with the recommendations and rulings of the DSB. Finally, I examine the factors affecting the determination of the reasonable period of time in this dispute, including the steps in the implementation process, as well as circumstances particular to this dispute that the United States has asked me to take into account in reaching my determination.

3.2   Mandate of the Arbitrator under Article 21.3(c) of the DSU

3.4   Article 21.3 of the DSU provides, in relevant part:

> If it is impracticable to comply immediately with the recommendations and rulings [of the DSB], the Member concerned shall have a reasonable period of time in which to do so. The reasonable period of time shall be:
>
> ...
>
> (c)   a period of time determined through binding arbitration within 90 days after the date of adoption of the recommendations and rulings. In such arbitration, a guideline for the arbitrator should be that the reasonable period of time to implement panel or Appellate Body recommendations should not exceed 15 months from the date of adoption

---

[8]   United States' submission, paras. 9 and 55.
[9]   China's submission, para. 7.
[10]   China's submission, paras. 1 and 28.

of a panel or Appellate Body report. However, that time may be shorter or longer, depending upon the particular circumstances.[11]

3.5   The mandate of the arbitrator, pursuant to Article 21.3(c) of the DSU, is therefore to determine the time period within which the implementing Member must comply with the recommendations and rulings of the DSB.[12]

3.6   Article 21.3(c) provides a guideline for the arbitrator that the period of implementation should not exceed 15 months. According to the last sentence of Article 21.3(c), the "particular circumstances" of the dispute may affect the length of the reasonable period of time, making it "shorter or longer". Other provisions of the DSU also shed light on the mandate of an arbitrator. Article 21.1 states that "prompt compliance" with the DSB's recommendations and rulings "is essential in order to ensure effective resolution of disputes". Moreover, the introductory clause of Article 21.3 stipulates that a reasonable period of time for implementation shall be available only "[i]f it is impracticable to comply immediately with the [DSB's] recommendations and rulings". Article 21.2 directs an arbitrator to pay "particular attention … to matters affecting the interests of developing country Members with respect to measures which have been subject to dispute settlement".

3.7   The means of implementation chosen by the Member concerned is relevant to the determination of the reasonable period of time. As noted in past awards, "*when* a Member must comply cannot be determined in isolation from the means used for implementation."[13] Therefore, "to determine *when* a Member must comply, it may be necessary to consider *how* a Member proposes to do

---

[11]   Footnotes 12-13 omitted.

[12]   In response to questioning at the hearing in this arbitration, both the United States and China agreed that the following principles are relevant for the determination of the reasonable period of time for implementation:

The implementing Member has discretion to select the means of implementation that it deems most appropriate.

The implementing Member's discretion is not unfettered. Rather, the chosen method of implementation:

-    must be such that it could be implemented within a reasonable period of time in accordance with the guidelines contained in Article 21.3(c);
-    must be apt in form, nature, and content to effect compliance; and
-    should otherwise be consistent with the covered agreements.

The "particular circumstances" of a dispute may affect the arbitrator's calculation of the reasonable period of time, and may make it "shorter or longer".

While a Member is not required to utilize extraordinary procedures to bring its measures into compliance, it must nevertheless utilize all the flexibilities and discretion available within its legal and administrative system in order to implement within the shortest period of time possible.

[13]   Award of the Arbitrator, *US – COOL (Article 21.3(c))*, para. 68. (emphasis original)

so."[14] Consistent with previous awards of arbitrators under Article 21.3(c), the implementing Member has a measure of discretion in choosing the means of implementation that it deems most appropriate. This discretion, however, "is not an 'unfettered' right to choose any method of implementation".[15] Rather, it is relevant to consider, in particular, "whether the implementing action falls within the range of permissible actions that can be taken in order to implement the DSB's recommendations and rulings".[16] Thus, the chosen method of implementation must be apt in form, nature, and content to bring the Member into compliance with its WTO obligations.[17]

3.8   Inasmuch as they elaborate on those aspects of the measure at issue that were found to be inconsistent with WTO obligations, the findings by the panel in the underlying dispute offer guidance for determining whether the proposed implementing measures are apt to achieve compliance, as well as how long is reasonably needed to do so.[18] It is nevertheless beyond the mandate of an arbitrator under Article 21.3(c) to determine the consistency with the covered agreements of the measure that the implementing Member envisages to adopt in order to comply with the DSB's recommendations and rulings. This question, should it arise, is to be addressed in proceedings conducted pursuant to Article 21.5 of the DSU.[19] Arbitration under Article 21.3(c) of the DSU is limited to determining the period of time within which implementation of the recommendations and rulings of the DSB is to occur.[20]

3.9   As regards the length of the reasonable period of time, as noted above, Article 21.3(c) of the DSU provides a guideline for the arbitrator that this "should not exceed 15 months from the date of adoption of a panel or Appellate Body report". As set out above, Article 21.1 of the DSU provides that "prompt compliance" is essential for the effective resolution of WTO disputes, and the first clause of Article 21.3 stipulates that a "reasonable period of time" for implementation shall be available only "[i]f it is impracticable to comply immediately with the recommendations and rulings" of the DSB. According to the last sentence of Article 21.3(c), the "particular circumstances" of a dispute

---

[14]   Award of the Arbitrator, *Japan – DRAMs (Korea) (Article 21.3(c))*, para. 26. (emphasis original) See also Awards of the Arbitrators, *US – COOL (Article 21.3(c))*, para. 68; *US – Washing Machines (Article 21.3(c))*, para. 3.8.

[15]   Award of the Arbitrator, *Colombia – Ports of Entry (Article 21.3(c))*, para. 36.

[16]   Awards of the Arbitrators, *Brazil – Retreaded Tyres (Article 21.3(c)), para. 48; Japan – DRAMs (Korea) (Article 21.3(c))*, para. 27; *US – Stainless Steel (Mexico) (Article 21.3(c))*, para. 42.

[17]   See Awards of the Arbitrators, *Colombia – Ports of Entry (Article 21.3(c))*, para. 64; *China – GOES (Article 21.3(c))*, para. 3.2; *US – Countervailing Measures (China) (Article 21.3(c))*, para. 3.3; *Colombia □ Textiles (Article 21.3(c))*, para. 3.4; *US – Washing Machines (Article 21.3(c))*, para. 3.8.

[18]   See Award of the Arbitrator, *Colombia – Textiles (Article 21.3(c))*, paras. 3.5 and 3.39-3.40.

[19]   See Awards of the Arbitrators, *Japan – DRAMs (Korea) (Article 21.3(c))*, para. 27; *US – Countervailing Measures (China) (Article 21.3(c))*, para. 3.4; *Colombia – Textiles (Article 21.3(c))*, para. 3.6.

[20]   See Awards of the Arbitrators, *China – GOES (Article 21.3(c))*, para. 3.2; *US – Countervailing Measures (China) (Article 21.3(c))*, para. 3.4; *Peru – Agricultural Products (Article 21.3(c))*, para. 3.6; *US – Washing Machines (Article 21.3(c))*, para. 3.8.

may affect the length of the reasonable period of time, making it "shorter or longer". In this respect, previous arbitrators have considered that the reasonable period of time for implementation should, in principle, be the shortest period possible within the legal system of the implementing Member[21] that will enable it to achieve effective implementation of the DSB's recommendations and rulings[22], taking account of the "particular circumstances" of the dispute.[23]

3.10   In considering the "particular circumstances" under Article 21.3(c), previous arbitrators have found that the complexity of the implementation process and the nature of the steps to be taken for implementation are relevant to the determination of the reasonable period of time.[24] Previous arbitrators have also highlighted that the objective of "prompt compliance" calls for the implementing Member to utilize the flexibilities available within its legal system in implementing the relevant recommendations and rulings of the DSB in the shortest period of time possible.[25] However, an implementing Member is not expected to utilize "extraordinary procedures" to bring its measure into compliance[26], and implementation "must be effected in a transparent and efficient manner that affords due process to all interested parties".[27]

3.11   With regard to the burden of proof, it is well established that the implementing Member bears the overall burden to prove that the time period requested for implementation constitutes a "reasonable period of time".[28] However, this does not "absolve" the complaining Member of its duty to provide

---

[21]   See Awards of the Arbitrators, *EC – Hormones (Article 21.3(c))*, para. 26; *Japan – DRAMs (Korea) (Article 21.3(c))*, para. 25; *China – GOES (Article 21.3(c))*, para. 3.3; *US – Countervailing Measures (China) (Article 21.3(c))*, para. 3.5.

[22]   See Award of the Arbitrator, *US – Stainless Steel (Mexico) (Article 21.3(c))*, para. 53.

[23]   See Awards of the Arbitrators, *China – GOES (Article 21.3(c))*, para. 3.3; *US – Countervailing Measures (China) (Article 21.3(c))*, para. 3.5.

[24]   See Awards of the Arbitrators, *EC – Bananas III (Article 21.3(c))*, para. 19; *EC – Tariff Preferences (Article 21.3(c))*, para. 53; *US – Oil Country Tubular Goods Sunset Reviews (Article 21.3(c))*, para. 26; *US – Countervailing Measures (China) (Article 21.3(c))*, para. 3.19.

[25]   See Awards of the Arbitrators, *US □ Offset Act (Byrd Amendment) (Article 21.3(c))*, para. 64; *Japan – DRAMs (Korea) (Article 21.3(c))*, para. 25; *Brazil – Retreaded Tyres (Article 21.3(c))*, para. 48; *US – Stainless Steel (Mexico) (Article 21.3(c))*, para. 42; *China – GOES (Article 21.3(c))*, para. 3.4; *US – Countervailing Measures (China) (Article 21.3(c))*, para. 3.5; *US – Shrimp II (Viet Nam) (Article 21.3(c))*, para. 3.5; *Colombia – Textiles (Article 21.3(c))*, paras. 3.51-3.53.

[26]   See Awards of the Arbitrators, *US – Offset Act (Byrd Amendment) (Article 21.3(c))*, para. 74; *Japan – DRAMs (Korea) (Article 21.3(c))*, para. 25; *Brazil – Retreaded Tyres (Article 21.3(c))*, para. 48; *US – Stainless Steel (Mexico) (Article 21.3(c))*, para. 42; *US – COOL (Article 21.3(c))*, para. 70; *China – GOES (Article 21.3(c))*, para. 3.4; *US – Countervailing Measures (China) (Article 21.3(c))*, para. 3.5; *US – Washing Machines (Article 21.3(c))*, para. 3.9.

[27]   Award of the Arbitrator, *China – GOES (Article 21.3(c))*, para. 3.46. See also Awards of the Arbitrators, *US – Oil Country Tubular Goods Sunset Reviews (Article 21.3(c))*, para. 51; *Japan – DRAMS (Korea) (Article 21.3(c))*, para. 51; *US – Shrimp II (Viet Nam) (Article 21.3(c))*, para. 3.36.

[28]   See Awards of the Arbitrators, *Canada – Pharmaceutical Patents (Article 21.3(c))*, para. 47; *US – 1916 Act (Article 21.3(c))*, para. 33; *EC – Tariff Preferences (Article 21.3(c))*, para. 27; *China – GOES (Article 21.3(c))*, para. 3.5; *US – Countervailing Measures (China) (Article 21.3(c))*, para. 3.6; *US – Washing Machines (Article 21.3(c))*, para. 3.10.

evidence supporting why it disagrees with the period of time proposed by the implementing Member, and to substantiate its view that any shorter period of time for implementation that it proposes is reasonable.[29]

3.3 Measures to be Brought Into Conformity

3.12 The dispute underlying this arbitration concerns China's challenge of certain methodologies and their use by the USDOC in a number of anti-dumping proceedings. At the hearing, the parties accepted that the United States' implementing obligations relate to the findings made by the Panel that are set forth in paragraphs 8.1.a through 8.1.c of the Panel Report, and that the measures at issue could generally be summarized as follows[30]:

    a.   in respect of the Single Rate Presumption (SRP):

        i.   the USDOC's presumption that, in anti-dumping proceedings involving a non-market economy (NME), exporters form part of an NME-wide entity and are assigned a single anti-dumping duty rate unless each exporter demonstrates, through the fulfilment of the criteria set out in the "Separate Rate Test", an absence of *de jure* and *de facto* governmental control of its export activities[31]; and

        ii.   the USDOC's determinations to apply the SRP in the 38 anti-dumping determinations challenged by China (namely, 13 original investigations and 25 administrative reviews)[32];

    b.   in respect of the weighted average-to-transaction (W-T) methodology applied in three of the 38 anti-dumping determinations challenged by China (namely, three original investigations):

        i.   the USDOC's determinations to apply the W-T methodology on the basis of:

            -    its identification of a pattern of export prices which differ significantly among different purchasers, regions or time periods[33]; and

---

[29] Awards of the Arbitrators, *Colombia – Ports of Entry (Article 21.3(c))*, para. 67; *US – Washing Machines (Article 21.3(c))*, para. 3.10.
[30] At the hearing, China also referred to paragraph 6.7 of the Appellate Body Report in this dispute, where the Appellate Body declared certain Panel statements moot. However, China accepted that this finding does not create an additional implementation obligation for the United States.
[31] Panel Report, paras. 7.311 and 8.1.c.ii.
[32] Panel Report, para. 8.1.c.iii.
[33] Panel Report, para. 8.1.a.i. I note that the Panel's finding on this point pertains to two of the three original investigations at issue.

-    its explanation as to why such differences could not be taken into account by the comparison methodologies that are normally to be used[34];

ii.   the USDOC's application of the W-T methodology to all export transactions[35]; and

iii.   the USDOC's use of zeroing under the W-T methodology[36]; and

c.   the USDOC's use of zeroing under the W-T methodology in one of the 38 anti-dumping determinations challenged by China (namely, one administrative review).[37]

3.13   In ruling on the claims raised by China against these measures, the Panel found:

a.   the SRP to be inconsistent "as such" with Article 6.10 and Article 9.2 of the Anti-Dumping Agreement[38];

b.   the United States to have acted inconsistently with Article 6.10 and Article 9.2 of the Anti-Dumping Agreement because the USDOC applied the SRP in the 38 anti-dumping determinations challenged by China[39];

c.   the United States to have acted inconsistently with Article 2.4.2 of the Anti-Dumping Agreement because of certain steps taken by the USDOC in relation to the W-T methodology and its use of zeroing under the W-T methodology in three original anti-dumping investigations[40]; and

d.   the United States to have acted inconsistently with Article 2.4.2 of the Anti-Dumping Agreement and Article VI:2 of the GATT 1994 because of the USDOC's use of zeroing under the W-T methodology in one administrative review.[41]

3.14   Accordingly, for purposes of this arbitration, the United States' implementation obligations pertain to the recommendations and rulings of the DSB with respect to one finding of "as such" inconsistency pertaining to the SRP, as well as several findings of "as applied" inconsistency pertaining to the USDOC's use of the SRP in 38 anti-dumping determinations and the USDOC's use of the W-T methodology, including its use of zeroing under that methodology, in four of these 38 anti-dumping determinations.

---

[34]   Panel Report, para. 8.1.a.ii.
[35]   Panel Report, para. 8.1.a.iii.
[36]   Panel Report, para. 8.1.a.iv.
[37]   Panel Report, para. 8.1.b.
[38]   Panel Report, para. 8.1.c.ii.
[39]   Panel Report, para. 8.1.c.iii.
[40]   Panel Report, paras. 8.1.a.i-8.1.a.iv.
[41]   Panel Report, para. 8.1.b.

3.4   Factors Affecting the Determination of the Reasonable Period of time

3.15   The United States considers that I should determine that 24 months is a reasonable period of time for implementing the DSB's recommendations and rulings in this dispute, due to "the number and magnitude of modifications to the challenged measures, the procedural requirements under U.S. law, the complexity of the issues involved, and the current resource demands and constraints on the USDOC".[42] The United States highlights "the breadth and complexity of the DSB's recommendations", in particular in light of the "as applied" findings, which relate to 38 anti-dumping determinations, and "the significant additional analysis that the USDOC likely will be required to undertake".[43] Regarding the chosen means of implementation, the United States intends to undertake two distinct sets of proceedings: (i) one proceeding pursuant to Section 123(g) of the Uruguay Round Agreements Act (URAA)[44] to address the "as such" recommendations and rulings of the DSB pertaining to the SRP; and (ii) 38 separate proceedings pursuant to Section 129(b) of the URAA[45] to address the DSB's "as applied" recommendations and rulings relating to the USDOC's use of the SRP in 38 anti-dumping determinations, as well as its use of the W-T methodology, and zeroing under that methodology, in certain of those determinations.[46] According to the United States, while these two sets of proceedings must be undertaken sequentially, there can be "a small degree of overlap" between them.[47] In particular, the United States proposes to commence the Section 129 proceedings once the preliminary determination in the Section 123 proceeding has been issued.[48]

3.16   China does not question the USDOC's recourse to proceedings under Section 123 and Section 129 of the URAA for purposes of implementation in this dispute.[49] In particular, China does not question that a Section 123 proceeding is an appropriate way to implement the DSB's "as such" recommendations and rulings pertaining to the SRP. Nor does China object to the degree of overlap between these proceedings that the United States indicates would occur. Rather, China accepts as reasonable the United States' proposal to commence the proceedings pursuant to Section 129 once the preliminary determination pursuant to Section 123 has been issued.[50] China nevertheless

---

[42]   United States' submission, para. 10.

[43]   United States' submission, para. 9.

[44]   Codified as *United States Code*, Title 19, Section 3533(g) (contained in Exhibit USA-1).

[45]   Codified as *United States Code*, Title 19, Section 3538(b) (contained in Exhibit USA-2).

[46]   United States' submission, para. 30. The United States refers to the Section 123 proceeding and the Section 129 proceedings as "Phase I" and "Phase II" of the implementation process, respectively. (*Ibid.*, paras. 7 and 18)

[47]   United States' submission, para. 26. See also para. 49 (United States' proposed timetable).

[48]   United States' submission, paras. 7 and 26.

[49]   China's submission, paras. 35-36; opening statement and response to questioning at the hearing.

[50]   China's submission, paras. 27, 36, and 38; opening statement and response to questioning at the hearing.

argues that the amount of time sought by the United States, both for its Section 123 proceeding and for the multiple Section 129 proceedings, is "unreasonably long" in the circumstances of this case.[51]

3.17 In my analysis below, I first address the parties' arguments concerning the specific steps to be taken by the United States in proceedings under Section 123 and Section 129, as well as the period of time that is reasonably required to complete such steps. I then address the particular circumstances of this dispute alleged by the parties to be relevant to my determination of the reasonable period of time.

3.4.1 Steps in the implementation process

3.18 As indicated above, the parties agree that the implementation of the DSB's "as such" recommendations and rulings can and should take place through a proceeding under Section 123 of the URAA and that the implementation of the DSB's "as applied" recommendations and rulings pertaining to the 38 anti-dumping determinations challenged by China can and should take place through separate proceedings under Section 129 of the URAA. The parties disagree, however, on the time period necessary to conduct such proceedings. The subsections below address, in turn, the implementation of the DSB's "as such" recommendations and rulings through a Section 123 proceeding concerning the SRP, and the implementation of the DSB's "as applied" recommendations and rulings concerning the 38 anti-dumping determinations at issue through separate Section 129 proceedings.

3.4.1.1 Implementation of the DSB's "as such" recommendations and rulings pertaining to the SRP

3.19 In order to implement the DSB's recommendations and rulings pertaining to the Panel's "as such" finding regarding the SRP, the United States intends to utilize the process set out in Section 123(g) of the URAA. In addition, the United States indicates that, prior to the commencement of this process, it needs time to conduct "inter-agency consultations" and related activity[52] so as to allow the USTR and the USDOC to consider the options available for implementation.[53] In considering the period of time required to complete both, the initial period of inter-agency consultations and related activity, and the

---

[51] China's submission, para. 36.

[52] In its proposed timetable, the United States explains that, during this period, the USTR and the USDOC consult, "pre-commencement analysis preparation" is undertaken, and the USDOC "begins devising methodologies to implement adverse findings in preparation for commencement of section 123 and section 129 proceedings". (United States' submission, para. 49)

[53] United States' submission, para. 32. In its proposed timetable, the United States indicates that this preliminary step took place from May to December 2017 (i.e. approximately 7 months following the adoption of the Panel and Appellate Body Reports on 22 May 2017). (*Ibid.*, para. 49)

Section 123 proceeding, the United States emphasizes the "complexity" of the issues involved and the "far-reaching impact" of the implementation process.[54] In total, the United States claims that 15 months are required to address the DSB's "as such" recommendations and rulings pertaining to the SRP.[55] According to the United States, this amount of time is to be allocated as follows: approximately 7 months for the initial inter-agency consultations and related activity; approximately 4 months to issue the preliminary determination once the Section 123 proceeding has commenced; and approximately 4 months to issue the final determination in the Section 123 proceeding.[56]

3.20   China disputes that the implementation of the DSB's "as such" recommendations and rulings is nearly as complicated as the United States suggests.[57] In this context, China contends that the reasonable period of time should not include any time after the adoption of the Panel and Appellate Body Reports for preparatory work because the USTR and the USDOC had at least 7 months prior to the adoption of those reports to undertake such work.[58] Moreover, China contests the amount of time that the United States claims it requires to issue the preliminary and the final determinations. China submits that, in the present dispute, the United States requires only 15 days to issue a preliminary determination[59] and that the additional time allocated for the United States to issue the final determination "should be brief".[60]

3.21   Section 123(g)(1) and (2) of the URAA reads[61]:

(g)   Requirements for agency action

(1)   Changes in agency regulations or practice

In any case in which a dispute settlement panel or the Appellate Body finds in its report that a regulation or practice of a department or agency of the United States is inconsistent with any of the Uruguay Round Agreements, that regulation or practice may not be amended, rescinded, or otherwise modified in the implementation of such report unless and until—

---

[54]   United States' submission, para. 35. See also heading II:B of that submission, where the United States refers to the "legal and technical complexity of this matter".
[55]   United States' submission, paras. 24 and 36.
[56]   United States' submission, para. 49.
[57]   China's submission, para. 34.
[58]   China's submission, para. 25. See also para. 39.
[59]   China's submission, paras. 44 and 46.
[60]   China's submission, para. 47.
[61]   Section 123(g)(1) and (2) of the URAA (contained in Exhibit USA-1).

(A)   the appropriate congressional committees have been consulted under subsection (f)[62];

(B)   the Trade Representative has sought advice regarding the modification from relevant private sector advisory committees established under section 135 of the Trade Act of 1974 (19 U.S.C. 2155);

(C)   the head of the relevant department or agency has provided an opportunity for public comment by publishing in the Federal Register the proposed modification and the explanation for the modification;

(D)   the Trade Representative has submitted to the appropriate congressional committees a report describing the proposed modification, the reasons for the modification, and a summary of the advice obtained under subparagraph (B) with respect to the modification;

(E)   the Trade Representative and the head of the relevant department or agency have consulted with the appropriate congressional committees on the proposed contents of the final rule or other modification; and

(F)   the final rule or other modification has been published in the Federal Register.

(2)   Effective date of modification

A final rule or other modification to which paragraph (1) applies may not go into effect before the end of the 60-day period beginning on the date on which consultations under paragraph (1)(E) begin, unless the president determines that an earlier effective date is in the national interest.

---

[62]   Subsection (f) refers to "[a]ctions upon circulation of reports" and requires that:
Promptly after the circulation of a report of a panel or of the Appellate Body to WTO members in a proceeding described in subsection (d) of this section, the Trade Representative shall—
(1) notify the appropriate congressional committees of the report;
(2) in the case of a report of a panel, consult with the appropriate congressional committees concerning the nature of any appeal that may be taken of the report; and
(3) if the report is adverse to the United States, consult with the appropriate congressional committees concerning whether to implement the report's recommendation and, if so, the manner of such implementation and the period of time needed for such implementation.
(Section 123(f) of the URAA (contained in Exhibit USA-1))

3.22   Pursuant to Section 123(g)(1), proceedings under that section are used to amend, rescind, or otherwise modify regulations or practices of a department or agency of the United States in response to a WTO dispute settlement panel or Appellate Body report. In the present dispute, the Panel found the SRP to be a norm of general and prospective application that could be challenged "as such" in WTO dispute settlement.[63] In reaching this conclusion, the Panel stressed, *inter alia*, the "consistent application" of the SRP since 1991, demonstrating "a pattern of conduct by the USDOC that one can reasonably expect will be followed in the future".[64] I understand the parties to agree that Section 123(g) can and should be used to address the Panel's "as such" finding of inconsistency pertaining to the SRP.[65]

3.23   The parties further agree that subparagraphs (A) through (F) of Section 123(g)(1) above identify the steps involved in a Section 123 proceeding.[66] I note that the only prescribed time period is found in Section 123(g)(2), which provides that, normally, the final rule or modification may not go into effect until at least 60 days after the USTR and the USDOC have consulted with the relevant congressional committees on the proposed modification. As confirmed by the United States at the hearing, there are no other prescribed time periods for a proceeding under Section 123 or for the individual steps involved. I understand from the parties' explanations at the hearing that some of the steps of a Section 123 proceeding can take place concurrently. According to the United States, whereas a necessary first step of the process is for the USTR to begin consulting with the appropriate congressional committees in line with the requirements of subparagraph (A), the USTR is able to seek advice from relevant private sector advisory committees at the same time that the public is afforded an opportunity to comment on the proposal, as provided for in steps (B) and (C).[67] The United States nevertheless stressed that step (D), which involves preparing a report for the relevant congressional committees, can take place only after steps (B) and (C) are completed, since the report in question must summarize the results of the private sector consultations and public comments on the proposed modification. It also seems logical that the consultations with congressional committees foreseen in step (E) could be expected to occur only after submission of the report referenced in step (D). I further understand that no public notice is given of the date of commencement of a Section 123 proceeding (step (A)), and that step (C), which involves publishing the proposed modification and the explanation for the modification in the Federal Register, corresponds to the

---

[63]   Panel Report, paras. 7.339 and 8.1.c.ii.
[64]   Panel Report, paras. 7.336 and 7.337, respectively.
[65]   United States' submission, para. 7; China's submission, para. 36; parties' responses to questioning at the hearing.
[66]   United States' submission, para. 31; China's submission, para. 37; parties' responses to questioning at the hearing.
[67]   By contrast, China considers that all of the steps described in subparagraphs (A), (B), and (C) can be conducted concurrently. (China's response to questioning at the hearing)

"preliminary determination" referred to by the parties in their submissions.[68] I note that the date by which step (C) can reasonably be completed in the context of the present dispute is of particular significance since the parties agree that the implementation of the DSB's "as applied" recommendations and rulings through proceedings under Section 129 of the URAA should commence upon issuance of the preliminary determination under Section 123.

3.24   The parties disagree on the time necessary to complete the process under Section 123 in implementing the DSB's "as such" recommendations and rulings in this dispute and, in particular, on the time that is required for preparatory work and until issuance of a preliminary determination under Section 123. As set out above, the United States indicates that it requires 7 months from the adoption of the Panel and Appellate Body Reports to conduct inter-agency consultations and related activity prior to commencing a Section 123 proceeding. Regarding the time required to issue the preliminary determination once the proceeding under Section 123 has commenced, the United States submits that approximately 4 months are required. In support of these proposed time periods, the United States highlights the complexity of the issues at hand in this dispute, in particular since it is the first time that the United States is required to conduct such a modification of the SRP.[69]

3.25   By contrast, China maintains that no time after the DSB's adoption of the Panel and Appellate Body Reports should be awarded for inter-agency consultations and related activity.[70] China argues that the United States had ample time to conduct inter-agency consultations and analysis preparation prior to the adoption of these reports.[71] Similarly, according to China, 15 days are sufficient to issue the preliminary determination in light of the United States' awareness of the WTO-inconsistency of the SRP prior to the adoption of the Panel and Appellate Body Reports.[72]

3.26   Thus, in setting out their respective positions as to the time periods required to conduct inter-agency consultations and related activity, and to issue the preliminary determination, the parties mainly disagree on the complexity of implementing the "as such" recommendations and rulings of the DSB and the steps that the United States could and should have undertaken prior to the adoption of the Panel and Appellate Body Reports.

3.27   I first address China's argument that the United States should have begun taking steps towards implementation prior to the adoption of the Panel and Appellate Body Reports, whether in the form of inter-agency consultations or

---

[68]   Similarly, I understand that step (F), which involves publishing the final rule or other modification in the Federal Register, corresponds to the "final determination" referred to by the parties in their submissions.
[69]   United States' response to questioning at the hearing.
[70]   China's submission, para. 25.
[71]   China's submission, paras. 39-40. See also para. 25.
[72]   China's submission, para. 46; opening statement and response to questioning at the hearing.

other preparatory work prior to the commencement of the Section 123 process, or under Section 123 after the process had commenced.[73] In its written submission, China emphasizes that, although the reasonable period of time for implementation is measured as from the date of adoption of the panel and Appellate Body reports[74], to date, the United States "has not commenced any proceedings to revise or repeal its WTO-inconsistent measures and does not intend to begin to do so until [December 2017]".[75] Yet, China points out that the United States has known that the SRP is WTO-inconsistent since November 2014, when the panel report in *US – Shrimp II (Viet Nam)* was circulated. China highlights that the panel in that dispute also found the SRP to be WTO-inconsistent, and the United States did not appeal that finding.[76] China adds that, at the latest, the United States has known that it would have to bring certain of its measures, including the SRP, into conformity with the WTO agreements since November 2016, when the United States decided not to appeal the findings of inconsistency contained in the Panel Report in this dispute.[77] China also relies on Section 123(f)(3) of the URAA, which requires the USTR to consult with the appropriate congressional committees as to the manner of implementation "promptly after the circulation" of a panel or Appellate Body report. According to China, the USTR was thus required to enter into such consultations after the United States' decision not to appeal the Panel Report in November 2016.[78]

3.28   As an initial matter, I note that previous arbitrators have considered consultations within government agencies to be a typical aspect of "law-making", and that, regardless of whether they are mandated by law, the time needed to undertake such consultations should be taken into account in determining a reasonable period of time for implementation.[79] In the specific context of this dispute, taking appropriate time for preparatory work – whether in the form of inter-agency consultations, other preparatory work, or consultations with appropriate congressional committees under Section 123(g)(1)(A) – could serve a useful and important purpose in ensuring that the resulting methodology will be consistent with the covered agreements. In

---

[73]   China's submission, paras. 42-43 and 46.
[74]   China's submission, para. 3.
[75]   China's submission, para. 5 (referring to United States' submission, para. 49 (United States' proposed timetable)). See also para. 22 and fn 28 thereto.
[76]   China's submission, para. 4 (referring to Panel Report, *US – Shrimp II (Viet Nam)*, para. 8.1.c).
[77]   China's submission, para. 4.
[78]   China's submission, para. 42. The United States argued at the hearing that Section 123(f)(3) does not require it to start implementation upon circulation of the relevant reports, and reiterated that implementation obligations arise as of the date of the DSB's recommendations and rulings. The United States further explained that consultations with Congress that take place prior to the adoption of the relevant reports pertain mainly to whether the United States will declare its intention to implement the reports' findings. (United States' response to questioning at the hearing)
[79]   Award of the Arbitrator, *Chile – Price Band System (Article 21.3(c))*, para. 42. See Awards of the Arbitrators, *Chile – Alcoholic Beverages (Article 21.3(c))*, para. 43; *US – Hot-Rolled Steel*, para. 38.

particular, such preparatory work could facilitate (and therefore reduce the time required to undertake) subsequent steps in the implementation process.

3.29   Like previous arbitrators, I consider that formal implementation steps need only be taken after the adoption of the relevant panel and Appellate Body reports. .[80] By the time of the hearing in this arbitration, over 6 months had elapsed since the DSB's adoption of the Panel and Appellate Body Reports in this dispute. According to the United States, it has taken implementation steps in the form of inter-agency consultations during that time.[81] In addition, the United States indicated at the hearing that consultations with the relevant congressional committees required by Section 123(g)(1)(A) are ongoing.[82] The United States also clarified that there are no public records of these preliminary steps.[83] I accept that some degree of consultation among the USDOC, the USTR, and the relevant congressional committees has already occurred. Nonetheless, in the absence of specific information from the United States about these consultations, the nature and timing of this preparatory work is unclear.

3.30   Whereas implementation obligations arise as of the date of the DSB's recommendations and rulings, I consider that circumstances pre-dating the adoption of the relevant panel or Appellate Body reports may in some instances bear on the determination of the reasonable period of time.[84] I am aware that the United States did not appeal the Panel's finding of "as such" inconsistency pertaining to the SRP. Therefore, the United States was, at least to a certain extent, in a position to begin considering its options for implementation prior to the adoption of the Panel and Appellate Body Reports in this dispute.[85] Moreover, as I will explain below, I am not persuaded that the implementation options available to the United States are especially numerous or complex. Thus, while I accept that preparatory work in the form of "inter-agency consultations" between the USDOC and the USTR or consultations with "appropriate congressional committees" is justified and, indeed, may well contribute to expediting the remaining steps in the implementation process, I do not consider

---

[80]   Award of the Arbitrator, *US – Countervailing Measures (China) (Article 21.3(c))*, para. 3.44. The parties agree that the reasonable period of time for implementation is measured as from the date of adoption of the relevant panel and Appellate Body reports. (United States' submission, para. 49; China's submission, para. 3)

[81]   United States' submission, para. 32. See also para. 49 (United States' proposed timetable).

[82]   In this respect, I note that, pursuant to Section 123(f)(3) of the URAA, the USTR shall consult with the appropriate congressional committees as to the manner of implementation of the report "promptly after the circulation" of a panel or Appellate Body report. (See *supra*, fn 62)

[83]   United States' response to questioning at the hearing.

[84]   See also Awards of the Arbitrators, *US – COOL (Article 21.3(c))*, para. 84; *China – GOES (Article 21.3(c))*, para. 3.30.

[85]   I also note that, in *US – Shrimp II (Viet Nam) (Article 21.3(c))*, the United States indicated that consultations and other preparatory work had been undertaken in relation to the panel's "as such" finding. (Award of the Arbitrator, *US – Shrimp II (Viet Nam) (Article 21.3(c))*, para. 3.33) In that case, the panel's "as such" finding at issue equally related to the USDOC's rebuttable presumption that all companies within an NME country belong to a single, NME-wide entity and that a single rate is assigned to that entity. (Panel Report, *US – Shrimp II (Viet Nam)*, para. 7.122)

that as many months are needed for these initial steps as the United States contends. I understand, as well, that these consultations in any event continue while the Section 123 process is ongoing.[86] I further recall that Article 21.1 of the DSU expressly identifies prompt compliance with the recommendations and rulings of the DSB as "essential in order to ensure effective resolution of disputes to the benefit of all Members" and that implementing Members are expected to use the flexibilities available to them within their domestic legal system to achieve such prompt compliance.

3.31   I now turn to the United States' argument that implementing the DSB's "as such" recommendations and rulings in this dispute is particularly complex.[87] In this context, the United States emphasizes that it has several options for implementing the DSB's "as such" recommendations and rulings. According to the United States, the USDOC may need to consider, *inter alia*: (i) the kind and quantity of evidence required to establish governmental control over the exporters' export activities; (ii) the bases for requesting information from examined exporters regarding government ownership and control; and (iii) procedural matters associated with the collection and examination of such information.[88] At the hearing, the United States further emphasized the importance of background work in considering these options during the Section 123 process.[89] China takes issue with the alleged complexity of the implementation of the DSB's "as such" recommendations and rulings regarding the SRP. China contends that implementation is "straightforward" given that the United States is merely required to withdraw its practice of applying the SRP.[90]

3.32   I recall that, in the present dispute, the DSB's "as such" recommendations and rulings pertain to one Panel finding regarding the SRP. I further recall that, under the SRP, the USDOC presumes that, in anti-dumping proceedings involving an NME, exporters form part of an NME-wide entity and are assigned a single anti-dumping duty rate unless each exporter demonstrates an absence of *de jure* and *de facto* governmental control of its export activities.[91] I am not convinced that implementation in this case is necessarily straightforward, as China contends. Although the Panel found the SRP to be inconsistent "as such"

---

[86]   At the hearing, the United States explained that background substantive work continues throughout the Section 123 process. (United States' response to questioning at the hearing)

[87]   In its written submission, the United States also refers to the "novelty" of the issues in the present dispute. (United States' submission, para. 35) However, at the hearing, the United States acknowledged that this was not the first time that a presumption similar to the SRP was found to be inconsistent "as such" with Articles 6.10 and 9.2 of the Anti-Dumping Agreement. The United States further clarified that its argument regarding any alleged novelty was in fact one relating to the complexity of addressing its implementation obligations in this dispute given that this is the first time that the United States is required to revise the SRP. (United States' response to questioning at the hearing)

[88]   United States' submission, paras. 23 and 32.

[89]   United States' response to questioning at the hearing.

[90]   China's submission, para. 47.

[91]   See Panel Report, para. 7.311.

with Articles 6.10 and 9.2 of the Anti-Dumping Agreement, it also agreed with the Appellate Body in *EC – Fasteners (China)* that "an investigating authority may treat multiple exporters as a single entity if it finds, through an objective affirmative determination, that there exists a situation that would signal that two or more legally distinct exporters are in such a relationship that they should be treated as a single entity."[92] Importantly, as noted above, the implementing Member has discretion in choosing the means of implementation it deems most appropriate. Moreover, while Article 3.7 of the DSU refers to the "withdrawal" of an inconsistent measure, it is clear that the obligation to bring a measure into conformity can also be met through modification of the measure found to be WTO-inconsistent.[93]

3.33   At the same time, I do not consider that implementation will necessarily be as complicated as the United States suggests. The United States explained at the hearing that it is considering the numerous possible options available to address the DSB's "as such" recommendations and rulings.[94] The United States views the development of an alternative analysis for single-exporter treatment as a WTO-consistent option for implementation in this dispute, and adds that this might entail a move from a presumption to a fact-based, case-by-case analysis.[95] In my view, while there may be a number of factors to be considered under such an option, there is a limit to the possible parameters that may be identified as relevant to the conduct of a case-specific factual analysis of this nature.[96] I also recall that no specific time periods are prescribed for any of the steps preceding the issuance of a preliminary determination under Section 123(g). Moreover, I note that Section 123 proceedings have been utilized by the United States in a

---

[92]   Panel Report, para. 7.361 (referring to Appellate Body Report, *EC – Fasteners (China)*, para. 376).

[93]   Awards of the Arbitrators, *US – Offset Act (Byrd Amendment) (Article 21.3(c))*, para. 50; *Japan – DRAMs (Korea) (Article 21.3(c))*, para. 27; *Brazil – Retreaded Tyres (Article 21.3(c))*, para. 71; *US – COOL (Article 21.3(c))*, para. 77; *US – Countervailing Measures (China) (Article 21.3(c))*, para. 3.18.

[94]   United States' opening statement at the hearing. See also United States' submission, para. 23.

[95]   United States' opening statement and response to questioning at the hearing.

[96]   In this context, I also note the United States' use of the Separate Rate Test as part of the SRP. As set out by the Panel, in order to overcome the presumption of governmental control and be eligible for a separate dumping margin and duty rate, the SRP requires individual exporters to make a specific request to that effect and to pass the Separate Rate Test, which contains certain conditions aimed to establish *de jure* and *de facto* independence from governmental control. With respect to *de jure* governmental control, the USDOC evaluates the relevant laws, regulations, and other enactments in order to ascertain whether there is: (a) an absence of restrictive stipulations associated with an individual exporter's business and export licences; (b) any legislative enactments decentralizing control of companies; and (c) any other formal measures by the central and/or local government decentralizing control of companies. As for *de facto* governmental control, the USDOC assesses whether: (a) the export prices are set by, or subject to the approval of, government authority; (b) the exporter has the authority to negotiate and sign contracts and other agreements; (c) the exporter has autonomy from the government in making decisions regarding the selection of management; and (d) the exporter retains the proceeds of its export sales and makes independent decisions regarding the disposition of profits or financing of losses. (Panel Report, para. 7.361 and fn 587 to para. 7.311)

---

number of prior disputes for purposes of implementing the DSB's recommendations and rulings and that, on some occasions, the United States indicated that a much shorter period of time would be sufficient to complete the entire process.[97]

3.34   On the basis of the foregoing, I consider that the United States could reasonably conduct the necessary preparatory work and issue the preliminary determination under Section 123 in respect of the DSB's "as such" recommendations and rulings concerning the SRP in significantly less time than the 11 months it claims are needed. As the same time, I do not consider that the United States can reasonably be expected to issue this preliminary determination within the 15 days proposed by China.

3.35   Finally, I recall that the parties disagree on the length of time that the United States requires to complete the Section 123 process through the issuance of a final determination. The United States' proposed timetable indicates that, once the preliminary determination is issued, it requires approximately 4 additional months to issue the final determination under Section 123.[98] The United States emphasized that this time period is necessary to, *inter alia*, consider and address all comments received in response to its proposal before it can publish a final modification in the Federal Register.[99] China disagrees and submits that the allocated time "should be brief and the process should consist mostly of formalities".[100] At the hearing, China explained that it had not proposed a particular length of time for this step given that both parties agree that the Section 129 proceedings to implement the DSB's "as applied" recommendations and rulings will commence as from the issuance of the preliminary determination in the Section 123 proceeding.[101]

3.36   As a general matter, the full timeframe within which a Section 123 proceeding can be completed is relevant to the determination of the reasonable period of time for implementation by the United States pursuant to that provision. In this dispute, however, as the final stage of the Section 123 proceeding will proceed in parallel with the Section 129 proceedings, the date by which the Section 123 proceeding may reasonably be completed is not relevant to the determination of the reasonable period of time. This is because of the overlap between the Section 123 and Section 129 proceedings. Both parties agree that the Section 129 proceedings should begin upon issuance of the preliminary Section 123 determination. Both parties also agree that the time reasonably needed to undertake the Section 129 proceedings will inevitably exceed the time needed between the preliminary and final Section 123

---

[97]   See Awards of the Arbitrators, *US – Oil Country Tubular Goods Sunset Review (Article 21.3(c))*, para. 7; *US – Stainless Steel (Mexico) (Article 21.3(c))*, para. 56.
[98]   United States' submission, para. 49.
[99]   United States' submission, para. 35.
[100]   China's submission, para. 47.
[101]   China's response to questioning at the hearing.

determinations. Put differently, it is clear that it is the end of the Section 129 proceedings that will determine the end of the reasonable period of time for implementation in this dispute, and it is also clear that the Section 123 proceeding will be completed before the end of the Section 129 proceedings. For these reasons, I do not consider it necessary to address further how much time should reasonably be allocated for the USDOC to issue the final determination in the Section 123 proceeding.

3.4.1.2   Implementation of the DSB's "as applied" recommendations and rulings pertaining to the 38 anti-dumping determinations at issue

3.37   As indicated above, the United States plans to address the DSB's recommendations and rulings regarding the Panel's "as applied" findings through multiple proceedings under Section 129 of the URAA. These findings concern the USDOC's use of the SRP in 38 anti-dumping determinations, as well as its use of the W-T methodology, and zeroing under that methodology, in certain of those determinations.[102] The United States claims that it will need approximately 13 months to complete these proceedings[103], as from the date of issuance of the preliminary determination in the proceeding under Section 123 of the URAA.

3.38   Section 129(b) and (d) of the URAA states[104]:

(b)   Action by administering authority

(1)   Consultations with administering authority and congressional committees

Promptly after a report by a dispute settlement panel or the Appellate Body is issued that contains findings that an action by the administering authority in a proceeding under title VII of the Tariff Act of 1930 is not in conformity with the obligations of the United States under the Antidumping Agreement or the Agreement on Subsidies and Countervailing Measures, the Trade Representative shall consult with the administering authority and the congressional committees on the matter.

(2)   Determination by administering authority

Notwithstanding any provision of the Tariff Act of 1930, the administering authority shall, within 180 days after receipt of a written request from the Trade Representative, issue a determination in connection with the particular proceeding that would render the administering authority's action described in

---

[102]   The United States refers to the Section 129 proceedings as "Phase II" of its implementation process. (United States' submission, paras. 7 and 18)
[103]   United States' submission, para. 49.
[104]   Section 129(b) and (d) of the URAA (contained in Exhibit USA-2).

paragraph (1) not inconsistent with the findings of the panel or the Appellate Body.

(3)   Consultations before implementation

Before the administering authority implements any determination under paragraph (2), the Trade Representative shall consult with the administering authority and the congressional committees with respect to such determination.

(4)   Implementation of recommendation

The Trade Representative may, after consulting with the administering authority and the congressional committees under paragraph (3), direct the administering authority to implement, in whole or in part, the determination made under paragraph (2).

...

(d)   Opportunity for comment by interested parties

Prior to issuing a determination under this section, the administering authority or the Commission, as the case may be, shall provide interested parties with an opportunity to submit written comments and, in appropriate cases, may hold a hearing, with respect to the determination.

3.39   The parties agree that Section 129 proceedings, in which the USDOC will carry out "redeterminations", are an appropriate means under US law for implementing the DSB's "as applied" recommendations and rulings with respect to the 38 anti-dumping determinations.[105] They both also accept that subparagraphs (1) through (4) above identify the steps involved in a Section 129 proceeding[106] and that these four steps are carried out sequentially. I also understand both parties to accept that, in this dispute, the USDOC's "redeterminations" should commence once the preliminary determination in the Section 123 proceeding has been issued.[107] The parties' views, however, diverge on the extent to which the multiple redeterminations that are needed can be conducted concurrently, and on the time required for these steps, notably with respect to: (i) the significance of the reference to a period of 180 days in Section 129(b)(2); and (ii) whether my determination of the reasonable period of time for implementation should account for the time that may be needed for the USDOC to conduct hearings and verifications in the Section 129 proceedings.

---

[105] United States' submission, paras. 6-7; China's submission, para. 36; China's response to questioning at the hearing.
[106] United States' submission, paras. 38-39; China's submission, para. 49; parties' responses to questioning at the hearing.
[107] United States' submission, paras. 7 and 26; China's submission, paras. 27, 36 and 38; China's response to questioning at the hearing.

3.40   The United States' proposed timetable for implementation indicates that the Section 129 proceedings will commence in April 2018, once the preliminary determination in the Section 123 proceedings has been issued.[108] The United States contends that a separate Section 129 proceeding will be needed for each of the 38 anti-dumping determinations found to be WTO-inconsistent.[109] Furthermore, given the number of redeterminations to be carried out pursuant to Section 129, the United States anticipates that the USDOC will need to divide these 38 proceedings into three distinct tranches. The United States explains that the rationale for this "staggered" approach is due to the administrative burden on the USDOC, as well as overlapping deadlines for interested parties and the USDOC.[110] The commencement of the three tranches is expected in April, May, and June of 2018, respectively. The United States' proposed timetable[111] suggests that, between April and November 2018, the USDOC will: (i) "finalize [its] staggered schedule, considering, for example, whether tranches are staggered by product or by type of determination, e.g., investigation rather than administrative review"; (ii) collect additional information through, *inter alia*, the development, finalization, and issuance of questionnaires and/or information requests, the receipt of comments upon the responses received, and the development and issuance of possible follow-up questions and comments[112]; and (iii) determine the approach to be used for the first tranche of preliminary Section 129 determinations. According to the United States, the USDOC will continue to work in tranches until December 2018, by when preliminary determinations in all three tranches will have been issued. The United States adds that, between October 2018 and March 2019, the USDOC will afford interested parties the opportunity to comment on these preliminary determinations; that the USDOC may need to hold hearings and/or conduct verifications; and that the USDOC will also analyse comments received. According to the United States, the USDOC will be able to complete its work on the three tranches, including issuance of the final Section 129 determinations and addressing any ministerial error allegations relating to them, in the 3-month period ending in May 2019. Also in May 2019, the United States expects the USTR and the USDOC to engage in consultations with congressional

---

[108]   United States' submission, para. 49.

[109]   United States' submission, para. 40; response to questioning at the hearing. In its submission, the United States notes that the Section 129 proceedings for each of the 38 determinations, including the 13 original investigations and 25 administrative reviews, "likely" would need to be separate. (United States' submission, para. 40) At the hearing, the United States clarified that the use of the term "likely" is to denote a future occurrence and is not meant to suggest that it is contemplating anything different.

[110]   At the hearing, the United States clarified that these overlapping deadlines occur as interested parties often have the same private counsel. (United States' response to questioning at the hearing)

[111]   United States' submission, para. 49.

[112]   The United States explains that the USDOC will need to solicit this additional information so as to determine, based on positive evidence, whether the relevant exporters or producers are separate legal entities. (United States' submission, para. 27)

committees, and the USTR to direct the USDOC to implement the final determinations in all of the Section 129 proceedings. Based on these considerations, the United States indicates that it will need approximately 13 months – from the issuance of the preliminary Section 123 determination in April 2018 through May 2019 – to complete the Section 129 proceedings.[113]

3.41   China contends that the United States should be able to complete the Section 129 proceedings within 5 and a half months.[114] In China's view, all of the Section 129 proceedings should be run in parallel. China highlights that, while this dispute technically concerns 38 anti-dumping determinations, it in fact concerns 13 anti-dumping cases, some of which consist of multiple-segment proceedings.[115] According to China, the redeterminations could be streamlined because the USDOC could concurrently conduct multiple determinations with respect to the same investigation, and the analysis required would be simpler and the time needed shorter with respect to subsequent administrative reviews that raise the same issue, for example with respect to the SRP.[116] China argues that the United States' proposal to undertake the implementation of the DSB's "as applied" recommendations and rulings in 13 months is in "gross violation" of Section 129 of the URAA given that this provision imposes a maximum of 180 days to issue a redetermination.[117] According to China, this period of 180 days includes all fact-finding, verifications, hearings, and preliminary determinations.[118] China also suggests that, in ascertaining the time period that would be reasonable for completion of the Section 129 redeterminations, I look for "guidance" from the provisions of US law that govern anti-dumping determinations. According to China, under the relevant regulations, the USDOC is permitted 215 days "to undertake an anti-dumping determination from

---

[113] I understand this 13-month period to be reflected in the United States' proposed timetable as follows: (i) approximately 6 months for the USDOC to issue preliminary determinations; (ii) approximately 3 months for interested parties to submit briefs to the USDOC and for the USDOC to hold hearings, conduct verifications, as well as analyse and prepare responses to comments from interested parties; (iii) approximately 2 months for the USDOC to issue final determinations and for the USTR to issue a letter directing the USDOC to implement the final determinations; and (iv) approximately 2 additional months due to the fact that the USDOC's conduct of the redeterminations will be staggered in three tranches. (United States' submission, para. 49)

[114] China's submission, para. 27. See also paras. 54-56. China highlights that a Section 129 proceeding involves three stages: (i) a consultation stage, which is to be conducted "'promptly' after the circulation of the report"; (ii) a determination stage, which is to take place within 180 days; and (iii) a final consultation stage. According to China, the first consultation stage should have taken place after the circulation of the Panel Report in this dispute. China further submits that the determination stage can be completed within 5 months, and that the final consultation stage can be completed within 15 days. (Ibid., paras. 51-56)

[115] China's submission, para. 61.

[116] China's submission, paras. 55 and 61; response to questioning at the hearing.

[117] China's submission, para. 57. See also paras. 52 and 55.

[118] China's response to questioning at the hearing.

scratch".[119] In this regard, China underlines that the nearly 400-day period proposed by the United States to conduct the Section 129 proceedings in this dispute is almost double the length prescribed for original investigations.[120] China adds that this goes against the reasoning of previous arbitrators under Article 21.3(c) of the DSU, who have recognized that a redetermination should be shorter than an original investigation because the implementing Member is "only required to conduct a re-determination to implement a limited number of DSB rulings of inconsistency."[121] China also argues that no additional time should be granted for on-site verifications given that such verifications are not required under Section 129 of the URAA and seldom carried out by the USDOC in redetermination processes.[122] In further support of its proposed 5 and a half month period for the Section 129 proceedings, China refers to information published in relation to the Section 129 proceedings undertaken in response to the DSB's recommendations and rulings in *US – Shrimp and Sawblades*, showing that the USDOC completed its redetermination in that dispute in 180 days and that the USTR directed implementation of that determination 18 days later.[123]

3.42   I begin by considering the United States' proposed approach to the various Section 129 proceedings, including whether these proceedings need to be staggered or conducted concurrently. As noted above, the United States identifies the large number of redeterminations needed, as well as the associated administrative workload and due process considerations, as key reasons for staggering the Section 129 proceedings in tranches.

3.43   China asserts that the United States' argument regarding the USDOC workload is not a relevant consideration in determining the reasonable period of time, and that, in any event, the USDOC is capable of handling a large number of investigations and reviews in parallel.[124] I recall that several previous arbitrators have considered that, in principle, the workload of the implementing authority is not relevant to the determination of the reasonable period of time for implementation of the DSB's recommendations and rulings.[125] I share that view. I further note that, in its submission, the United States sets out a possible

---

[119]   China's submission, para. 58. See also China's opening statement at the hearing. As explained at para. 3.46 and fn 135 below, the United States disputes that the USDOC is required by law to complete original investigations within 215 days.

[120]   China's submission, para. 58.

[121]   China's submission, para. 58 (quoting Awards of the Arbitrators, *Japan – DRAMS (Article 21.3(c))*, para. 48; *US – Washing Machines (Article 21.3(c))*, para. 3.50).

[122]   According to China, the USDOC conducted verifications in only three of 20 recent Section 129 proceedings. (China's submission, para. 59 and fn 67 thereto)

[123]   China's response to questioning at the hearing (referring to the dispute in *US – Shrimp and Sawblades* (DS422)).

[124]   China's submission, para. 64.

[125]   Awards of the Arbitrators, *US – 1916 Act (Article 21.3(c))*, para. 38; *US – Countervailing Measures (China) (Article 21.3(c))*, para. 3.49; *US – Shrimp II (Viet Nam) (Article 21.3(c))*, para. 3.55; *US – Washing Machines (Article 21.3(c))*, para. 3.63.

division of the redeterminations into three tranches: one tranche for the redeterminations in respect of 13 investigations, a second tranche for the redeterminations in respect of 13 administrative reviews, and a third tranche for the redeterminations to be made in respect of the remaining 12 administrative reviews. At the same time, the United States explains that this proposed division of work is merely "illustrative", and that the USDOC expects to consider other possible ways of grouping redeterminations into tranches, for example by product or by type of determination (investigation or administrative review).[126] In my view, the proposed approach of addressing the redeterminations in tranches is a matter for the US authorities. In this regard, previous arbitrators have said that an implementing Member has a measure of discretion in choosing the means of implementation that it deems most appropriate.[127] Indeed, it is just this type of flexibility, within their respective legal systems, that Members are expected to utilize in order to achieve prompt compliance with DSB recommendations and rulings. I note that the commonality in the issues to be considered and the relationship between original investigations and subsequent administrative reviews for the same products are such that it may be possible for the USDOC to expedite its work for many of the redeterminations.

3.44   As regards the 180-day period referred to in Section 129(b)(2) of the URAA, the United States contests China's assertions that this provision constrains the USDOC to carry out all aspects of a redetermination within a maximum of 180 days and that, therefore, the 13-month period proposed by the United States is inconsistent with its own statute.[128] The United States explains that Section 129(b)(2) does not set any overall limit on the length of time that may be used to complete all of the steps involved in a redetermination, because the 180-day period to which it refers is triggered not when the USDOC begins its work pursuant to Section 129, but only when the USTR makes a written request to the USDOC relating to the redetermination. The United States adds that nothing in the statute precludes the USDOC from commencing a Section 129 proceeding prior to receipt of a written request from the USTR, and beginning, for example to issue questionnaires to parties prior to the receipt of such a request, as has been done in prior implementation proceedings. The United States recognizes that there have been cases where an entire Section 129 proceeding could be completed within 180 days; however, whether this can be done or not is decided on a case-by-case basis.[129] The United States rejects, therefore, China's invocation in this dispute of the time taken for the Section 129 proceedings undertaken in response to the DSB's recommendations and rulings in *US – Shrimp and Sawblades*. The United States explains that the

---

[126]   United States' submission, fn 10 to para. 7. See also para. 49.
[127]   Awards of the Arbitrators, *Brazil – Retreaded Tyres (Article 21.3(c))*, para. 48; *China – GOES (Article 21.3(c))*, para. 3.4; *US – Countervailing Measures (China) (Article 21.3(c))*, para. 3.3; *US – Washing Machines (Article 21.3(c))*, para. 3.8.
[128]   United States' response to questioning at the hearing.
[129]   *Ibid.*

implementation required in this case is very different from that in *US □ Shrimp and Sawblades*, given that here the USDOC will be applying a new methodology and presumably gathering information about the relationship between importers and exporters.[130]

3.45   I note that the period of 180 days specified in the text of Section 129(b)(2) of the URAA refers to the period within which, following the receipt of a written request from the USTR, the USDOC must issue a determination implementing the recommendations and rulings of the DSB. As the United States points out, it is the USDOC's receipt of a written request from the USTR, rather than the commencement of a Section 129 proceeding, that triggers the start of the 180-day period. Such request could, in principle, be received before or after the USDOC begins its work on the redetermination. Moreover, subparagraphs (1), (3), and (4) of Section 129(b) set out other actions involving the USTR, the USDOC, and Congress that are to be carried out both before and after the written request has been made pursuant to Section 129(b)(2). I am therefore not persuaded by China's assertion that Section 129(b)(2) establishes a maximum time period within which all steps of a Section 129 redetermination must be completed. Instead, as previous arbitrators have done[131], I accept the United States' explanations regarding the scope of this provision. This is, of course, without prejudice to the question of how much time is reasonably needed to conduct the Section 129 proceedings in this dispute.

3.46   I turn next to the question of the relevance, for the reasonable period of time for implementation, of the relative scope of original investigations and administrative reviews, on the one hand, and redeterminations, on the other hand. Relying on the reasoning of previous arbitrators, China argues that, since the scope of the redeterminations needed is much more limited, these proceedings require significantly less time than the time required in original proceedings.[132] I accept the logic of this proposition. At the same time, I am mindful that the length of time needed for original investigations under US law is contested. While China asserts that such proceedings may take a maximum of 215 days[133], the United States contends that they may take up to 355 days.[134]

---

[130]   *Ibid.*
[131]   Awards of the Arbitrators, *US – Countervailing Measures (China) (Article 21.3(c))*, para. 3.41; *US – Shrimp II (Viet Nam) (Article 21.3(c))*; para. 3.46; *US – Washing Machines (Article 21.3(c))*, para. 3.47.
[132]   China's submission, para. 58 (referring to Awards of the Arbitrators, *Japan – DRAMS (Korea) (Article 21.3(c))*, para. 48; *US – Washing Machines (Article 21.3(c))*, para. 3.50).
[133]   China's submission, para. 58; opening statement at the hearing.
[134]   The United States explained at the hearing that US law allows for the possibility of extension of the deadlines for the issuance of the preliminary and final determinations in an anti-dumping investigation. The United States added that, when account is also taken of the time needed to deal with any potential ministerial errors, an entire investigation may take 355 days. (United States' opening statement at the hearing)

3.47   In considering the time that is reasonably necessary to conduct the requisite Section 129 proceedings in this dispute, I note that, as clarified by the United States at the hearing, there is no provision of US law that mandates that all steps taken in original investigations must also be taken in Section 129 redeterminations.[135] Moreover, the Section 129 redeterminations may well be more limited in scope than the proceedings in which the original, WTO-inconsistent determinations were made. Yet, as noted above, the United States views the development of an alternative analysis for single-exporter treatment as a WTO-consistent option for implementation in this dispute, and adds that this might entail a move from a presumption to a fact-based, case-by-case analysis.[136] I consider that this renders it less likely that the USDOC will be able to make all of the required re-determinations without re-opening its factual record in at least some of the relevant proceedings.

3.48   These considerations are also relevant to the disagreement between the parties on whether or not my determination of the reasonable period of time should account for the time that may be needed for the USDOC to hold hearings and conduct verifications as part of the Section 129 proceedings. It is undisputed that: (i) the USDOC is not required to conduct verifications in such proceedings; (ii) pursuant to Section 129(d), the USDOC may, "in appropriate cases", hold a hearing; and (iii) in practice, the USDOC often does not take either of these steps in a Section 129 proceeding. Nevertheless, bearing in mind the nature of the implementation that the United States proposes to undertake in these redeterminations, and mindful that investigated exporters and producers themselves benefit from the opportunity to defend their interests in hearings and through the process of verification, I would be reluctant to determine any period of time for implementation that would foreclose the possibility that such procedural steps could be taken if and when warranted. Lastly, with respect to the 1 month that the United States indicates is usually taken for correction of any ministerial errors[137], the United States accepted at the hearing that the process of addressing ministerial errors can be conducted concurrently with the process of consulting Congress.[138]

3.49   On the basis of the foregoing, I consider that the United States could reasonably complete all of the Section 129 redeterminations in respect of the DSB's "as applied" recommendations and rulings concerning the 38 anti-dumping determinations found to be WTO-inconsistent in significantly less time than the 13-month period it has proposed. At the same time, I believe that the Section 129 redeterminations to be undertaken in this dispute will require more than the 5 and a half months proposed by China.

---

[135]   United States' response to questioning at the hearing.
[136]   United States' opening statement and response to questioning at the hearing.
[137]   United States' submission, para. 46.
[138]   United States' response to questioning at the hearing.

3.4.2   Particular circumstances of this dispute

3.50   The United States identifies the following as "particular circumstances" of this dispute that, in its view, weigh in favour of a longer period of time for implementation: (i) the number and magnitude of modifications to the challenged measures; (ii) the procedural requirements under its domestic law; (iii) the complexity and novelty of the issues involved; (iv) the current workload of the USDOC; and (v) the continuing formation of the US administration and the fact that many key positions at the USDOC have yet to be filled.[139] The United States also points to the agreement reached by China and the European Union in *EC – Fasteners (China)*, setting the reasonable period of time for implementation by the European Union at 14 months and 2 weeks.[140] The United States highlights the "similarity of one of the major substantive issues" in *EC – Fasteners (China)* and this dispute[141], and adds that "the significantly larger number of administrative determinations" in the present dispute[142] warrants a substantially longer reasonable period of time.[143] In addition, the United States emphasizes that China made a "choice" to bring "as applied" claims against 38 distinct anti-dumping determinations.[144] For the United States, when a complaining Member chooses to bring a dispute of this magnitude, it must recognize that the responding Member will need more time to implement the DSB's recommendations and rulings.[145]

3.51   For its part, China contends that I should take account of what it alleges to be the United States' record of failing to meet previous reasonable period of time deadlines in reaching my determination of the reasonable period of time in this dispute.[146]

3.52   I have addressed several of these circumstances above. With respect to the remaining circumstances advanced by the United States, China argues that any additional workload arising from the DSB's recommendations and rulings in

---

[139]   United States' submission, paras. 10 and 50-54. With respect to the current workload of the USDOC, the United States argues that the USDOC recently experienced "a significant increase in new anti-dumping and countervailing duty petitions covering an array of different products and countries" and that, as of 8 November 2017, there were 77 ongoing anti-dumping and countervailing duty investigations, 129 ongoing periodic reviews, and seven ongoing new shipper reviews. (*Ibid.*, paras. 51-52)

[140]   United States' submission, para. 11.

[141]   United States' submission, para. 12.

[142]   The United States contends that the reasonable period of time should account for the need to conduct "significant additional analysis" on its part, owing to the 38 determinations that China chose to challenge in this dispute, as opposed to one determination in *EC – Fasteners (China)*. (United States' submission, paras. 9 and 12-13)

[143]   United States' submission, para. 12.

[144]   United States' submission, para. 13.

[145]   *Ibid.*

[146]   China's opening statement at the hearing. China also submits that I should take into account the United States' early awareness of its implementing obligations in my determination of the reasonable period of time. (China's submission, paras. 31, 40, 42 and 46) I have addressed this issue at paragraphs 3.27-3.30 above.

this dispute and practical challenges the USDOC may face in handling that workload are not relevant to the determination of the reasonable period of time for implementation of the DSB's recommendations and rulings.[147] China also disagrees that the reasonable period of time agreed by the parties in *EC – Fasteners (China)* is relevant to my determination of the reasonable period of time in this dispute. In particular, China argues that, contrary to the present dispute, the DSB's recommendations and rulings in *EC □ Fasteners (China)* required implementation through legislative means, which is more time-consuming than the means of implementation proposed by the United States in this dispute. In addition, China contends that the USDOC is capable of conducting all relevant redeterminations in parallel and that China's "choice" to challenge 38 anti-dumping determinations reflects the USDOC's widespread use of WTO-inconsistent measures and does not warrant the grant of a longer period of time for implementation.[148]

3.53   With respect to the allegedly heavy workload of the USDOC, the United States argues that my determination of the reasonable period of time should account for the administrative burden associated with the addition of 38 implementation proceedings on top of the USDOC's existing heavy workload.[149] As I have noted above, previous arbitrators have declined to find that the workload of the implementing authority warranted a longer period of time for implementation.[150] In this dispute, the United States has neither demonstrated the impact that the implementation process would have on the USDOC's workload, nor explained how such workload should be taken into account in my determination of the reasonable period of time. Moreover, I recall that the implementing Member is expected to use all available flexibilities within its legal system to ensure "prompt compliance" with the DSB's recommendations and rulings in accordance with Article 21 of the DSU.[151] In my view, prioritizing compliance action in respect of the DSB's recommendations and rulings at issue in these proceedings would constitute an exercise of flexibility available to the USDOC, which it would be expected to utilize.[152] Accordingly, I do not consider the USDOC's workload to be relevant to my determination of the reasonable period of time for implementation in this dispute.

---

[147]   China's submission, paras. 66-68. See also para. 64.

[148]   China's submission, paras. 30-32 and 65.

[149]   United States' submission, para. 52; response to questioning at the hearing.

[150]   Awards of the Arbitrators, *US – 1916 Act (Article 21.3(c))*, para. 38; *US – Countervailing Measures (China) (Article 21.3(c))*, para. 3.49; *US – Shrimp II (Viet Nam) (Article 21.3(c))*, para. 3.55; *US – Washing Machines (Article 21.3(c))*, para. 3.63.

[151]   See Awards of the Arbitrators, *US – Offset Act (Byrd Amendment) (Article 21.3(c))*, para. 64; *Japan – DRAMs (Korea) (Article 21.3(c))*, para. 25; *Brazil – Retreaded Tyres (Article 21.3(c))*, para. 73; *US – Stainless Steel (Mexico) (Article 21.3(c))*, para. 42; *China – GOES (Article 21.3(c))*, para. 3.4; *US □ Countervailing Measures (China) (Article 21.3(c))*, para. 3.49; *US – Shrimp II (Viet Nam) (Article 21.3(c))*, para. 3.55; *Colombia – Textiles (Article 21.3(c))*, paras. 3.51-3.53; *US – Washing Machines (Article 21.3(c))*, para. 3.9.

[152]   Award of the Arbitrator, *US – Shrimp II (Viet Nam) (Article 21.3(c))*, para. 3.55.

3.54   Regarding the continuing formation of the US administration and the fact that certain key positions at the USDOC remain vacant, the United States explained at the hearing that, even though an "extra month here or there" has not been added to its proposed schedule for this reason, this factor was nevertheless taken into account in developing that schedule.[153] The United States added that, while this "particular circumstance" affects both proceedings under Section 123 and Section 129 of the URAA, the former is affected relatively more, given that it is a policy process.[154] Although the United States has clarified, to some extent, the stages of the implementation process where this factor could have an impact, it has not persuaded me that the USDOC would not be able to use the flexibilities and the staff available to it to act with appropriate dispatch in achieving compliance with its WTO obligations in this dispute. Therefore, I do not consider this to be a particular circumstance relevant to the determination of the reasonable period of time for implementation in this dispute.

3.55   I am similarly unpersuaded that I should take account of the reasonable period of time agreed by the parties in *EC – Fasteners (China)*. The DSB recommendations and rulings in that dispute did not apply to the United States. Rather, they concerned a measure taken by another WTO Member, and implementation was undertaken in a different legal system.[155] For these reasons, I consider that the reasonable period of time agreed by China and the European Union in *EC – Fasteners (China)* is not relevant to my determination in this arbitration.

3.56   Finally, with respect to China's argument regarding the United States' alleged record of failing to comply within applicable reasonable periods of time in previous disputes, I note that the United States contests the existence of such a track-record.[156] I am also mindful that each dispute, and the implementation process that may follow the DSB's recommendations and rulings, embody their own set of facts and context. Thus, I do not consider any such alleged track-record to be a particular circumstance relevant to my determination of the reasonable period of time for implementation in this dispute.

4.   AWARD

4.1   In light of the foregoing considerations, the "reasonable period of time" for the United States to implement the recommendations and rulings of the DSB in this dispute is 15 months, from 22 May 2017, that is, from the date on which the DSB adopted the Panel and Appellate Body Reports in this dispute. The reasonable period of time for implementation will expire on 22 August 2018.

---

[153]   United States' response to questioning at the hearing.
[154]   *Ibid.*
[155]   See Award of the Arbitrator, *US – Shrimp II (Viet Nam) (Article 21.3(c))*, para. 3.38.
[156]   United States' response to questioning at the hearing.

ANNEX A

EXECUTIVE SUMMARY OF THE
UNITED STATES' SUBMISSION

1.   The amount of time a Member requires for implementation of DSB recommendations depends on the particular facts and circumstances of the dispute, including the scope of the recommendations and the types of procedures required under the Member's laws to make the necessary changes in the measures at issue. Specific circumstances identified in previous awards as relevant to the Arbitrator's determination of the RPT include: (1) the legal form of implementation; (2) the technical complexity of the measure the Member must draft, adopt, and implement; and (3) the period of time in which the implementing Member can achieve that proposed legal form of implementation in accordance with its system of government.

2.   The United States would draw the Arbitrator's attention to the reasonable period of time to which China agreed pursuant to Article 21.3(b) of the DSU in the *EC – Fasteners (China)* dispute. In that dispute, China reached agreement with the European Union on a reasonable period of time of 14 months and two weeks. While *EC – Fasteners (China)* involved an "as such" finding and "as applied" findings with respect to *one* antidumping determination, this dispute involves an "as such" finding on a very similar measure and "as applied" findings concerning *38 separate determinations*. This dispute also involves "as applied findings" with respect to four of those 38 determinations concerning the use of the alternative, average-to-transaction comparison methodology and "zeroing". The similarity of one of the major substantive issues in these two disputes, coupled with the significantly larger number of administrative determinations involved here, warrants a substantially longer compliance period in this dispute, as China logically should agree. When choosing to bring a dispute of this magnitude, the complaining Member must recognize that it will take more time for the responding Member to implement any and all adverse findings.

3.   Addressing the numerous findings in this dispute requires a multi-phase process. The most practical way under U.S. law to implement the recommendations of the DSB would be to conduct proceedings under both section 123 and section 129 of the *Uruguay Round Agreements Act* ("URAA"). First, the United States contemplates conducting a proceeding pursuant to section 123 of the URAA to address the Panel's "as such" findings under the AD Agreement. Second, the United States contemplates conducting proceedings pursuant to section 129 of the URAA to address the Panel's "as applied" findings as they relate to 13 original investigations and 25 administrative reviews. The United States anticipates that it will not be possible to commence the 38 section 129 proceedings (Phase II) until the section 123 proceeding (Phase I) has been

mostly completed. The United States expects that any approach to address the DSB recommendations concerning the Panel's "as such" findings under the AD Agreement will need to be developed through the section 123 proceeding before it could be applied or adapted in the 38 section 129 proceedings concerning the challenged determinations. Therefore, Phases I and II must be undertaken sequentially, although there could be a small degree of overlap in the two phases.

4.   Both parties, as well as the WTO dispute settlement system as a whole, have a strong interest in setting the RPT at a length that allows for an implementation process that takes account of all available information and uses a well-considered approach to implementing the findings in the Appellate Body and Panel reports. In this dispute, the RPT determined by the Arbitrator should be of sufficient length to allow the United States to address all of the various DSB recommendations in a manner consistent with relevant WTO obligations. Such a result would preserve the rights of the United States to have a reasonable time for compliance and to impose appropriate antidumping duties, while at the same time preserving China's rights to ensure that antidumping duties are imposed in accordance with WTO rules. If the RPT is too short to permit the United States to address the DSB's recommendations effectively, the likelihood of a "positive solution" to the dispute would be reduced.

5.   The volume and complexity of the DSB's recommendations – in particular the "as applied" findings related to the 38 separate determinations that China chose to challenge together in this one dispute – and U.S. legal requirements should be considered in determining the appropriate reasonable period of time to secure a "positive solution" for this dispute. For the reasons outlined in this submission, a period of no less than 24 months is a reasonable period of time for implementation.

ANNEX B

EXECUTIVE SUMMARY OF CHINA'S SUBMISSION

1.   The reasonable period of time ("RPT") for the United States to implement the recommendations and rulings of the Dispute Settlement Body ("DSB") in this dispute should be six months from the adoption of the Panel and Appellate body reports. Article 21 of the *Understanding on Rules and Procedures Governing the Settlement of Disputes* ("DSU") requires a Member to promptly comply with DSB recommendations, which, according to jurisprudence developed by arbitrators under Article 21.3(c), requires compliance within the shortest period possible within the legal system of the Member. The particular facts and circumstances of the dispute can bear on the arbitrator's finding of a reasonable period of time, but only to the extent they assist the arbitrator in determining the shortest period possible in which the Member can comply.

2.   The United States' 24 month-request ignores the United States' long period of inactivity after it became aware it would have to implement the Panel's findings. The United States knew its implementation obligations no later than November 2016, when it chose not to appeal the Panel report. It should have been preparing for compliance since that time, and under no circumstances should it be granted an RPT that includes time *after* the DSB's recommendations and rulings were adopted for pre-commencement planning and analysis. This is particularly true considering that China requested consultations with the United States nearly four years ago now, and its exporters have suffered under USDOC's WTO-inconsistent anti-dumping duties for the entire intervening time.

3.   The United States reliance on the reasonable period of time agreed to by China in *EC – Fasteners (China)* is misplaced. Contrary to the United States' contention, China believes that the RPT for this dispute should be substantially shorter than that in *EC – Fasteners (China)*. The jurisprudence makes clear that compliance action requiring legislative means will be more time consuming than implementation that can be conducted entirely administratively. The "as such" ruling in *EC – Fasteners (China)* concerned a statute, not an administrative measure, as here, suggesting the RPT in that dispute should be longer than here. Additionally, as the "as such" ruling in *EC – Fasteners (China)* was appealed, unlike here, the European Union had far less time to prepare for implementation prior to the issuance of the DSB's recommendations than the United States has had in this dispute, again suggesting the need for a longer RPT. Finally, the number of "as applied" determinations that must be addressed is a red herring, as the USDOC is capable of running its redeterminations in parallel.

4.   The United States' request for 24 months overstates the complexity of compliance. China does not object to the United States' proposal to conduct a proceeding pursuant to section 123 of the *Uruguay Round Agreements Act* ("URAA") to address the Panel's "as such" findings under the *Anti-Dumping*

Agreement, and then to conduct proceedings pursuant to section 129 of the URAA to address the Panel's "as applied" findings. Nor does China object to the United States waiting to commence its section 129 proceedings until the preliminary determination in the section 123 proceeding has been issued. China, does, however, object to the time the United States proposes each of these processes should take. The USDOC should have concluded any and all "pre-commencement" preparatory work *prior* to the adoption of the recommendations and rulings, and should have been able to produce a preliminary determination under Section 123 in *two weeks*. The DSB's "as applied" recommendations relating to 13 original investigations and 25 administrative reviews undertaken by the USDOC likewise will not require anywhere near the 13 months requested by the United States, which in any case is more than is permitted under United States' law. Rather, this aspect of the United States' compliance obligations can be completed in five-and-a-half months.

5.   China's "choice" to challenge 38 separate USDOC determinations is a function of the widespread use of WTO-inconsistent measures by USDOC and should not be the basis for a longer RPT. To the extent the United States is arguing for a longer RPT on the basis that the supposedly large number of Section 129 proceedings will be work-intensive, previous arbitrators have consistently rejected the proposition that the workload faced by the implementing agency of the implementing Member is a relevant "particular circumstance" to be considered by the arbitrator in setting the RPT.

Cumulative List of Published Disputes